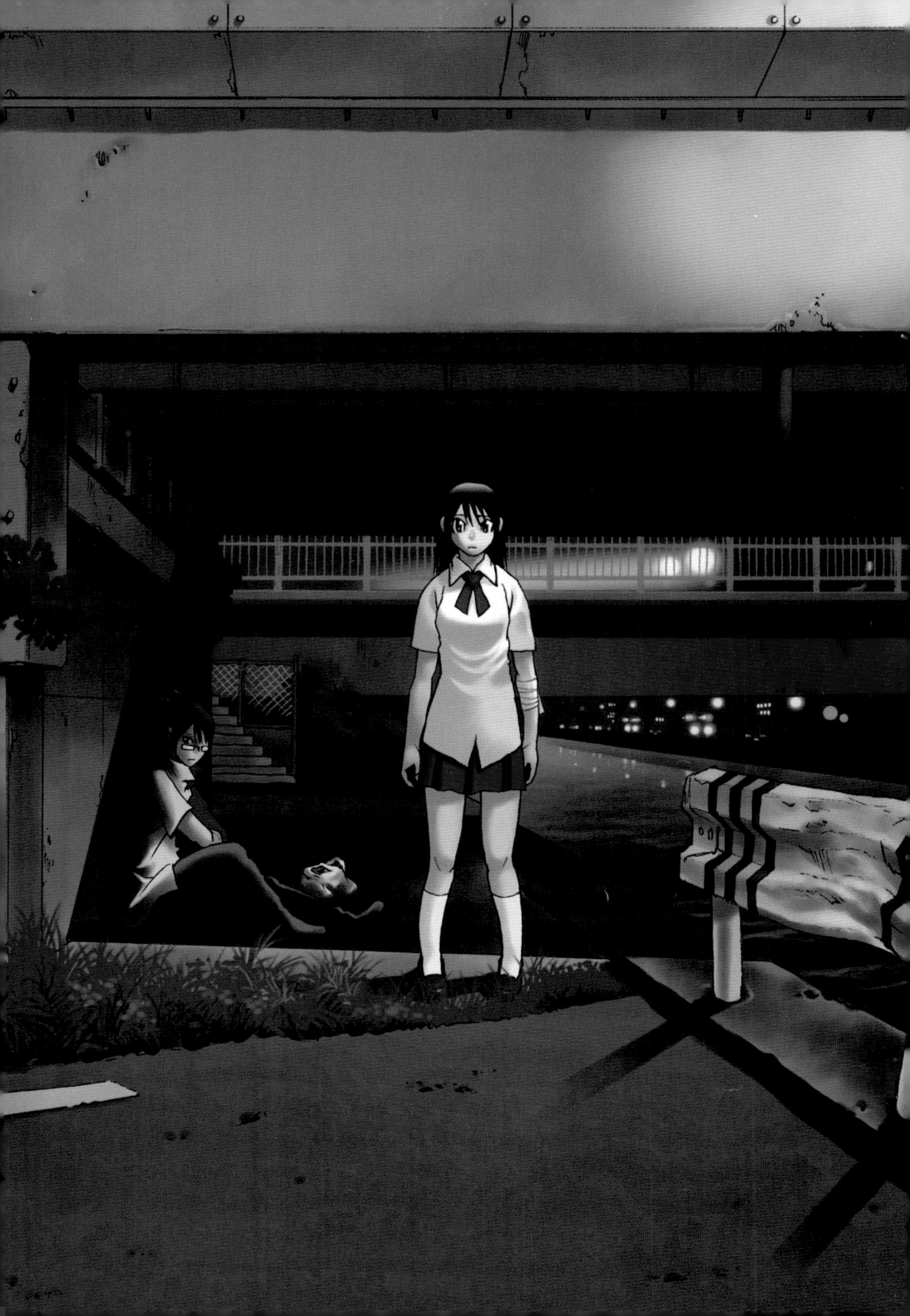

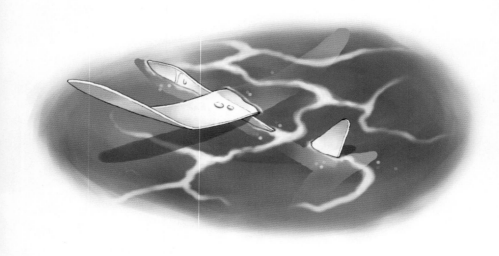

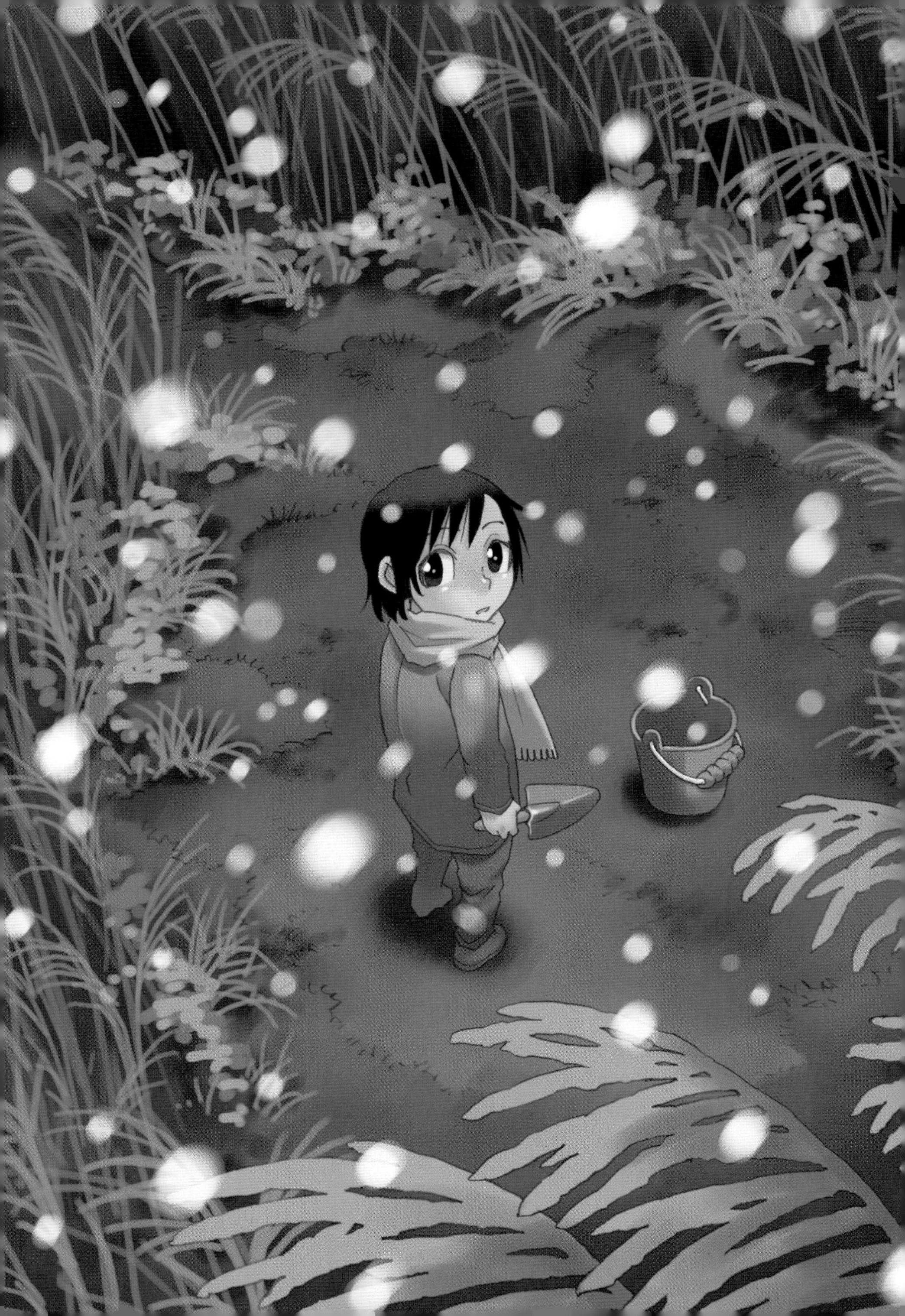

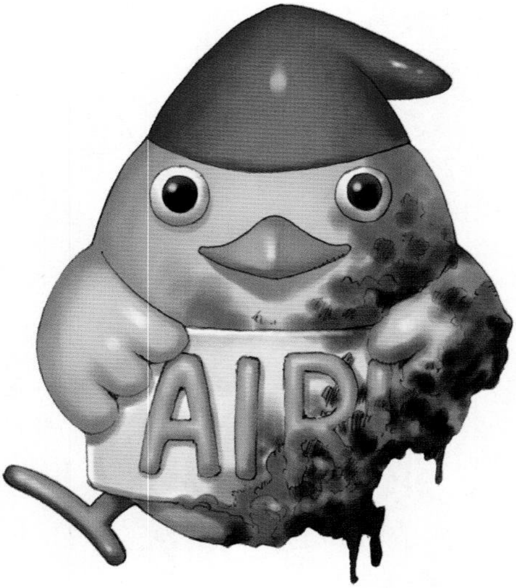
AIR

CONTENTS

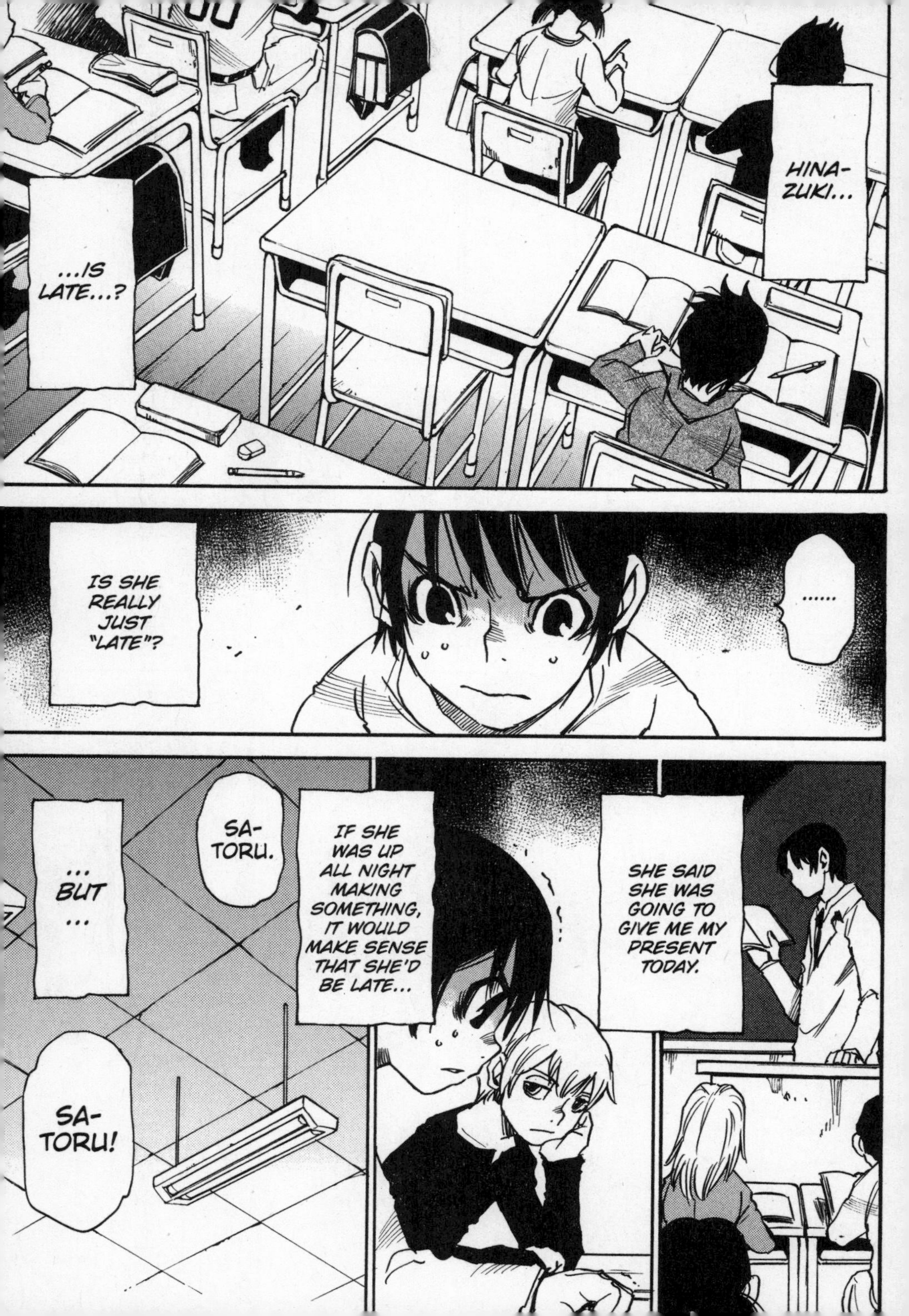
HINA-ZUKI...
...IS LATE...?
......
IS SHE REALLY JUST "LATE"?
SHE SAID SHE WAS GOING TO GIVE ME MY PRESENT TODAY.
IF SHE WAS UP ALL NIGHT MAKING SOMETHING, IT WOULD MAKE SENSE THAT SHE'D BE LATE...
...BUT...
SA-TORU.
SA-TORU!

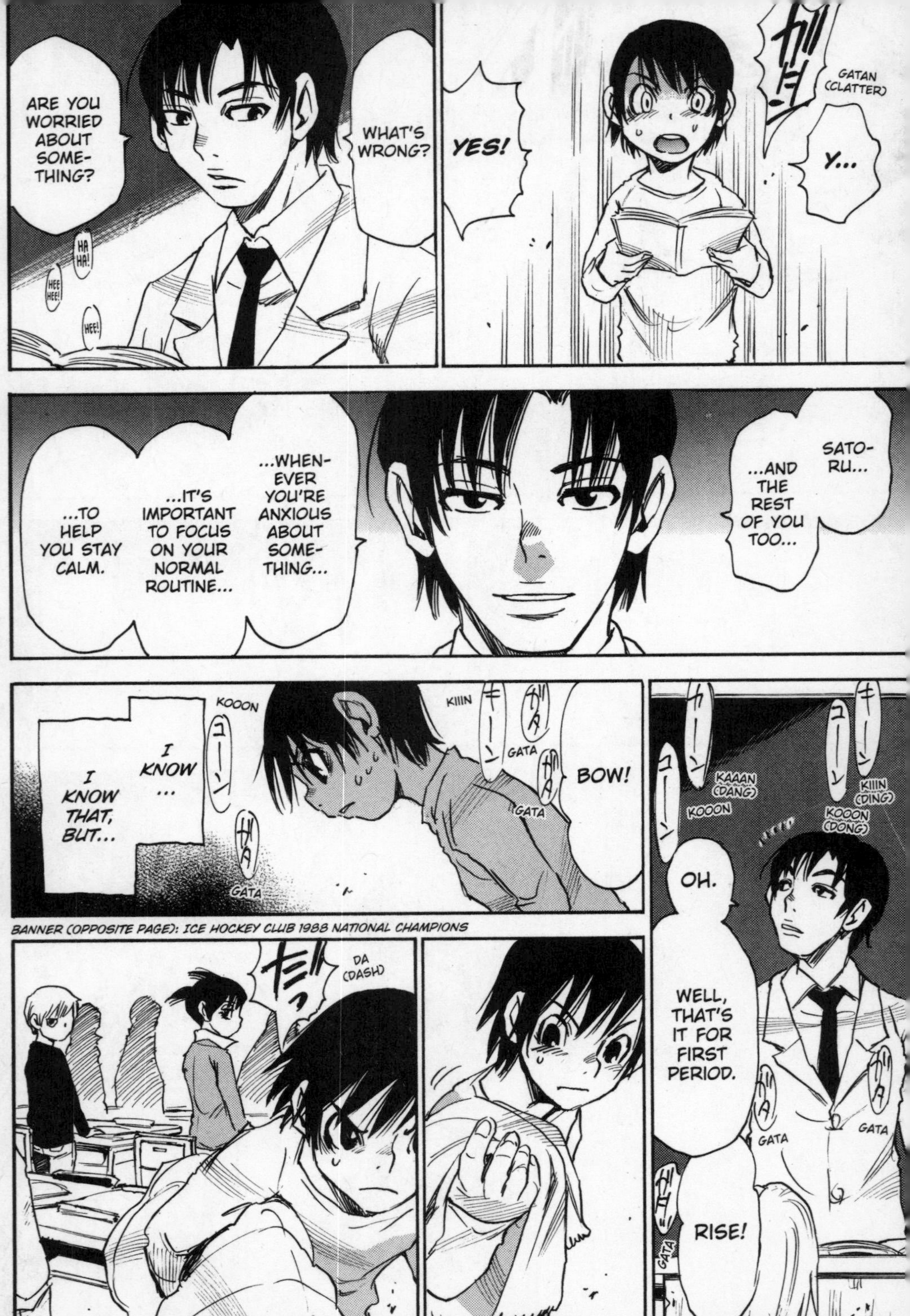
GATAN (CLATTER)
Y...
YES!
WHAT'S WRONG?
ARE YOU WORRIED ABOUT SOME-THING?
HA HA!
HEE HEE!
HEE!
SATO-RU...
...AND THE REST OF YOU TOO...
...WHEN-EVER YOU'RE ANXIOUS ABOUT SOME-THING...
...IT'S IMPORTANT TO FOCUS ON YOUR NORMAL ROUTINE...
...TO HELP YOU STAY CALM.
KIIIN (DING)
KOOON (DONG)
KAAAN (DANG)
KOOON
OH.
WELL, THAT'S IT FOR FIRST PERIOD.
GATA
GATA
RISE!
GATA
BOW!
KIIIN
GATA
GATA
KOOON
I KNOW...
I KNOW THAT, BUT...
GATA
DA (DASH)
BANNER (OPPOSITE PAGE): ICE HOCKEY CLUB 1988 NATIONAL CHAMPIONS

#13: Whiteout, March 1988

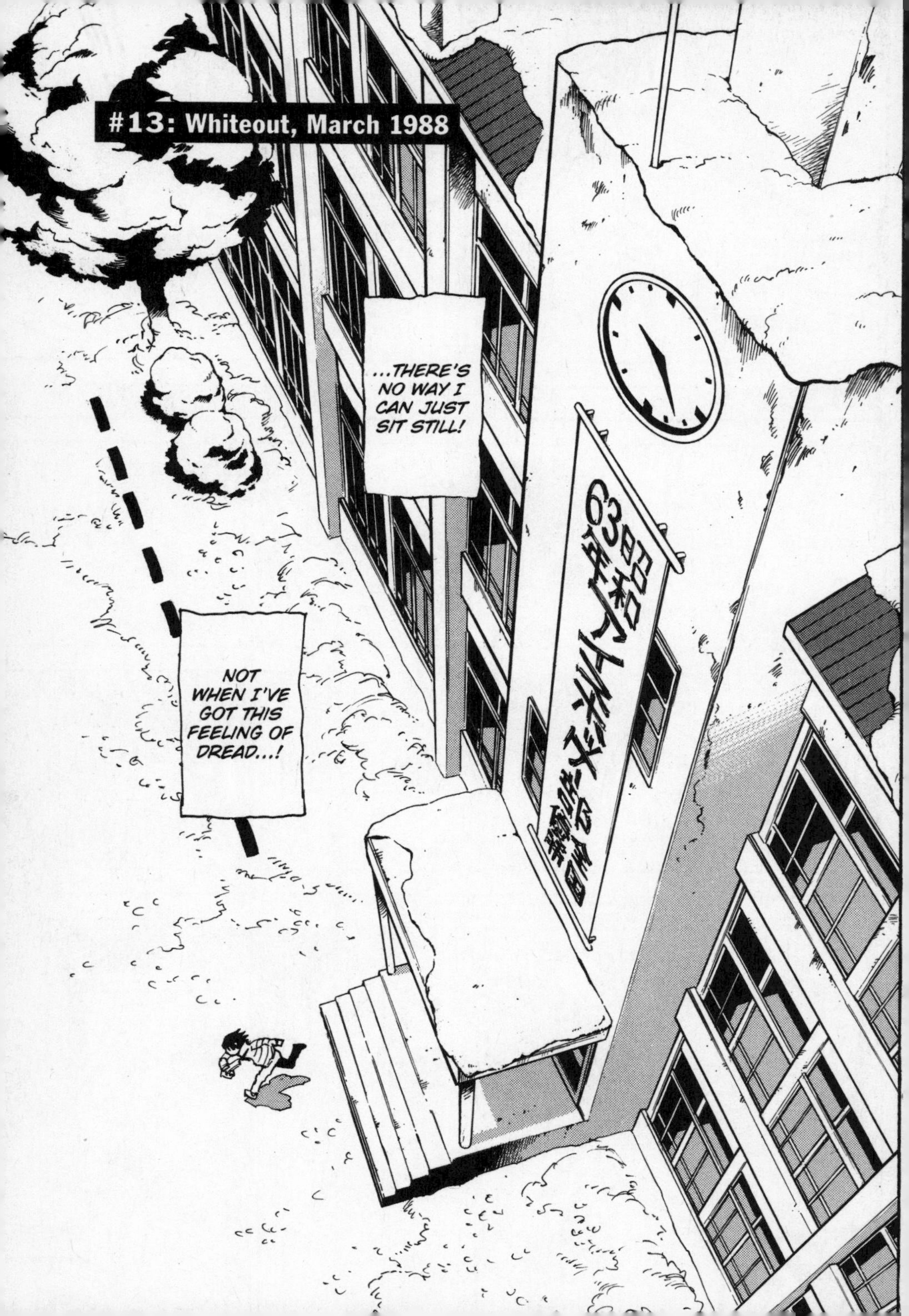
...THERE'S NO WAY I CAN JUST SIT STILL!
NOT WHEN I'VE GOT THIS FEELING OF DREAD...!

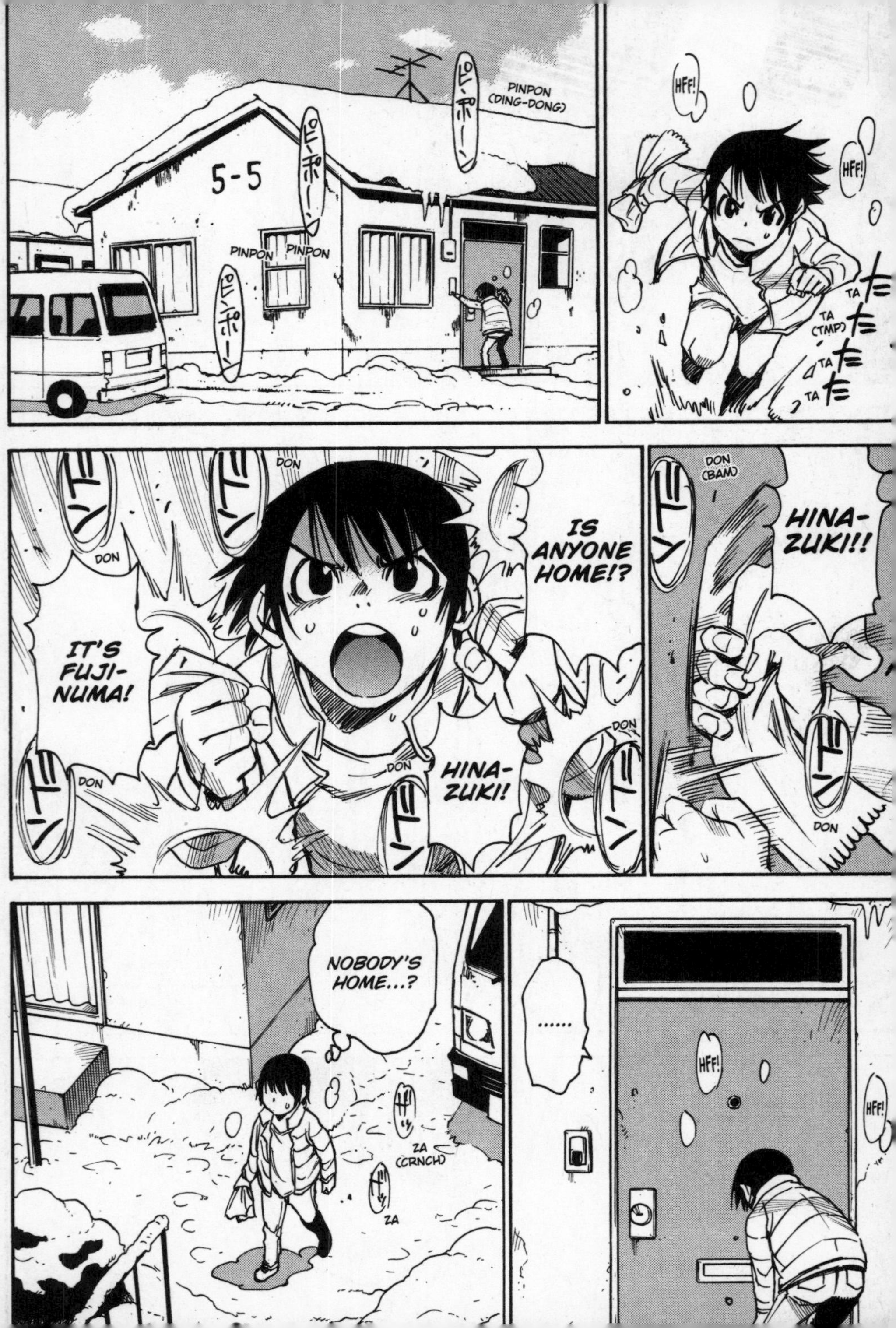
HFF!
HFF!
TA
TA (TMP)
TA
TA
PINPON (DING-DONG)
5-5
PINPON
PINPON
DON (BAM)
HINA-ZUKI!!
DON
DON
DON
IS ANYONE HOME!?
IT'S FUJI-NUMA!
DON
DON
HINA-ZUKI!
DON
......
HFF!
HFF!
NOBODY'S HOME...?
ZA (CRNCH)
ZA

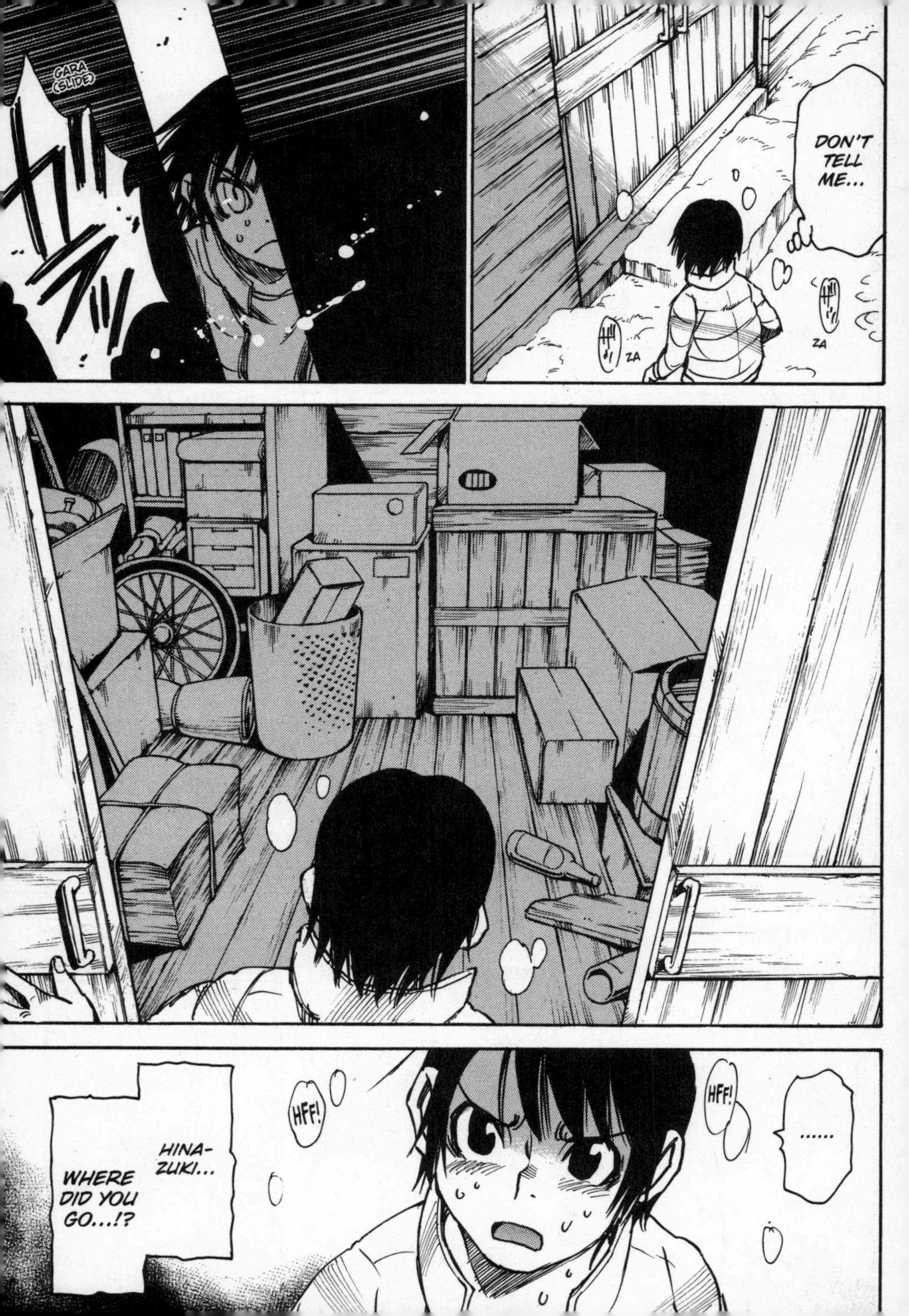
DON'T TELL ME...
ZA
ZA
GARA (SLIDE)
......
HFF!
HFF!
HINA-ZUKI...
WHERE DID YOU GO...!?

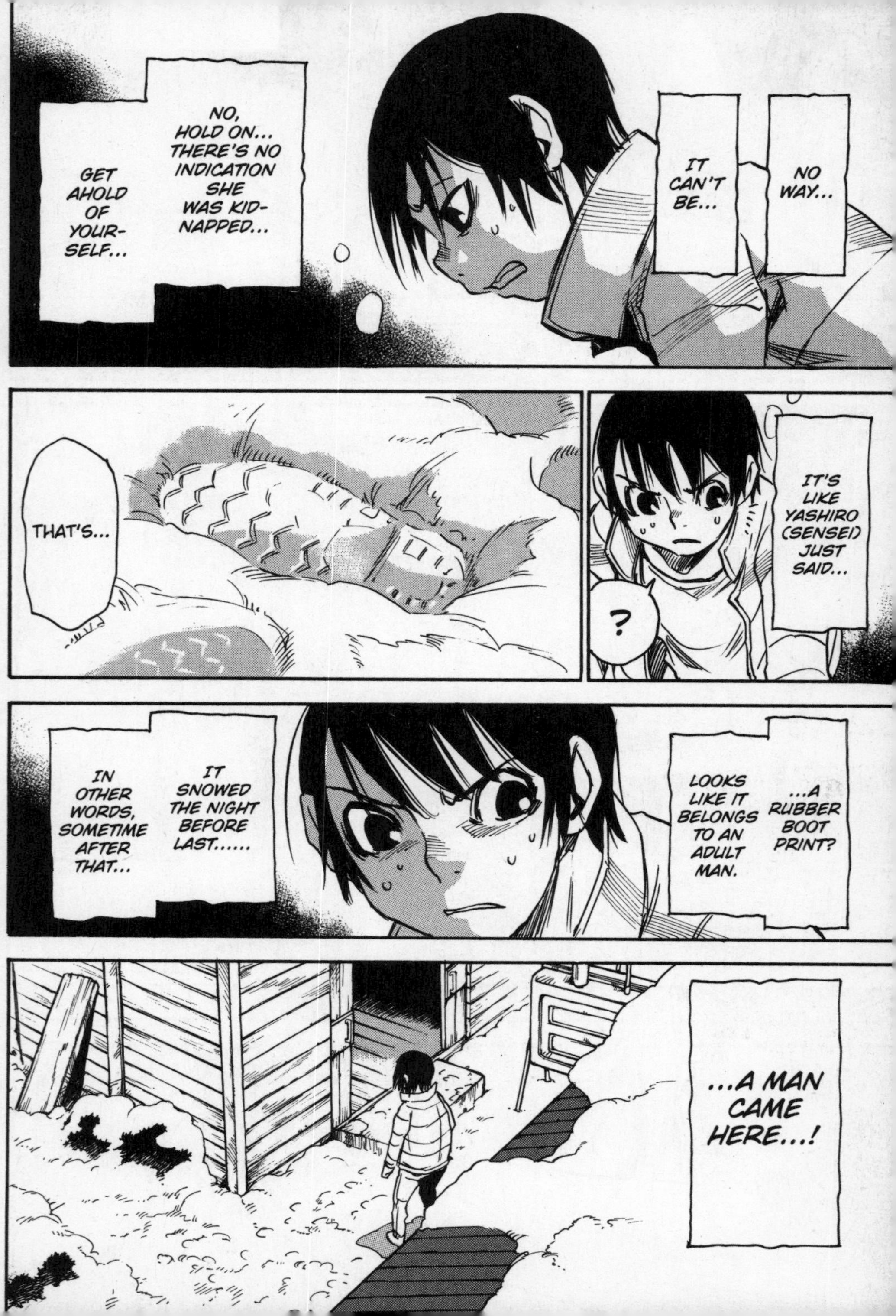
NO WAY...
IT CAN'T BE...
NO, HOLD ON... THERE'S NO INDICATION SHE WAS KID-NAPPED...
GET AHOLD OF YOUR-SELF...
IT'S LIKE YASHIRO (SENSEI) JUST SAID...
?
THAT'S...
...A RUBBER BOOT PRINT?
LOOKS LIKE IT BELONGS TO AN ADULT MAN.
IT SNOWED THE NIGHT BEFORE LAST......
IN OTHER WORDS, SOMETIME AFTER THAT...
...A MAN CAME HERE...!

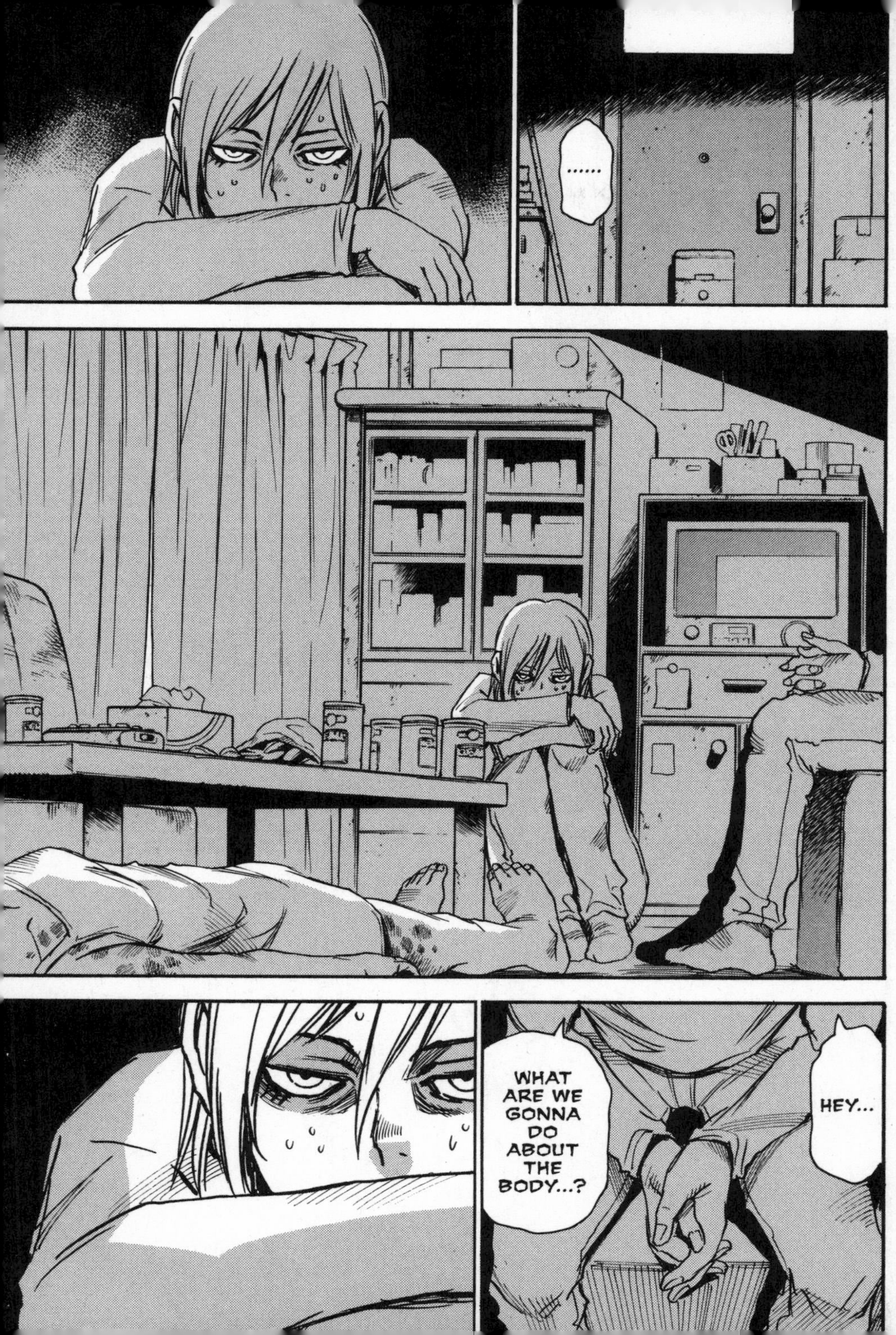
......
HEY...
WHAT ARE WE GONNA DO ABOUT THE BODY...?

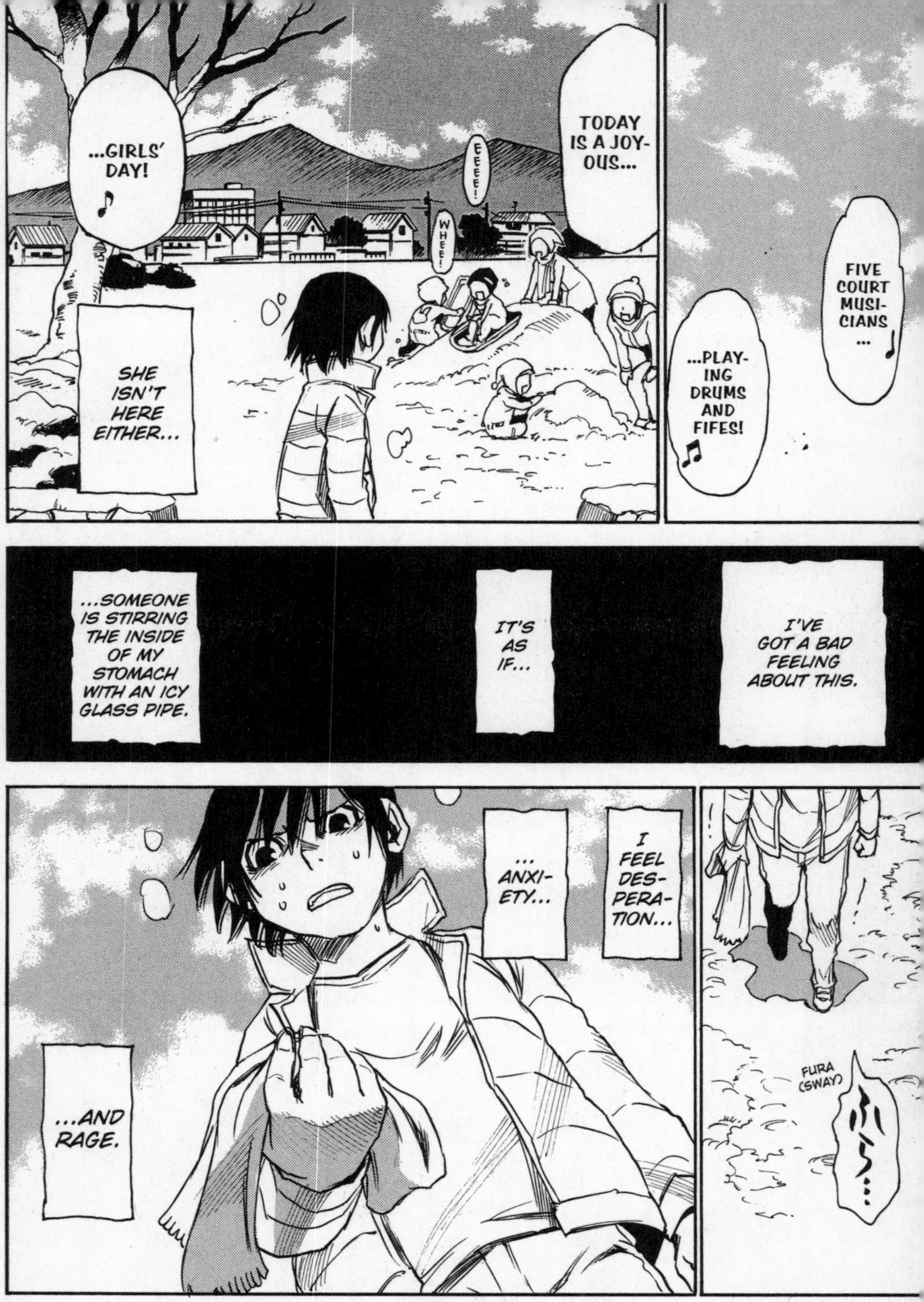
FIVE COURT MUSICIANS...
...PLAYING DRUMS AND FIFES!
TODAY IS A JOYOUS...
EEEE!
WHEE!
...GIRLS' DAY!
SHE ISN'T HERE EITHER...
I'VE GOT A BAD FEELING ABOUT THIS.
IT'S AS IF...
...SOMEONE IS STIRRING THE INSIDE OF MY STOMACH WITH AN ICY GLASS PIPE.
FURA (SWAY)
ふら…
I FEEL DESPERATION...
...ANXIETY...
...AND RAGE.

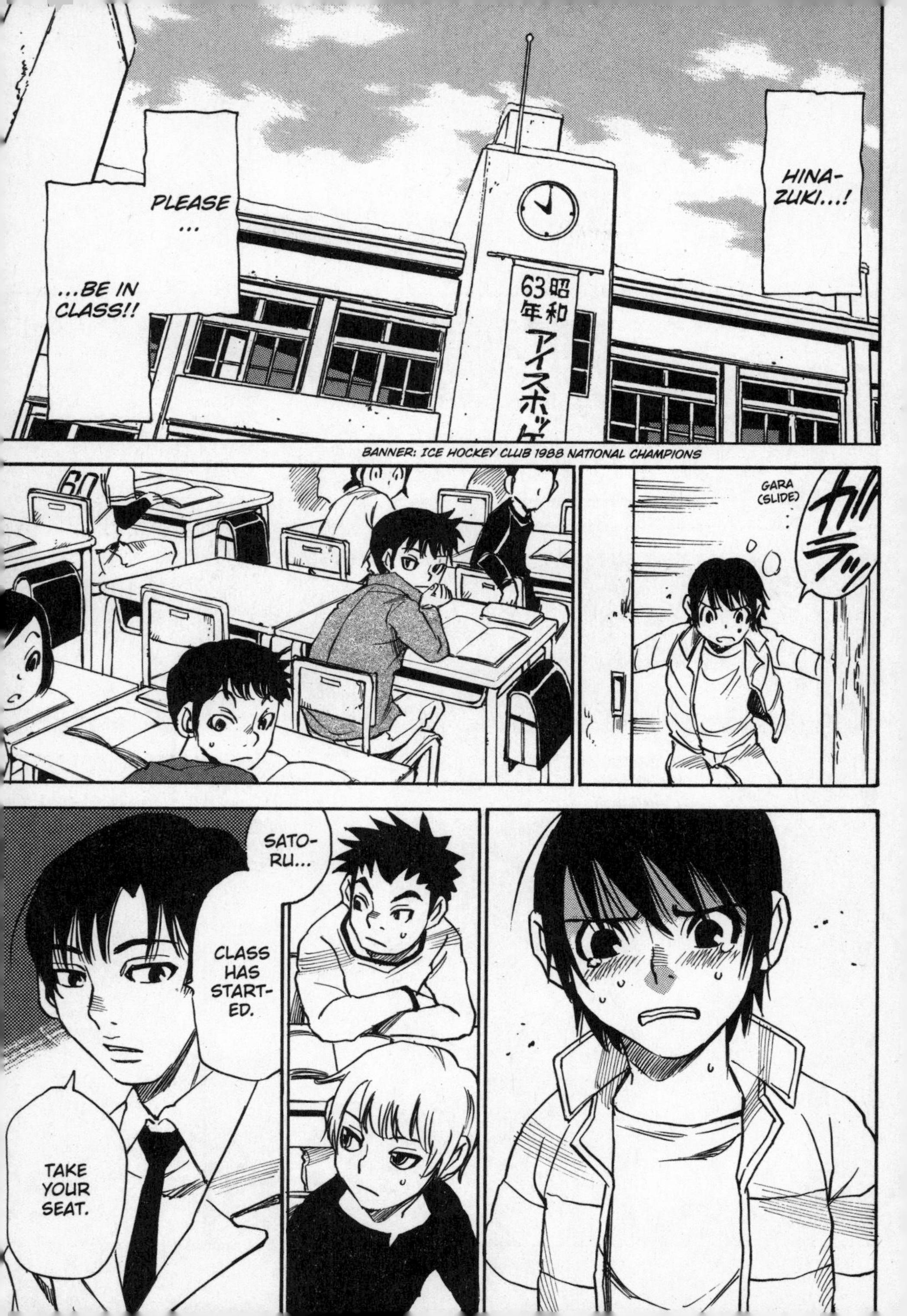
HINA-ZUKI...!
PLEASE ...
...BE IN CLASS!!
昭和63年
アイスホッ
BANNER: ICE HOCKEY CLUB 1988 NATIONAL CHAMPIONS
GARA (SLIDE)
ガラッ
SATO-RU...
CLASS HAS START-ED.
TAKE YOUR SEAT.

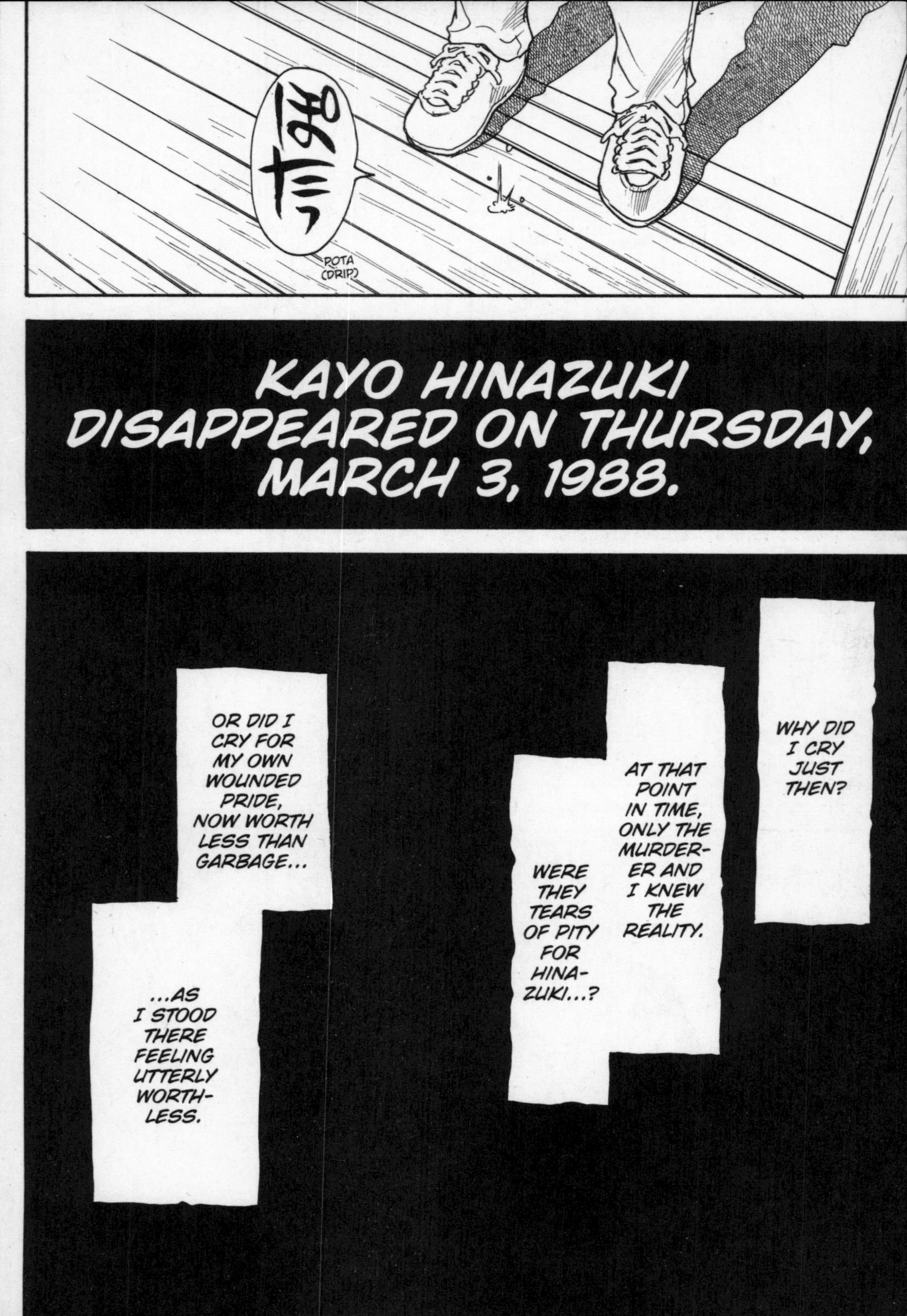
ぽたっ
POTA (DRIP)
KAYO HINAZUKI DISAPPEARED ON THURSDAY, MARCH 3, 1988.
WHY DID I CRY JUST THEN?
AT THAT POINT IN TIME, ONLY THE MURDERER AND I KNEW THE REALITY.
WERE THEY TEARS OF PITY FOR HINAZUKI...?
OR DID I CRY FOR MY OWN WOUNDED PRIDE, NOW WORTH LESS THAN GARBAGE...
...AS I STOOD THERE FEELING UTTERLY WORTHLESS.

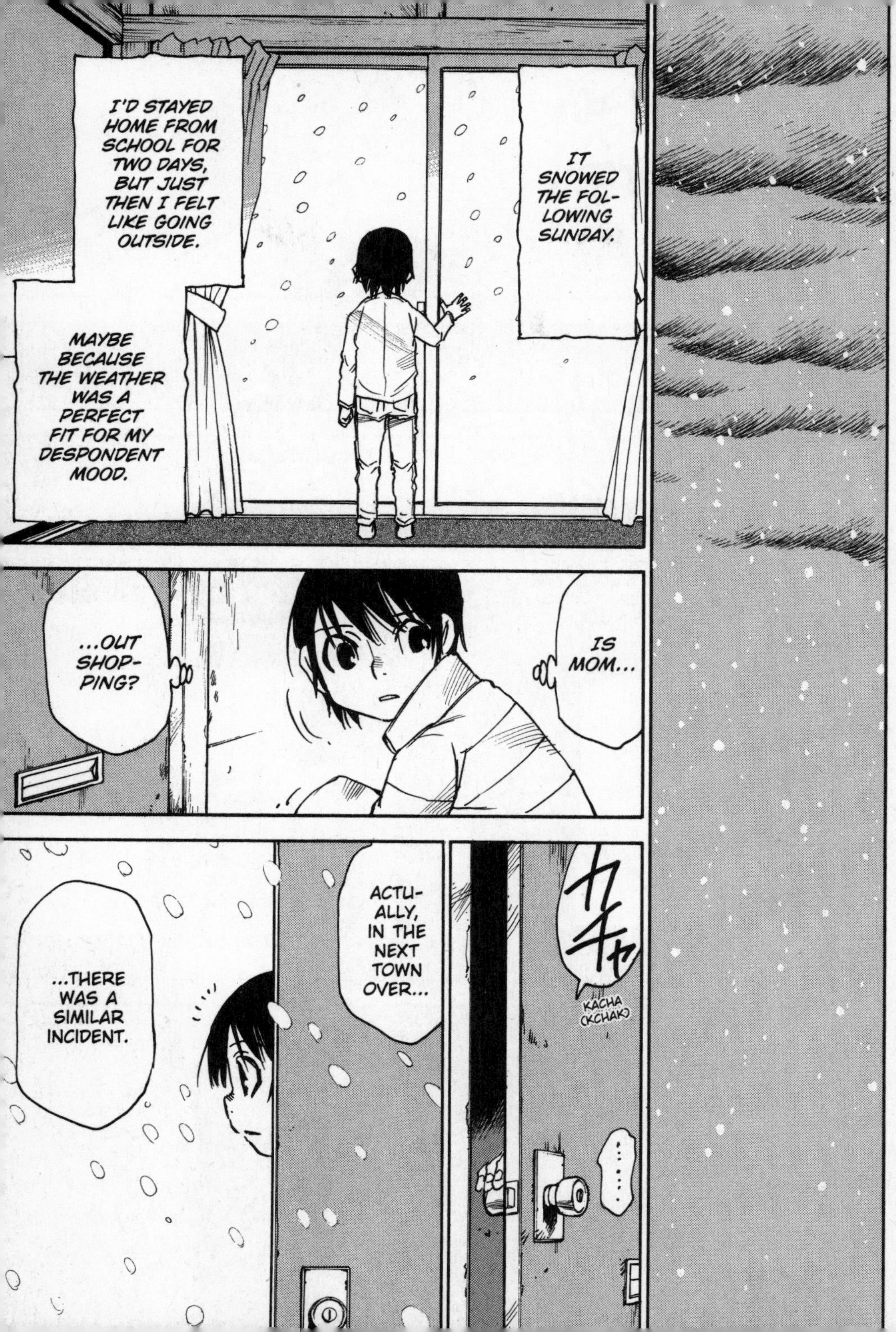
IT SNOWED THE FOL-LOWING SUNDAY.
I'D STAYED HOME FROM SCHOOL FOR TWO DAYS, BUT JUST THEN I FELT LIKE GOING OUTSIDE.
MAYBE BECAUSE THE WEATHER WAS A PERFECT FIT FOR MY DESPONDENT MOOD.
IS MOM...
...OUT SHOP-PING?
カチャ
KACHA (KCHAK)
......
ACTU-ALLY, IN THE NEXT TOWN OVER...
...THERE WAS A SIMILAR INCIDENT.

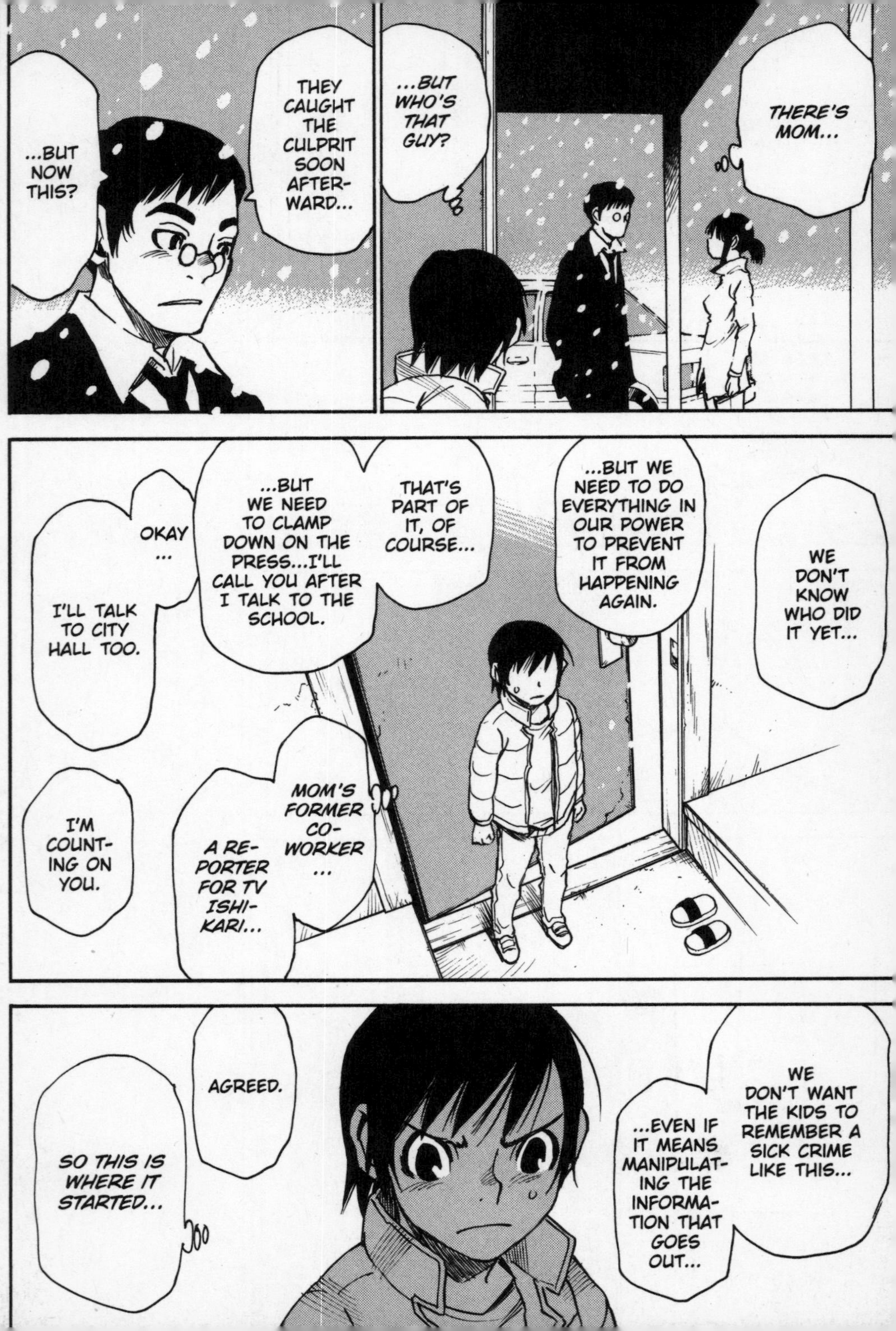
THERE'S MOM...
...BUT WHO'S THAT GUY?
THEY CAUGHT THE CULPRIT SOON AFTER-WARD...
...BUT NOW THIS?
WE DON'T KNOW WHO DID IT YET...
...BUT WE NEED TO DO EVERYTHING IN OUR POWER TO PREVENT IT FROM HAPPENING AGAIN.
THAT'S PART OF IT, OF COURSE...
...BUT WE NEED TO CLAMP DOWN ON THE PRESS...I'LL CALL YOU AFTER I TALK TO THE SCHOOL.
OKAY ...
I'LL TALK TO CITY HALL TOO.
MOM'S FORMER CO-WORKER ...
A RE-PORTER FOR TV ISHI-KARI...
I'M COUNT-ING ON YOU.
WE DON'T WANT THE KIDS TO REMEMBER A SICK CRIME LIKE THIS...
...EVEN IF IT MEANS MANIPULAT-ING THE INFORMA-TION THAT GOES OUT...
AGREED.
SO THIS IS WHERE IT STARTED...

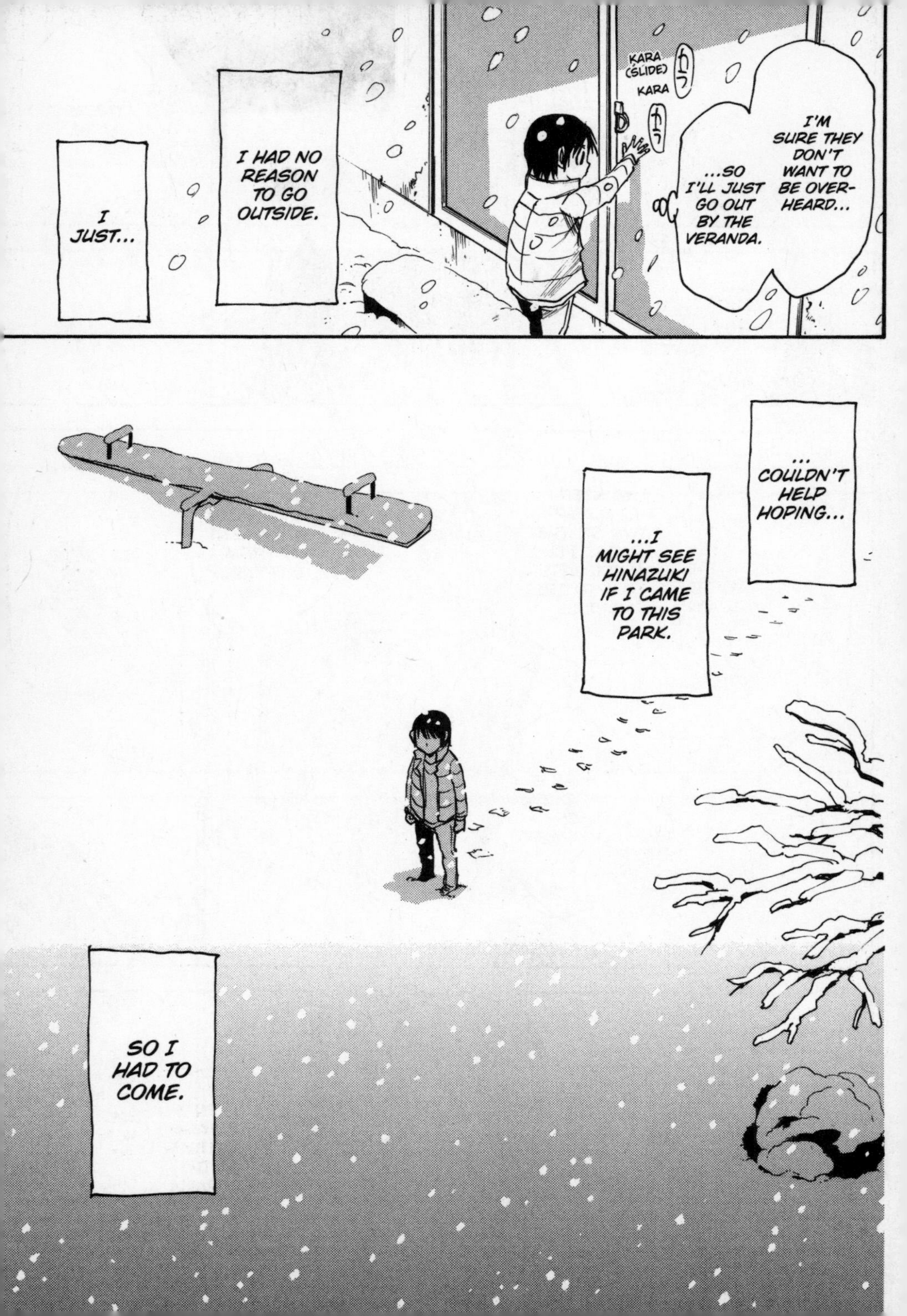
I'M SURE THEY DON'T WANT TO BE OVER-HEARD...
...SO I'LL JUST GO OUT BY THE VERANDA.
KARA (SLIDE) KARA
I HAD NO REASON TO GO OUTSIDE.
I JUST...
... COULDN'T HELP HOPING...
...I MIGHT SEE HINAZUKI IF I CAME TO THIS PARK.
SO I HAD TO COME.

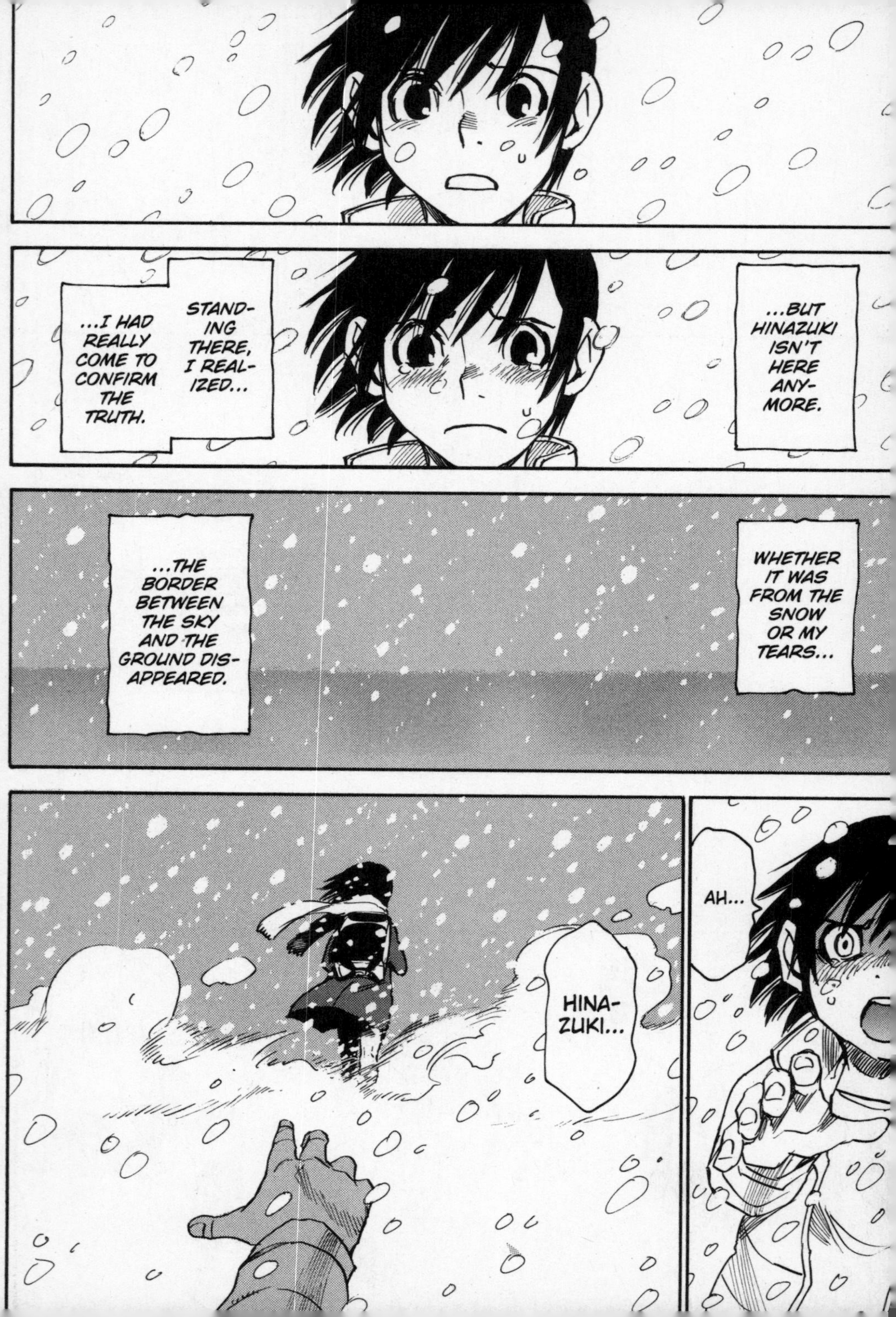
...BUT HINAZUKI ISN'T HERE ANYMORE.
STANDING THERE, I REALIZED...
...I HAD REALLY COME TO CONFIRM THE TRUTH.
WHETHER IT WAS FROM THE SNOW OR MY TEARS...
...THE BORDER BETWEEN THE SKY AND THE GROUND DISAPPEARED.
AH...
HINAZUKI...

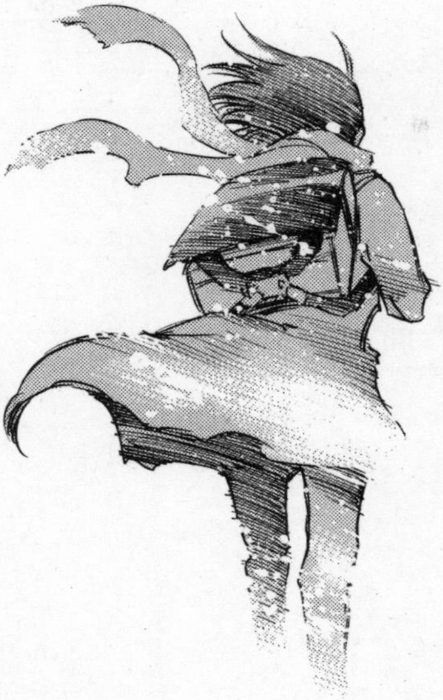

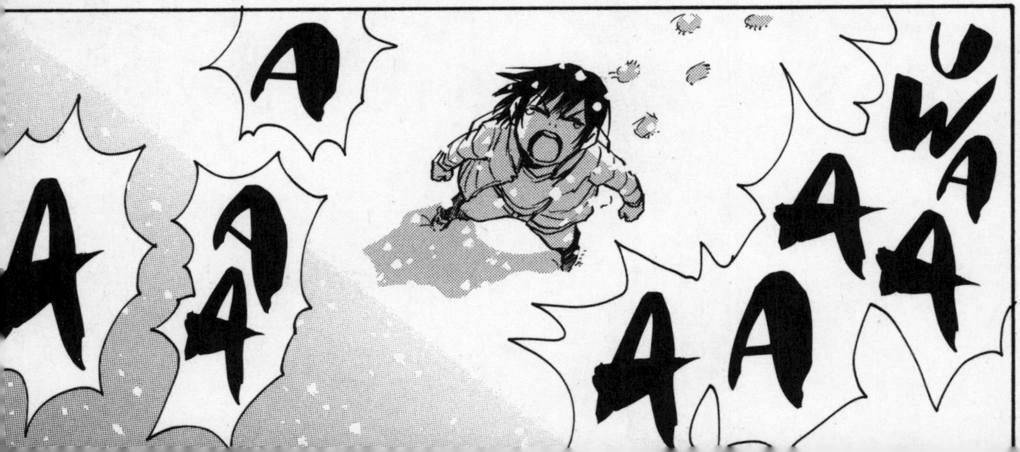
UWAAAAAA
AAAA

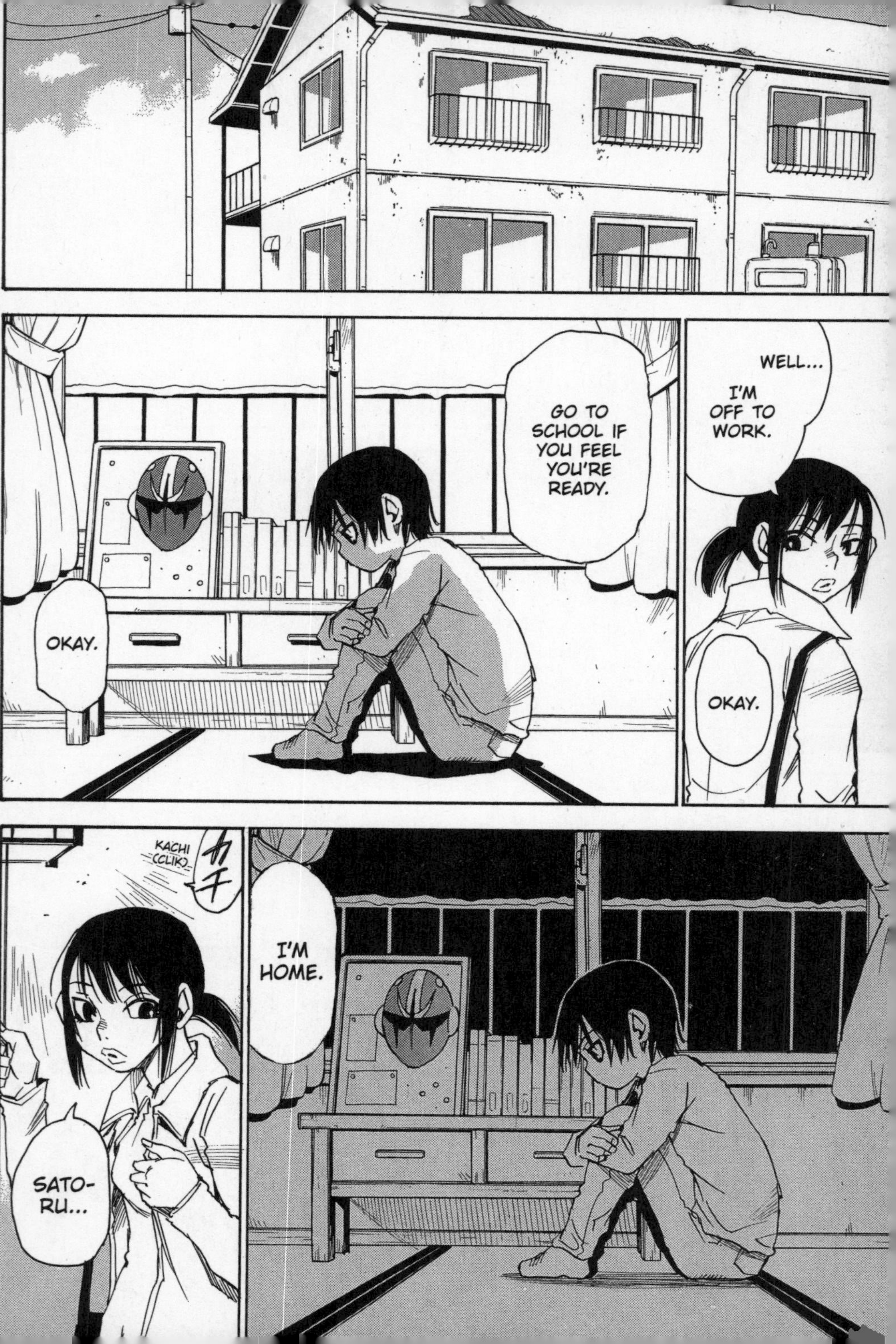
WELL... I'M OFF TO WORK.
OKAY.
GO TO SCHOOL IF YOU FEEL YOU'RE READY.
OKAY.
I'M HOME.
カチ
KACHI (CLIK)
SATO-RU...

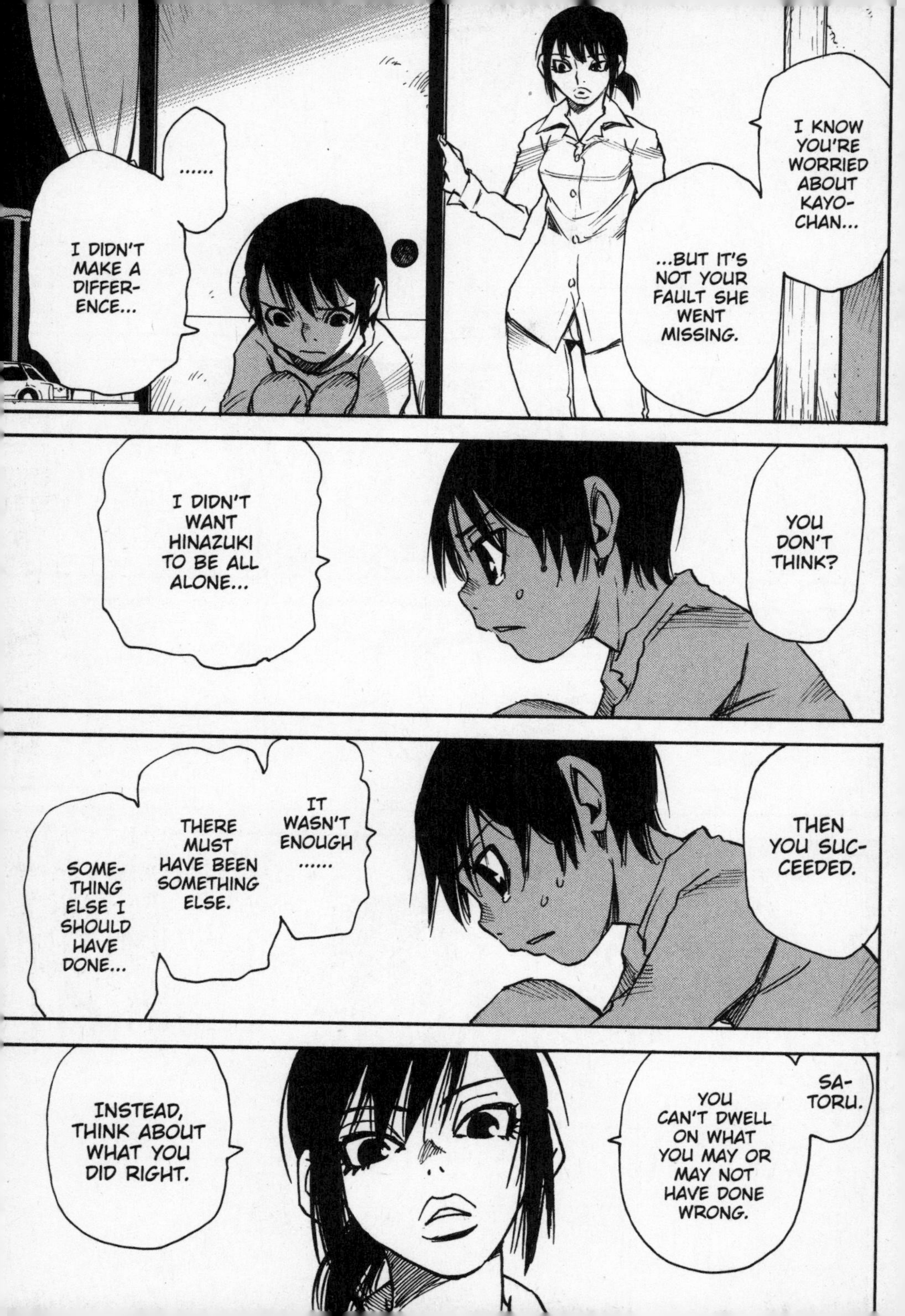
I KNOW YOU'RE WORRIED ABOUT KAYO-CHAN...
...BUT IT'S NOT YOUR FAULT SHE WENT MISSING.
......
I DIDN'T MAKE A DIFFERENCE...
YOU DON'T THINK?
I DIDN'T WANT HINAZUKI TO BE ALL ALONE...
THEN YOU SUCCEEDED.
IT WASN'T ENOUGH ......
THERE MUST HAVE BEEN SOMETHING ELSE.
SOMETHING ELSE I SHOULD HAVE DONE...
SATORU.
YOU CAN'T DWELL ON WHAT YOU MAY OR MAY NOT HAVE DONE WRONG.
INSTEAD, THINK ABOUT WHAT YOU DID RIGHT.

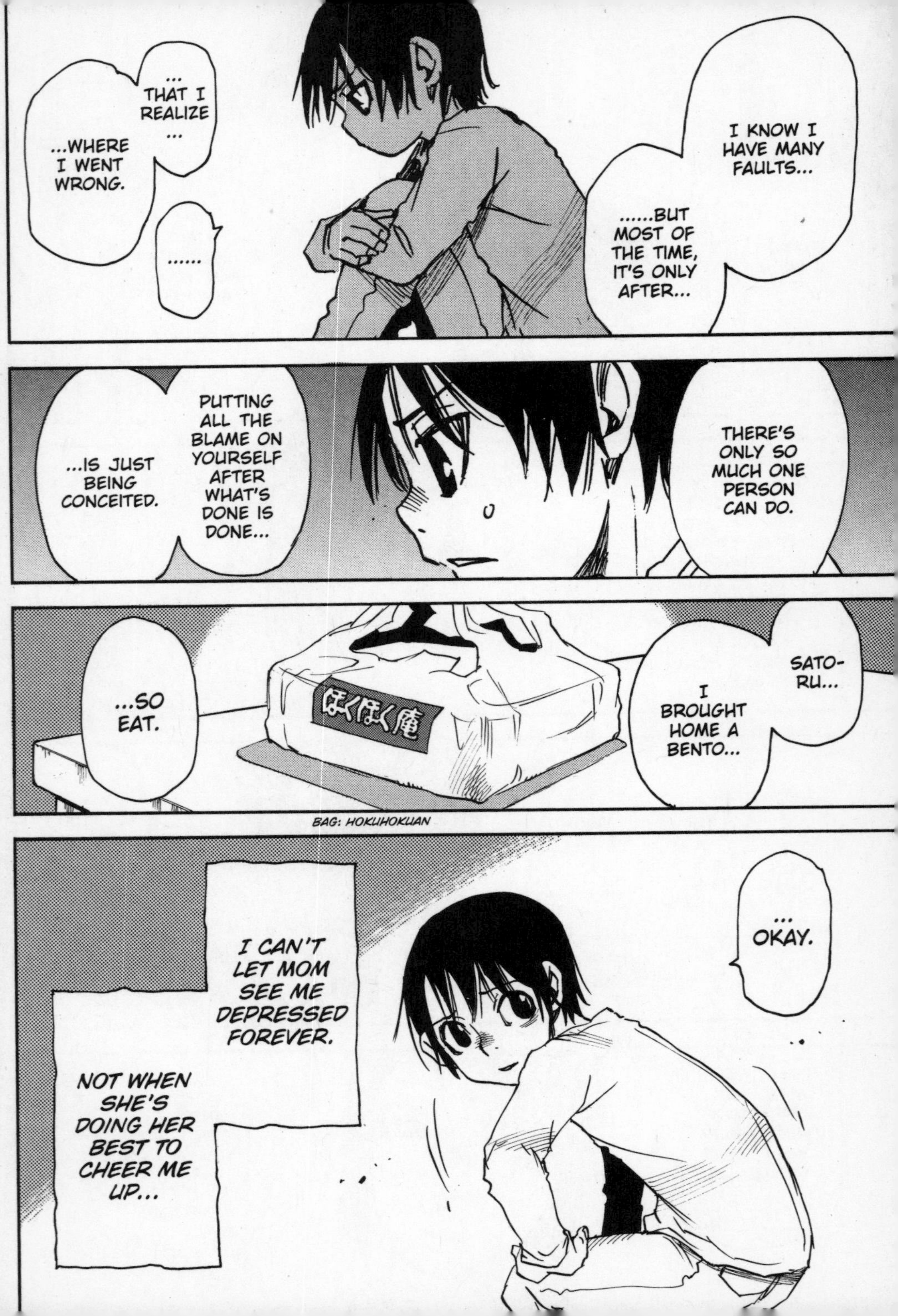
I KNOW I HAVE MANY FAULTS...
......BUT MOST OF THE TIME, IT'S ONLY AFTER...
... THAT I REALIZE ...
...WHERE I WENT WRONG.
......
THERE'S ONLY SO MUCH ONE PERSON CAN DO.
PUTTING ALL THE BLAME ON YOURSELF AFTER WHAT'S DONE IS DONE...
...IS JUST BEING CONCEITED.
SATO-RU...
I BROUGHT HOME A BENTO...
ほくほく庵
...SO EAT.
BAG: HOKUHOKUAN
... OKAY.
I CAN'T LET MOM SEE ME DEPRESSED FOREVER.
NOT WHEN SHE'S DOING HER BEST TO CHEER ME UP...

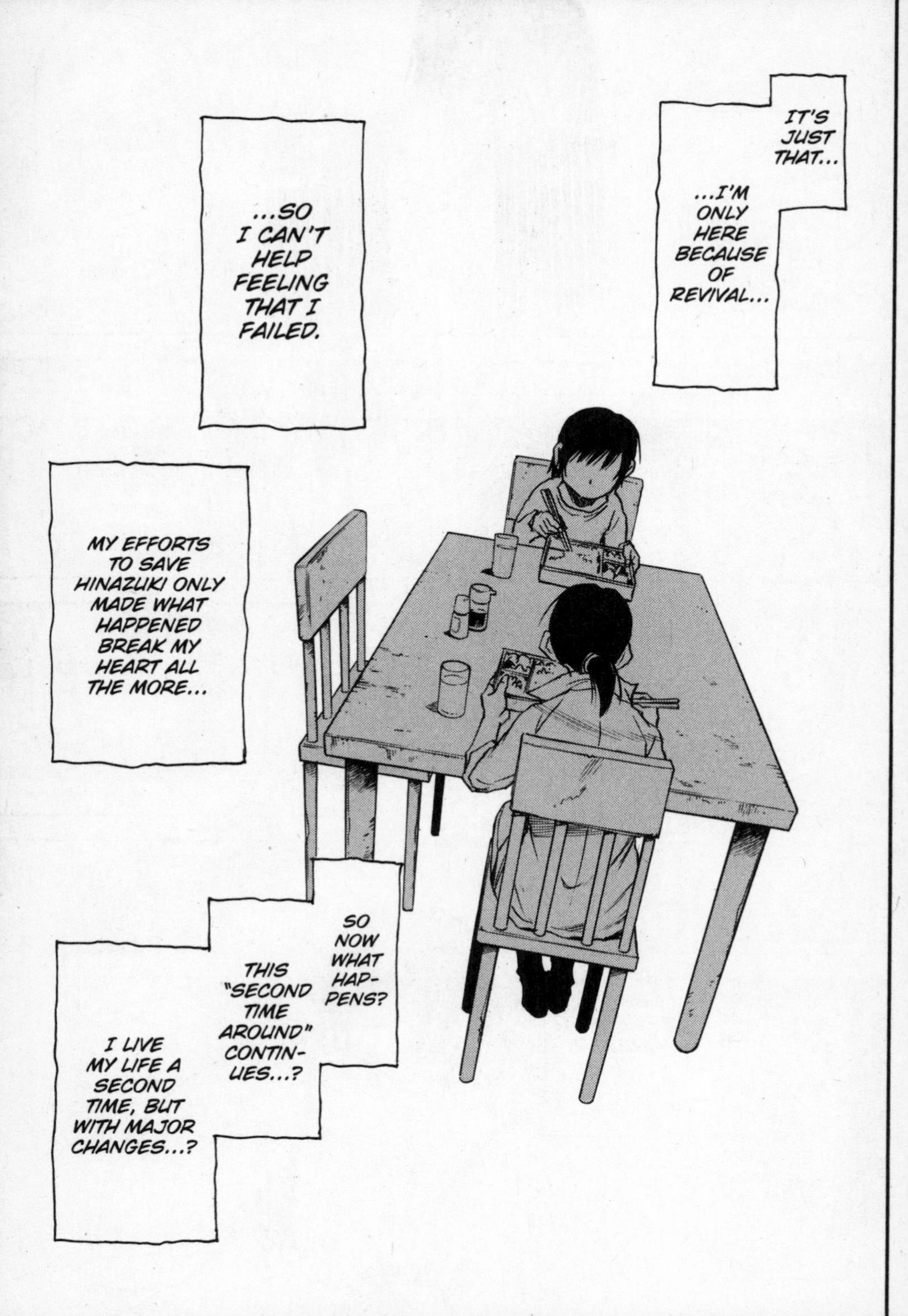
IT'S JUST THAT...
...I'M ONLY HERE BECAUSE OF REVIVAL...
...SO I CAN'T HELP FEELING THAT I FAILED.
MY EFFORTS TO SAVE HINAZUKI ONLY MADE WHAT HAPPENED BREAK MY HEART ALL THE MORE...
SO NOW WHAT HAP-PENS?
THIS "SECOND TIME AROUND" CONTIN-UES...?
I LIVE MY LIFE A SECOND TIME, BUT WITH MAJOR CHANGES...?

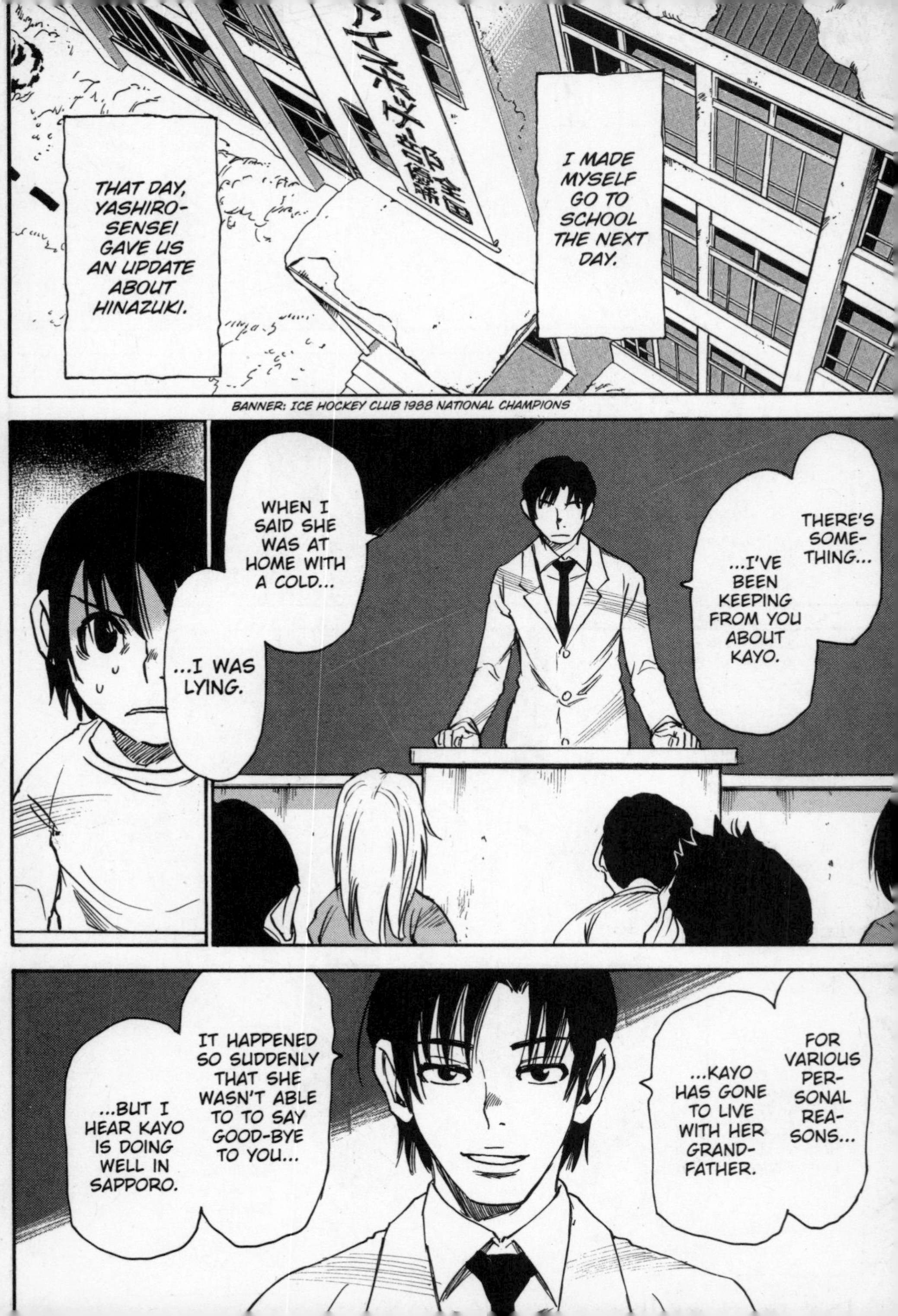
I MADE MYSELF GO TO SCHOOL THE NEXT DAY.
THAT DAY, YASHIRO-SENSEI GAVE US AN UPDATE ABOUT HINAZUKI.
BANNER: ICE HOCKEY CLUB 1988 NATIONAL CHAMPIONS
THERE'S SOMETHING...
...I'VE BEEN KEEPING FROM YOU ABOUT KAYO.
WHEN I SAID SHE WAS AT HOME WITH A COLD...
...I WAS LYING.
FOR VARIOUS PERSONAL REASONS...
...KAYO HAS GONE TO LIVE WITH HER GRANDFATHER.
IT HAPPENED SO SUDDENLY THAT SHE WASN'T ABLE TO TO SAY GOOD-BYE TO YOU...
...BUT I HEAR KAYO IS DOING WELL IN SAPPORO.

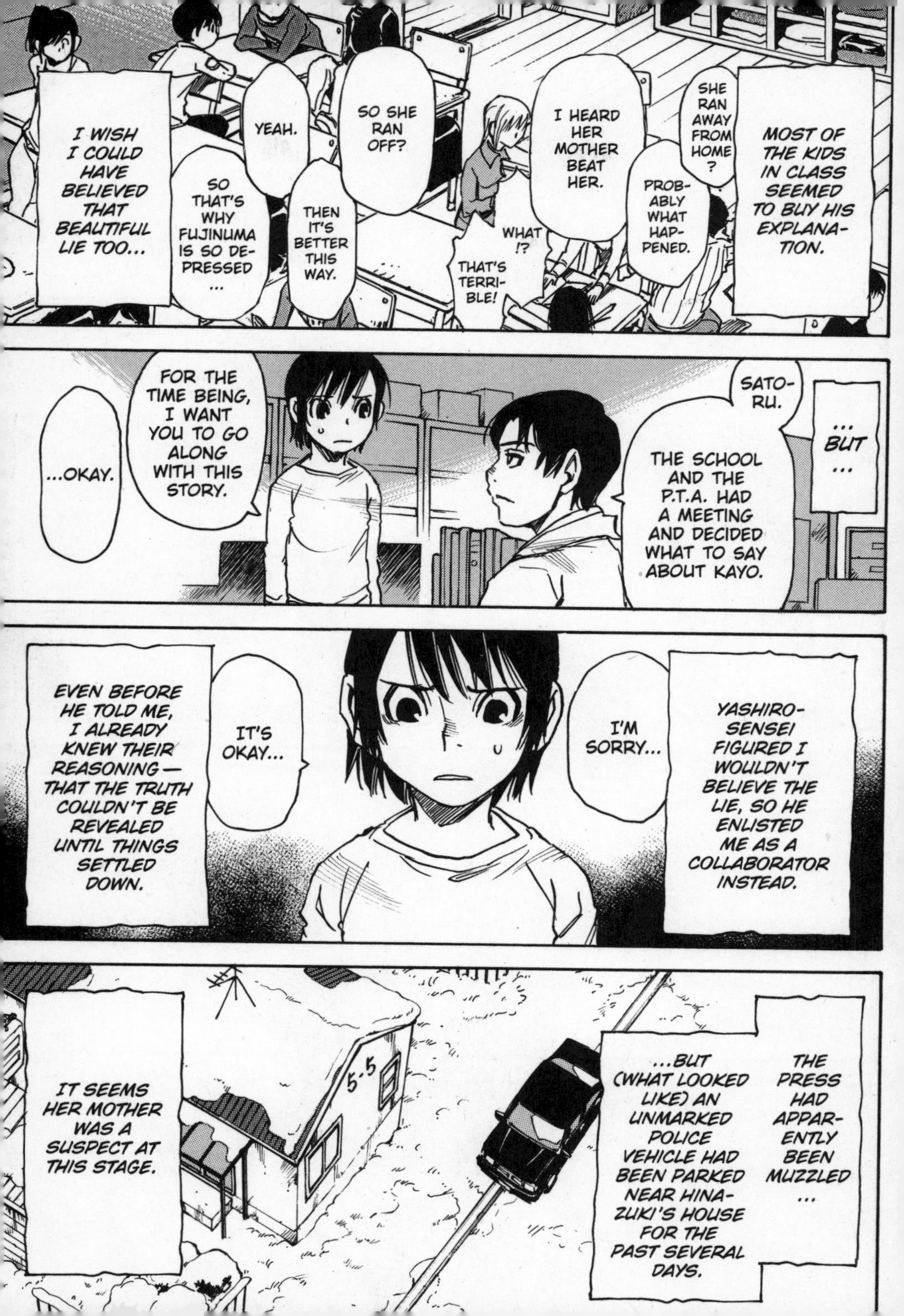
MOST OF THE KIDS IN CLASS SEEMED TO BUY HIS EXPLANATION.
SHE RAN AWAY FROM HOME?
PROBABLY WHAT HAPPENED.
I HEARD HER MOTHER BEAT HER.
WHAT!?
THAT'S TERRIBLE!
SO SHE RAN OFF?
YEAH.
THEN IT'S BETTER THIS WAY.
...
SO THAT'S WHY FUJINUMA IS SO DEPRESSED...
I WISH I COULD HAVE BELIEVED THAT BEAUTIFUL LIE TOO...
...BUT...
SATORU.
THE SCHOOL AND THE P.T.A. HAD A MEETING AND DECIDED WHAT TO SAY ABOUT KAYO.
FOR THE TIME BEING, I WANT YOU TO GO ALONG WITH THIS STORY.
...OKAY.
YASHIRO-SENSEI FIGURED I WOULDN'T BELIEVE THE LIE, SO HE ENLISTED ME AS A COLLABORATOR INSTEAD.
I'M SORRY...
IT'S OKAY...
EVEN BEFORE HE TOLD ME, I ALREADY KNEW THEIR REASONING—THAT THE TRUTH COULDN'T BE REVEALED UNTIL THINGS SETTLED DOWN.
THE PRESS HAD APPARENTLY BEEN MUZZLED...
...BUT (WHAT LOOKED LIKE) AN UNMARKED POLICE VEHICLE HAD BEEN PARKED NEAR HINAZUKI'S HOUSE FOR THE PAST SEVERAL DAYS.
IT SEEMS HER MOTHER WAS A SUSPECT AT THIS STAGE.

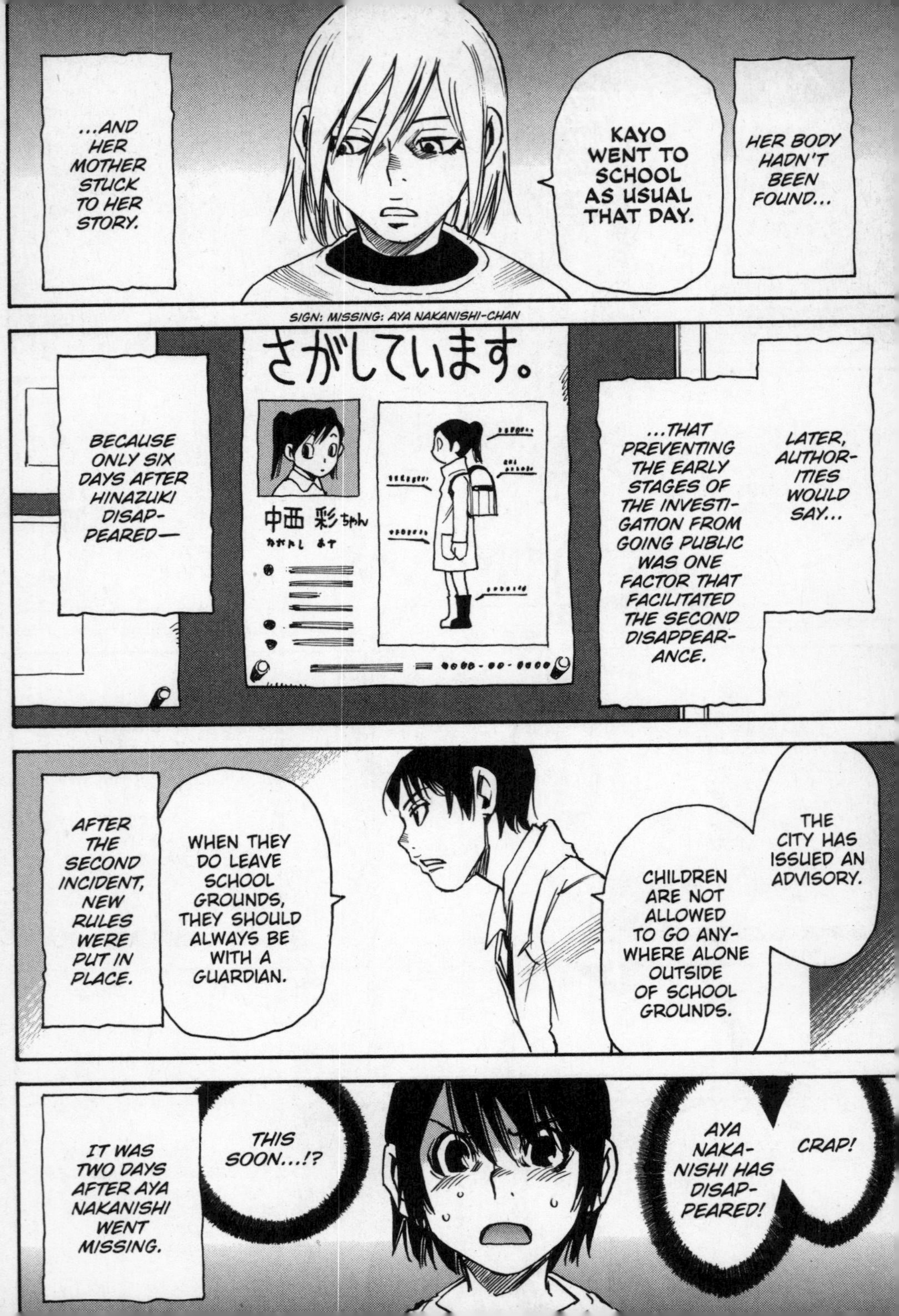
HER BODY HADN'T BEEN FOUND...
KAYO WENT TO SCHOOL AS USUAL THAT DAY.
...AND HER MOTHER STUCK TO HER STORY.
SIGN: MISSING: AYA NAKANISHI-CHAN
LATER, AUTHOR-ITIES WOULD SAY...
...THAT PREVENTING THE EARLY STAGES OF THE INVESTI-GATION FROM GOING PUBLIC WAS ONE FACTOR THAT FACILITATED THE SECOND DISAPPEAR-ANCE.
さがしています。
中西 彩ちゃん
BECAUSE ONLY SIX DAYS AFTER HINAZUKI DISAP-PEARED—
THE CITY HAS ISSUED AN ADVISORY.
CHILDREN ARE NOT ALLOWED TO GO ANY-WHERE ALONE OUTSIDE OF SCHOOL GROUNDS.
WHEN THEY DO LEAVE SCHOOL GROUNDS, THEY SHOULD ALWAYS BE WITH A GUARDIAN.
AFTER THE SECOND INCIDENT, NEW RULES WERE PUT IN PLACE.
CRAP!
AYA NAKA-NISHI HAS DISAP-PEARED!
THIS SOON...!?
IT WAS TWO DAYS AFTER AYA NAKANISHI WENT MISSING.

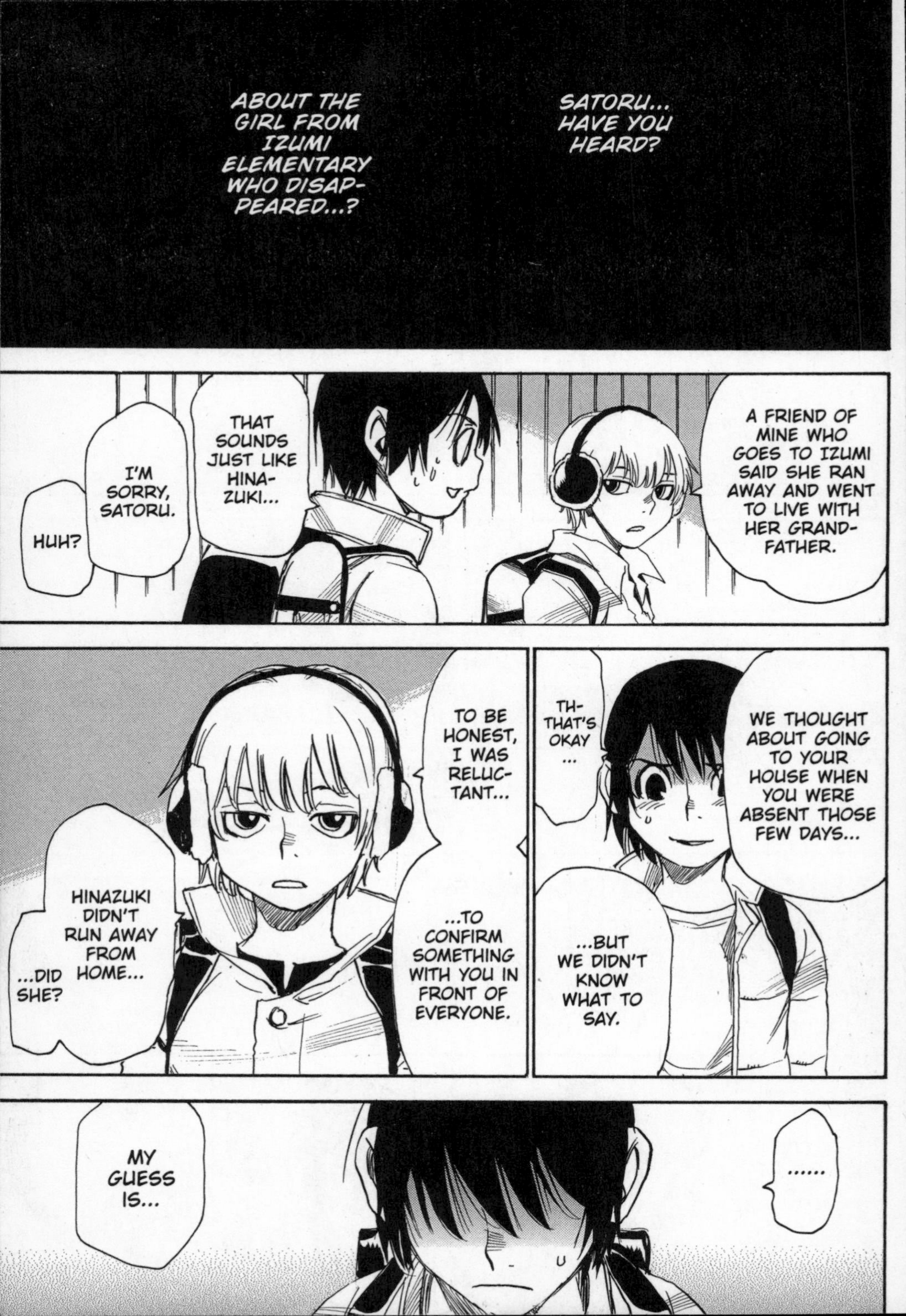
SATORU... HAVE YOU HEARD?
ABOUT THE GIRL FROM IZUMI ELEMENTARY WHO DISAP-PEARED...?
A FRIEND OF MINE WHO GOES TO IZUMI SAID SHE RAN AWAY AND WENT TO LIVE WITH HER GRAND-FATHER.
THAT SOUNDS JUST LIKE HINA-ZUKI...
I'M SORRY, SATORU.
HUH?
WE THOUGHT ABOUT GOING TO YOUR HOUSE WHEN YOU WERE ABSENT THOSE FEW DAYS...
TH-THAT'S OKAY ...
...BUT WE DIDN'T KNOW WHAT TO SAY.
TO BE HONEST, I WAS RELUC-TANT...
...TO CONFIRM SOMETHING WITH YOU IN FRONT OF EVERYONE.
HINAZUKI DIDN'T RUN AWAY FROM HOME...
...DID SHE?
......
MY GUESS IS...

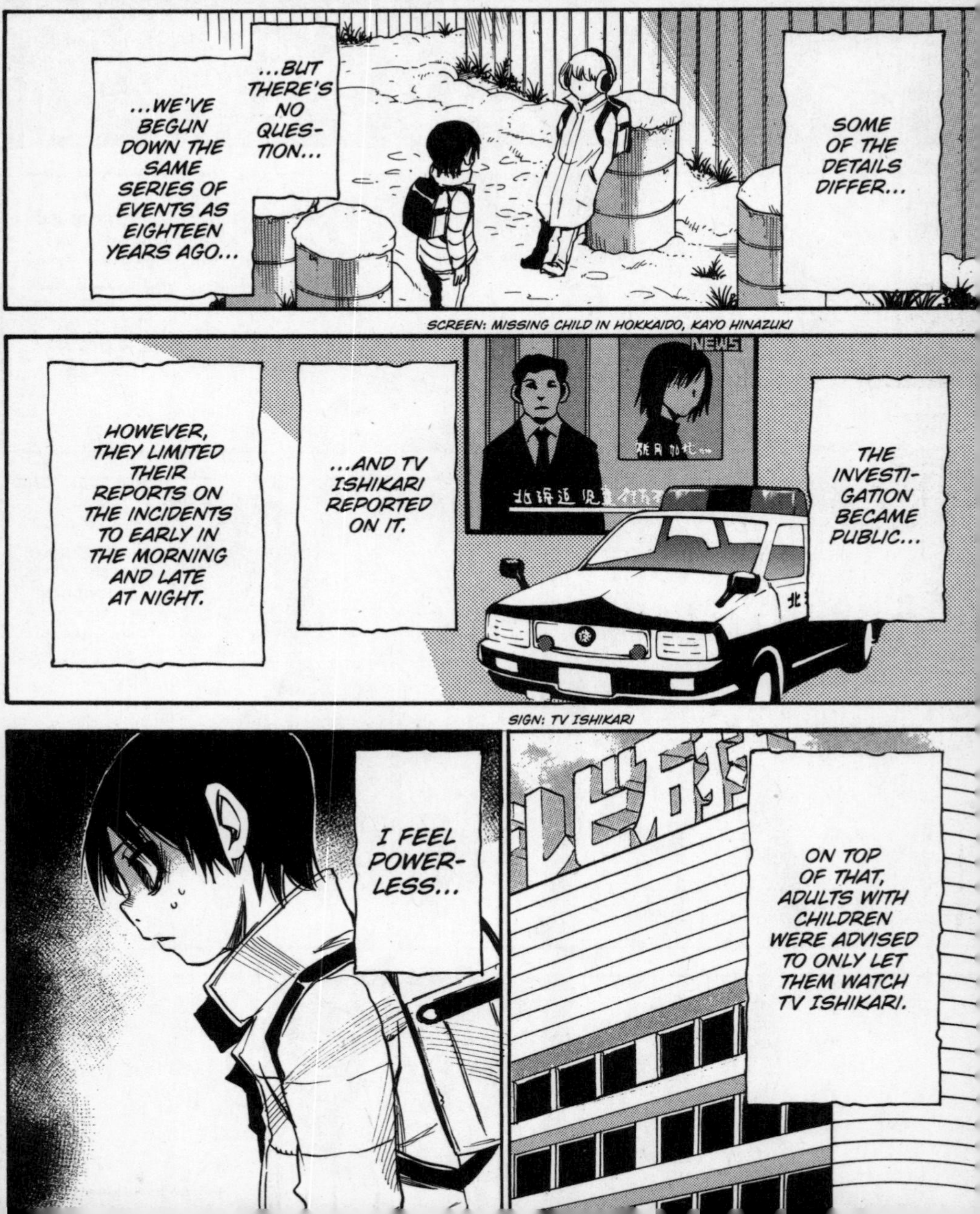
SOME OF THE DETAILS DIFFER...
...BUT THERE'S NO QUESTION...
...WE'VE BEGUN DOWN THE SAME SERIES OF EVENTS AS EIGHTEEN YEARS AGO...
SCREEN: MISSING CHILD IN HOKKAIDO, KAYO HINAZUKI
THE INVESTIGATION BECAME PUBLIC...
...AND TV ISHIKARI REPORTED ON IT.
HOWEVER, THEY LIMITED THEIR REPORTS ON THE INCIDENTS TO EARLY IN THE MORNING AND LATE AT NIGHT.
SIGN: TV ISHIKARI
ON TOP OF THAT, ADULTS WITH CHILDREN WERE ADVISED TO ONLY LET THEM WATCH TV ISHIKARI.
I FEEL POWERLESS...

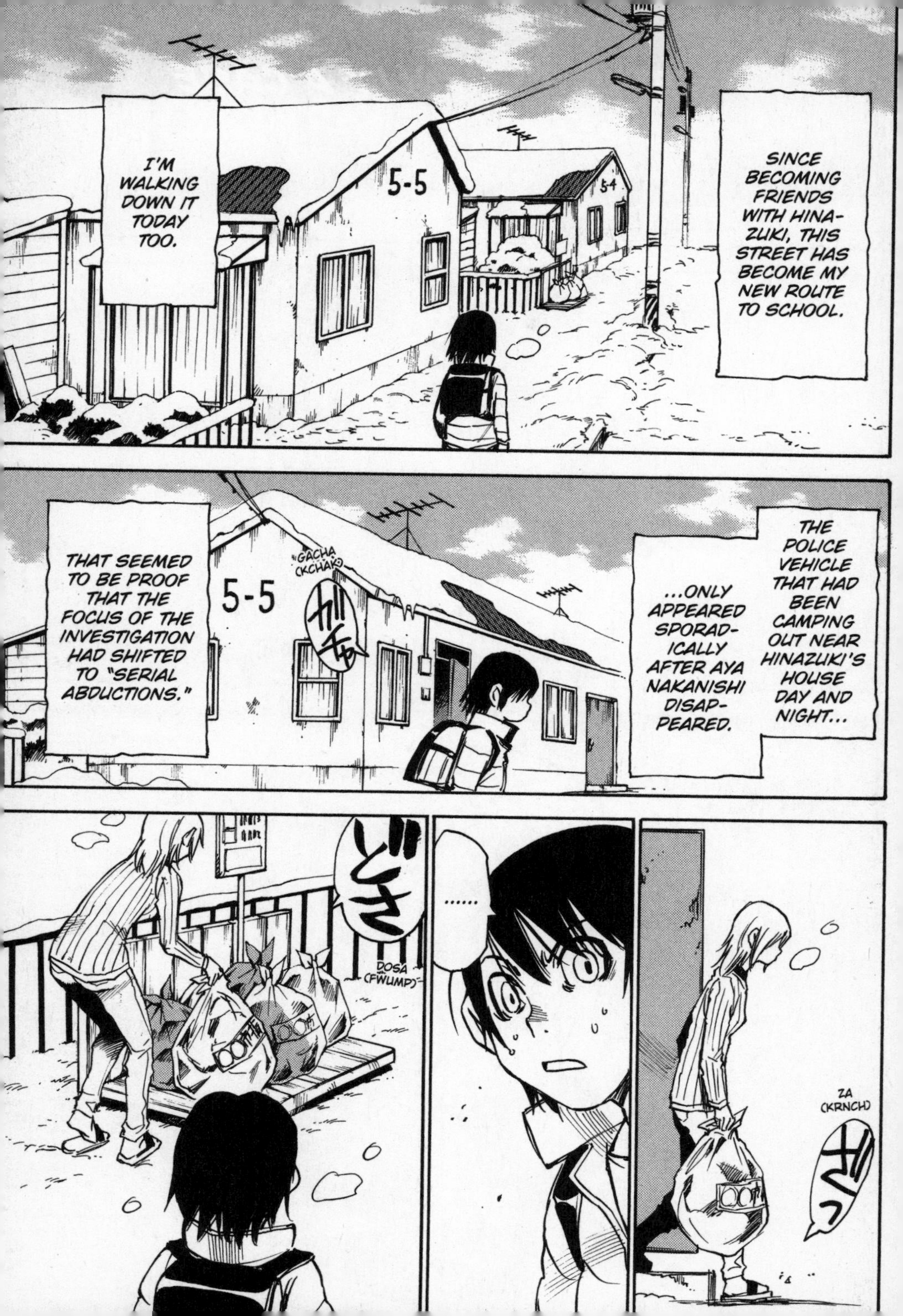
SINCE BECOMING FRIENDS WITH HINA-ZUKI, THIS STREET HAS BECOME MY NEW ROUTE TO SCHOOL.
I'M WALKING DOWN IT TODAY TOO.
THE POLICE VEHICLE THAT HAD BEEN CAMPING OUT NEAR HINAZUKI'S HOUSE DAY AND NIGHT...
...ONLY APPEARED SPORAD-ICALLY AFTER AYA NAKANISHI DISAP-PEARED.
GACHA (KCHAK)
THAT SEEMED TO BE PROOF THAT THE FOCUS OF THE INVESTIGATION HAD SHIFTED TO "SERIAL ABDUCTIONS."
ZA (KRNCH)
......
DOSA (FWUMP)

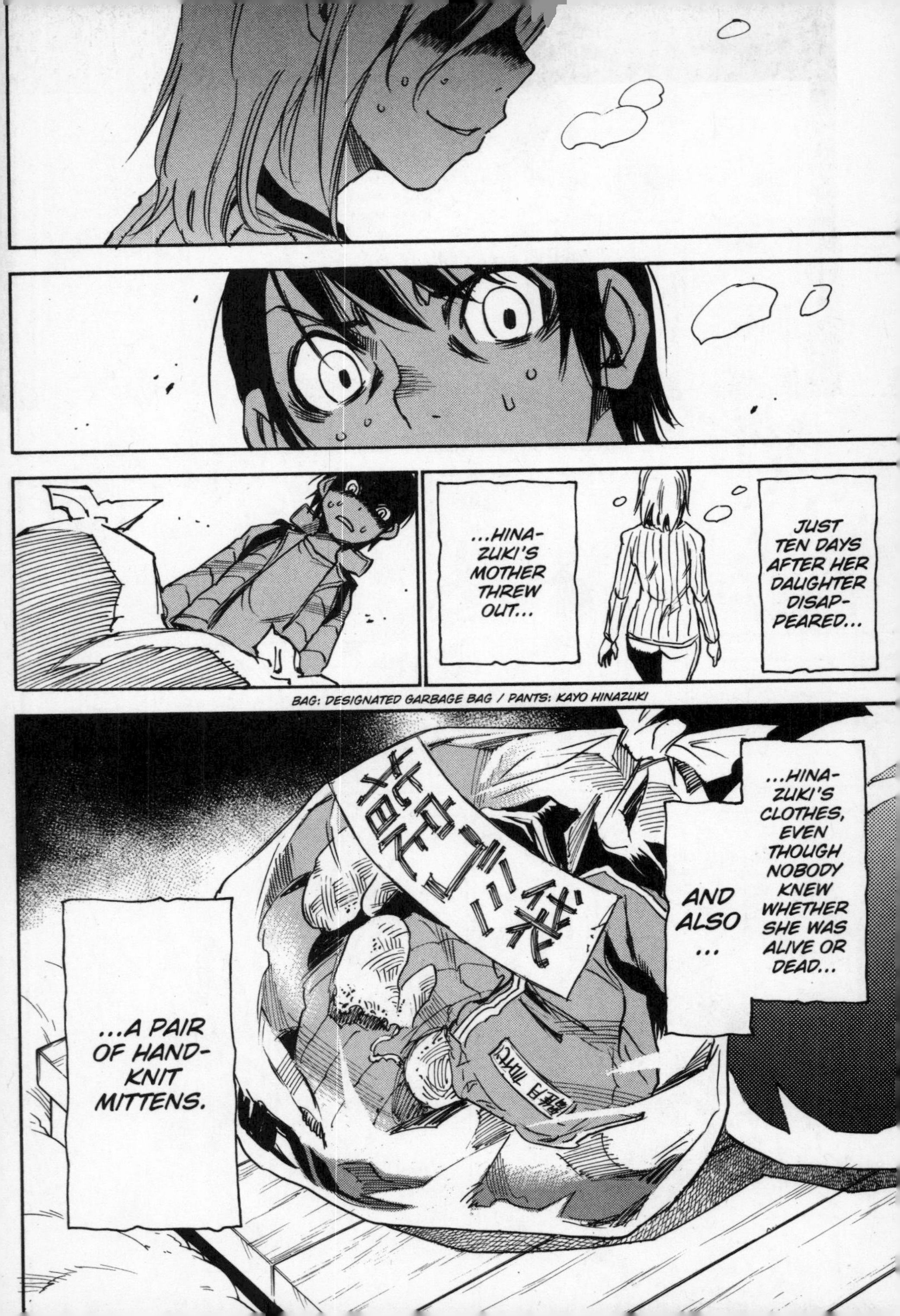
JUST TEN DAYS AFTER HER DAUGHTER DISAP-PEARED...
...HINA-ZUKI'S MOTHER THREW OUT...
BAG: DESIGNATED GARBAGE BAG / PANTS: KAYO HINAZUKI
...HINA-ZUKI'S CLOTHES, EVEN THOUGH NOBODY KNEW WHETHER SHE WAS ALIVE OR DEAD...
AND ALSO...
...A PAIR OF HAND-KNIT MITTENS.
指定ゴミ袋

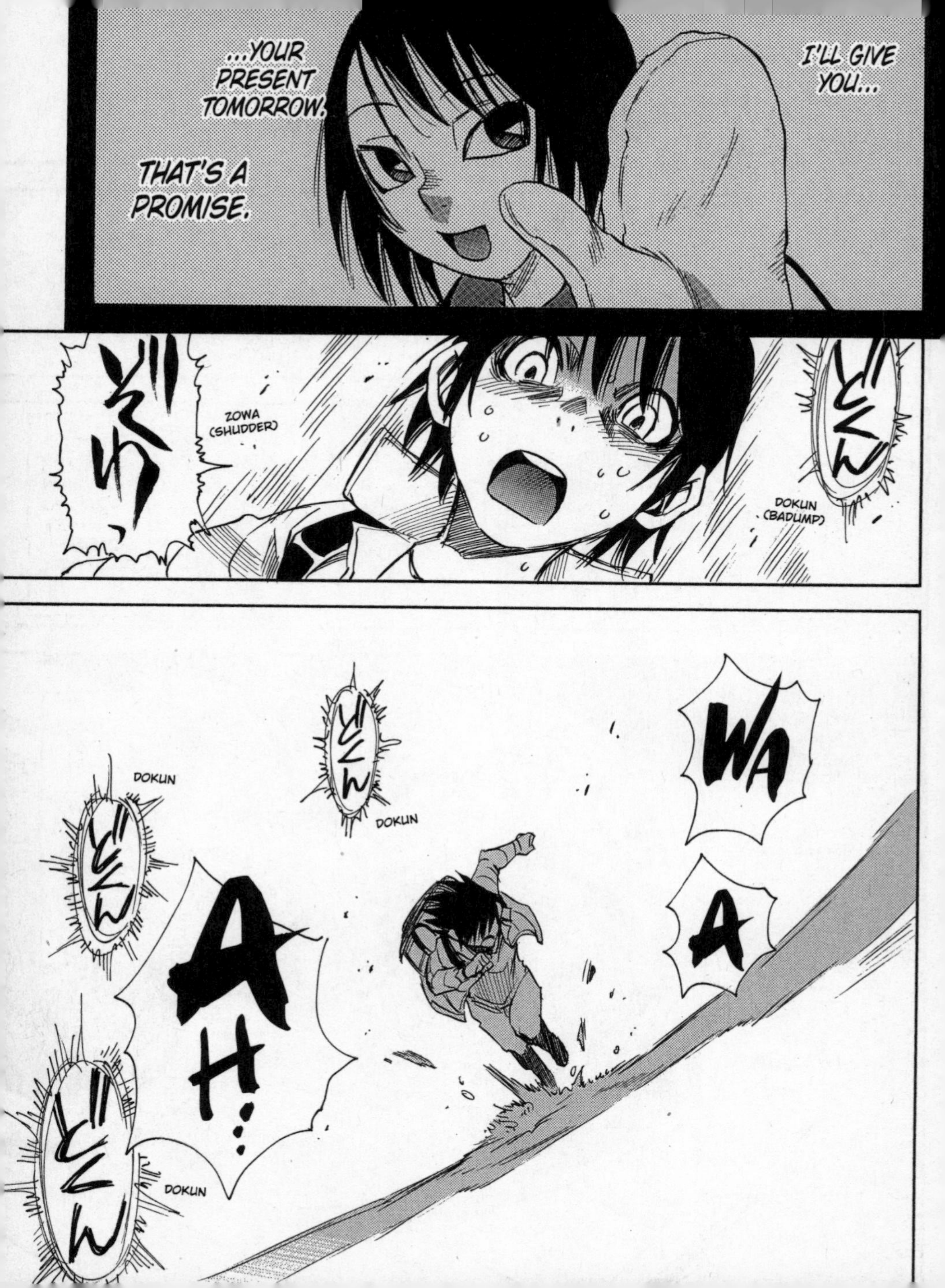
I'LL GIVE YOU...
...YOUR PRESENT TOMORROW.
THAT'S A PROMISE.
どくん
DOKUN (BADUMP)
ぞわっ
ZOWA (SHUDDER)
WA
A
どくん
DOKUN
AH!!
どくん
DOKUN
どくん
DOKUN

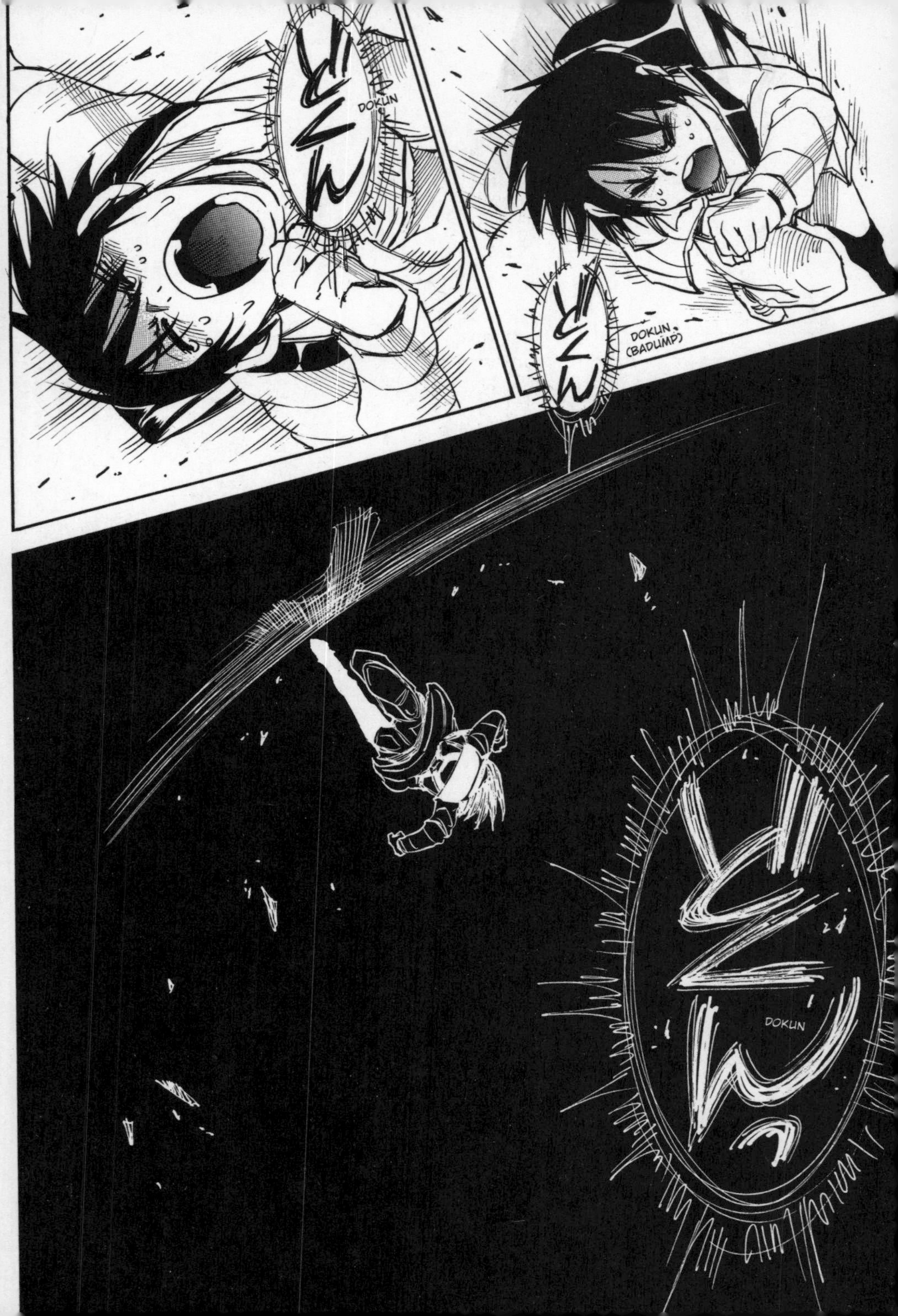
DOKUN
(BADUMP)
DOKUN
DOKUN

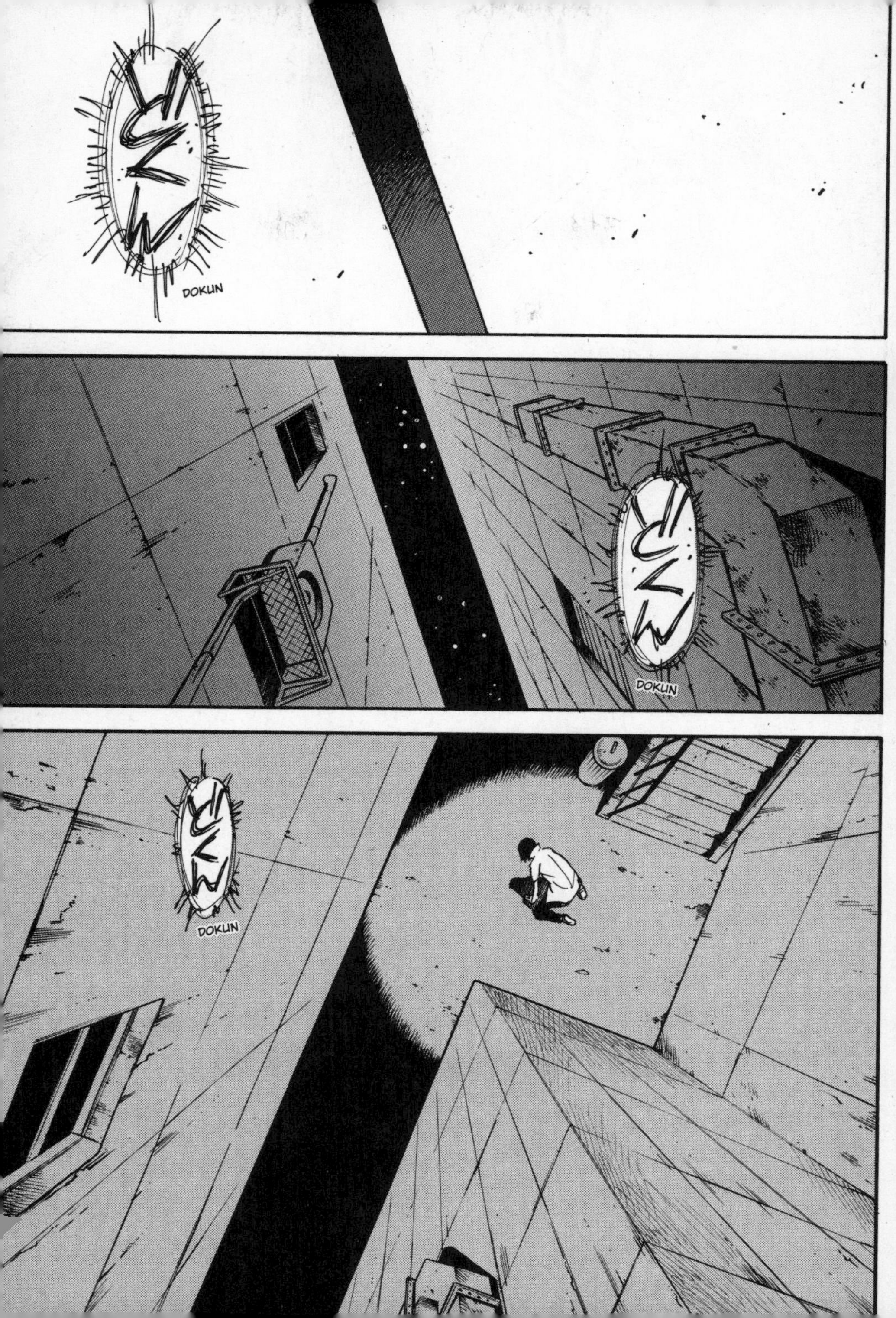
DOKUN
DOKUN
DOKUN

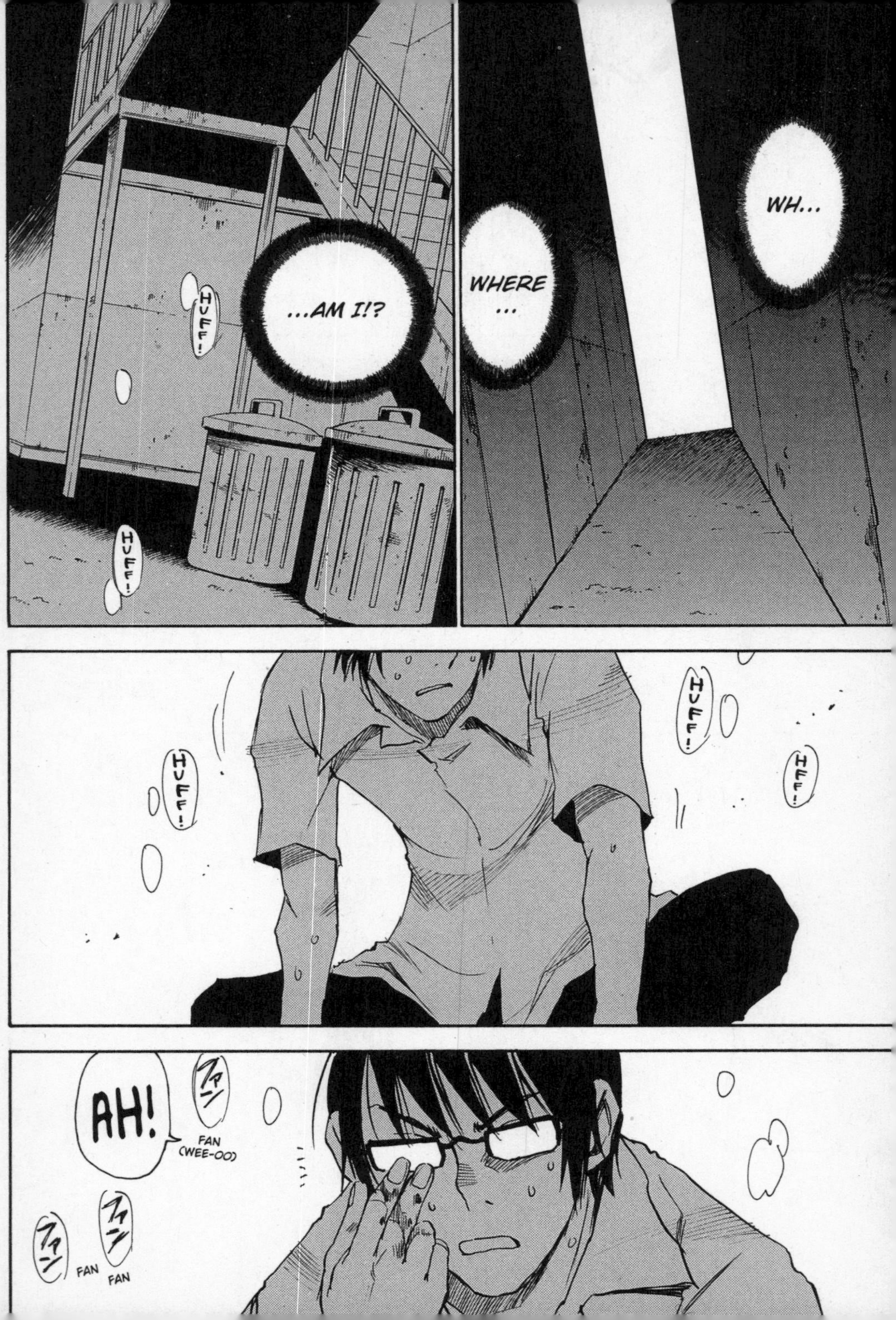
WH...
WHERE ...
...AM I!?
HUFF!
HUFF!
HUFF!
HFF!
HUFF!
AH!
FAN (WEE-OO)
FAN
FAN

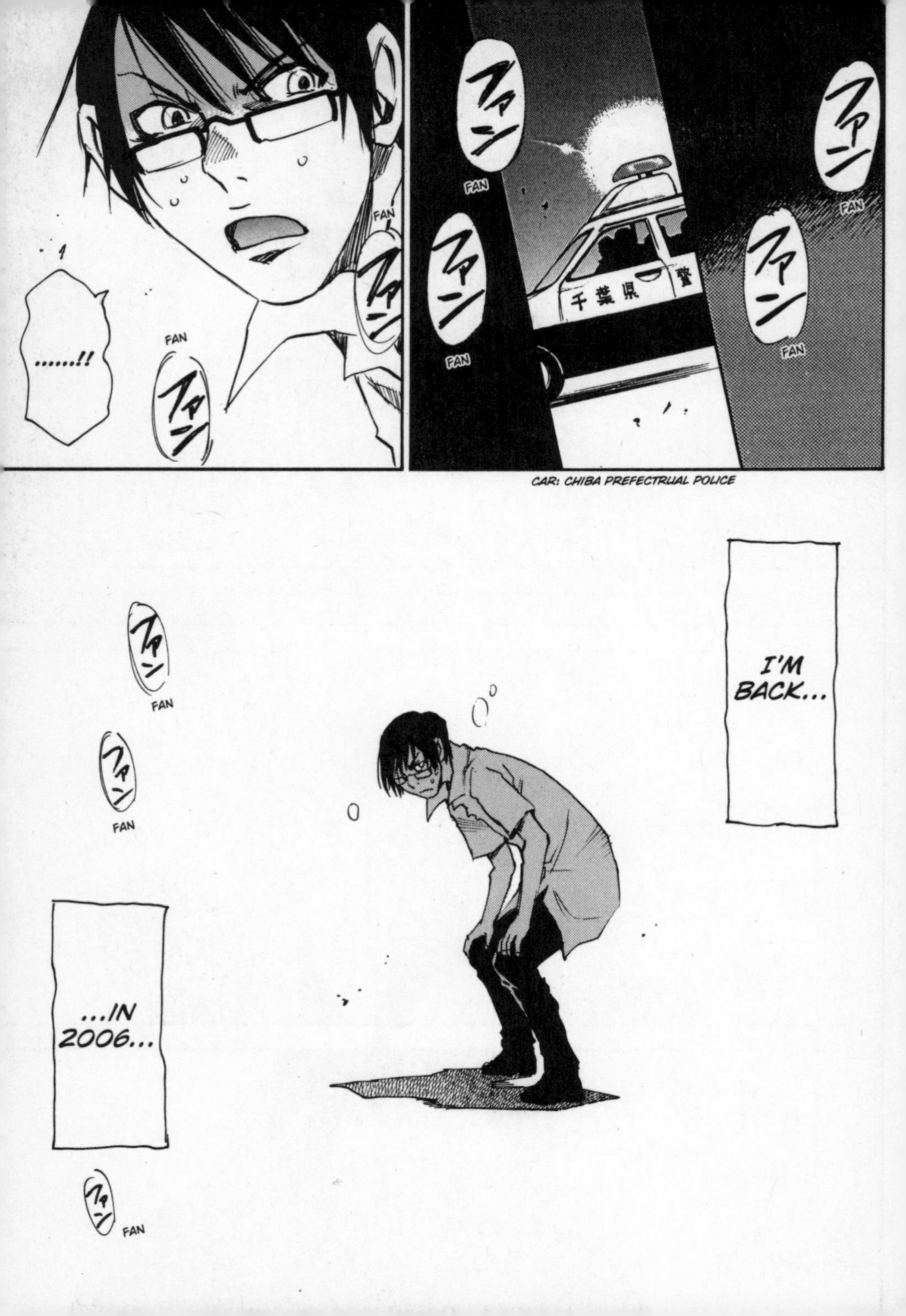
ファン
FAN
ファン
FAN
ファン
FAN
ファン
FAN
千葉県警
FAN
ファン
......!!
FAN
ファン
I'M BACK...
ファン
FAN
ファン
FAN
...IN 2006...
ファン
FAN

CAR: CHIBA PREFECTRUAL POLICE

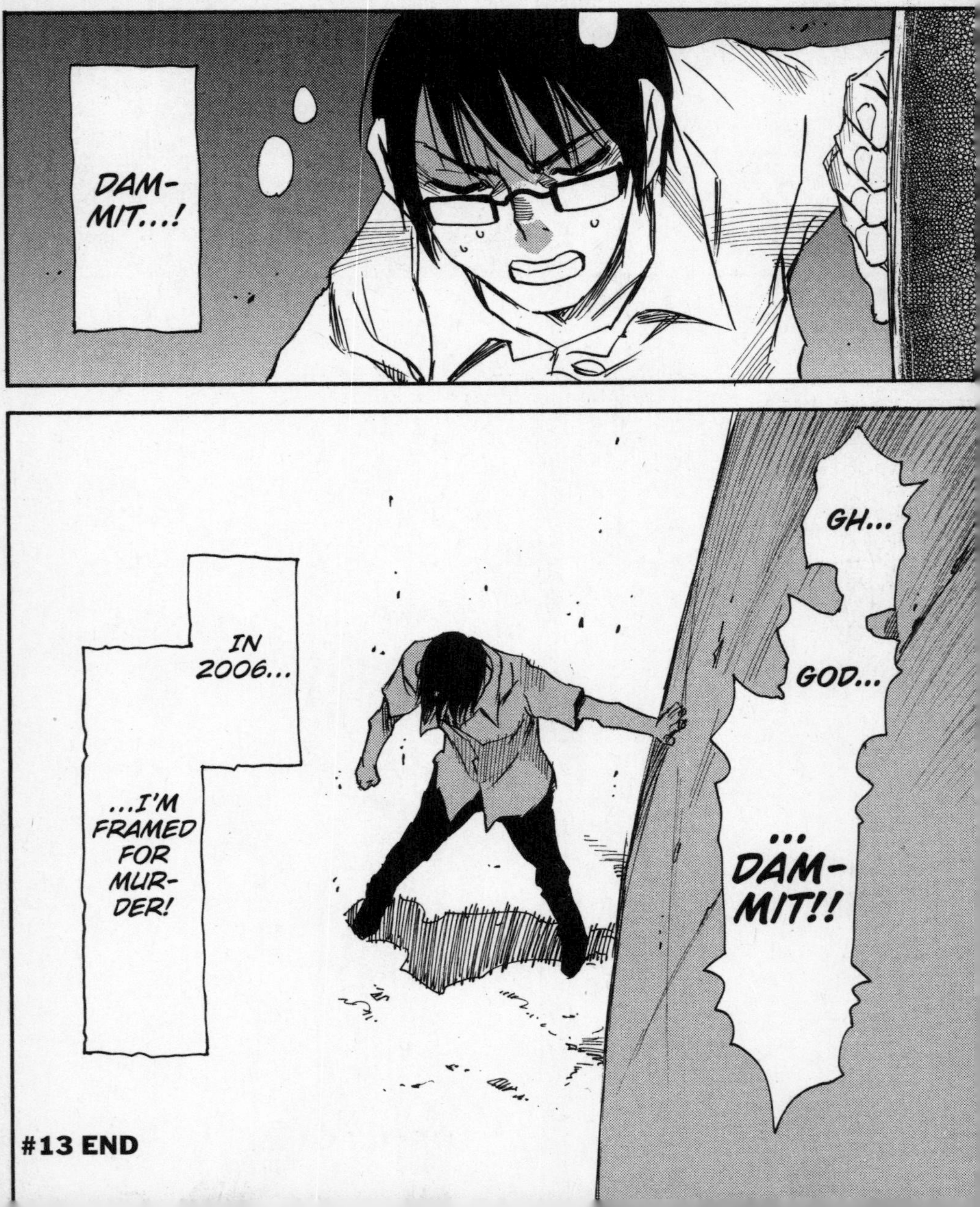
DAM-
MIT...!
GH...
GOD...
...DÄM-
MIT!!
IN
2006...
...I'M
FRAMED
FOR
MUR-
DER!
#13 END

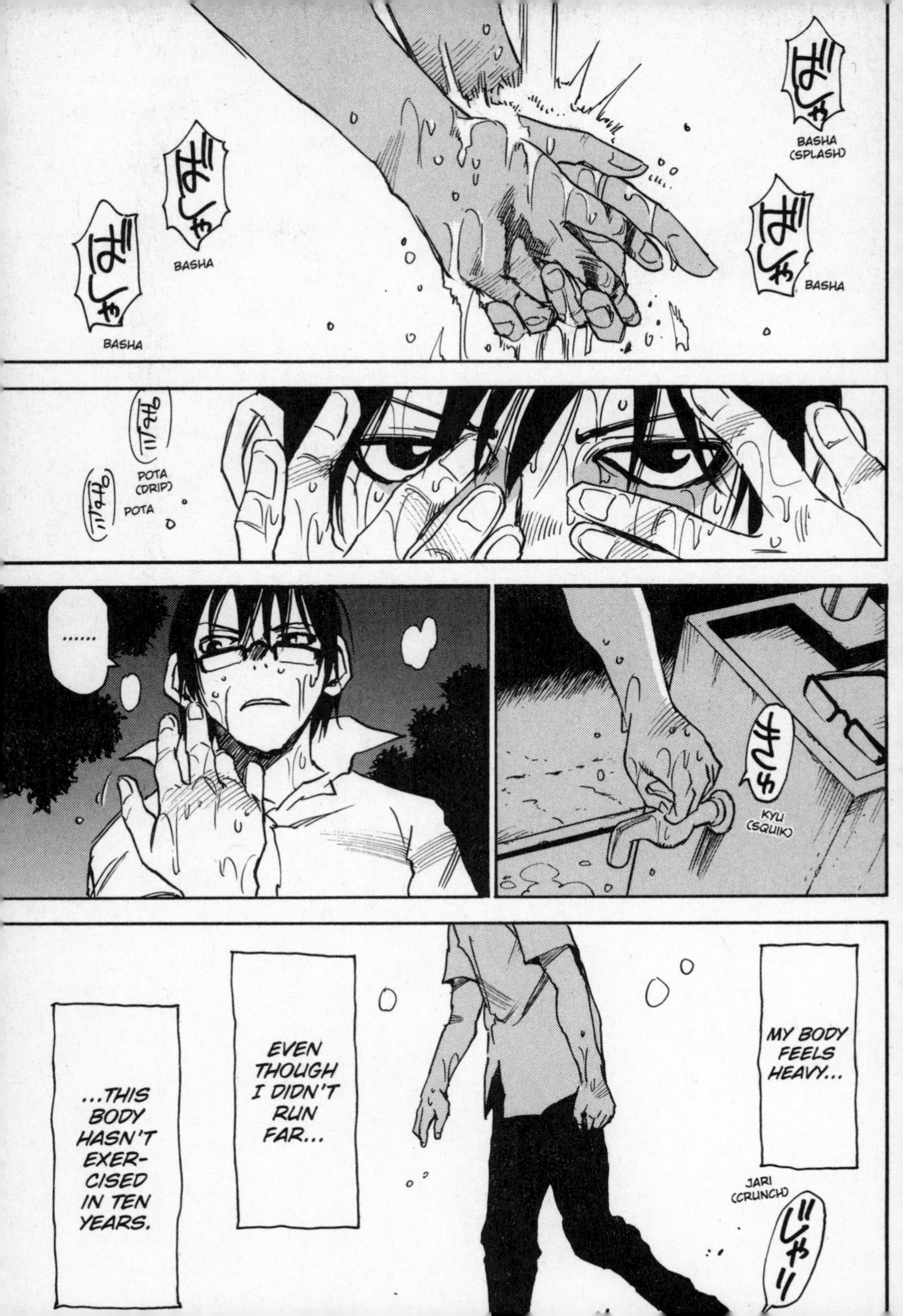

ばしゃ
BASHA (SPLASH)
ばしゃ
BASHA
ばしゃ
BASHA
ばしゃ
BASHA
ぽた
POTA (DRIP)
ぽた
POTA
きゅ
KYU (SQUIK)
......
MY BODY FEELS HEAVY...
JARI (CRUNCH)
じゃり
EVEN THOUGH I DIDN'T RUN FAR...
...THIS BODY HASN'T EXER-CISED IN TEN YEARS.

#14: Under Siege, May 2006

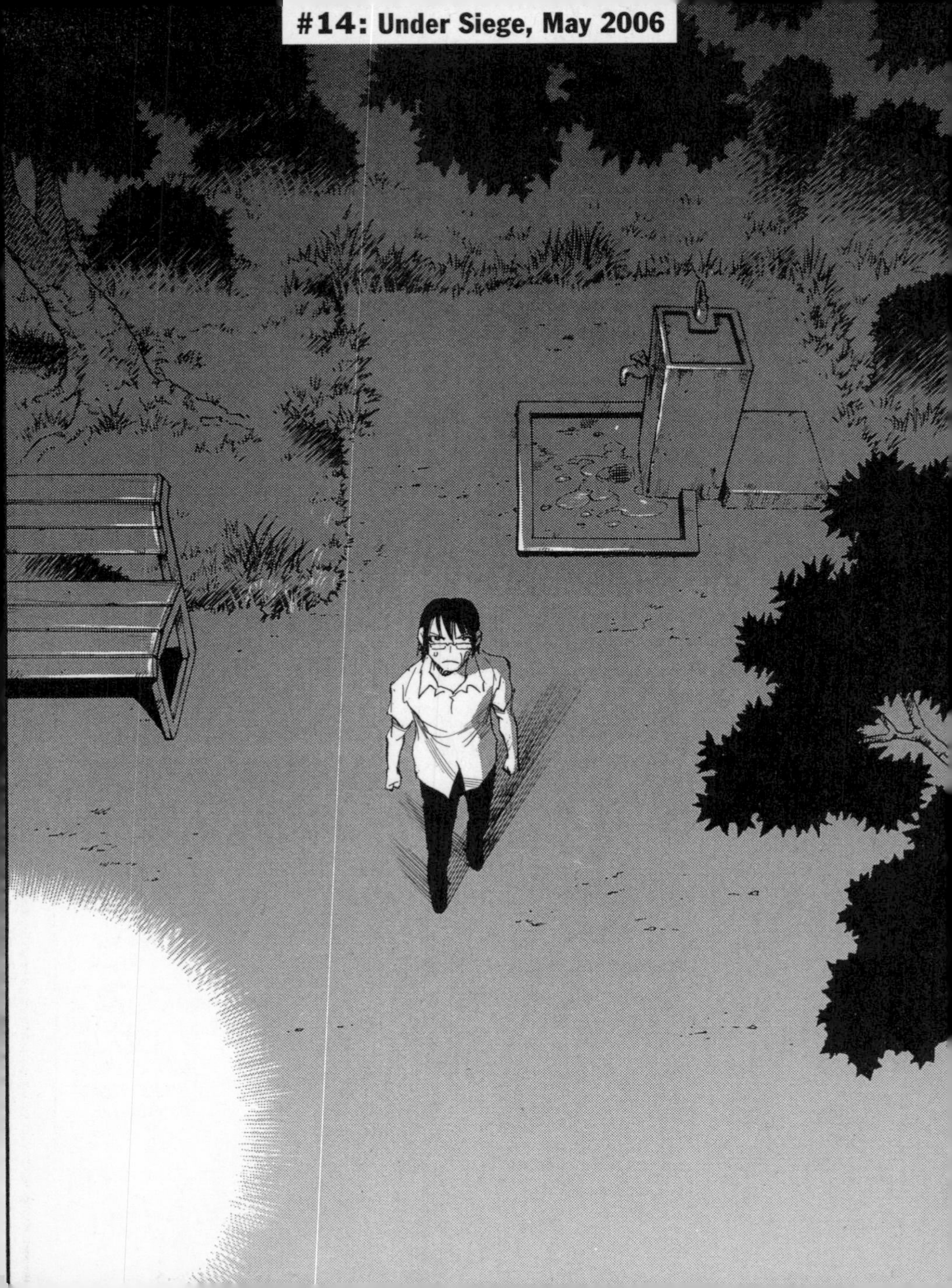

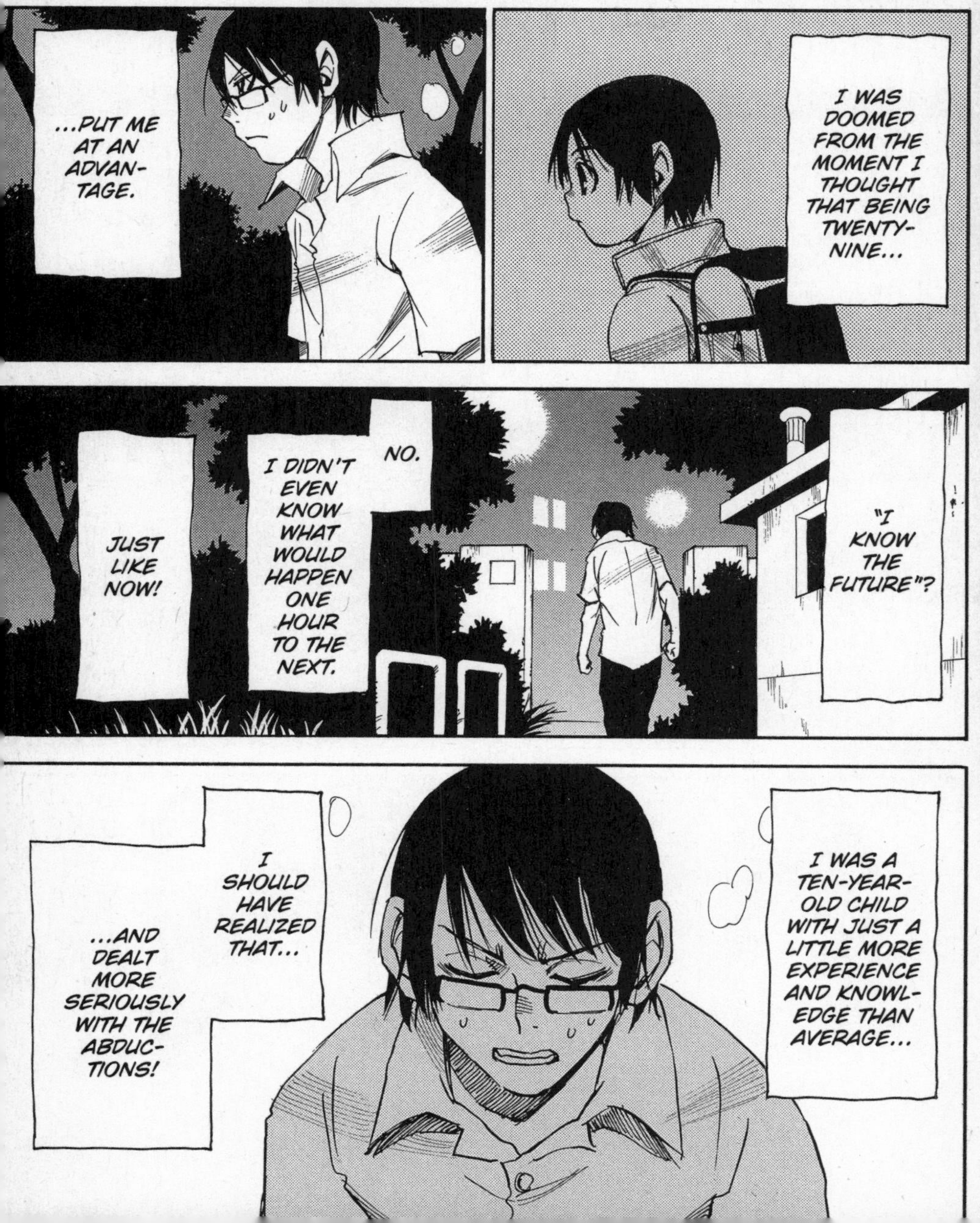
I WAS DOOMED FROM THE MOMENT I THOUGHT THAT BEING TWENTY-NINE...
...PUT ME AT AN ADVANTAGE.
"I KNOW THE FUTURE"?
NO.
I DIDN'T EVEN KNOW WHAT WOULD HAPPEN ONE HOUR TO THE NEXT.
JUST LIKE NOW!
I WAS A TEN-YEAR-OLD CHILD WITH JUST A LITTLE MORE EXPERIENCE AND KNOWLEDGE THAN AVERAGE...
I SHOULD HAVE REALIZED THAT...
...AND DEALT MORE SERIOUSLY WITH THE ABDUCTIONS!

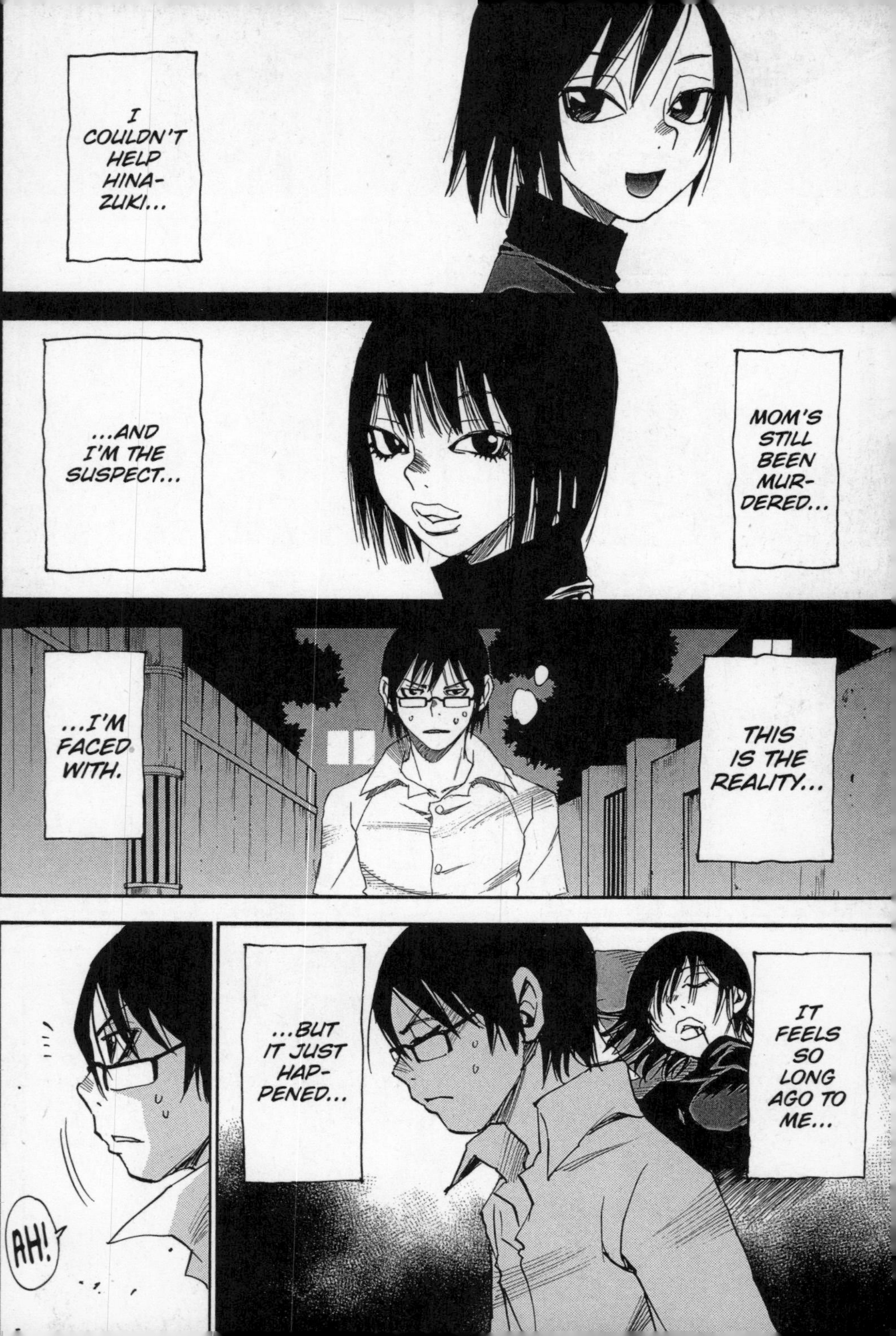
I COULDN'T HELP HINA-ZUKI...
MOM'S STILL BEEN MUR-DERED...
...AND I'M THE SUSPECT...
THIS IS THE REALITY...
...I'M FACED WITH.
IT FEELS SO LONG AGO TO ME...
...BUT IT JUST HAP-PENED...
AH!

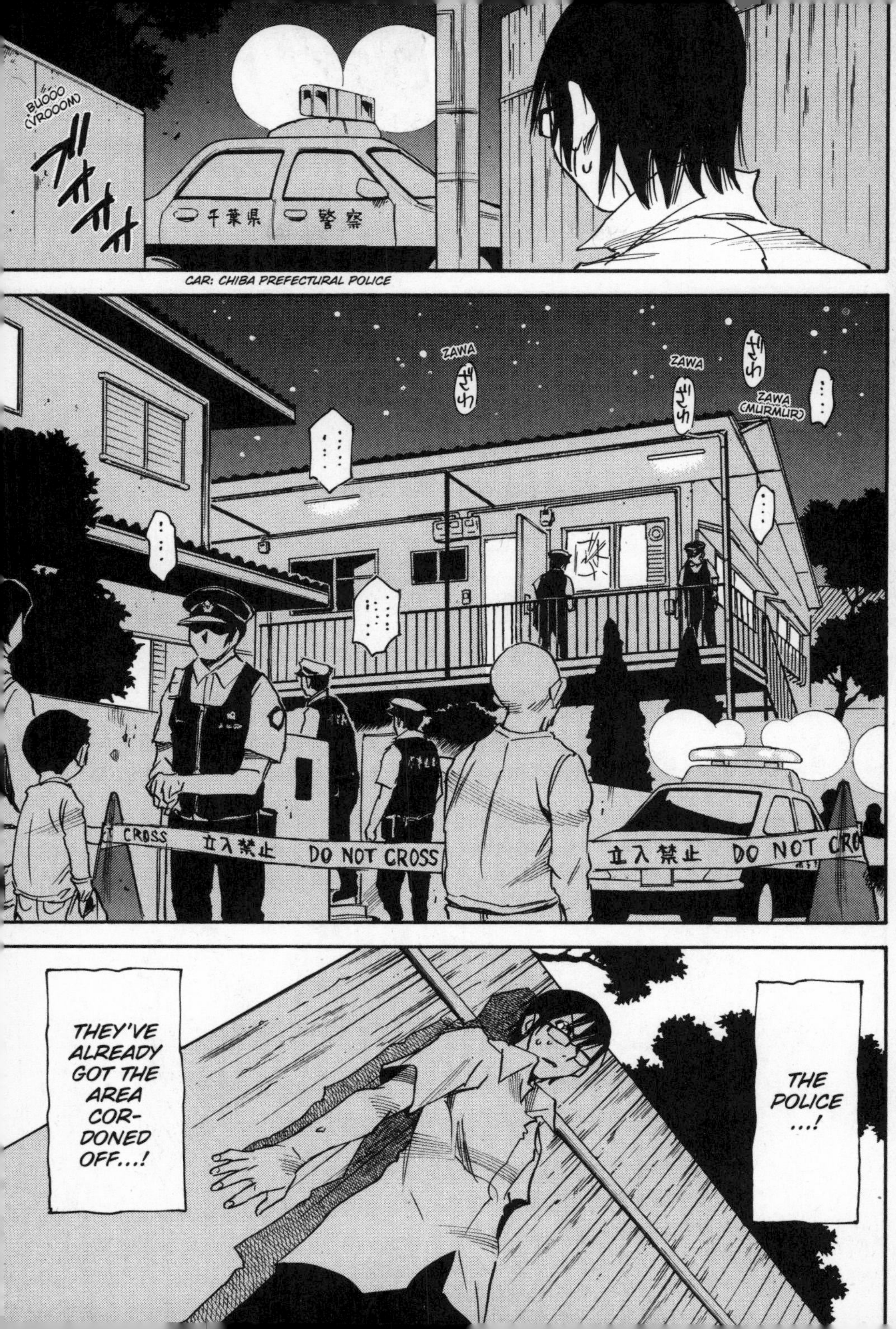
BUOOO (VROOOM)
ブォォォ
千葉県 警察
CAR: CHIBA PREFECTURAL POLICE
ざわ ZAWA
ざわ ZAWA
ざわ ZAWA (MURMUR)
CROSS 立入禁止 DO NOT CROSS
立入禁止 DO NOT CRO
THE POLICE ...!
THEY'VE ALREADY GOT THE AREA CORDONED OFF...!

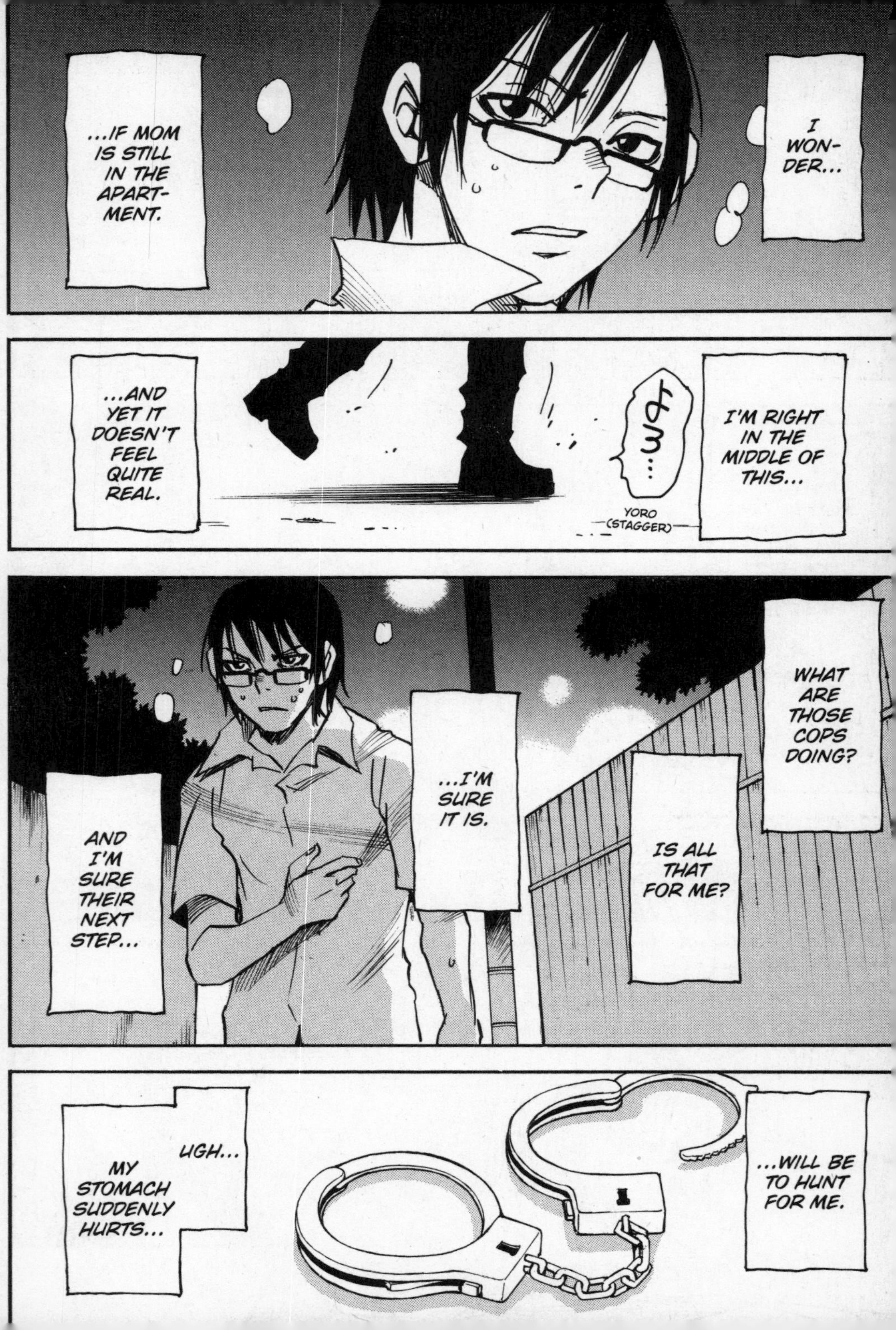
I WONDER...
...IF MOM IS STILL IN THE APARTMENT.
I'M RIGHT IN THE MIDDLE OF THIS...
よろ...
YORO (STAGGER)
...AND YET IT DOESN'T FEEL QUITE REAL.
WHAT ARE THOSE COPS DOING?
IS ALL THAT FOR ME?
...I'M SURE IT IS.
AND I'M SURE THEIR NEXT STEP...
...WILL BE TO HUNT FOR ME.
UGH...
MY STOMACH SUDDENLY HURTS...

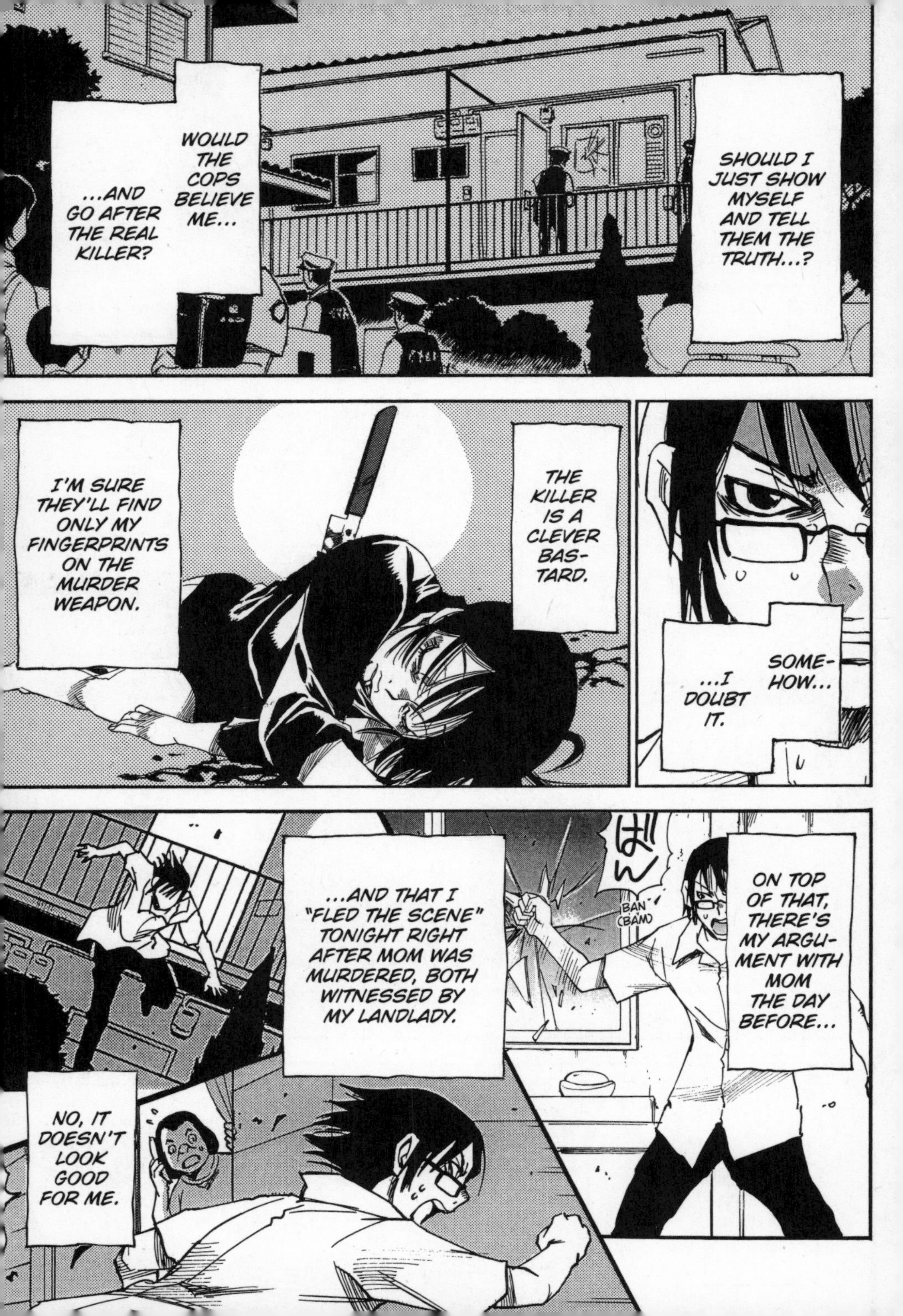
SHOULD I JUST SHOW MYSELF AND TELL THEM THE TRUTH...?
WOULD THE COPS BELIEVE ME...
...AND GO AFTER THE REAL KILLER?
SOME-HOW...
...I DOUBT IT.
THE KILLER IS A CLEVER BAS-TARD.
I'M SURE THEY'LL FIND ONLY MY FINGERPRINTS ON THE MURDER WEAPON.
ON TOP OF THAT, THERE'S MY ARGU-MENT WITH MOM THE DAY BEFORE...
ばん
BAN (BAM)
...AND THAT I "FLED THE SCENE" TONIGHT RIGHT AFTER MOM WAS MURDERED, BOTH WITNESSED BY MY LANDLADY.
NO, IT DOESN'T LOOK GOOD FOR ME.

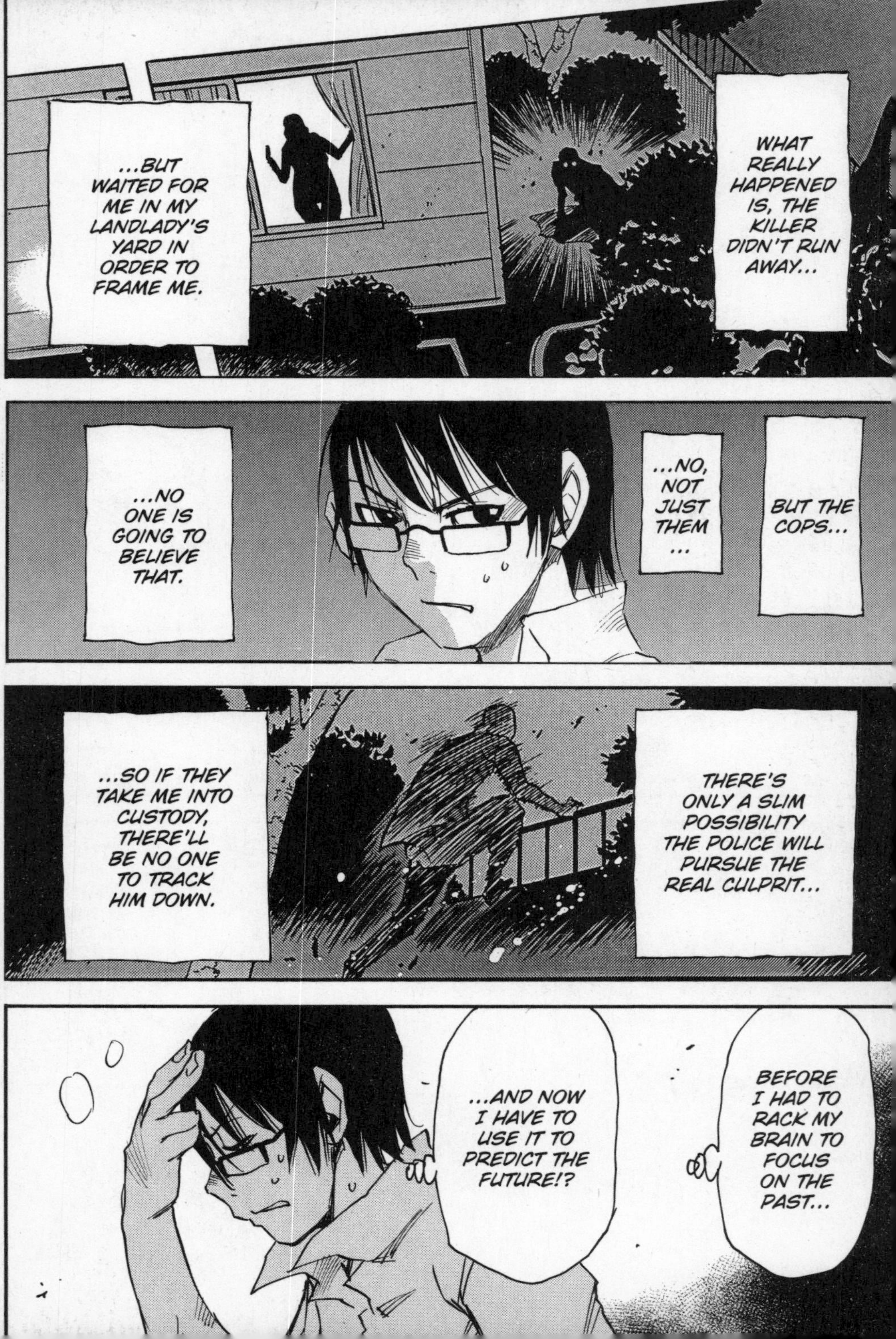
WHAT REALLY HAPPENED IS, THE KILLER DIDN'T RUN AWAY...
...BUT WAITED FOR ME IN MY LANDLADY'S YARD IN ORDER TO FRAME ME.
BUT THE COPS...
...NO, NOT JUST THEM ...
...NO ONE IS GOING TO BELIEVE THAT.
THERE'S ONLY A SLIM POSSIBILITY THE POLICE WILL PURSUE THE REAL CULPRIT...
...SO IF THEY TAKE ME INTO CUSTODY, THERE'LL BE NO ONE TO TRACK HIM DOWN.
BEFORE I HAD TO RACK MY BRAIN TO FOCUS ON THE PAST...
...AND NOW I HAVE TO USE IT TO PREDICT THE FUTURE!?

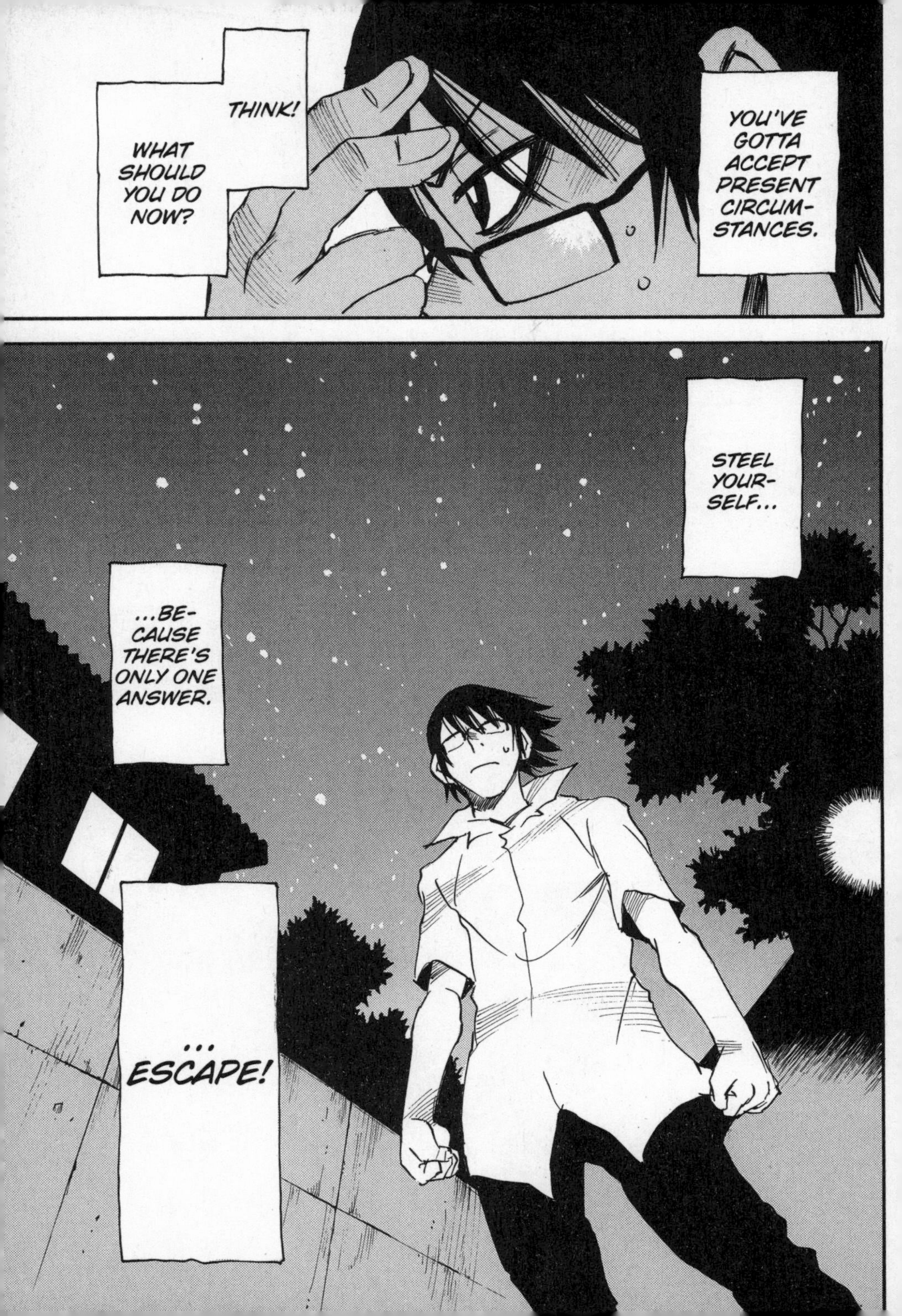
YOU'VE GOTTA ACCEPT PRESENT CIRCUM-STANCES.
THINK!
WHAT SHOULD YOU DO NOW?
STEEL YOUR-SELF...
...BE-CAUSE THERE'S ONLY ONE ANSWER.
...ESCAPE!

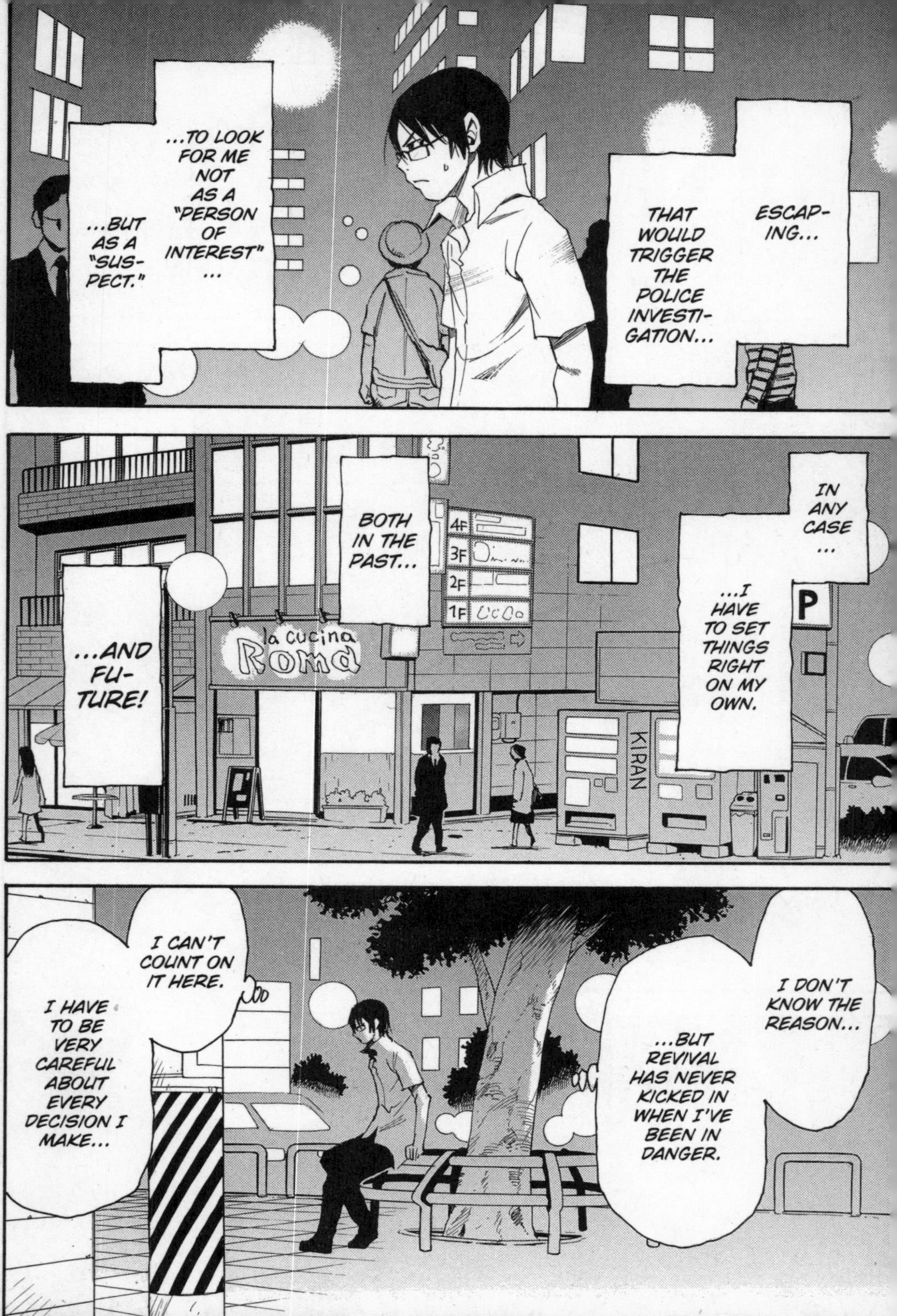
ESCAPING...
THAT WOULD TRIGGER THE POLICE INVESTIGATION...
...TO LOOK FOR ME NOT AS A "PERSON OF INTEREST"...
...BUT AS A "SUSPECT."
IN ANY CASE...
...I HAVE TO SET THINGS RIGHT ON MY OWN.
P
KIRAN
4F
3F
2F
1F
BOTH IN THE PAST...
la cucina Roma
...AND FUTURE!
I DON'T KNOW THE REASON...
...BUT REVIVAL HAS NEVER KICKED IN WHEN I'VE BEEN IN DANGER.
I CAN'T COUNT ON IT HERE.
I HAVE TO BE VERY CAREFUL ABOUT EVERY DECISION I MAKE...

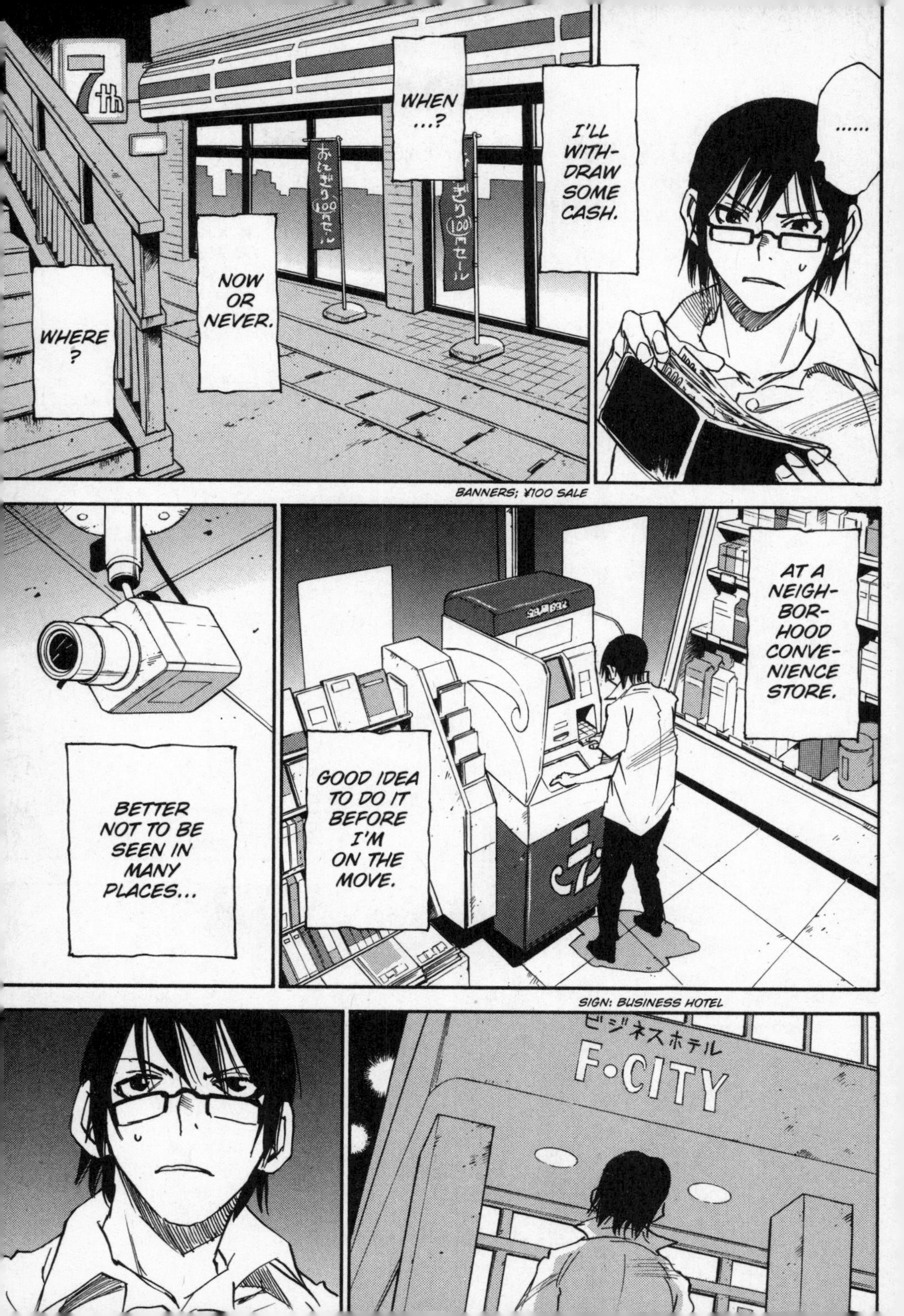
......
I'LL WITH-DRAW SOME CASH.
WHEN ...?
NOW OR NEVER.
WHERE ?
BANNERS: ¥100 SALE
AT A NEIGH-BOR-HOOD CONVE-NIENCE STORE.
GOOD IDEA TO DO IT BEFORE I'M ON THE MOVE.
BETTER NOT TO BE SEEN IN MANY PLACES...
SIGN: BUSINESS HOTEL
ビジネスホテル
F・CITY

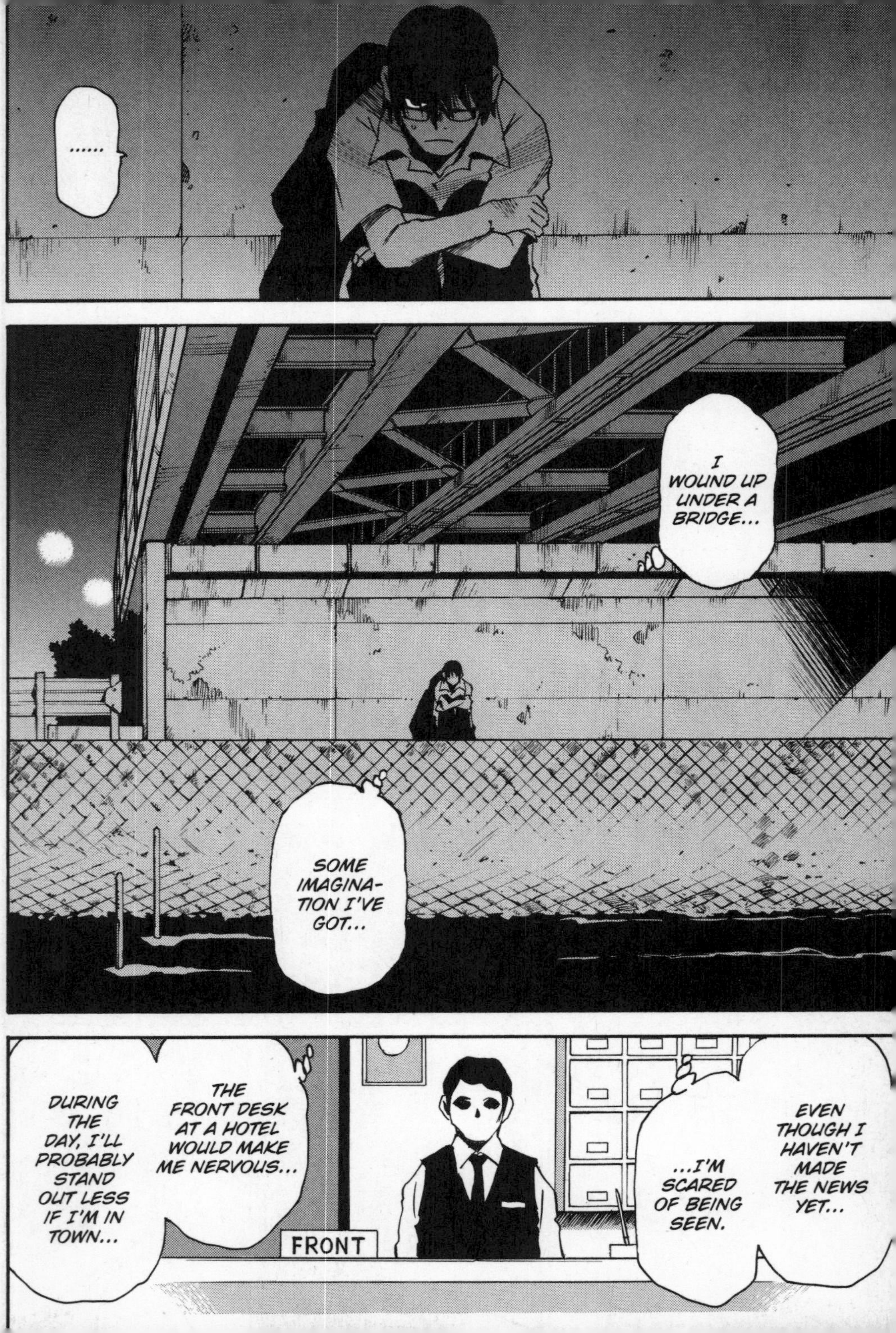
......
I WOUND UP UNDER A BRIDGE...
SOME IMAGINATION I'VE GOT...
EVEN THOUGH I HAVEN'T MADE THE NEWS YET...
...I'M SCARED OF BEING SEEN.
THE FRONT DESK AT A HOTEL WOULD MAKE ME NERVOUS...
FRONT
DURING THE DAY, I'LL PROBABLY STAND OUT LESS IF I'M IN TOWN...

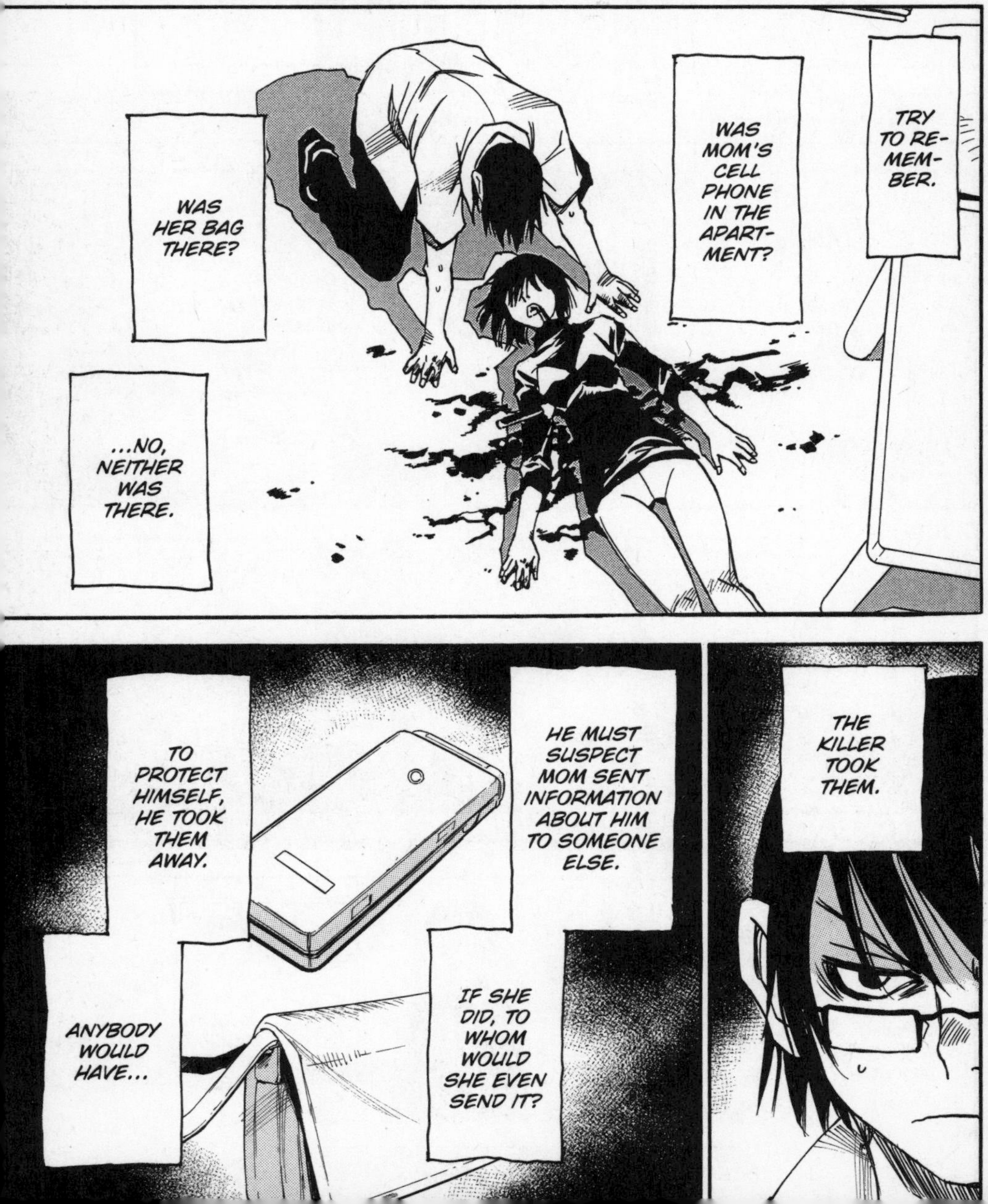
TRY TO RE-MEMBER.
WAS MOM'S CELL PHONE IN THE APARTMENT?
WAS HER BAG THERE?
...NO, NEITHER WAS THERE.
THE KILLER TOOK THEM.
HE MUST SUSPECT MOM SENT INFORMATION ABOUT HIM TO SOMEONE ELSE.
TO PROTECT HIMSELF, HE TOOK THEM AWAY.
IF SHE DID, TO WHOM WOULD SHE EVEN SEND IT?
ANYBODY WOULD HAVE...

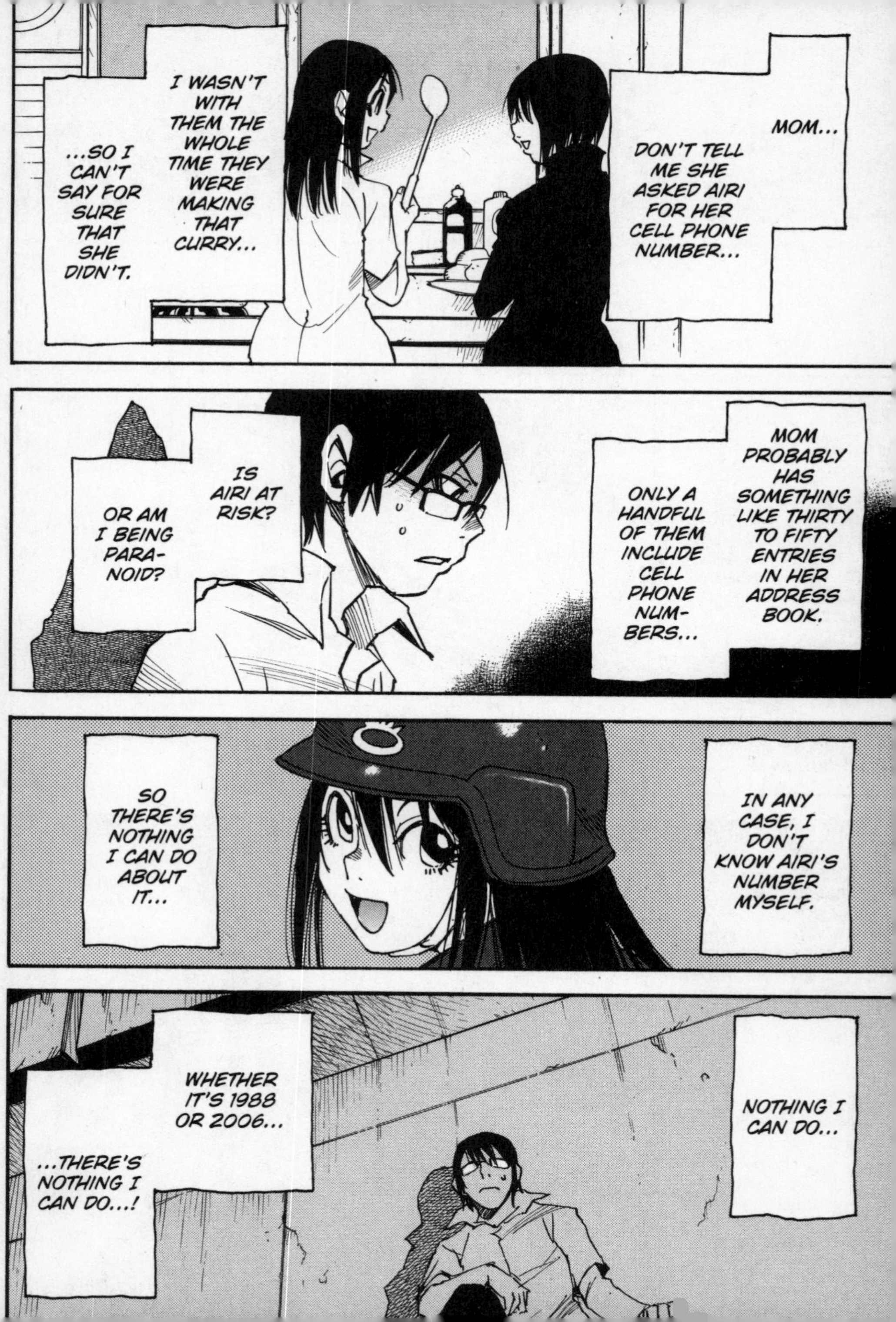
MOM...
DON'T TELL ME SHE ASKED AIRI FOR HER CELL PHONE NUMBER...
I WASN'T WITH THEM THE WHOLE TIME THEY WERE MAKING THAT CURRY...
...SO I CAN'T SAY FOR SURE THAT SHE DIDN'T.
MOM PROBABLY HAS SOMETHING LIKE THIRTY TO FIFTY ENTRIES IN HER ADDRESS BOOK.
ONLY A HANDFUL OF THEM INCLUDE CELL PHONE NUMBERS...
IS AIRI AT RISK?
OR AM I BEING PARANOID?
IN ANY CASE, I DON'T KNOW AIRI'S NUMBER MYSELF.
SO THERE'S NOTHING I CAN DO ABOUT IT...
NOTHING I CAN DO...
WHETHER IT'S 1988 OR 2006...
...THERE'S NOTHING I CAN DO...!

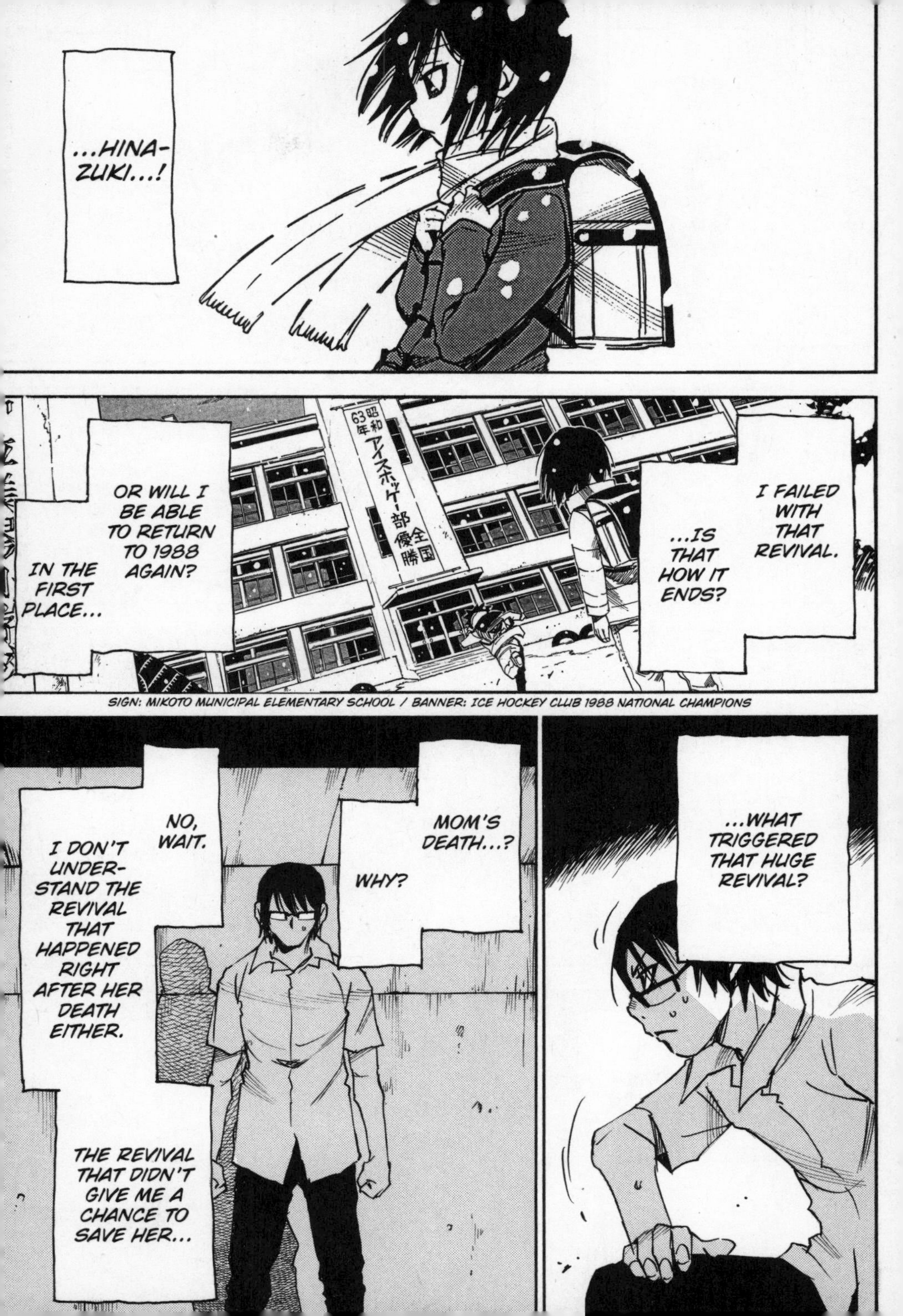
...HINA-ZUKI...!
I FAILED WITH THAT REVIVAL.
...IS THAT HOW IT ENDS?
昭和63年 アイスホッケー部 全国優勝
OR WILL I BE ABLE TO RETURN TO 1988 AGAIN?
IN THE FIRST PLACE...
SIGN: MIKOTO MUNICIPAL ELEMENTARY SCHOOL / BANNER: ICE HOCKEY CLUB 1988 NATIONAL CHAMPIONS
...WHAT TRIGGERED THAT HUGE REVIVAL?
MOM'S DEATH...?
WHY?
NO, WAIT.
I DON'T UNDER-STAND THE REVIVAL THAT HAPPENED RIGHT AFTER HER DEATH EITHER.
THE REVIVAL THAT DIDN'T GIVE ME A CHANCE TO SAVE HER...

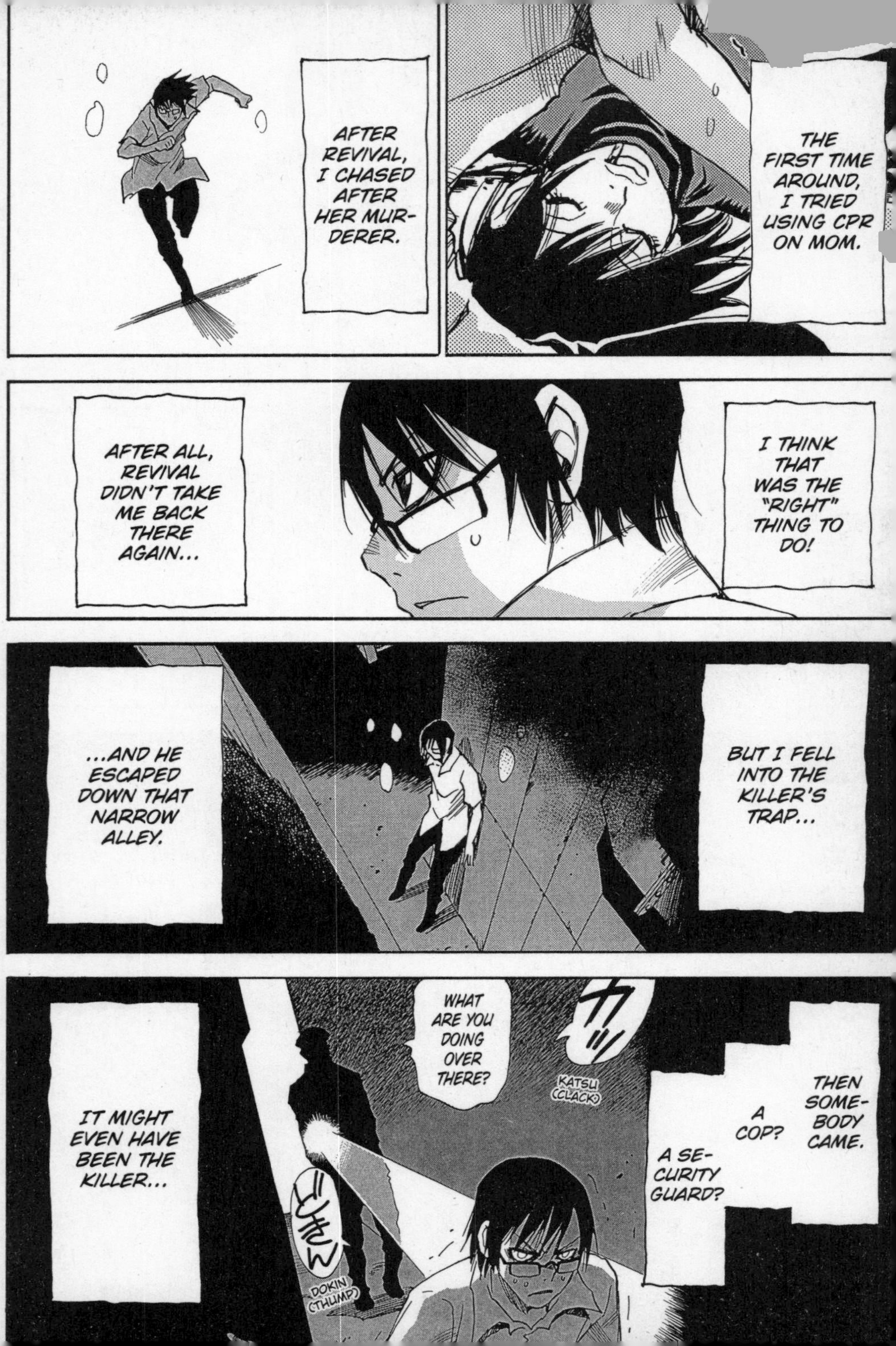
THE FIRST TIME AROUND, I TRIED USING CPR ON MOM.
AFTER REVIVAL, I CHASED AFTER HER MURDERER.
I THINK THAT WAS THE "RIGHT" THING TO DO!
AFTER ALL, REVIVAL DIDN'T TAKE ME BACK THERE AGAIN...
BUT I FELL INTO THE KILLER'S TRAP...
...AND HE ESCAPED DOWN THAT NARROW ALLEY.
THEN SOMEBODY CAME.
A COP?
A SECURITY GUARD?
カッ
KATSU (CLACK)
WHAT ARE YOU DOING OVER THERE?
どきん
DOKIN (THUMP)
IT MIGHT EVEN HAVE BEEN THE KILLER...

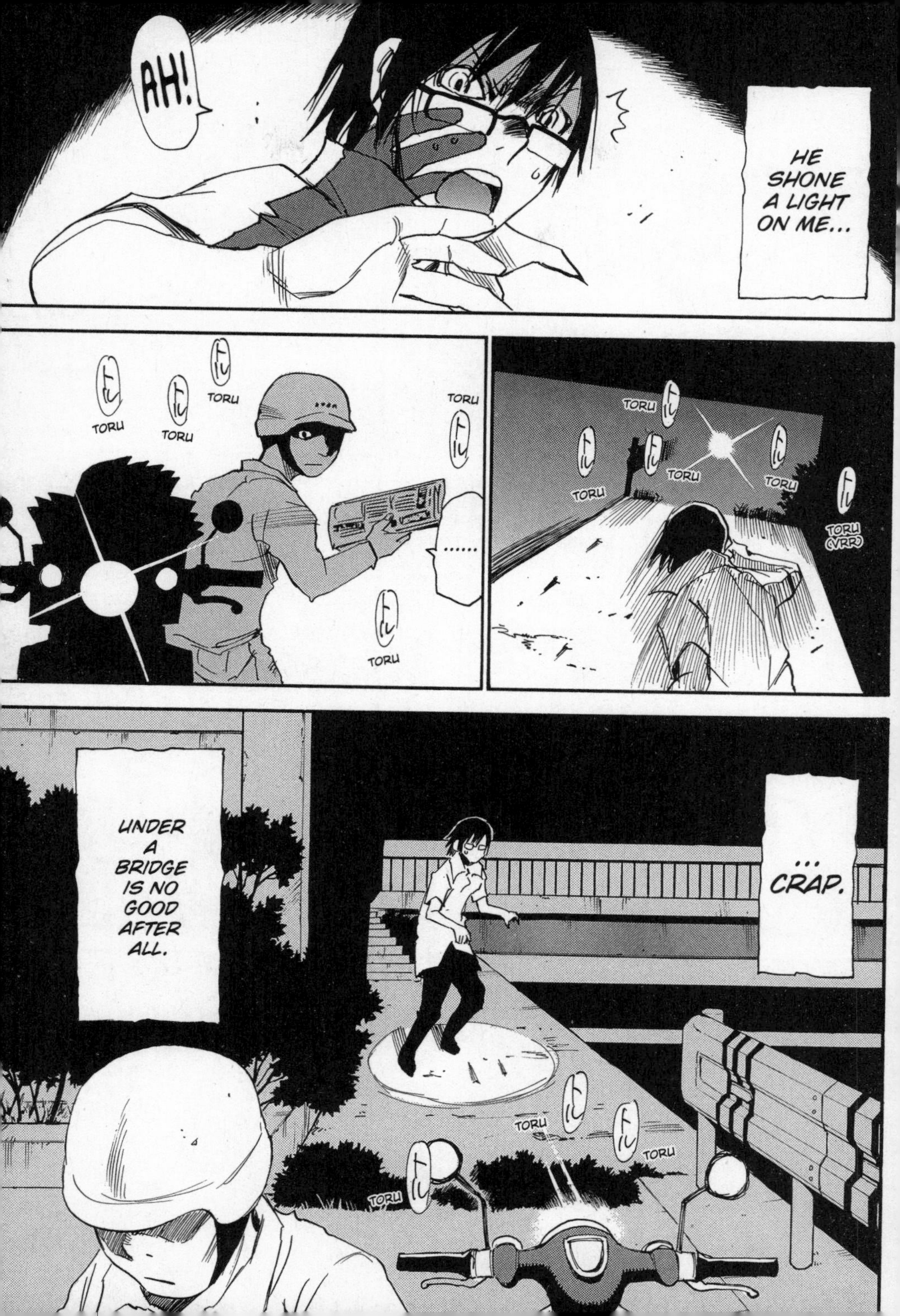

HE SHONE A LIGHT ON ME...
AH!
TORU
TORU
TORU
TORU
TORU
TORU (VRR)
TORU
TORU
TORU
TORU
......
TORU
... CRAP.
UNDER A BRIDGE IS NO GOOD AFTER ALL.
TORU
TORU
TORU

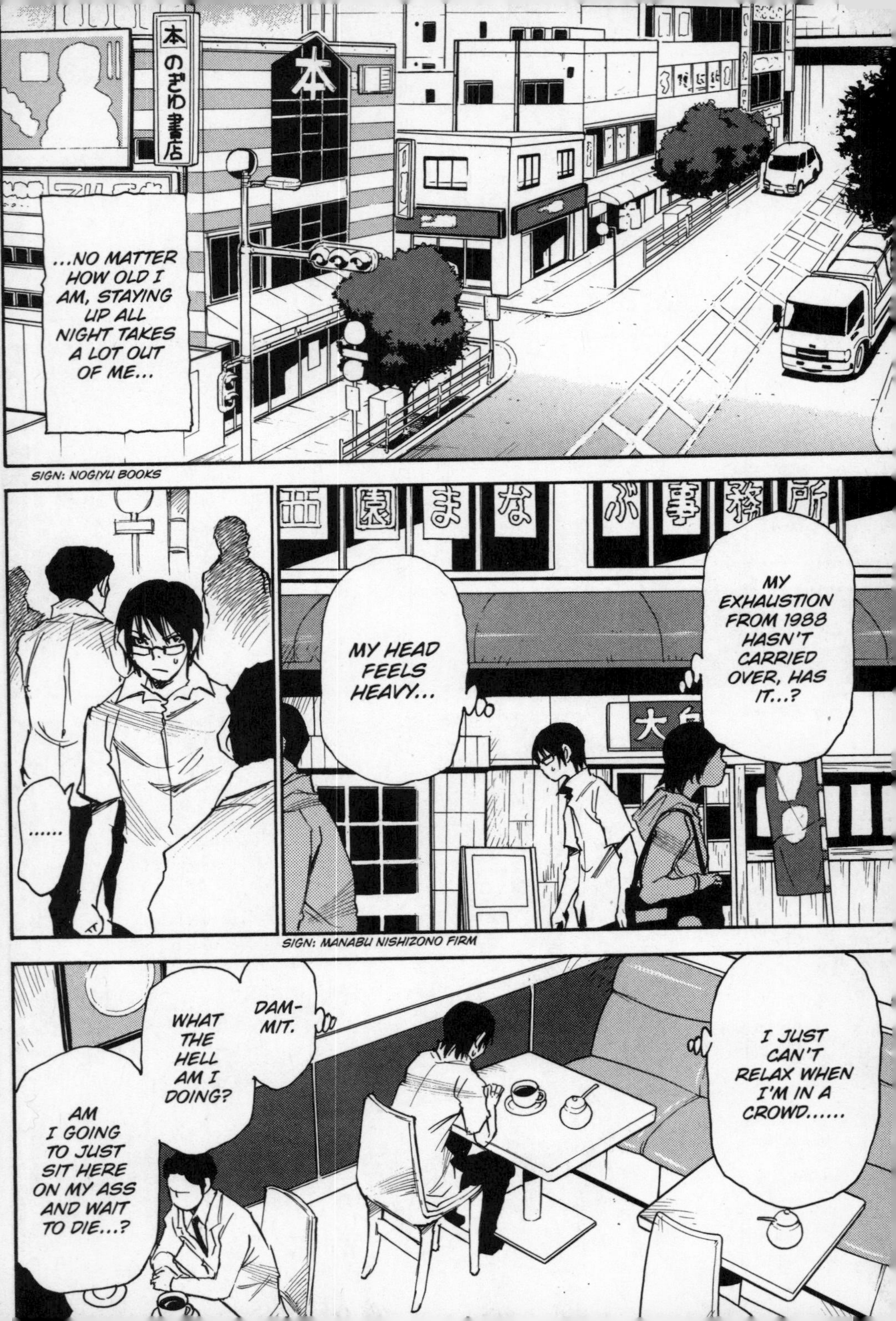
本
のぎゆ書店
...NO MATTER HOW OLD I AM, STAYING UP ALL NIGHT TAKES A LOT OUT OF ME...
SIGN: NOGIYU BOOKS
西園まなぶ事務所
MY EXHAUSTION FROM 1988 HASN'T CARRIED OVER, HAS IT...?
MY HEAD FEELS HEAVY...
......
SIGN: MANABU NISHIZONO FIRM
I JUST CAN'T RELAX WHEN I'M IN A CROWD......
DAM-MIT.
WHAT THE HELL AM I DOING?
AM I GOING TO JUST SIT HERE ON MY ASS AND WAIT TO DIE...?

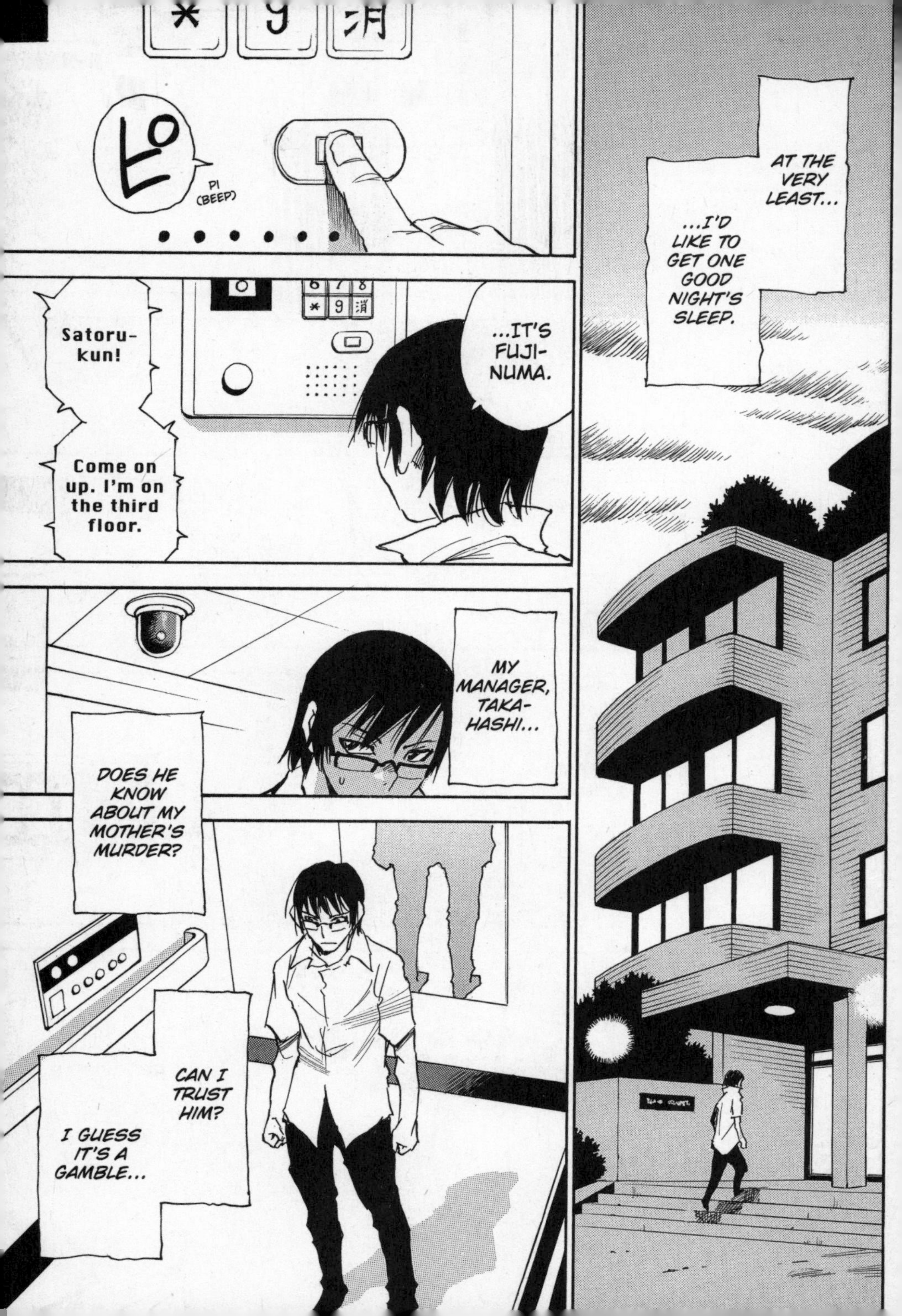

AT THE VERY LEAST...
...I'D LIKE TO GET ONE GOOD NIGHT'S SLEEP.
ピ
PI (BEEP)
...IT'S FUJI-NUMA.
Satoru-kun!
Come on up. I'm on the third floor.
MY MANAGER, TAKA-HASHI...
DOES HE KNOW ABOUT MY MOTHER'S MURDER?
CAN I TRUST HIM?
I GUESS IT'S A GAMBLE...

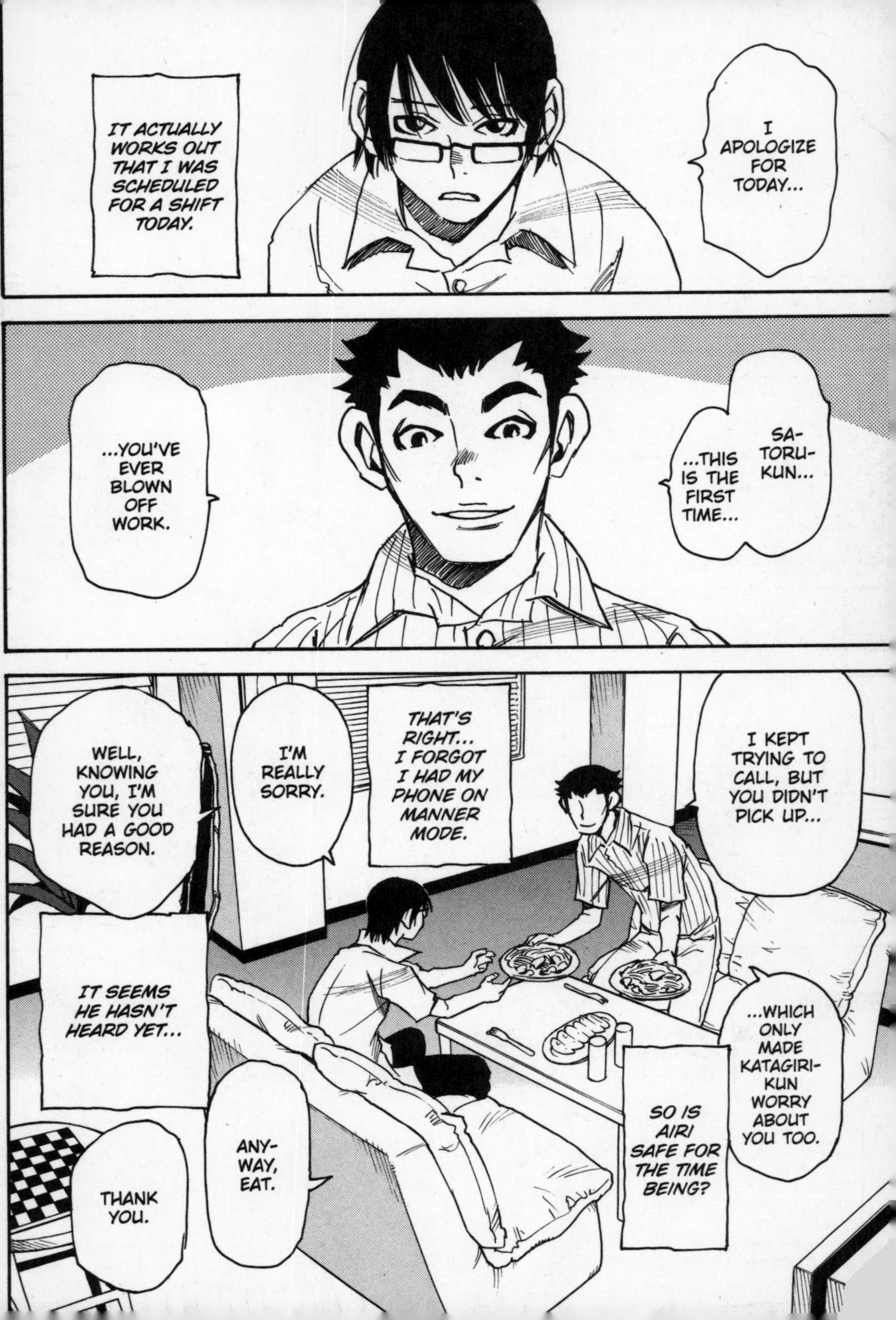
I APOLOGIZE FOR TODAY...
IT ACTUALLY WORKS OUT THAT I WAS SCHEDULED FOR A SHIFT TODAY.
SA-TORU-KUN...
...THIS IS THE FIRST TIME...
...YOU'VE EVER BLOWN OFF WORK.
I KEPT TRYING TO CALL, BUT YOU DIDN'T PICK UP...
THAT'S RIGHT... I FORGOT I HAD MY PHONE ON MANNER MODE.
I'M REALLY SORRY.
WELL, KNOWING YOU, I'M SURE YOU HAD A GOOD REASON.
...WHICH ONLY MADE KATAGIRI-KUN WORRY ABOUT YOU TOO.
SO IS AIRI SAFE FOR THE TIME BEING?
IT SEEMS HE HASN'T HEARD YET...
ANY-WAY, EAT.
THANK YOU.

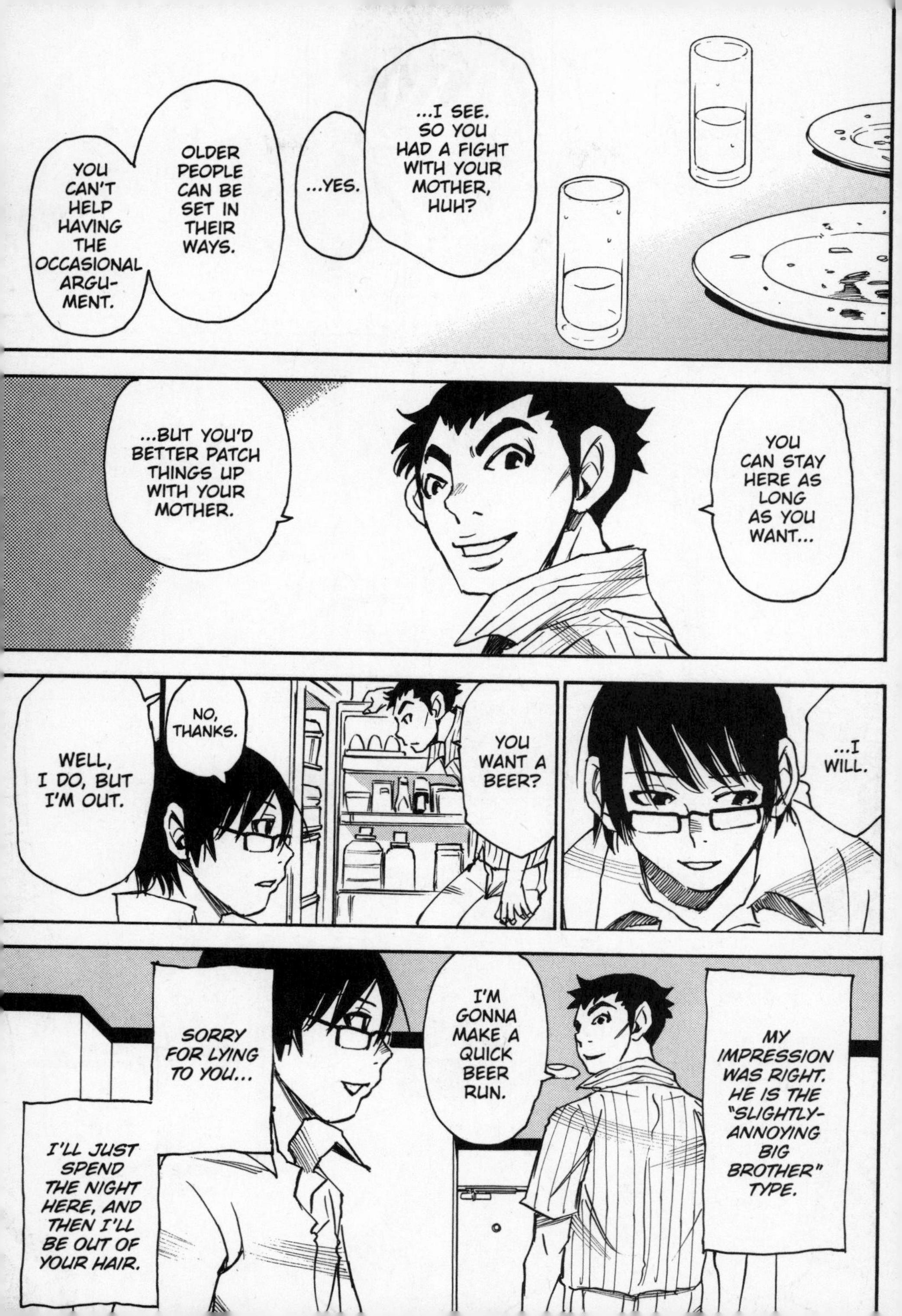
...I SEE. SO YOU HAD A FIGHT WITH YOUR MOTHER, HUH?
...YES.
OLDER PEOPLE CAN BE SET IN THEIR WAYS.
YOU CAN'T HELP HAVING THE OCCASIONAL ARGUMENT.
YOU CAN STAY HERE AS LONG AS YOU WANT...
...BUT YOU'D BETTER PATCH THINGS UP WITH YOUR MOTHER.
...I WILL.
YOU WANT A BEER?
NO, THANKS.
WELL, I DO, BUT I'M OUT.
MY IMPRESSION WAS RIGHT. HE IS THE "SLIGHTLY-ANNOYING BIG BROTHER" TYPE.
I'M GONNA MAKE A QUICK BEER RUN.
SORRY FOR LYING TO YOU...
I'LL JUST SPEND THE NIGHT HERE, AND THEN I'LL BE OUT OF YOUR HAIR.

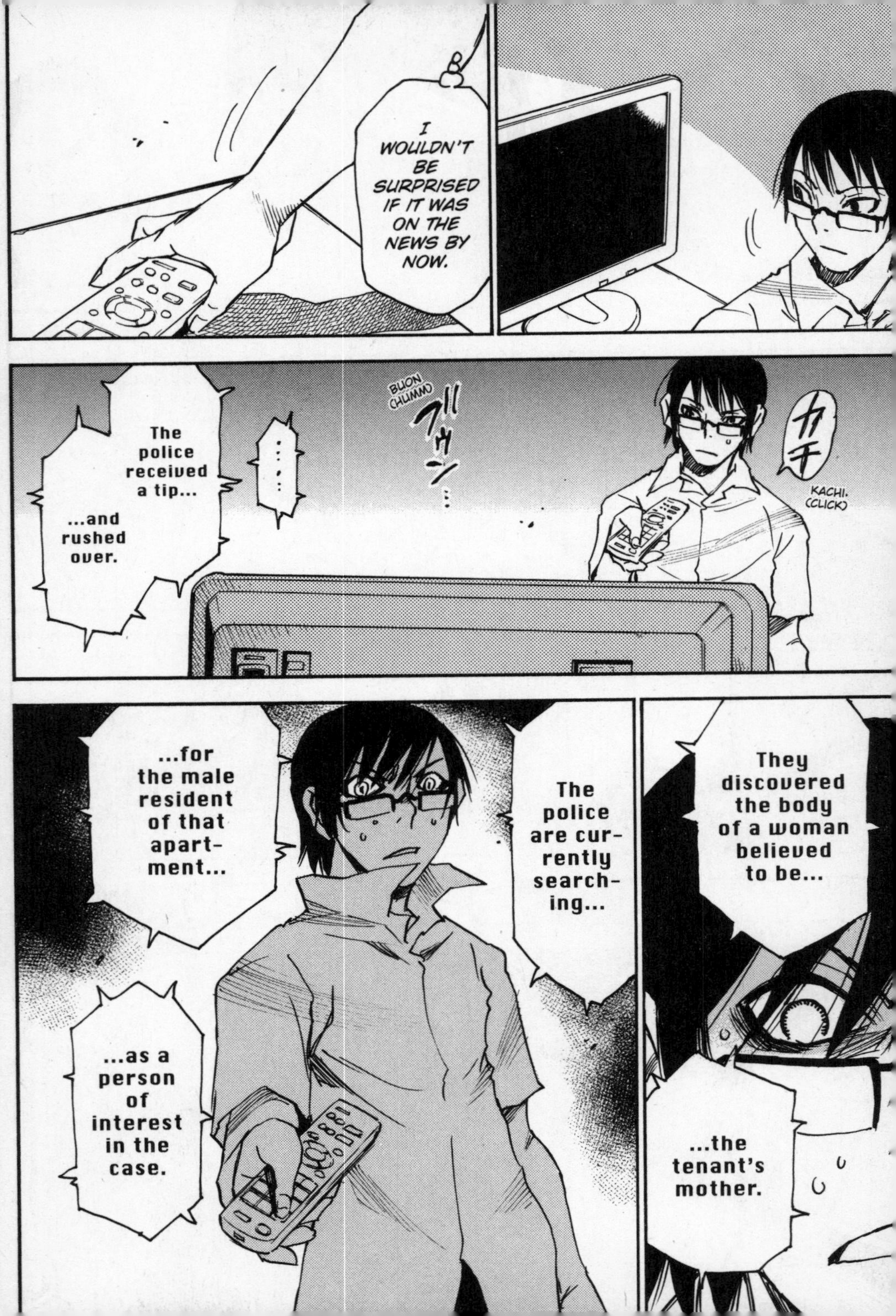
I WOULDN'T BE SURPRISED IF IT WAS ON THE NEWS BY NOW.
カチ
KACHI. (CLICK)
ブゥン…
BUON (HUMM)
……
The police received a tip...
...and rushed over.
They discovered the body of a woman believed to be...
...the tenant's mother.
The police are cur-rently search-ing...
...for the male resident of that apart-ment...
...as a person of interest in the case.

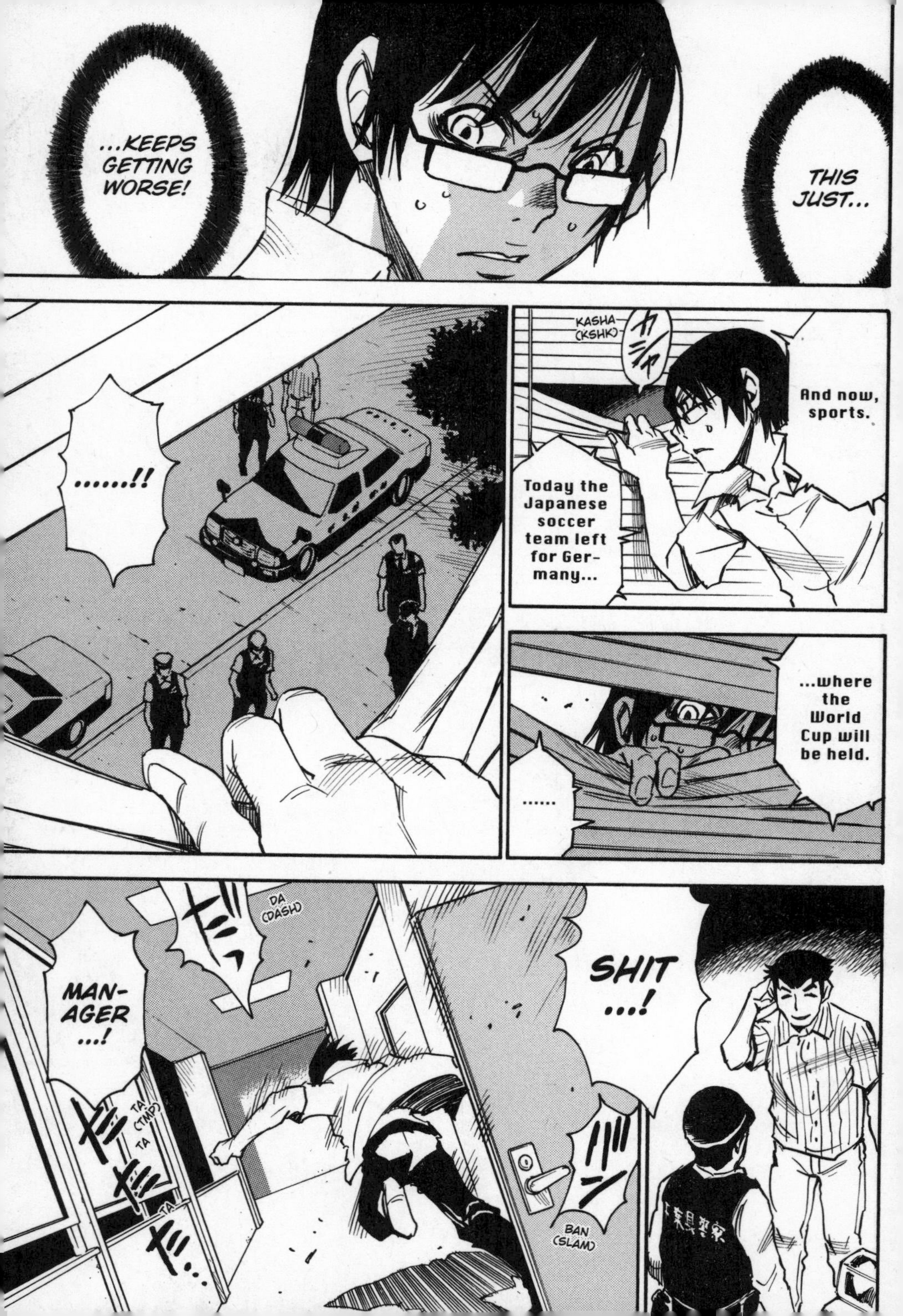
THIS JUST...
...KEEPS GETTING WORSE!
KASHA (KSHK)
And now, sports.
Today the Japanese soccer team left for Ger-many...
...where the World Cup will be held.
......
......!!
SHIT ...!
BAN (SLAM)
DA (DASH)
MAN-AGER ...!
TA (TMP)
TA
TA

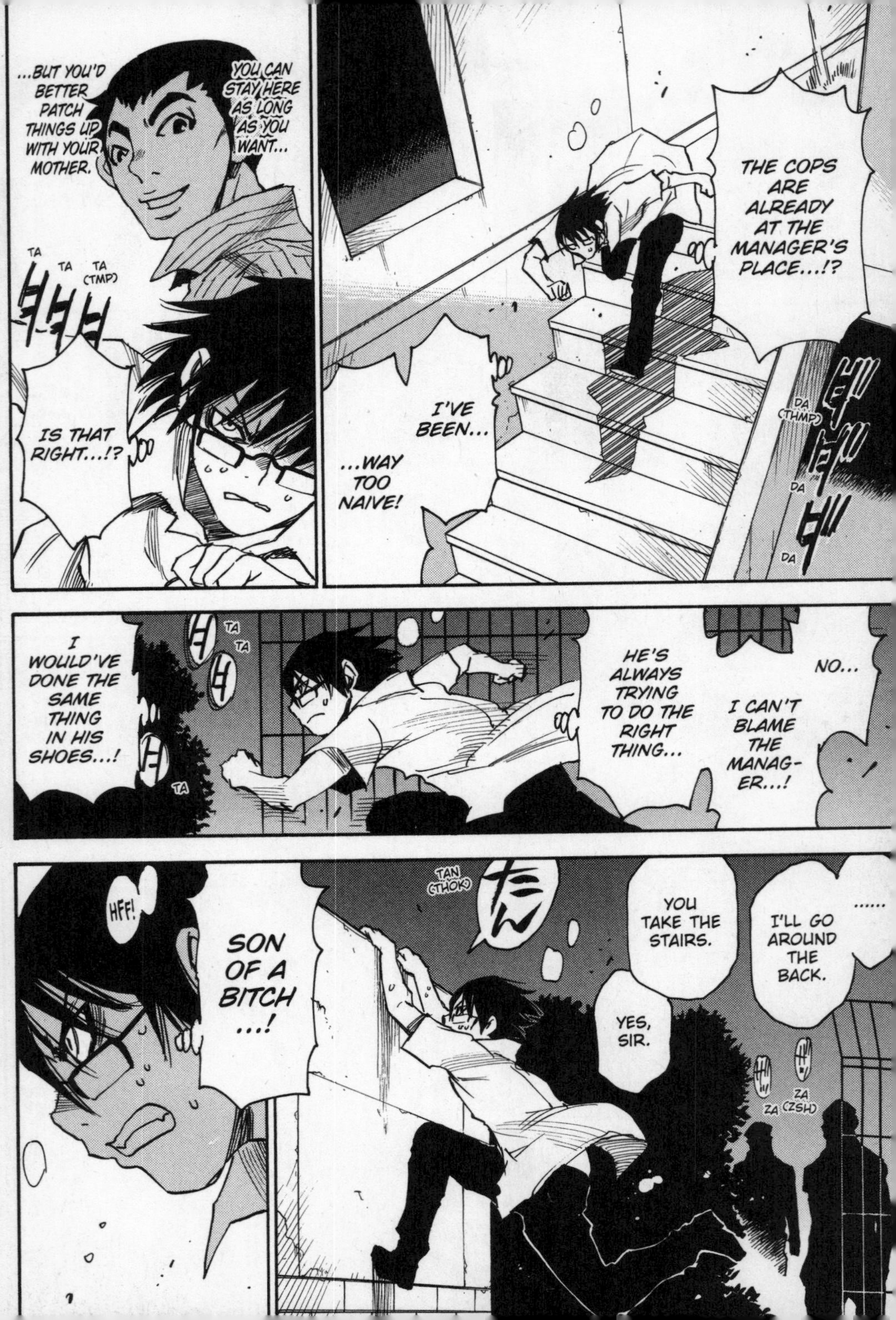
THE COPS ARE ALREADY AT THE MANAGER'S PLACE...!?
DA (THMP)
DA
DA
I'VE BEEN...
...WAY TOO NAIVE!
YOU CAN STAY HERE AS LONG AS YOU WANT...
...BUT YOU'D BETTER PATCH THINGS UP WITH YOUR MOTHER.
TA
TA
TA (TMP)
IS THAT RIGHT...!?
NO...
I CAN'T BLAME THE MANAGER...!
HE'S ALWAYS TRYING TO DO THE RIGHT THING...
TA
TA
I WOULD'VE DONE THE SAME THING IN HIS SHOES...!
TA
......
I'LL GO AROUND THE BACK.
YOU TAKE THE STAIRS.
YES, SIR.
ZA
ZA (ZSH)
TAN (THOK)
SON OF A BITCH...!
HFF!

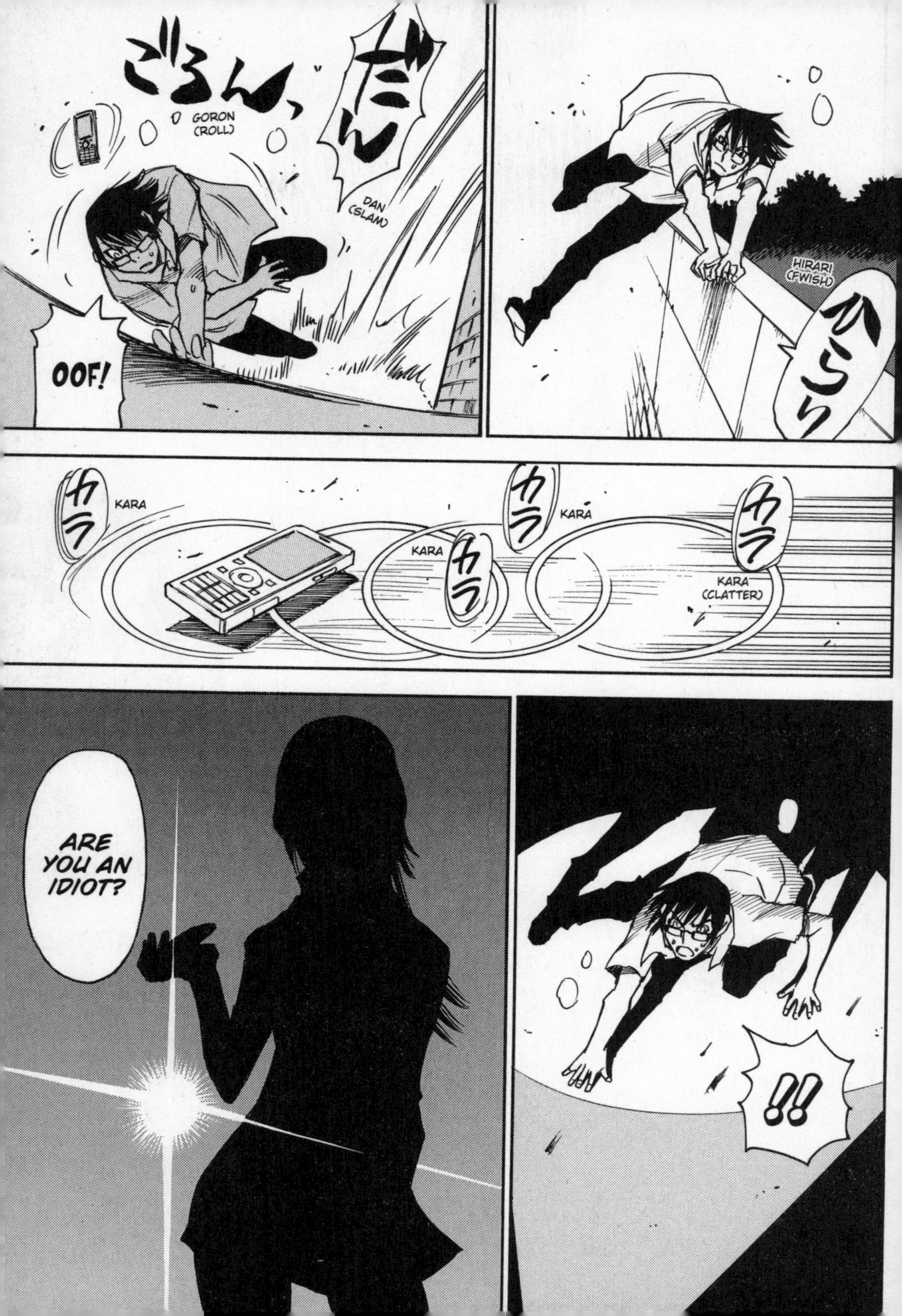
ひらり
HIRARI (FWISH)
だん
DAN (SLAM)
ごろん
GORON (ROLL)
OOF!
カラ
KARA (CLATTER)
カラ
KARA
カラ
KARA
カラ
KARA
!!
ARE YOU AN IDIOT?

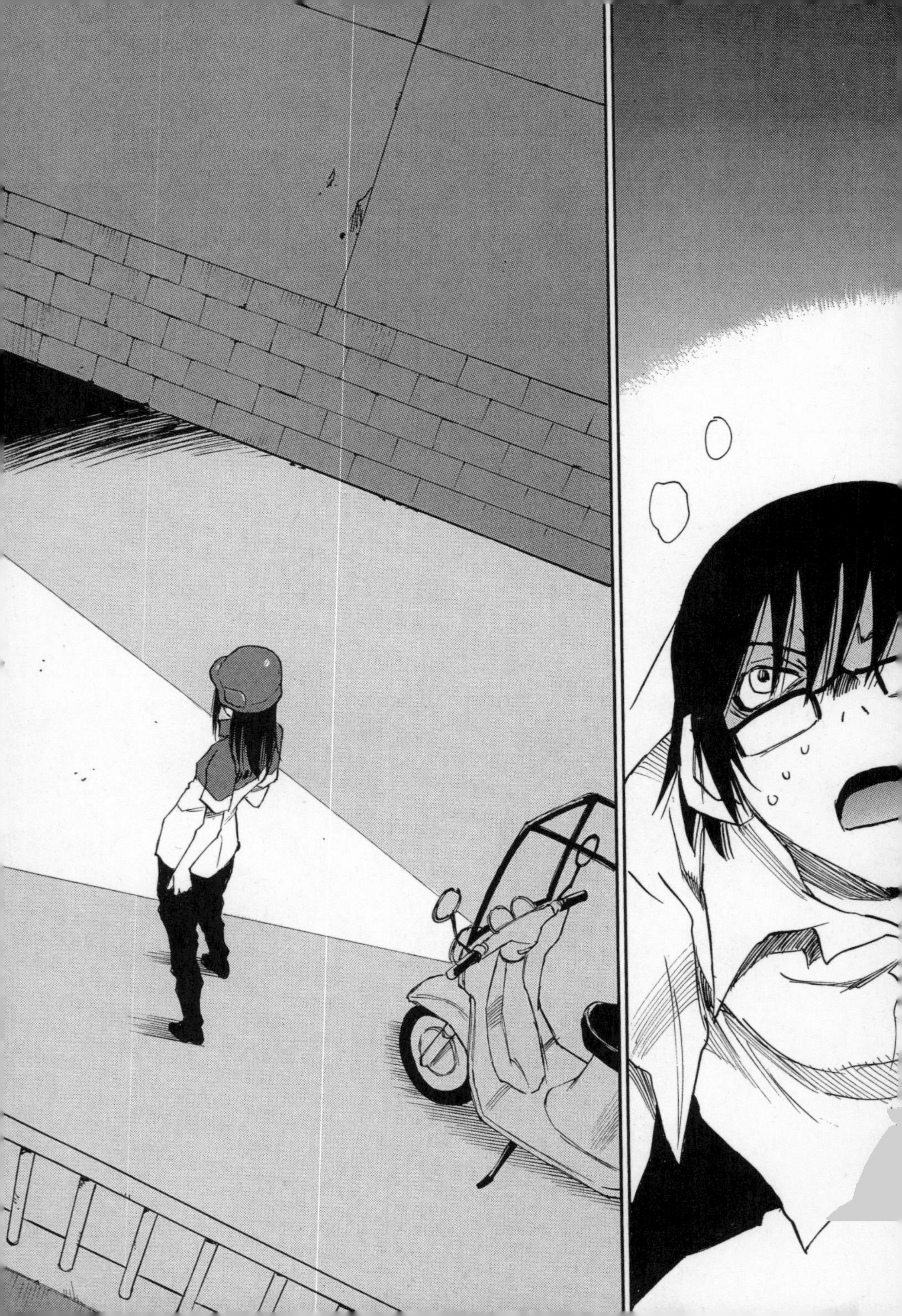

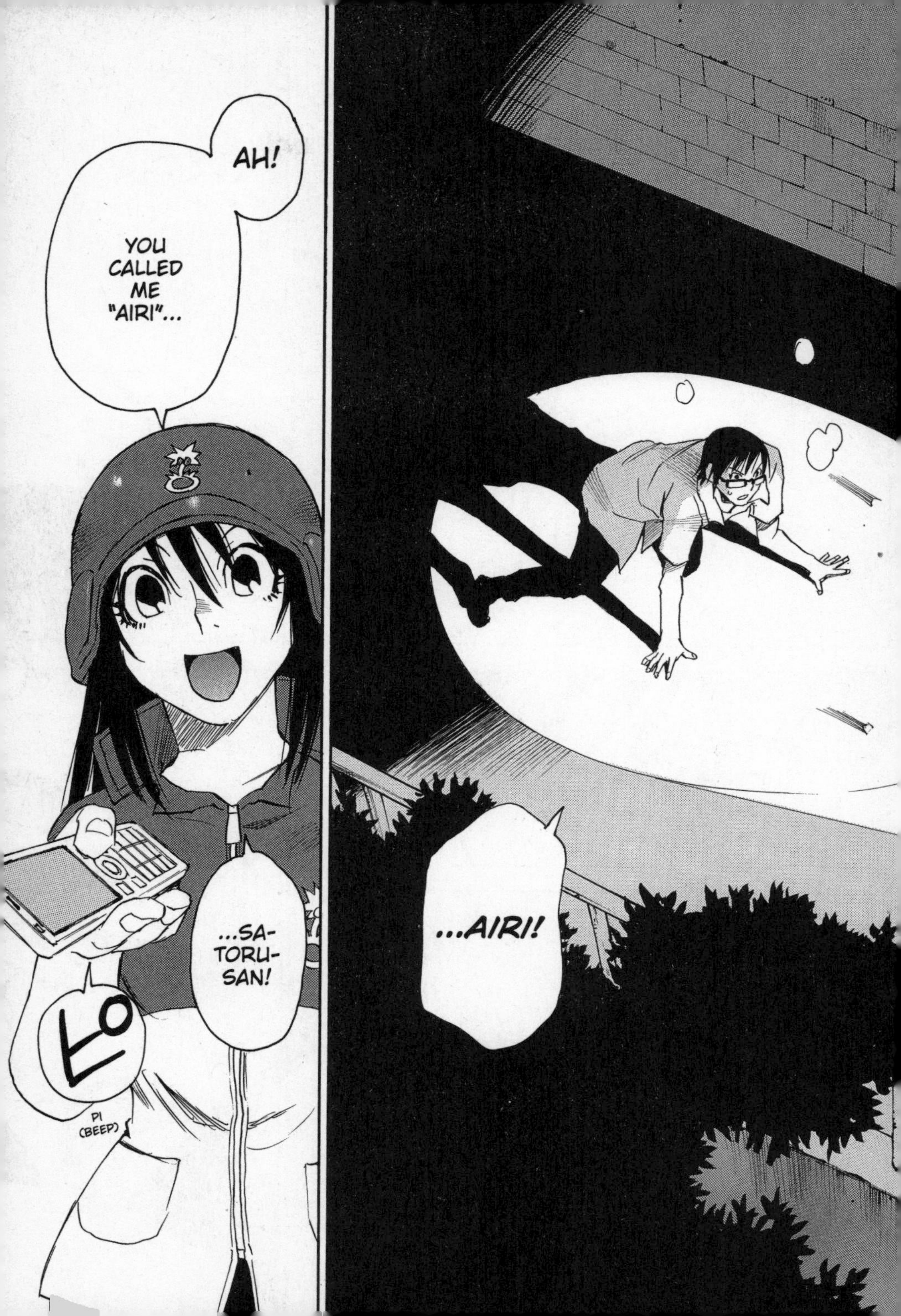
...AIRI!
AH!
YOU CALLED ME "AIRI"...
...SA-TORU-SAN!
ピ
PI (BEEP)

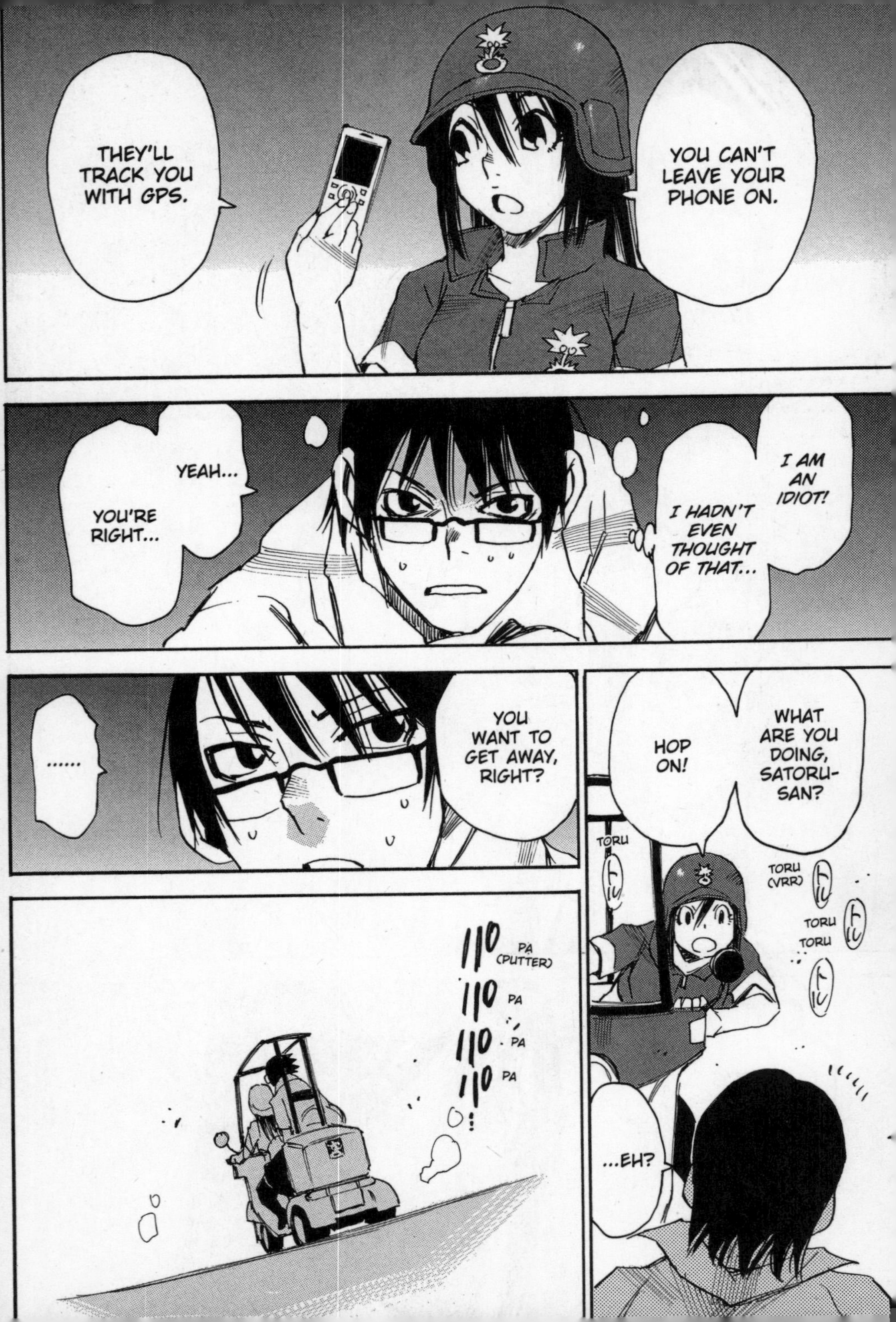
YOU CAN'T LEAVE YOUR PHONE ON.
THEY'LL TRACK YOU WITH GPS.
I AM AN IDIOT!
I HADN'T EVEN THOUGHT OF THAT...
YEAH...
YOU'RE RIGHT...
WHAT ARE YOU DOING, SATORU-SAN?
HOP ON!
TORU
TORU (VRR)
TORU
TORU
...EH?
YOU WANT TO GET AWAY, RIGHT?
......
PA (PUTTER)
PA
PA
PA

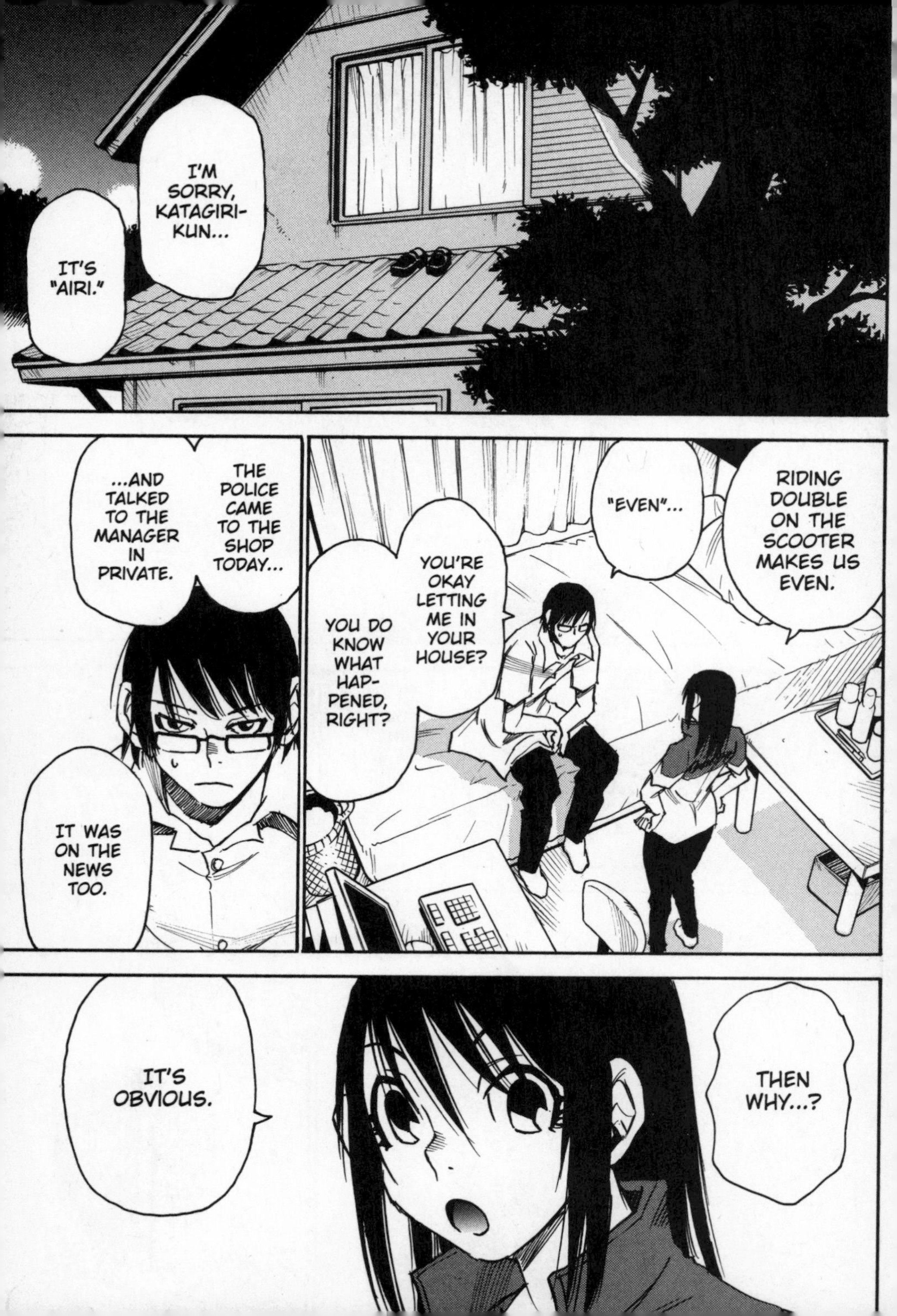
I'M SORRY, KATAGIRI-KUN...
IT'S "AIRI."
RIDING DOUBLE ON THE SCOOTER MAKES US EVEN.
"EVEN"...
YOU'RE OKAY LETTING ME IN YOUR HOUSE?
YOU DO KNOW WHAT HAP-PENED, RIGHT?
THE POLICE CAME TO THE SHOP TODAY...
...AND TALKED TO THE MANAGER IN PRIVATE.
IT WAS ON THE NEWS TOO.
THEN WHY...?
IT'S OBVIOUS.

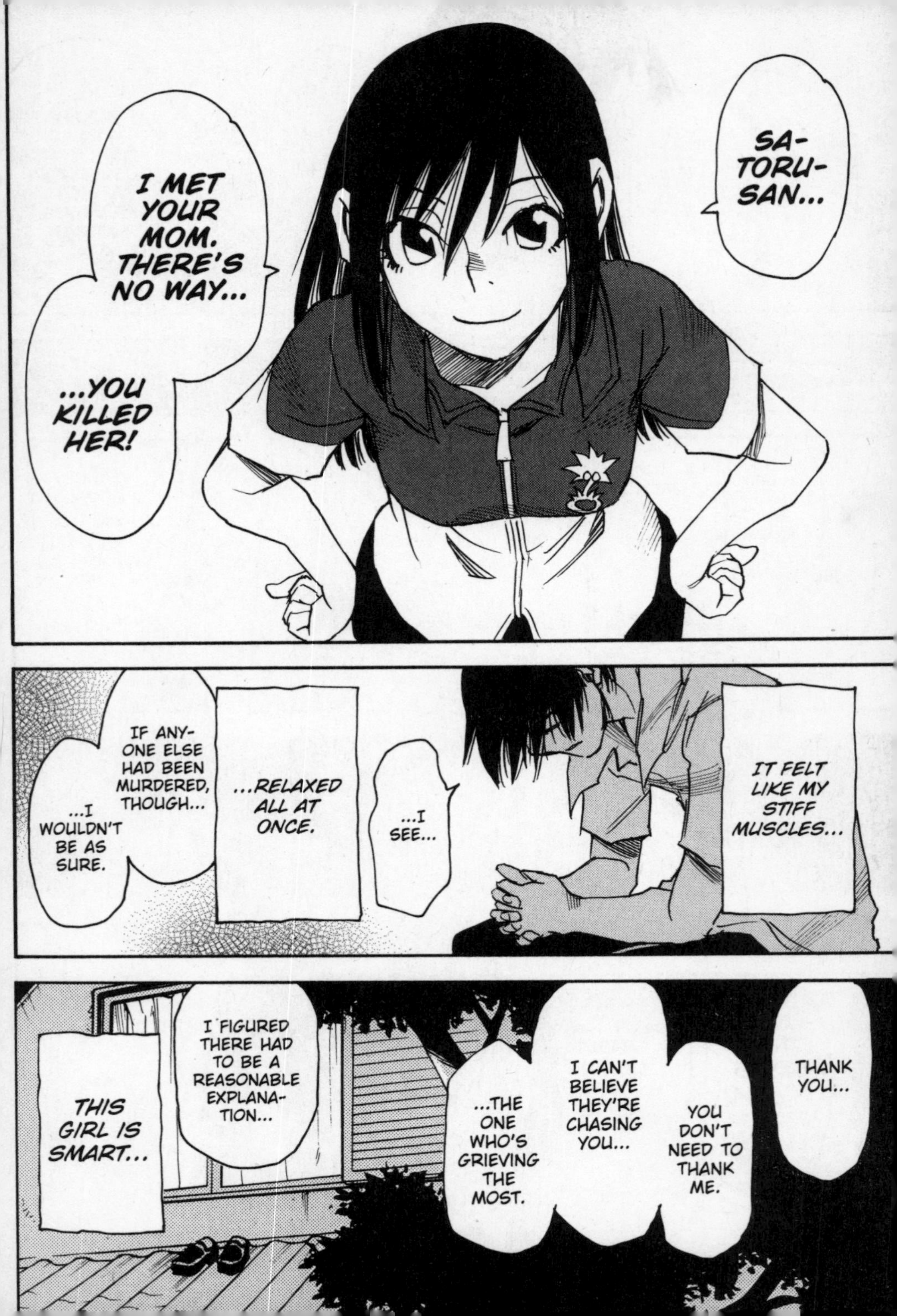
SA-TORU-SAN...
I MET YOUR MOM. THERE'S NO WAY...
...YOU KILLED HER!
IT FELT LIKE MY STIFF MUSCLES...
...I SEE...
...RELAXED ALL AT ONCE.
IF ANY-ONE ELSE HAD BEEN MURDERED, THOUGH...
...I WOULDN'T BE AS SURE.
THANK YOU...
YOU DON'T NEED TO THANK ME.
I CAN'T BELIEVE THEY'RE CHASING YOU...
...THE ONE WHO'S GRIEVING THE MOST.
I FIGURED THERE HAD TO BE A REASONABLE EXPLANA-TION...
THIS GIRL IS SMART...

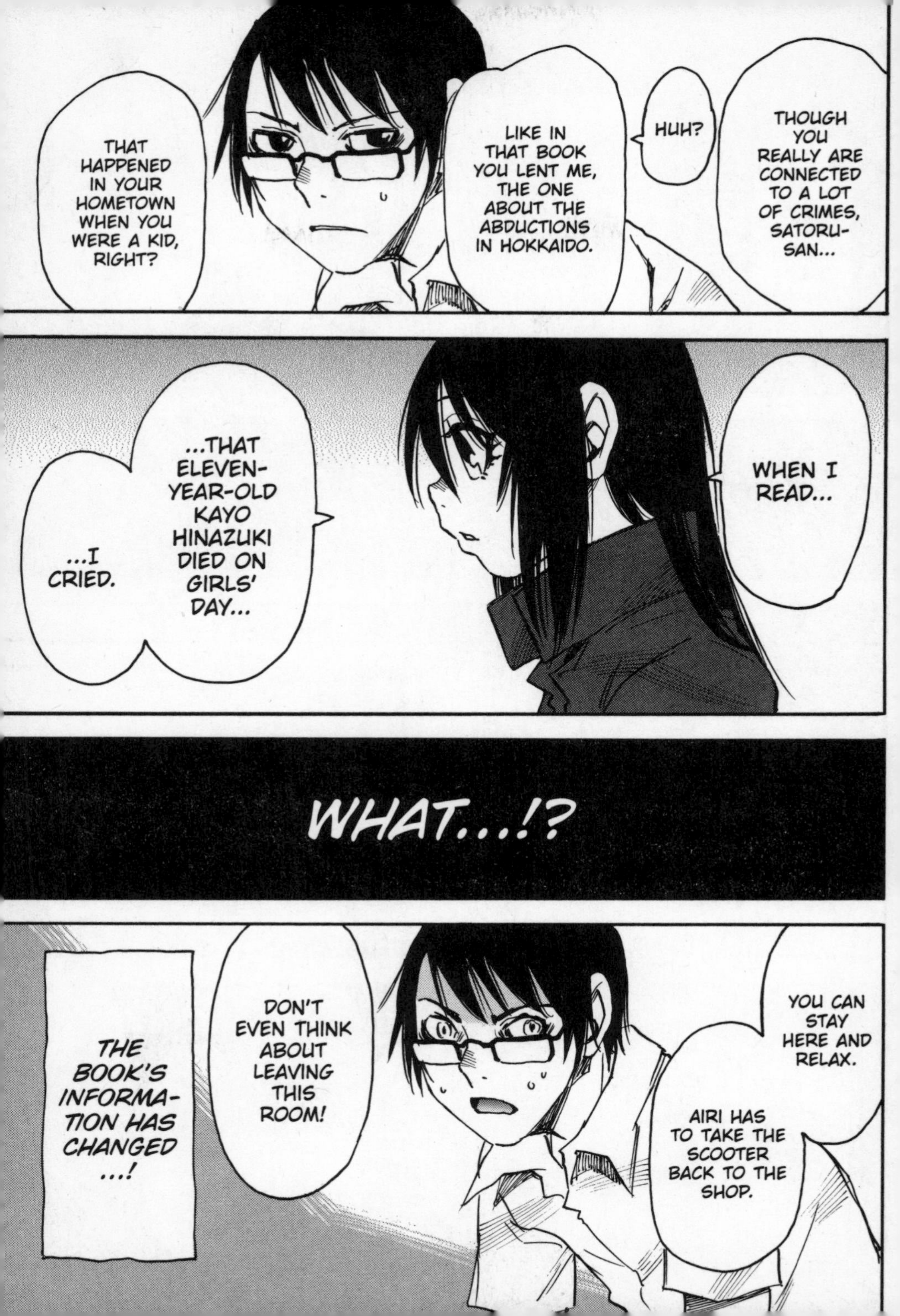
THOUGH YOU REALLY ARE CONNECTED TO A LOT OF CRIMES, SATORU-SAN...
HUH?
LIKE IN THAT BOOK YOU LENT ME, THE ONE ABOUT THE ABDUCTIONS IN HOKKAIDO.
THAT HAPPENED IN YOUR HOMETOWN WHEN YOU WERE A KID, RIGHT?
WHEN I READ...
...THAT ELEVEN-YEAR-OLD KAYO HINAZUKI DIED ON GIRLS' DAY...
...I CRIED.
WHAT...!?
YOU CAN STAY HERE AND RELAX.
AIRI HAS TO TAKE THE SCOOTER BACK TO THE SHOP.
DON'T EVEN THINK ABOUT LEAVING THIS ROOM!
THE BOOK'S INFORMATION HAS CHANGED...!

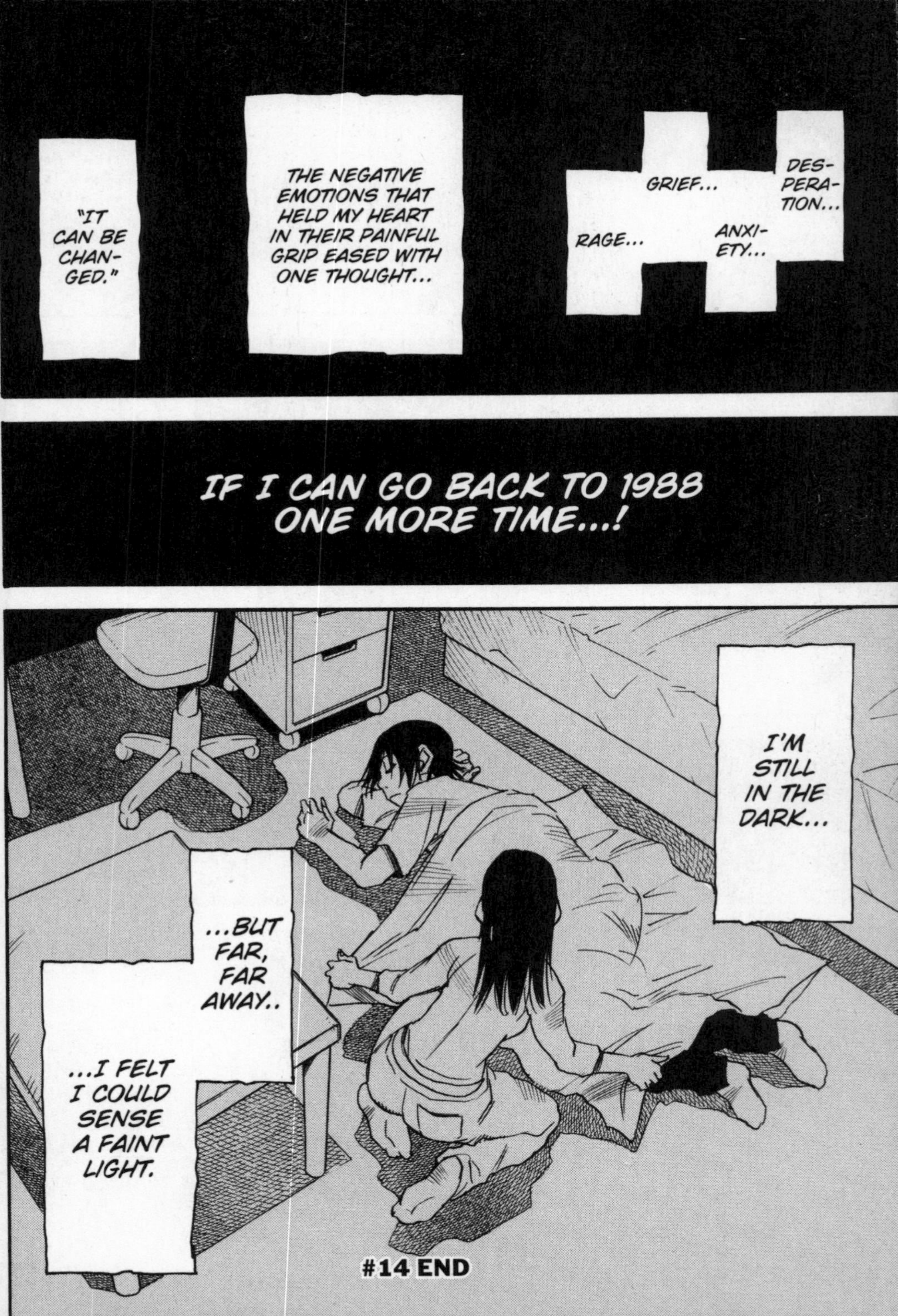
DES-PERA-TION...
GRIEF...
ANXI-ETY...
RAGE...
THE NEGATIVE EMOTIONS THAT HELD MY HEART IN THEIR PAINFUL GRIP EASED WITH ONE THOUGHT...
"IT CAN BE CHAN-GED."
IF I CAN GO BACK TO 1988 ONE MORE TIME...!
I'M STILL IN THE DARK...
...BUT FAR, FAR AWAY..
...I FELT I COULD SENSE A FAINT LIGHT.
#14 END

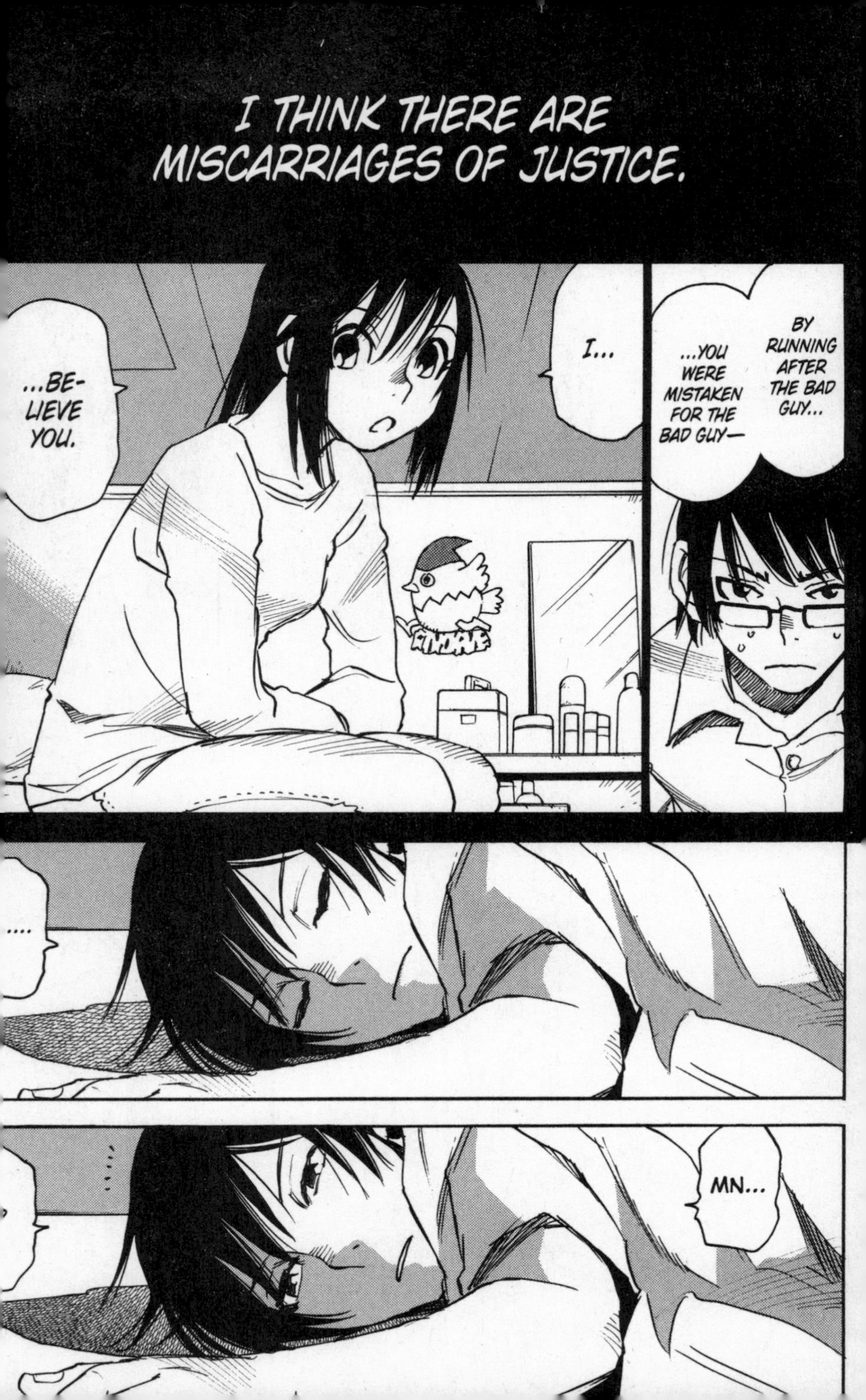
I THINK THERE ARE MISCARRIAGES OF JUSTICE.
BY RUNNING AFTER THE BAD GUY...
...YOU WERE MISTAKEN FOR THE BAD GUY—
I...
...BE-LIEVE YOU.
....
MN...
....

#15: I Want to Believe, May 2006

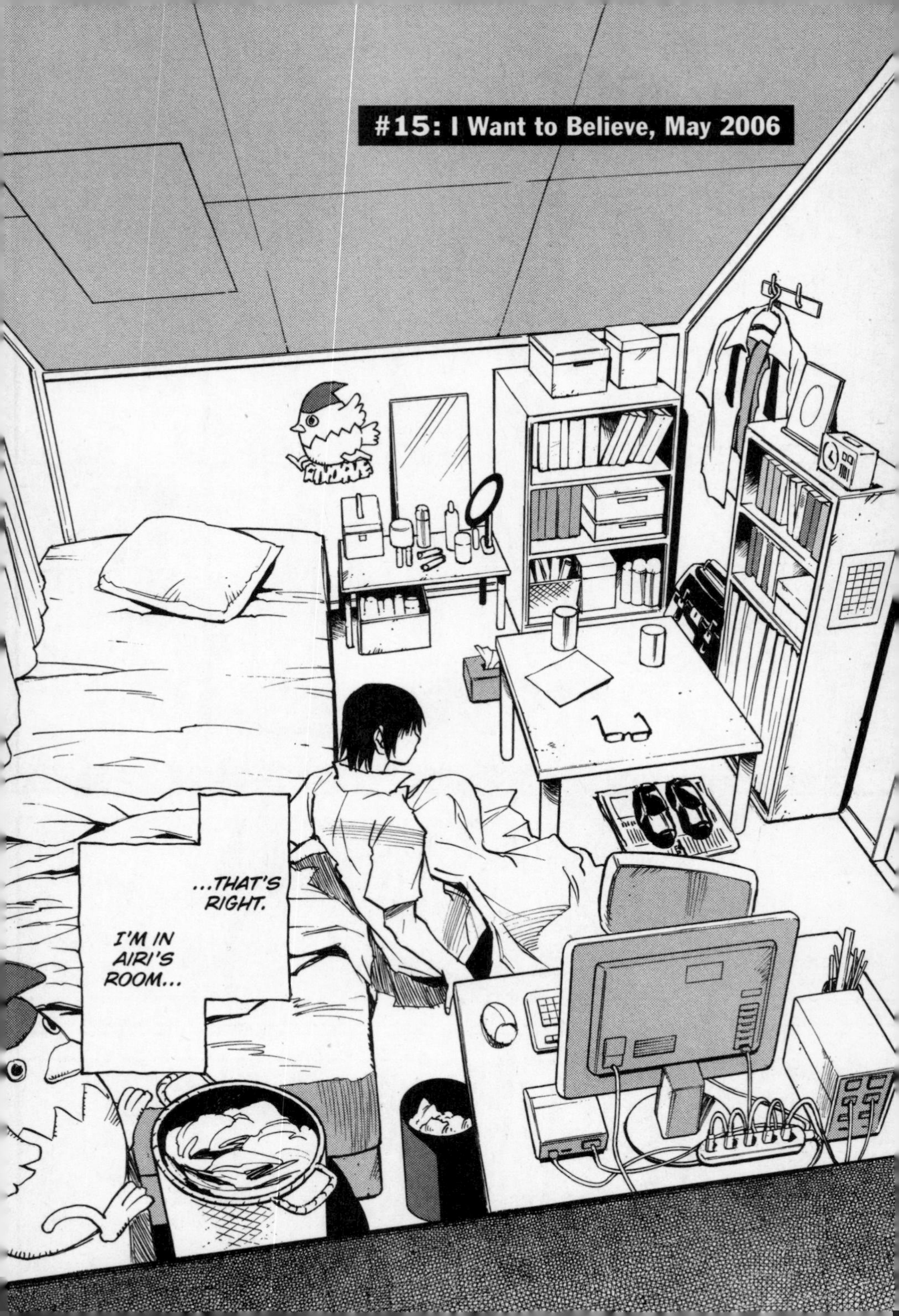
...THAT'S RIGHT.
I'M IN AIRI'S ROOM...

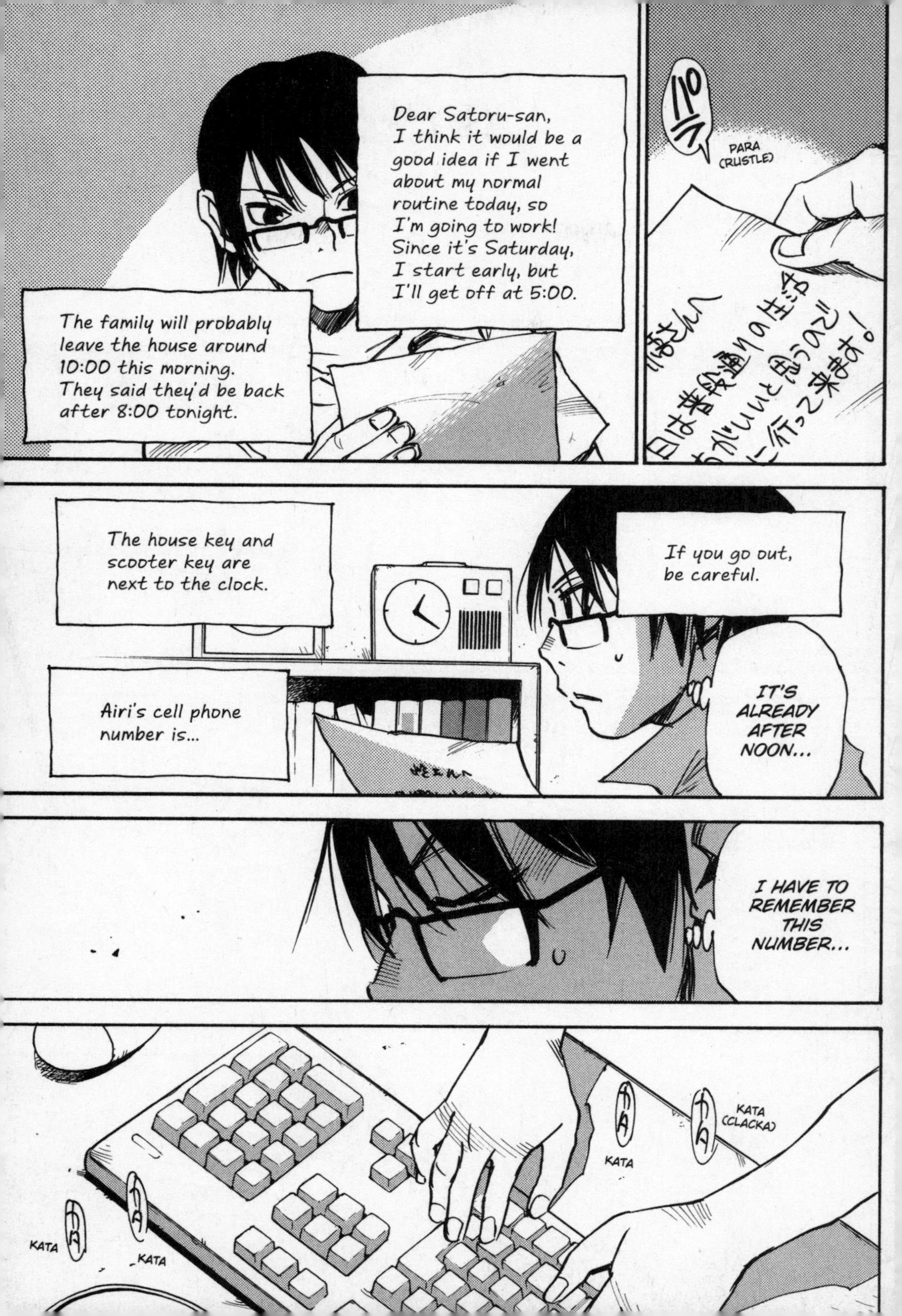

PARA (RUSTLE)
Dear Satoru-san, I think it would be a good idea if I went about my normal routine today, so I'm going to work! Since it's Saturday, I start early, but I'll get off at 5:00.
The family will probably leave the house around 10:00 this morning. They said they'd be back after 8:00 tonight.
If you go out, be careful.
The house key and scooter key are next to the clock.
IT'S ALREADY AFTER NOON...
Airi's cell phone number is...
I HAVE TO REMEMBER THIS NUMBER...
KATA (CLACKA)
KATA
KATA
KATA

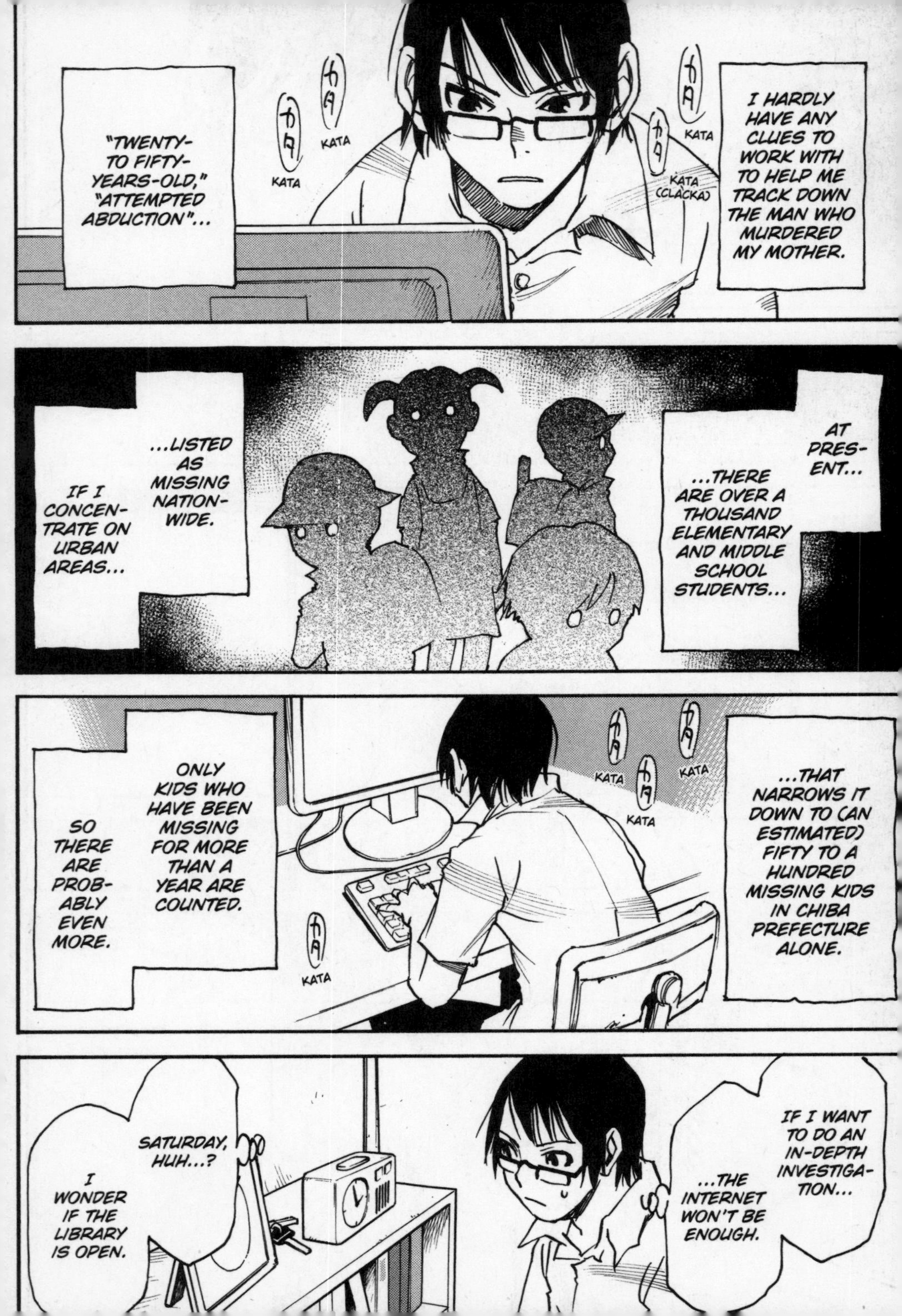

I HARDLY HAVE ANY CLUES TO WORK WITH TO HELP ME TRACK DOWN THE MAN WHO MURDERED MY MOTHER.
KATA
KATA (CLACKA)
KATA
KATA
"TWENTY- TO FIFTY-YEARS-OLD," "ATTEMPTED ABDUCTION"...
AT PRESENT...
...THERE ARE OVER A THOUSAND ELEMENTARY AND MIDDLE SCHOOL STUDENTS...
...LISTED AS MISSING NATIONWIDE.
IF I CONCENTRATE ON URBAN AREAS...
...THAT NARROWS IT DOWN TO (AN ESTIMATED) FIFTY TO A HUNDRED MISSING KIDS IN CHIBA PREFECTURE ALONE.
KATA
KATA
KATA
KATA
ONLY KIDS WHO HAVE BEEN MISSING FOR MORE THAN A YEAR ARE COUNTED.
SO THERE ARE PROBABLY EVEN MORE.
IF I WANT TO DO AN IN-DEPTH INVESTIGATION...
...THE INTERNET WON'T BE ENOUGH.
SATURDAY, HUH...?
I WONDER IF THE LIBRARY IS OPEN.

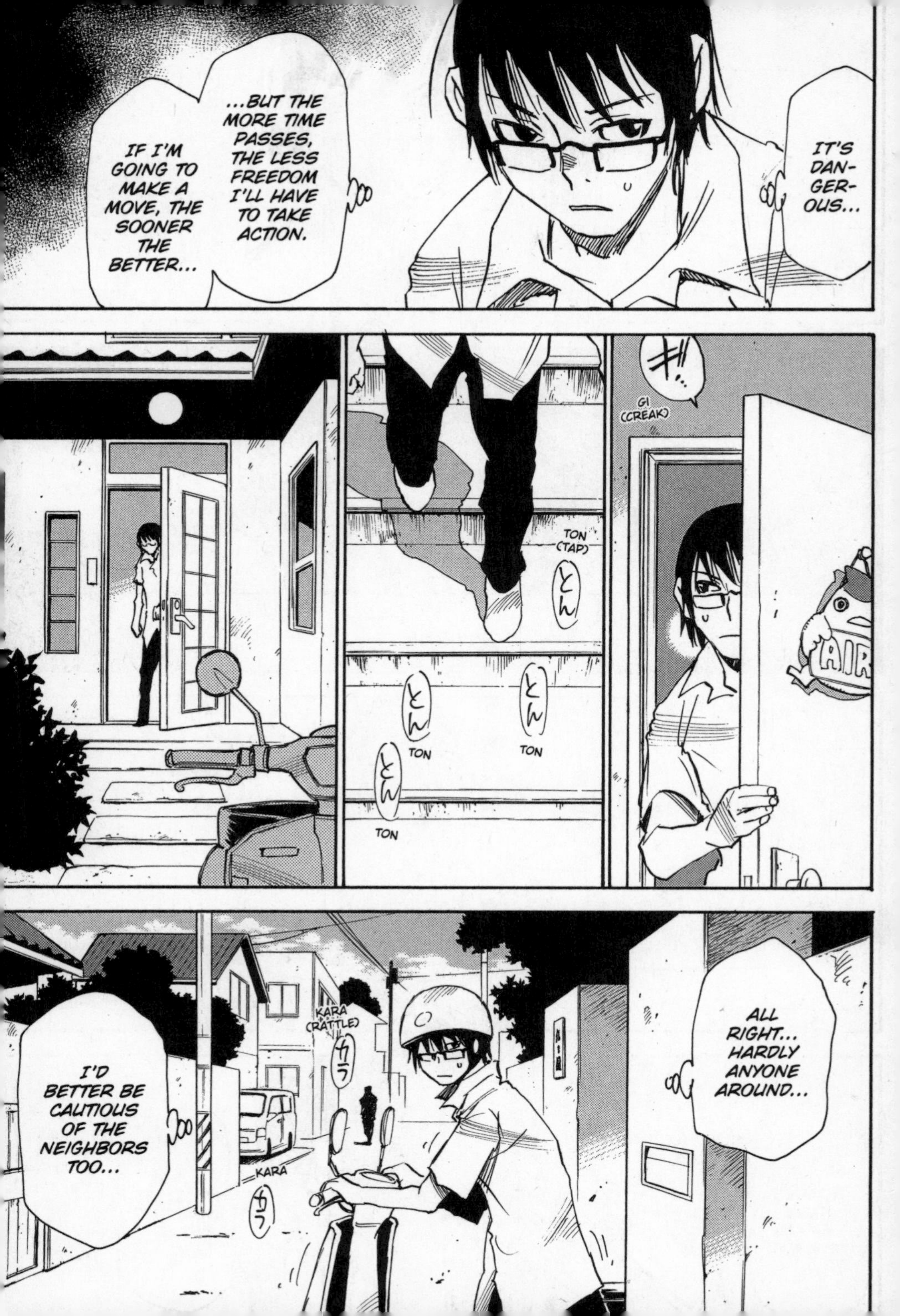
IT'S DAN-GER-OUS...
...BUT THE MORE TIME PASSES, THE LESS FREEDOM I'LL HAVE TO TAKE ACTION.
IF I'M GOING TO MAKE A MOVE, THE SOONER THE BETTER...
ギ!!
GI (CREAK)
とん
TON (TAP)
とん
TON
とん
TON
とん
TON
ALL RIGHT... HARDLY ANYONE AROUND...
カラ
KARA (RATTLE)
カラ
KARA
I'D BETTER BE CAUTIOUS OF THE NEIGHBORS TOO...

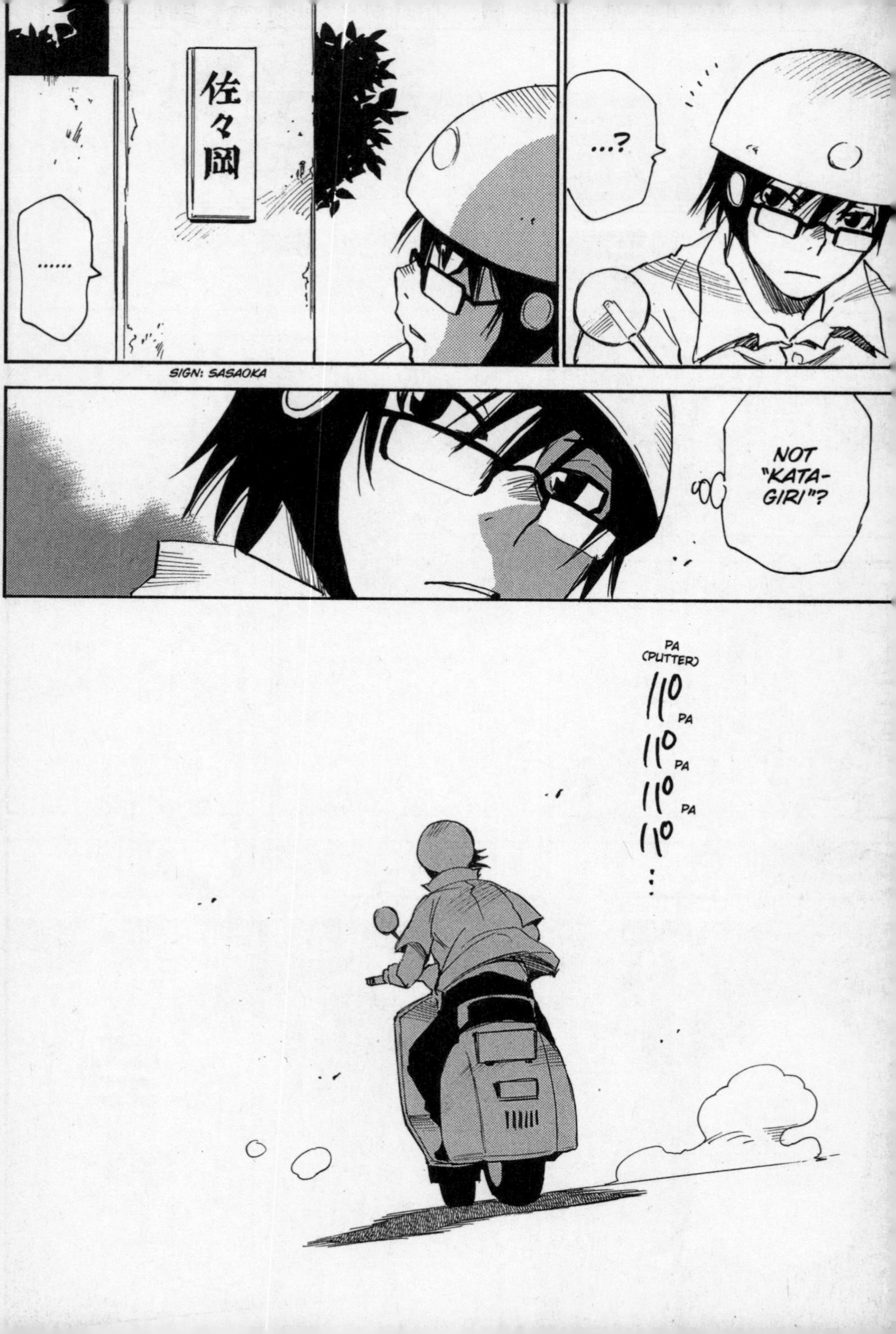
...?
佐々岡
......
SIGN: SASAOKA
NOT "KATA-GIRI"?
PA (PUTTER)
PA
PA
PA
...

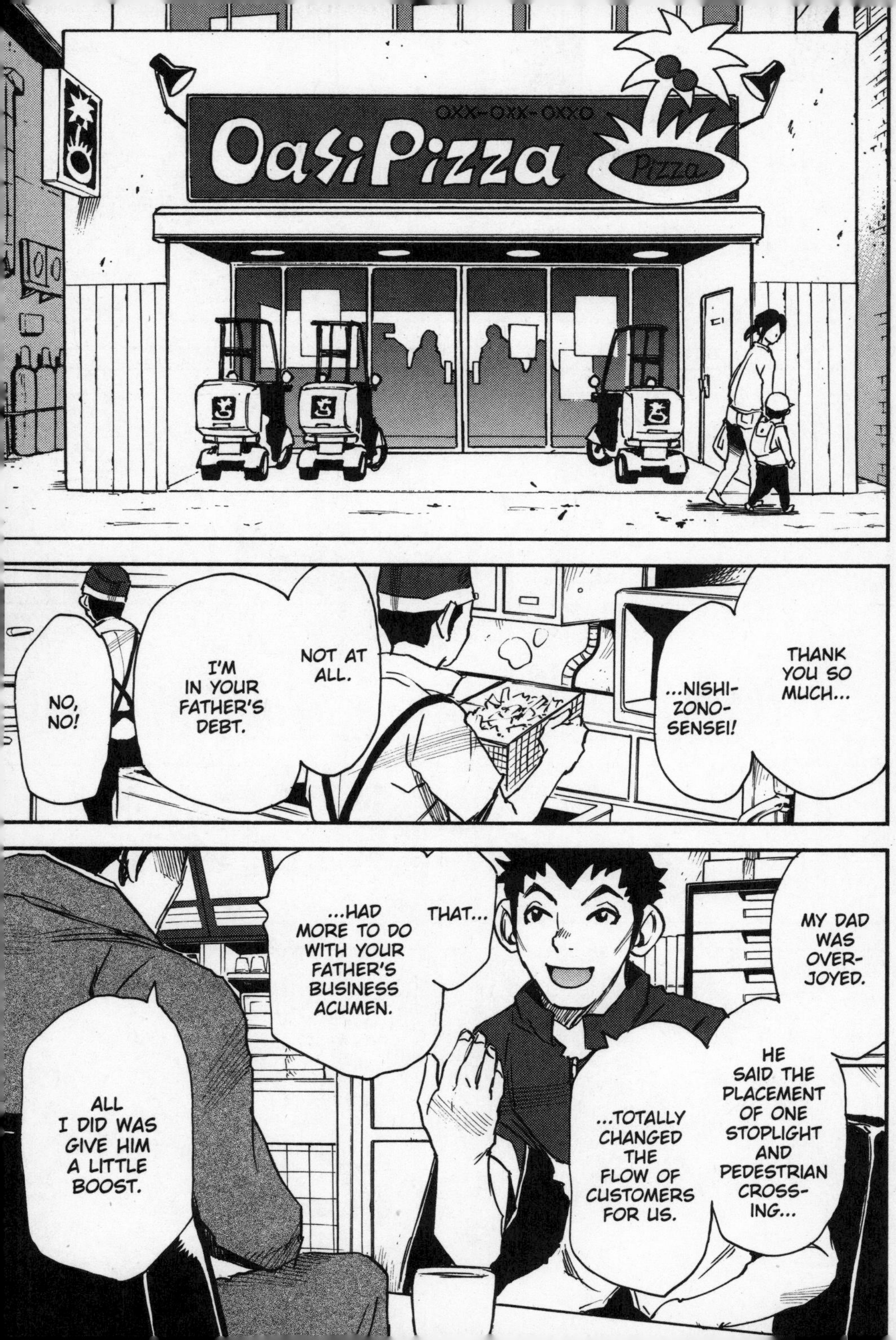
OXX-OXX-OXXO
OasiPizza
Pizza
THANK YOU SO MUCH...
...NISHI-ZONO-SENSEI!
NOT AT ALL.
I'M IN YOUR FATHER'S DEBT.
NO, NO!
MY DAD WAS OVER-JOYED.
THAT...
...HAD MORE TO DO WITH YOUR FATHER'S BUSINESS ACUMEN.
HE SAID THE PLACEMENT OF ONE STOPLIGHT AND PEDESTRIAN CROSS-ING...
...TOTALLY CHANGED THE FLOW OF CUSTOMERS FOR US.
ALL I DID WAS GIVE HIM A LITTLE BOOST.

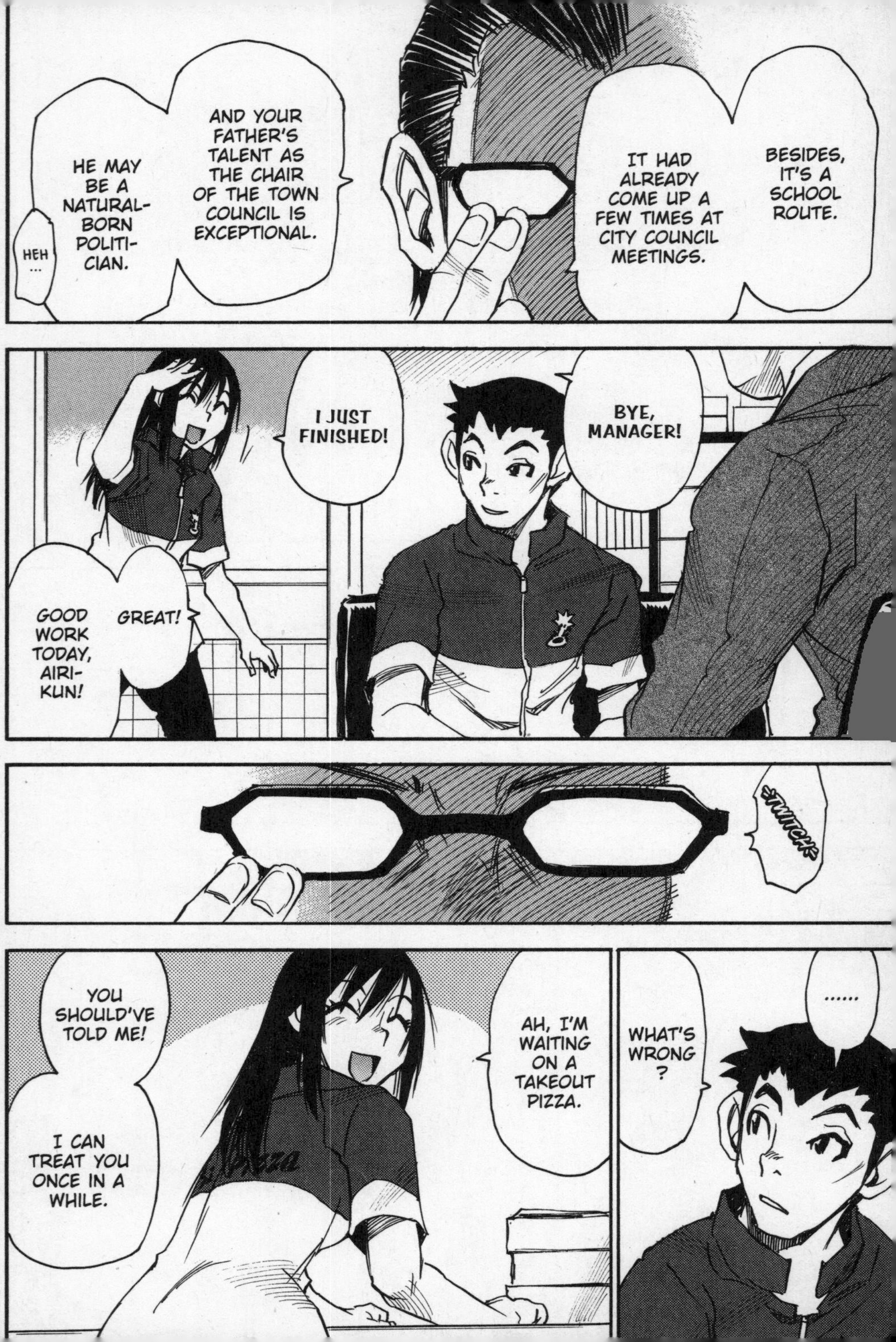
BESIDES, IT'S A SCHOOL ROUTE.
IT HAD ALREADY COME UP A FEW TIMES AT CITY COUNCIL MEETINGS.
AND YOUR FATHER'S TALENT AS THE CHAIR OF THE TOWN COUNCIL IS EXCEPTIONAL.
HE MAY BE A NATURAL-BORN POLITI-CIAN.
HEH...
BYE, MANAGER!
I JUST FINISHED!
GREAT!
GOOD WORK TODAY, AIRI-KUN!
TWITCH
......
WHAT'S WRONG?
AH, I'M WAITING ON A TAKEOUT PIZZA.
YOU SHOULD'VE TOLD ME!
I CAN TREAT YOU ONCE IN A WHILE.

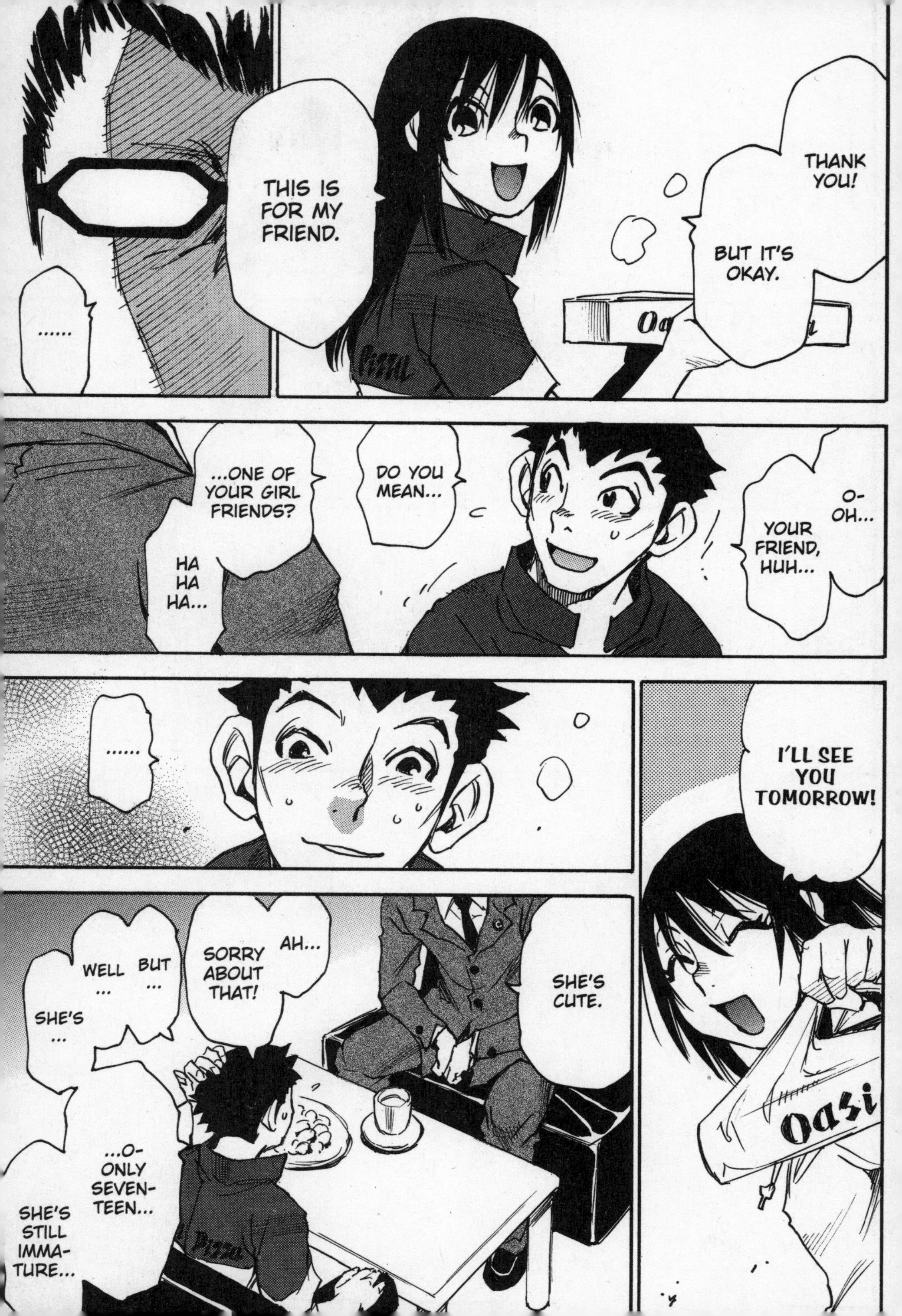
THANK YOU!
BUT IT'S OKAY.
THIS IS FOR MY FRIEND.
......
O-OH...
YOUR FRIEND, HUH...
DO YOU MEAN...
...ONE OF YOUR GIRL FRIENDS?
HA HA HA...
I'LL SEE YOU TOMORROW!
......
SHE'S CUTE.
AH...
SORRY ABOUT THAT!
BUT ...
WELL ...
SHE'S ...
...O-ONLY SEVENTEEN...
SHE'S STILL IMMATURE...

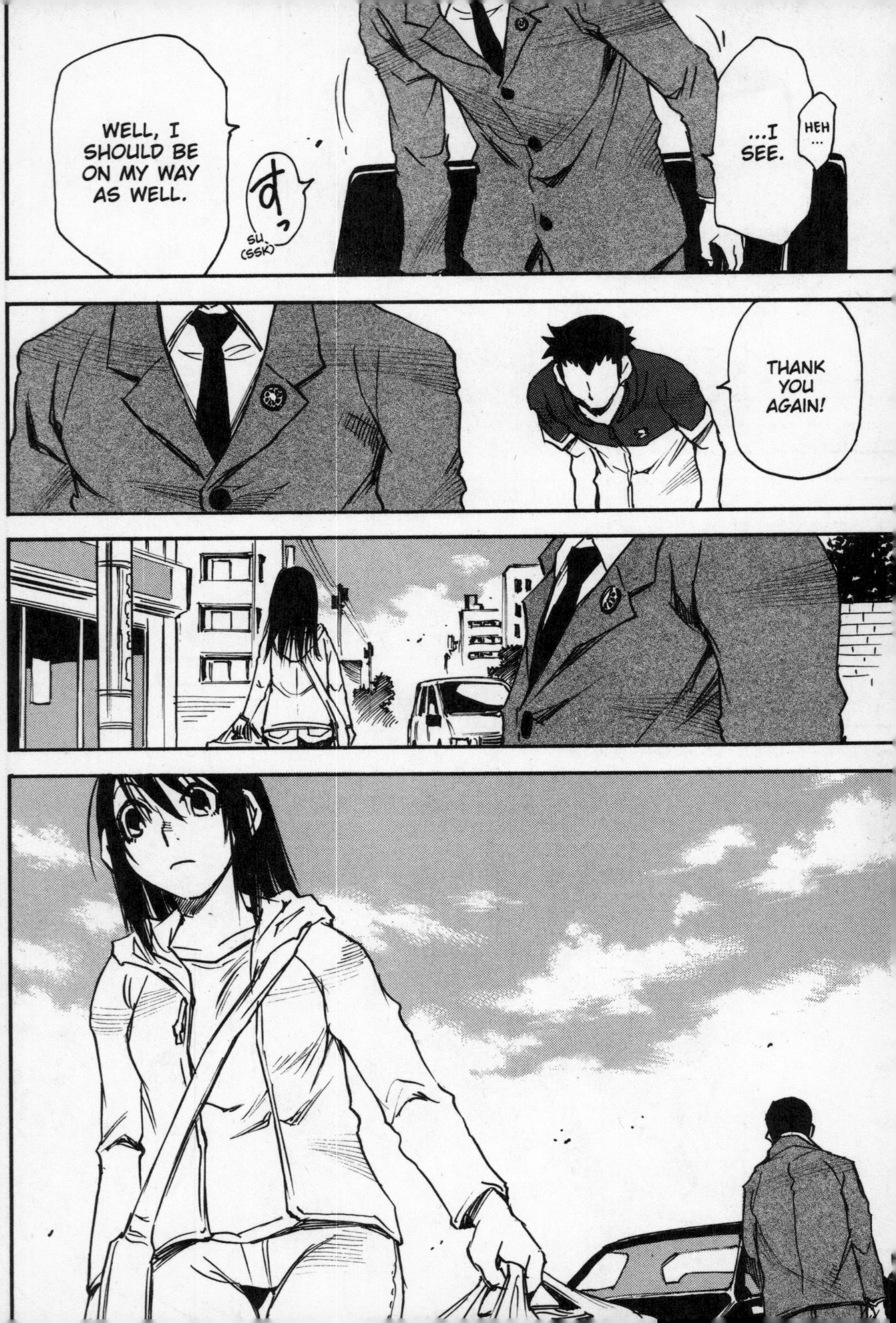
HEH...
...I SEE.
すっ
SU (SSK)
WELL, I SHOULD BE ON MY WAY AS WELL.
THANK YOU AGAIN!

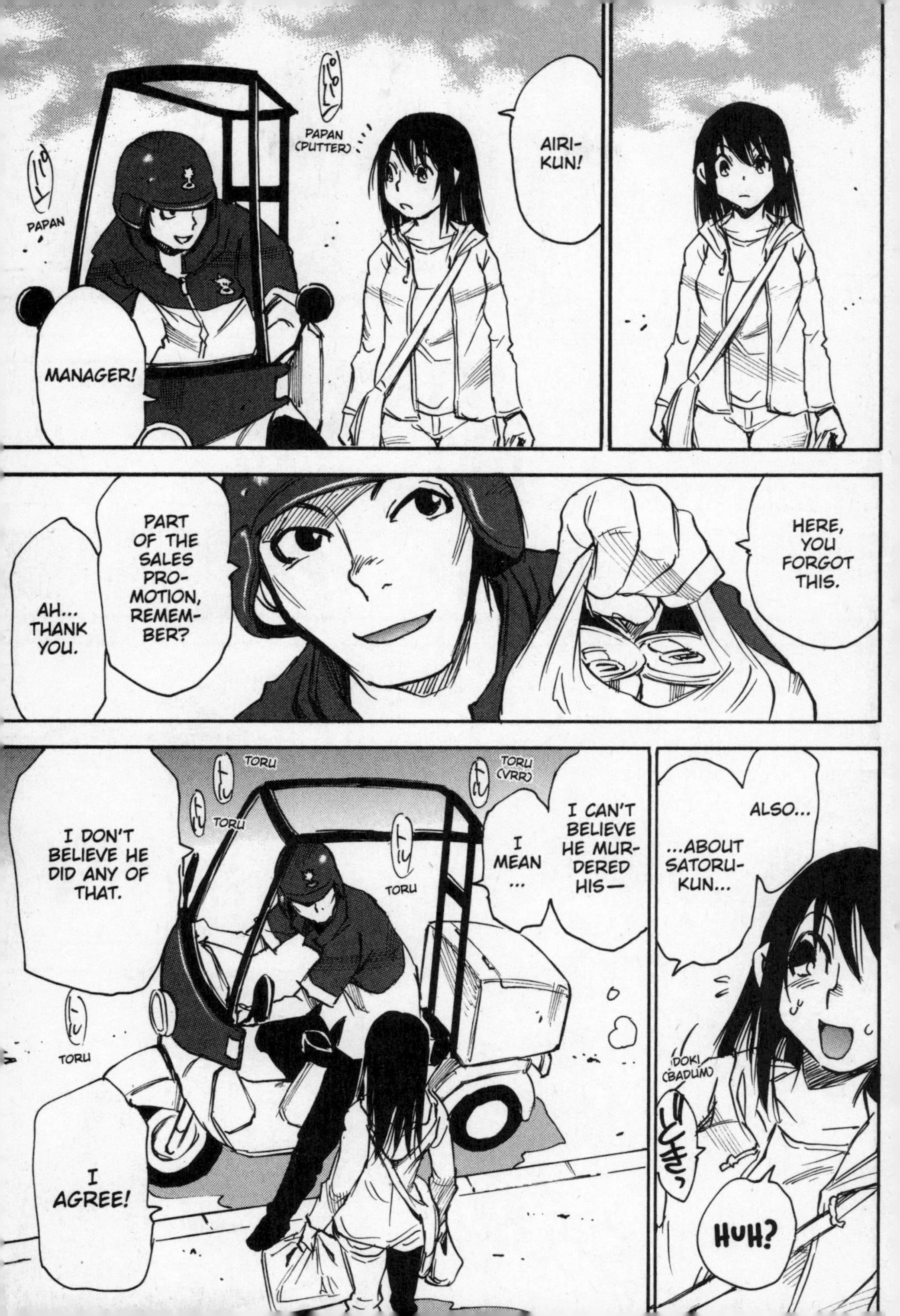

AIRI-KUN!
PAPAN (PUTTER)
PAPAN
MANAGER!
HERE, YOU FORGOT THIS.
PART OF THE SALES PROMOTION, REMEMBER?
AH... THANK YOU.
ALSO...
...ABOUT SATORU-KUN...
DOKI (BADUM)
HUH?
TORU (VRR)
I CAN'T BELIEVE HE MURDERED HIS—
I MEAN ...
TORU
TORU
TORU
I DON'T BELIEVE HE DID ANY OF THAT.
TORU
I AGREE!

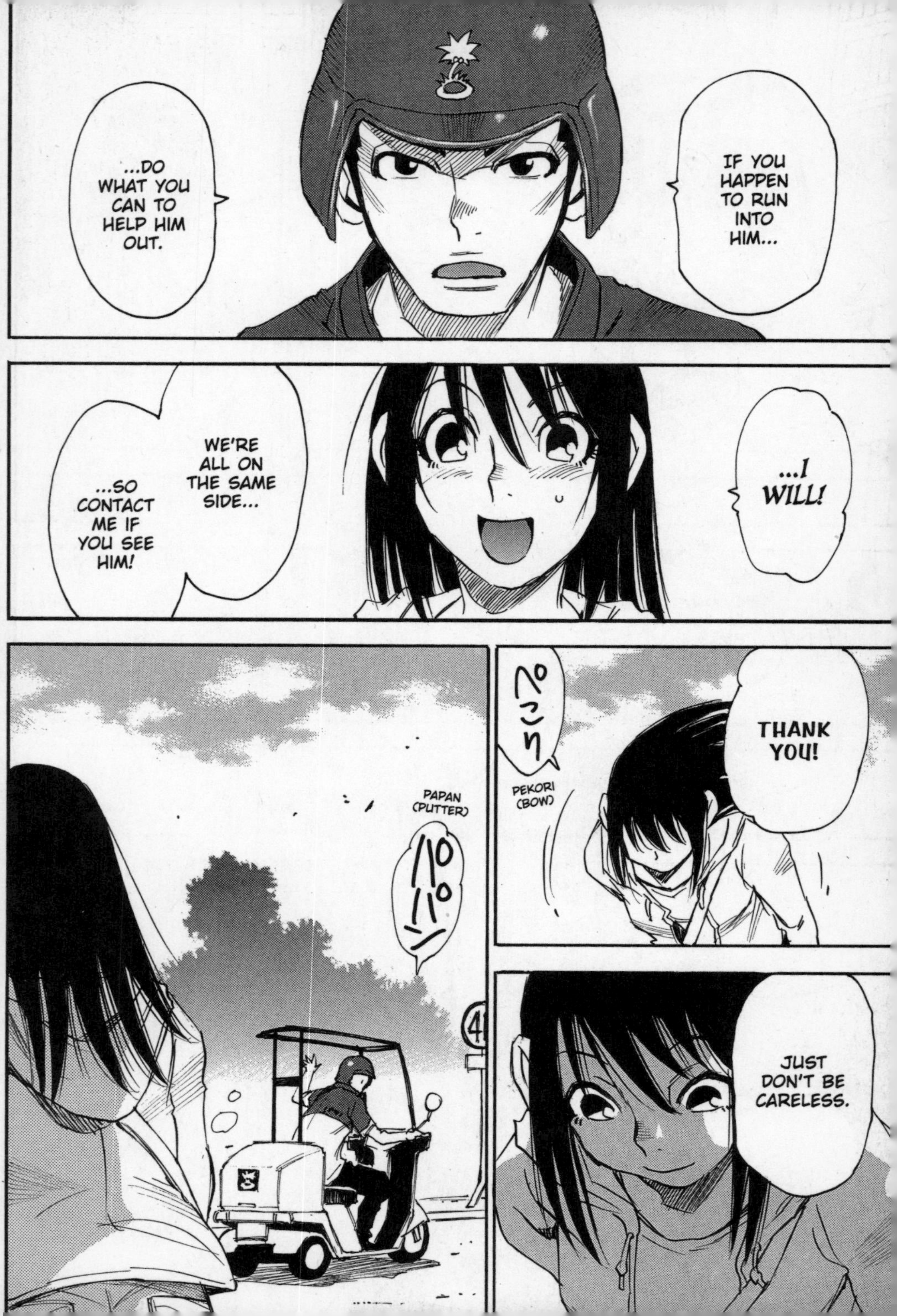
IF YOU HAPPEN TO RUN INTO HIM...
...DO WHAT YOU CAN TO HELP HIM OUT.
...I WILL!
WE'RE ALL ON THE SAME SIDE...
...SO CONTACT ME IF YOU SEE HIM!
THANK YOU!
ぺこり
PEKORI (BOW)
JUST DON'T BE CARELESS.
パパン
PAPAN (PUTTER)

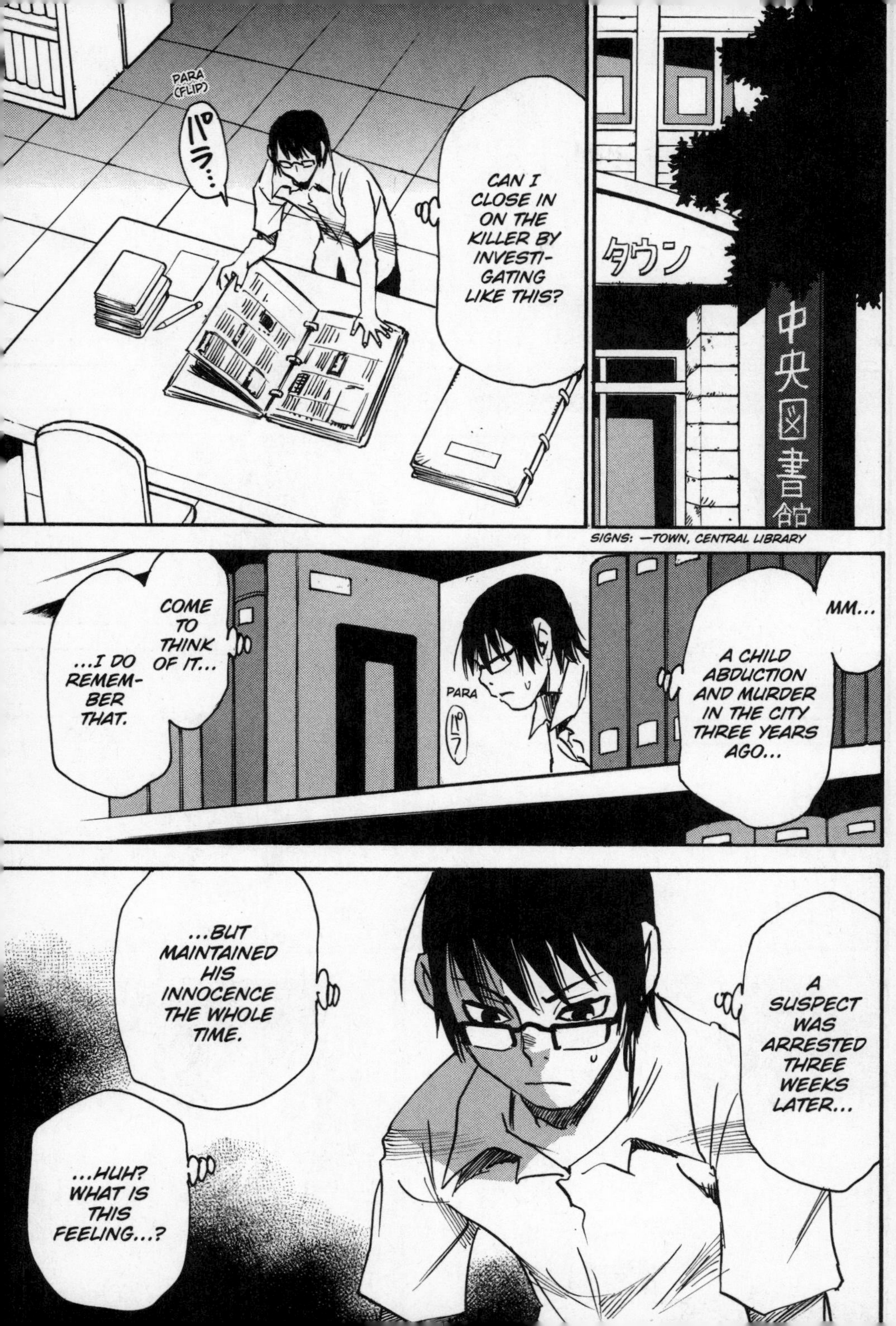
タウン
中央図書館
SIGNS: —TOWN, CENTRAL LIBRARY
CAN I CLOSE IN ON THE KILLER BY INVESTIGATING LIKE THIS?
PARA (FLIP)
パラ…
MM…
A CHILD ABDUCTION AND MURDER IN THE CITY THREE YEARS AGO…
PARA
パラ
COME TO THINK OF IT…
…I DO REMEMBER THAT.
A SUSPECT WAS ARRESTED THREE WEEKS LATER…
…BUT MAINTAINED HIS INNOCENCE THE WHOLE TIME.
…HUH? WHAT IS THIS FEELING…?

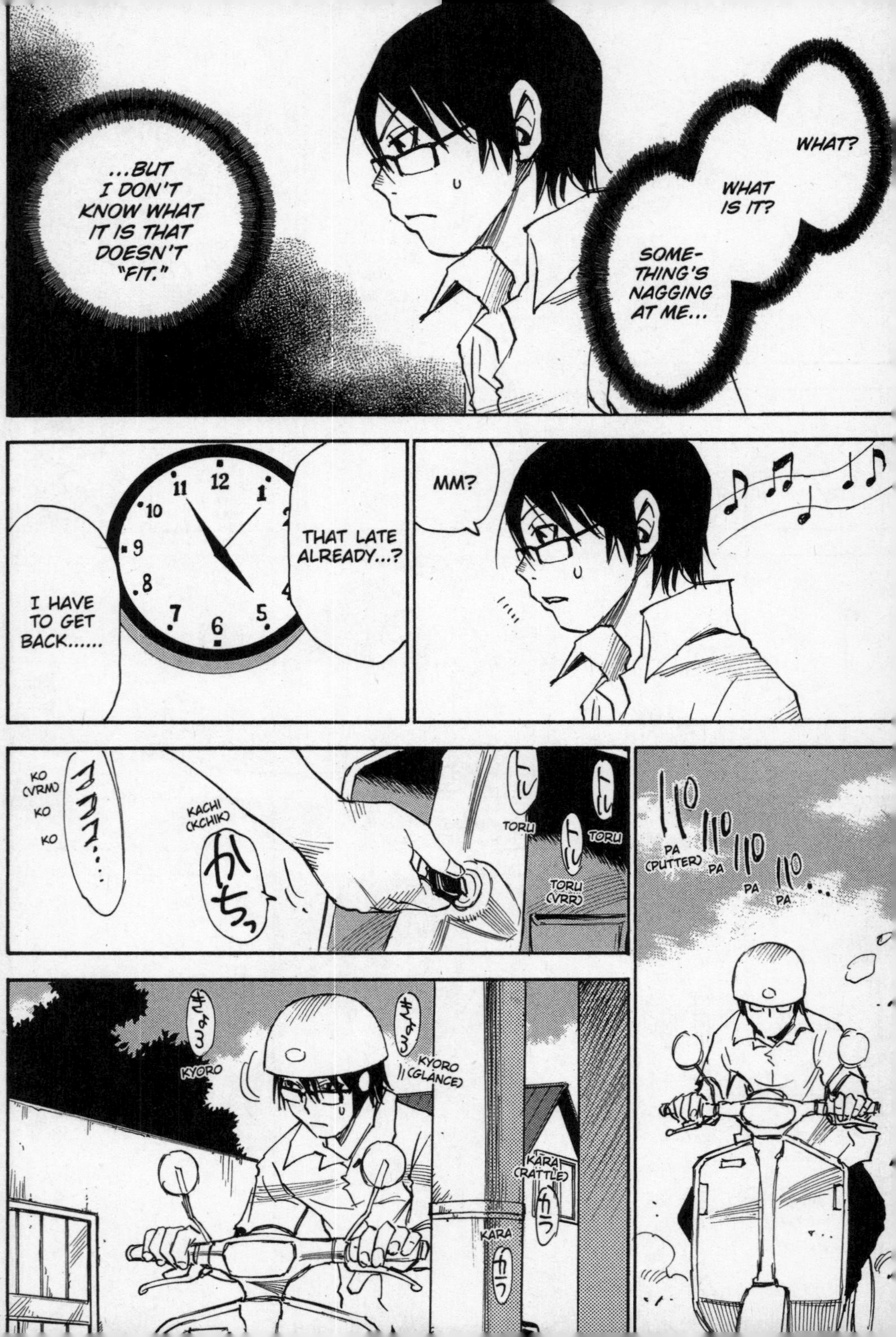

WHAT?
WHAT IS IT?
SOME-THING'S NAGGING AT ME...
...BUT I DON'T KNOW WHAT IT IS THAT DOESN'T "FIT."
MM?
THAT LATE ALREADY...?
I HAVE TO GET BACK......
PA (PUTTER) PA PA PA...
TORU TORU
TORU (VRR)
KACHI (KCHIK)
かちっ
KO (VRM) KO KO
KARA (RATTLE) KARA
KYORO (GLANCE)
KYORO

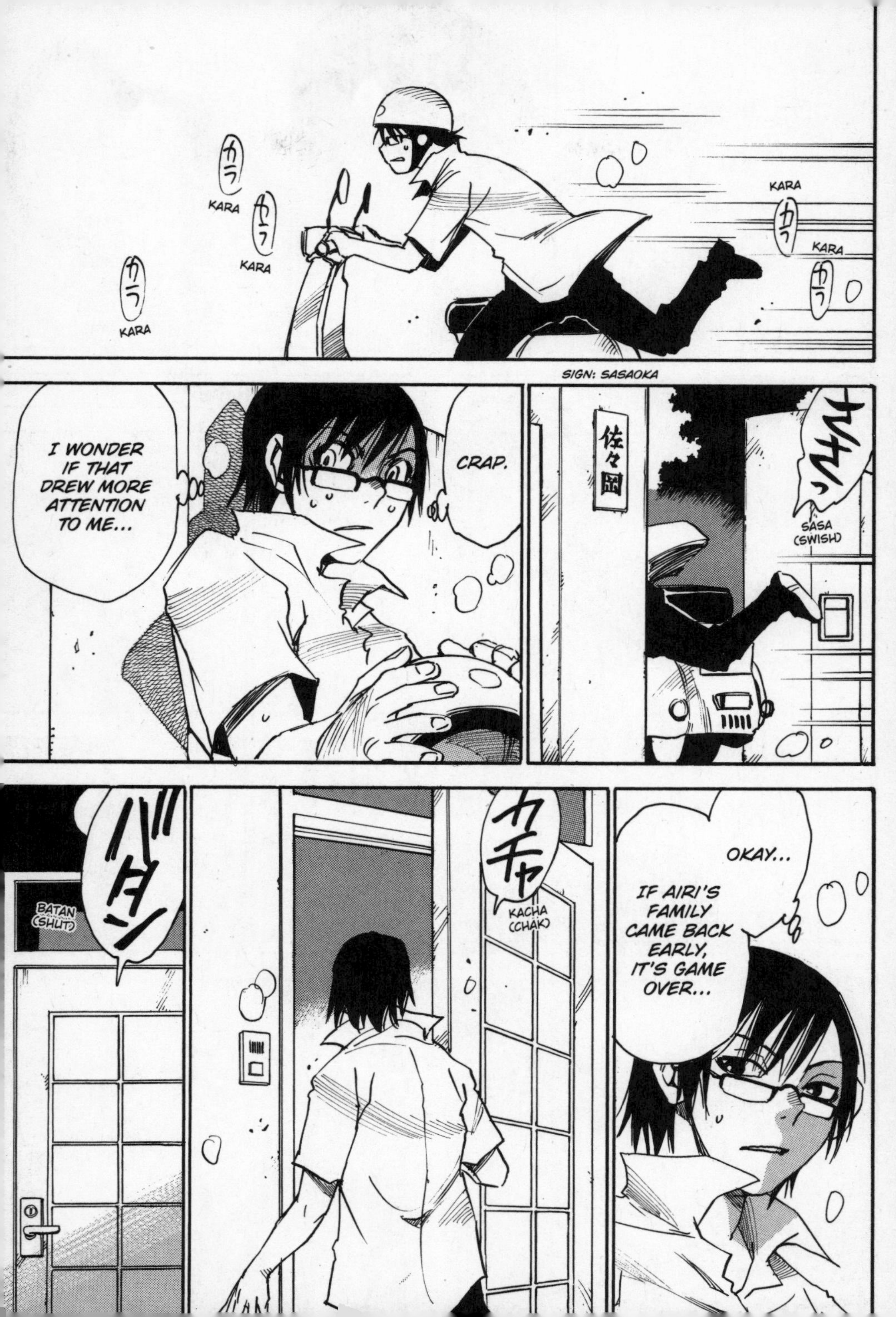

KARA
カラ
KARA
カラ
カラ
KARA
カラ
KARA
カラ
KARA
SIGN: SASAOKA
佐々岡
ささっ
SASA (SWISH)
CRAP.
I WONDER IF THAT DREW MORE ATTENTION TO ME...
OKAY...
IF AIRI'S FAMILY CAME BACK EARLY, IT'S GAME OVER...
カチャ
KACHA (CHAK)
バタン
BATAN (SHUT)

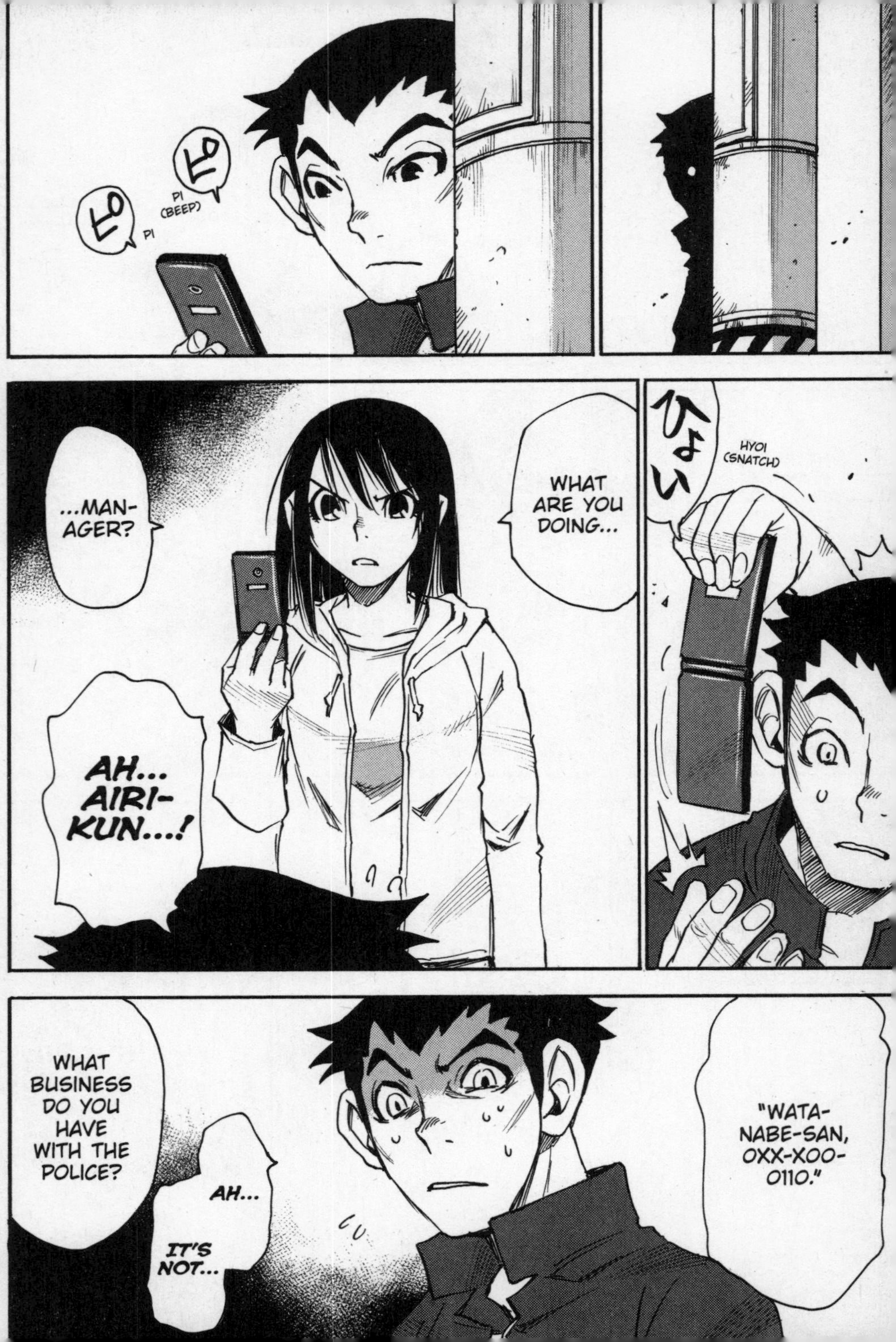
ピ
PI (BEEP)
ピ
PI
ひょい
HYOI (SNATCH)
WHAT ARE YOU DOING...
...MAN-AGER?
AH... AIRI-KUN...!
"WATA-NABE-SAN, OXX-XOO-0110."
WHAT BUSINESS DO YOU HAVE WITH THE POLICE?
AH...
IT'S NOT...

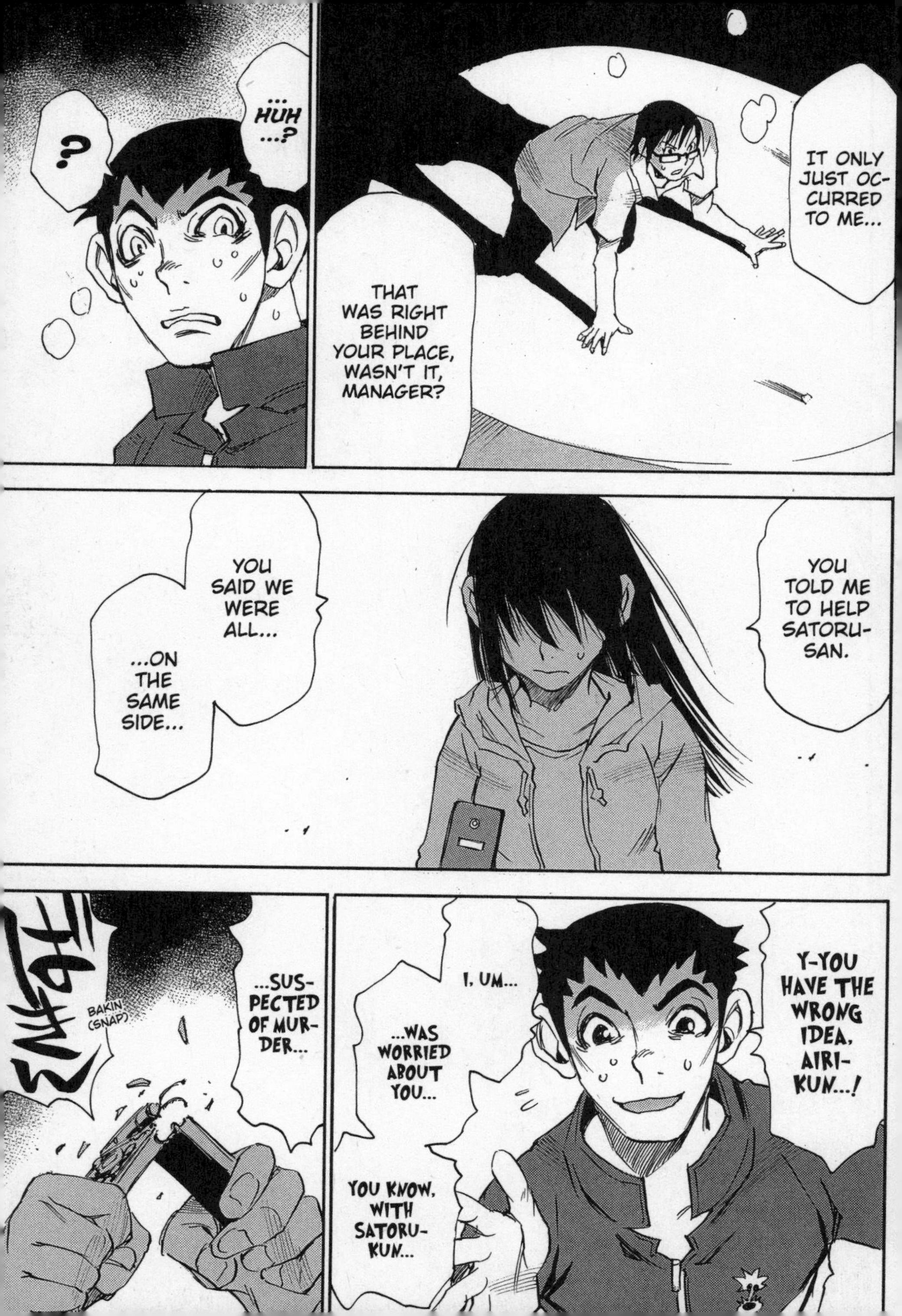
IT ONLY JUST OC-CURRED TO ME...
THAT WAS RIGHT BEHIND YOUR PLACE, WASN'T IT, MANAGER?
...HUH...?
?
YOU TOLD ME TO HELP SATORU-SAN.
YOU SAID WE WERE ALL...
...ON THE SAME SIDE...
Y-YOU HAVE THE WRONG IDEA, AIRI-KUN...!
I, UM...
...WAS WORRIED ABOUT YOU...
YOU KNOW, WITH SATORU-KUN...
...SUS-PECTED OF MUR-DER...
BAKIN (SNAP)

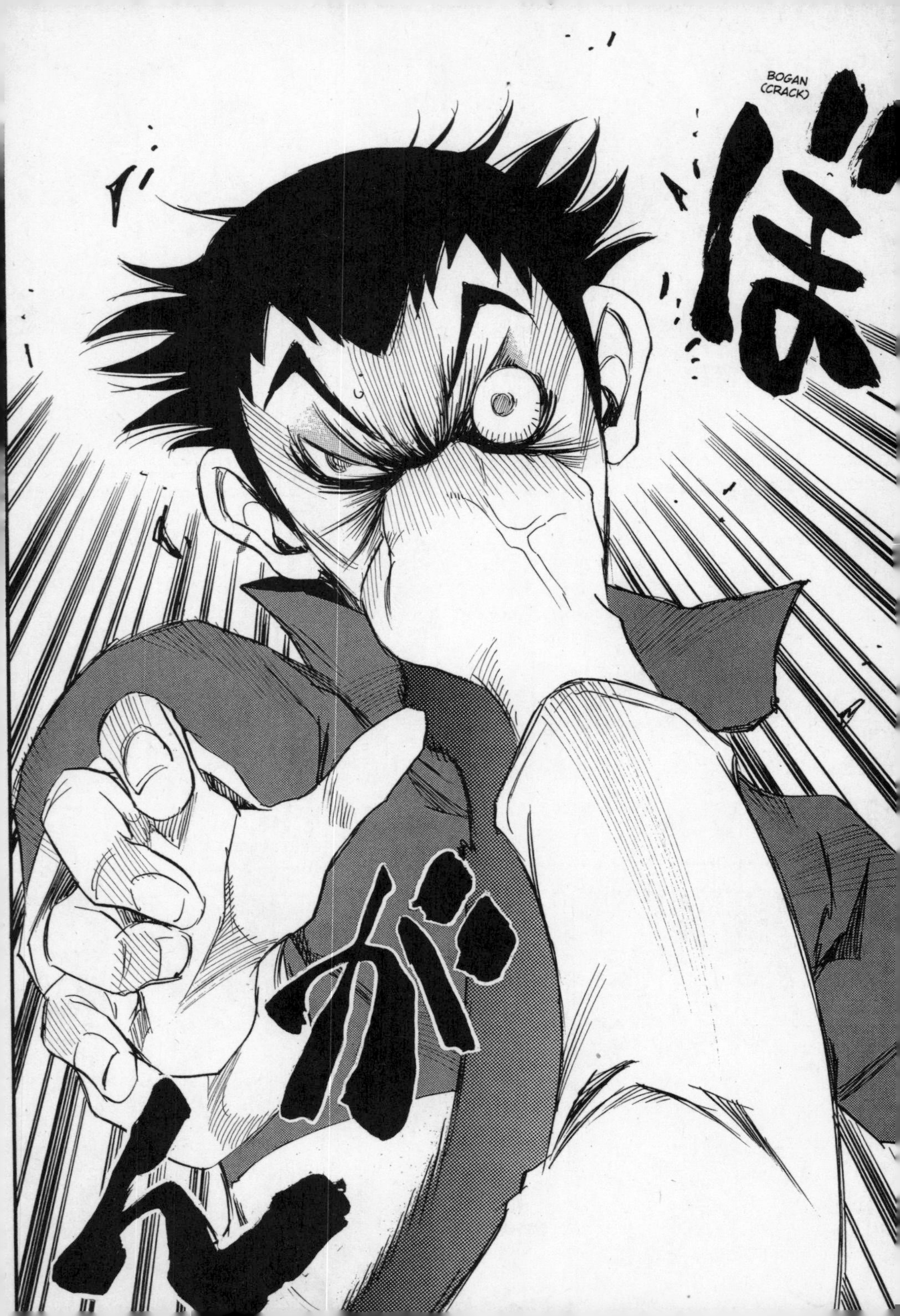
ぼ
BOGAN (CRACK)
がん

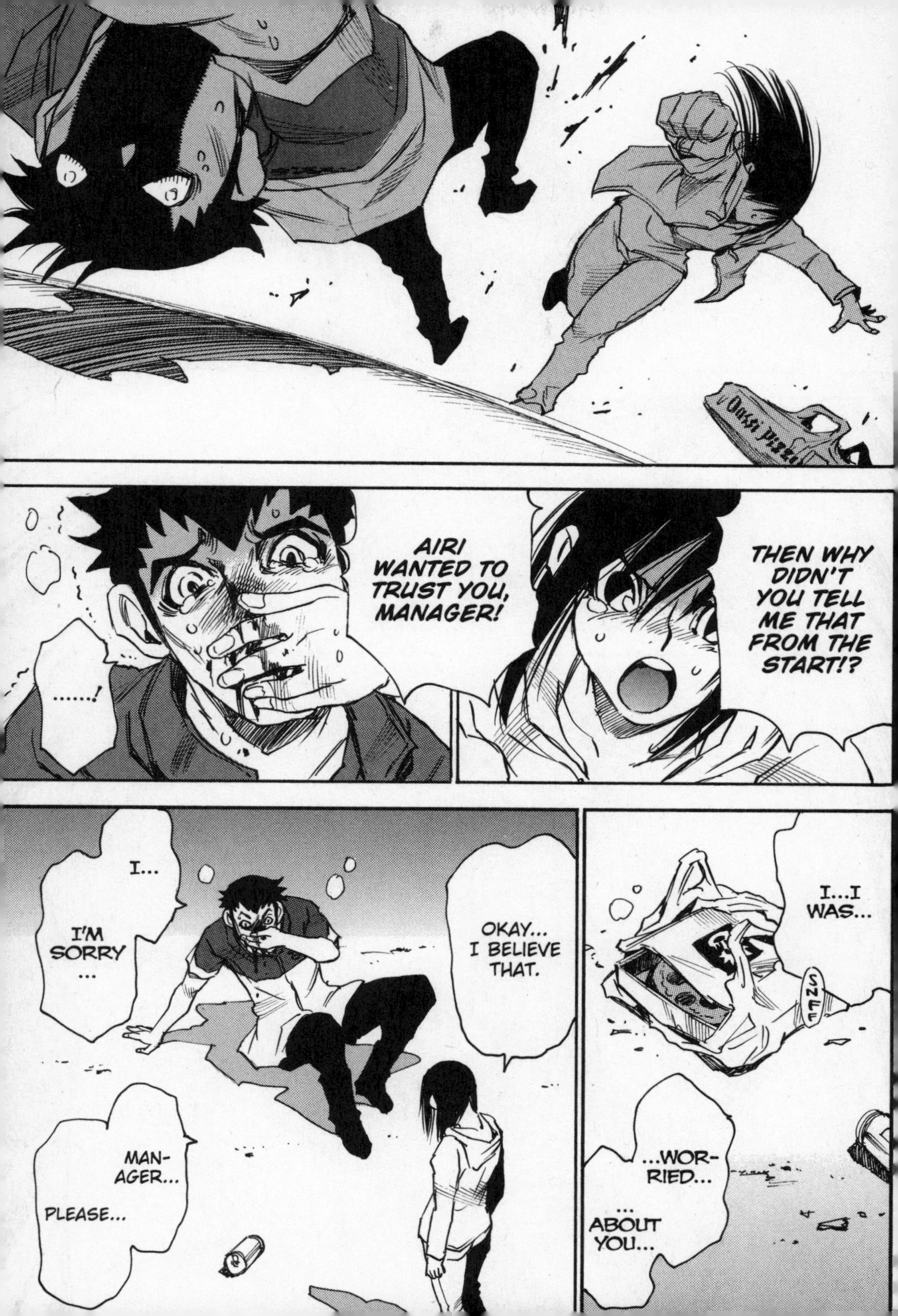
THEN WHY DIDN'T YOU TELL ME THAT FROM THE START!?
AIRI WANTED TO TRUST YOU, MANAGER!
......!
I...I WAS...
SNFF
...WOR-RIED...
...ABOUT YOU...
OKAY... I BELIEVE THAT.
I...
I'M SORRY ...
MAN-AGER...
PLEASE...

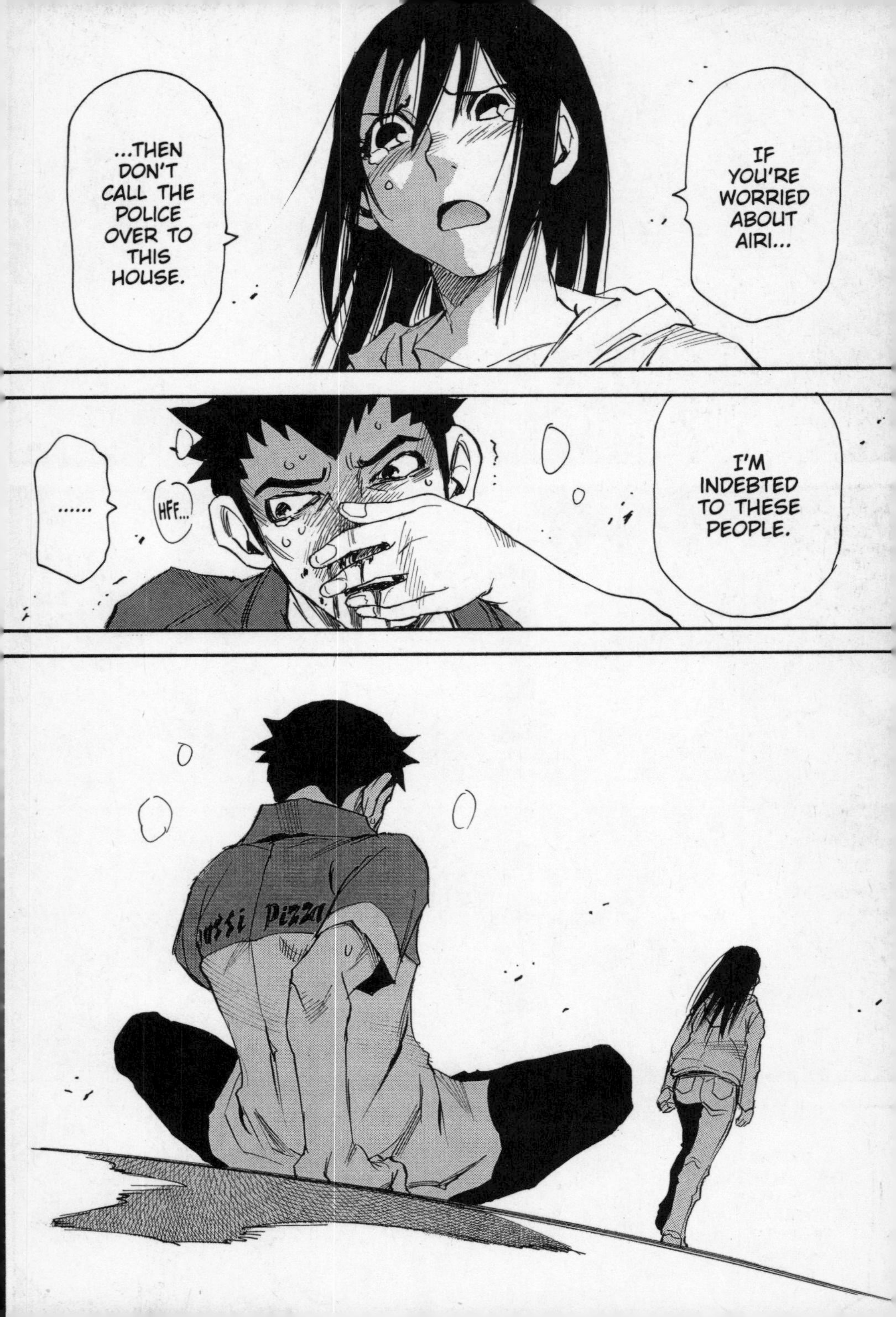
IF YOU'RE WORRIED ABOUT AIRI...
...THEN DON'T CALL THE POLICE OVER TO THIS HOUSE.
I'M INDEBTED TO THESE PEOPLE.
HFF...
......

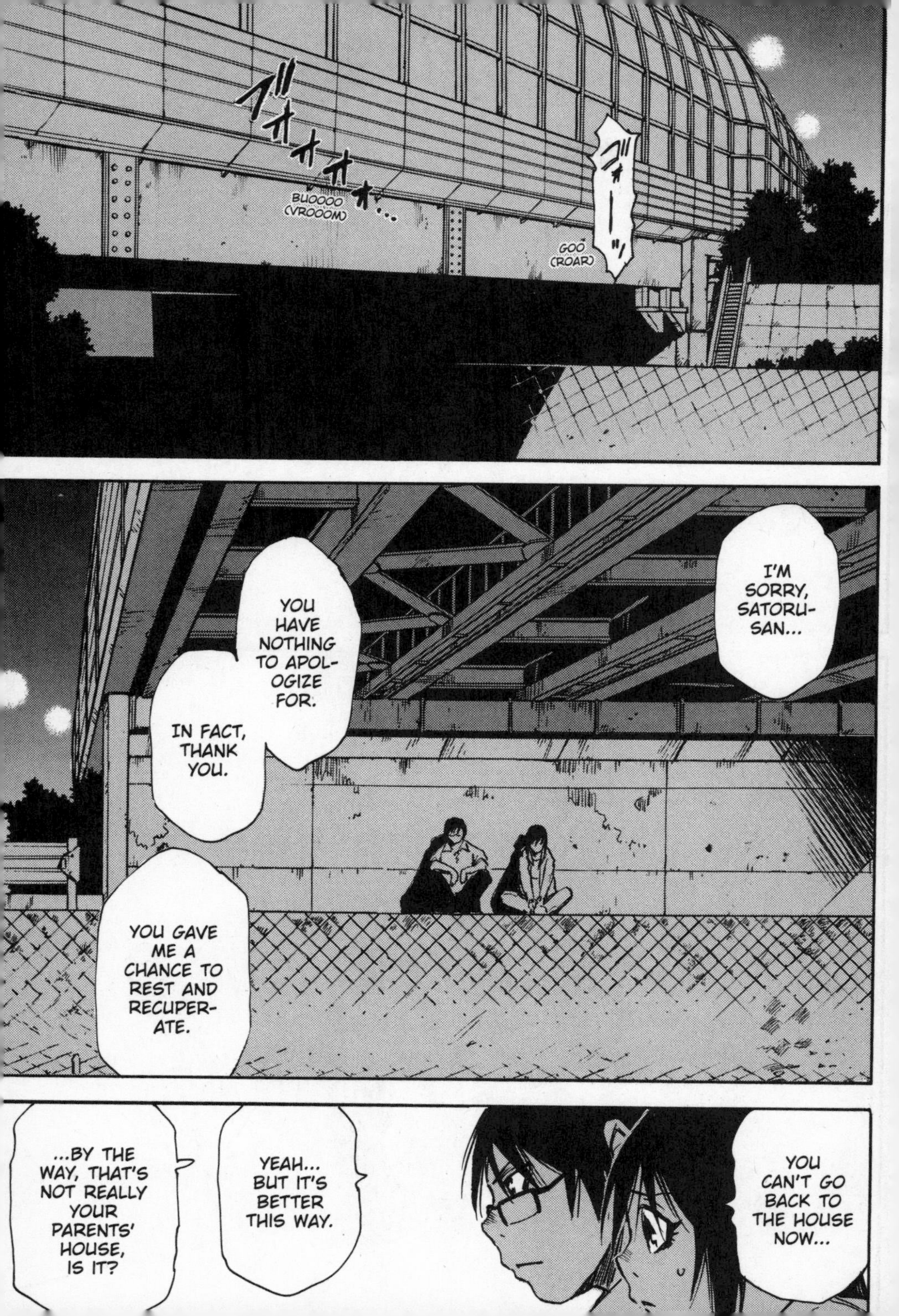
GOO (ROAR)
BUOOOO (VROOOM)
I'M SORRY, SATORU-SAN...
YOU HAVE NOTHING TO APOLOGIZE FOR.
IN FACT, THANK YOU.
YOU GAVE ME A CHANCE TO REST AND RECUPERATE.
YOU CAN'T GO BACK TO THE HOUSE NOW...
YEAH... BUT IT'S BETTER THIS WAY.
...BY THE WAY, THAT'S NOT REALLY YOUR PARENTS' HOUSE, IS IT?

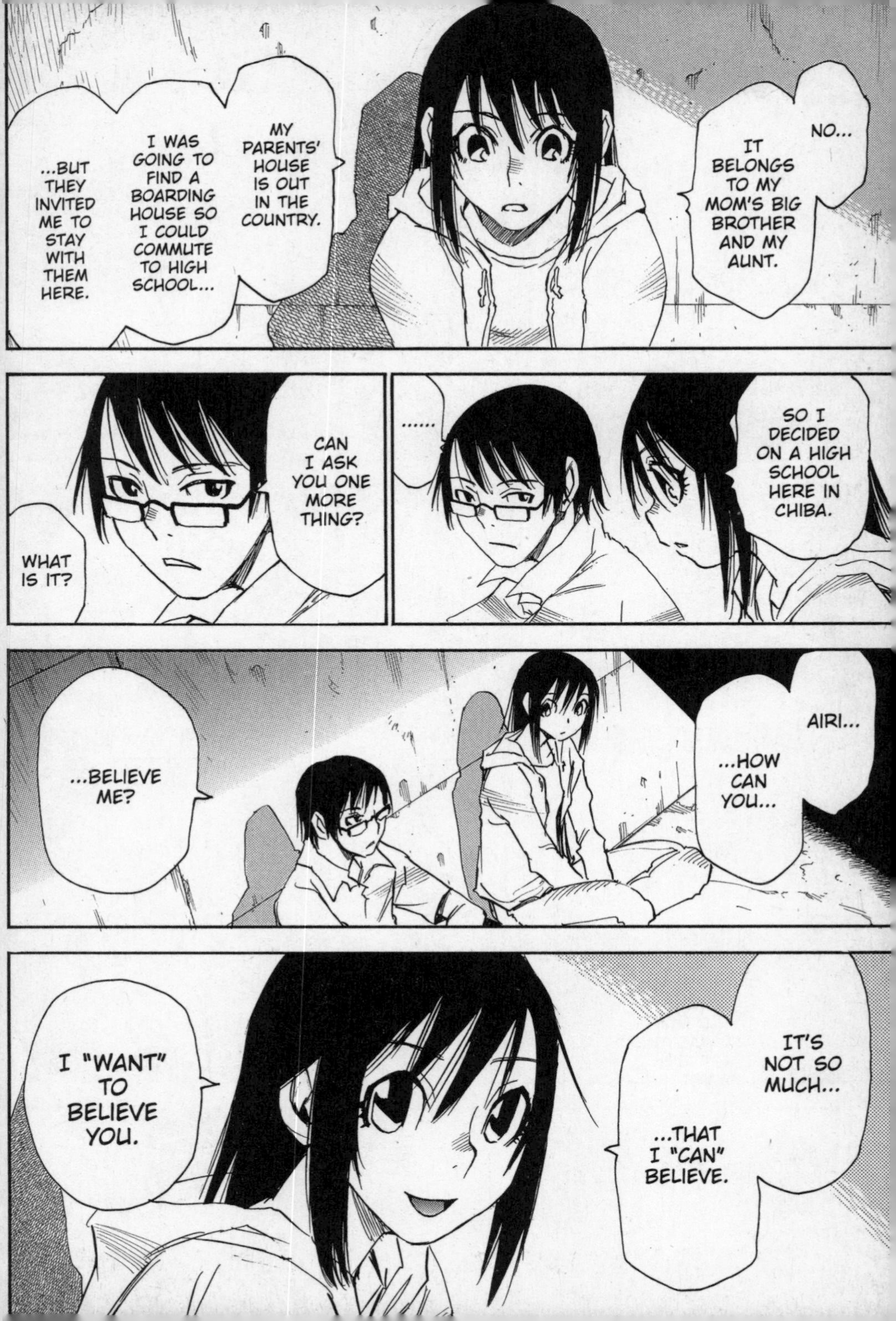
NO...
IT BELONGS TO MY MOM'S BIG BROTHER AND MY AUNT.
MY PARENTS' HOUSE IS OUT IN THE COUNTRY.
I WAS GOING TO FIND A BOARDING HOUSE SO I COULD COMMUTE TO HIGH SCHOOL...
...BUT THEY INVITED ME TO STAY WITH THEM HERE.
SO I DECIDED ON A HIGH SCHOOL HERE IN CHIBA.
......
CAN I ASK YOU ONE MORE THING?
WHAT IS IT?
AIRI...
...HOW CAN YOU...
...BELIEVE ME?
IT'S NOT SO MUCH...
...THAT I "CAN" BELIEVE.
I "WANT" TO BELIEVE YOU.

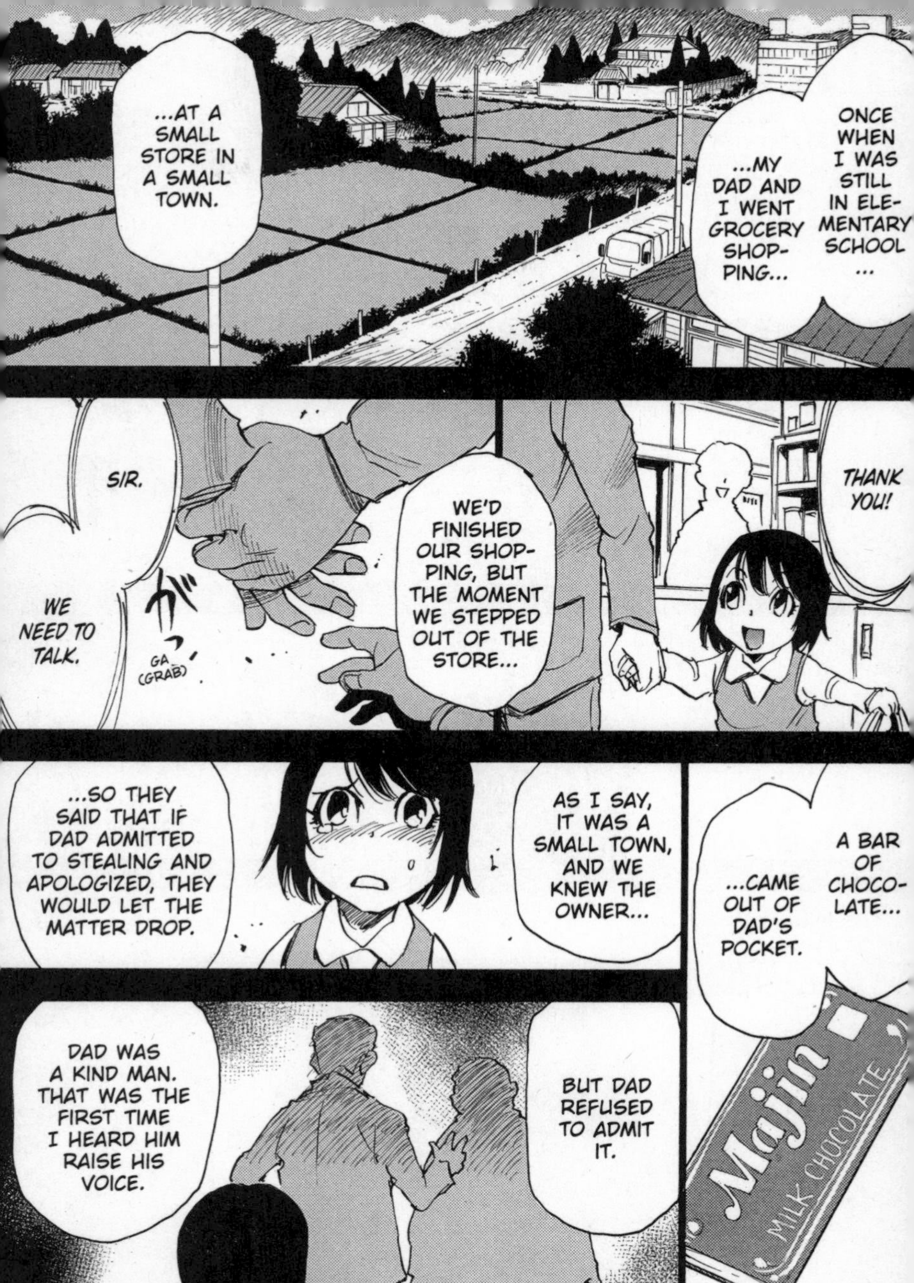
ONCE WHEN I WAS STILL IN ELEMENTARY SCHOOL...
...MY DAD AND I WENT GROCERY SHOPPING...
...AT A SMALL STORE IN A SMALL TOWN.
THANK YOU!
WE'D FINISHED OUR SHOPPING, BUT THE MOMENT WE STEPPED OUT OF THE STORE...
GA (GRAB)
SIR.
WE NEED TO TALK.
A BAR OF CHOCOLATE...
...CAME OUT OF DAD'S POCKET.
Majin MILK CHOCOLATE
AS I SAY, IT WAS A SMALL TOWN, AND WE KNEW THE OWNER...
...SO THEY SAID THAT IF DAD ADMITTED TO STEALING AND APOLOGIZED, THEY WOULD LET THE MATTER DROP.
BUT DAD REFUSED TO ADMIT IT.
DAD WAS A KIND MAN. THAT WAS THE FIRST TIME I HEARD HIM RAISE HIS VOICE.

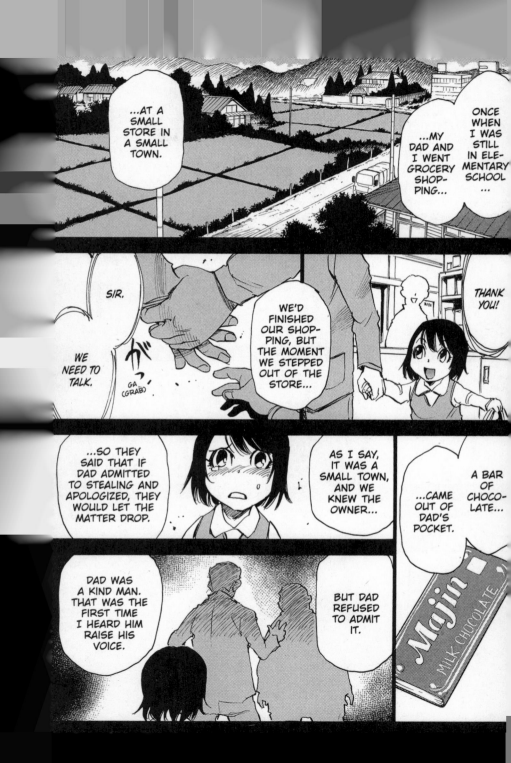

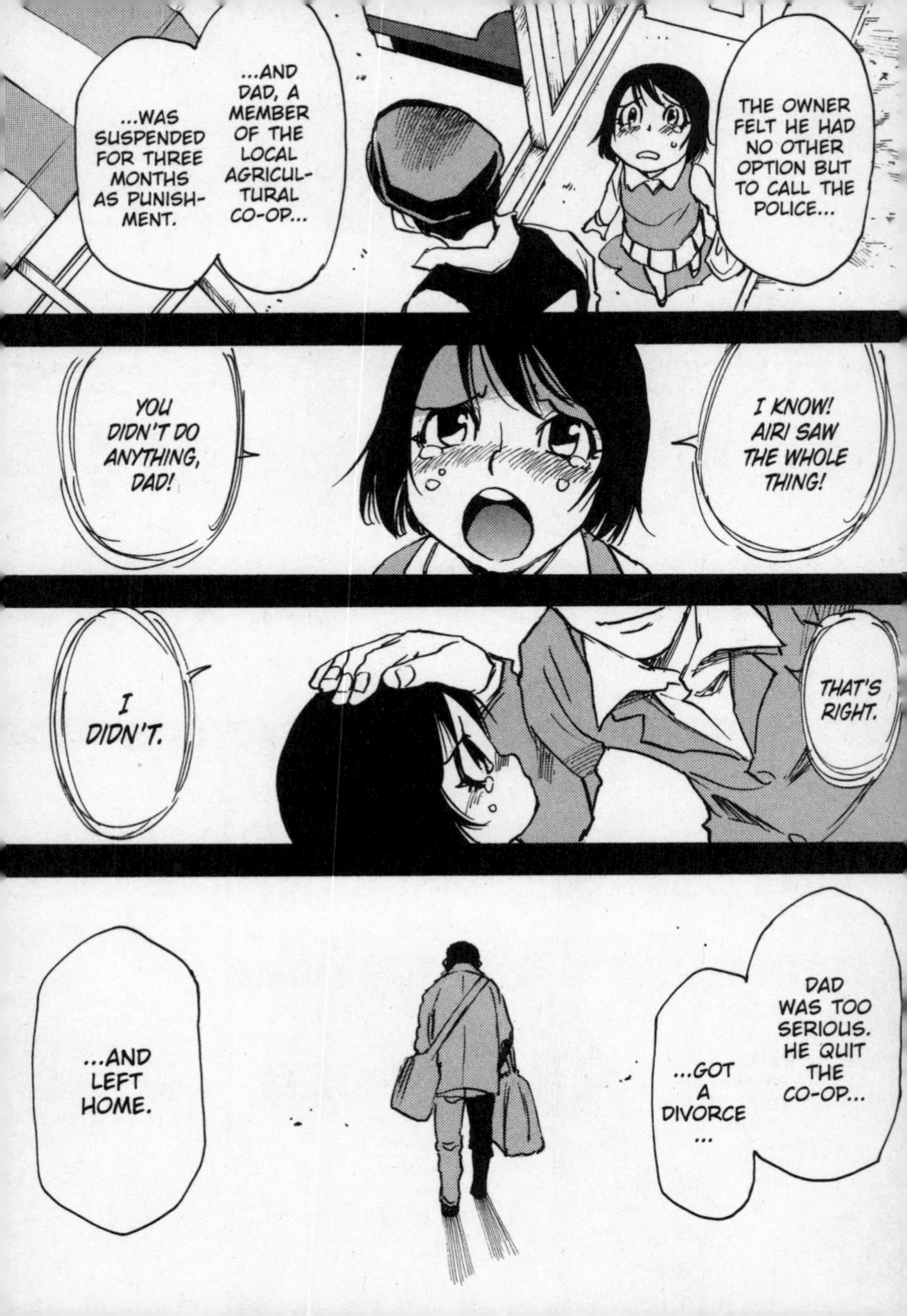
THE OWNER FELT HE HAD NO OTHER OPTION BUT TO CALL THE POLICE...
...AND DAD, A MEMBER OF THE LOCAL AGRICULTURAL CO-OP...
...WAS SUSPENDED FOR THREE MONTHS AS PUNISHMENT.
I KNOW! AIRI SAW THE WHOLE THING!
YOU DIDN'T DO ANYTHING, DAD!
THAT'S RIGHT.
I DIDN'T.
DAD WAS TOO SERIOUS. HE QUIT THE CO-OP...
...GOT A DIVORCE...
...AND LEFT HOME.

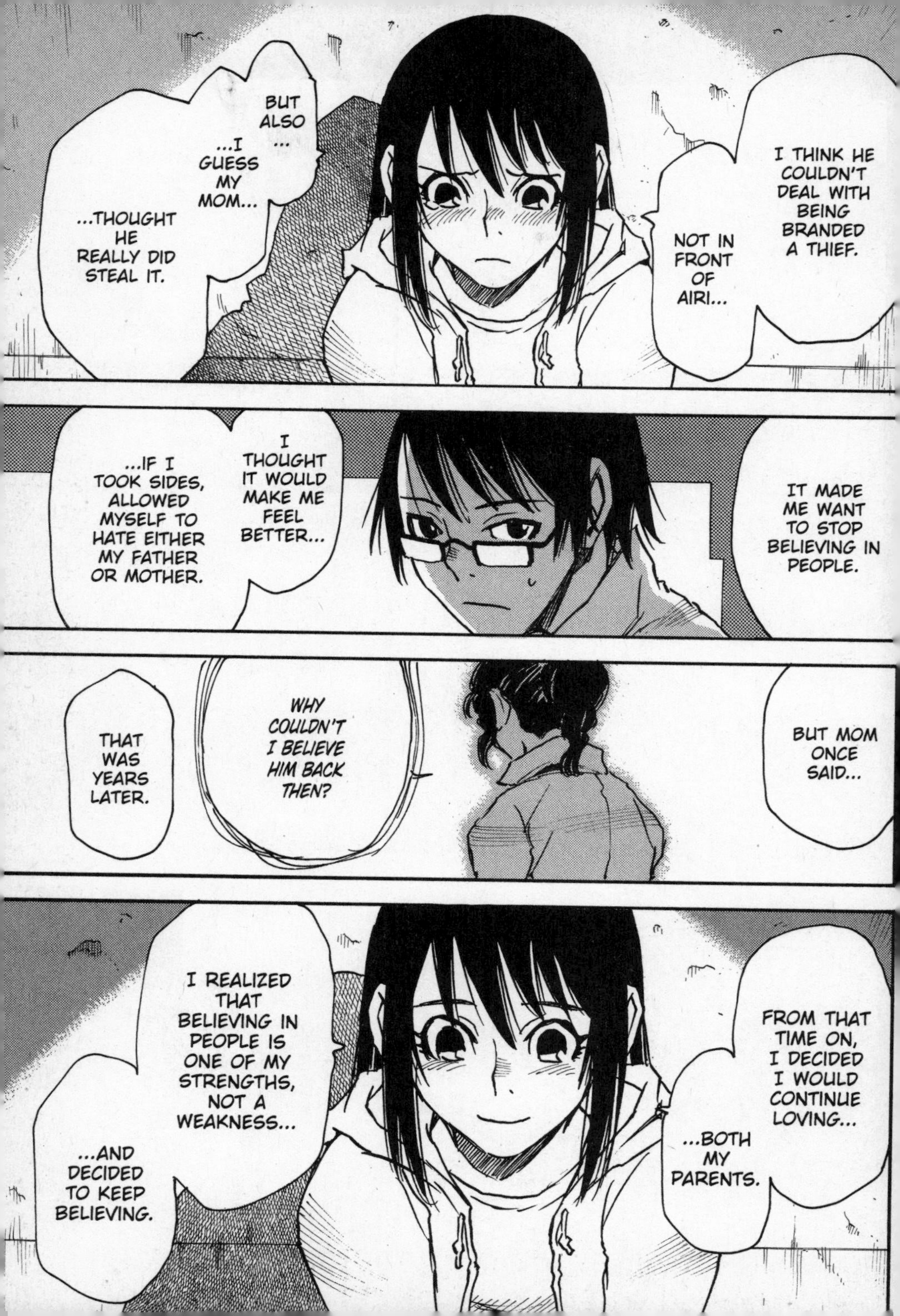
I THINK HE COULDN'T DEAL WITH BEING BRANDED A THIEF.
NOT IN FRONT OF AIRI...
BUT ALSO ...
...I GUESS MY MOM...
...THOUGHT HE REALLY DID STEAL IT.
IT MADE ME WANT TO STOP BELIEVING IN PEOPLE.
I THOUGHT IT WOULD MAKE ME FEEL BETTER...
...IF I TOOK SIDES, ALLOWED MYSELF TO HATE EITHER MY FATHER OR MOTHER.
BUT MOM ONCE SAID...
WHY COULDN'T I BELIEVE HIM BACK THEN?
THAT WAS YEARS LATER.
FROM THAT TIME ON, I DECIDED I WOULD CONTINUE LOVING...
...BOTH MY PARENTS.
I REALIZED THAT BELIEVING IN PEOPLE IS ONE OF MY STRENGTHS, NOT A WEAKNESS...
...AND DECIDED TO KEEP BELIEVING.

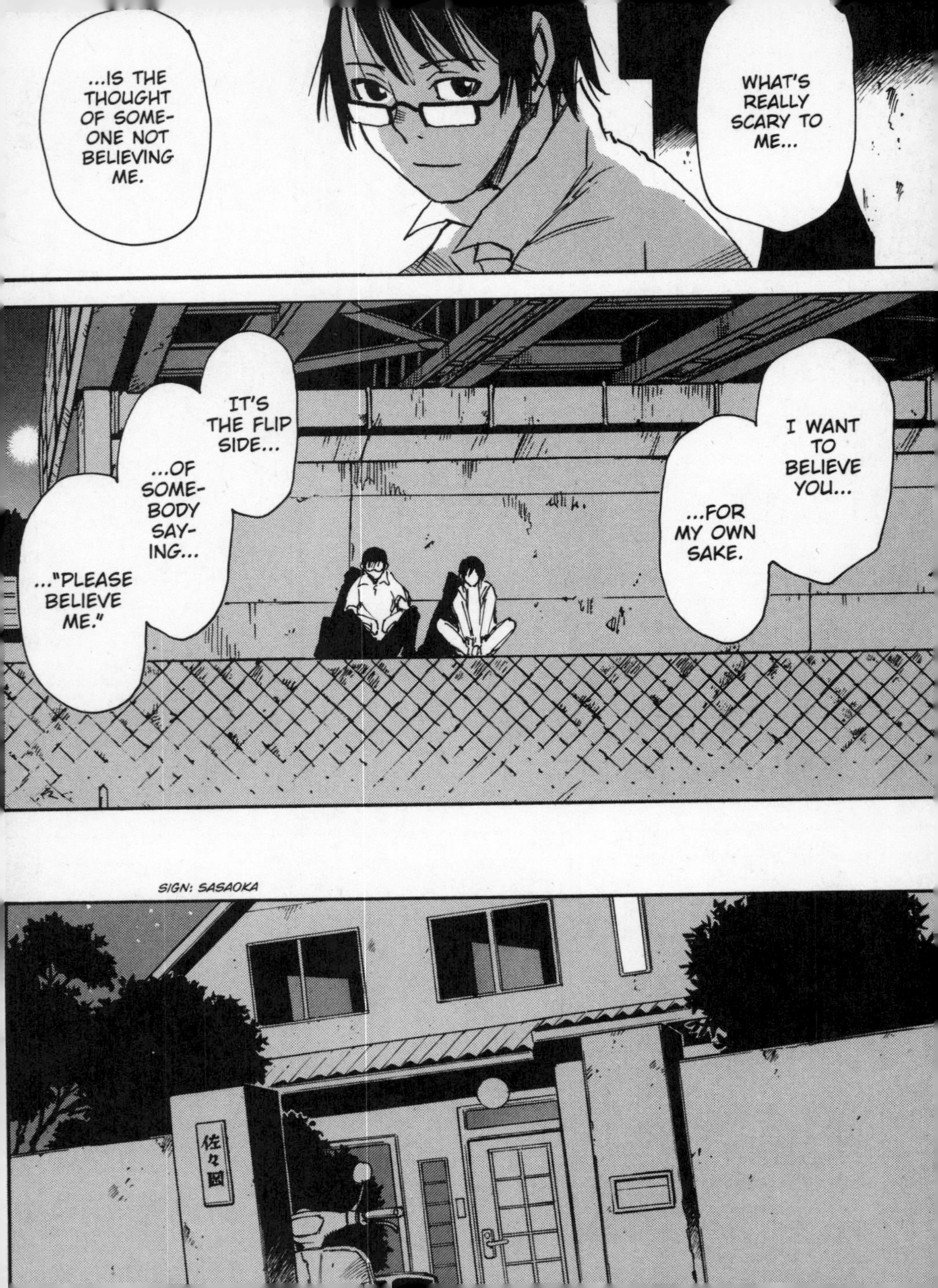
WHAT'S REALLY SCARY TO ME...
...IS THE THOUGHT OF SOME-ONE NOT BELIEVING ME.
I WANT TO BELIEVE YOU...
...FOR MY OWN SAKE.
IT'S THE FLIP SIDE...
...OF SOME-BODY SAY-ING...
..."PLEASE BELIEVE ME."
SIGN: SASAOKA
佐々岡

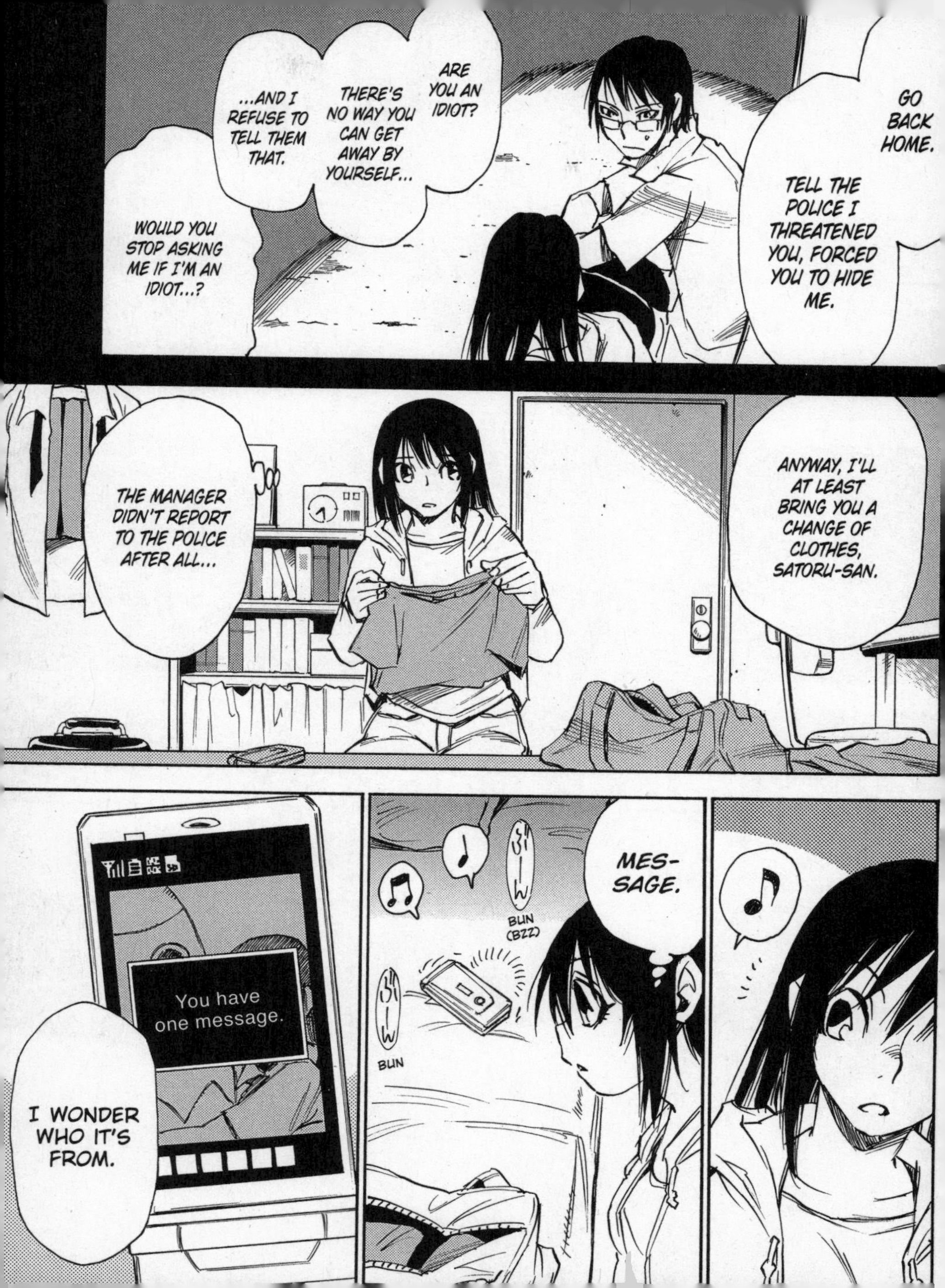
GO BACK HOME.
TELL THE POLICE I THREATENED YOU, FORCED YOU TO HIDE ME.
ARE YOU AN IDIOT?
THERE'S NO WAY YOU CAN GET AWAY BY YOURSELF...
...AND I REFUSE TO TELL THEM THAT.
WOULD YOU STOP ASKING ME IF I'M AN IDIOT...?
ANYWAY, I'LL AT LEAST BRING YOU A CHANGE OF CLOTHES, SATORU-SAN.
THE MANAGER DIDN'T REPORT TO THE POLICE AFTER ALL...
MES-SAGE.
BUN (BZZ)
BUN
You have one message.
I WONDER WHO IT'S FROM.

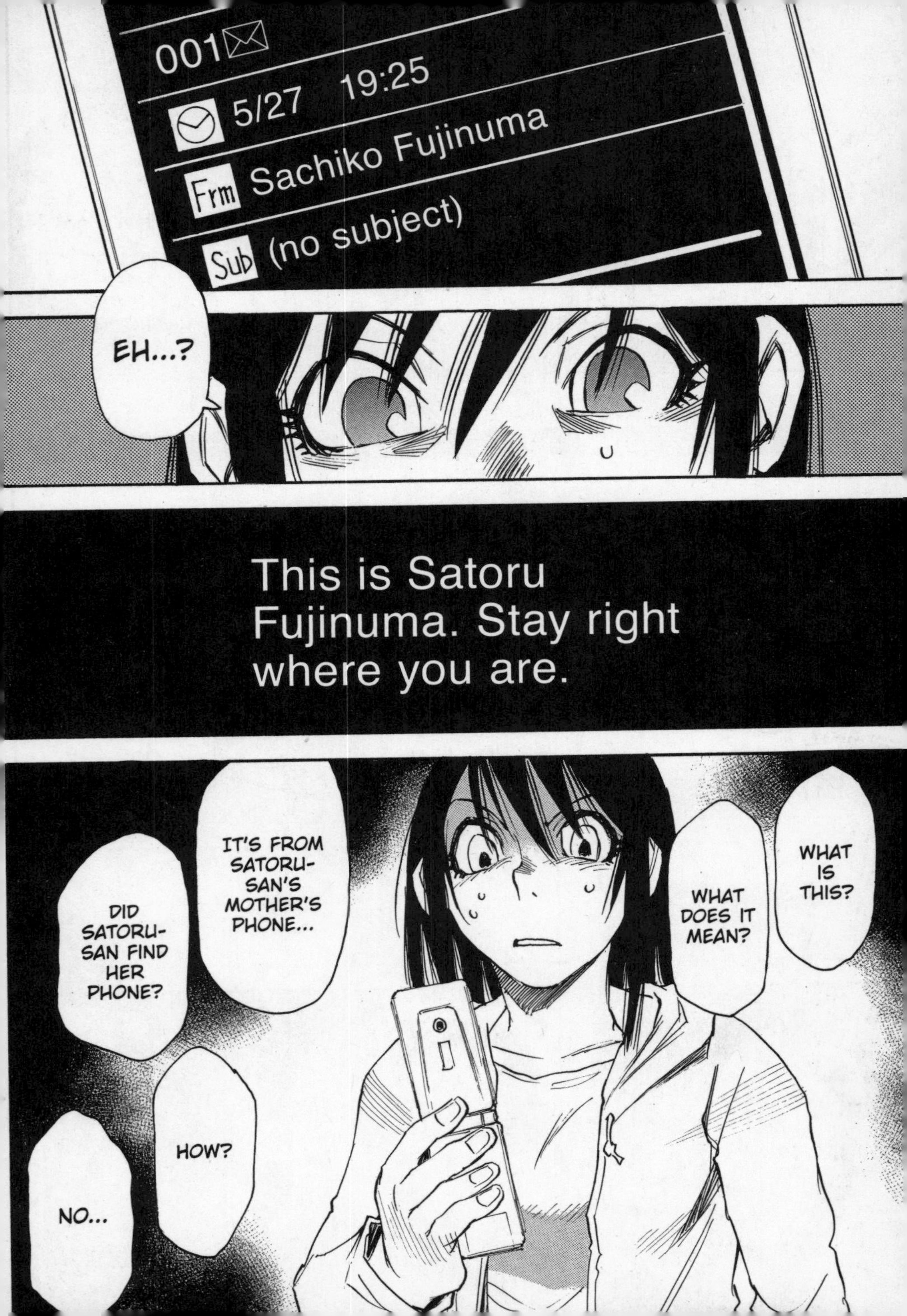
001
5/27 19:25
Frm Sachiko Fujinuma
Sub (no subject)
EH...?
This is Satoru Fujinuma. Stay right where you are.
WHAT IS THIS?
WHAT DOES IT MEAN?
IT'S FROM SATORU-SAN'S MOTHER'S PHONE...
DID SATORU-SAN FIND HER PHONE?
HOW?
NO...

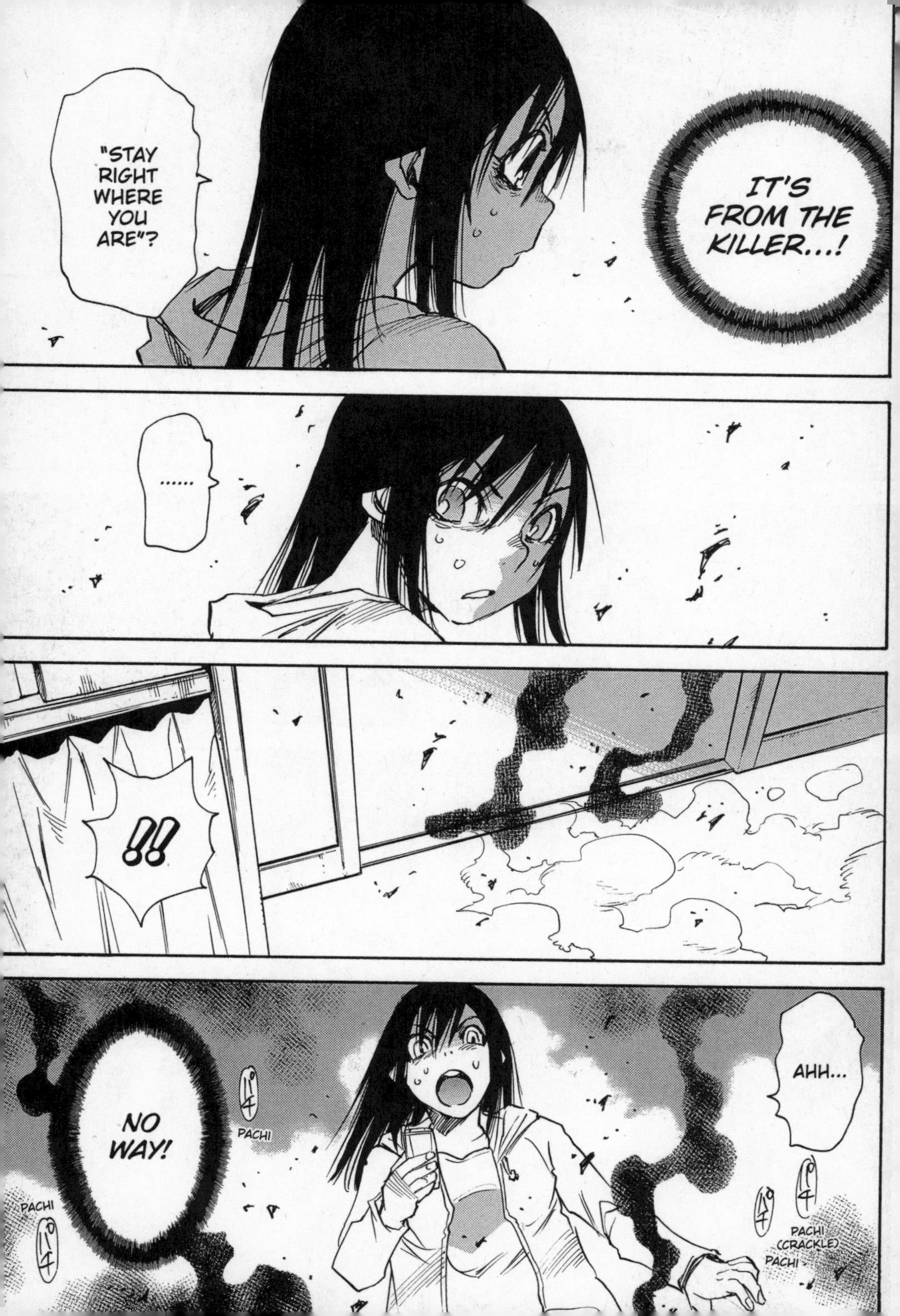
IT'S FROM THE KILLER...!
"STAY RIGHT WHERE YOU ARE"?
......
!!
AHH...
パチ
パチ
PACHI (CRACKLE)
PACHI
パチ
PACHI
NO WAY!
パチ
PACHI

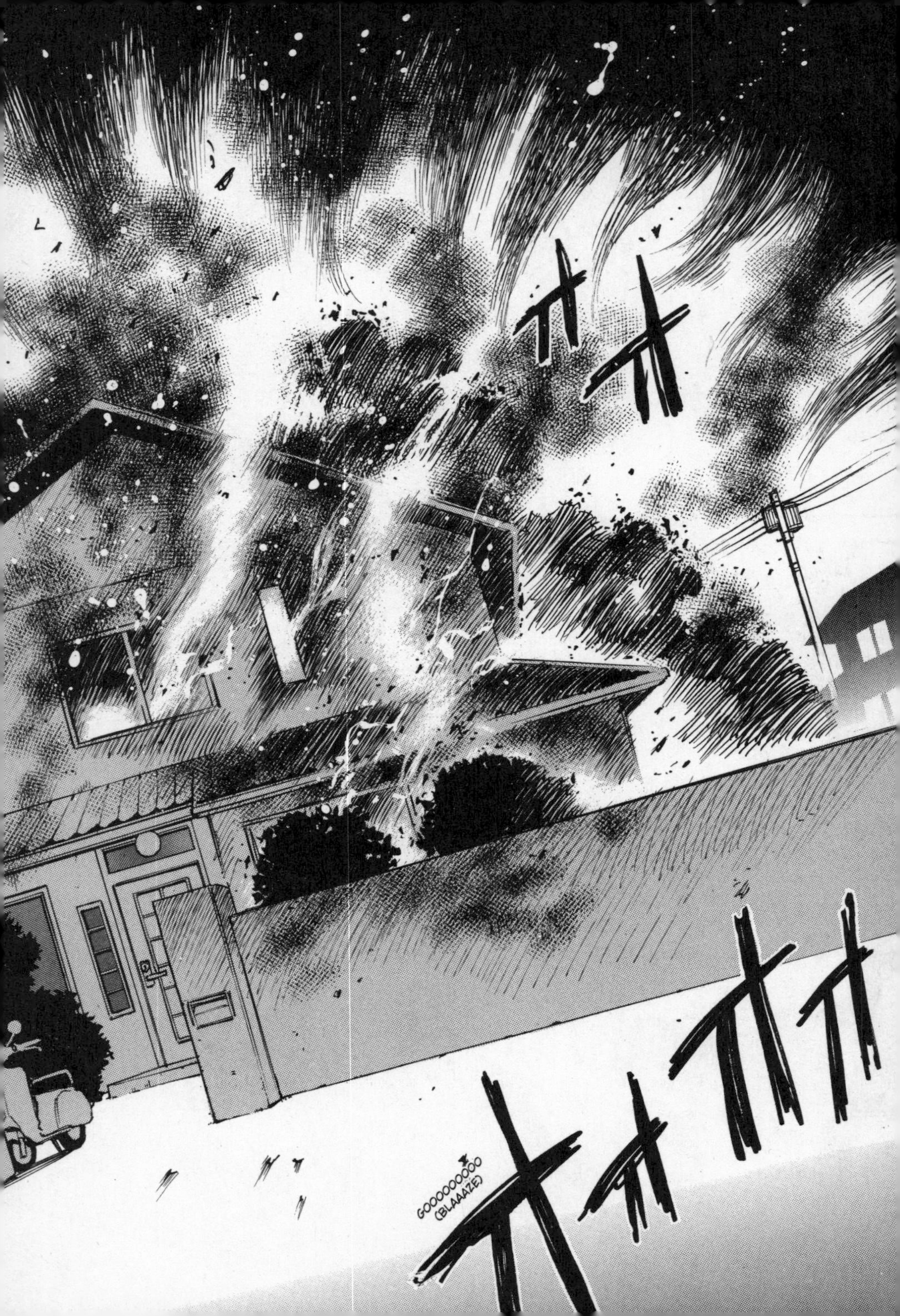
GOOOOOOOOO
(BLAAAZE)

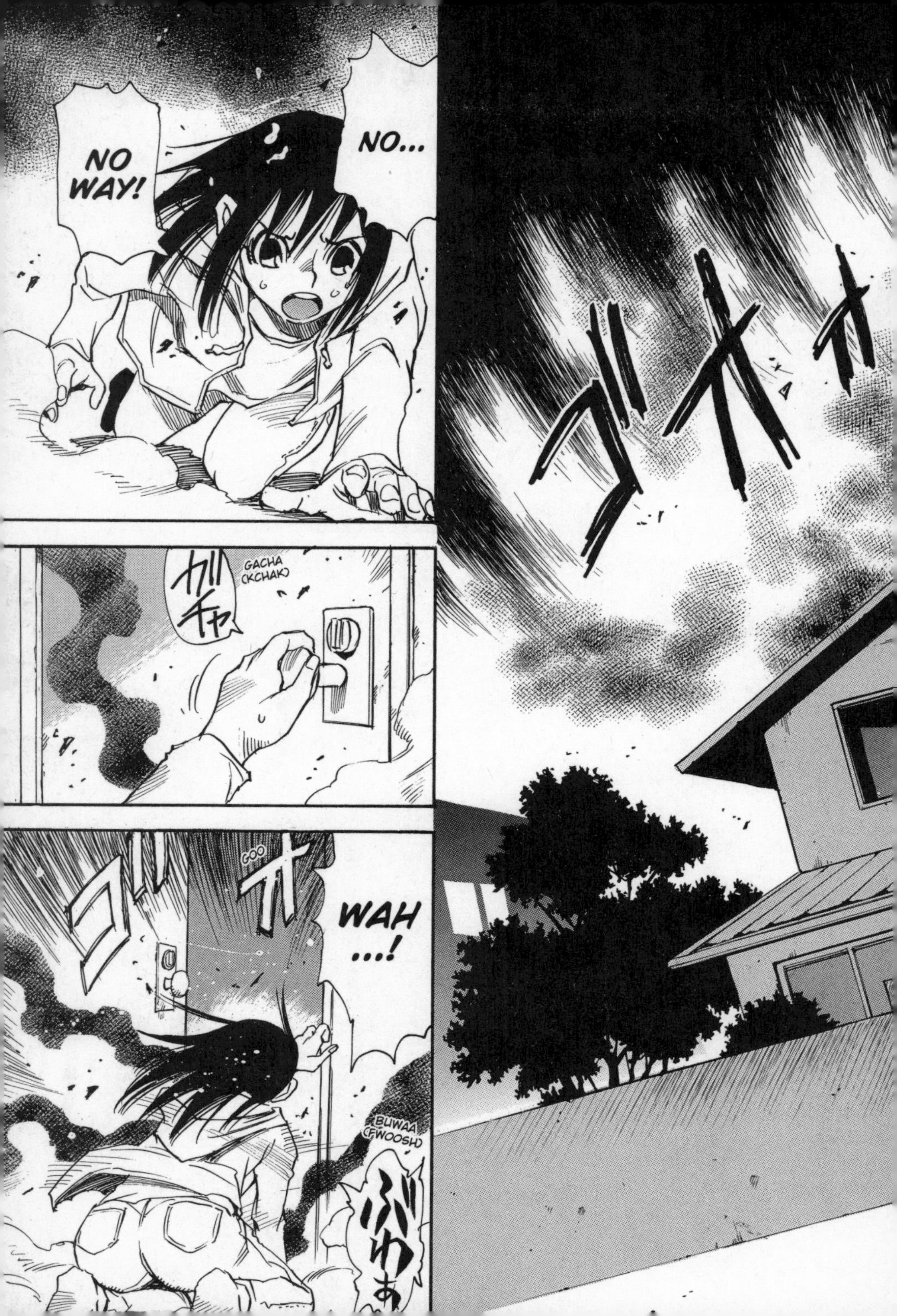
ゴオォ
NO...
NO WAY!
カチャ
GACHA (KCHAK)
ゴオ
GOO
WAH ...!
BUWAA (FWOOSH)
ぶわあ

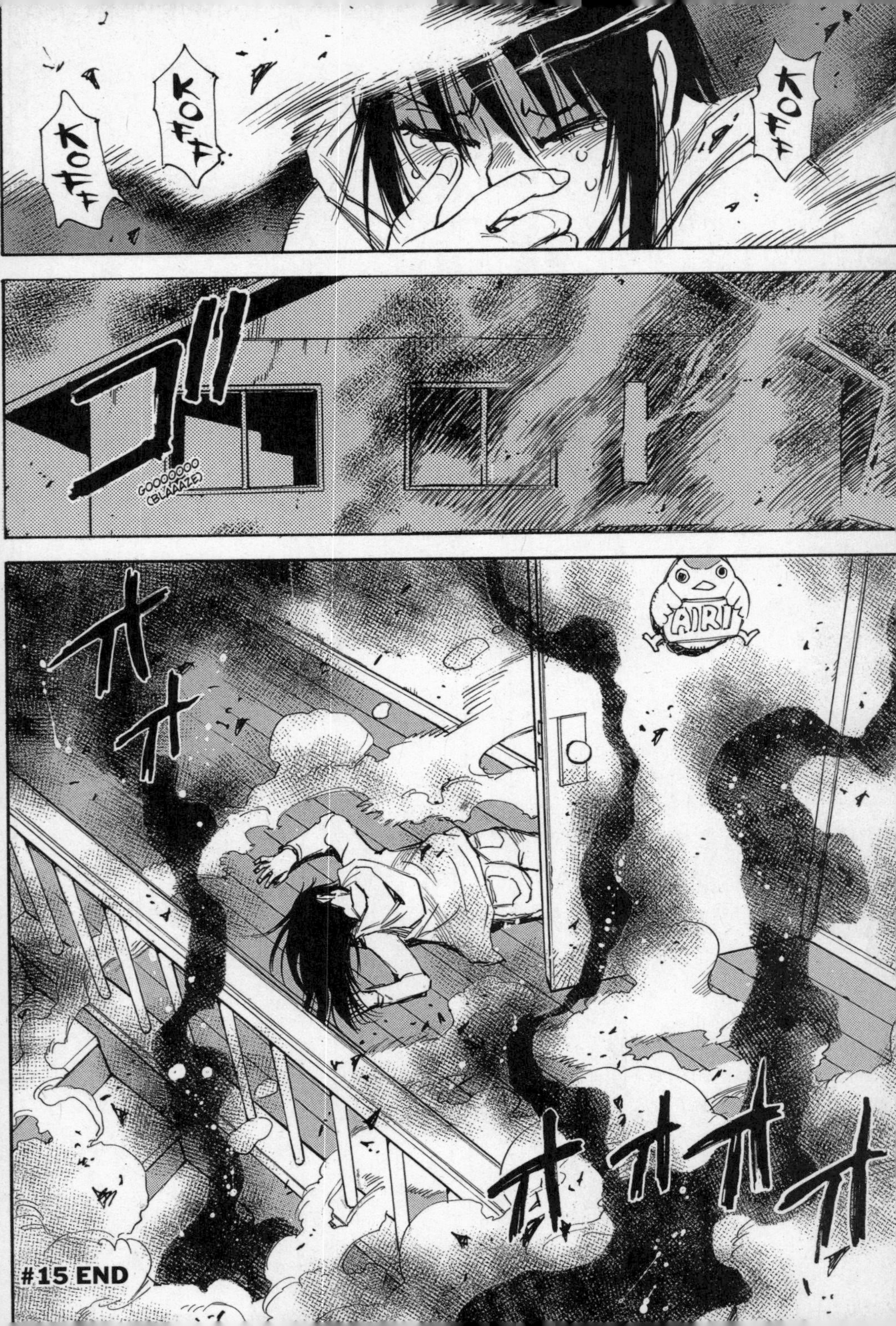
KOFF
KOFF
KOFF
ゴ
GOOOOOOO (BLAAAZE)
AIRI
オオ
オオオオ
#15 END

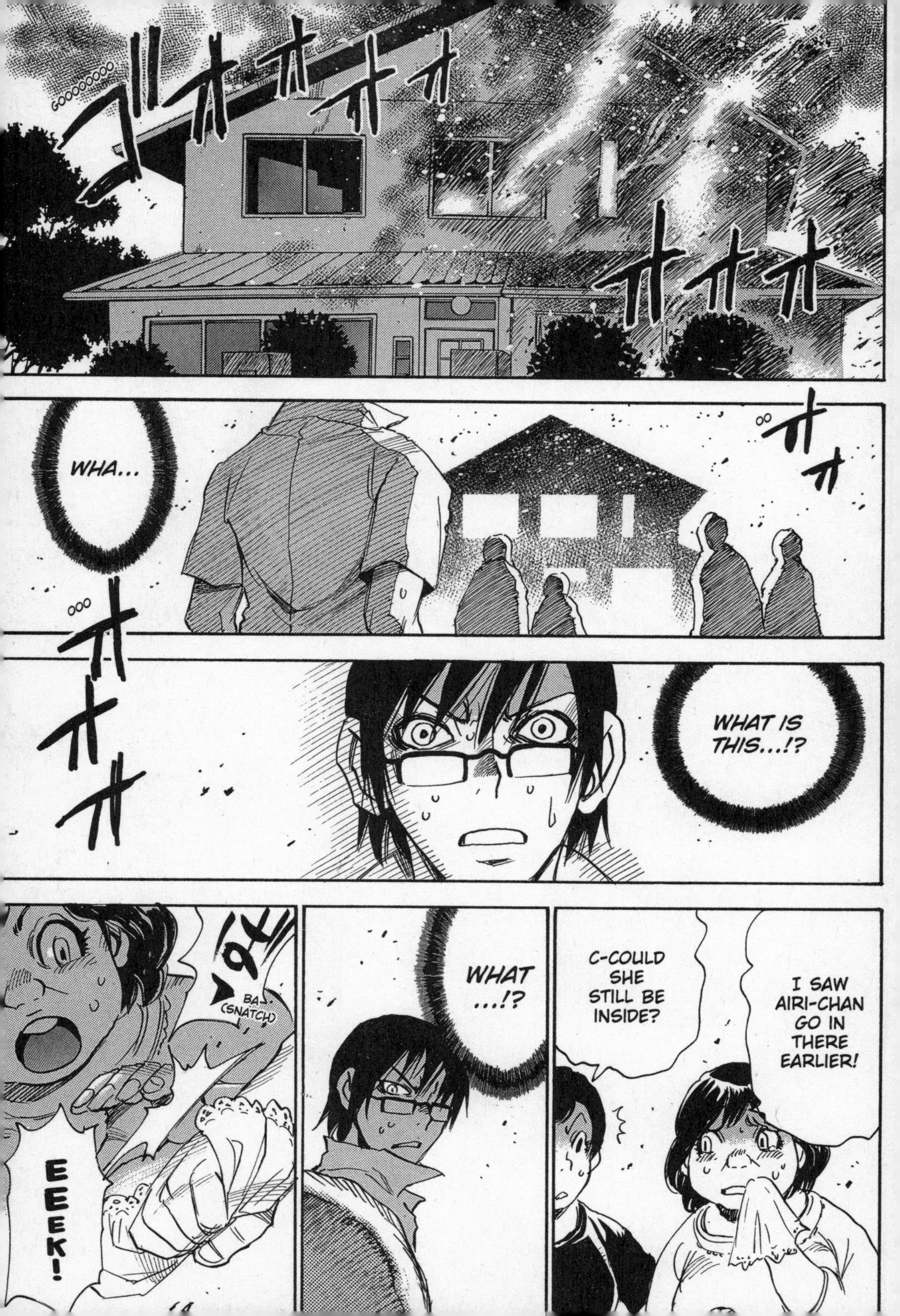
GOOOOOOOO
OO
WHA...
OOO
WHAT IS THIS...!?
I SAW AIRI-CHAN GO IN THERE EARLIER!
C-COULD SHE STILL BE INSIDE?
WHAT ...!?
BA- (SNATCH)
EEEK!

#16: Mother, May 2006

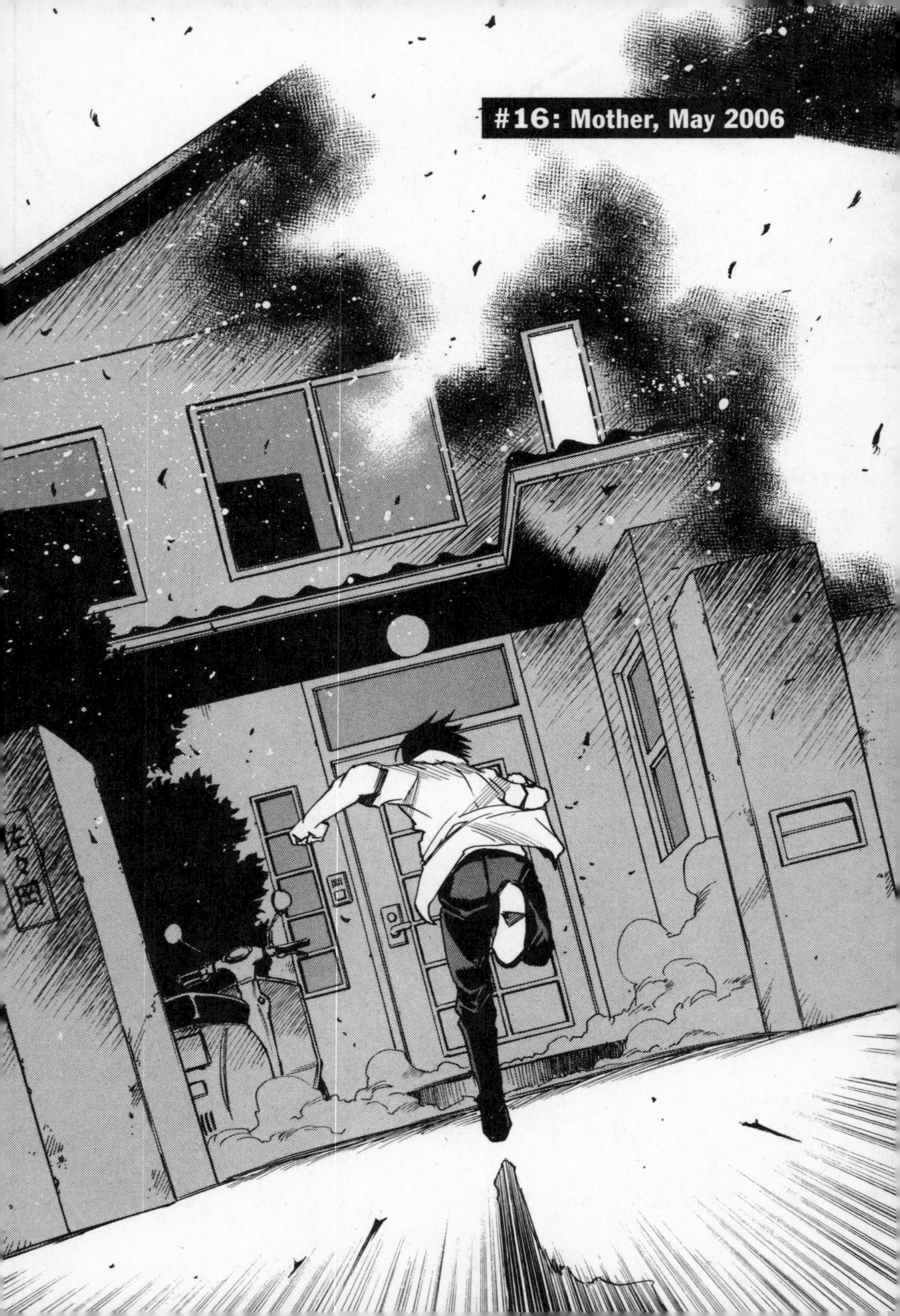

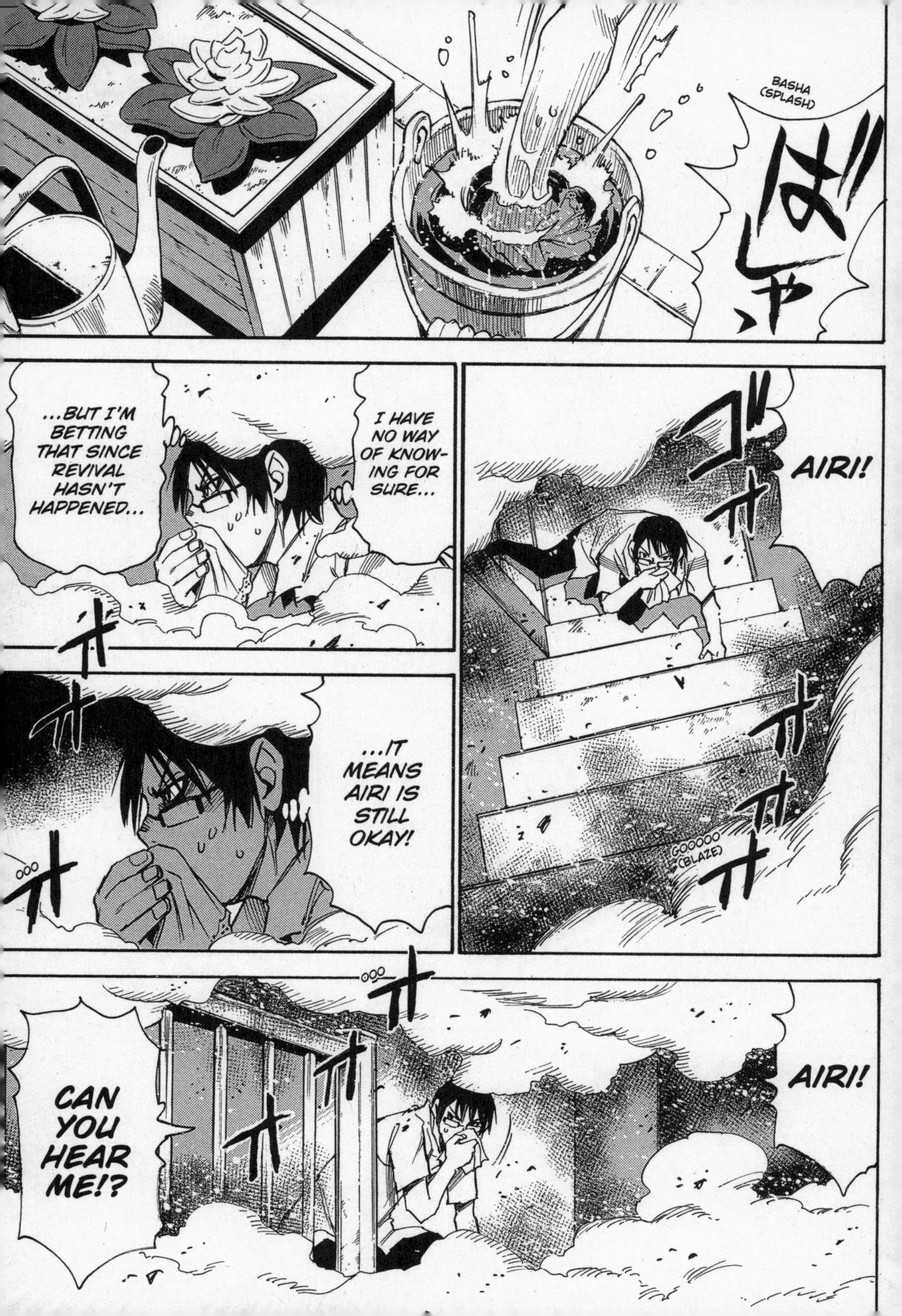
BASHA (SPLASH)
AIRI!
GOOOOO (BLAZE)
I HAVE NO WAY OF KNOW-ING FOR SURE...
...BUT I'M BETTING THAT SINCE REVIVAL HASN'T HAPPENED...
...IT MEANS AIRI IS STILL OKAY!
AIRI!
CAN YOU HEAR ME!?

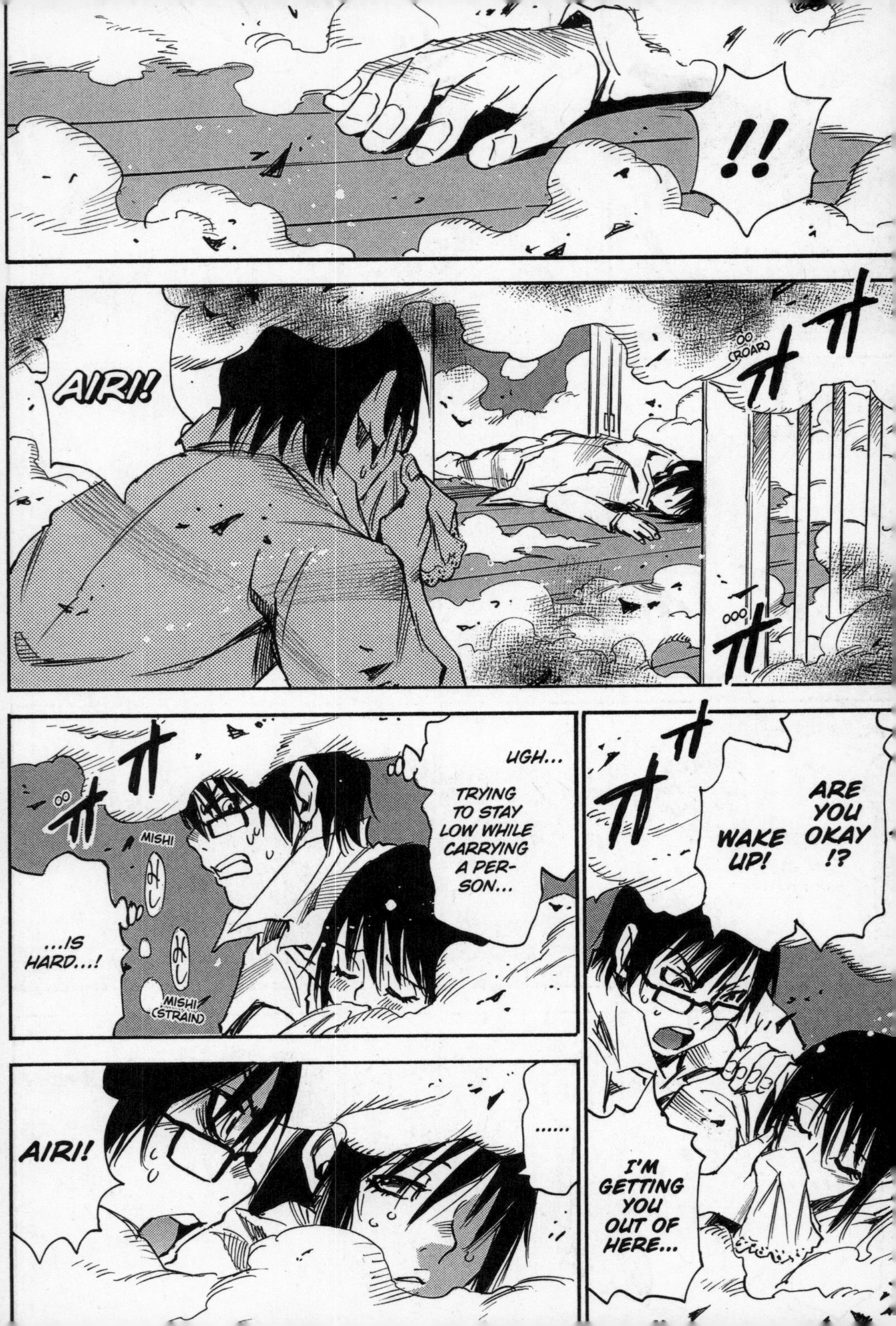

!!
OO (ROAR)
AIRI!
OOO
ARE YOU OKAY!?
WAKE UP!
UGH...
TRYING TO STAY LOW WHILE CARRYING A PER-SON...
OO
MISHI
みし
みし
MISHI (STRAIN)
...IS HARD...!
I'M GETTING YOU OUT OF HERE...
......
AIRI!

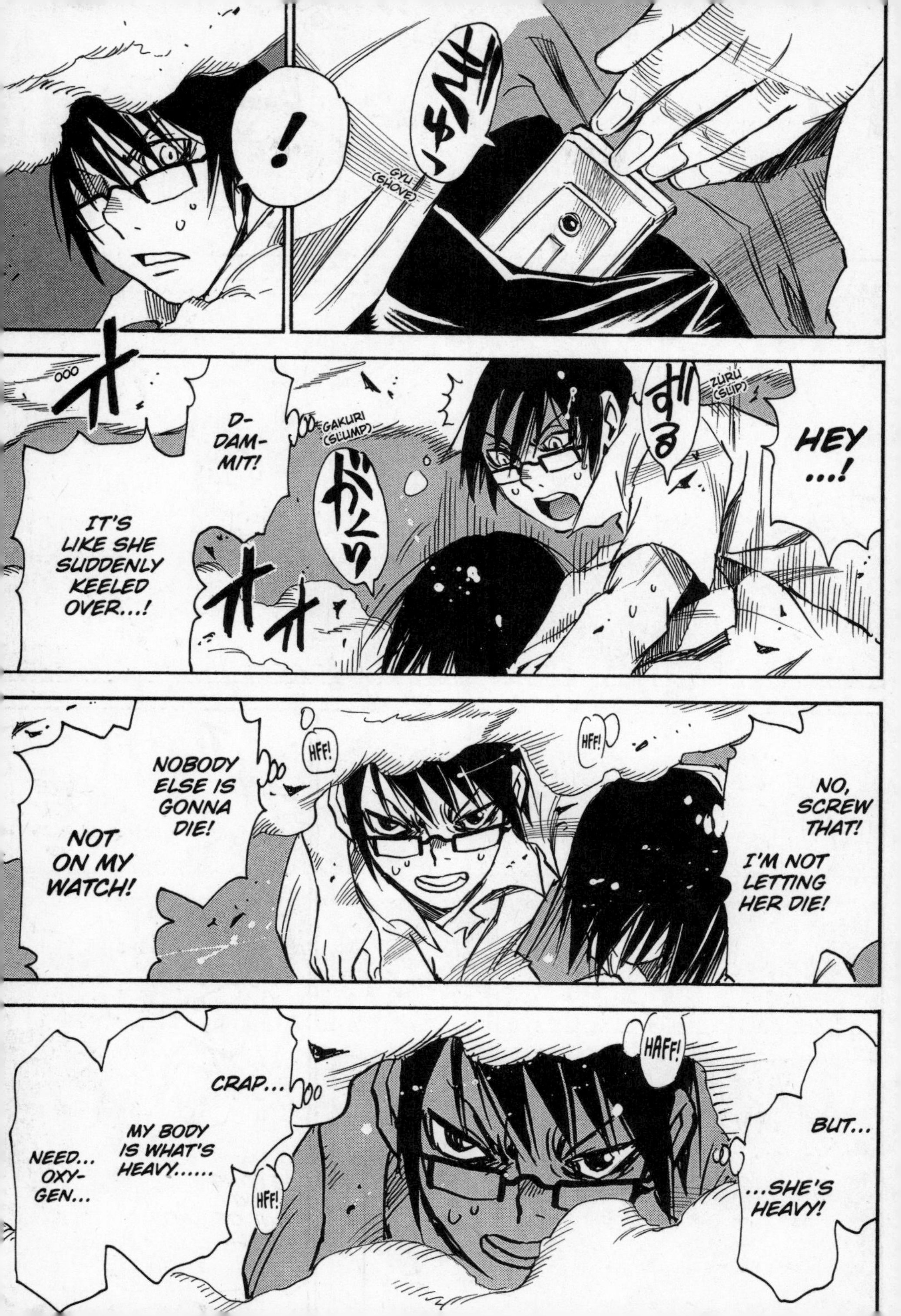
GYU (SHOVE)
!
HEY ...!
ZURU (SLIP)
GAKURI (SLUMP)
D-DAMMIT!
IT'S LIKE SHE SUDDENLY KEELED OVER...!
OOO
NO, SCREW THAT!
I'M NOT LETTING HER DIE!
HFF!
HFF!
NOBODY ELSE IS GONNA DIE!
NOT ON MY WATCH!
BUT...
...SHE'S HEAVY!
HAFF!
CRAP...
MY BODY IS WHAT'S HEAVY......
HFF!
NEED... OXYGEN...

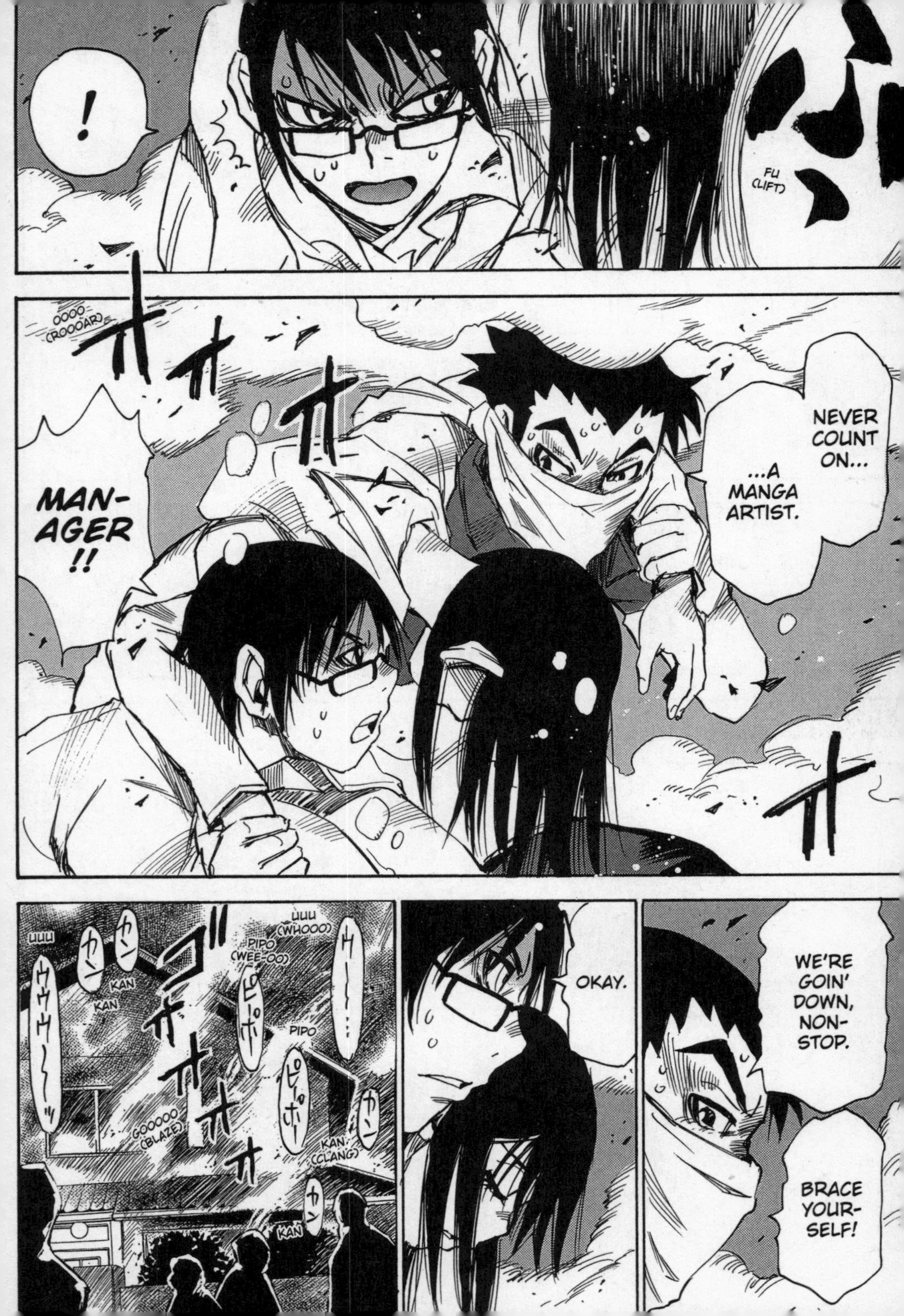
FU (LIFT)
!
NEVER COUNT ON...
...A MANGA ARTIST.
OOOO (ROOOAR)
MAN-AGER!!
WE'RE GOIN' DOWN, NON-STOP.
BRACE YOURSELF!
OKAY.
UUU (WHOOO)
PIPO (WEE-OO)
PIPO
KAN (CLANG)
KAN
GOOOOO (BLAZE)
KAN
KAN
UUU

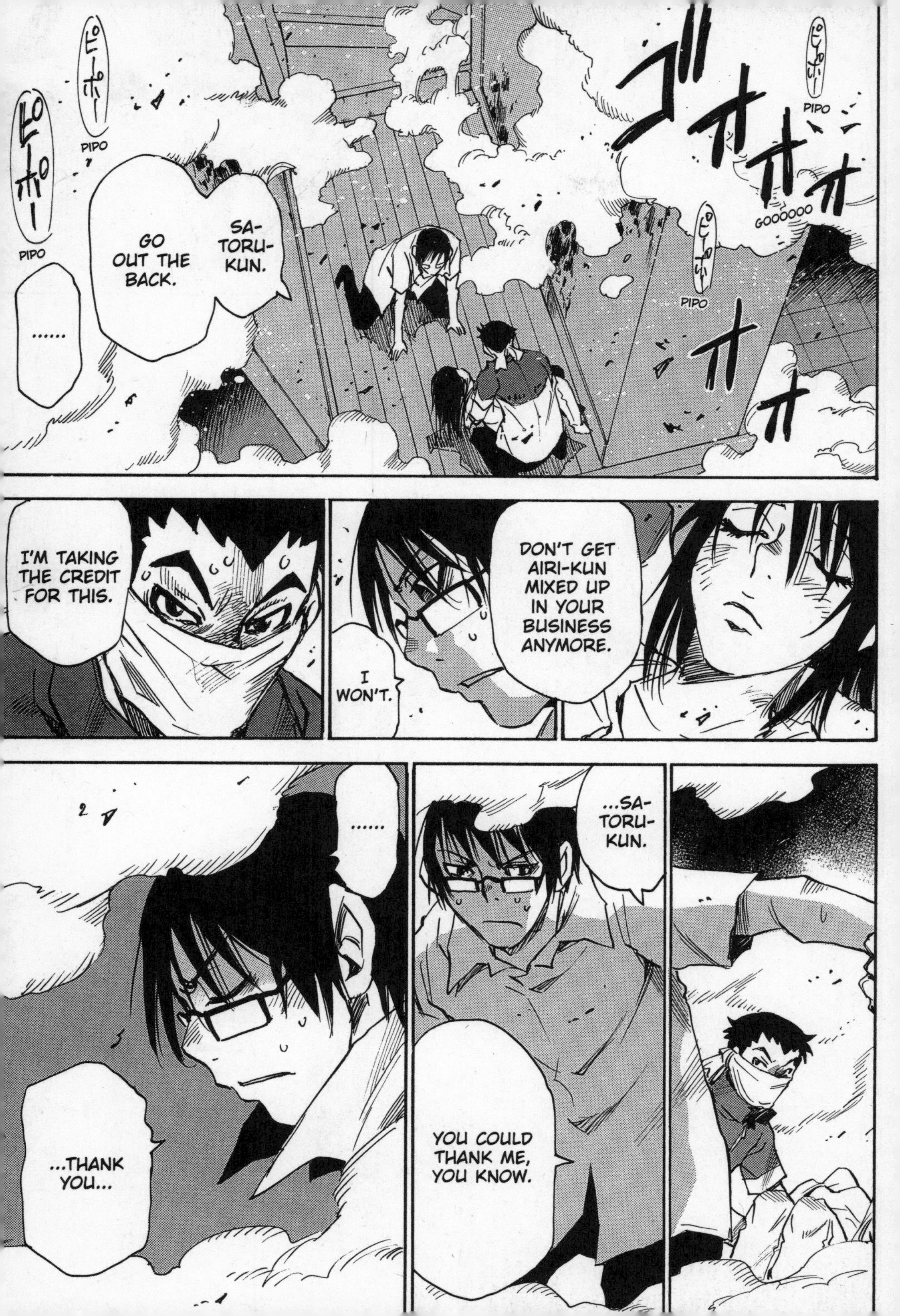
ピーポー
PIPO
ゴオオオ
GOOOOOO
ピーポー
PIPO
SA-TORU-KUN.
GO OUT THE BACK.
ピーポー
PIPO
ピーポー
PIPO
......
DON'T GET AIRI-KUN MIXED UP IN YOUR BUSINESS ANYMORE.
I WON'T.
I'M TAKING THE CREDIT FOR THIS.
...SA-TORU-KUN.
YOU COULD THANK ME, YOU KNOW.
......
...THANK YOU...

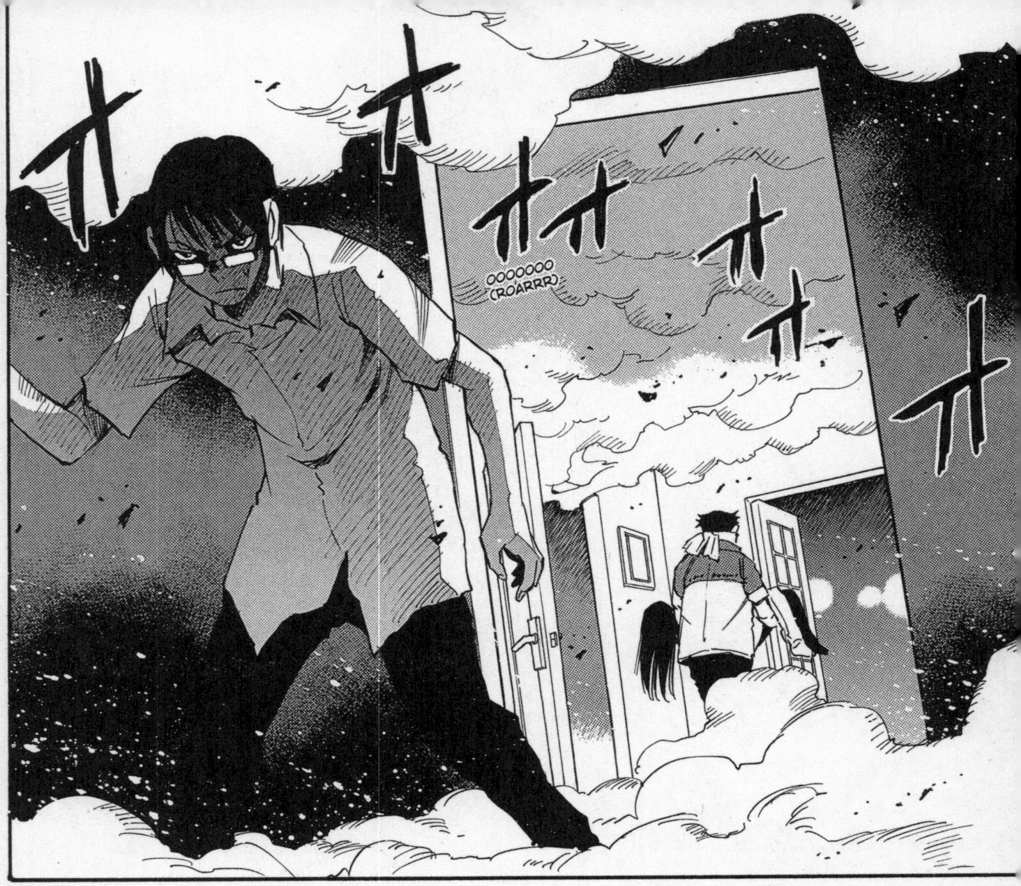
OOOOOOO
(ROARRR)

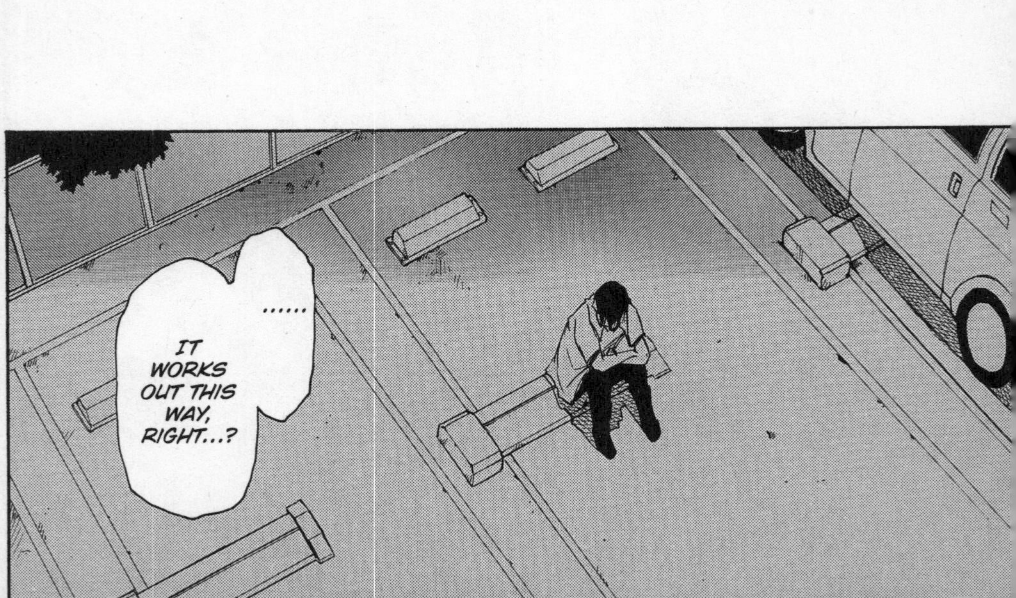
......
IT WORKS OUT THIS WAY, RIGHT...?

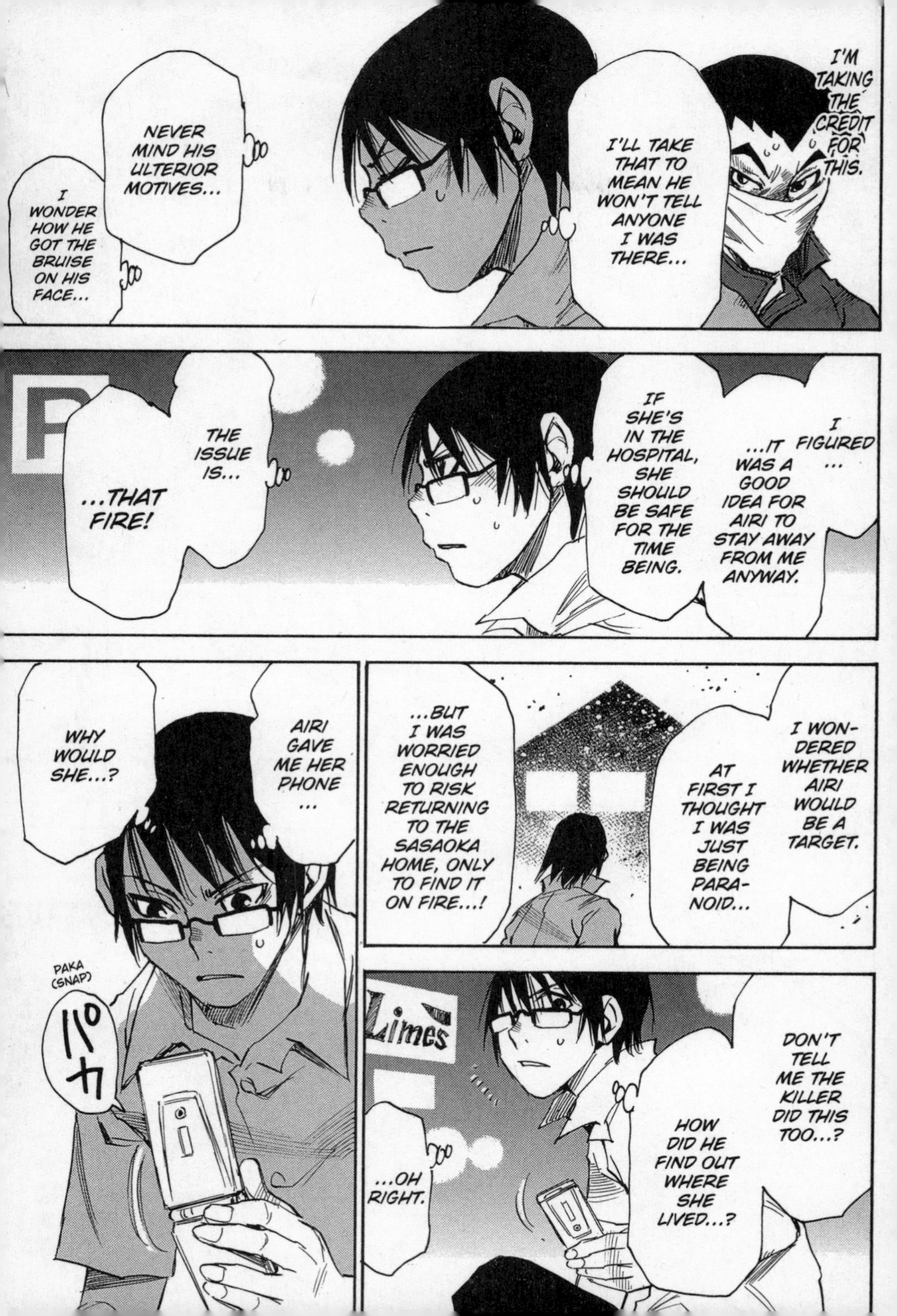

I'M TAKING THE CREDIT FOR THIS.
I'LL TAKE THAT TO MEAN HE WON'T TELL ANYONE I WAS THERE...
NEVER MIND HIS ULTERIOR MOTIVES...
I WONDER HOW HE GOT THE BRUISE ON HIS FACE...
I FIGURED...
...IT WAS A GOOD IDEA FOR AIRI TO STAY AWAY FROM ME ANYWAY.
IF SHE'S IN THE HOSPITAL, SHE SHOULD BE SAFE FOR THE TIME BEING.
THE ISSUE IS...
...THAT FIRE!
I WON-DERED WHETHER AIRI WOULD BE A TARGET.
AT FIRST I THOUGHT I WAS JUST BEING PARA-NOID...
...BUT I WAS WORRIED ENOUGH TO RISK RETURNING TO THE SASAOKA HOME, ONLY TO FIND IT ON FIRE...!
DON'T TELL ME THE KILLER DID THIS TOO...?
HOW DID HE FIND OUT WHERE SHE LIVED...?
...OH RIGHT.
Limes
AIRI GAVE ME HER PHONE...
WHY WOULD SHE...?
パカ
PAKA (SNAP)

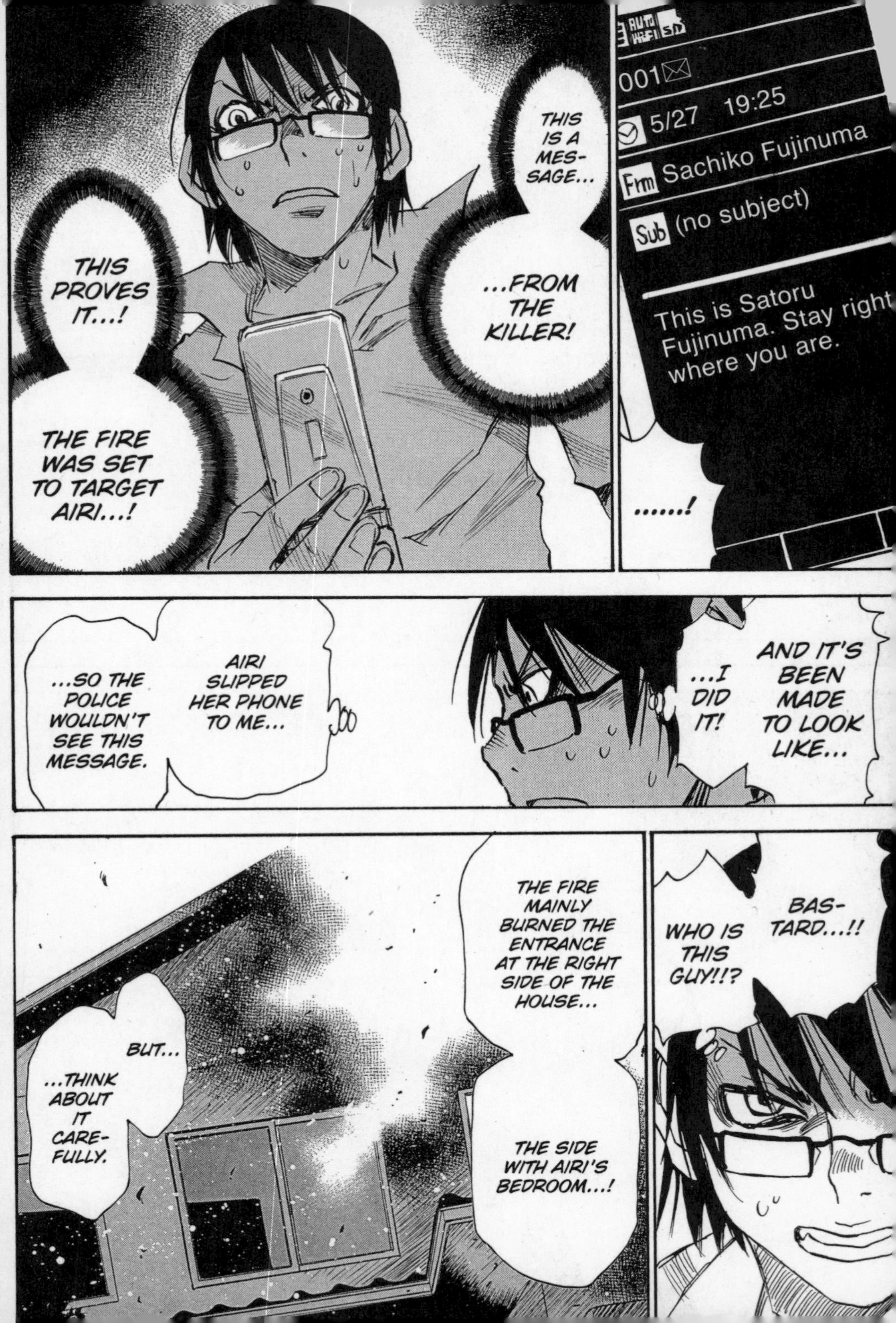
001
5/27 19:25
Frm Sachiko Fujinuma
Sub (no subject)
This is Satoru Fujinuma. Stay right where you are.
......!
THIS IS A MES-SAGE...
...FROM THE KILLER!
THIS PROVES IT...!
THE FIRE WAS SET TO TARGET AIRI...!
AND IT'S BEEN MADE TO LOOK LIKE...
...I DID IT!
AIRI SLIPPED HER PHONE TO ME...
...SO THE POLICE WOULDN'T SEE THIS MESSAGE.
BAS-TARD...!!
WHO IS THIS GUY!!?
THE FIRE MAINLY BURNED THE ENTRANCE AT THE RIGHT SIDE OF THE HOUSE...
THE SIDE WITH AIRI'S BEDROOM...!
BUT...
...THINK ABOUT IT CARE-FULLY.

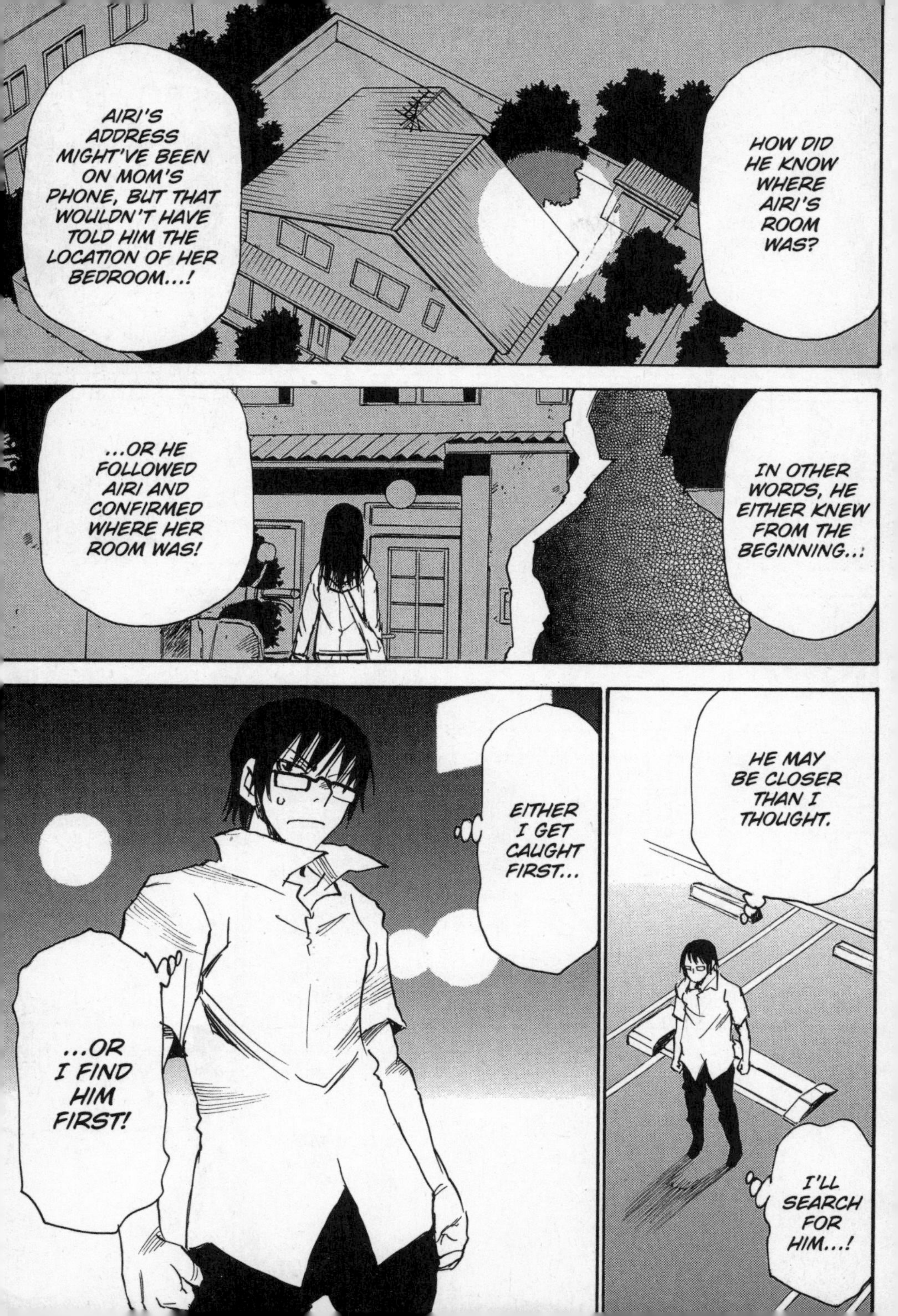
HOW DID HE KNOW WHERE AIRI'S ROOM WAS?
AIRI'S ADDRESS MIGHT'VE BEEN ON MOM'S PHONE, BUT THAT WOULDN'T HAVE TOLD HIM THE LOCATION OF HER BEDROOM...!
IN OTHER WORDS, HE EITHER KNEW FROM THE BEGINNING...
...OR HE FOLLOWED AIRI AND CONFIRMED WHERE HER ROOM WAS!
HE MAY BE CLOSER THAN I THOUGHT.
I'LL SEARCH FOR HIM...!
EITHER I GET CAUGHT FIRST...
...OR I FIND HIM FIRST!

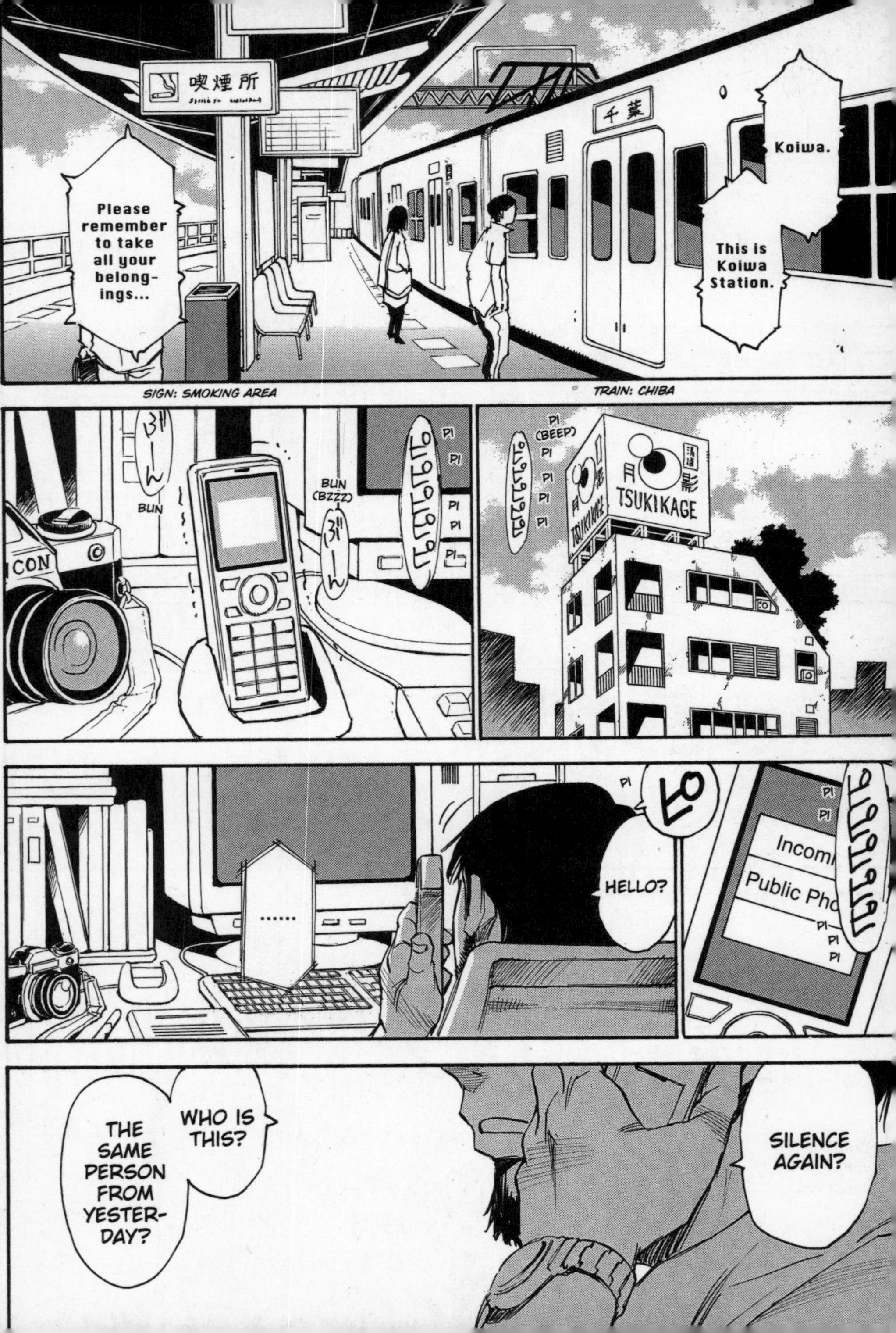

Koiwa.
This is Koiwa Station.
千葉
Please remember to take all your belongings...
喫煙所
SIGN: SMOKING AREA
TRAIN: CHIBA
PI (BEEP) PI PI PI PI PI
月影
TSUKIKAGE
ぶーん
BUN
BUN (BZZZ)
ぶーん
PI PI PI PI PI
CON
PI PI
Incomi
Public Pho
PI PI PI
ピ
PI
HELLO?
......
SILENCE AGAIN?
WHO IS THIS?
THE SAME PERSON FROM YESTERDAY?

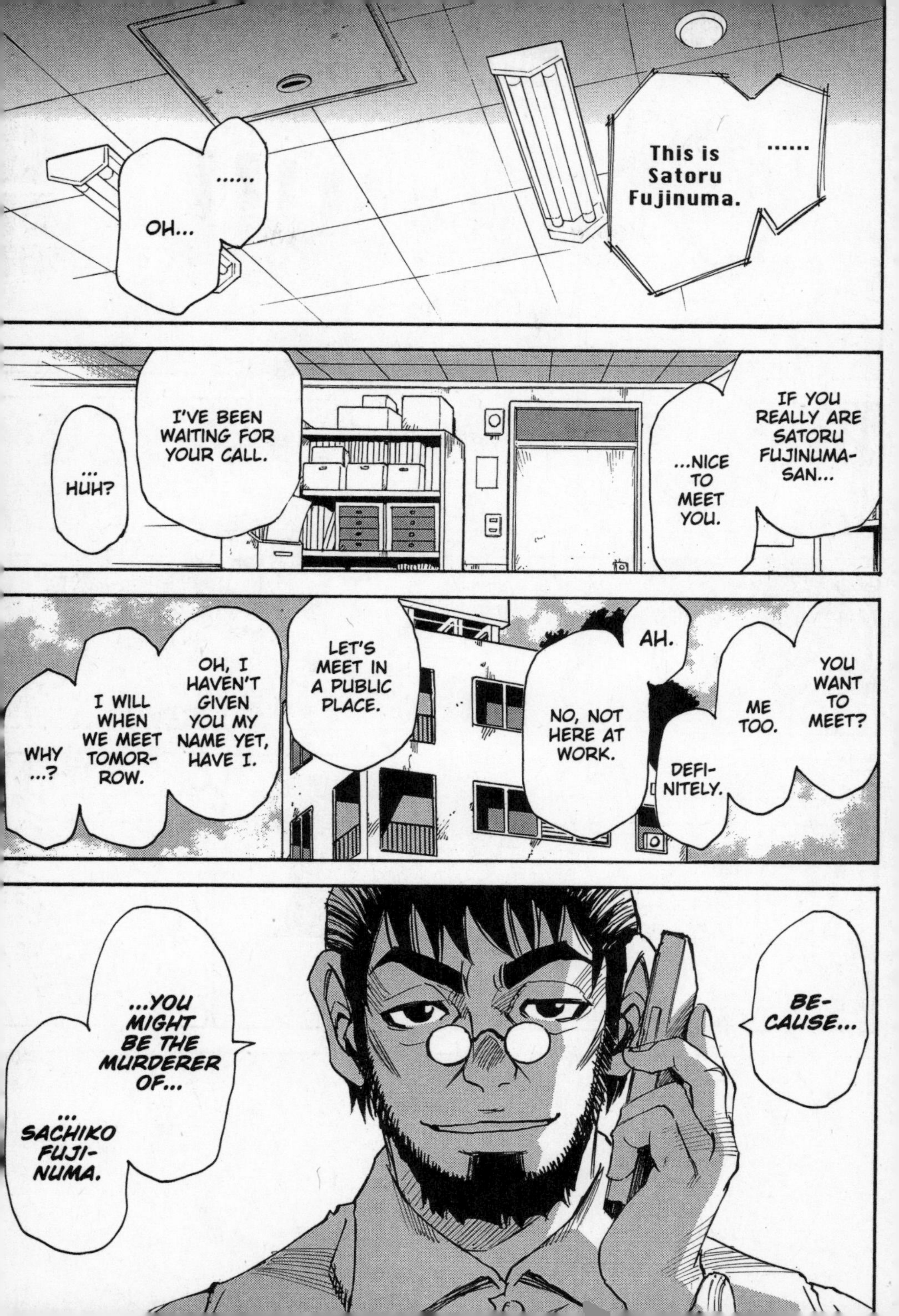
......
This is Satoru Fujinuma.
......
OH...
IF YOU REALLY ARE SATORU FUJINUMA-SAN...
...NICE TO MEET YOU.
I'VE BEEN WAITING FOR YOUR CALL.
...HUH?
YOU WANT TO MEET?
ME TOO.
DEFINITELY.
AH.
NO, NOT HERE AT WORK.
LET'S MEET IN A PUBLIC PLACE.
OH, I HAVEN'T GIVEN YOU MY NAME YET, HAVE I.
I WILL WHEN WE MEET TOMORROW.
WHY ...?
BECAUSE...
...YOU MIGHT BE THE MURDERER OF...
...SACHIKO FUJINUMA.

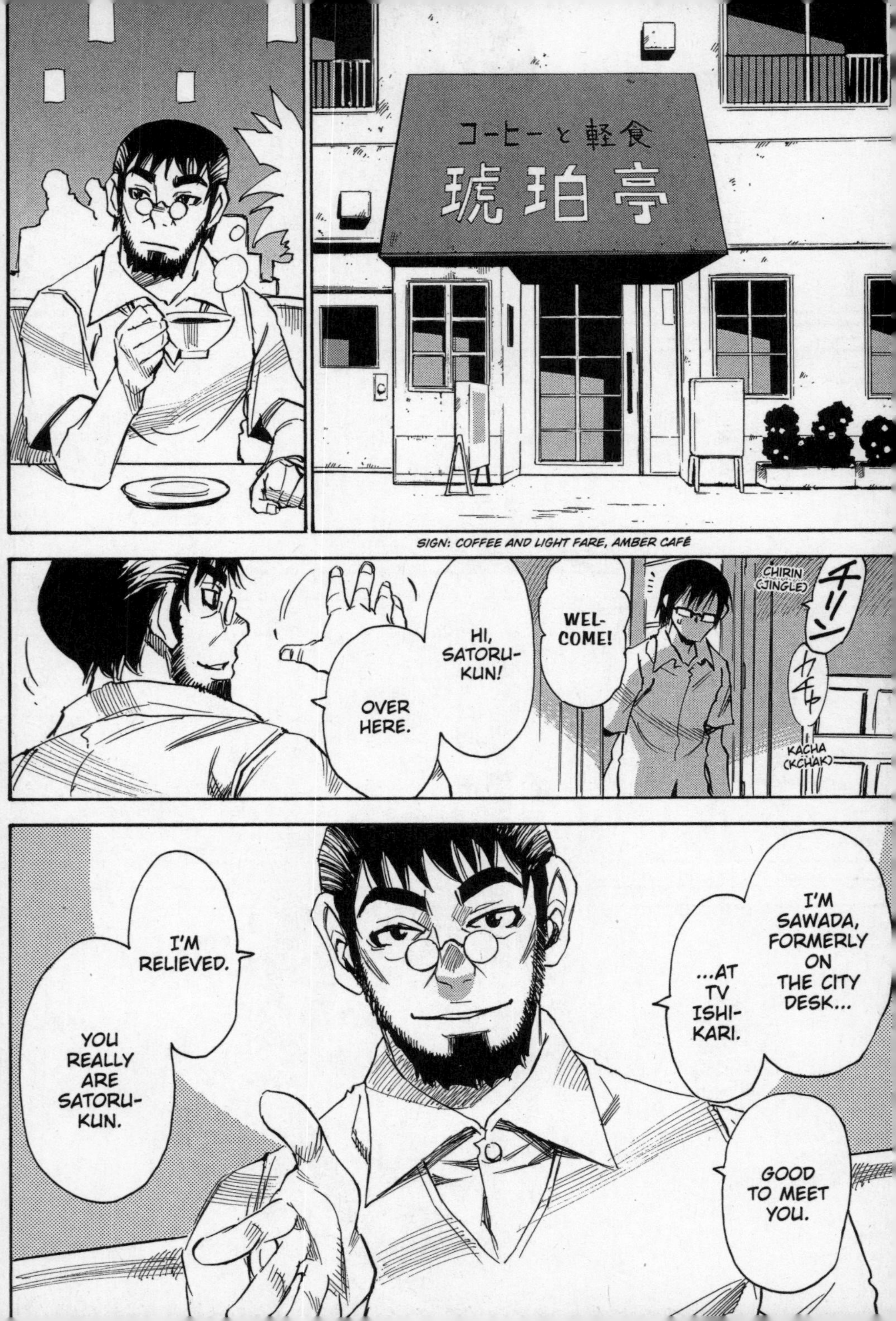
コーヒーと軽食
琥珀亭
SIGN: COFFEE AND LIGHT FARE, AMBER CAFÉ
チリン
CHIRIN (JINGLE)
カチャ
KACHA (KCHAK)
WEL-COME!
HI, SATORU-KUN!
OVER HERE.
I'M SAWADA, FORMERLY ON THE CITY DESK...
...AT TV ISHI-KARI.
GOOD TO MEET YOU.
I'M RELIEVED.
YOU REALLY ARE SATORU-KUN.

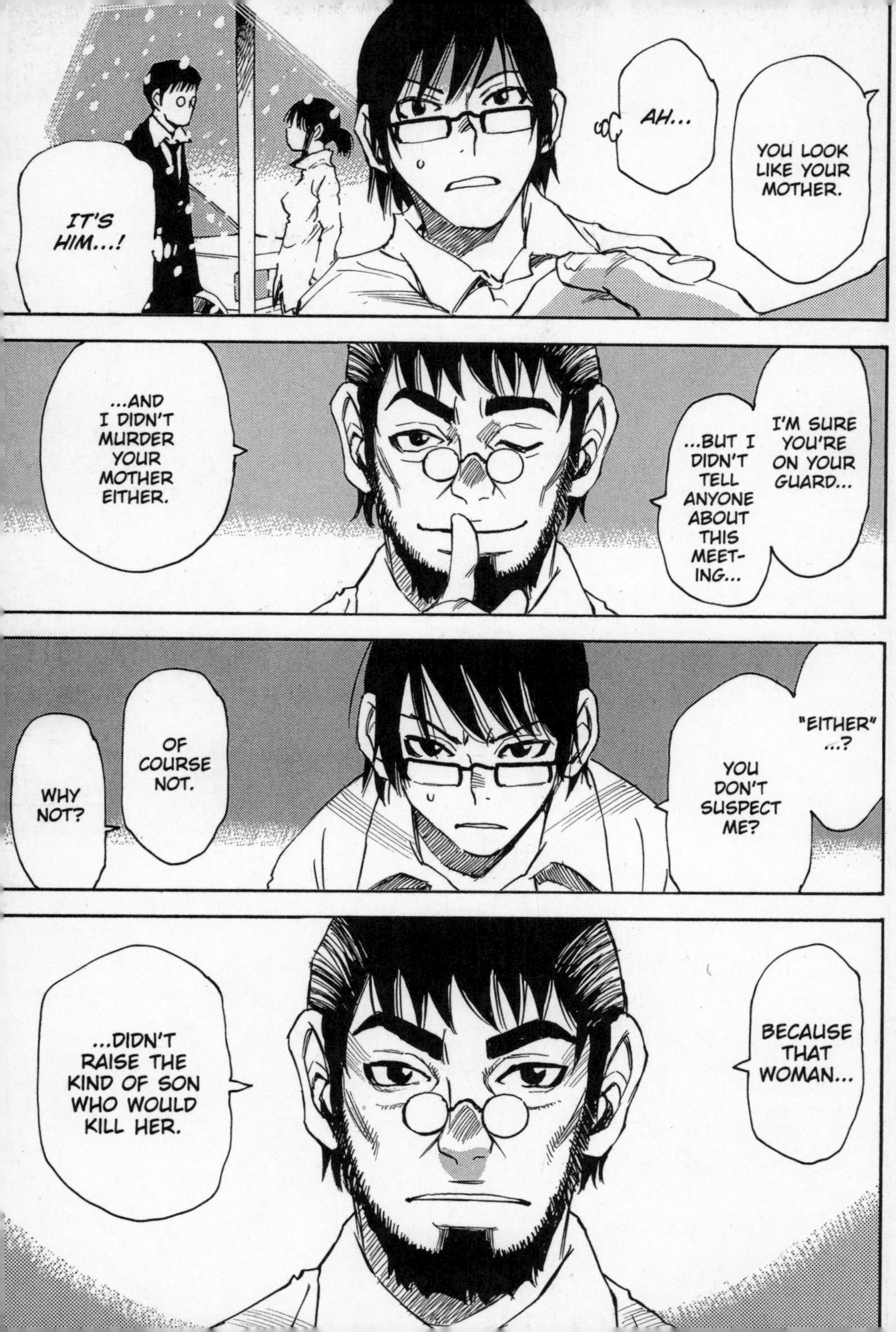
YOU LOOK LIKE YOUR MOTHER.
AH...
IT'S HIM...!
I'M SURE YOU'RE ON YOUR GUARD...
...BUT I DIDN'T TELL ANYONE ABOUT THIS MEET-ING...
...AND I DIDN'T MURDER YOUR MOTHER EITHER.
"EITHER" ...?
YOU DON'T SUSPECT ME?
OF COURSE NOT.
WHY NOT?
BECAUSE THAT WOMAN...
...DIDN'T RAISE THE KIND OF SON WHO WOULD KILL HER.

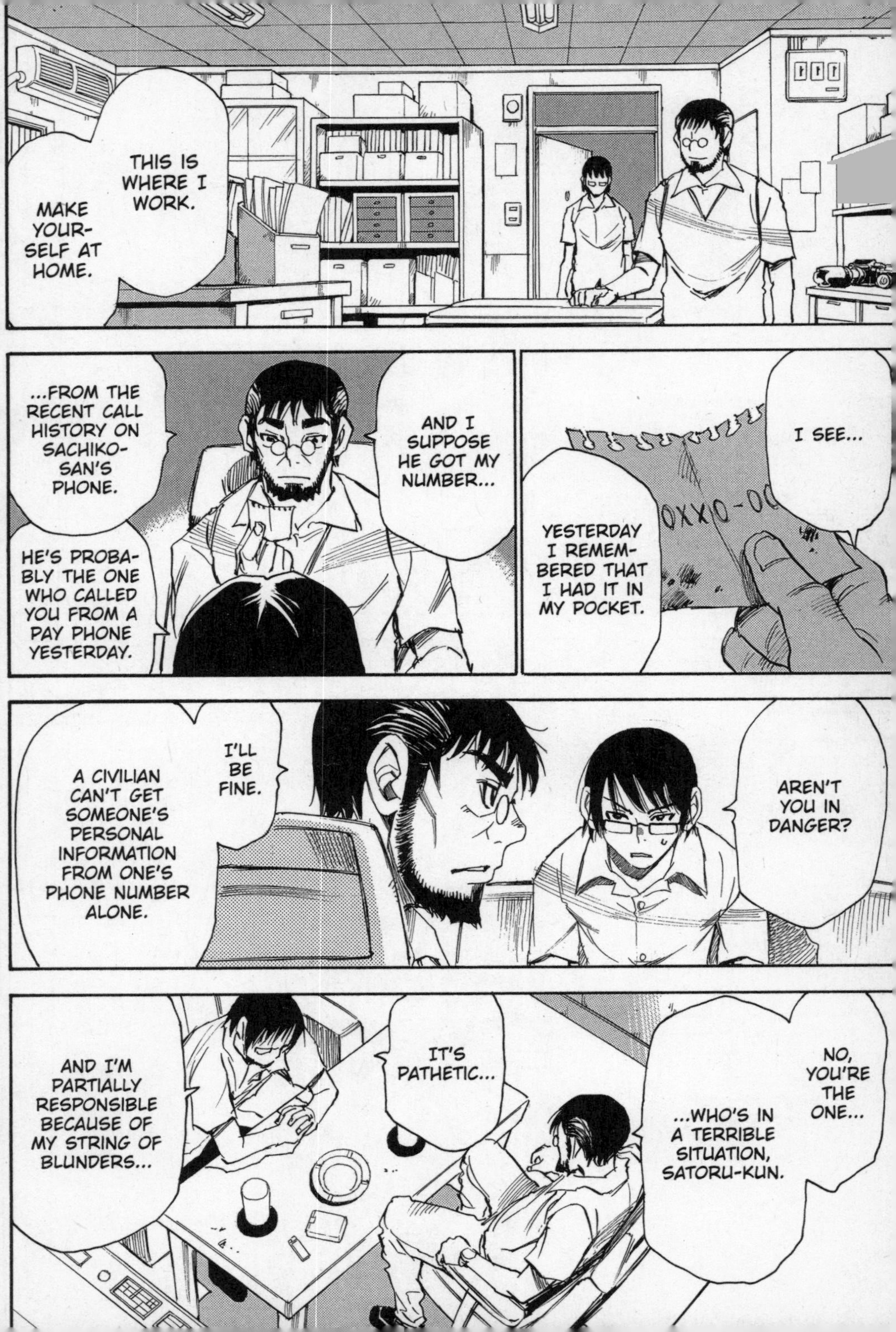
THIS IS WHERE I WORK.
MAKE YOURSELF AT HOME.
I SEE...
YESTERDAY I REMEMBERED THAT I HAD IT IN MY POCKET.
AND I SUPPOSE HE GOT MY NUMBER...
...FROM THE RECENT CALL HISTORY ON SACHIKO-SAN'S PHONE.
HE'S PROBABLY THE ONE WHO CALLED YOU FROM A PAY PHONE YESTERDAY.
AREN'T YOU IN DANGER?
I'LL BE FINE.
A CIVILIAN CAN'T GET SOMEONE'S PERSONAL INFORMATION FROM ONE'S PHONE NUMBER ALONE.
NO, YOU'RE THE ONE...
...WHO'S IN A TERRIBLE SITUATION, SATORU-KUN.
IT'S PATHETIC...
AND I'M PARTIALLY RESPONSIBLE BECAUSE OF MY STRING OF BLUNDERS...

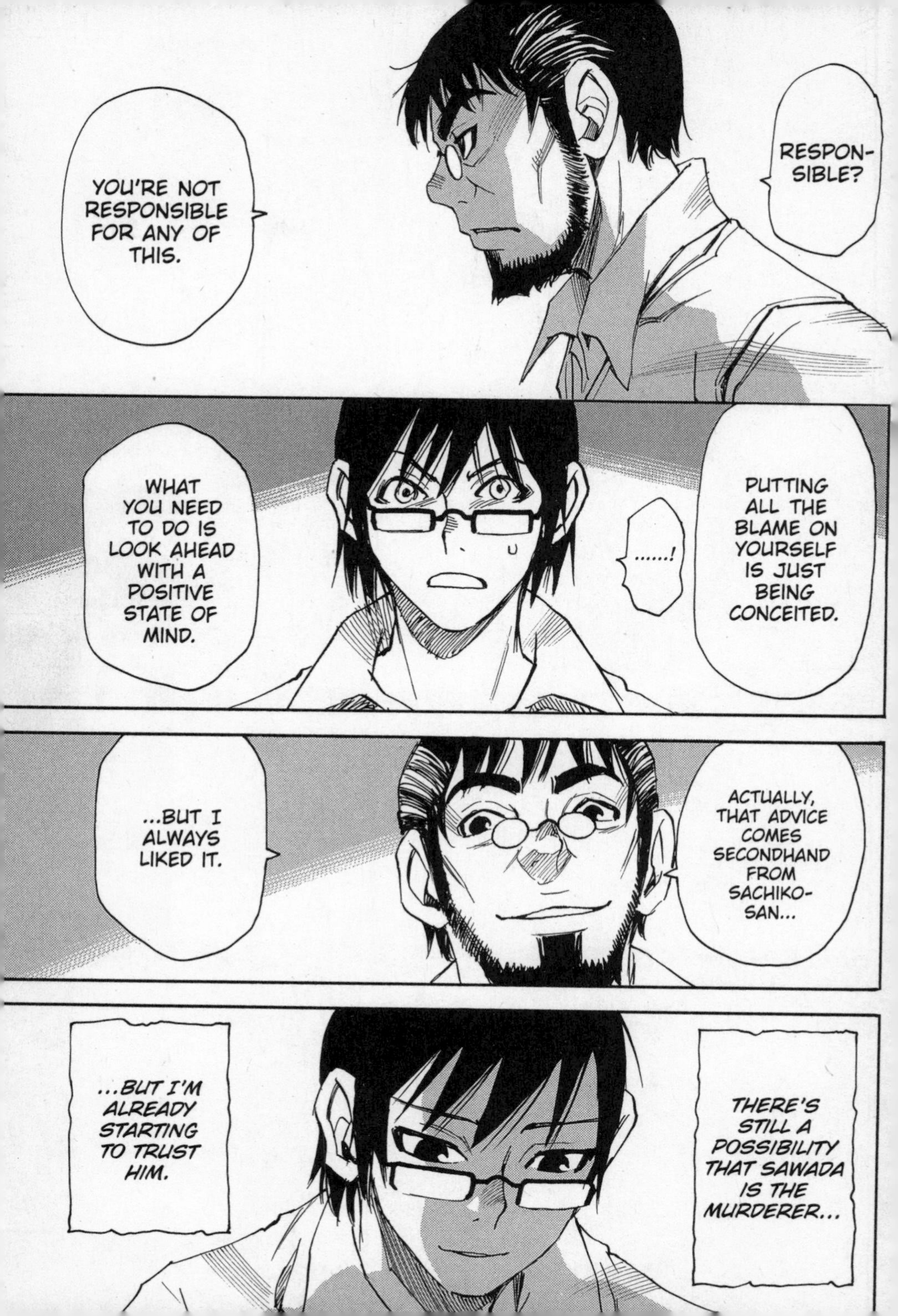
RESPON-SIBLE?
YOU'RE NOT RESPONSIBLE FOR ANY OF THIS.
PUTTING ALL THE BLAME ON YOURSELF IS JUST BEING CONCEITED.
......!
WHAT YOU NEED TO DO IS LOOK AHEAD WITH A POSITIVE STATE OF MIND.
ACTUALLY, THAT ADVICE COMES SECONDHAND FROM SACHIKO-SAN...
...BUT I ALWAYS LIKED IT.
THERE'S STILL A POSSIBILITY THAT SAWADA IS THE MURDERER...
...BUT I'M ALREADY STARTING TO TRUST HIM.

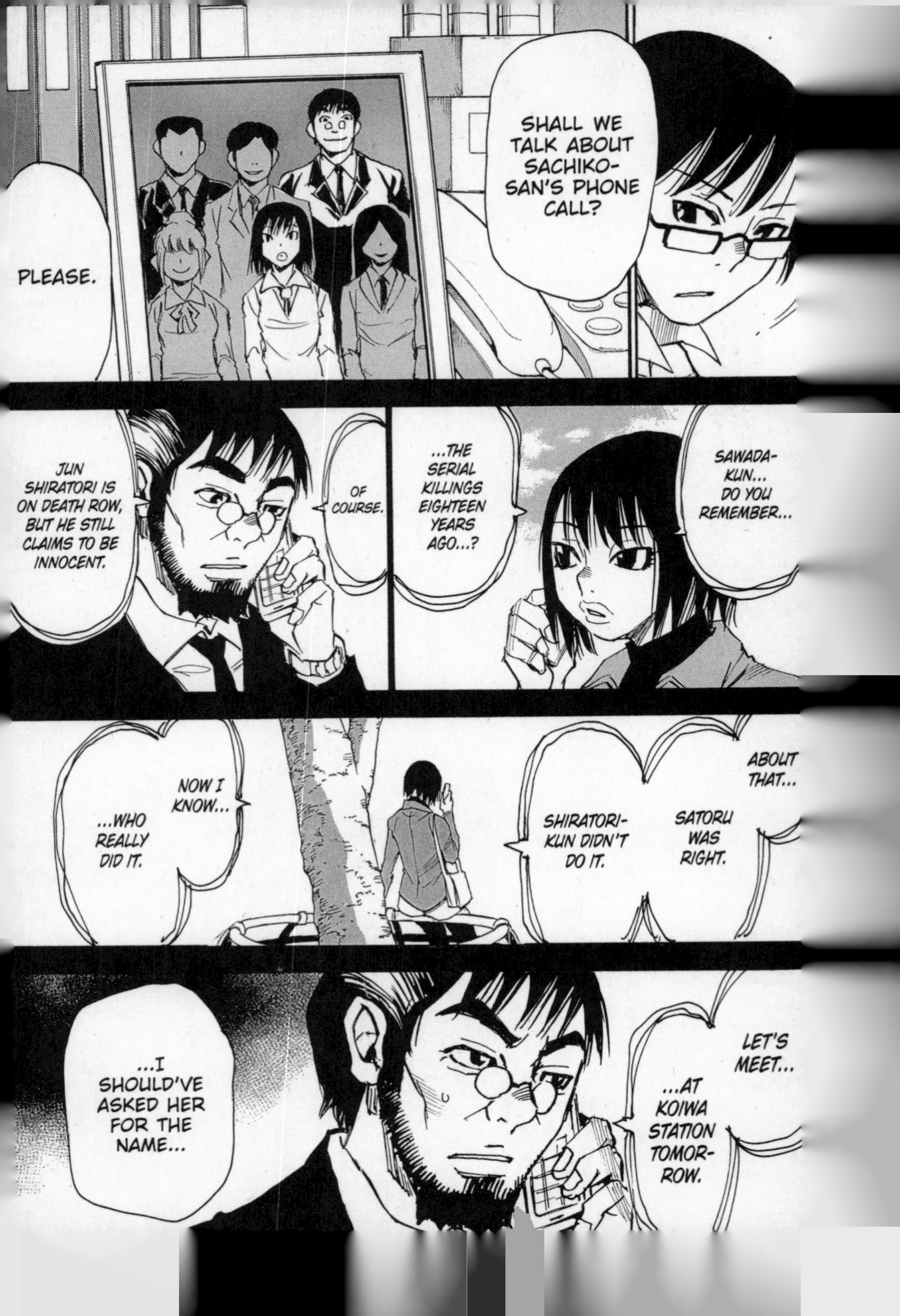
SHALL WE TALK ABOUT SACHIKO-SAN'S PHONE CALL?
PLEASE.
SAWADA-KUN... DO YOU REMEMBER...
...THE SERIAL KILLINGS EIGHTEEN YEARS AGO...?
OF COURSE.
JUN SHIRATORI IS ON DEATH ROW, BUT HE STILL CLAIMS TO BE INNOCENT.
ABOUT THAT...
SATORU WAS RIGHT.
SHIRATORI-KUN DIDN'T DO IT.
NOW I KNOW...
...WHO REALLY DID IT.
LET'S MEET...
...AT KOIWA STATION TOMORROW.
...I SHOULD'VE ASKED HER FOR THE NAME...

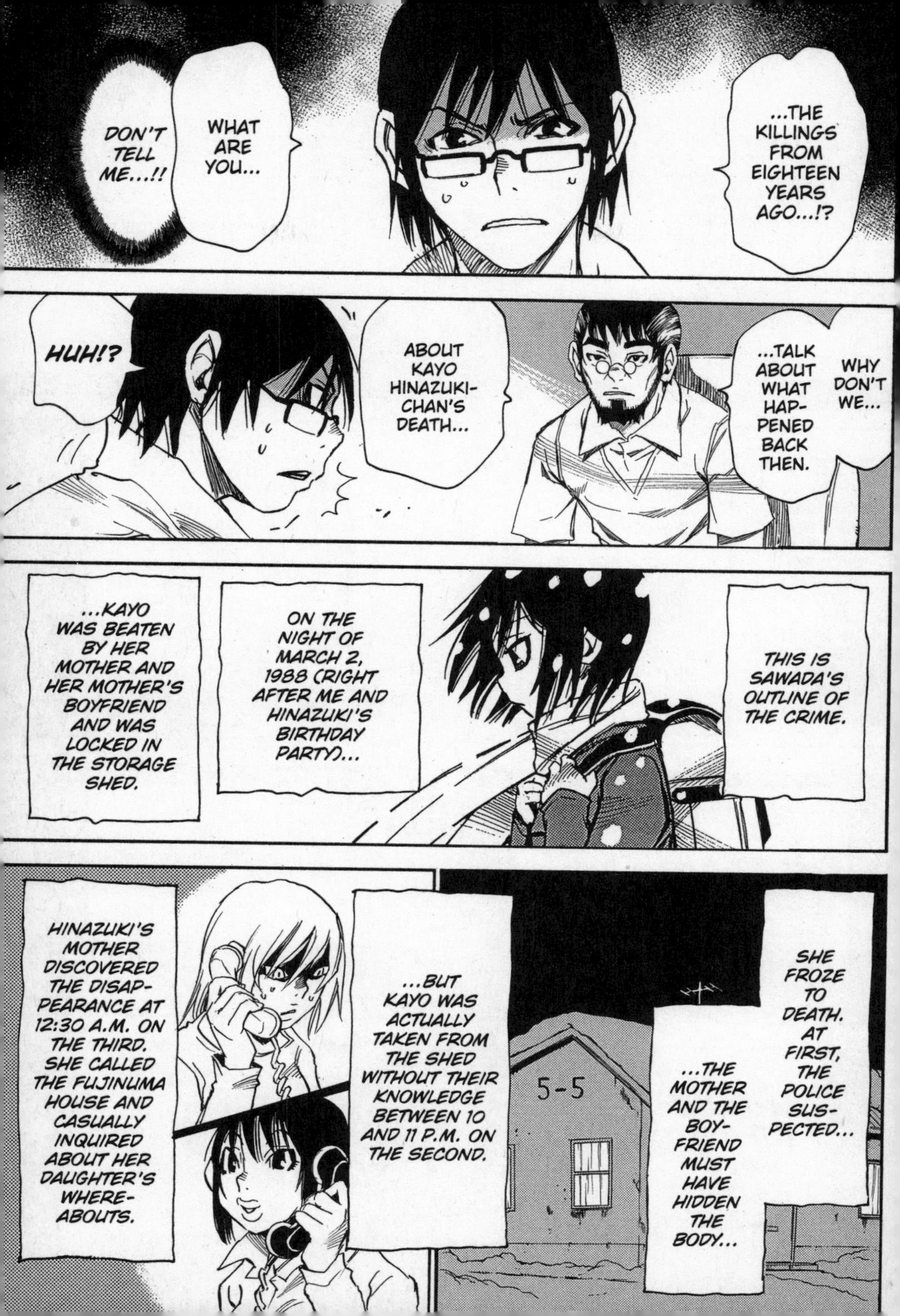
...THE KILLINGS FROM EIGHTEEN YEARS AGO...!?
WHAT ARE YOU...
DON'T TELL ME...!!
WHY DON'T WE...
...TALK ABOUT WHAT HAP-PENED BACK THEN.
ABOUT KAYO HINAZUKI-CHAN'S DEATH...
HUH!?
THIS IS SAWADA'S OUTLINE OF THE CRIME.
ON THE NIGHT OF MARCH 2, 1988 (RIGHT AFTER ME AND HINAZUKI'S BIRTHDAY PARTY)...
...KAYO WAS BEATEN BY HER MOTHER AND HER MOTHER'S BOYFRIEND AND WAS LOCKED IN THE STORAGE SHED.
SHE FROZE TO DEATH. AT FIRST, THE POLICE SUS-PECTED...
...THE MOTHER AND THE BOY-FRIEND MUST HAVE HIDDEN THE BODY...
5-5
...BUT KAYO WAS ACTUALLY TAKEN FROM THE SHED WITHOUT THEIR KNOWLEDGE BETWEEN 10 AND 11 P.M. ON THE SECOND.
HINAZUKI'S MOTHER DISCOVERED THE DISAP-PEARANCE AT 12:30 A.M. ON THE THIRD. SHE CALLED THE FUJINUMA HOUSE AND CASUALLY INQUIRED ABOUT HER DAUGHTER'S WHERE-ABOUTS.

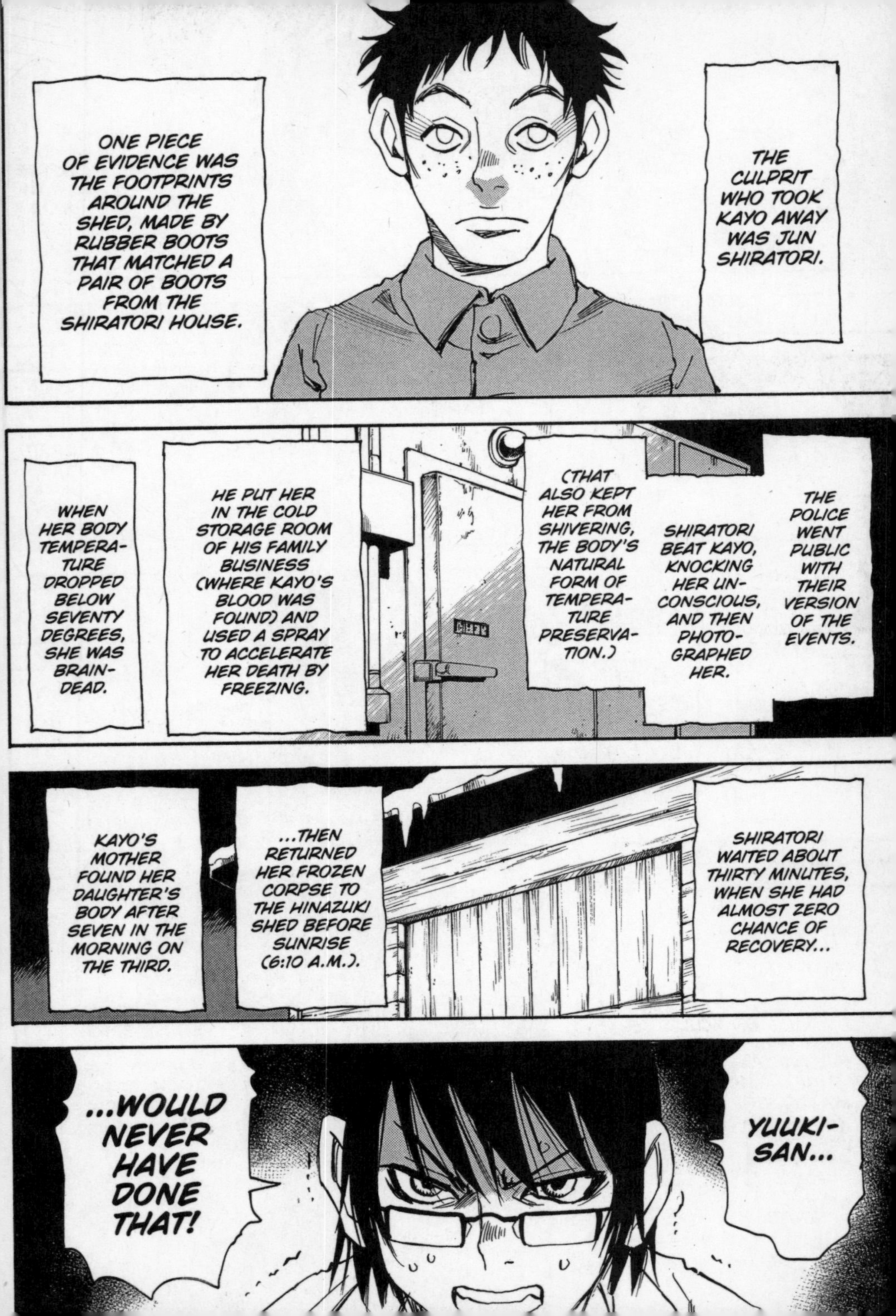
THE CULPRIT WHO TOOK KAYO AWAY WAS JUN SHIRATORI.
ONE PIECE OF EVIDENCE WAS THE FOOTPRINTS AROUND THE SHED, MADE BY RUBBER BOOTS THAT MATCHED A PAIR OF BOOTS FROM THE SHIRATORI HOUSE.
THE POLICE WENT PUBLIC WITH THEIR VERSION OF THE EVENTS.
SHIRATORI BEAT KAYO, KNOCKING HER UN-CONSCIOUS, AND THEN PHOTO-GRAPHED HER.
(THAT ALSO KEPT HER FROM SHIVERING, THE BODY'S NATURAL FORM OF TEMPERA-TURE PRESERVA-TION.)
HE PUT HER IN THE COLD STORAGE ROOM OF HIS FAMILY BUSINESS (WHERE KAYO'S BLOOD WAS FOUND) AND USED A SPRAY TO ACCELERATE HER DEATH BY FREEZING.
WHEN HER BODY TEMPERA-TURE DROPPED BELOW SEVENTY DEGREES, SHE WAS BRAIN-DEAD.
SHIRATORI WAITED ABOUT THIRTY MINUTES, WHEN SHE HAD ALMOST ZERO CHANCE OF RECOVERY...
...THEN RETURNED HER FROZEN CORPSE TO THE HINAZUKI SHED BEFORE SUNRISE (6:10 A.M.).
KAYO'S MOTHER FOUND HER DAUGHTER'S BODY AFTER SEVEN IN THE MORNING ON THE THIRD.
YUUKI-SAN...
...WOULD NEVER HAVE DONE THAT!

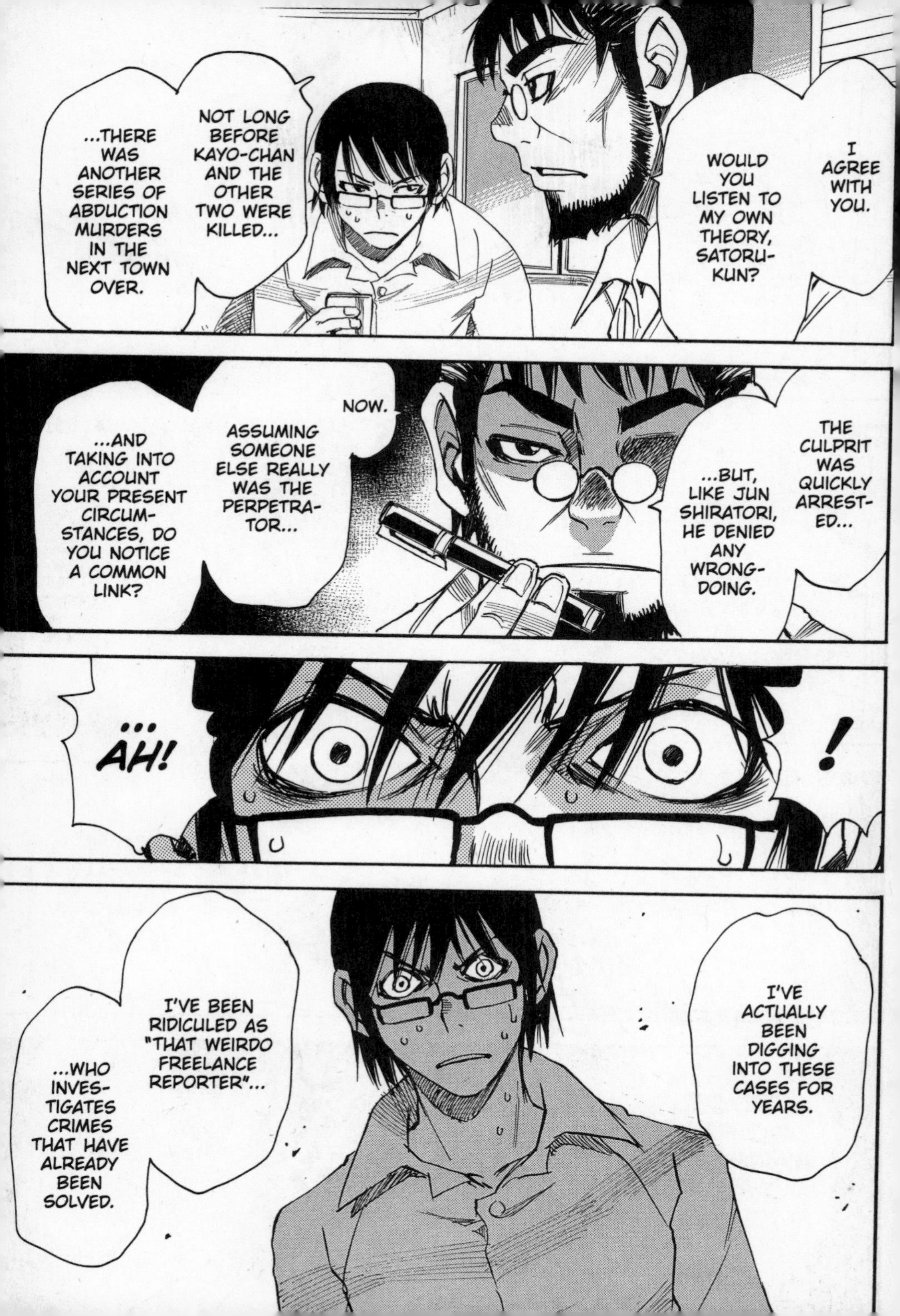
I AGREE WITH YOU.
WOULD YOU LISTEN TO MY OWN THEORY, SATORU-KUN?
NOT LONG BEFORE KAYO-CHAN AND THE OTHER TWO WERE KILLED...
...THERE WAS ANOTHER SERIES OF ABDUCTION MURDERS IN THE NEXT TOWN OVER.
THE CULPRIT WAS QUICKLY ARREST-ED...
...BUT, LIKE JUN SHIRATORI, HE DENIED ANY WRONG-DOING.
NOW.
ASSUMING SOMEONE ELSE REALLY WAS THE PERPETRA-TOR...
...AND TAKING INTO ACCOUNT YOUR PRESENT CIRCUM-STANCES, DO YOU NOTICE A COMMON LINK?
!
... AH!
I'VE ACTUALLY BEEN DIGGING INTO THESE CASES FOR YEARS.
I'VE BEEN RIDICULED AS "THAT WEIRDO FREELANCE REPORTER"...
...WHO INVES-TIGATES CRIMES THAT HAVE ALREADY BEEN SOLVED.

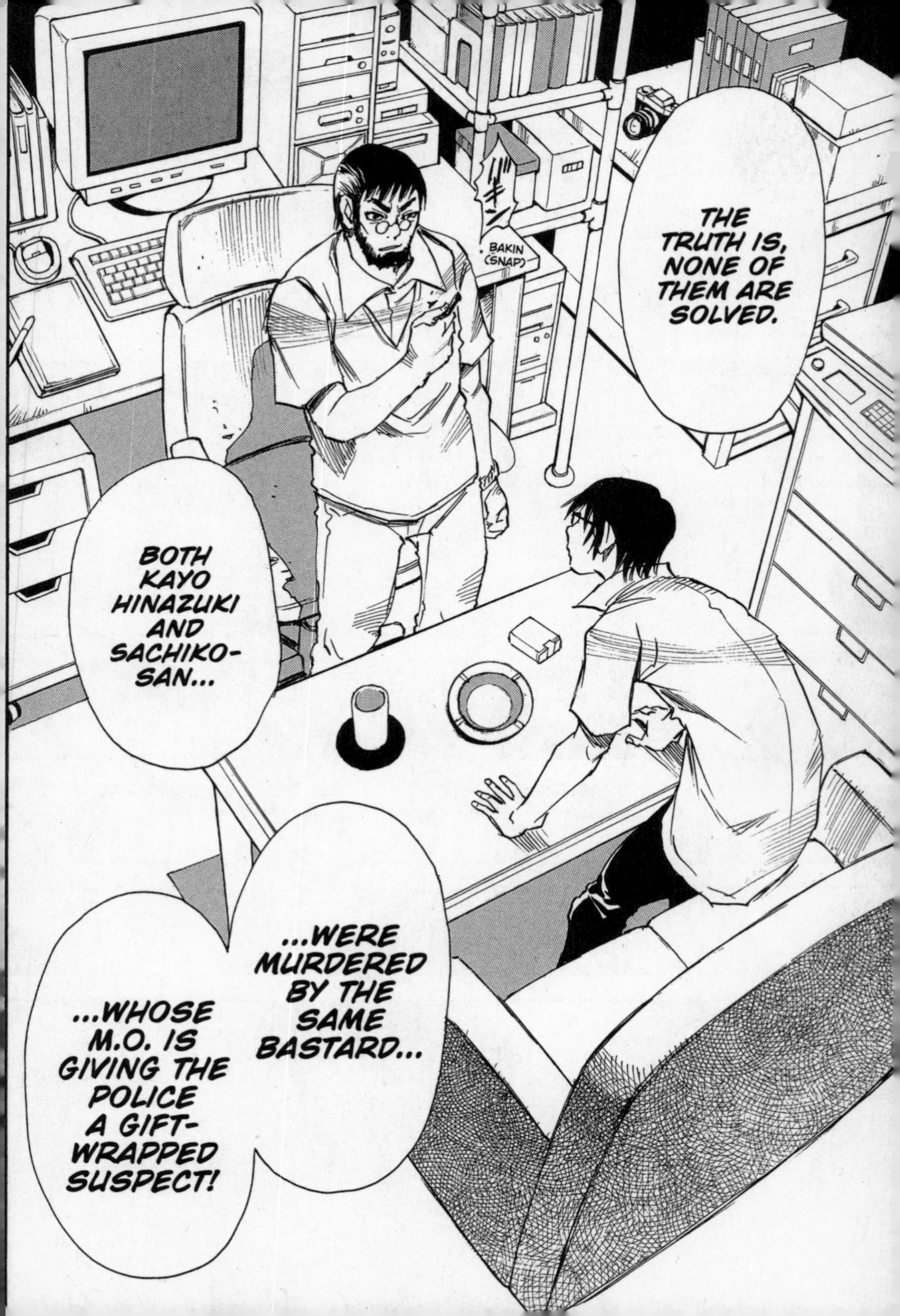
THE TRUTH IS, NONE OF THEM ARE SOLVED.
BAKIN (SNAP)
BOTH KAYO HINAZUKI AND SACHIKO-SAN...
...WERE MURDERED BY THE SAME BASTARD...
...WHOSE M.O. IS GIVING THE POLICE A GIFT-WRAPPED SUSPECT!

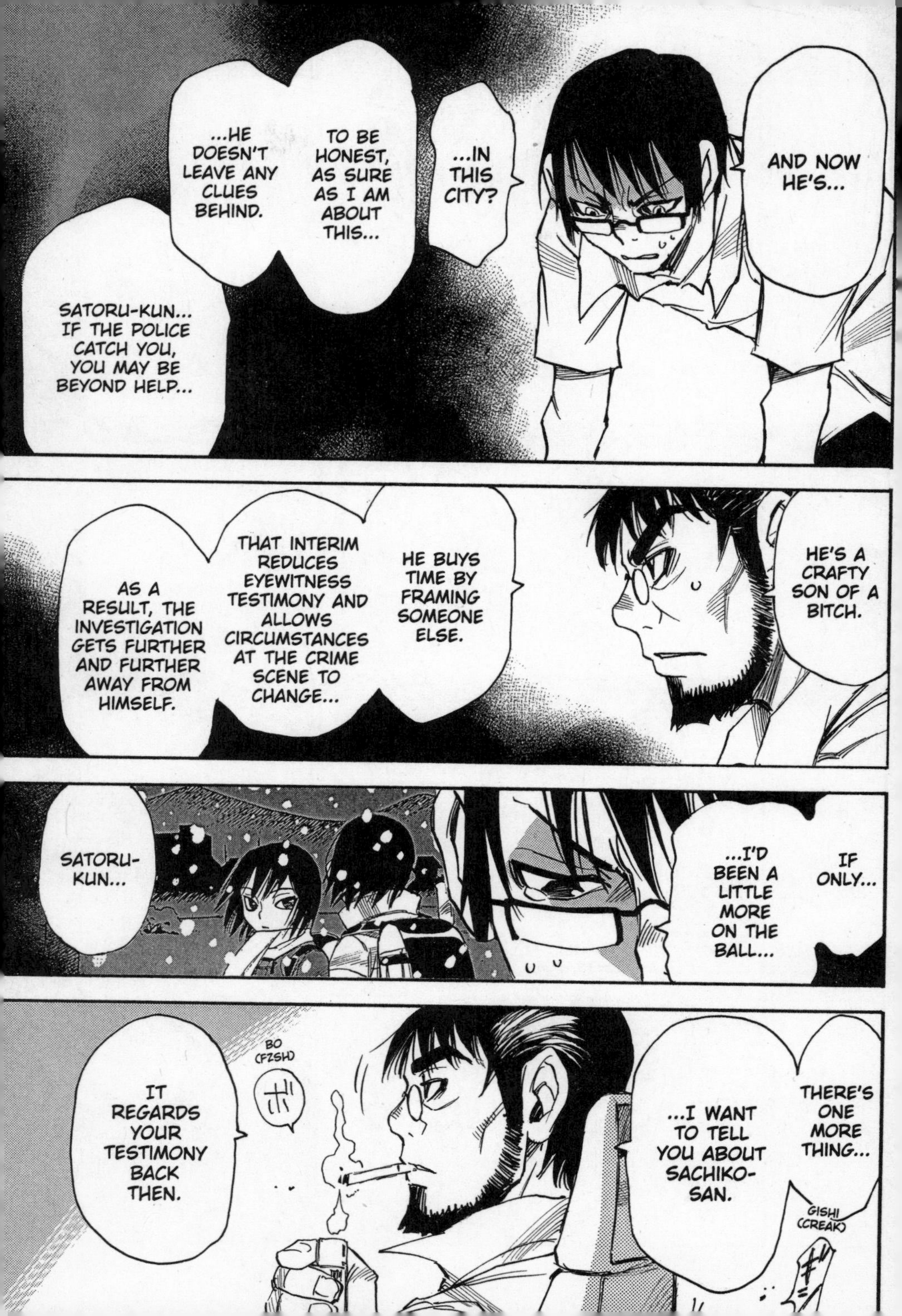
AND NOW HE'S...
...IN THIS CITY?
TO BE HONEST, AS SURE AS I AM ABOUT THIS...
...HE DOESN'T LEAVE ANY CLUES BEHIND.
SATORU-KUN... IF THE POLICE CATCH YOU, YOU MAY BE BEYOND HELP...
HE'S A CRAFTY SON OF A BITCH.
HE BUYS TIME BY FRAMING SOMEONE ELSE.
THAT INTERIM REDUCES EYEWITNESS TESTIMONY AND ALLOWS CIRCUMSTANCES AT THE CRIME SCENE TO CHANGE...
AS A RESULT, THE INVESTIGATION GETS FURTHER AND FURTHER AWAY FROM HIMSELF.
IF ONLY...
...I'D BEEN A LITTLE MORE ON THE BALL...
SATORU-KUN...
THERE'S ONE MORE THING...
GISHI (CREAK)
...I WANT TO TELL YOU ABOUT SACHIKO-SAN.
BO (FZSH)
IT REGARDS YOUR TESTIMONY BACK THEN.

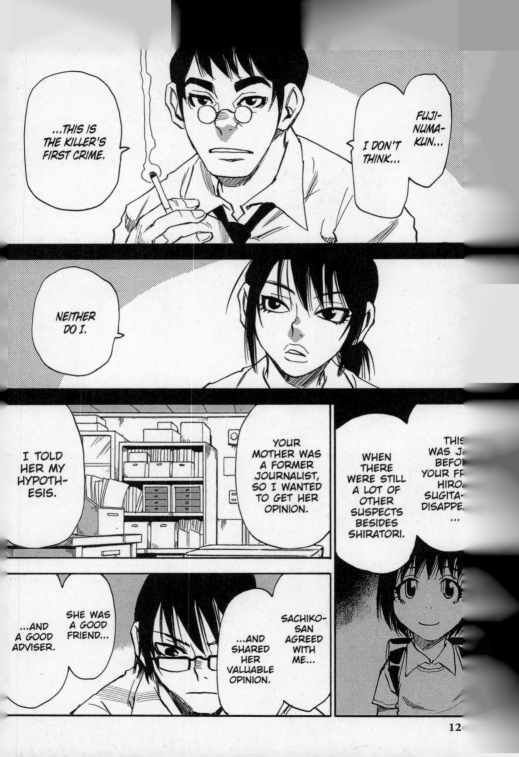

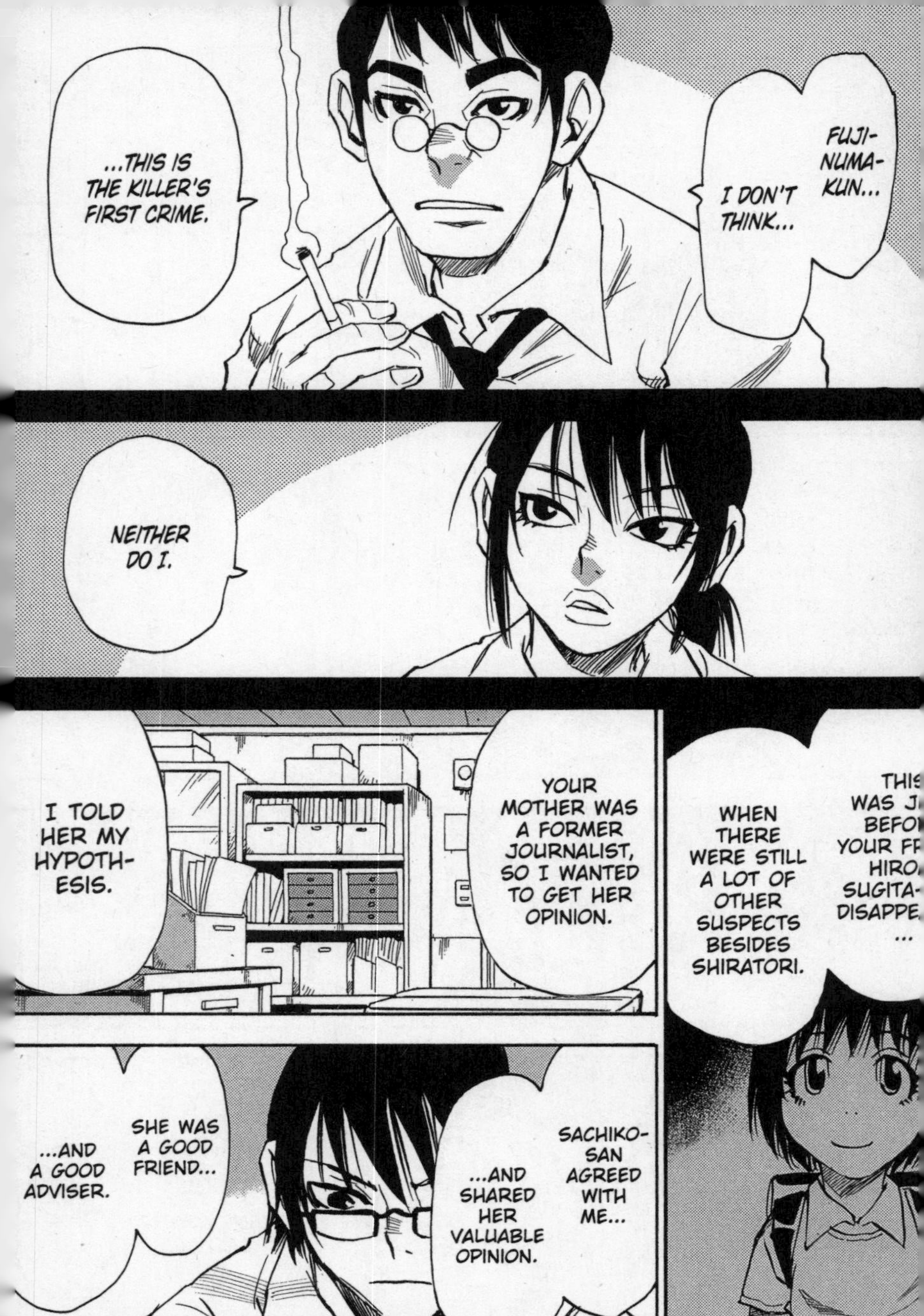
FUJI-NUMA-KUN...
I DON'T THINK...
...THIS IS THE KILLER'S FIRST CRIME.
NEITHER DO I.
THIS WAS J BEFO YOUR FR HIRO SUGITA- DISAPPE ...
WHEN THERE WERE STILL A LOT OF OTHER SUSPECTS BESIDES SHIRATORI.
YOUR MOTHER WAS A FORMER JOURNALIST, SO I WANTED TO GET HER OPINION.
I TOLD HER MY HYPOTHESIS.
SACHIKO-SAN AGREED WITH ME...
...AND SHARED HER VALUABLE OPINION.
SHE WAS A GOOD FRIEND...
...AND A GOOD ADVISER.

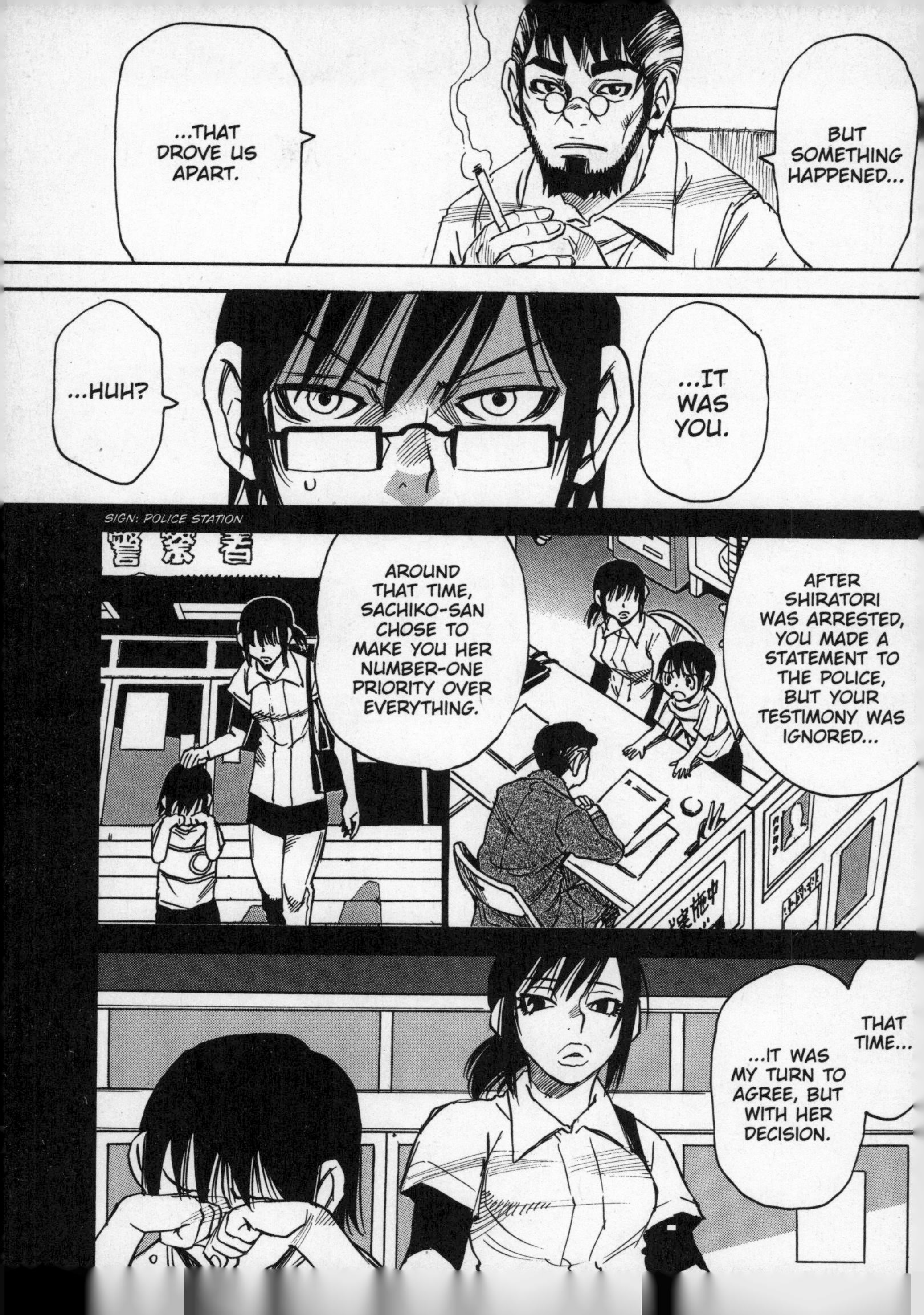
BUT SOMETHING HAPPENED...
...THAT DROVE US APART.
...IT WAS YOU.
...HUH?
SIGN: POLICE STATION
AFTER SHIRATORI WAS ARRESTED, YOU MADE A STATEMENT TO THE POLICE, BUT YOUR TESTIMONY WAS IGNORED...
AROUND THAT TIME, SACHIKO-SAN CHOSE TO MAKE YOU HER NUMBER-ONE PRIORITY OVER EVERYTHING.
THAT TIME...
...IT WAS MY TURN TO AGREE, BUT WITH HER DECISION.

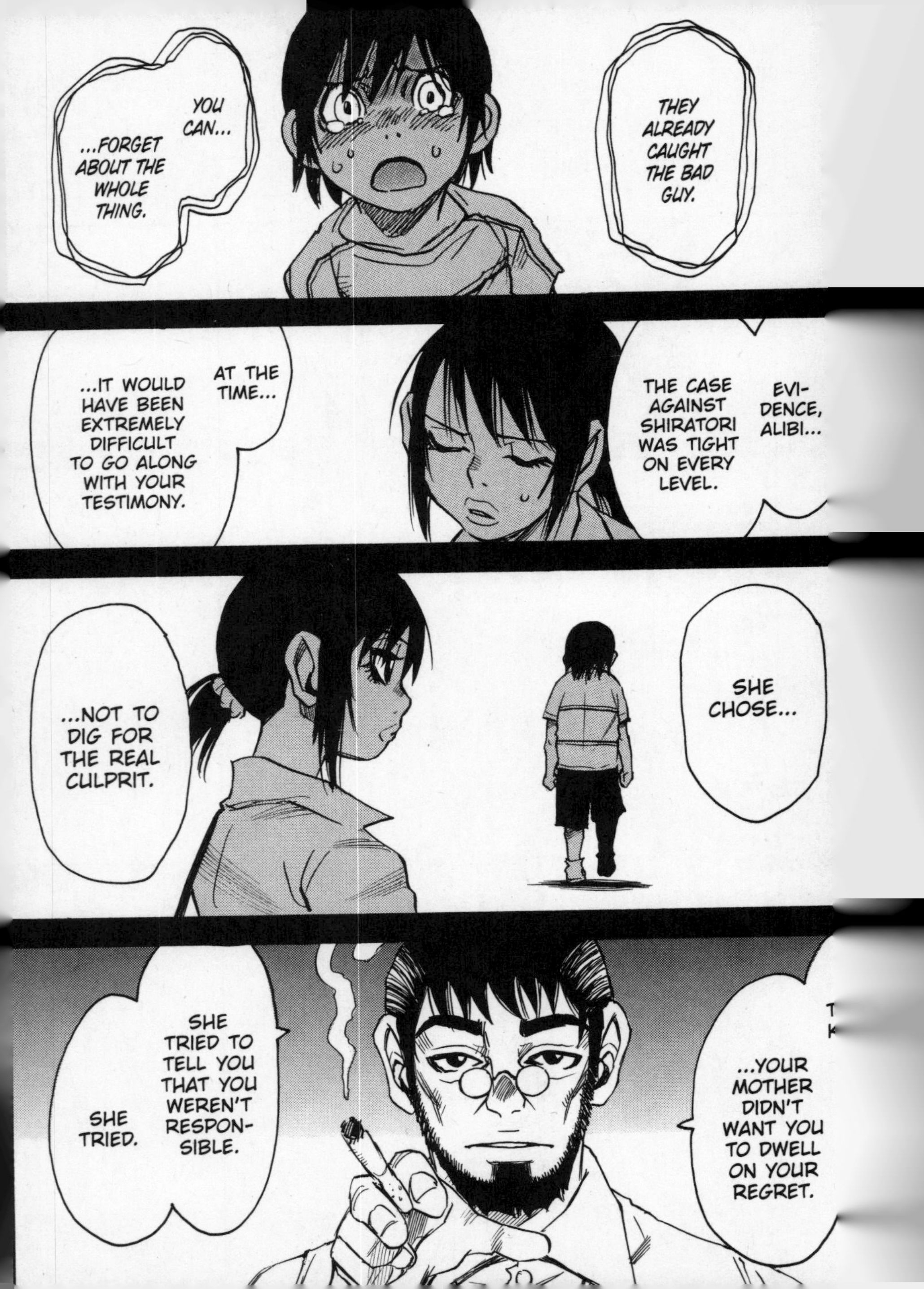
THEY ALREADY CAUGHT THE BAD GUY.
YOU CAN...
...FORGET ABOUT THE WHOLE THING.
EVI-DENCE, ALIBI...
THE CASE AGAINST SHIRATORI WAS TIGHT ON EVERY LEVEL.
AT THE TIME...
...IT WOULD HAVE BEEN EXTREMELY DIFFICULT TO GO ALONG WITH YOUR TESTIMONY.
SHE CHOSE...
...NOT TO DIG FOR THE REAL CULPRIT.
...YOUR MOTHER DIDN'T WANT YOU TO DWELL ON YOUR REGRET.
SHE TRIED TO TELL YOU THAT YOU WEREN'T RESPON-SIBLE.
SHE TRIED.

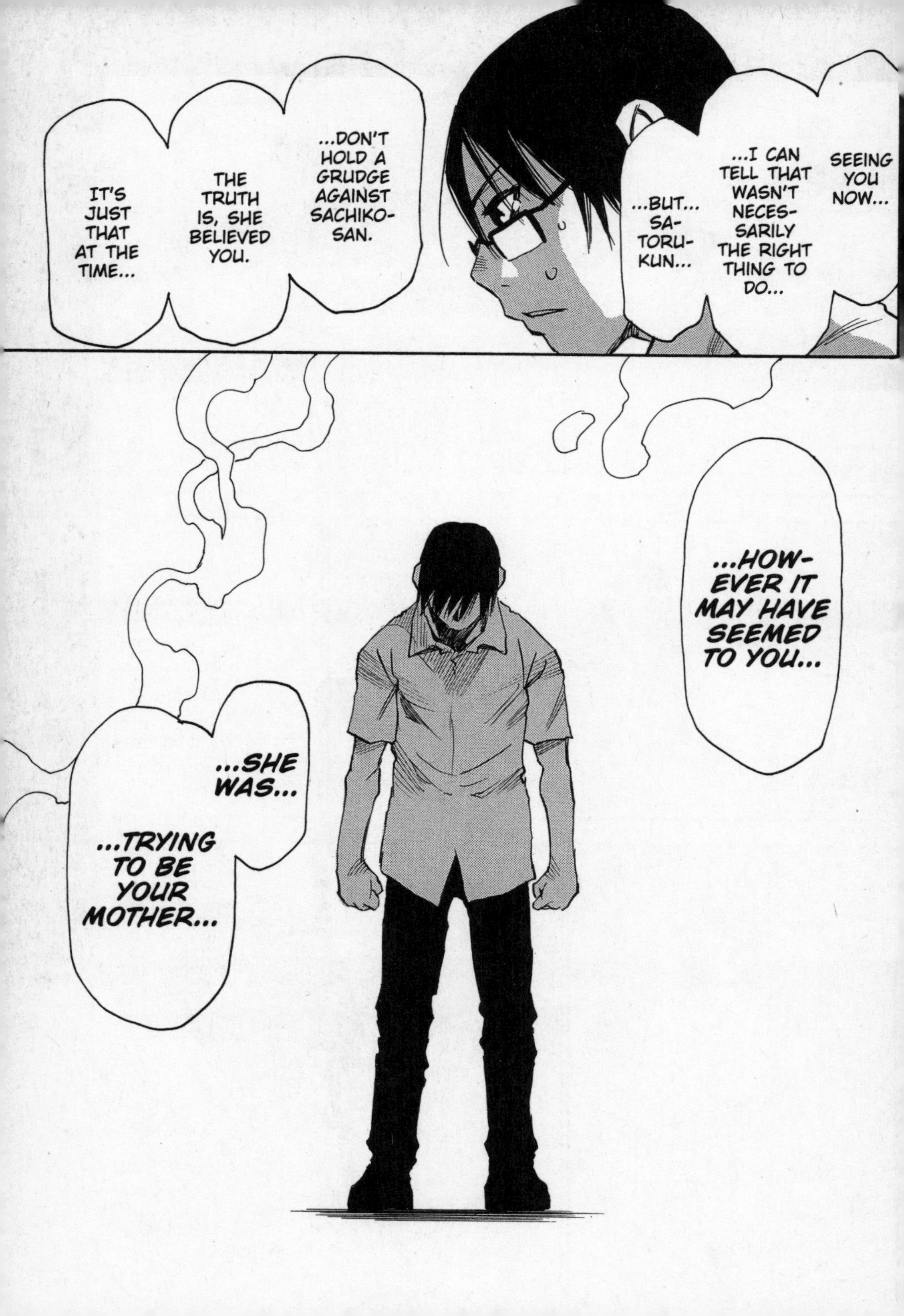
SEEING YOU NOW...
...I CAN TELL THAT WASN'T NECES-SARILY THE RIGHT THING TO DO...
...BUT... SA-TORU-KUN...
...DON'T HOLD A GRUDGE AGAINST SACHIKO-SAN.
THE TRUTH IS, SHE BELIEVED YOU.
IT'S JUST THAT AT THE TIME...
...HOW-EVER IT MAY HAVE SEEMED TO YOU...
...SHE WAS...
...TRYING TO BE YOUR MOTHER...

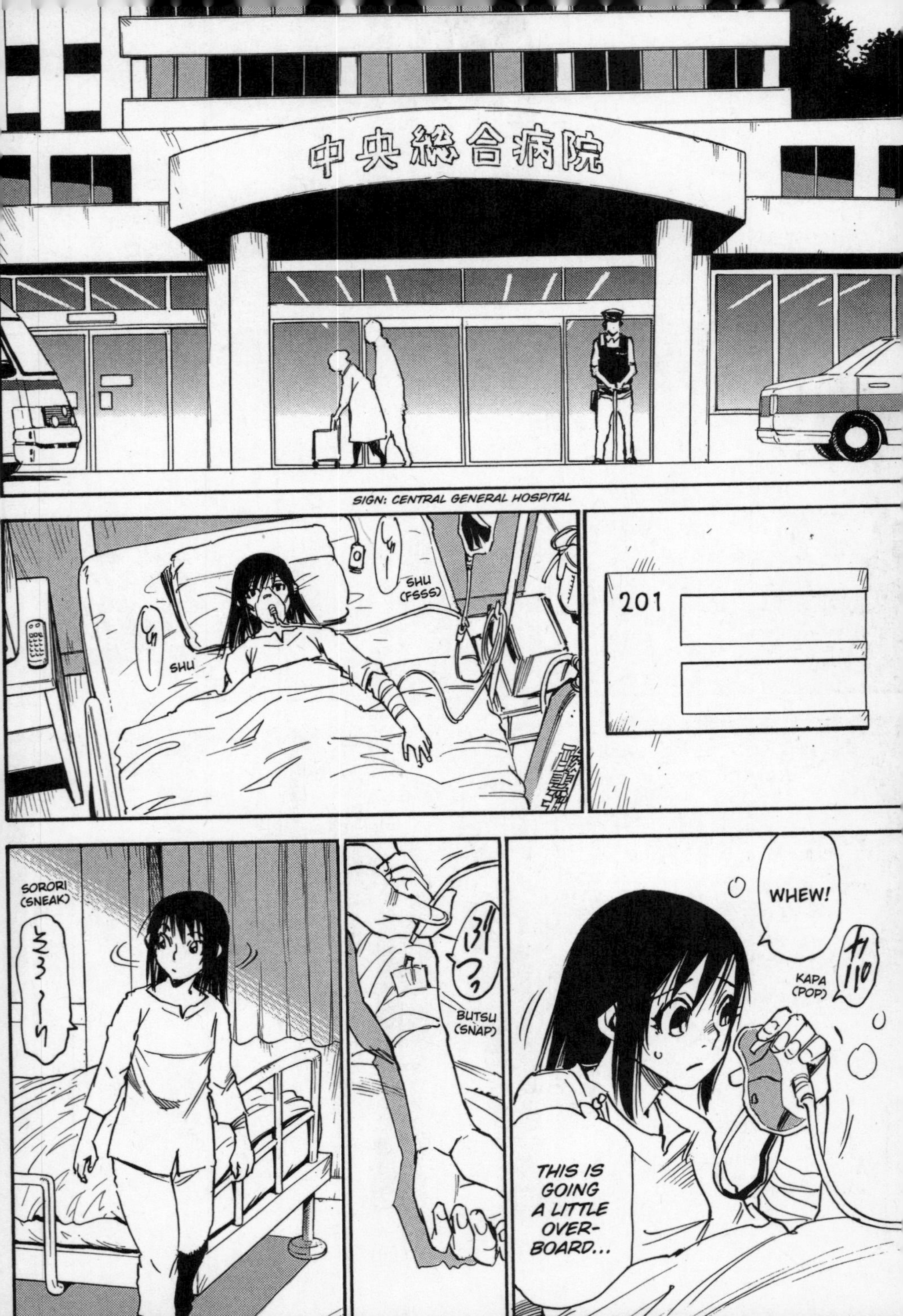
中央総合病院
SIGN: CENTRAL GENERAL HOSPITAL
201
SHU (FSSS)
SHU
WHEW!
KAPA (POP)
THIS IS GOING A LITTLE OVER-BOARD...
BUTSU (SNAP)
SORORI (SNEAK)

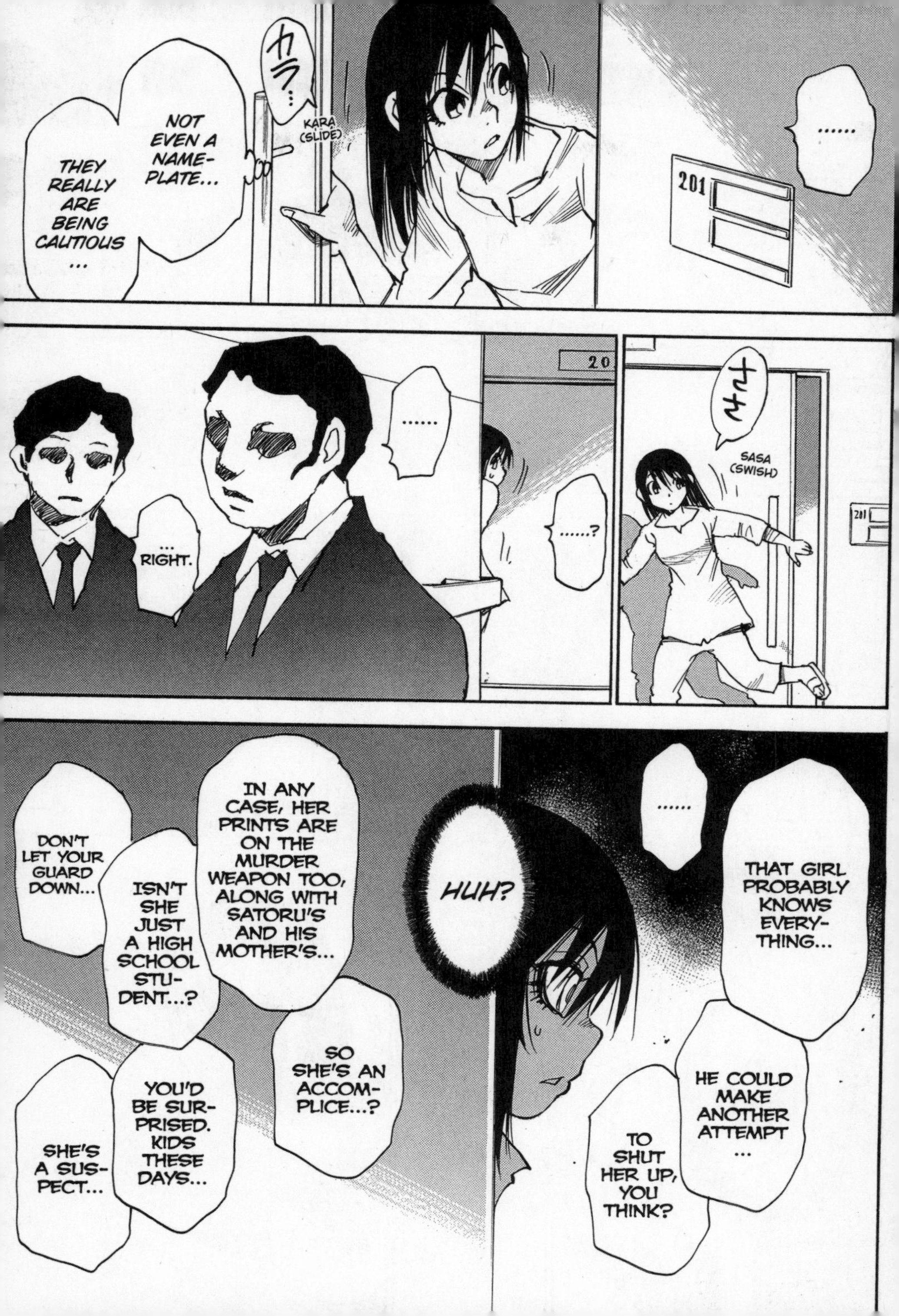
......
カラ…
KARA (SLIDE)
NOT EVEN A NAME-PLATE...
THEY REALLY ARE BEING CAUTIOUS ...
ささ
SASA (SWISH)
......?
......
... RIGHT.
......
THAT GIRL PROBABLY KNOWS EVERY-THING...
HUH?
HE COULD MAKE ANOTHER ATTEMPT ...
TO SHUT HER UP, YOU THINK?
IN ANY CASE, HER PRINTS ARE ON THE MURDER WEAPON TOO, ALONG WITH SATORU'S AND HIS MOTHER'S...
DON'T LET YOUR GUARD DOWN...
ISN'T SHE JUST A HIGH SCHOOL STU-DENT...?
SO SHE'S AN ACCOM-PLICE...?
YOU'D BE SUR-PRISED. KIDS THESE DAYS...
SHE'S A SUS-PECT...

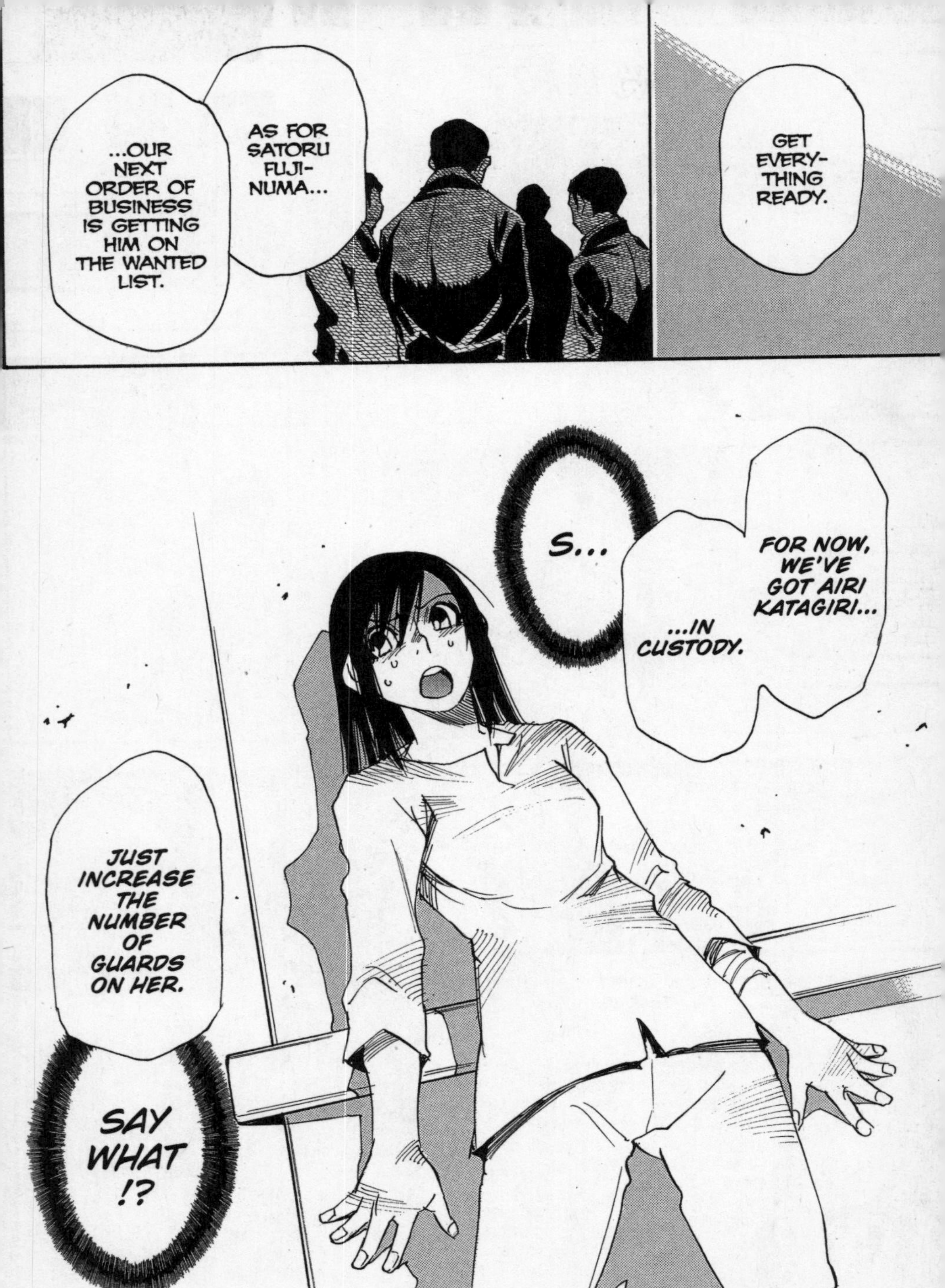
GET EVERYTHING READY.
AS FOR SATORU FUJI-NUMA...
...OUR NEXT ORDER OF BUSINESS IS GETTING HIM ON THE WANTED LIST.
FOR NOW, WE'VE GOT AIRI KATAGIRI...
...IN CUSTODY.
S...
JUST INCREASE THE NUMBER OF GUARDS ON HER.
SAY WHAT!?

#16 END

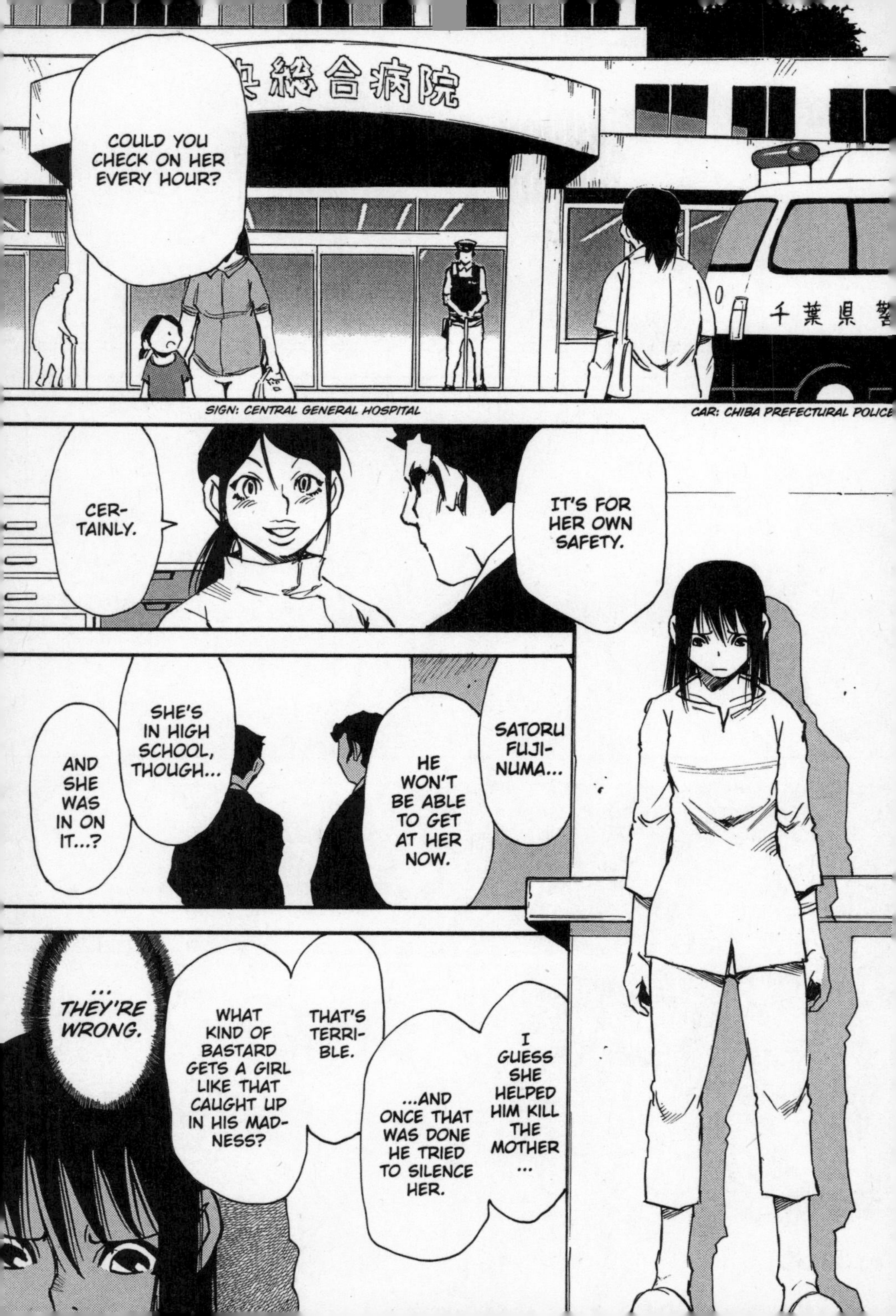
央総合病院
千葉県警
COULD YOU CHECK ON HER EVERY HOUR?
SIGN: CENTRAL GENERAL HOSPITAL
CAR: CHIBA PREFECTURAL POLICE
IT'S FOR HER OWN SAFETY.
CER-TAINLY.
SATORU FUJI-NUMA...
HE WON'T BE ABLE TO GET AT HER NOW.
SHE'S IN HIGH SCHOOL, THOUGH...
AND SHE WAS IN ON IT...?
I GUESS SHE HELPED HIM KILL THE MOTHER...
...AND ONCE THAT WAS DONE HE TRIED TO SILENCE HER.
THAT'S TERRI-BLE.
WHAT KIND OF BASTARD GETS A GIRL LIKE THAT CAUGHT UP IN HIS MAD-NESS?
...THEY'RE WRONG.

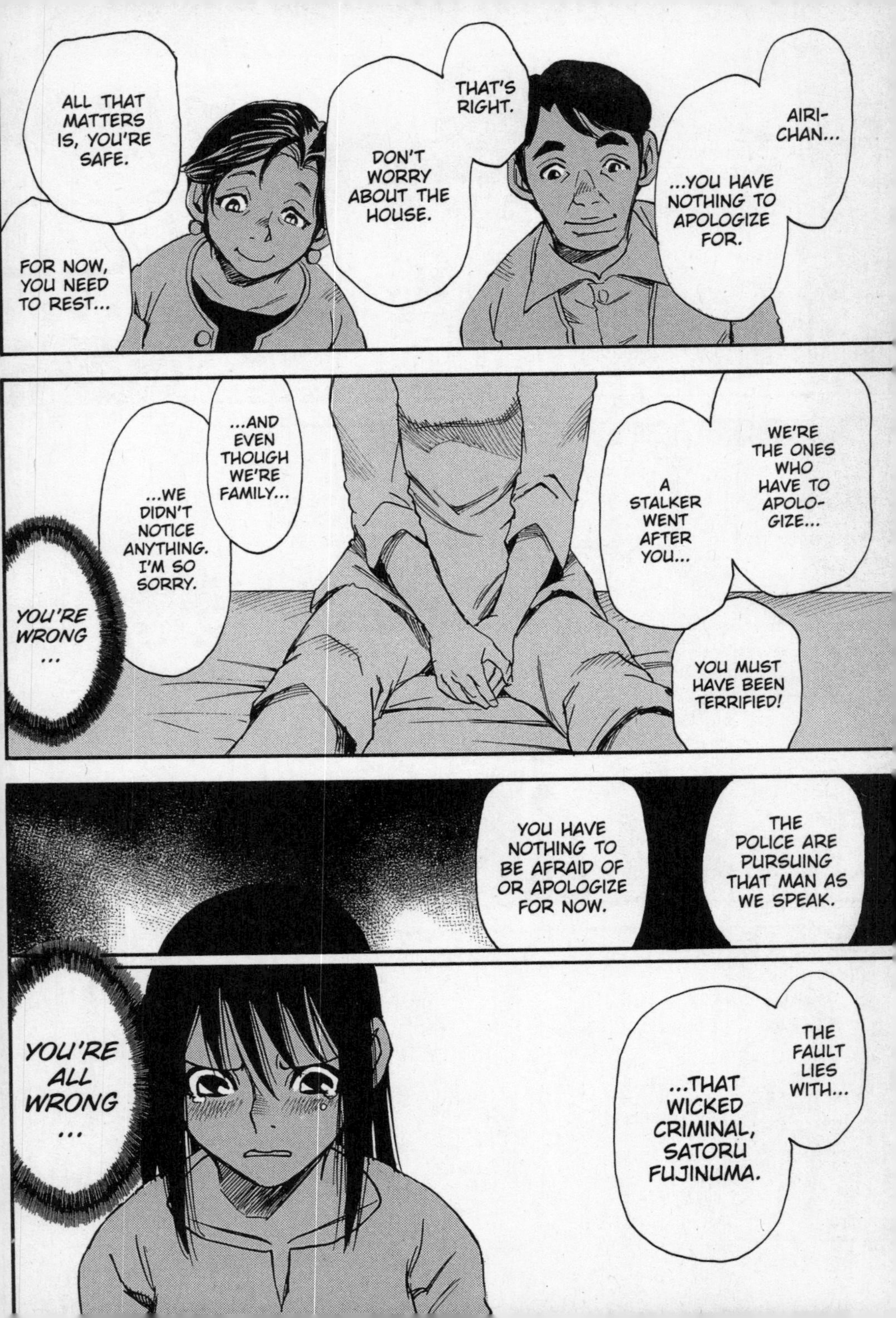
AIRI-CHAN...
...YOU HAVE NOTHING TO APOLOGIZE FOR.
THAT'S RIGHT.
DON'T WORRY ABOUT THE HOUSE.
ALL THAT MATTERS IS, YOU'RE SAFE.
FOR NOW, YOU NEED TO REST...
WE'RE THE ONES WHO HAVE TO APOLOGIZE...
A STALKER WENT AFTER YOU...
YOU MUST HAVE BEEN TERRIFIED!
...AND EVEN THOUGH WE'RE FAMILY...
...WE DIDN'T NOTICE ANYTHING. I'M SO SORRY.
YOU'RE WRONG...
THE POLICE ARE PURSUING THAT MAN AS WE SPEAK.
YOU HAVE NOTHING TO BE AFRAID OF OR APOLOGIZE FOR NOW.
THE FAULT LIES WITH...
...THAT WICKED CRIMINAL, SATORU FUJINUMA.
YOU'RE ALL WRONG...

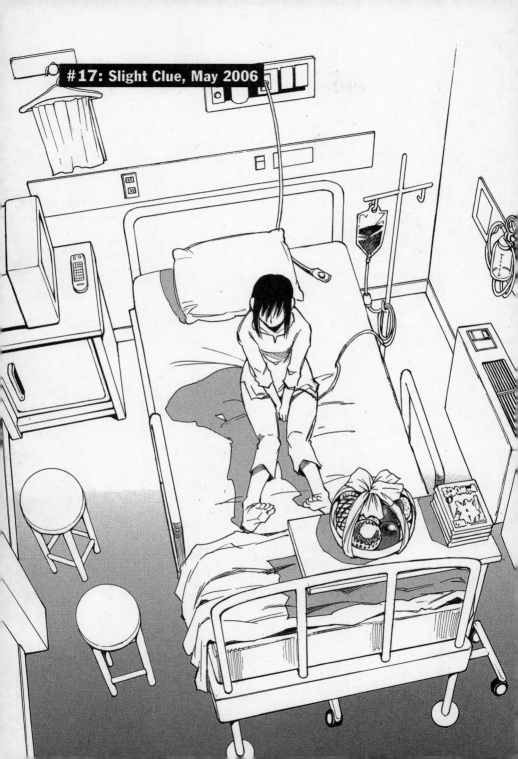

#17: Slight Clue, May 2006

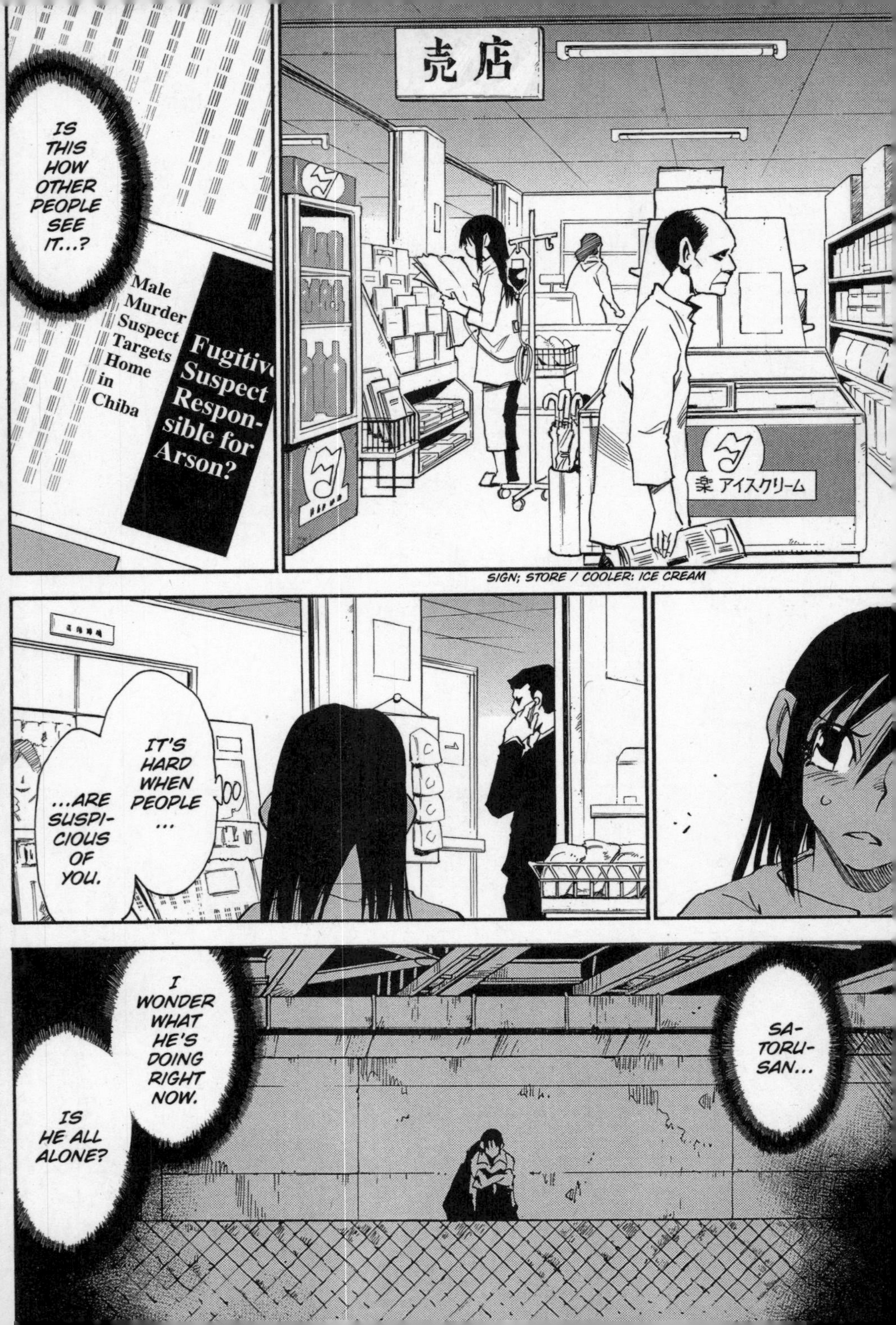
売店
楽 アイスクリーム
IS THIS HOW OTHER PEOPLE SEE IT...?
Fugitive Suspect Responsible for Arson?
Male Murder Suspect Targets Home in Chiba
SIGN; STORE / COOLER: ICE CREAM
IT'S HARD WHEN PEOPLE ...
...ARE SUSPICIOUS OF YOU.
SA-TORU-SAN...
I WONDER WHAT HE'S DOING RIGHT NOW.
IS HE ALL ALONE?

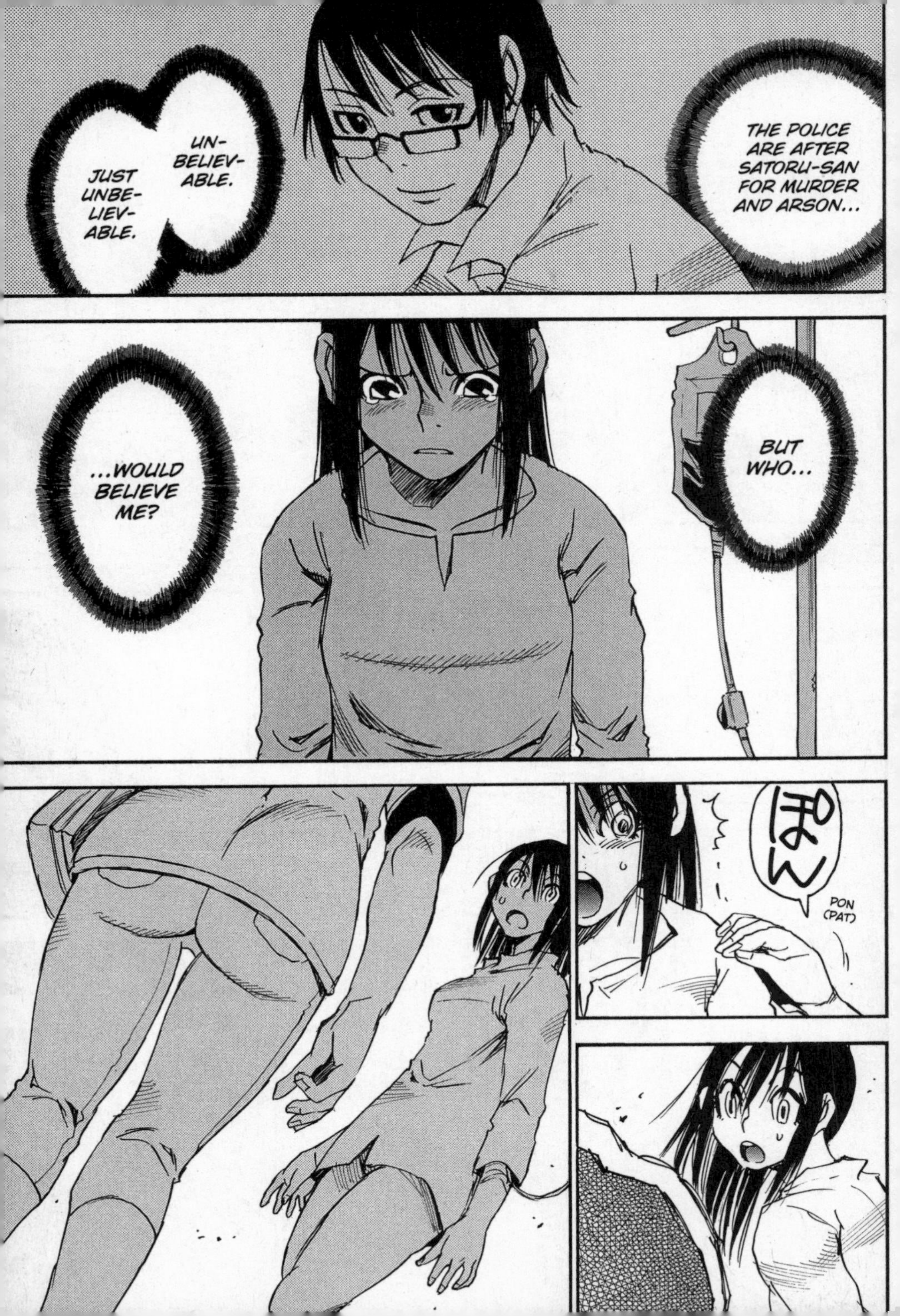
THE POLICE ARE AFTER SATORU-SAN FOR MURDER AND ARSON...
UN-BELIEV-ABLE.
JUST UNBE-LIEV-ABLE.
BUT WHO...
...WOULD BELIEVE ME?
ぽん
PON (PAT)

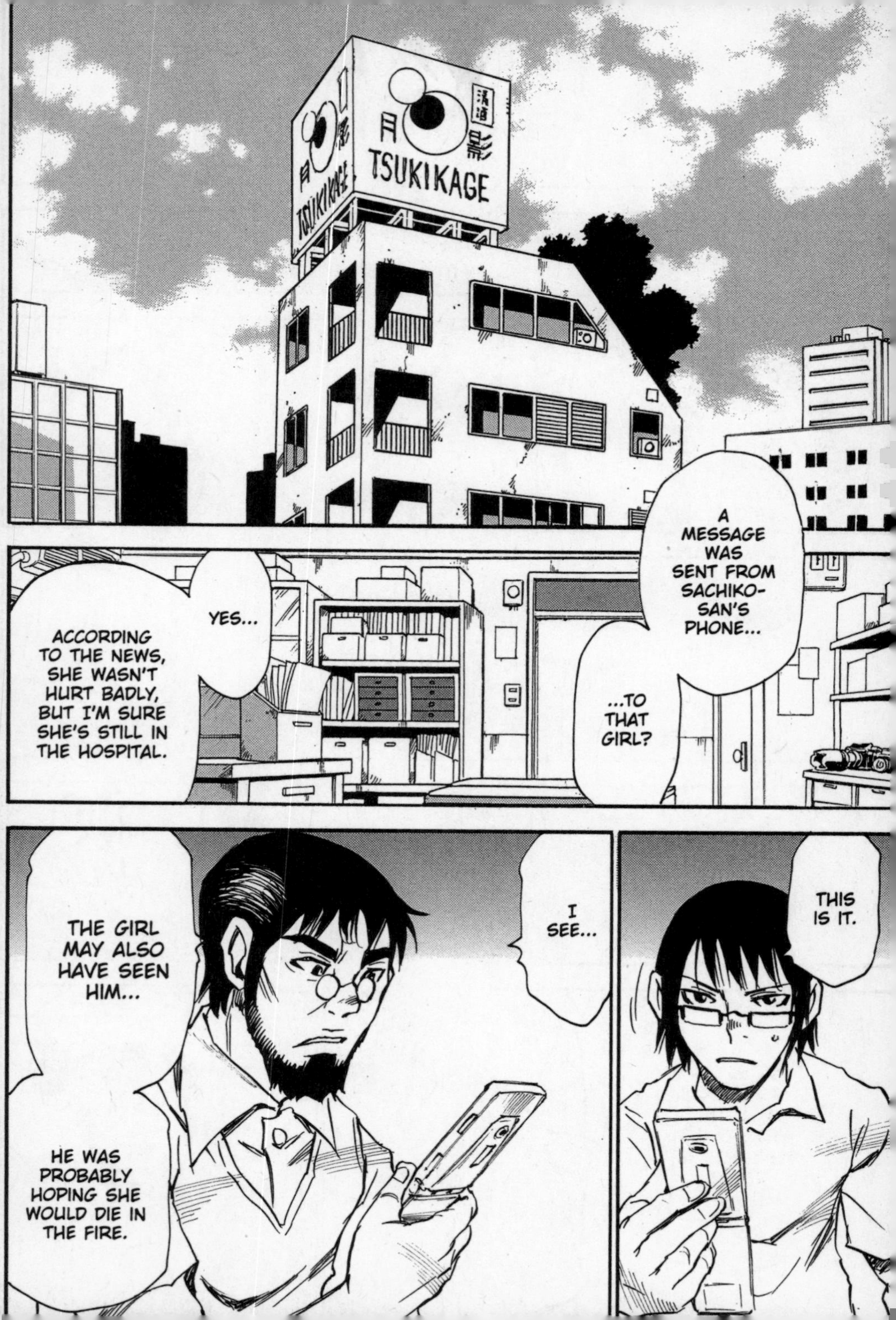
清酒
月影
TSUKIKAGE
A MESSAGE WAS SENT FROM SACHIKO-SAN'S PHONE...
...TO THAT GIRL?
YES...
ACCORDING TO THE NEWS, SHE WASN'T HURT BADLY, BUT I'M SURE SHE'S STILL IN THE HOSPITAL.
THIS IS IT.
I SEE...
THE GIRL MAY ALSO HAVE SEEN HIM...
HE WAS PROBABLY HOPING SHE WOULD DIE IN THE FIRE.

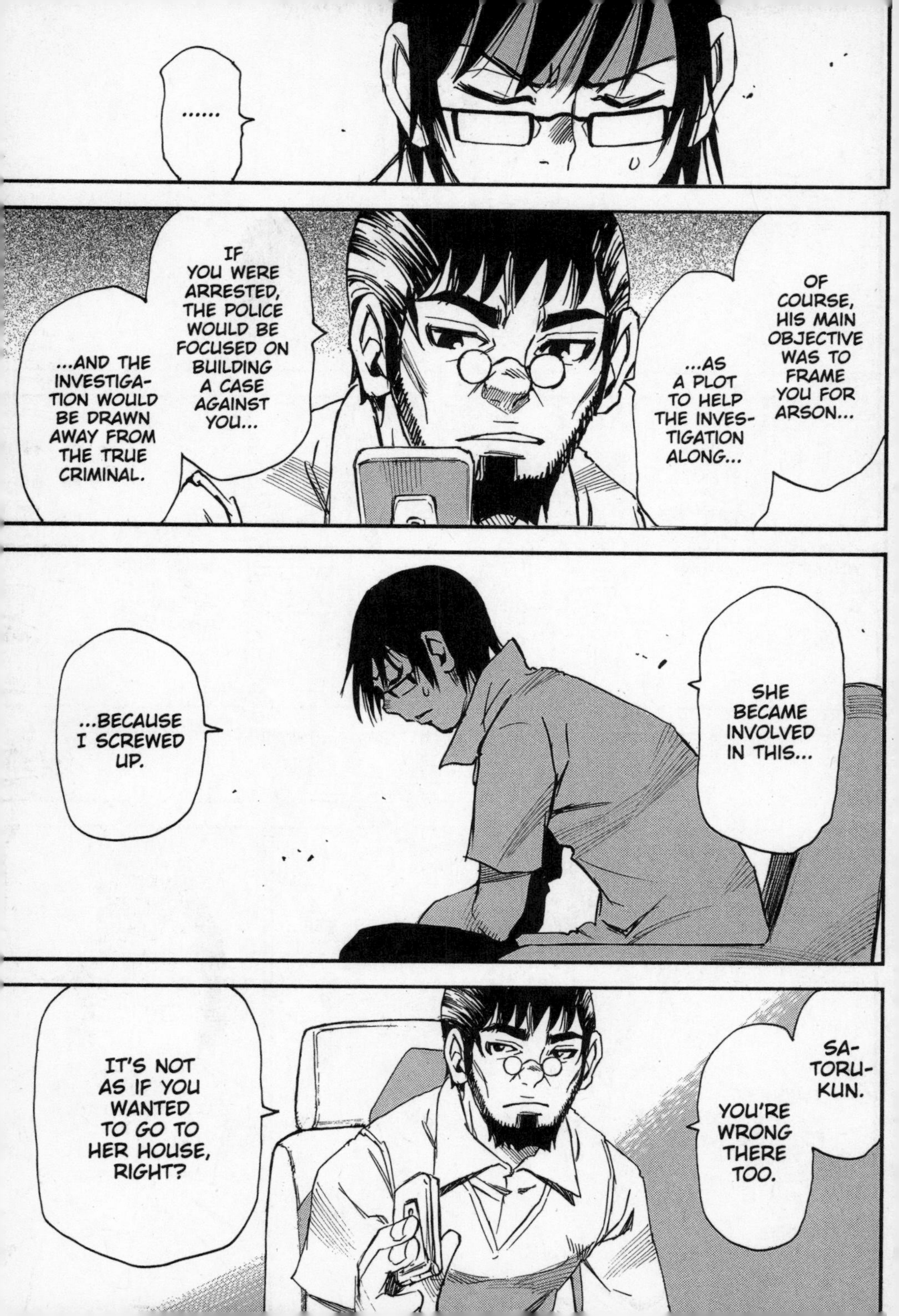
......
OF COURSE, HIS MAIN OBJECTIVE WAS TO FRAME YOU FOR ARSON...
...AS A PLOT TO HELP THE INVESTIGATION ALONG...
IF YOU WERE ARRESTED, THE POLICE WOULD BE FOCUSED ON BUILDING A CASE AGAINST YOU...
...AND THE INVESTIGATION WOULD BE DRAWN AWAY FROM THE TRUE CRIMINAL.
SHE BECAME INVOLVED IN THIS...
...BECAUSE I SCREWED UP.
SATORU-KUN.
YOU'RE WRONG THERE TOO.
IT'S NOT AS IF YOU WANTED TO GO TO HER HOUSE, RIGHT?

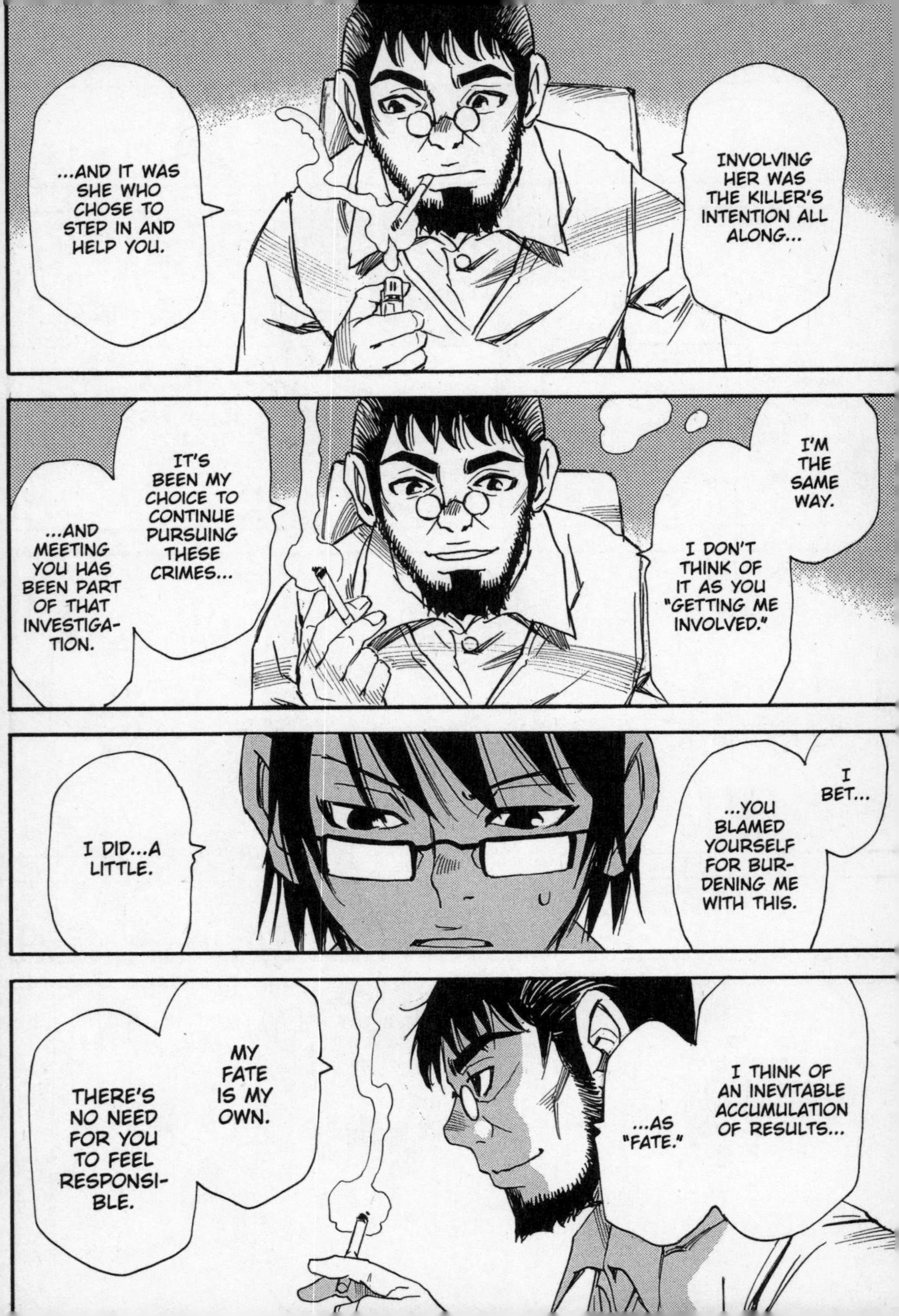
INVOLVING HER WAS THE KILLER'S INTENTION ALL ALONG...
...AND IT WAS SHE WHO CHOSE TO STEP IN AND HELP YOU.
I'M THE SAME WAY.
I DON'T THINK OF IT AS YOU "GETTING ME INVOLVED."
IT'S BEEN MY CHOICE TO CONTINUE PURSUING THESE CRIMES...
...AND MEETING YOU HAS BEEN PART OF THAT INVESTIGATION.
I BET...
...YOU BLAMED YOURSELF FOR BURDENING ME WITH THIS.
I DID...A LITTLE.
I THINK OF AN INEVITABLE ACCUMULATION OF RESULTS...
...AS "FATE."
MY FATE IS MY OWN.
THERE'S NO NEED FOR YOU TO FEEL RESPONSIBLE.

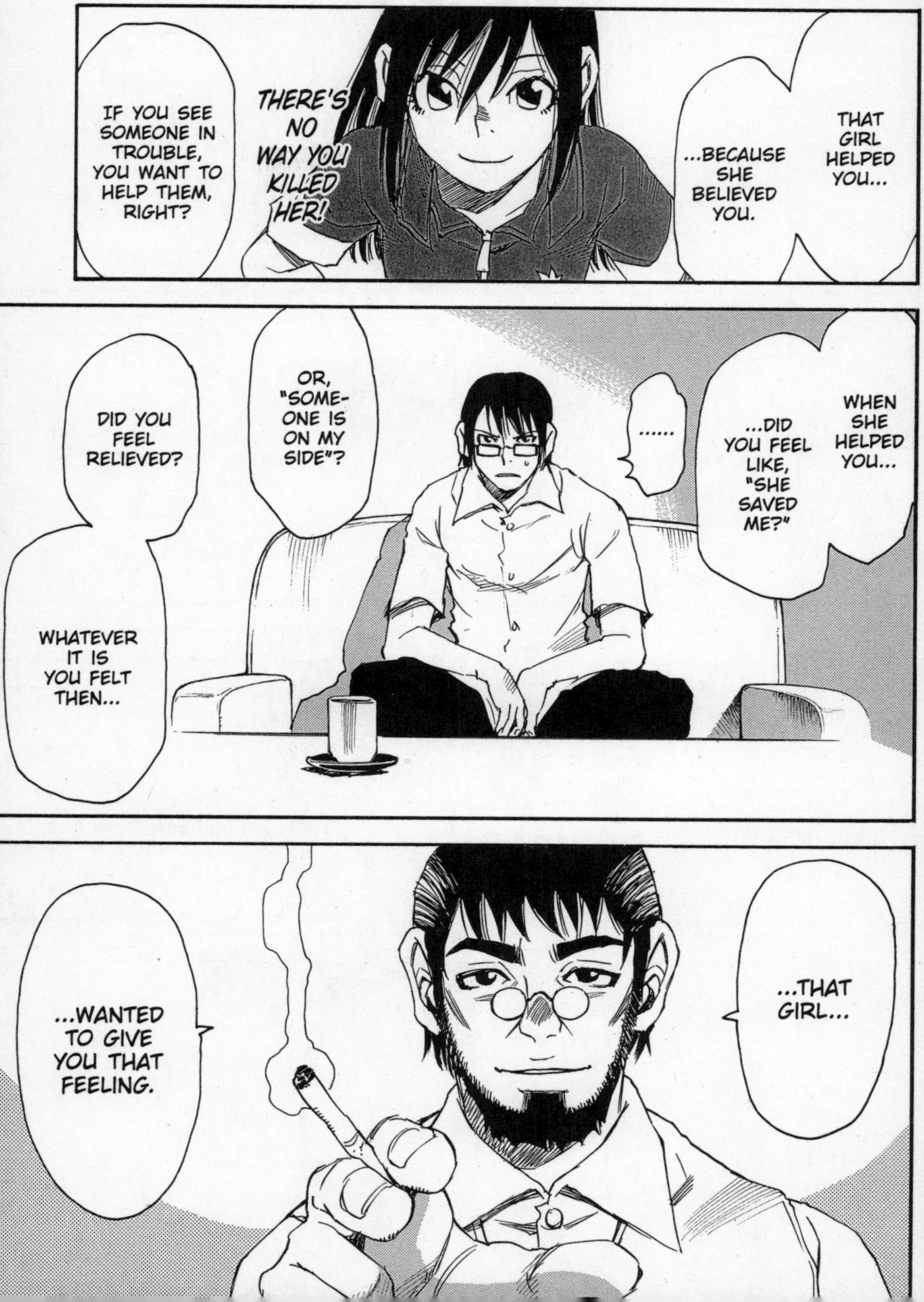
THAT GIRL HELPED YOU...
...BECAUSE SHE BELIEVED YOU.
THERE'S NO WAY YOU KILLED HER!
IF YOU SEE SOMEONE IN TROUBLE, YOU WANT TO HELP THEM, RIGHT?
WHEN SHE HELPED YOU...
...DID YOU FEEL LIKE, "SHE SAVED ME?"
......
OR, "SOME-ONE IS ON MY SIDE"?
DID YOU FEEL RELIEVED?
WHATEVER IT IS YOU FELT THEN...
...THAT GIRL...
...WANTED TO GIVE YOU THAT FEELING.

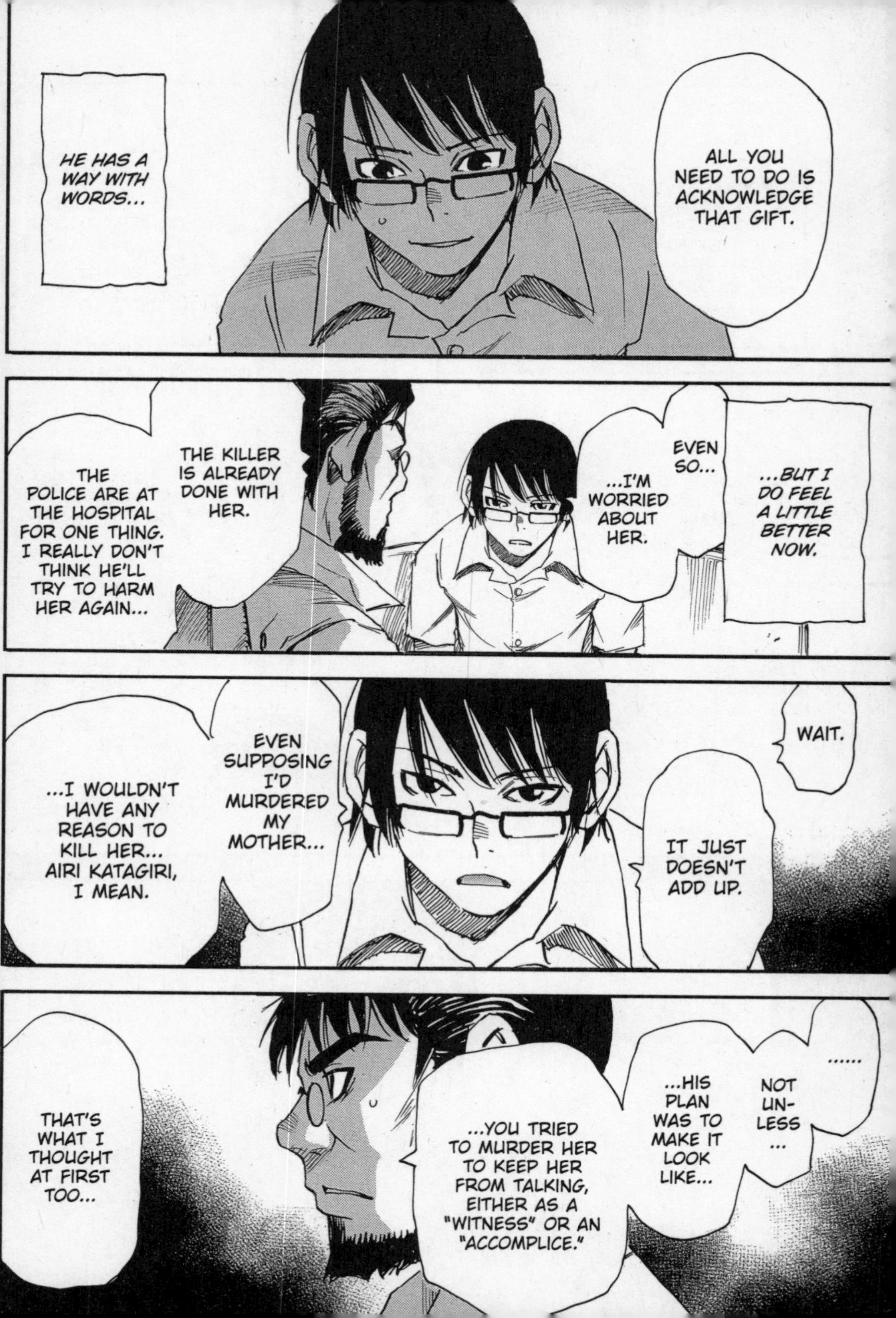
ALL YOU NEED TO DO IS ACKNOWLEDGE THAT GIFT.
HE HAS A WAY WITH WORDS...
...BUT I DO FEEL A LITTLE BETTER NOW.
EVEN SO...
...I'M WORRIED ABOUT HER.
THE KILLER IS ALREADY DONE WITH HER.
THE POLICE ARE AT THE HOSPITAL FOR ONE THING. I REALLY DON'T THINK HE'LL TRY TO HARM HER AGAIN...
WAIT.
IT JUST DOESN'T ADD UP.
EVEN SUPPOSING I'D MURDERED MY MOTHER...
...I WOULDN'T HAVE ANY REASON TO KILL HER... AIRI KATAGIRI, I MEAN.
......
NOT UN-LESS...
...HIS PLAN WAS TO MAKE IT LOOK LIKE...
...YOU TRIED TO MURDER HER TO KEEP HER FROM TALKING, EITHER AS A "WITNESS" OR AN "ACCOMPLICE."
THAT'S WHAT I THOUGHT AT FIRST TOO...

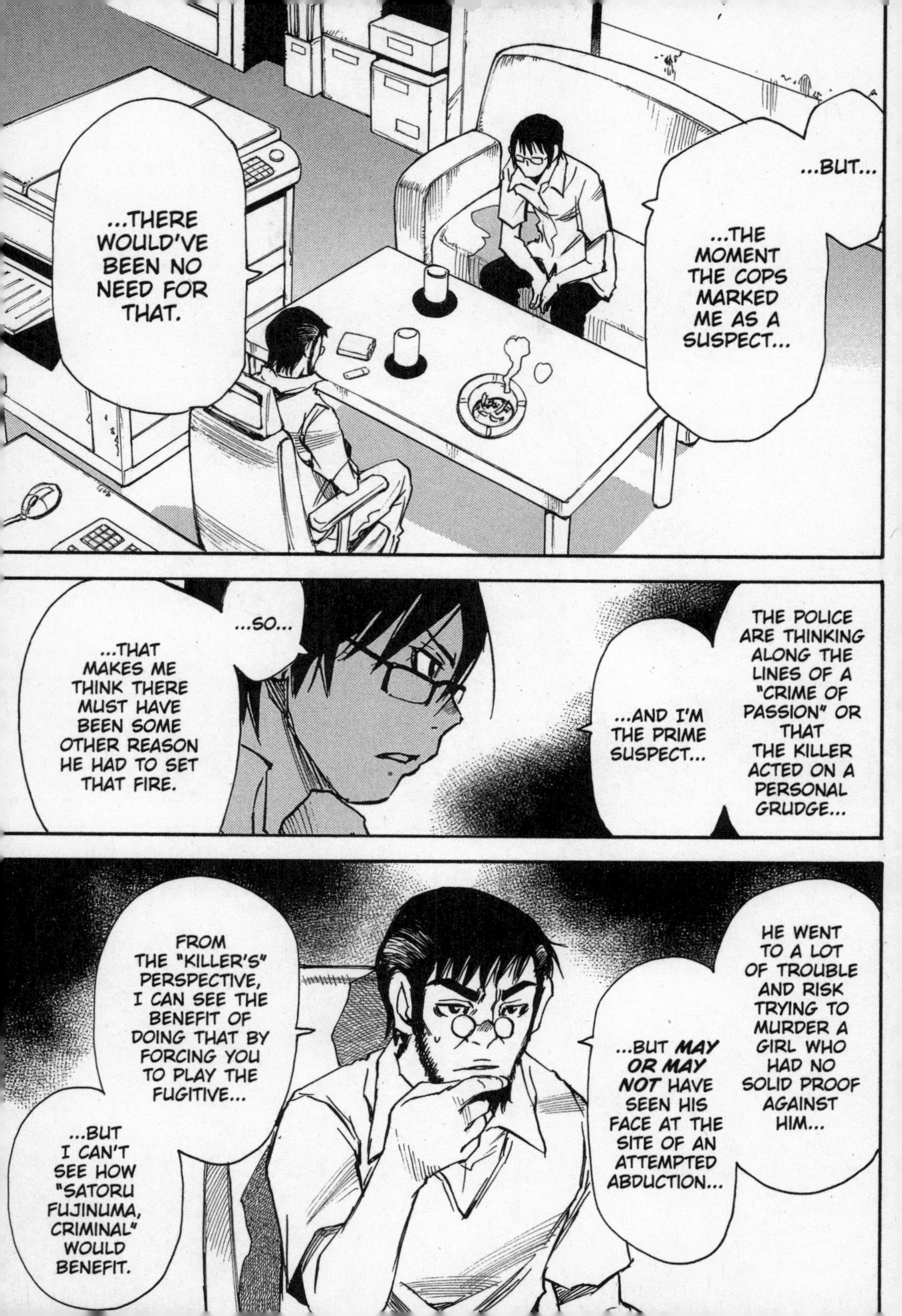
...BUT...
...THE MOMENT THE COPS MARKED ME AS A SUSPECT...
...THERE WOULD'VE BEEN NO NEED FOR THAT.
THE POLICE ARE THINKING ALONG THE LINES OF A "CRIME OF PASSION" OR THAT THE KILLER ACTED ON A PERSONAL GRUDGE...
...AND I'M THE PRIME SUSPECT...
...SO...
...THAT MAKES ME THINK THERE MUST HAVE BEEN SOME OTHER REASON HE HAD TO SET THAT FIRE.
HE WENT TO A LOT OF TROUBLE AND RISK TRYING TO MURDER A GIRL WHO HAD NO SOLID PROOF AGAINST HIM...
...BUT *MAY OR MAY NOT* HAVE SEEN HIS FACE AT THE SITE OF AN ATTEMPTED ABDUCTION...
FROM THE "KILLER'S" PERSPECTIVE, I CAN SEE THE BENEFIT OF DOING THAT BY FORCING YOU TO PLAY THE FUGITIVE...
...BUT I CAN'T SEE HOW "SATORU FUJINUMA, CRIMINAL" WOULD BENEFIT.

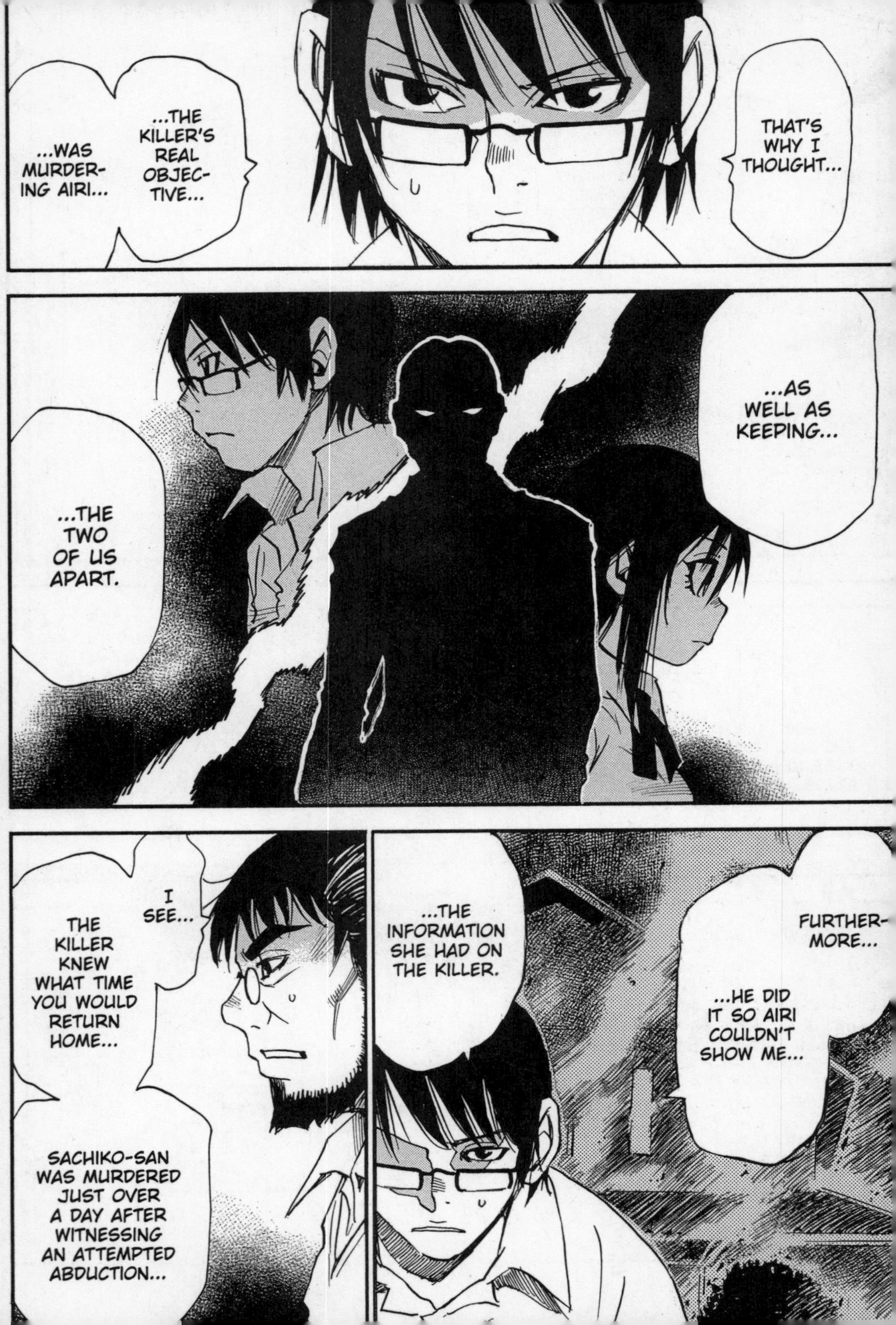
THAT'S WHY I THOUGHT...
...THE KILLER'S REAL OBJECTIVE...
...WAS MURDERING AIRI...
...AS WELL AS KEEPING...
...THE TWO OF US APART.
FURTHERMORE...
...HE DID IT SO AIRI COULDN'T SHOW ME...
...THE INFORMATION SHE HAD ON THE KILLER.
I SEE...
THE KILLER KNEW WHAT TIME YOU WOULD RETURN HOME...
SACHIKO-SAN WAS MURDERED JUST OVER A DAY AFTER WITNESSING AN ATTEMPTED ABDUCTION...

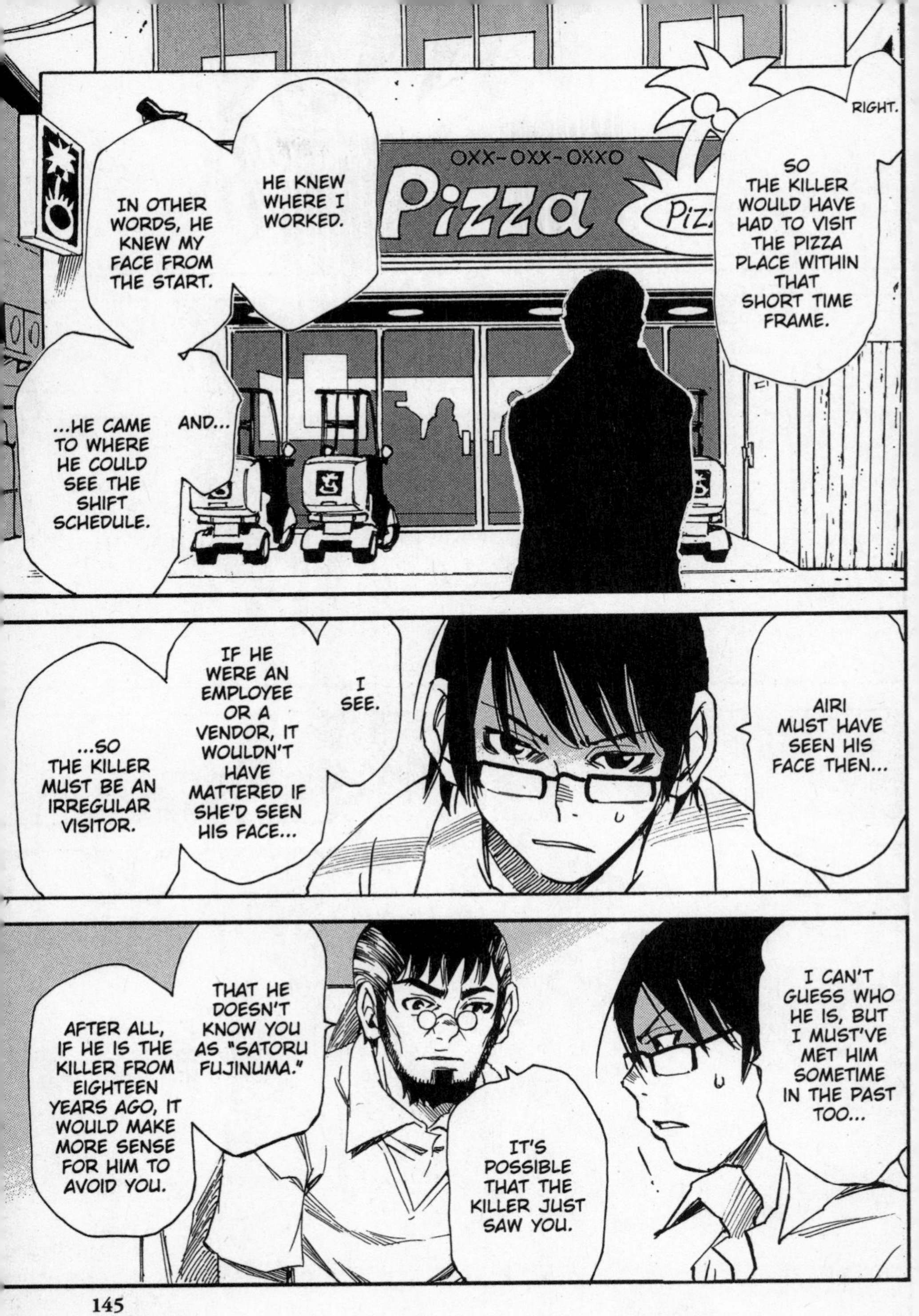
RIGHT.
SO THE KILLER WOULD HAVE HAD TO VISIT THE PIZZA PLACE WITHIN THAT SHORT TIME FRAME.
OXX-OXX-OXXO
Pizza
HE KNEW WHERE I WORKED.
IN OTHER WORDS, HE KNEW MY FACE FROM THE START.
AND...
...HE CAME TO WHERE HE COULD SEE THE SHIFT SCHEDULE.
AIRI MUST HAVE SEEN HIS FACE THEN...
I SEE.
IF HE WERE AN EMPLOYEE OR A VENDOR, IT WOULDN'T HAVE MATTERED IF SHE'D SEEN HIS FACE...
...SO THE KILLER MUST BE AN IRREGULAR VISITOR.
I CAN'T GUESS WHO HE IS, BUT I MUST'VE MET HIM SOMETIME IN THE PAST TOO...
IT'S POSSIBLE THAT THE KILLER JUST SAW YOU.
THAT HE DOESN'T KNOW YOU AS "SATORU FUJINUMA."
AFTER ALL, IF HE IS THE KILLER FROM EIGHTEEN YEARS AGO, IT WOULD MAKE MORE SENSE FOR HIM TO AVOID YOU.

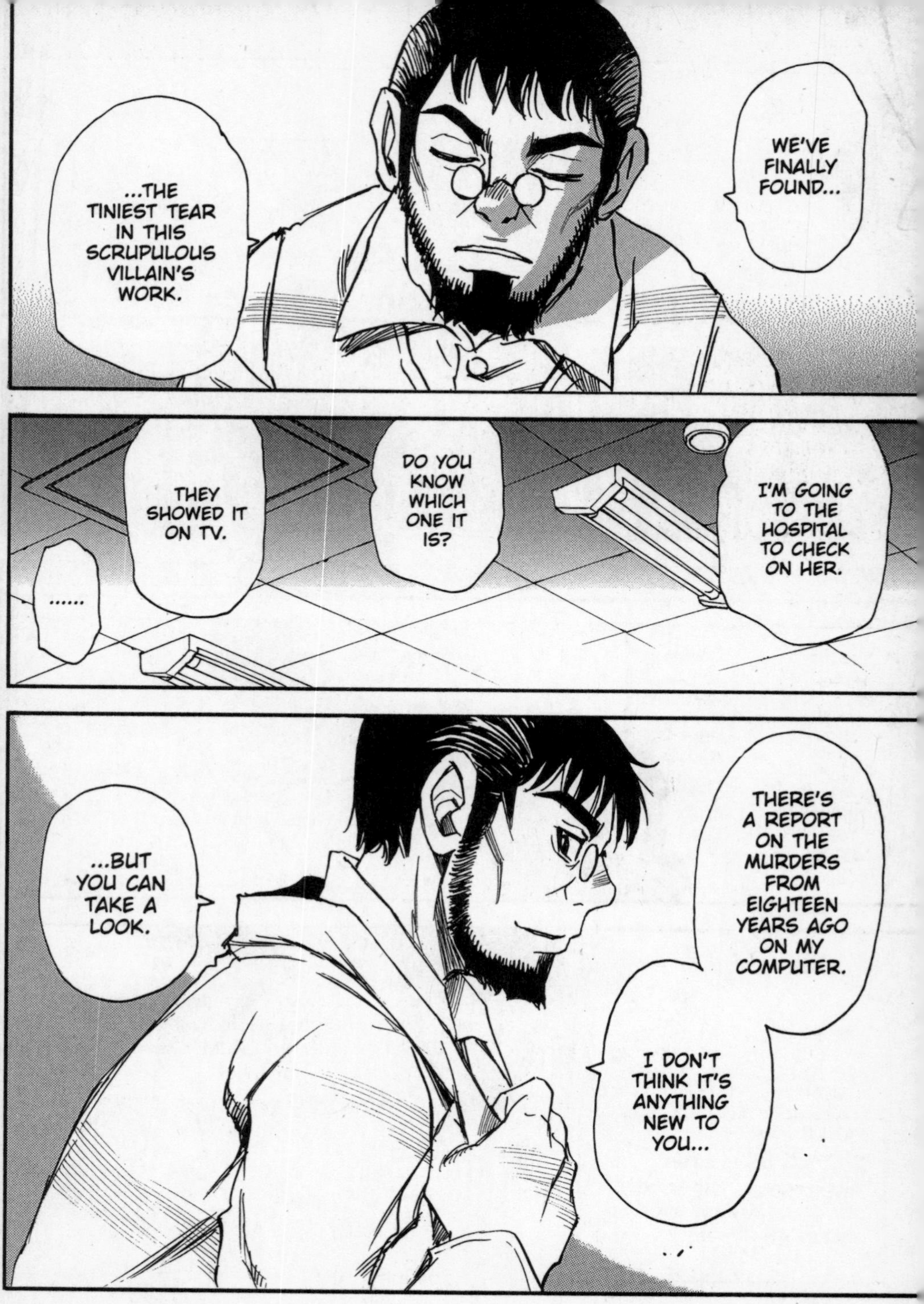
WE'VE FINALLY FOUND...
...THE TINIEST TEAR IN THIS SCRUPULOUS VILLAIN'S WORK.
I'M GOING TO THE HOSPITAL TO CHECK ON HER.
DO YOU KNOW WHICH ONE IT IS?
THEY SHOWED IT ON TV.
......
THERE'S A REPORT ON THE MURDERS FROM EIGHTEEN YEARS AGO ON MY COMPUTER.
I DON'T THINK IT'S ANYTHING NEW TO YOU...
...BUT YOU CAN TAKE A LOOK.

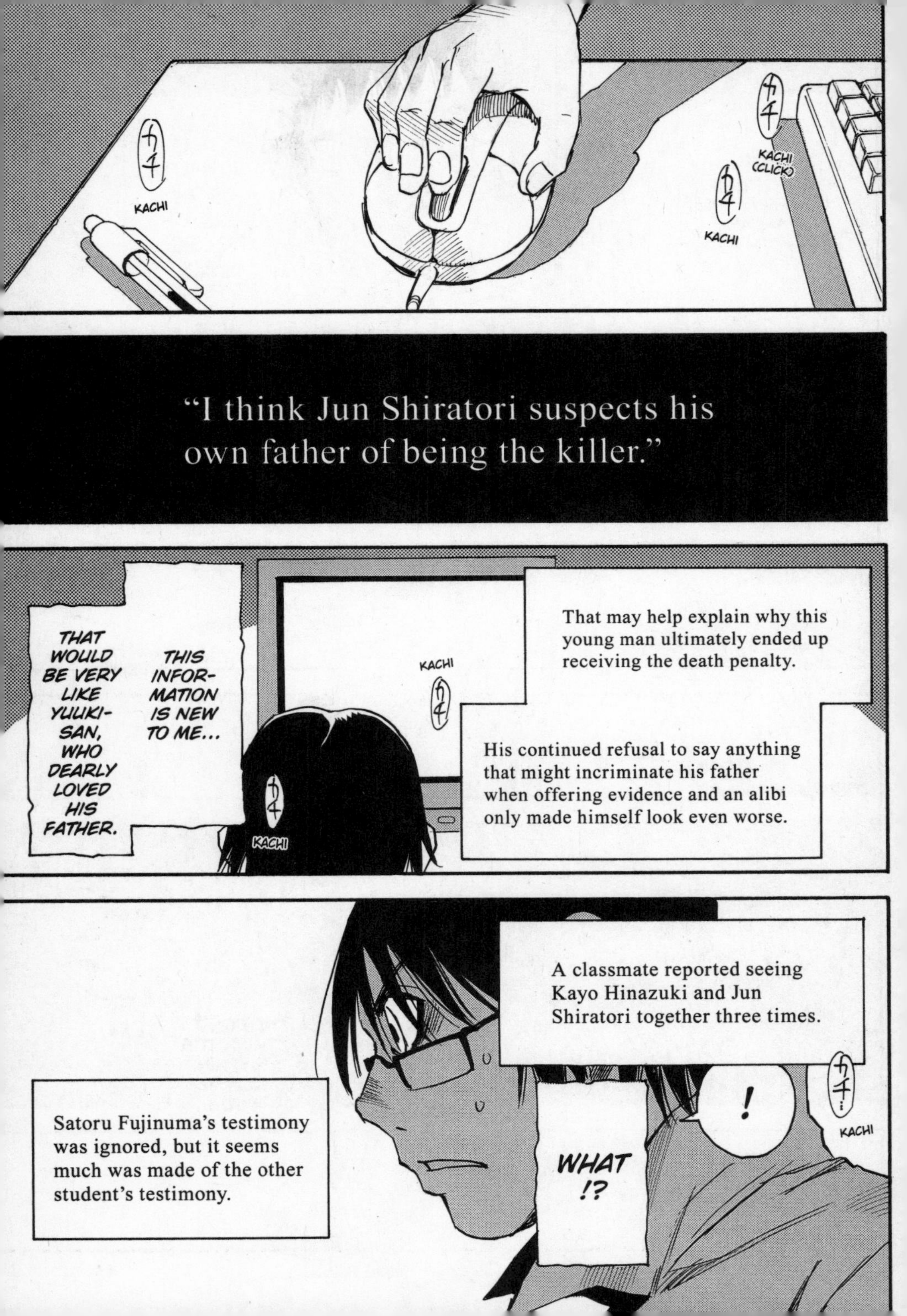
カチ
KACHI (CLICK)
カチ
KACHI
カチ
KACHI
"I think Jun Shiratori suspects his own father of being the killer."
That may help explain why this young man ultimately ended up receiving the death penalty.
His continued refusal to say anything that might incriminate his father when offering evidence and an alibi only made himself look even worse.
KACHI
カチ
THIS INFORMATION IS NEW TO ME...
THAT WOULD BE VERY LIKE YUUKI-SAN, WHO DEARLY LOVED HIS FATHER.
カチ
KACHI
カチ...
KACHI
A classmate reported seeing Kayo Hinazuki and Jun Shiratori together three times.
!
WHAT!?
Satoru Fujinuma's testimony was ignored, but it seems much was made of the other student's testimony.

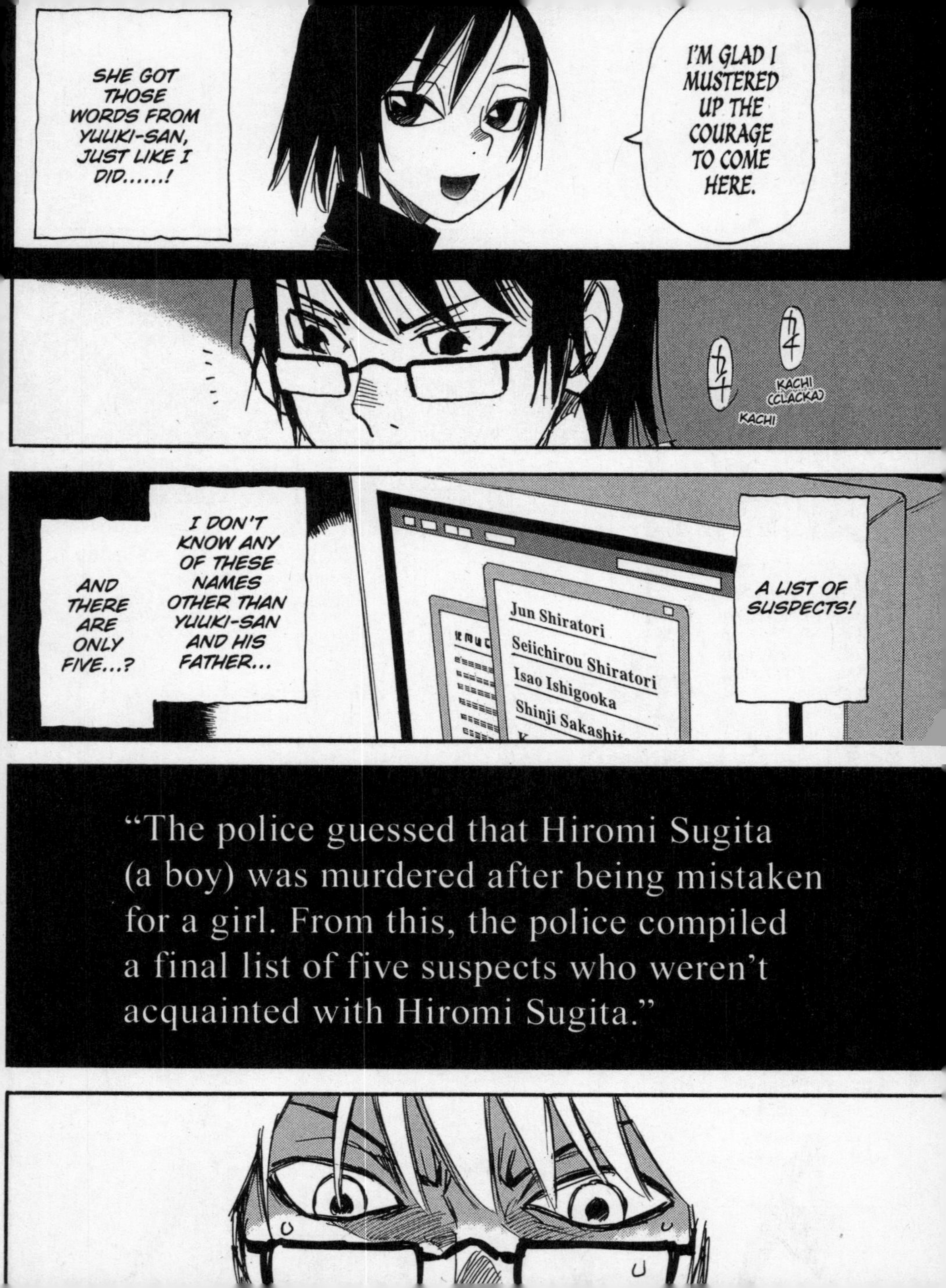
I'M GLAD I MUSTERED UP THE COURAGE TO COME HERE.
SHE GOT THOSE WORDS FROM YUUKI-SAN, JUST LIKE I DID......!
カチ
カチ
KACHI (CLACKA)
KACHI
A LIST OF SUSPECTS!
Jun Shiratori
Seiichirou Shiratori
Isao Ishigooka
Shinji Sakashit
I DON'T KNOW ANY OF THESE NAMES OTHER THAN YUUKI-SAN AND HIS FATHER...
AND THERE ARE ONLY FIVE...?
"The police guessed that Hiromi Sugita (a boy) was murdered after being mistaken for a girl. From this, the police compiled a final list of five suspects who weren't acquainted with Hiromi Sugita."

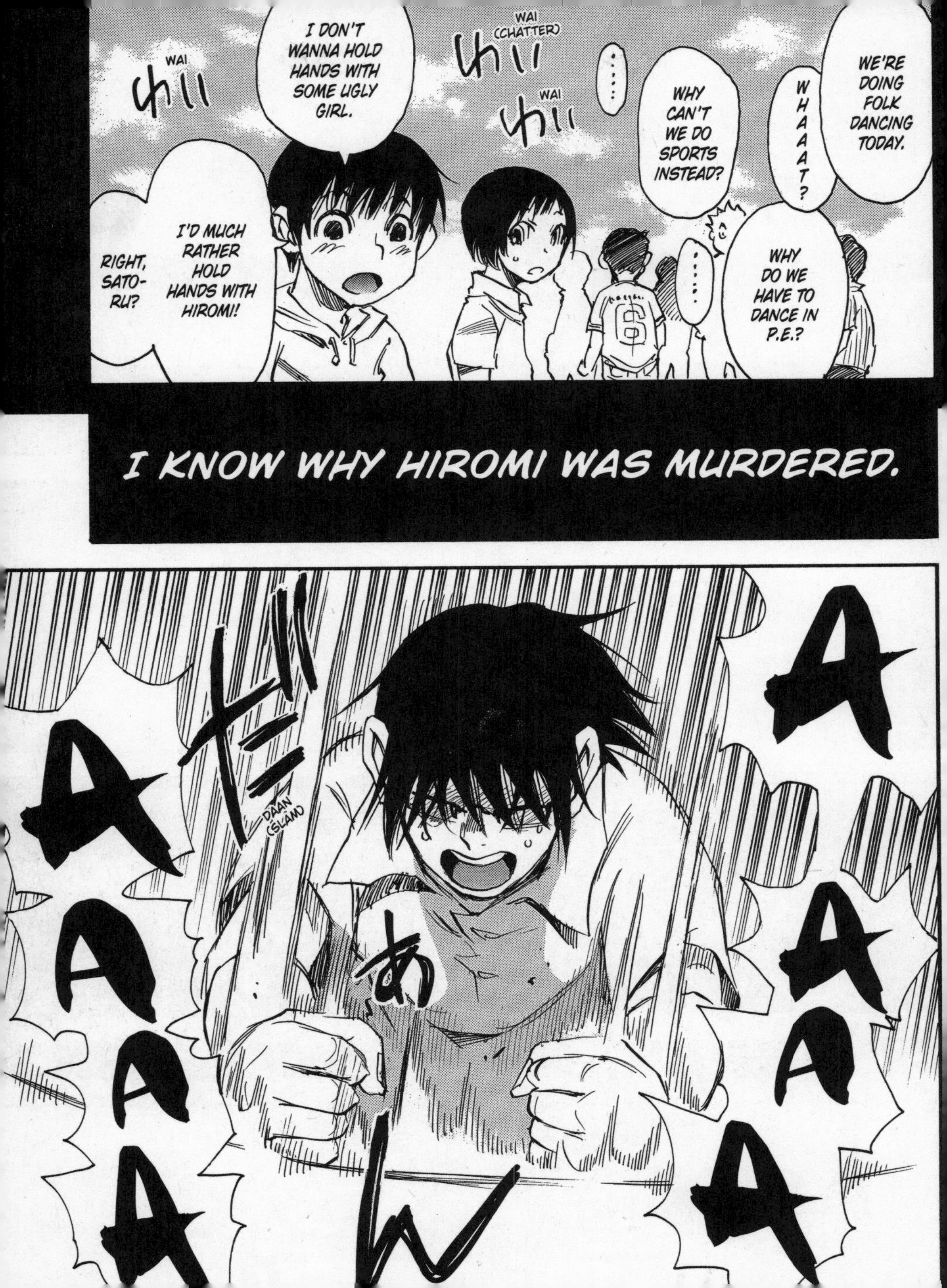
WE'RE DOING FOLK DANCING TODAY.
WHAAAT?
WHY CAN'T WE DO SPORTS INSTEAD?
WHY DO WE HAVE TO DANCE IN P.E.?
......
......
WAI (CHATTER)
WAI
I DON'T WANNA HOLD HANDS WITH SOME UGLY GIRL.
WAI
I'D MUCH RATHER HOLD HANDS WITH HIROMI!
RIGHT, SATO-RU?
I KNOW WHY HIROMI WAS MURDERED.
DAAN (SLAM)
A A A A A A A A
あ
W

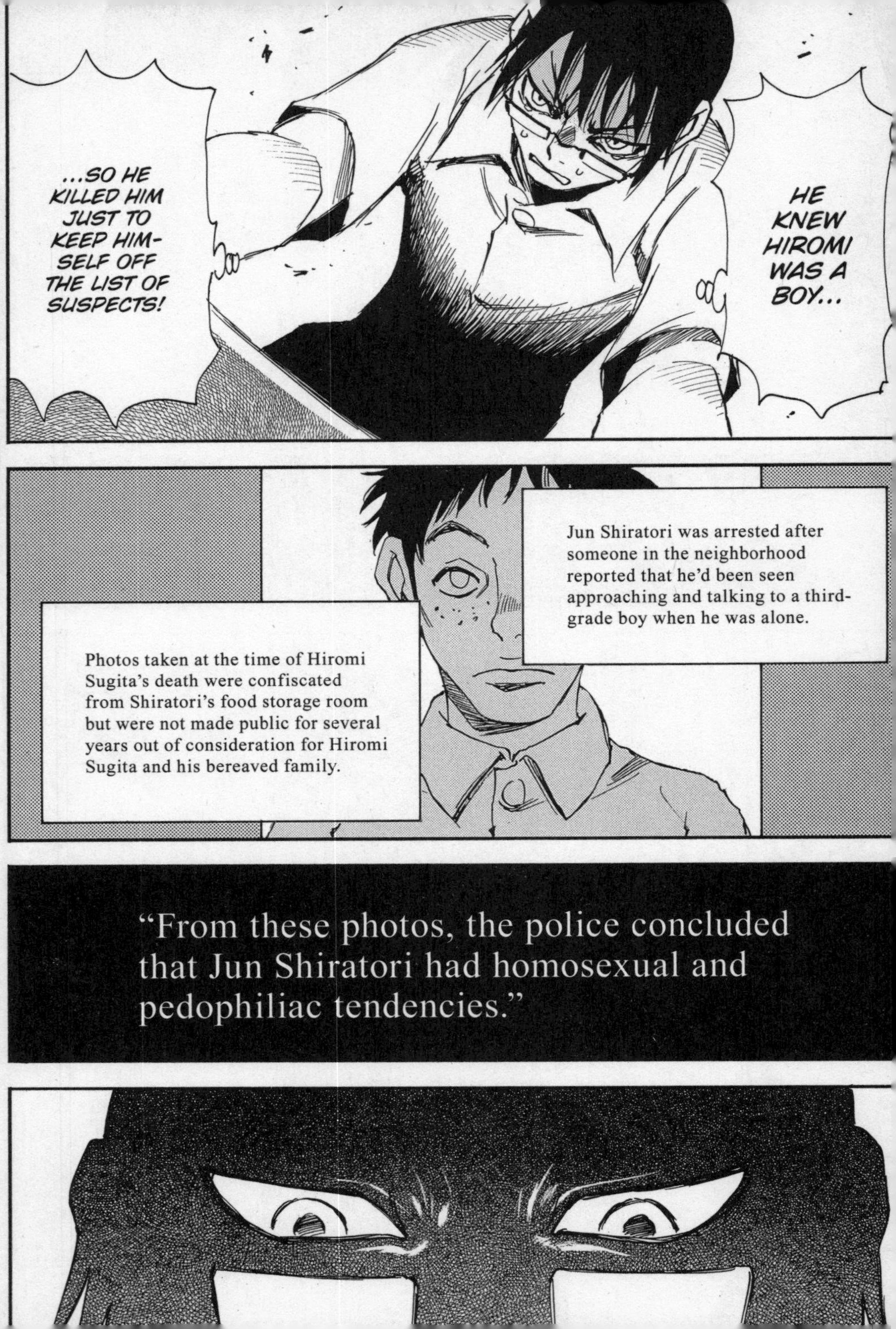
HE KNEW HIROMI WAS A BOY...
...SO HE KILLED HIM JUST TO KEEP HIM-SELF OFF THE LIST OF SUSPECTS!
Jun Shiratori was arrested after someone in the neighborhood reported that he'd been seen approaching and talking to a third-grade boy when he was alone.
Photos taken at the time of Hiromi Sugita's death were confiscated from Shiratori's food storage room but were not made public for several years out of consideration for Hiromi Sugita and his bereaved family.
"From these photos, the police concluded that Jun Shiratori had homosexual and pedophiliac tendencies."

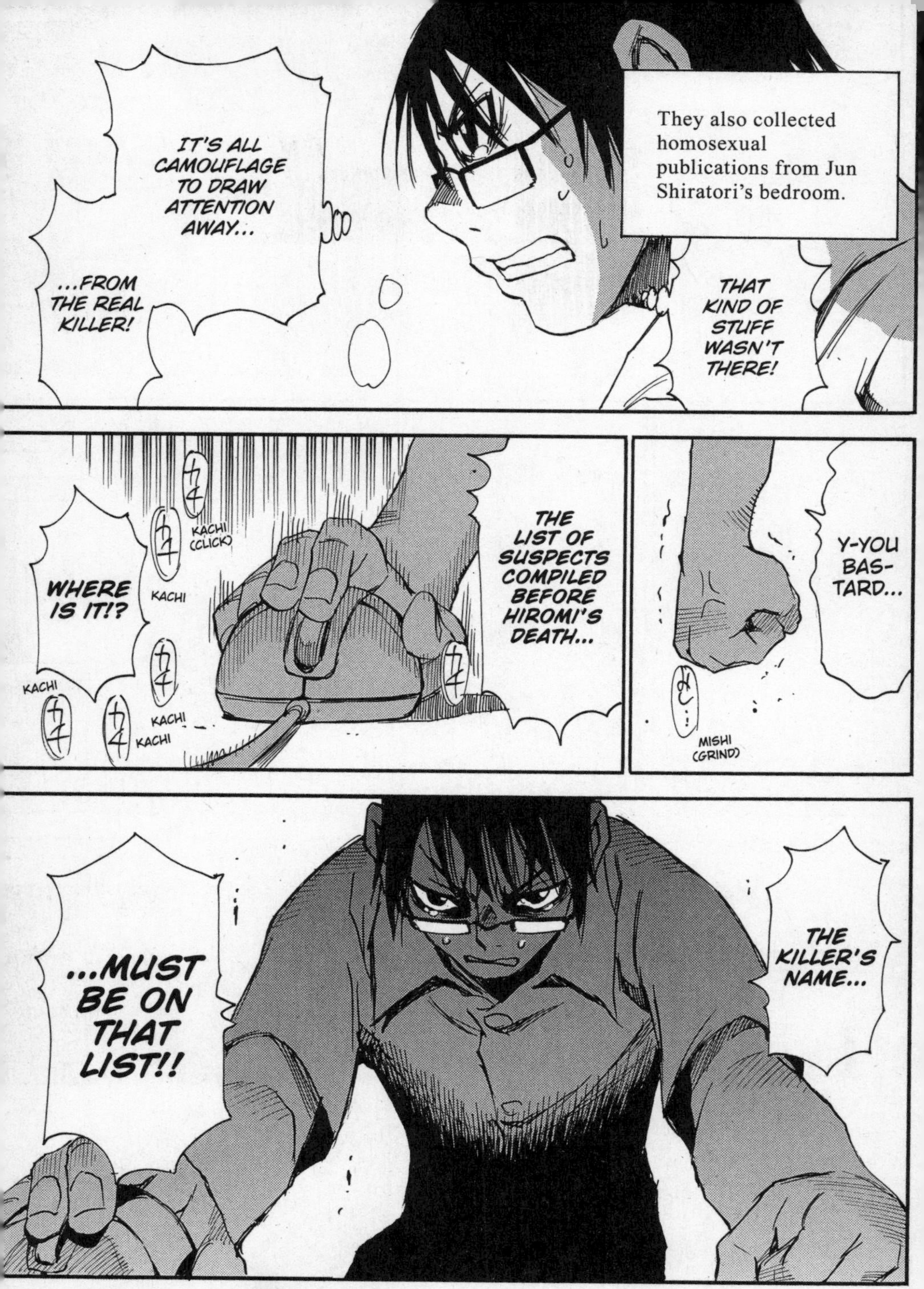
They also collected homosexual publications from Jun Shiratori's bedroom.
THAT KIND OF STUFF WASN'T THERE!
IT'S ALL CAMOUFLAGE TO DRAW ATTENTION AWAY...
...FROM THE REAL KILLER!
Y-YOU BASTARD...
MISHI (GRIND)
THE LIST OF SUSPECTS COMPILED BEFORE HIROMI'S DEATH...
KACHI (CLICK)
KACHI
WHERE IS IT!?
KACHI
KACHI
KACHI
THE KILLER'S NAME...
...MUST BE ON THAT LIST!!

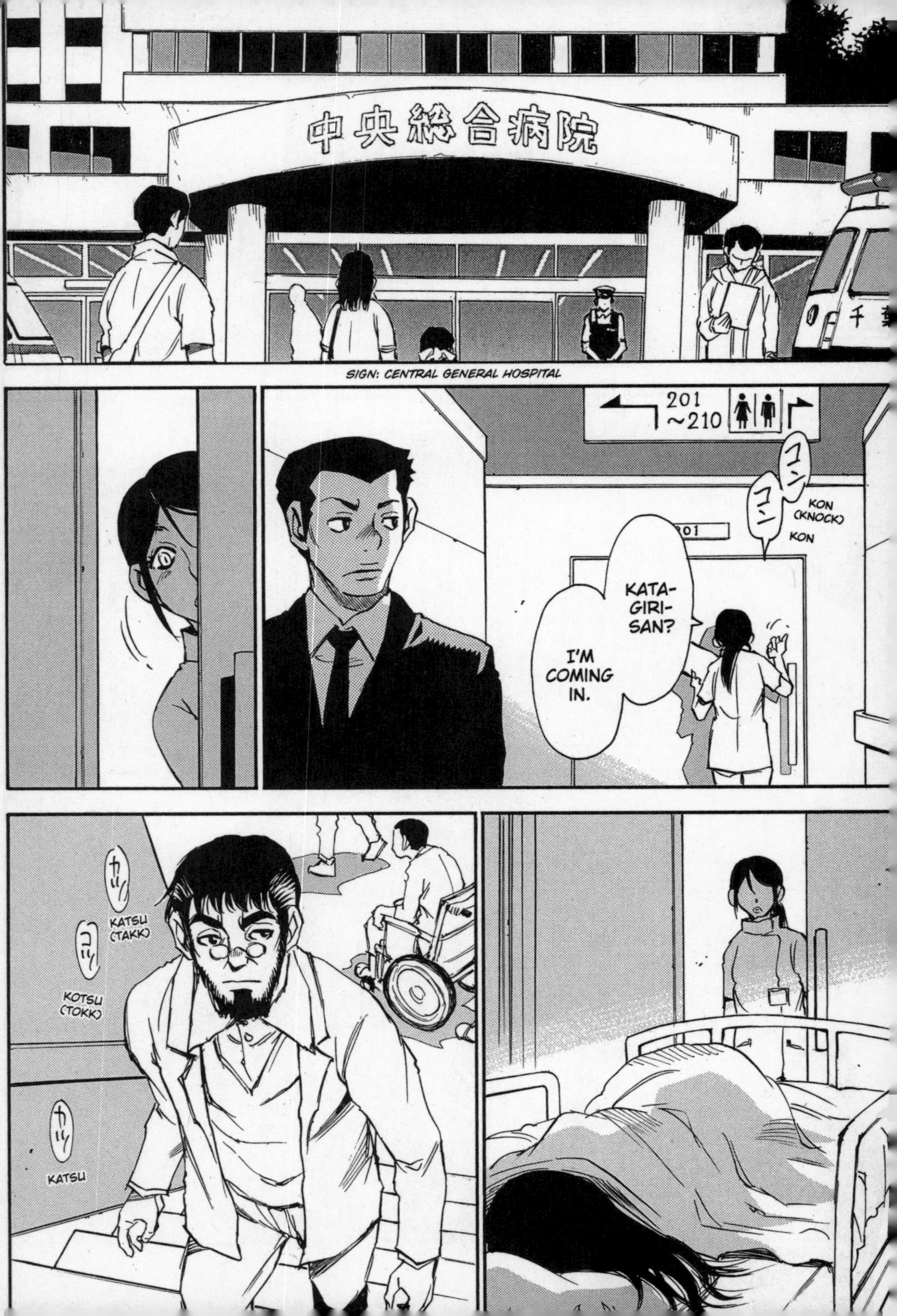
中央総合病院
SIGN: CENTRAL GENERAL HOSPITAL
201 ~210
コン コン
KON (KNOCK) KON
KATA-GIRI-SAN?
I'M COMING IN.
カッ
KATSU (TAKK)
コッ
KOTSU (TOKK)
カッ
KATSU

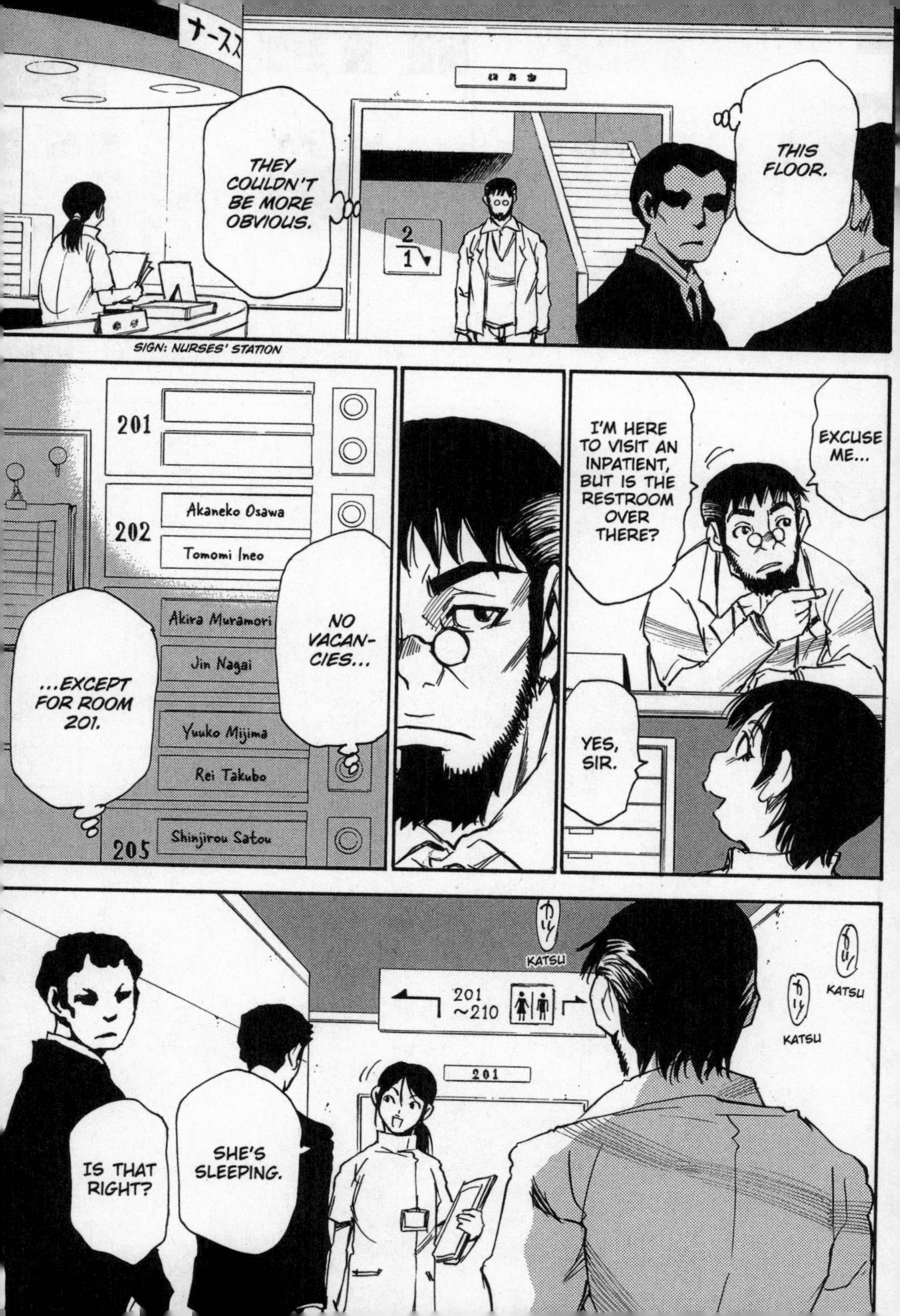
ナースス
THIS FLOOR.
THEY COULDN'T BE MORE OBVIOUS.
2
1
SIGN: NURSES' STATION
EXCUSE ME...
I'M HERE TO VISIT AN INPATIENT, BUT IS THE RESTROOM OVER THERE?
YES, SIR.
201
202
Akaneko Osawa
Tomomi Ineo
Akira Muramori
Jin Nagai
Yuuko Mijima
Rei Takubo
205
Shinjirou Satou
NO VACANCIES...
...EXCEPT FOR ROOM 201.
KATSU
KATSU
KATSU
201 ~210
201
SHE'S SLEEPING.
IS THAT RIGHT?

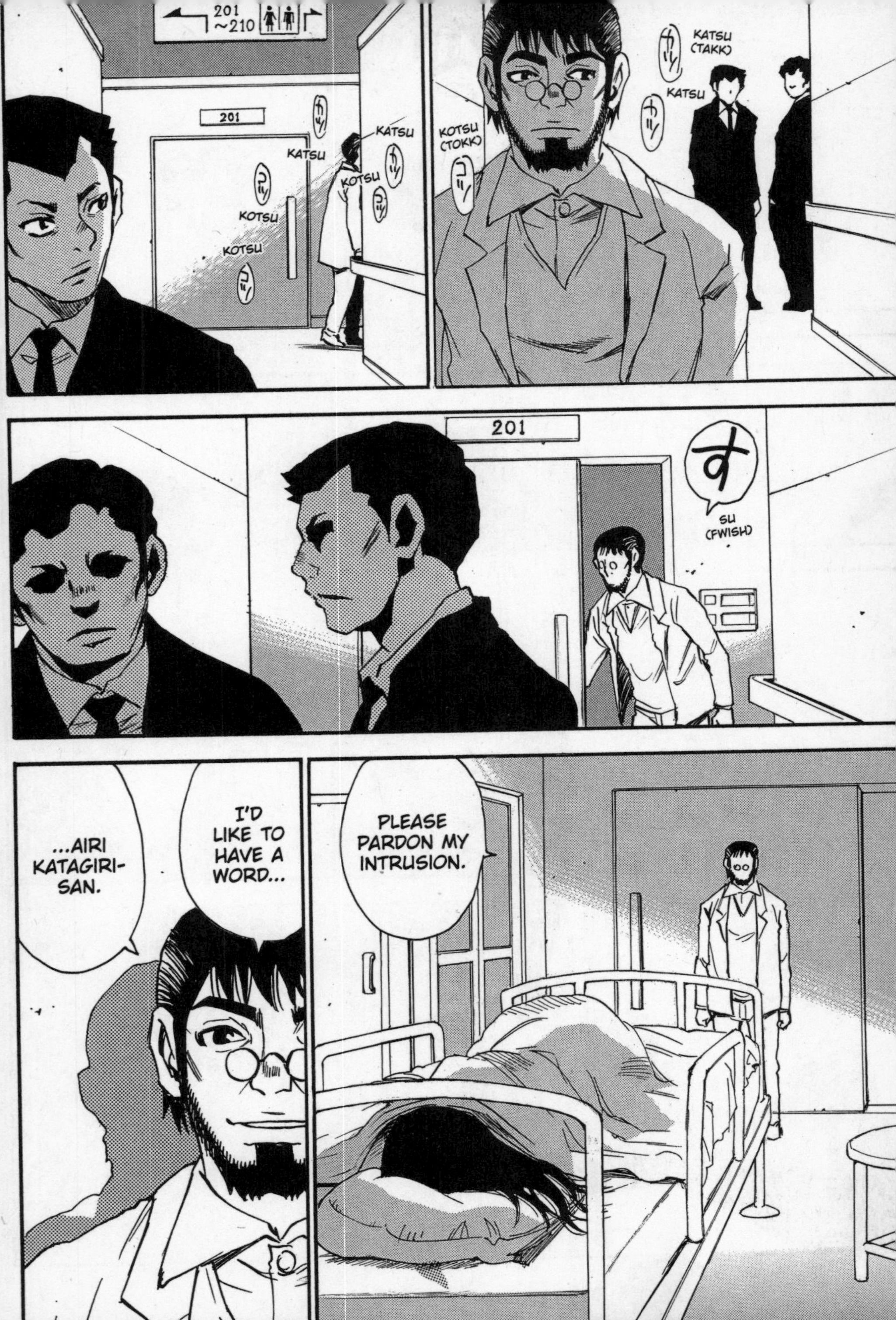
カツ
KATSU (TAKK)
カツ
KATSU
コツ
KOTSU (TOKK)
201 ~210
201
KATSU
カツ
KATSU
コツ
KOTSU
コツ
KOTSU
コツ
KOTSU
201
す
SU (FWISH)
PLEASE PARDON MY INTRUSION.
I'D LIKE TO HAVE A WORD...
...AIRI KATAGIRI-SAN.

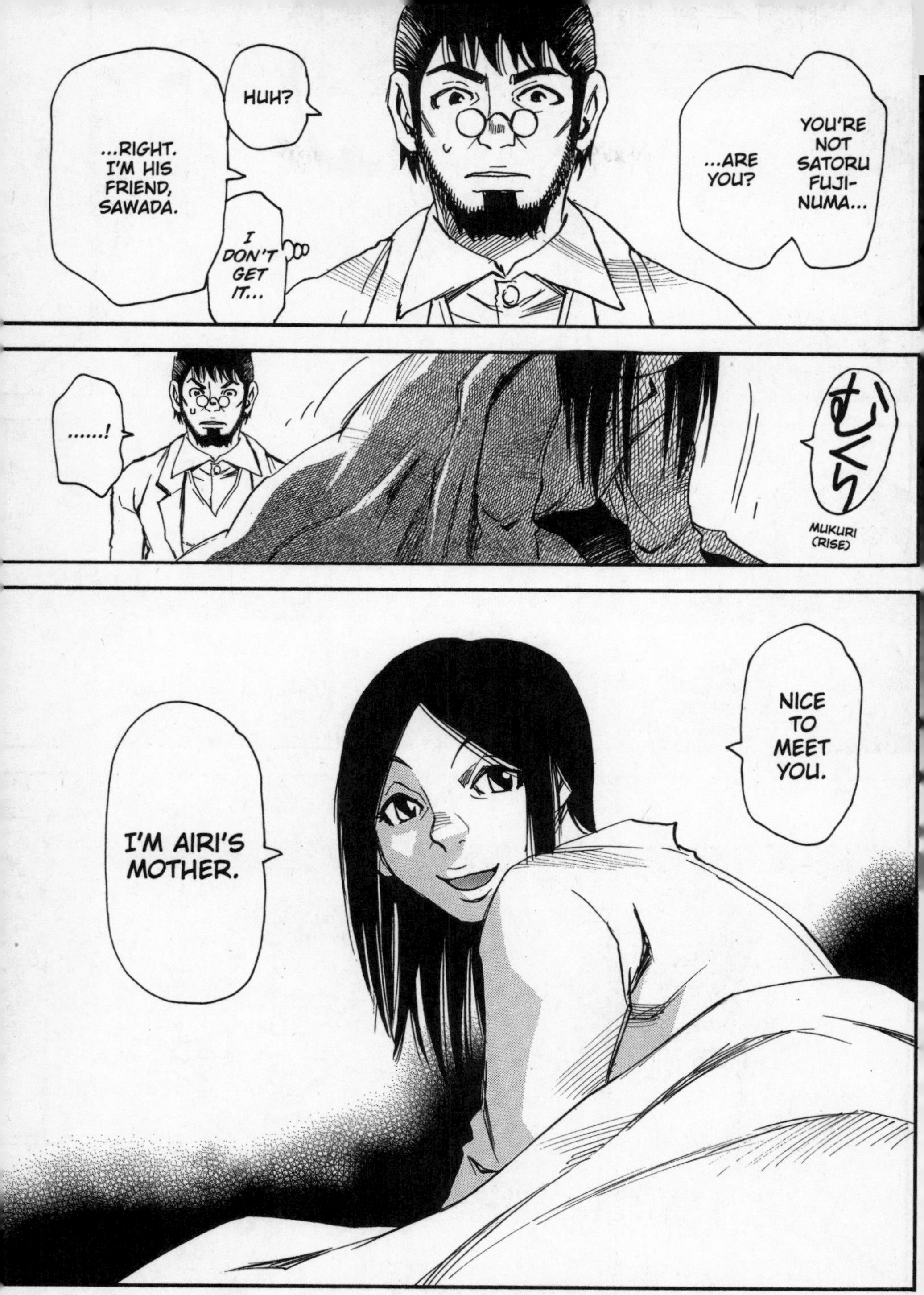
YOU'RE NOT SATORU FUJI-NUMA...
...ARE YOU?
HUH?
...RIGHT. I'M HIS FRIEND, SAWADA.
I DON'T GET IT...
むくり
MUKURI (RISE)
......!
NICE TO MEET YOU.
I'M AIRI'S MOTHER.

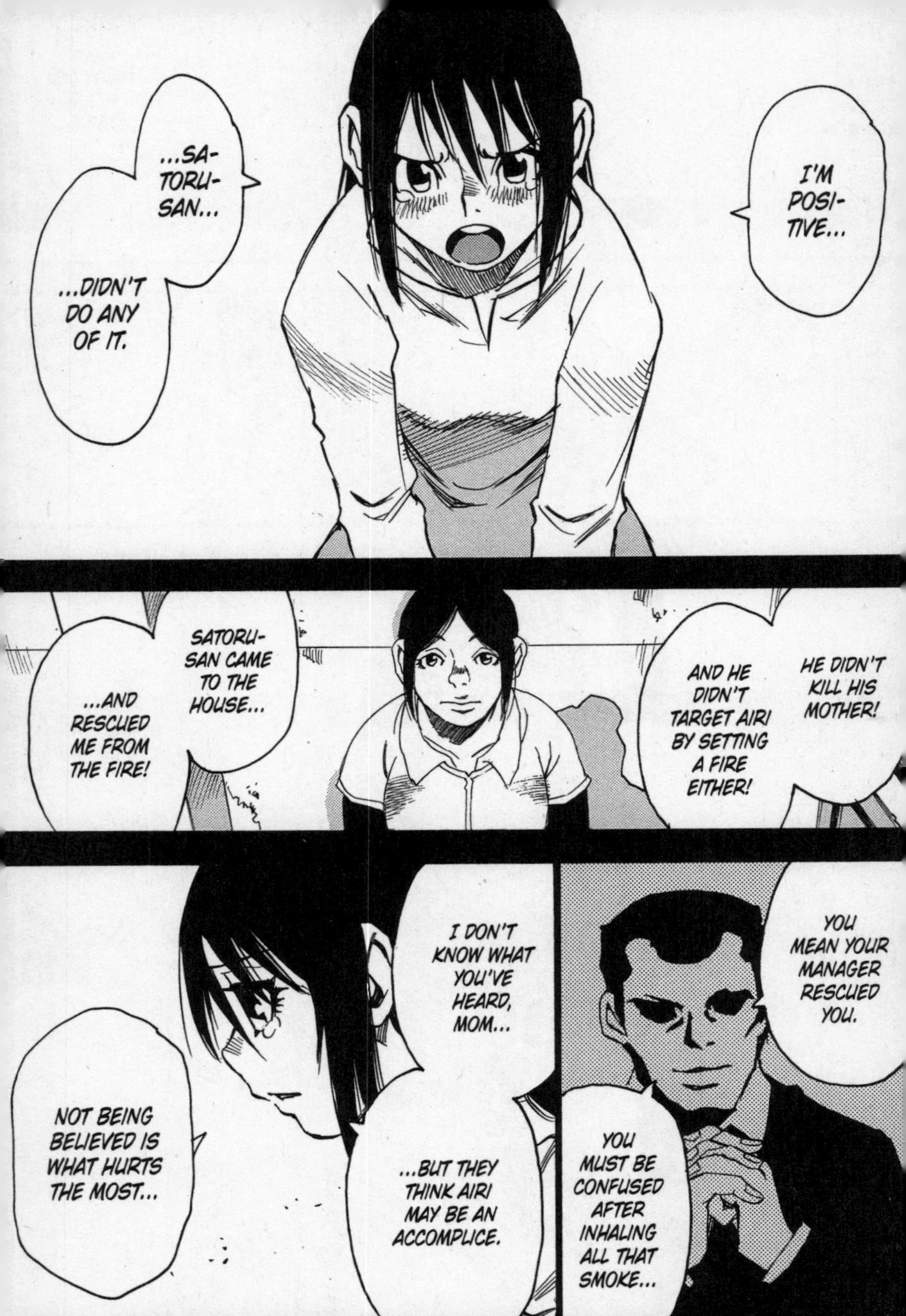
I'M POSITIVE...
...SATORU-SAN...
...DIDN'T DO ANY OF IT.
HE DIDN'T KILL HIS MOTHER!
AND HE DIDN'T TARGET AIRI BY SETTING A FIRE EITHER!
SATORU-SAN CAME TO THE HOUSE...
...AND RESCUED ME FROM THE FIRE!
YOU MEAN YOUR MANAGER RESCUED YOU.
YOU MUST BE CONFUSED AFTER INHALING ALL THAT SMOKE...
I DON'T KNOW WHAT YOU'VE HEARD, MOM...
...BUT THEY THINK AIRI MAY BE AN ACCOMPLICE.
NOT BEING BELIEVED IS WHAT HURTS THE MOST...

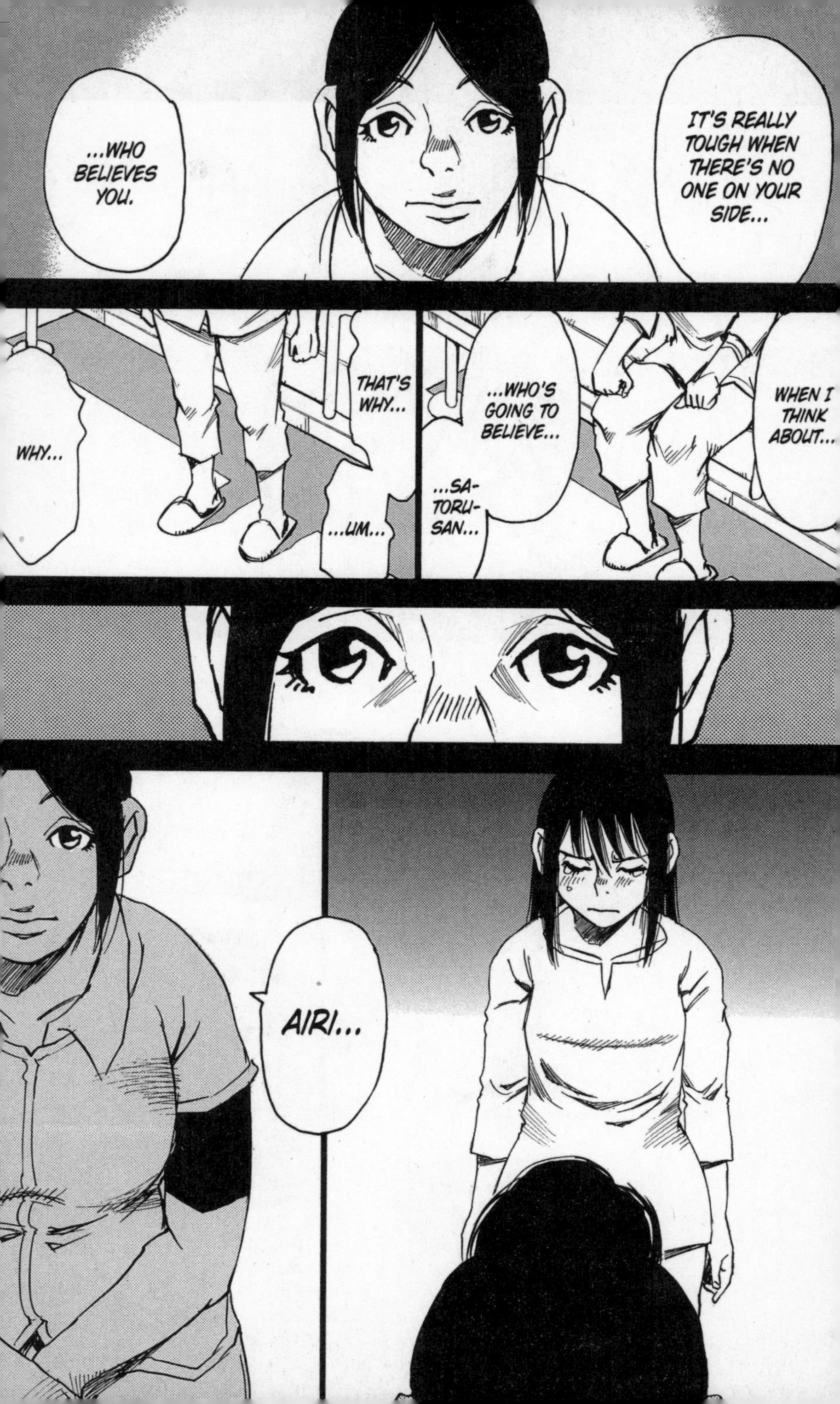
IT'S REALLY TOUGH WHEN THERE'S NO ONE ON YOUR SIDE...
...WHO BELIEVES YOU.
WHEN I THINK ABOUT...
...WHO'S GOING TO BELIEVE...
...SA-TORU-SAN...
THAT'S WHY...
...UM...
WHY...
AIRI...

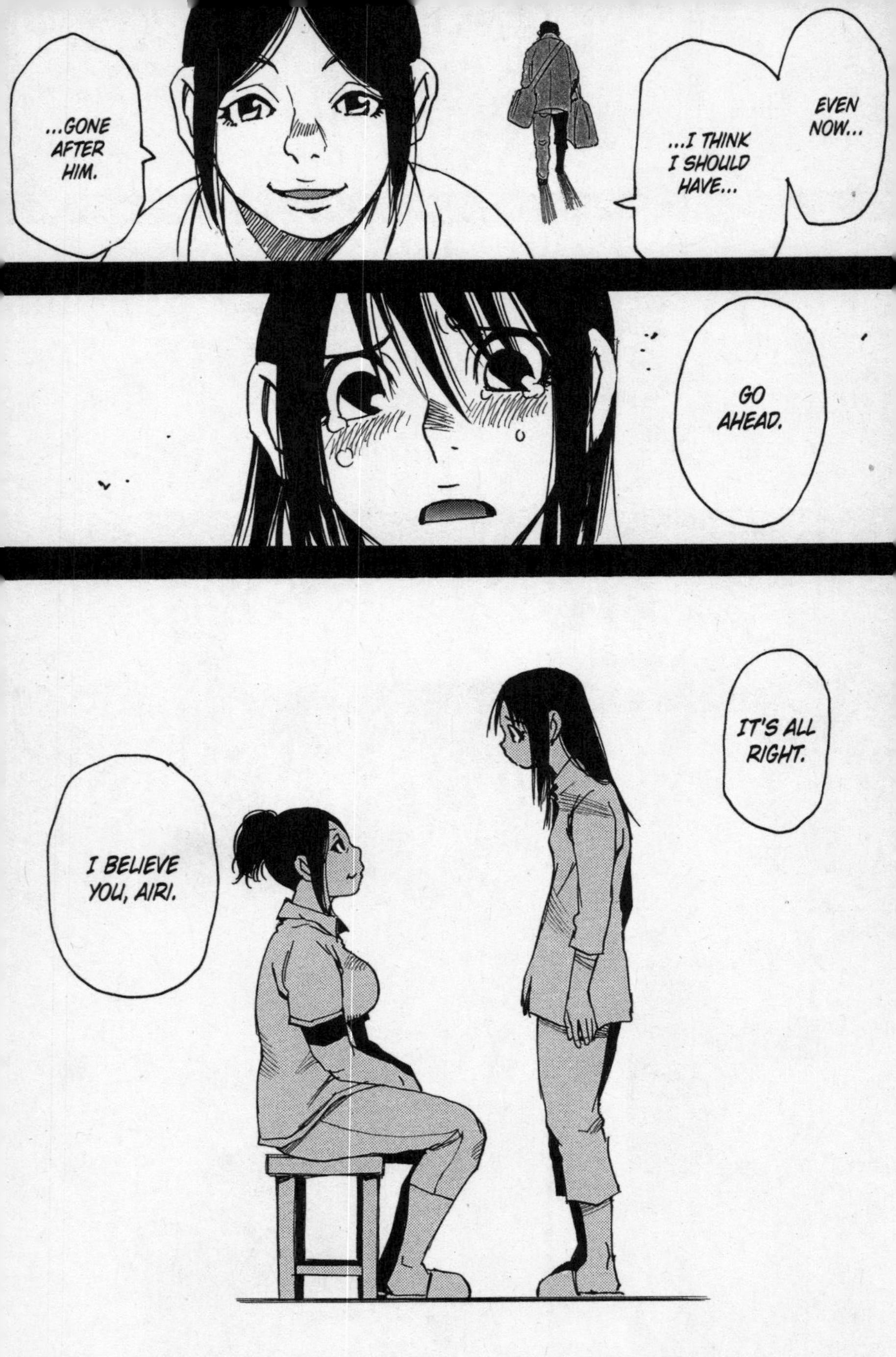
EVEN NOW...
...I THINK I SHOULD HAVE...
...GONE AFTER HIM.
GO AHEAD.
IT'S ALL RIGHT.
I BELIEVE YOU, AIRI.

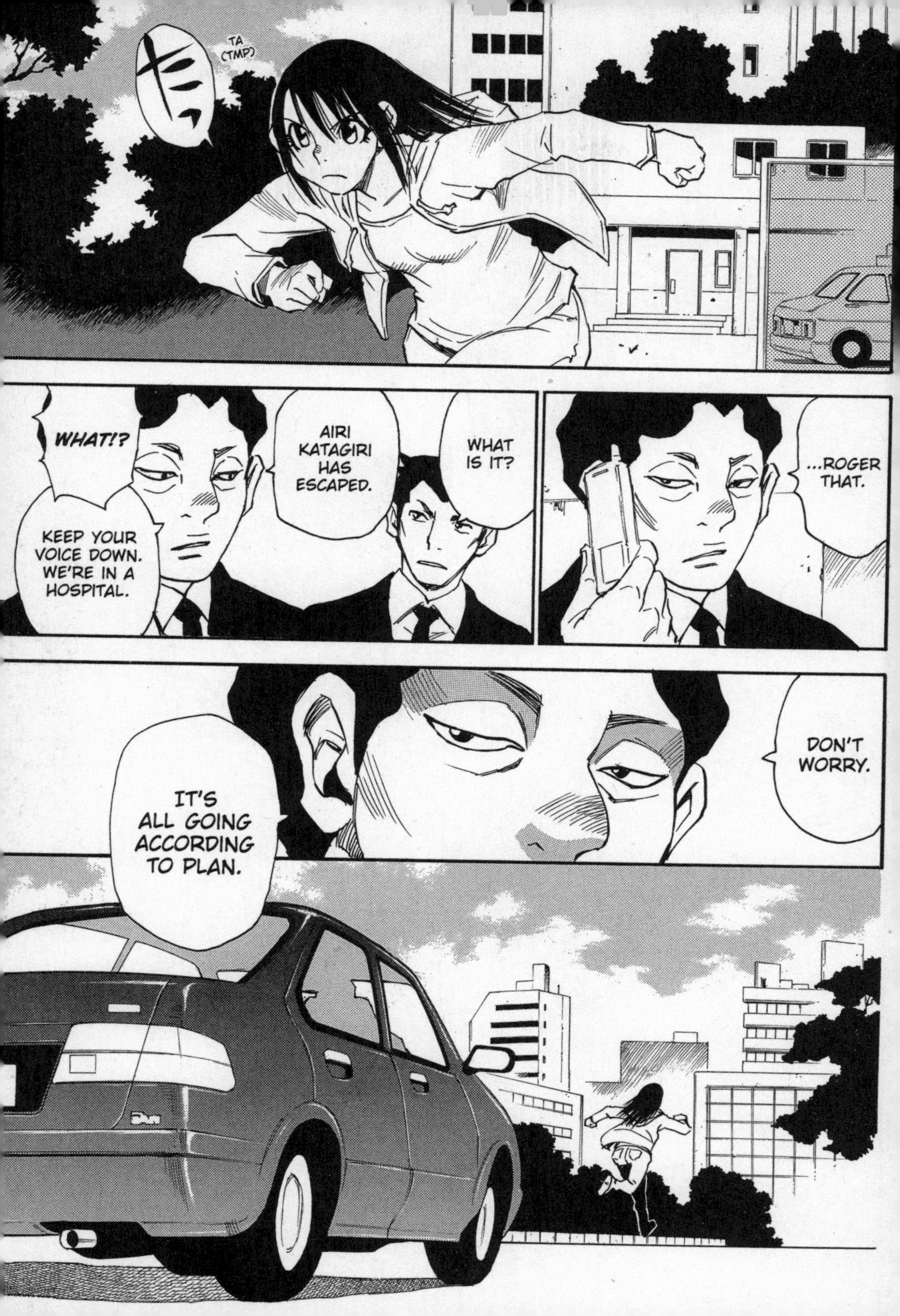
TA (TMP)
...ROGER THAT.
WHAT IS IT?
AIRI KATAGIRI HAS ESCAPED.
WHAT!?
KEEP YOUR VOICE DOWN. WE'RE IN A HOSPITAL.
DON'T WORRY.
IT'S ALL GOING ACCORDING TO PLAN.

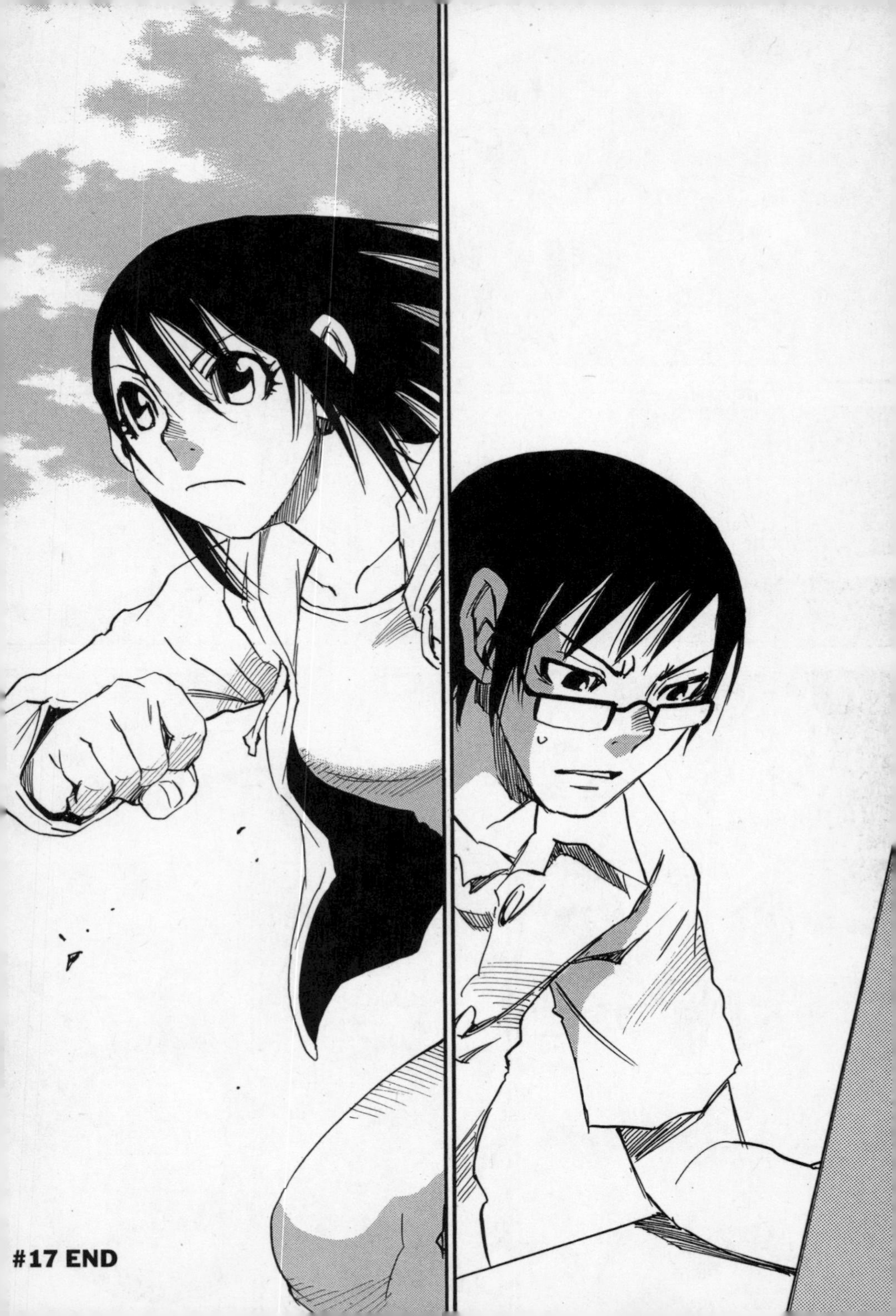
#17 END

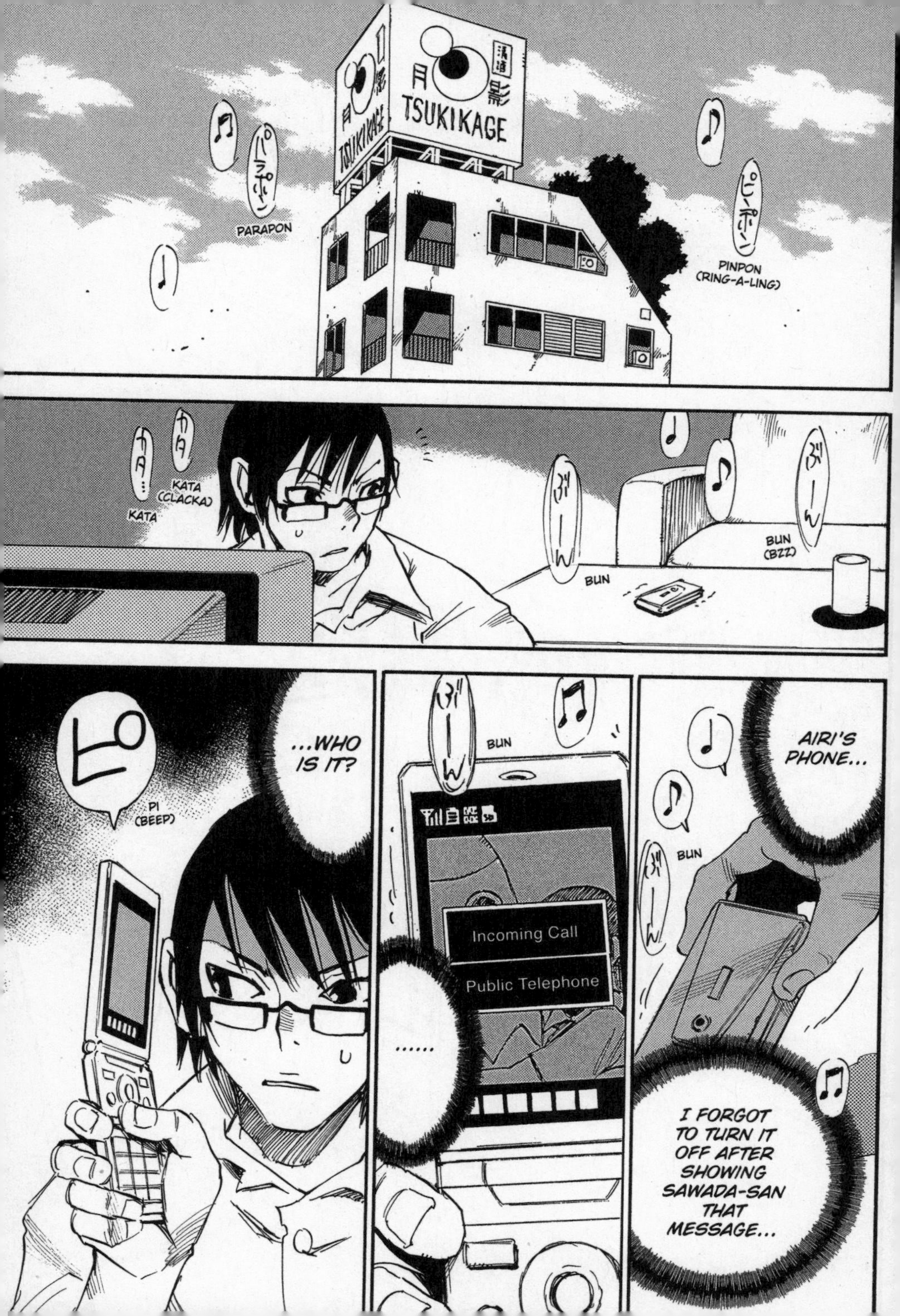

清酒
月影
TSUKIKAGE
ピンポン
PINPON (RING-A-LING)
パラポン
PARAPON
BUN (BZZ)
BUN
カタ
KATA (CLACKA)
カタ…
KATA
AIRI'S PHONE...
BUN
I FORGOT TO TURN IT OFF AFTER SHOWING SAWADA-SAN THAT MESSAGE...
BUN
Incoming Call
Public Telephone
......
...WHO IS IT?
ピ
PI (BEEP)

#18: Time for Farewell, May 2006

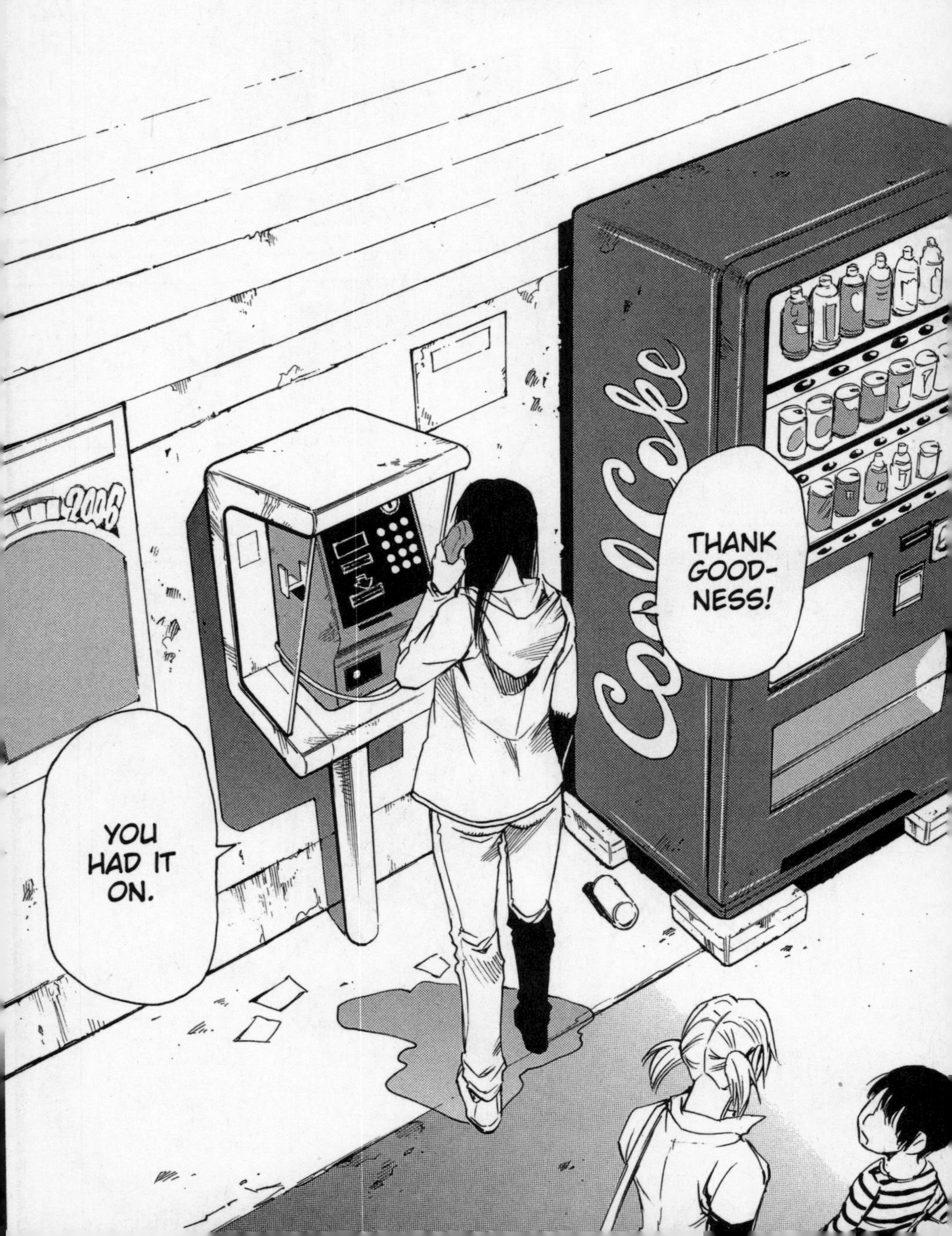
THANK GOODNESS!
YOU HAD IT ON.
2006

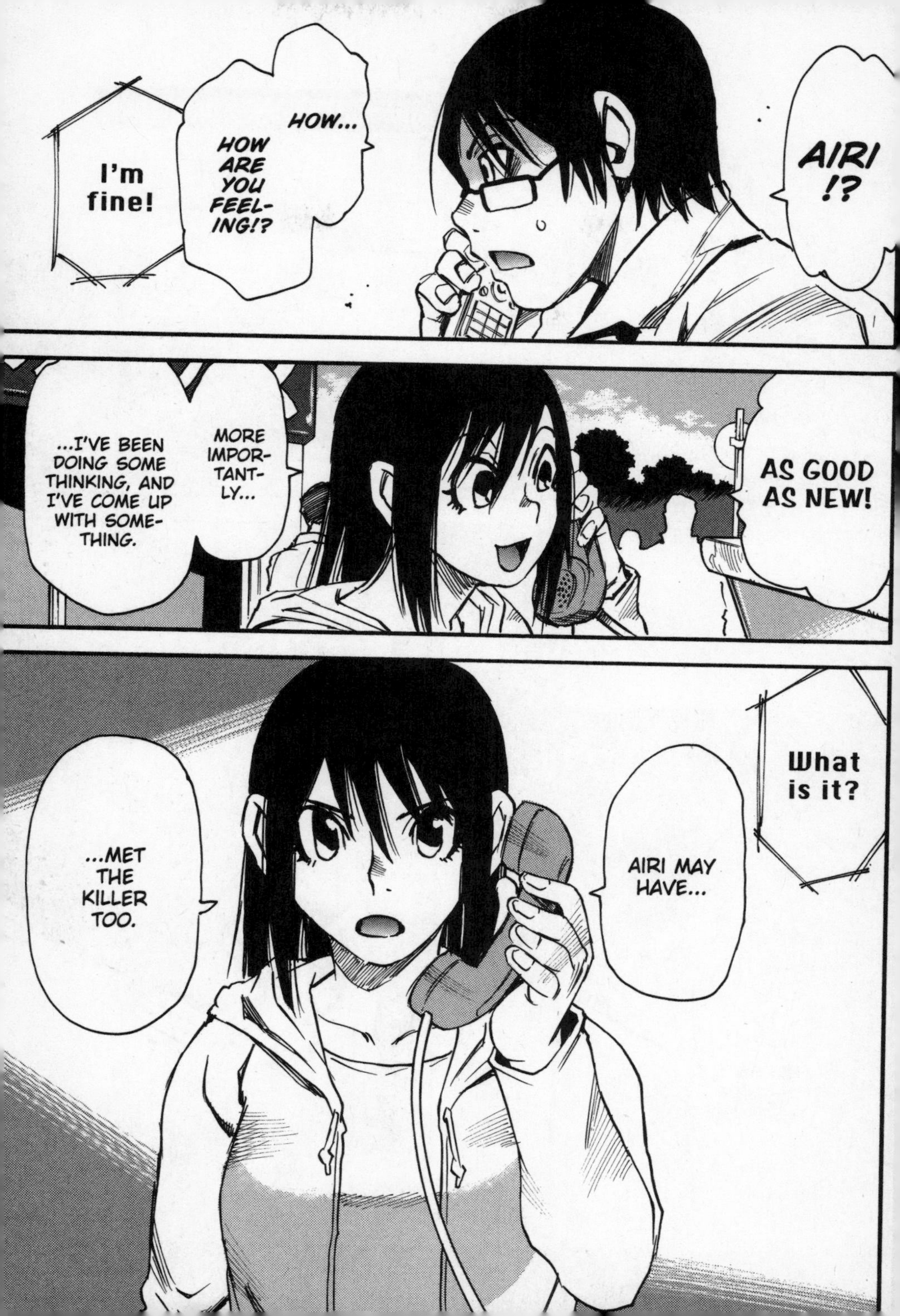
AIRI !?
HOW...
HOW ARE YOU FEEL-ING!?
I'm fine!
AS GOOD AS NEW!
MORE IMPOR-TANT-LY...
...I'VE BEEN DOING SOME THINKING, AND I'VE COME UP WITH SOME-THING.
What is it?
AIRI MAY HAVE...
...MET THE KILLER TOO.

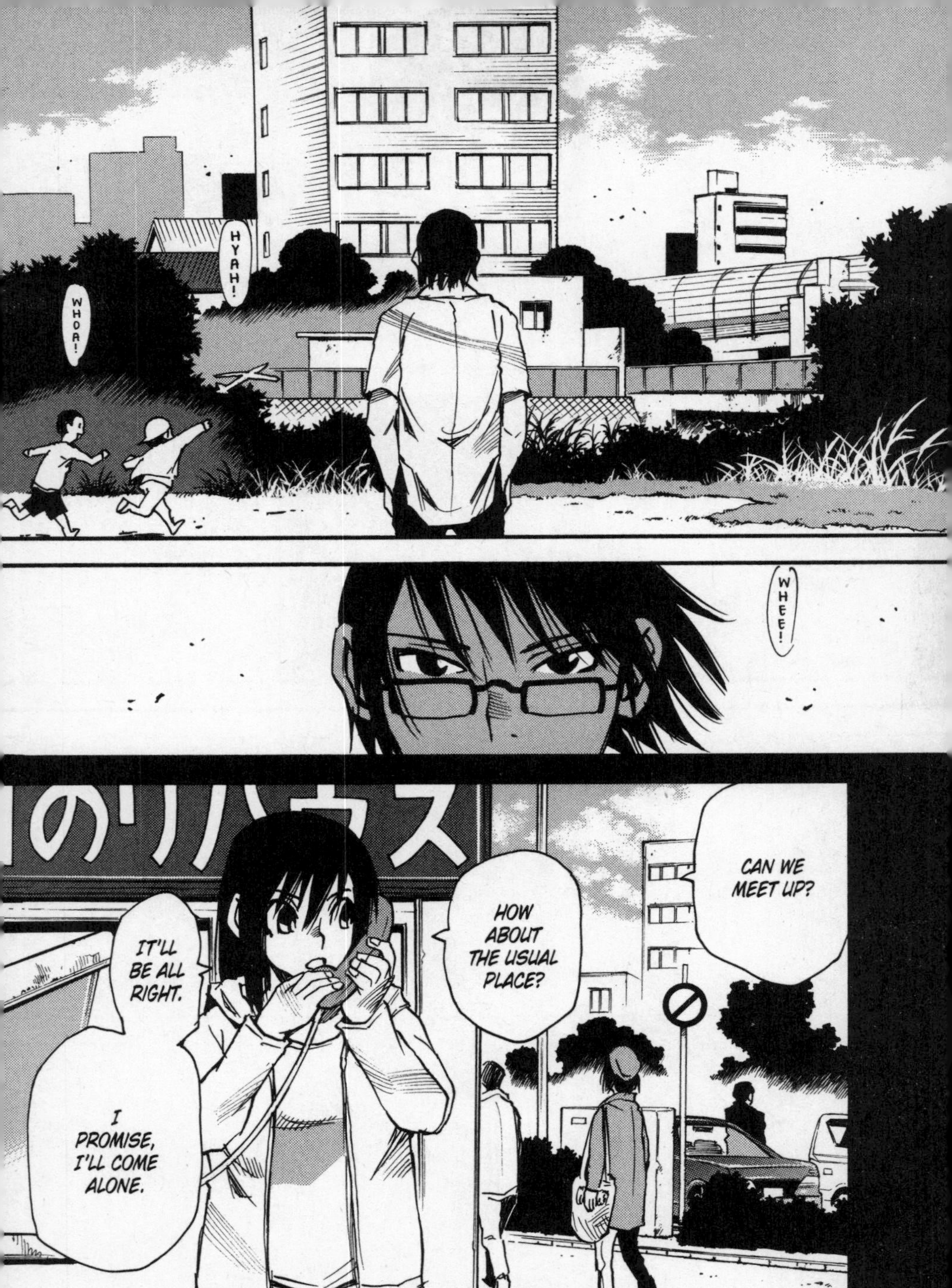
HYAH!
WHOA!
WHEE!
のリハウス
CAN WE MEET UP?
HOW ABOUT THE USUAL PLACE?
IT'LL BE ALL RIGHT.
I PROMISE, I'LL COME ALONE.

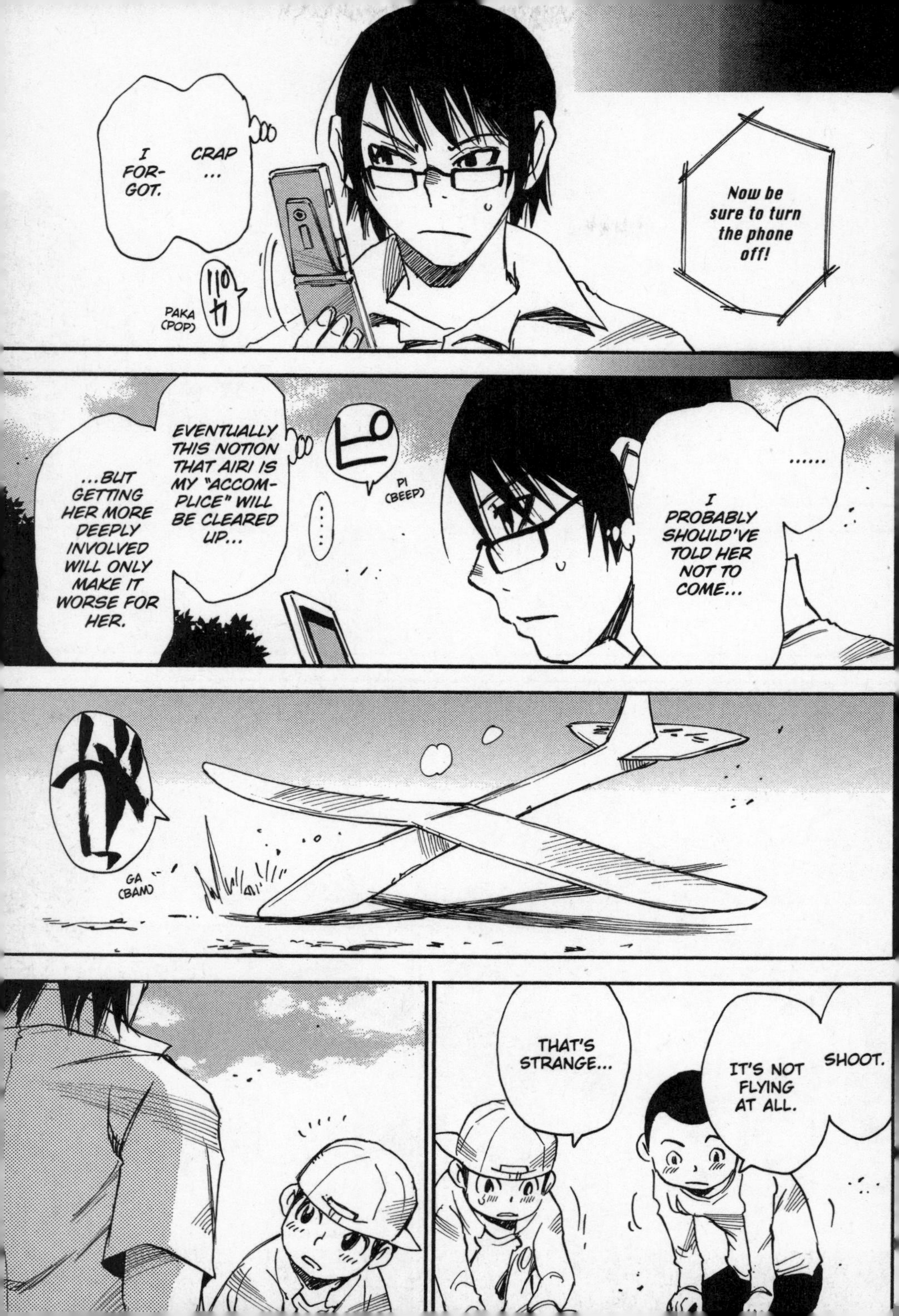

Now be sure to turn the phone off!
CRAP... I FORGOT.
PAKA (POP)
......
I PROBABLY SHOULD'VE TOLD HER NOT TO COME...
PI (BEEP)
......
EVENTUALLY THIS NOTION THAT AIRI IS MY "ACCOMPLICE" WILL BE CLEARED UP...
...BUT GETTING HER MORE DEEPLY INVOLVED WILL ONLY MAKE IT WORSE FOR HER.
GA (BAM)
SHOOT.
IT'S NOT FLYING AT ALL.
THAT'S STRANGE...

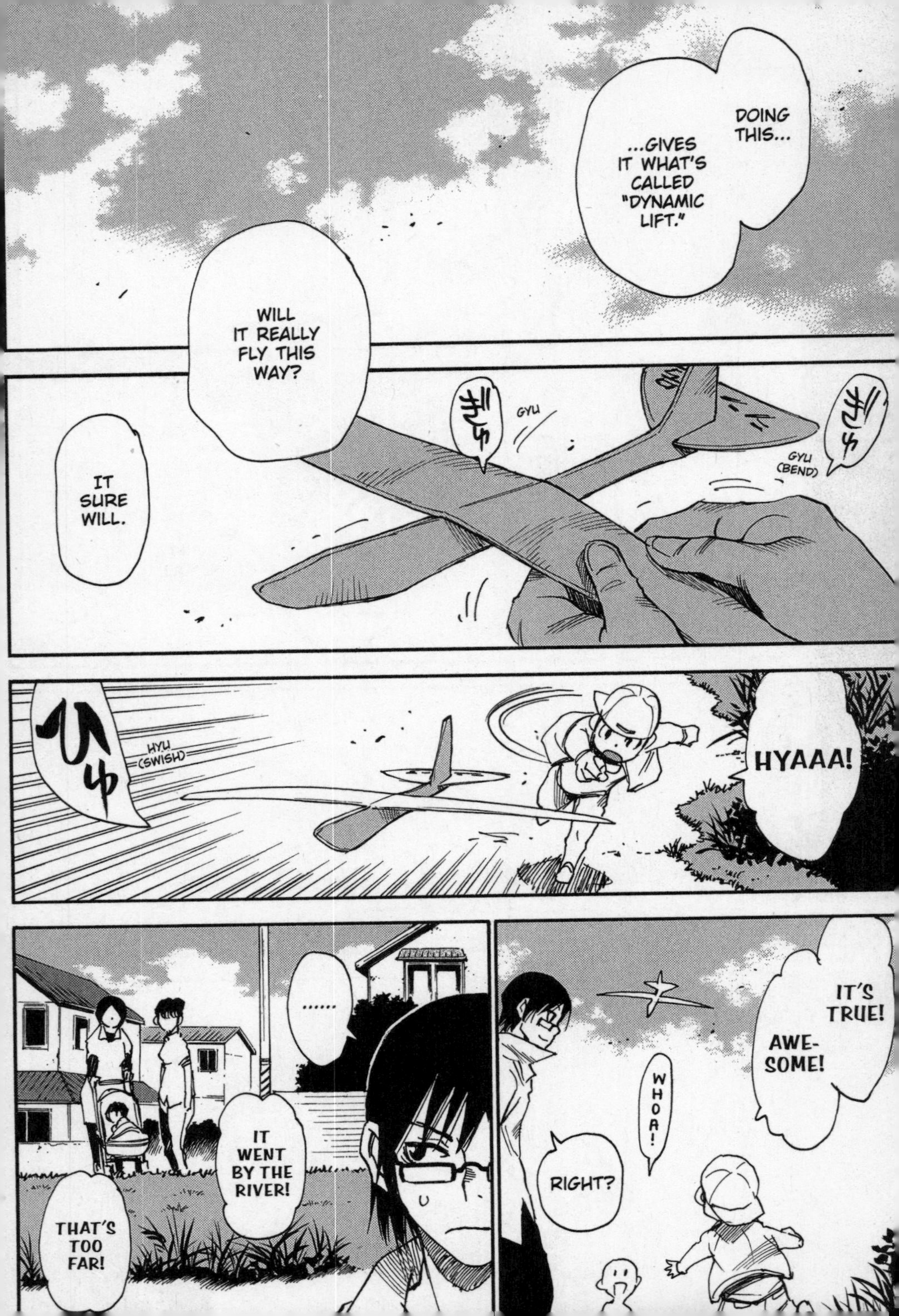
DOING THIS...
...GIVES IT WHAT'S CALLED "DYNAMIC LIFT."
WILL IT REALLY FLY THIS WAY?
ぎゅ
GYU (BEND)
ぎゅ
GYU
IT SURE WILL.
HYAAA!
ひゅ
HYU (SWISH)
IT'S TRUE!
AWE-SOME!
WHOA!
RIGHT?
......
IT WENT BY THE RIVER!
THAT'S TOO FAR!

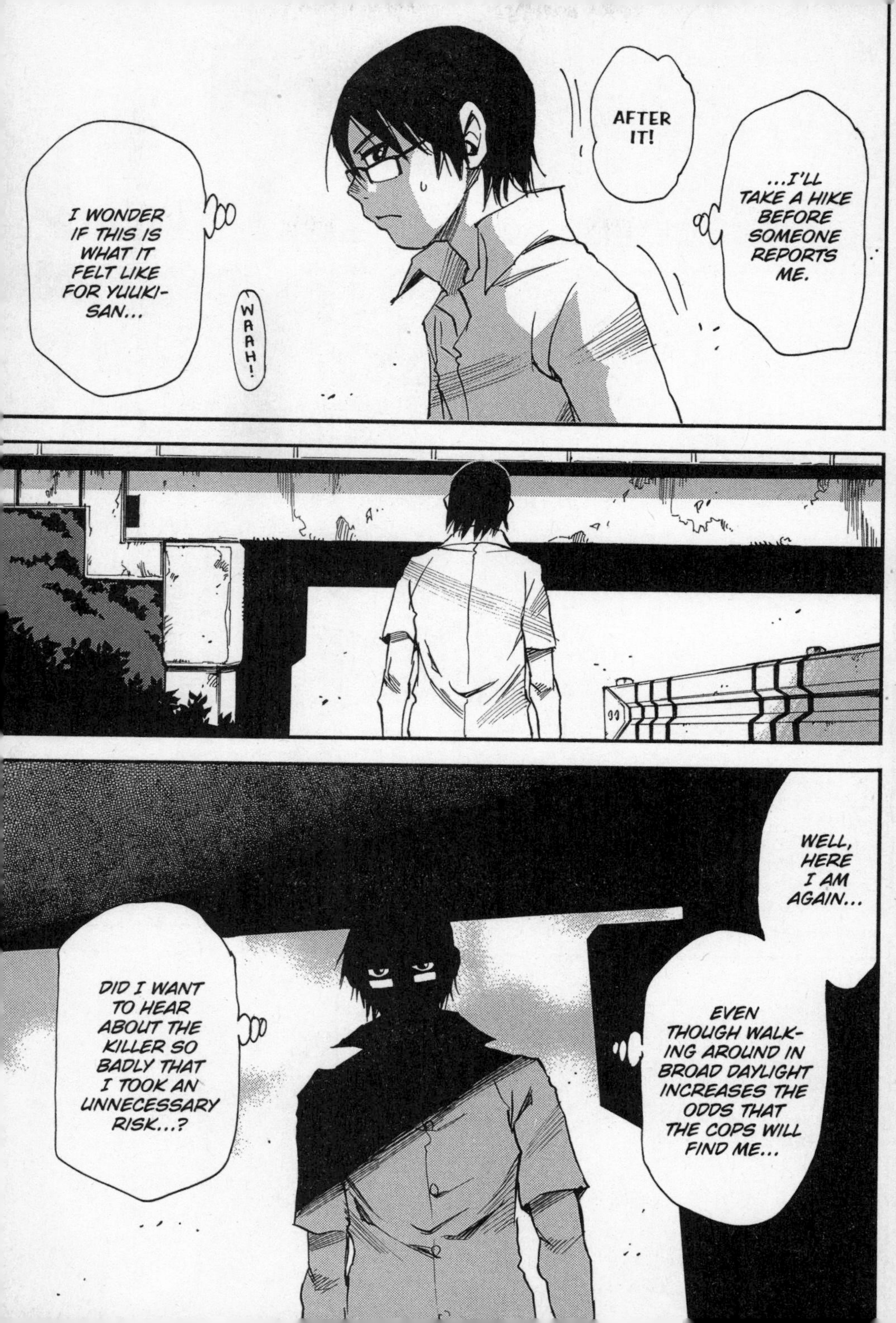
AFTER IT!
...I'LL TAKE A HIKE BEFORE SOMEONE REPORTS ME.
WAAH!
I WONDER IF THIS IS WHAT IT FELT LIKE FOR YUUKI-SAN...
WELL, HERE I AM AGAIN...
EVEN THOUGH WALKING AROUND IN BROAD DAYLIGHT INCREASES THE ODDS THAT THE COPS WILL FIND ME...
DID I WANT TO HEAR ABOUT THE KILLER SO BADLY THAT I TOOK AN UNNECESSARY RISK...?

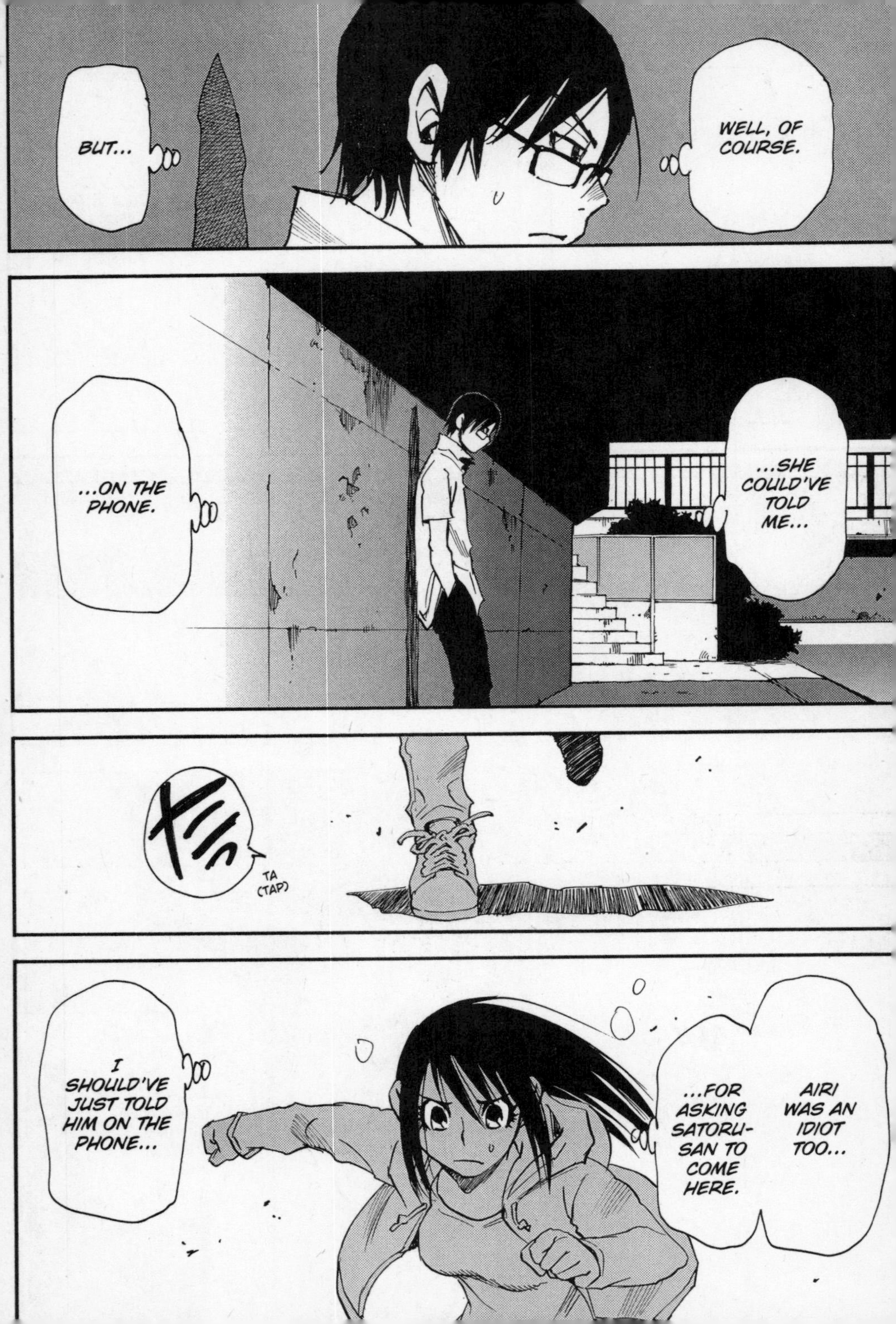
WELL, OF COURSE.
BUT...
...SHE COULD'VE TOLD ME...
...ON THE PHONE.
TA (TAP)
AIRI WAS AN IDIOT TOO...
...FOR ASKING SATORU-SAN TO COME HERE.
I SHOULD'VE JUST TOLD HIM ON THE PHONE...

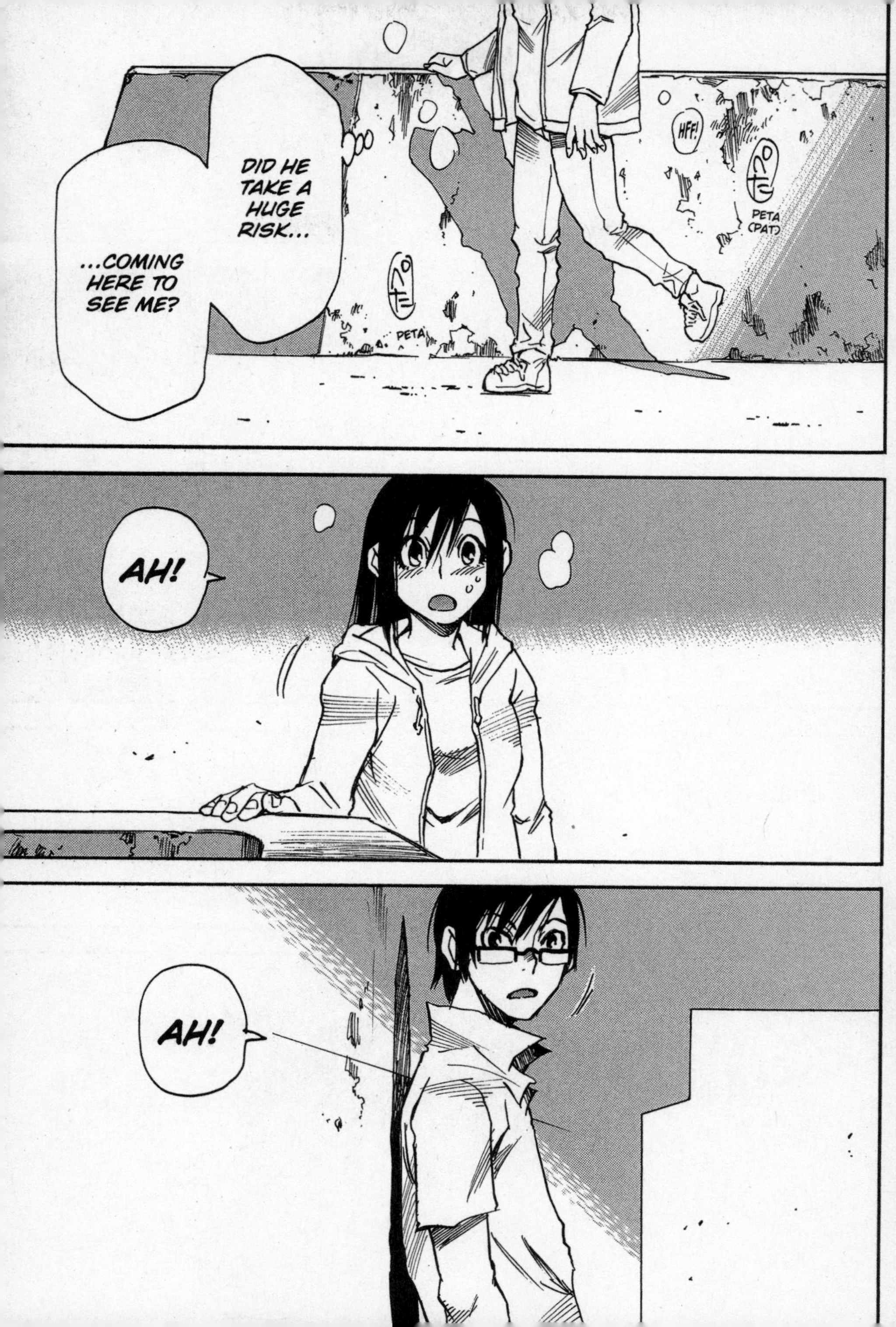
HFF!
PETA (PAT)
DID HE TAKE A HUGE RISK...
PETA
...COMING HERE TO SEE ME?
AH!
AH!

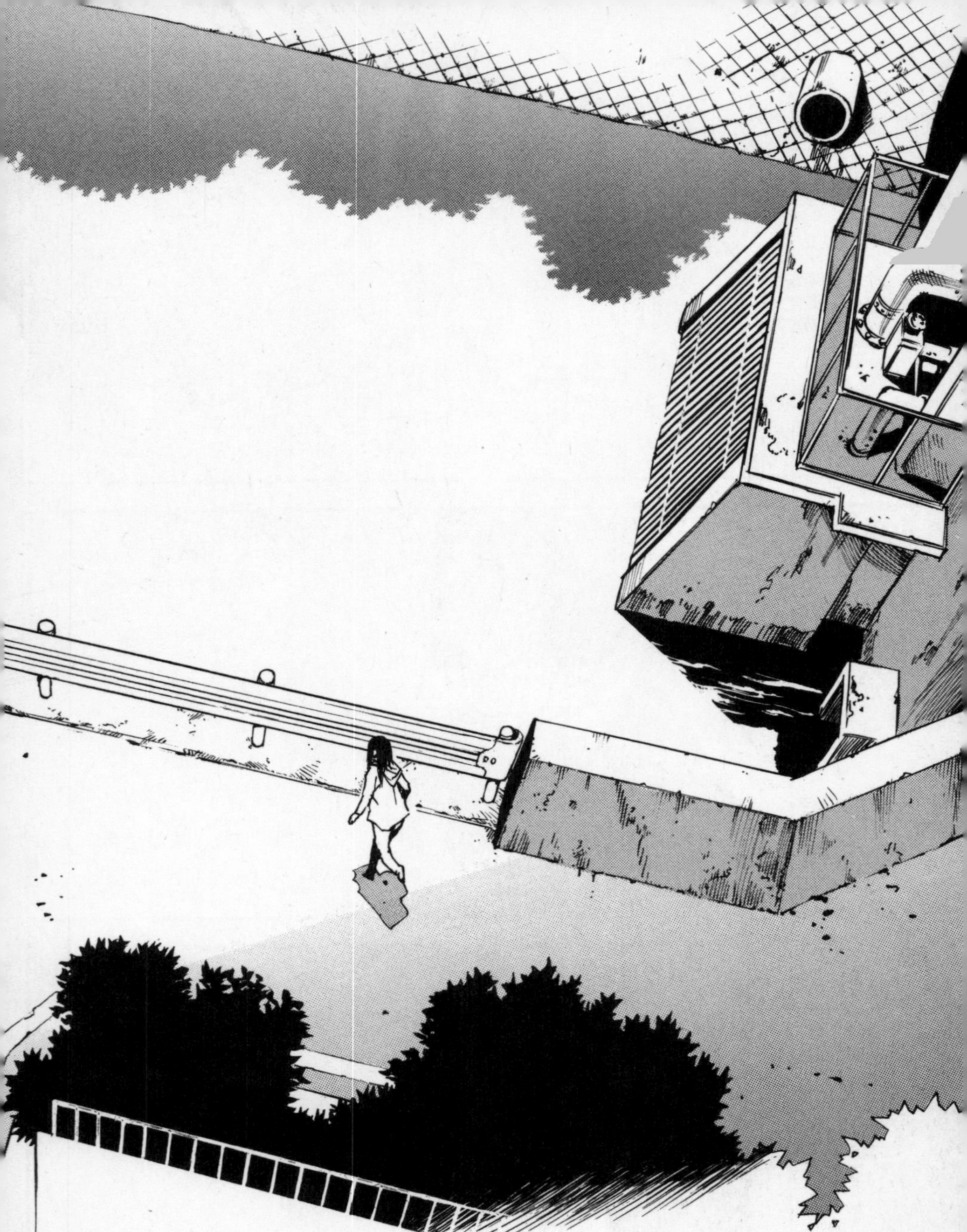

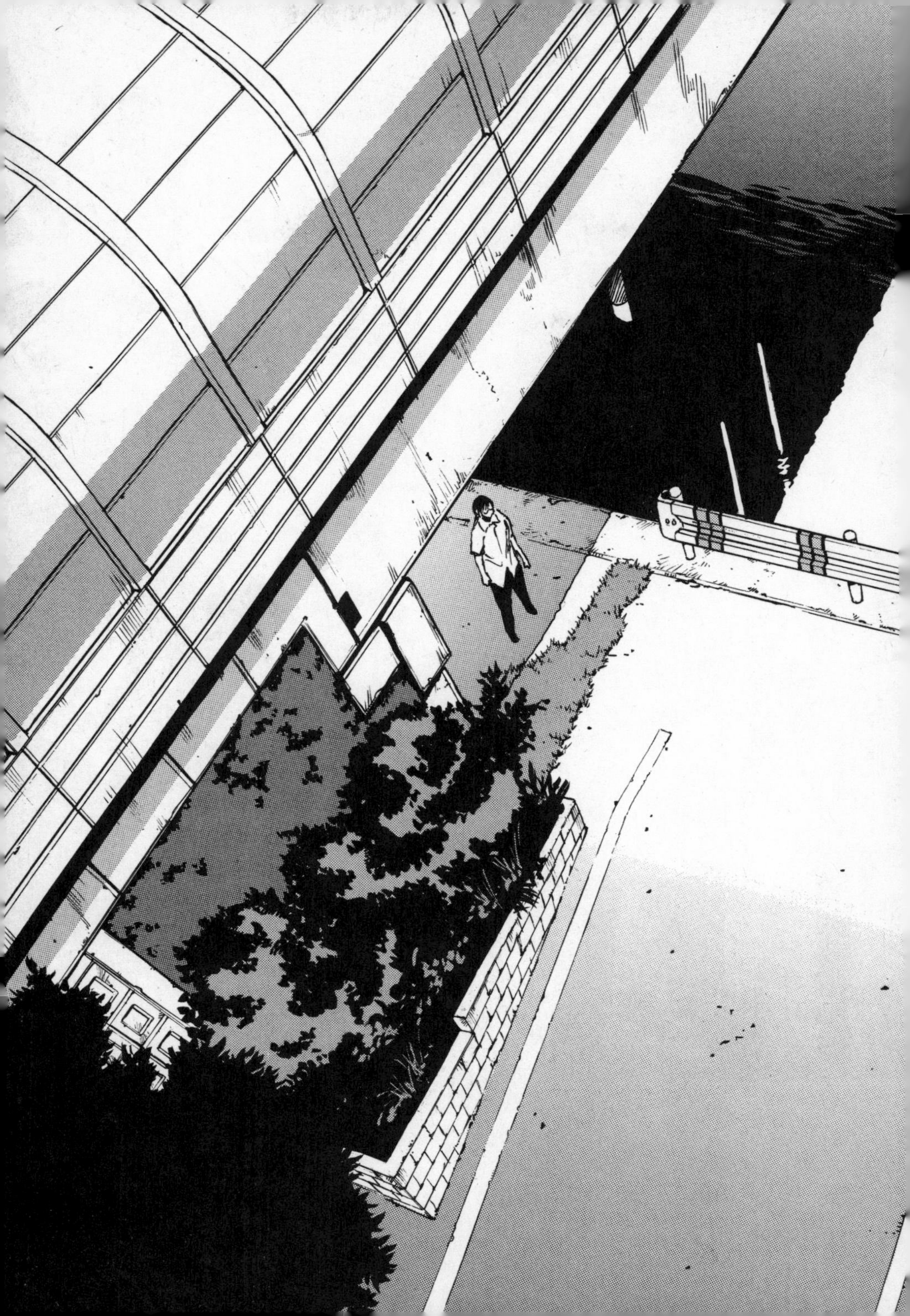

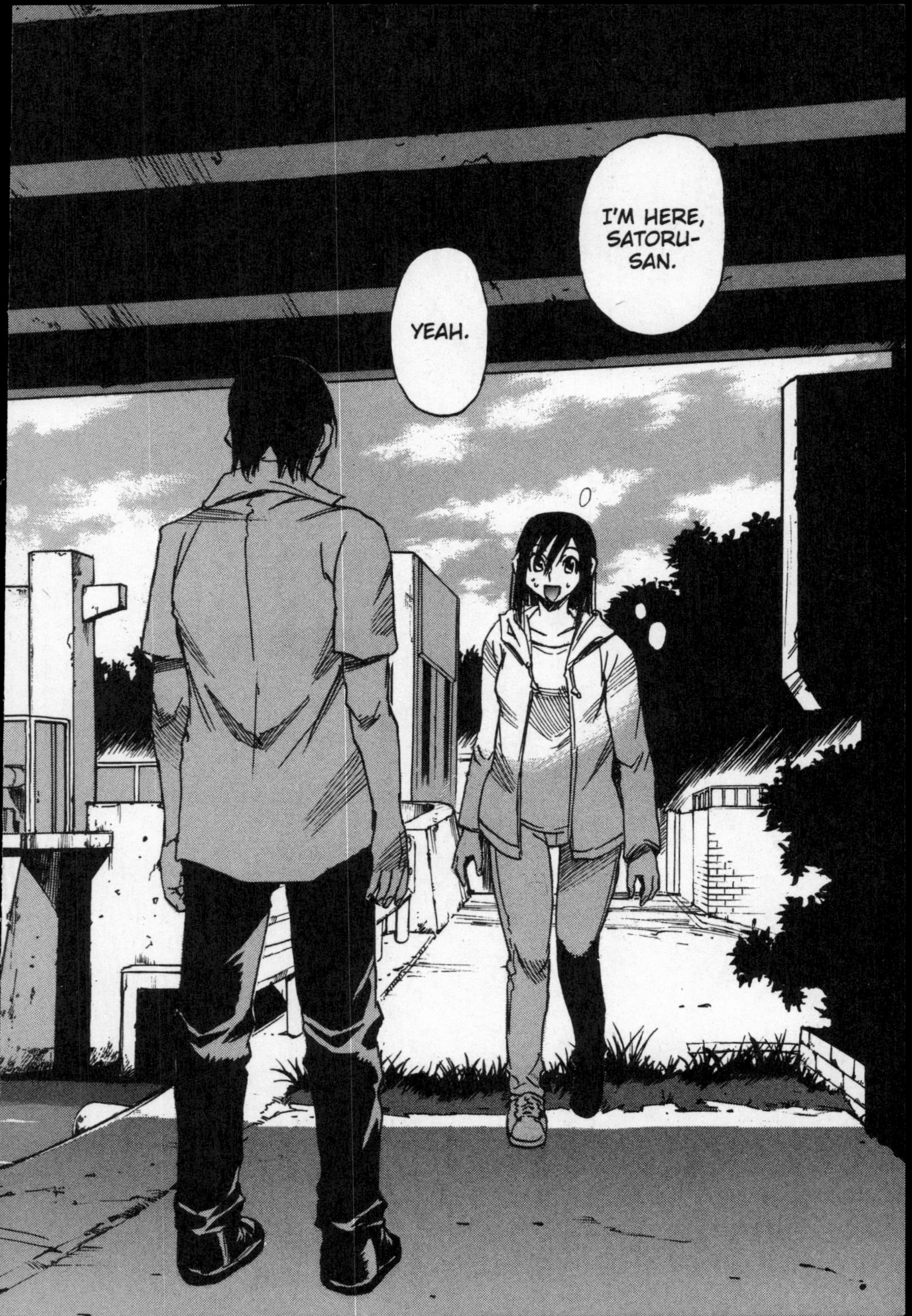
I'M HERE, SATORU-SAN.
YEAH.

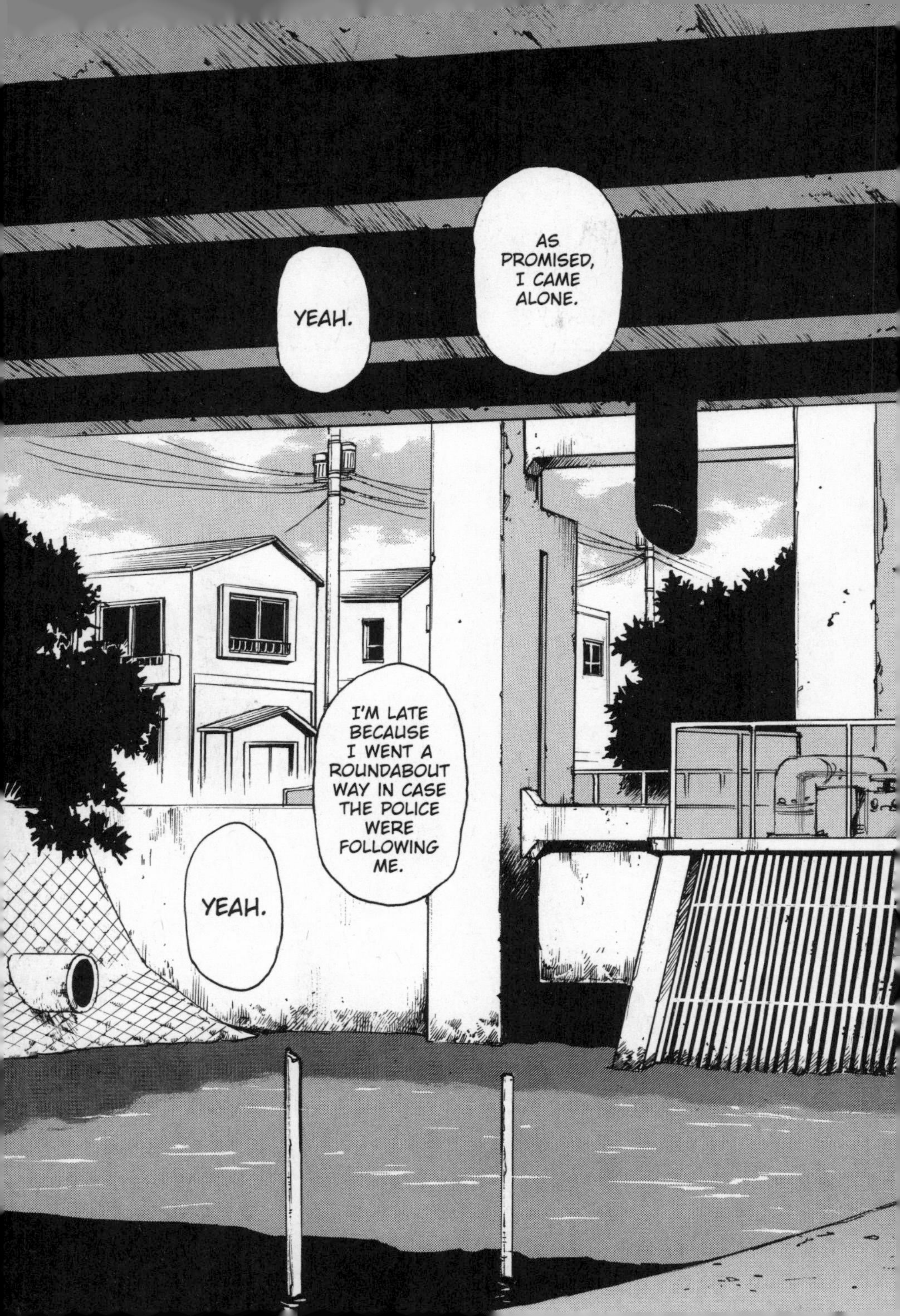
AS PROMISED, I CAME ALONE.
YEAH.
I'M LATE BECAUSE I WENT A ROUNDABOUT WAY IN CASE THE POLICE WERE FOLLOWING ME.
YEAH.

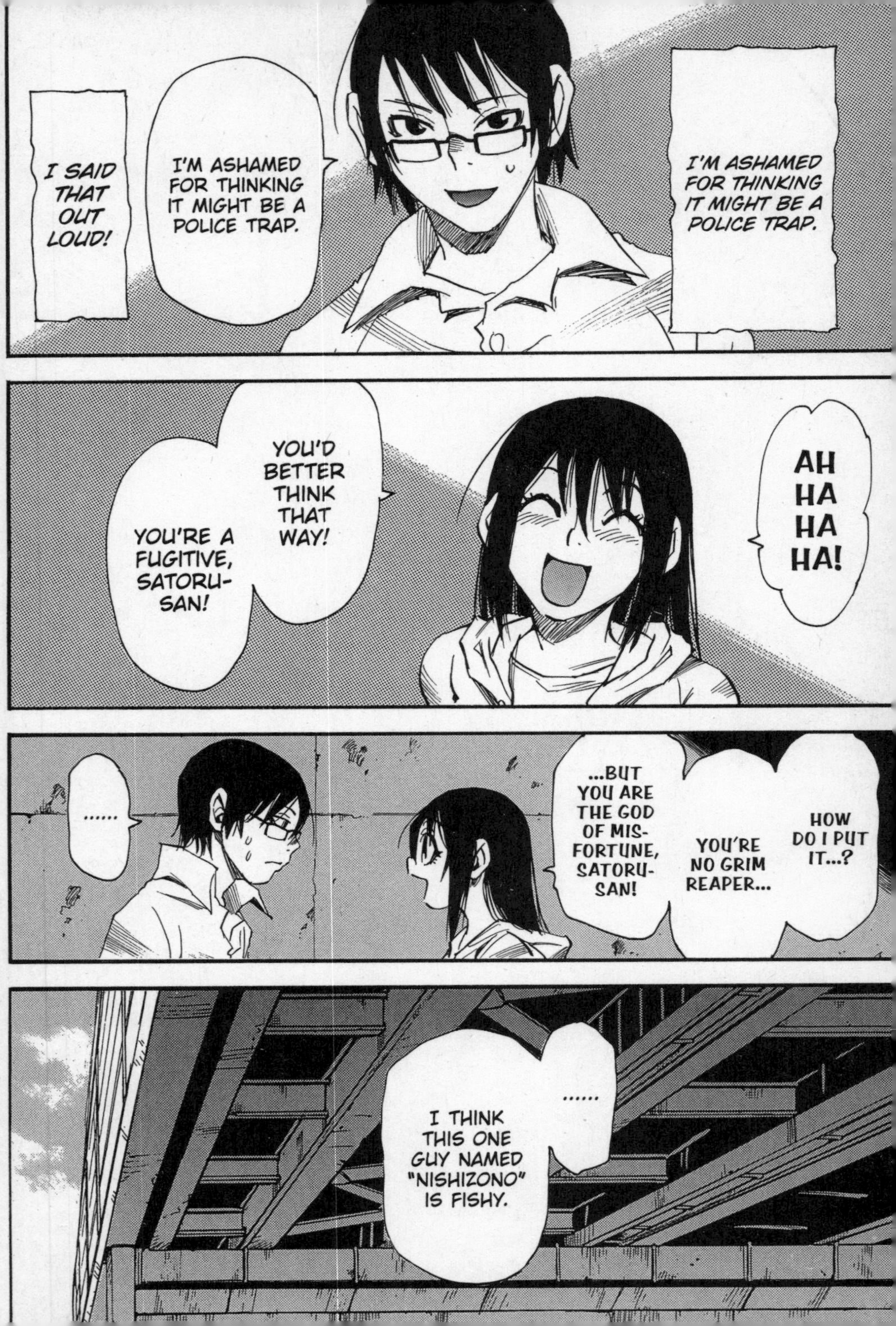
I'M ASHAMED FOR THINKING IT MIGHT BE A POLICE TRAP.
I'M ASHAMED FOR THINKING IT MIGHT BE A POLICE TRAP.
I SAID THAT OUT LOUD!
AH HA HA HA!
YOU'D BETTER THINK THAT WAY!
YOU'RE A FUGITIVE, SATORU-SAN!
HOW DO I PUT IT...?
YOU'RE NO GRIM REAPER...
...BUT YOU ARE THE GOD OF MIS-FORTUNE, SATORU-SAN!
......
......
I THINK THIS ONE GUY NAMED "NISHIZONO" IS FISHY.

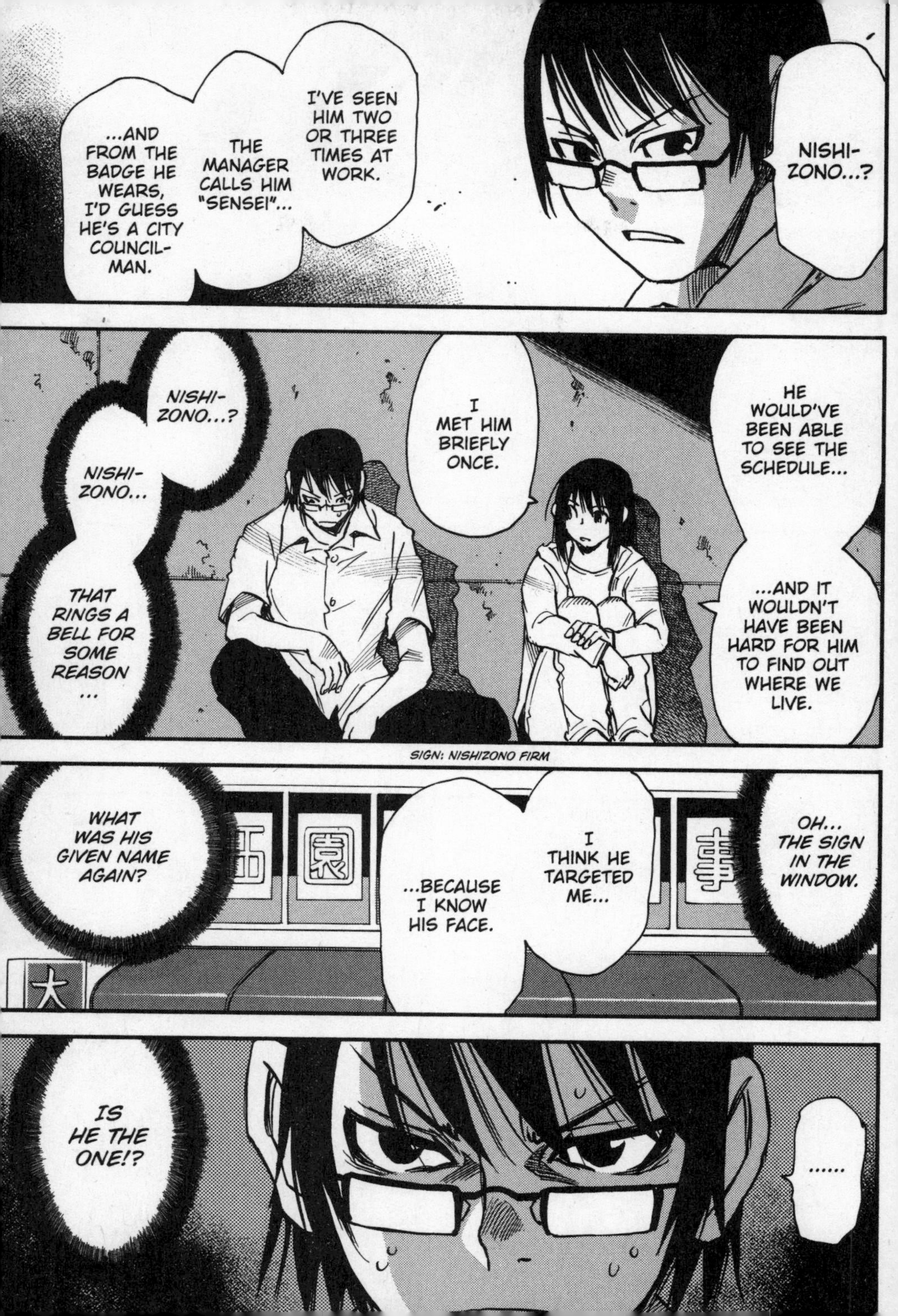
NISHI-ZONO...?
I'VE SEEN HIM TWO OR THREE TIMES AT WORK.
THE MANAGER CALLS HIM "SENSEI"...
...AND FROM THE BADGE HE WEARS, I'D GUESS HE'S A CITY COUNCIL-MAN.
HE WOULD'VE BEEN ABLE TO SEE THE SCHEDULE...
...AND IT WOULDN'T HAVE BEEN HARD FOR HIM TO FIND OUT WHERE WE LIVE.
I MET HIM BRIEFLY ONCE.
NISHI-ZONO...?
NISHI-ZONO...
THAT RINGS A BELL FOR SOME REASON...
SIGN: NISHIZONO FIRM
OH... THE SIGN IN THE WINDOW.
I THINK HE TARGETED ME...
...BECAUSE I KNOW HIS FACE.
WHAT WAS HIS GIVEN NAME AGAIN?
......
IS HE THE ONE!?

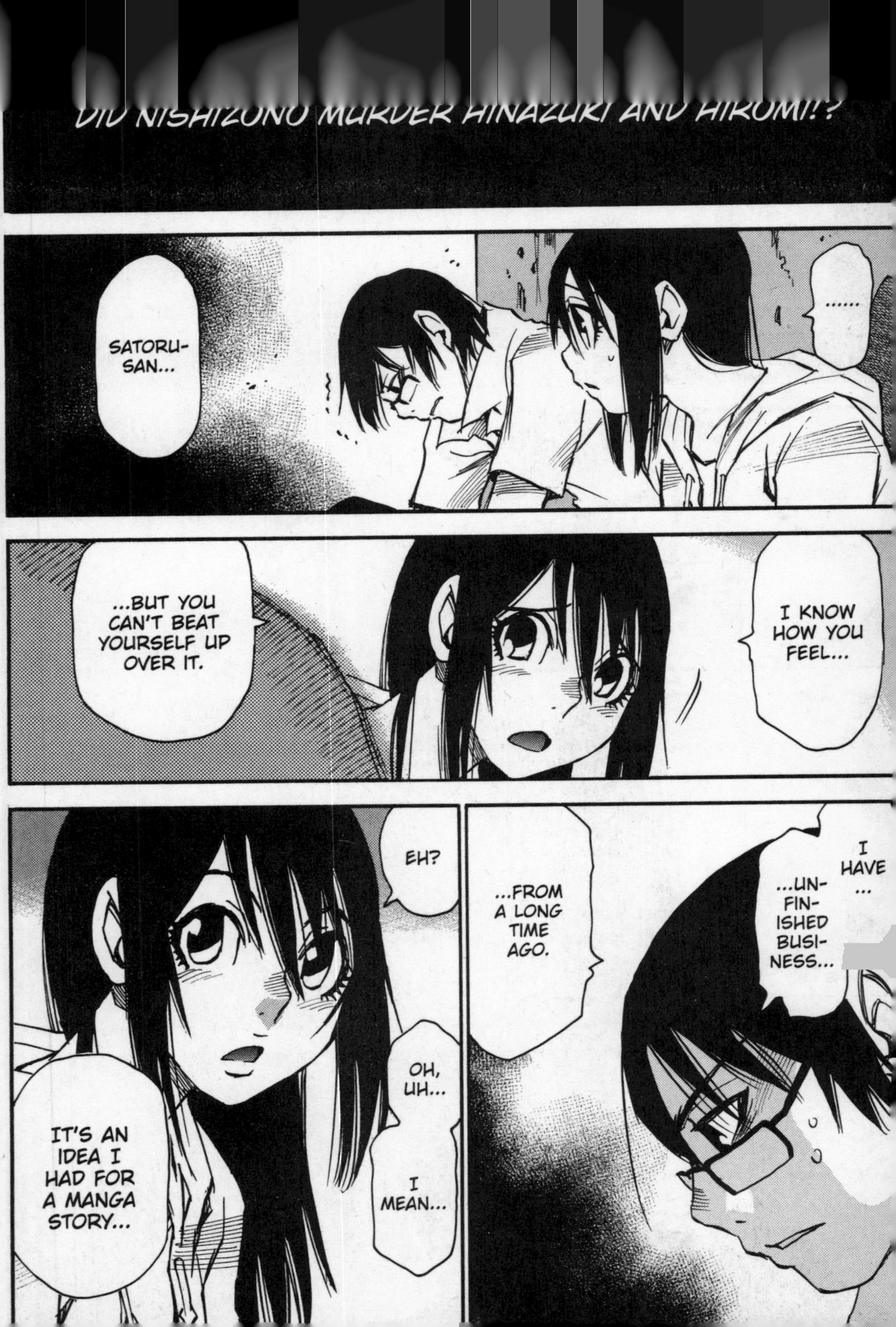
DID NISHIZONO MURDER HINAZUKI AND HIROMI!?
......
SATORU-SAN...
I KNOW HOW YOU FEEL...
...BUT YOU CAN'T BEAT YOURSELF UP OVER IT.
I HAVE ...
...UN-FIN-ISHED BUSI-NESS...
...FROM A LONG TIME AGO.
EH?
OH, UH...
I MEAN...
IT'S AN IDEA I HAD FOR A MANGA STORY...

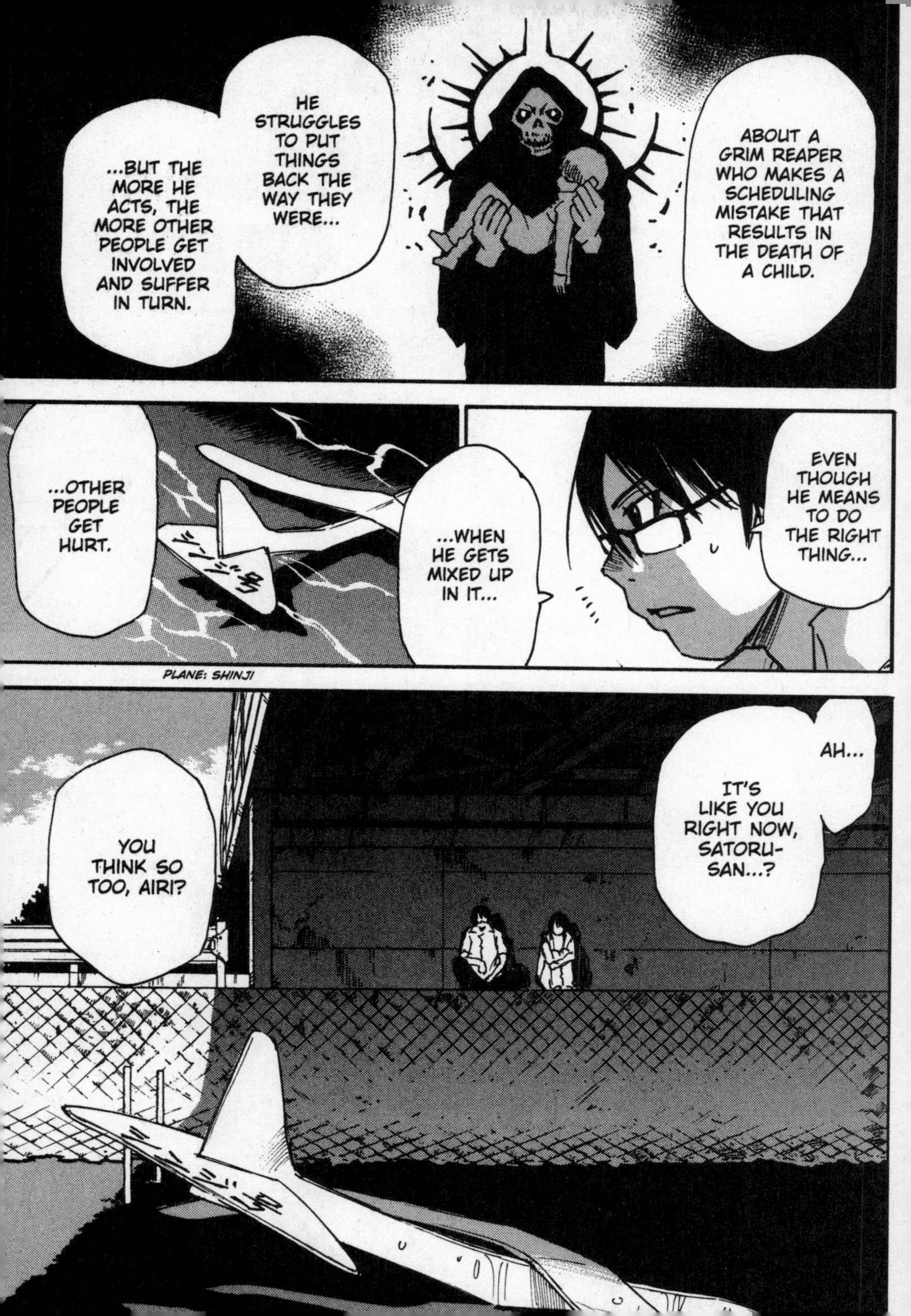
ABOUT A GRIM REAPER WHO MAKES A SCHEDULING MISTAKE THAT RESULTS IN THE DEATH OF A CHILD.
HE STRUGGLES TO PUT THINGS BACK THE WAY THEY WERE...
...BUT THE MORE HE ACTS, THE MORE OTHER PEOPLE GET INVOLVED AND SUFFER IN TURN.
EVEN THOUGH HE MEANS TO DO THE RIGHT THING...
...WHEN HE GETS MIXED UP IN IT...
...OTHER PEOPLE GET HURT.
PLANE: SHINJI
AH...
IT'S LIKE YOU RIGHT NOW, SATORU-SAN...?
YOU THINK SO TOO, AIRI?

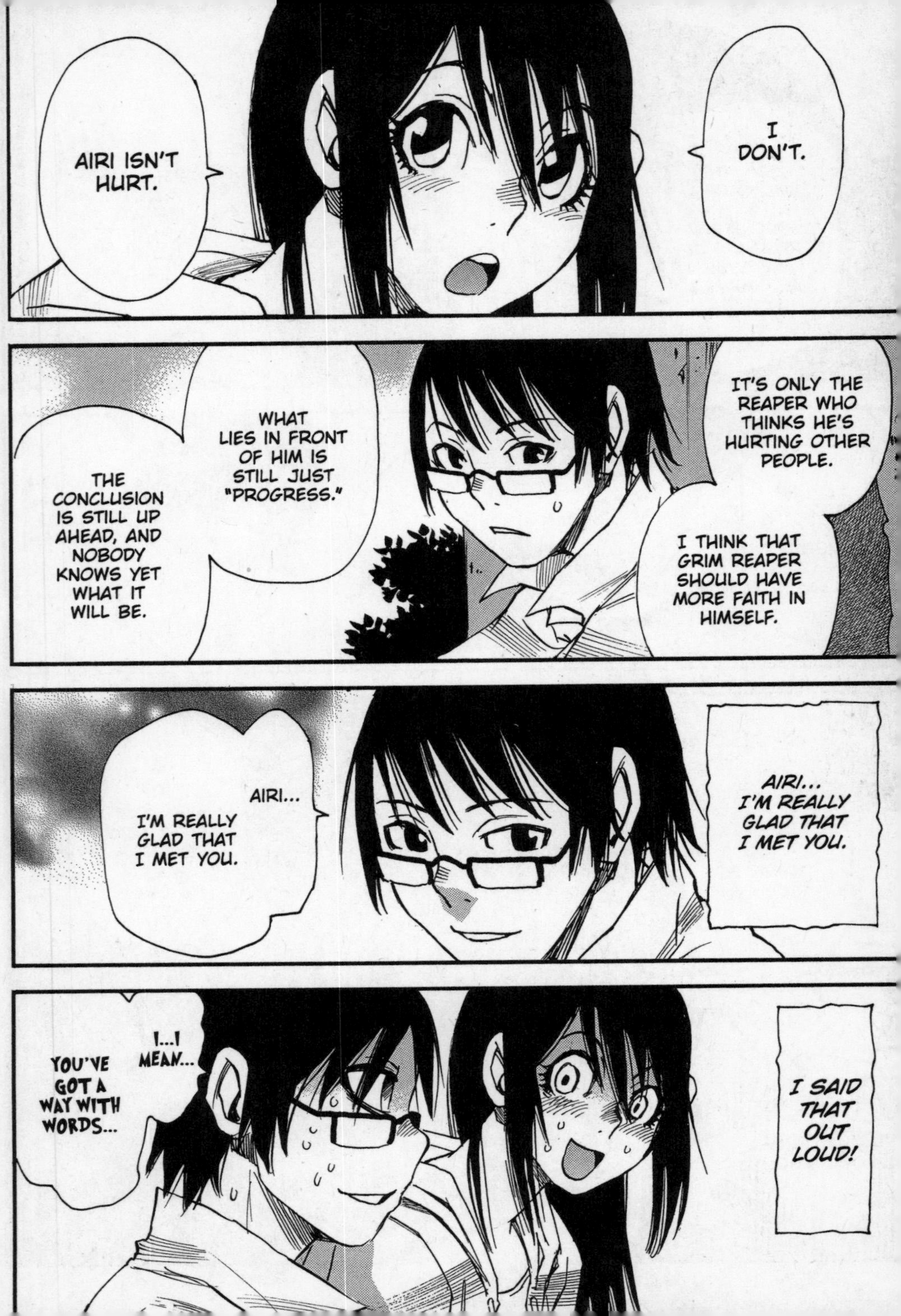
I DON'T.
AIRI ISN'T HURT.
IT'S ONLY THE REAPER WHO THINKS HE'S HURTING OTHER PEOPLE.
I THINK THAT GRIM REAPER SHOULD HAVE MORE FAITH IN HIMSELF.
WHAT LIES IN FRONT OF HIM IS STILL JUST "PROGRESS."
THE CONCLUSION IS STILL UP AHEAD, AND NOBODY KNOWS YET WHAT IT WILL BE.
AIRI... I'M REALLY GLAD THAT I MET YOU.
AIRI...
I'M REALLY GLAD THAT I MET YOU.
I SAID THAT OUT LOUD!
I...I MEAN...
YOU'VE GOT A WAY WITH WORDS...

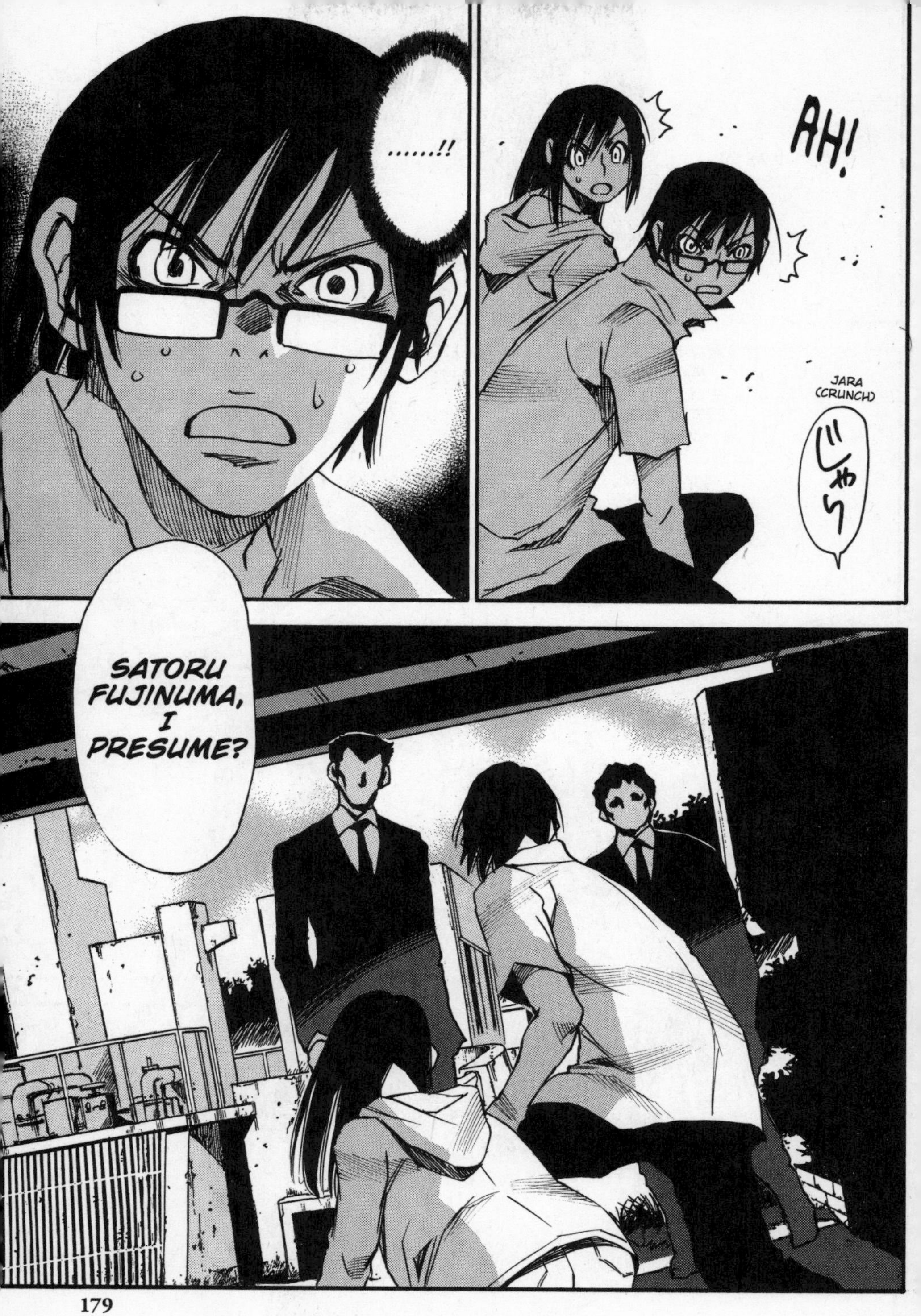
AH!
JARA (CRUNCH)
じゃら
......!!
SATORU FUJINUMA, I PRESUME?

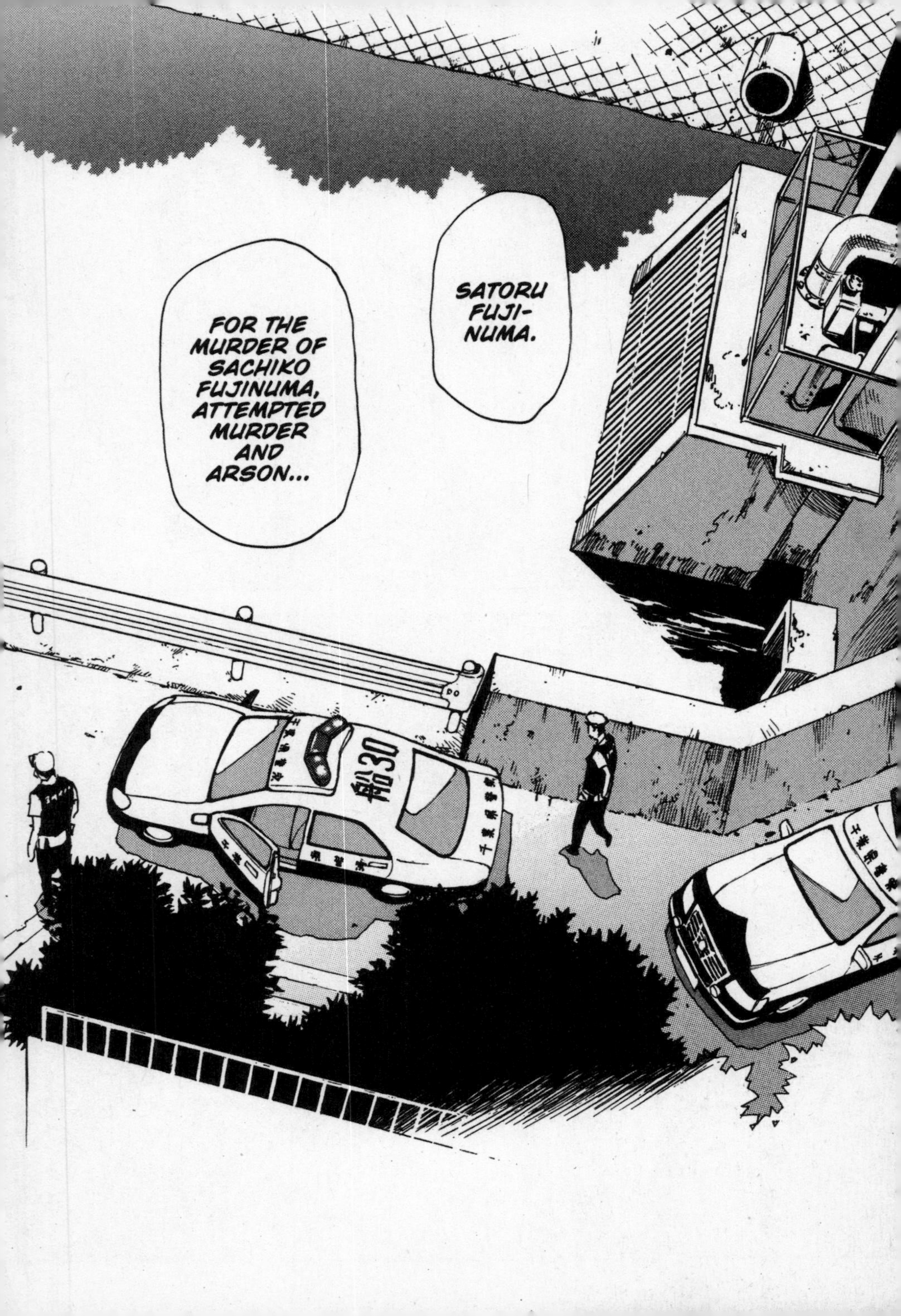
SATORU FUJI-NUMA.
FOR THE MURDER OF SACHIKO FUJINUMA, ATTEMPTED MURDER AND ARSON...

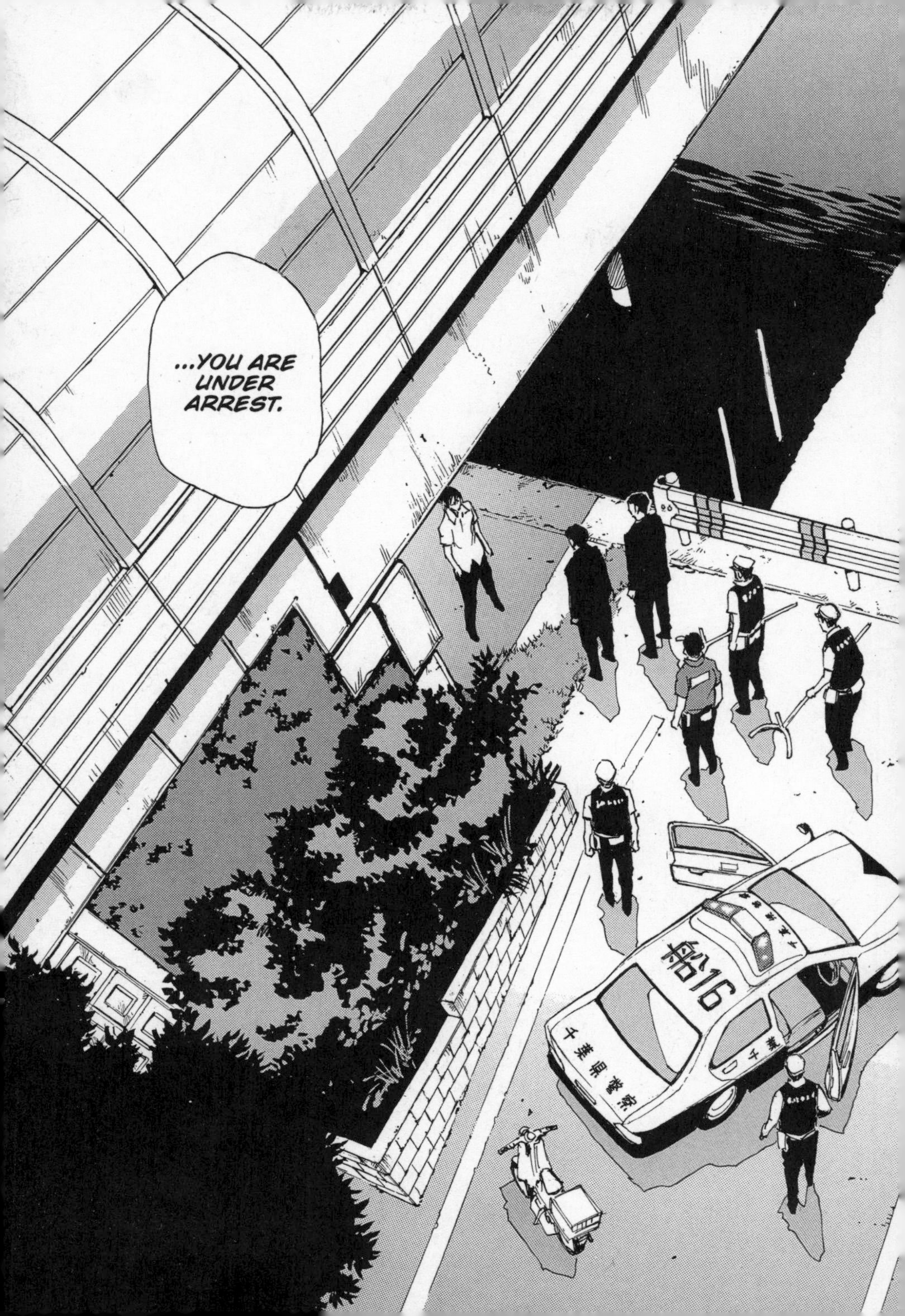
...YOU ARE UNDER ARREST.
船16
千葉県警察

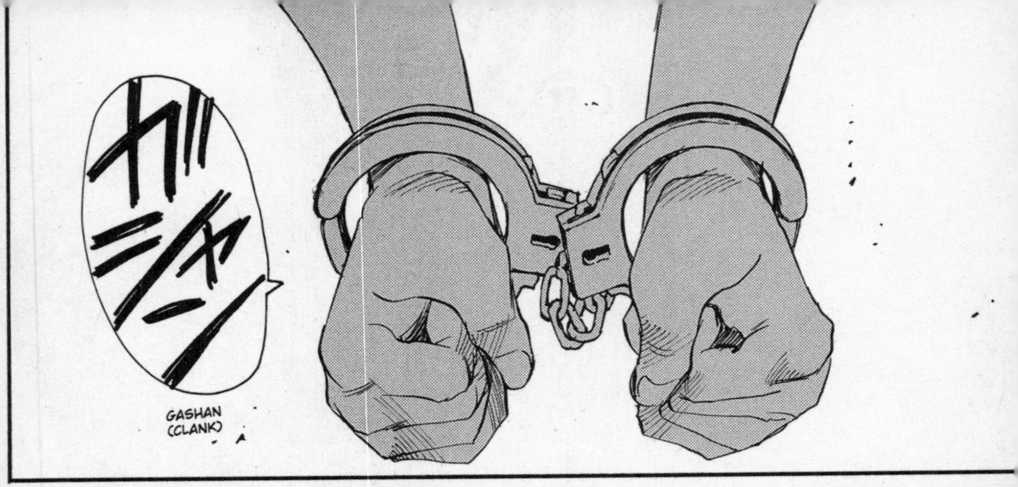
ガシャン
GASHAN (CLANK)
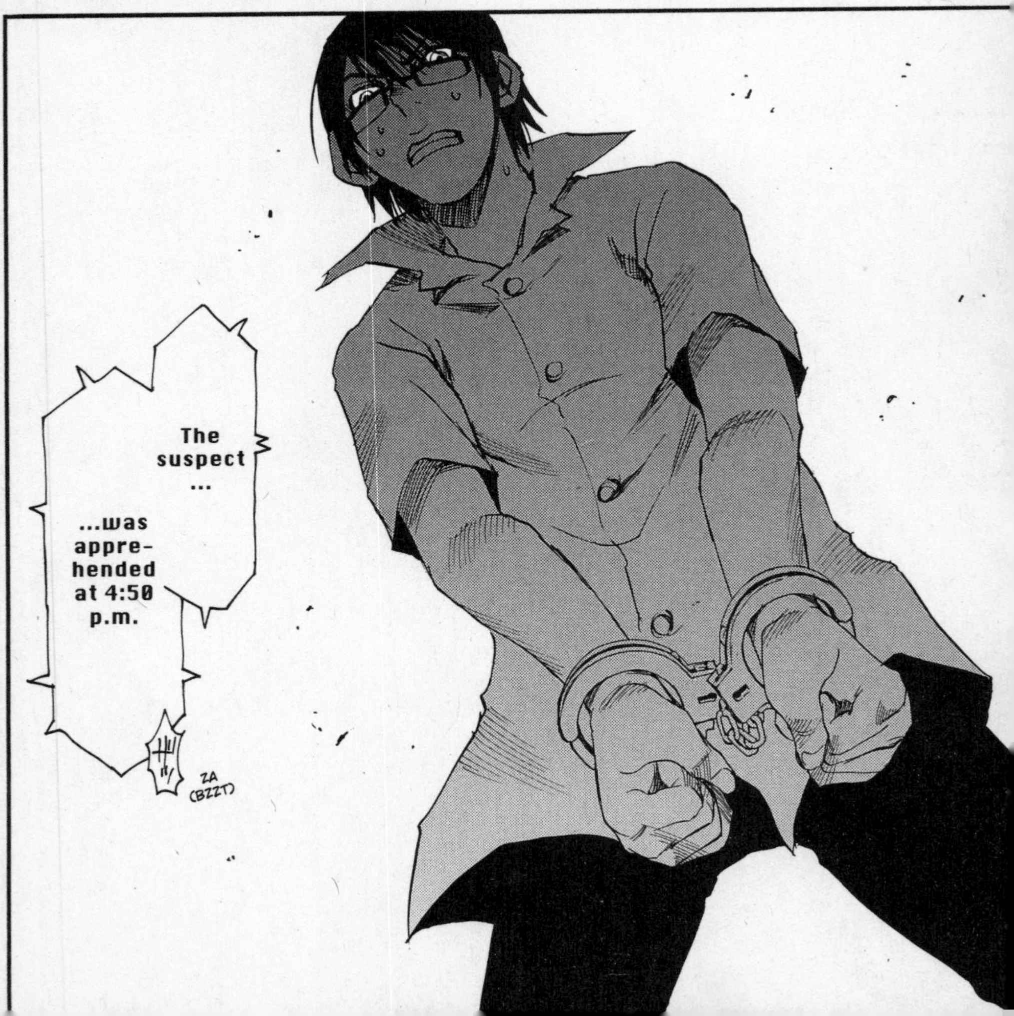
The suspect ...
...was apprehended at 4:50 p.m.
ザ
ZA (BZZT)

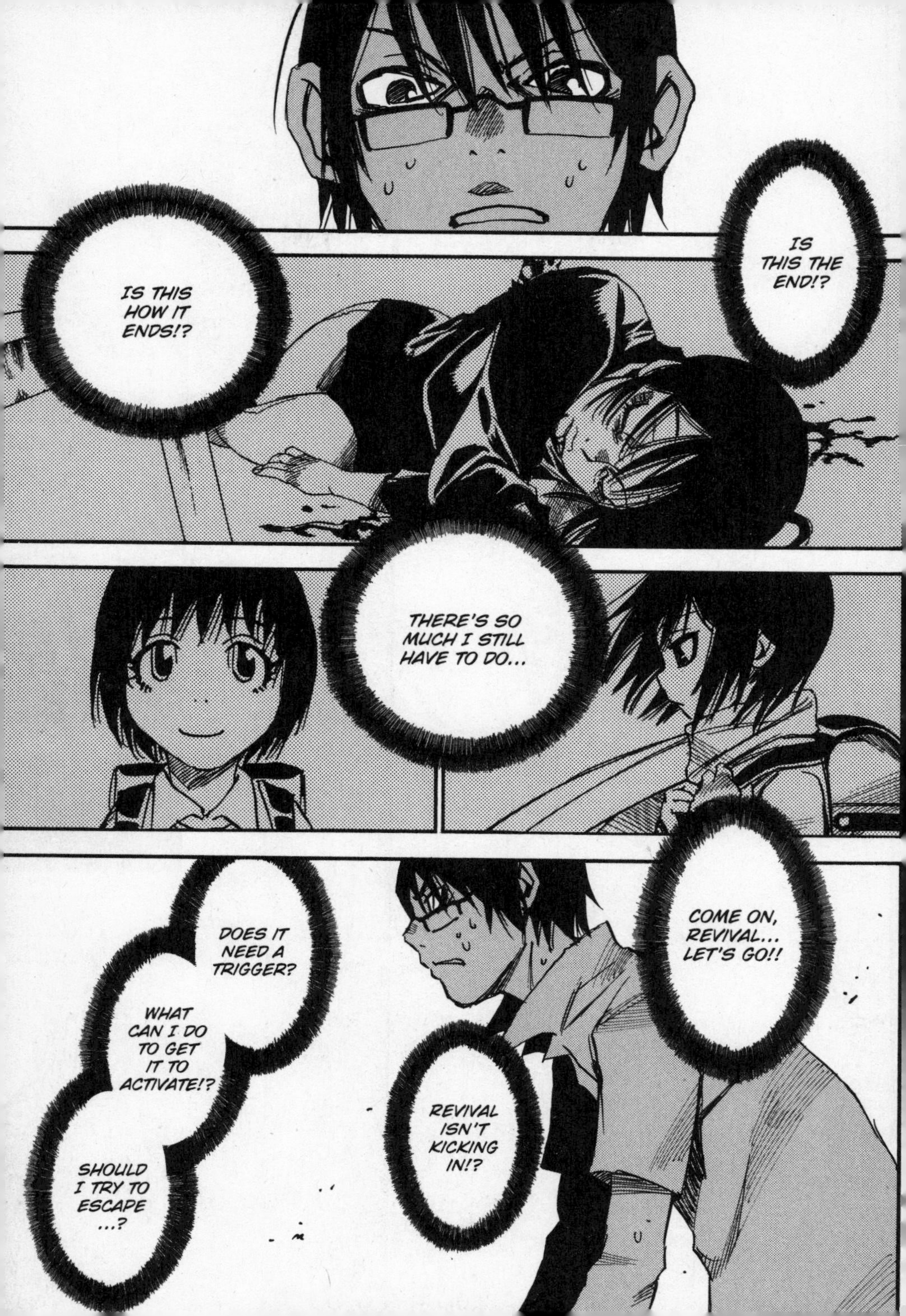
IS THIS THE END!?
IS THIS HOW IT ENDS!?
THERE'S SO MUCH I STILL HAVE TO DO...
COME ON, REVIVAL... LET'S GO!!
REVIVAL ISN'T KICKING IN!?
DOES IT NEED A TRIGGER?
WHAT CAN I DO TO GET IT TO ACTIVATE!?
SHOULD I TRY TO ESCAPE ...?

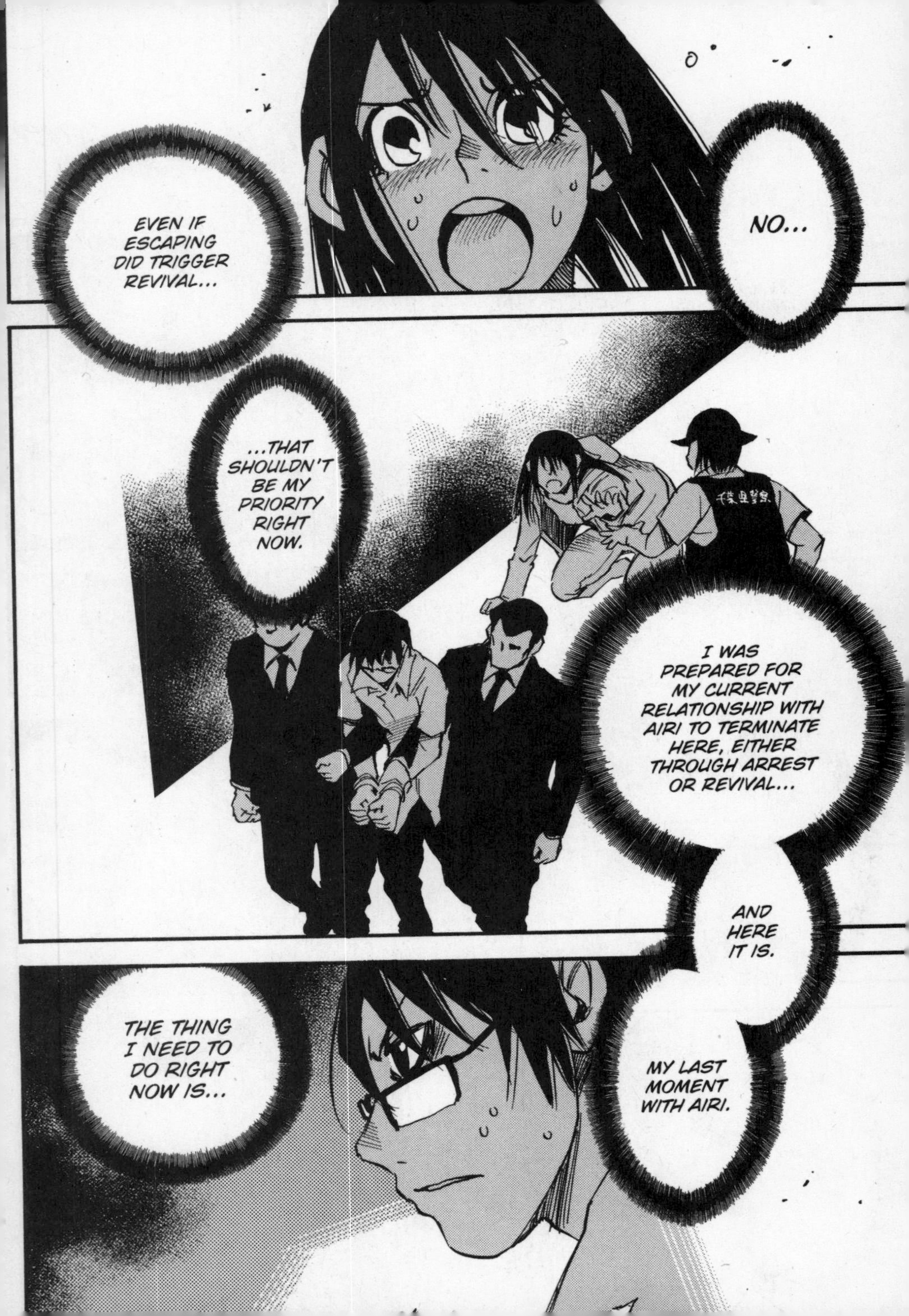
NO...
EVEN IF ESCAPING DID TRIGGER REVIVAL...
...THAT SHOULDN'T BE MY PRIORITY RIGHT NOW.
I WAS PREPARED FOR MY CURRENT RELATIONSHIP WITH AIRI TO TERMINATE HERE, EITHER THROUGH ARREST OR REVIVAL...
AND HERE IT IS.
THE THING I NEED TO DO RIGHT NOW IS...
MY LAST MOMENT WITH AIRI.

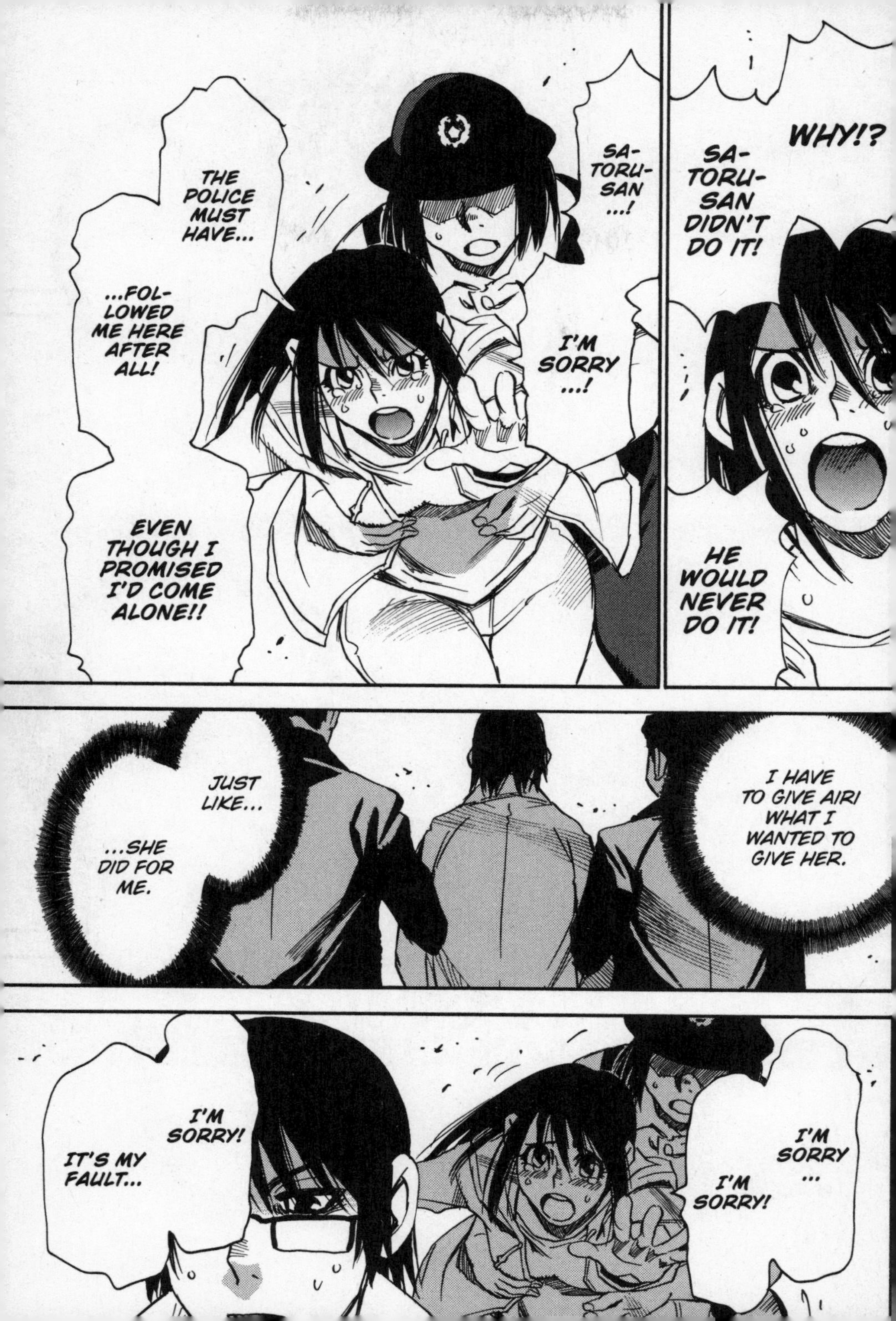
WHY!?
SA-TORU-SAN DIDN'T DO IT!
HE WOULD NEVER DO IT!
SA-TORU-SAN ...!
I'M SORRY ...!
THE POLICE MUST HAVE...
...FOL-LOWED ME HERE AFTER ALL!
EVEN THOUGH I PROMISED I'D COME ALONE!!
I HAVE TO GIVE AIRI WHAT I WANTED TO GIVE HER.
JUST LIKE...
...SHE DID FOR ME.
I'M SORRY ...
I'M SORRY!
I'M SORRY!
IT'S MY FAULT...

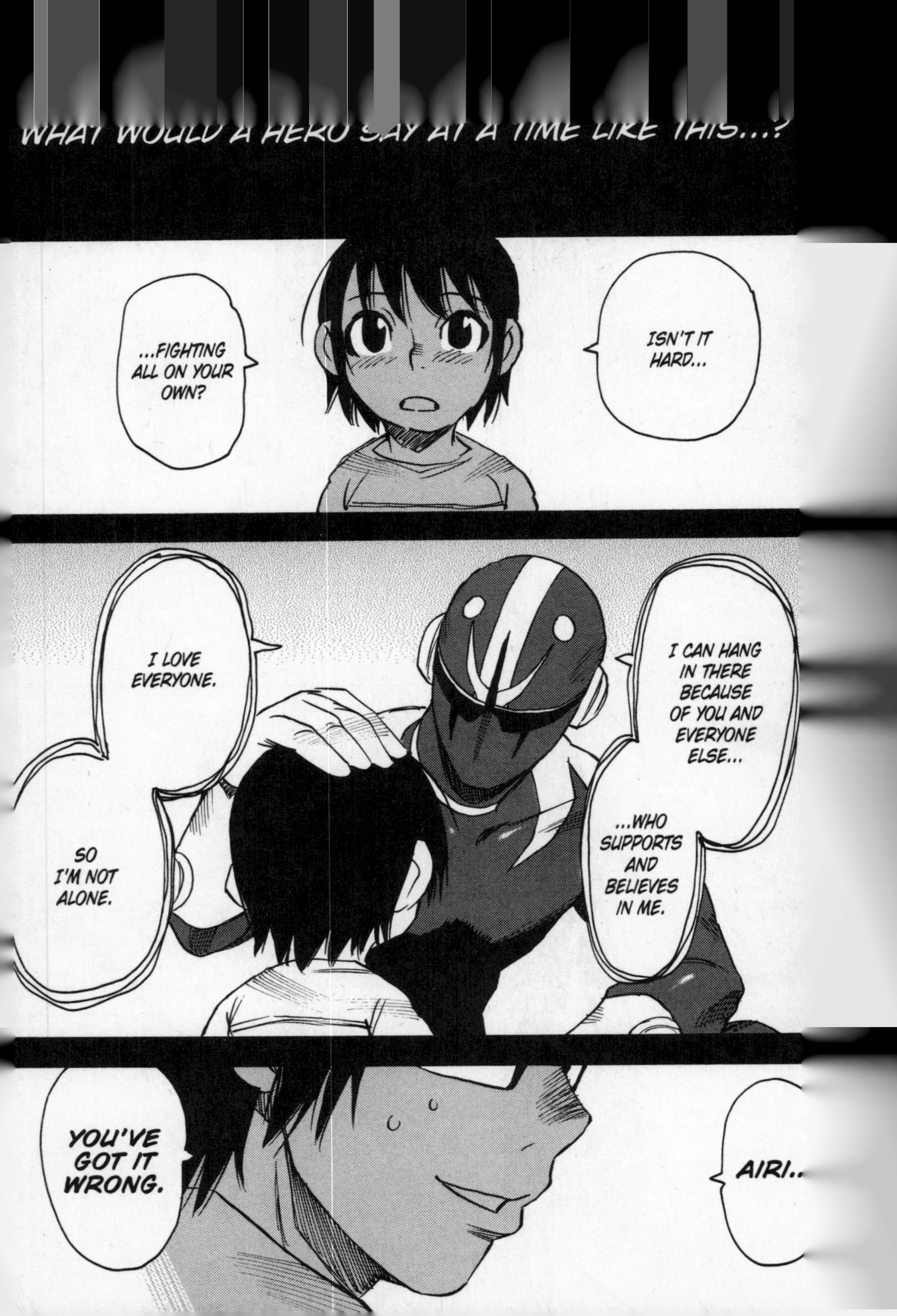
WHAT WOULD A HERO SAY AT A TIME LIKE THIS...?
ISN'T IT HARD...
...FIGHTING ALL ON YOUR OWN?
I CAN HANG IN THERE BECAUSE OF YOU AND EVERYONE ELSE...
...WHO SUPPORTS AND BELIEVES IN ME.
I LOVE EVERYONE.
SO I'M NOT ALONE.
AIRI...
YOU'VE GOT IT WRONG.

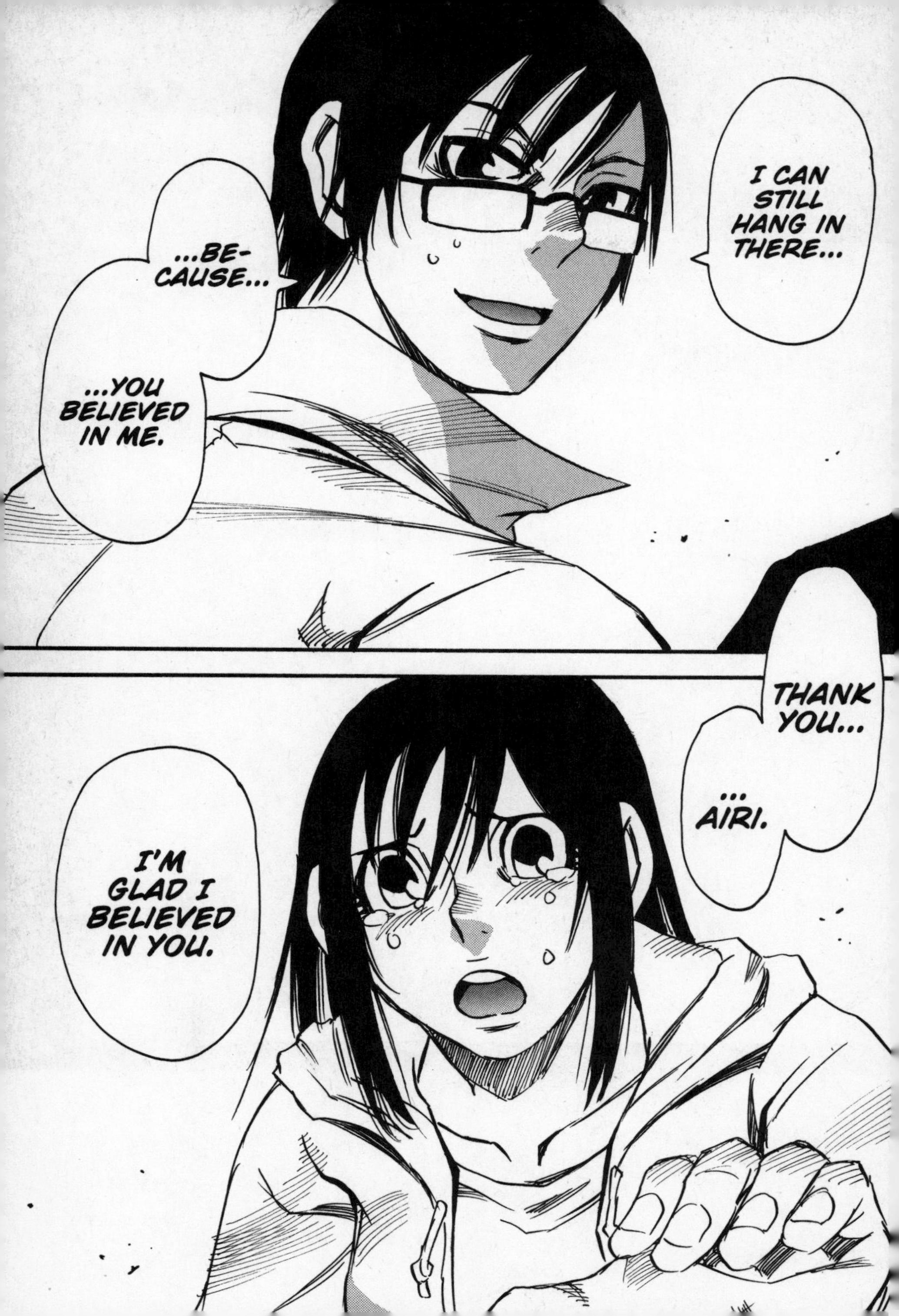
I CAN STILL HANG IN THERE...
...BE-CAUSE...
...YOU BELIEVED IN ME.
THANK YOU...
... AIRI.
I'M GLAD I BELIEVED IN YOU.

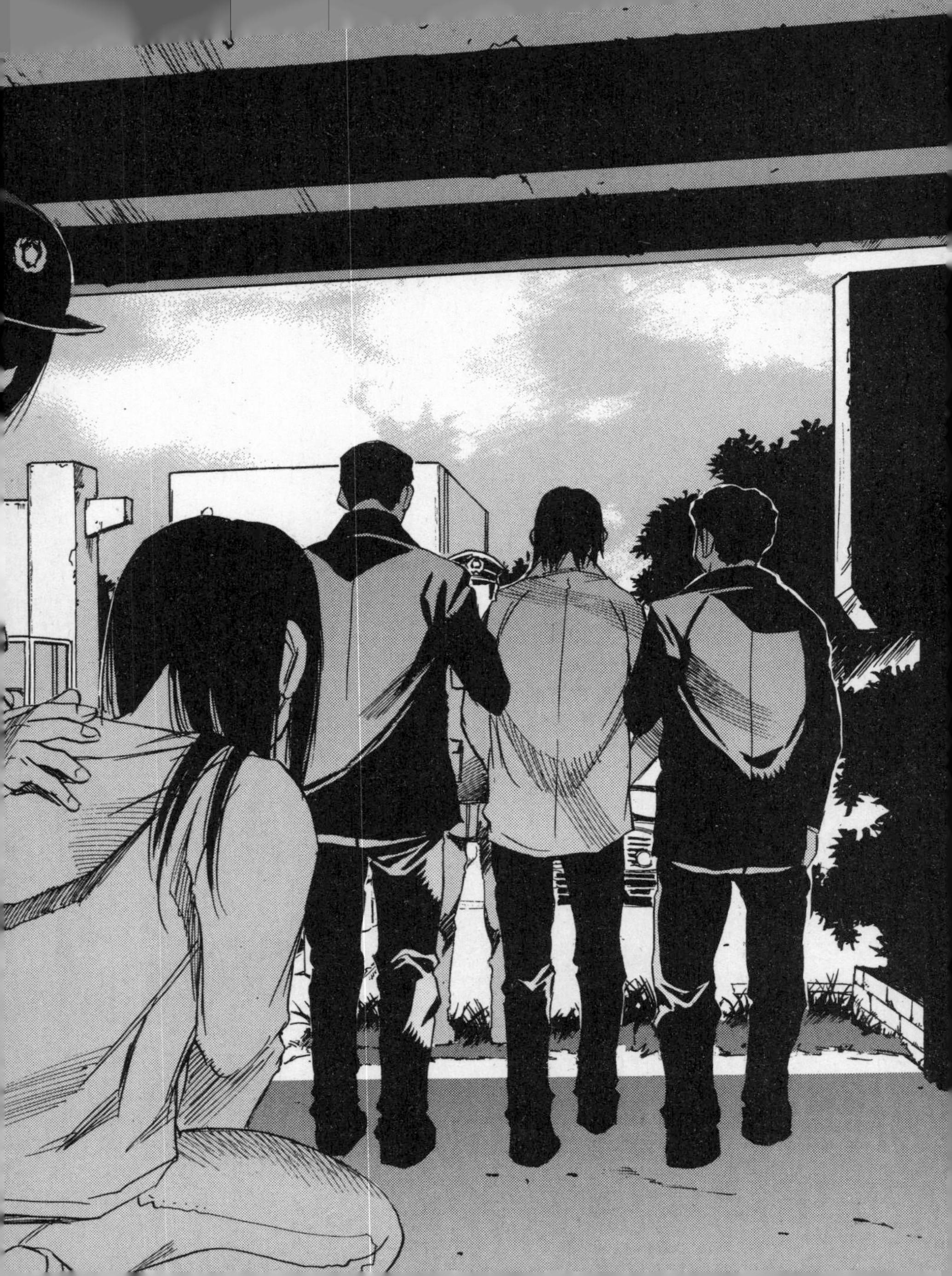

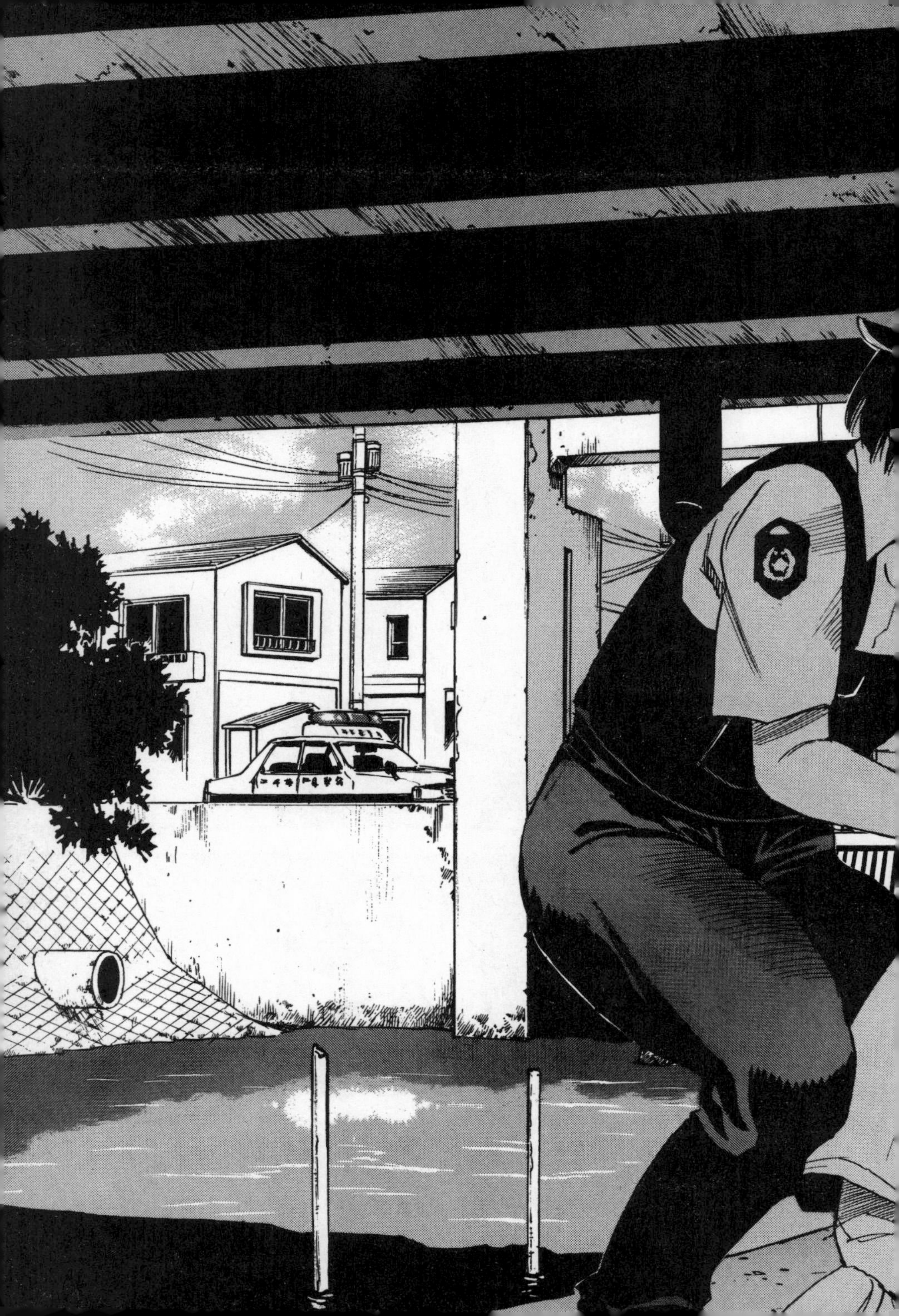

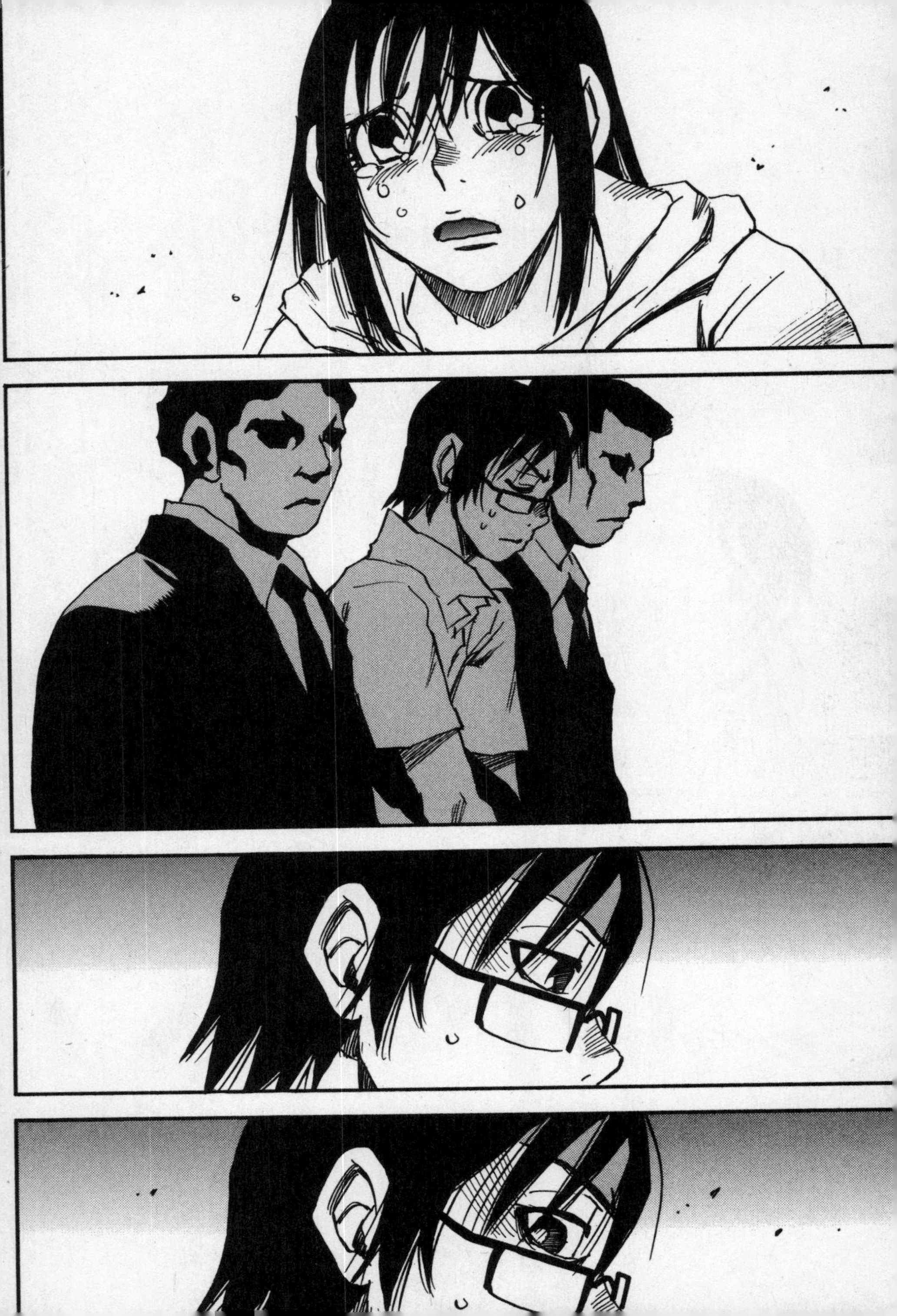

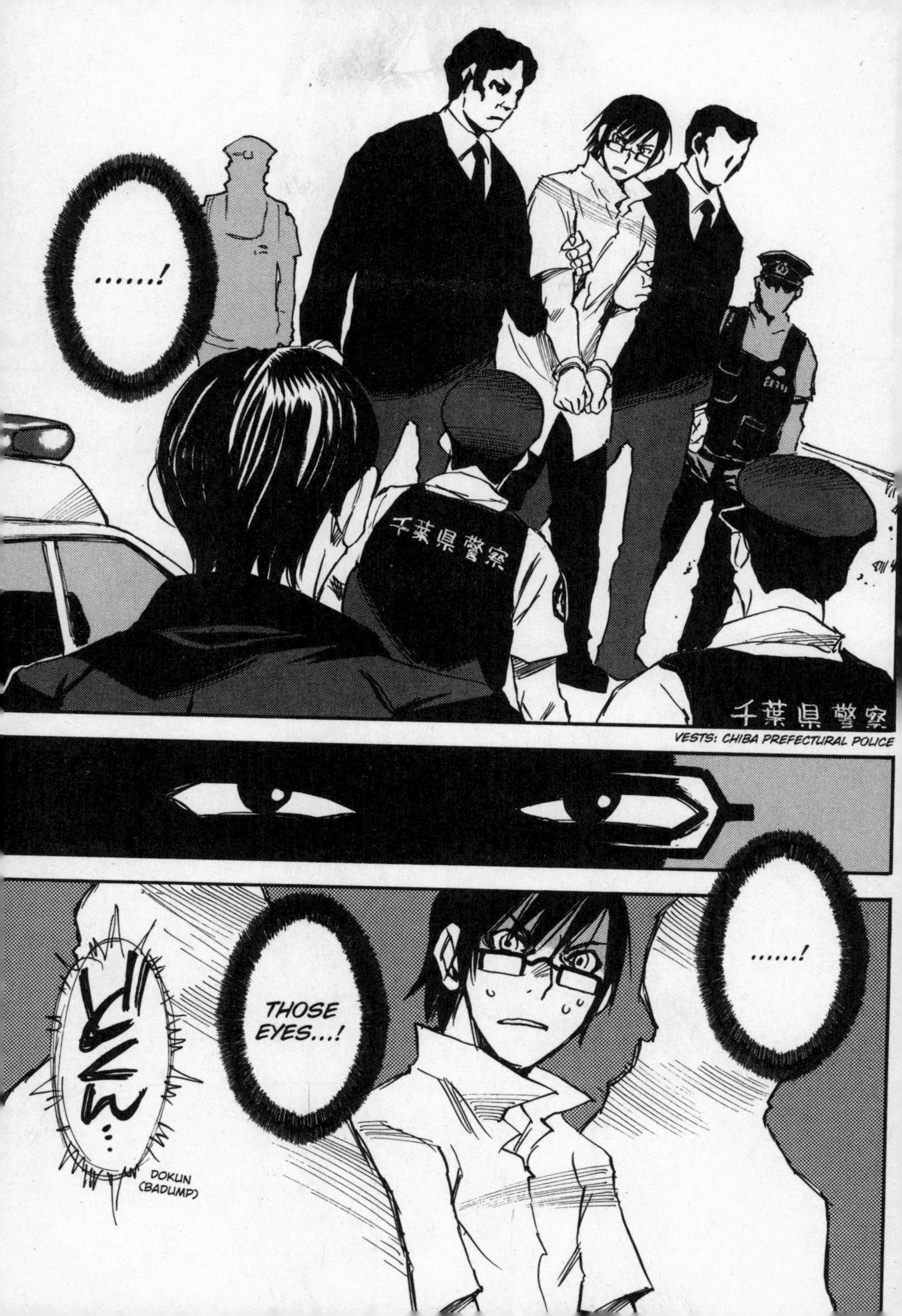
......!
千葉県警察
千葉県警察
VESTS: CHIBA PREFECTURAL POLICE
......!
THOSE EYES...!
どくん...
DOKUN (BADUMP)

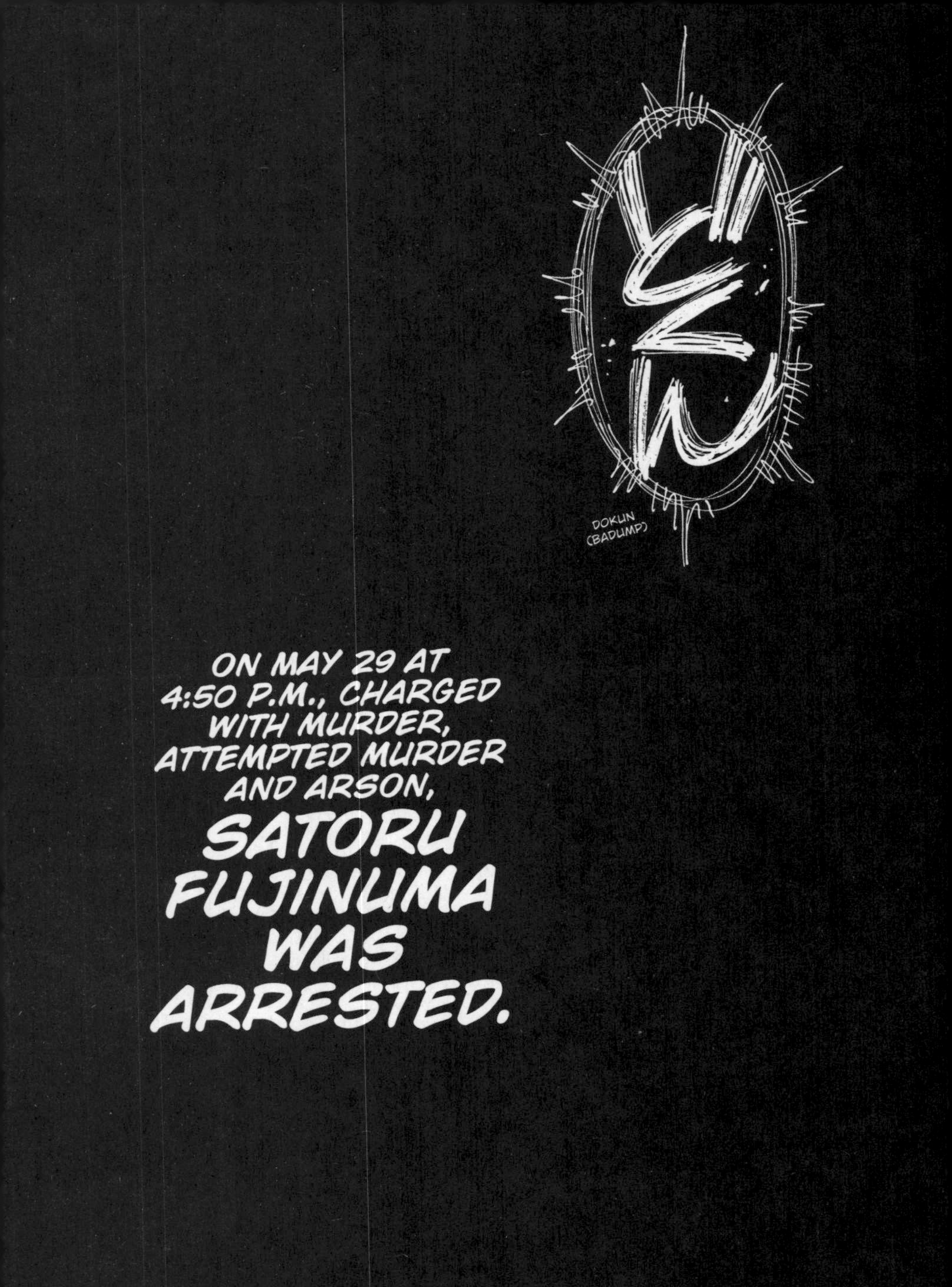
DOKUN (BADUMP)
ON MAY 29 AT 4:50 P.M., CHARGED WITH MURDER, ATTEMPTED MURDER AND ARSON,
SATORU FUJINUMA WAS ARRESTED.

#18 END

STAFF

Kei Sanbe

Yoichiro Tomita
Manami 18-years-old
Shuuei Takagi
Zukku Ozaki
Kouji Kikuta

Keishi Kanesada

BOOK DESIGN
Yukio Hoshino
VOLARE inc.

EDITOR
Tsunenori Matsumiya

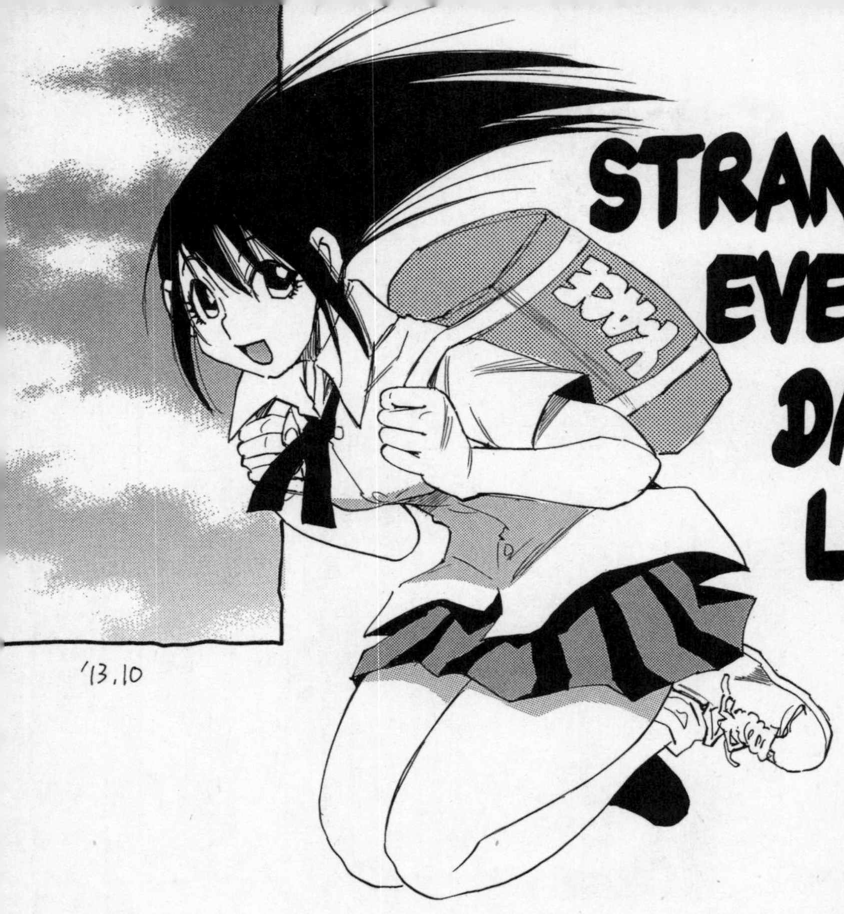

STRANGE, EVERY-DAY LIFE

'13.10

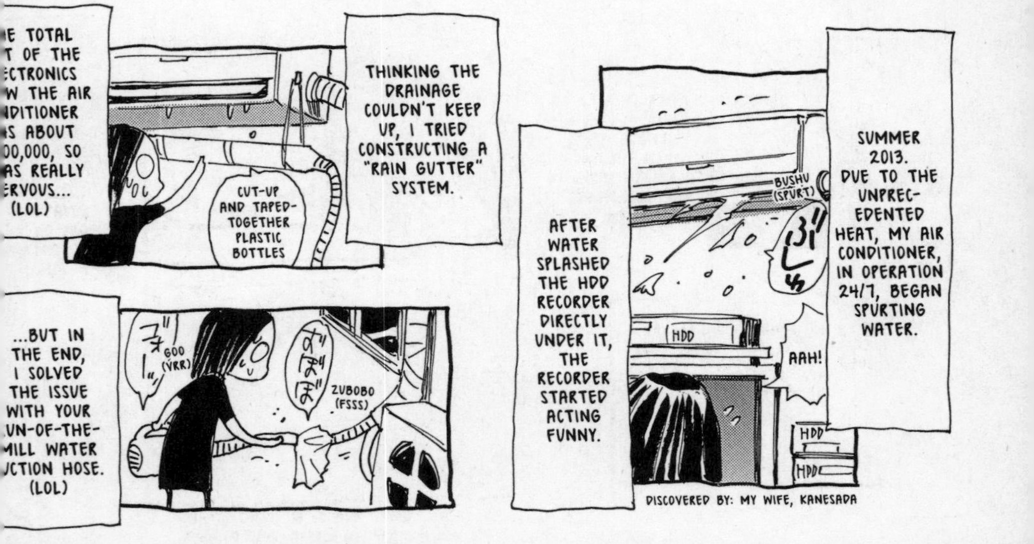

SUMMER 2013. DUE TO THE UNPREC-EDENTED HEAT, MY AIR CONDITIONER, IN OPERATION 24/7, BEGAN SPURTING WATER.
BUSHU (SPURT)
AAH!
HDD
HDD
HDD
AFTER WATER SPLASHED THE HDD RECORDER DIRECTLY UNDER IT, THE RECORDER STARTED ACTING FUNNY.
DISCOVERED BY: MY WIFE, KANESADA
THINKING THE DRAINAGE COULDN'T KEEP UP, I TRIED CONSTRUCTING A "RAIN GUTTER" SYSTEM.
CUT-UP AND TAPED-TOGETHER PLASTIC BOTTLES
E TOTAL T OF THE ECTRONICS W THE AIR NDITIONER S ABOUT 00,000, SO AS REALLY ERVOUS... (LOL)
ZUBOBO (FSSS)
GOO (VRR)
...BUT IN THE END, I SOLVED THE ISSUE WITH YOUR UN-OF-THE-MILL WATER UCTION HOSE. (LOL)

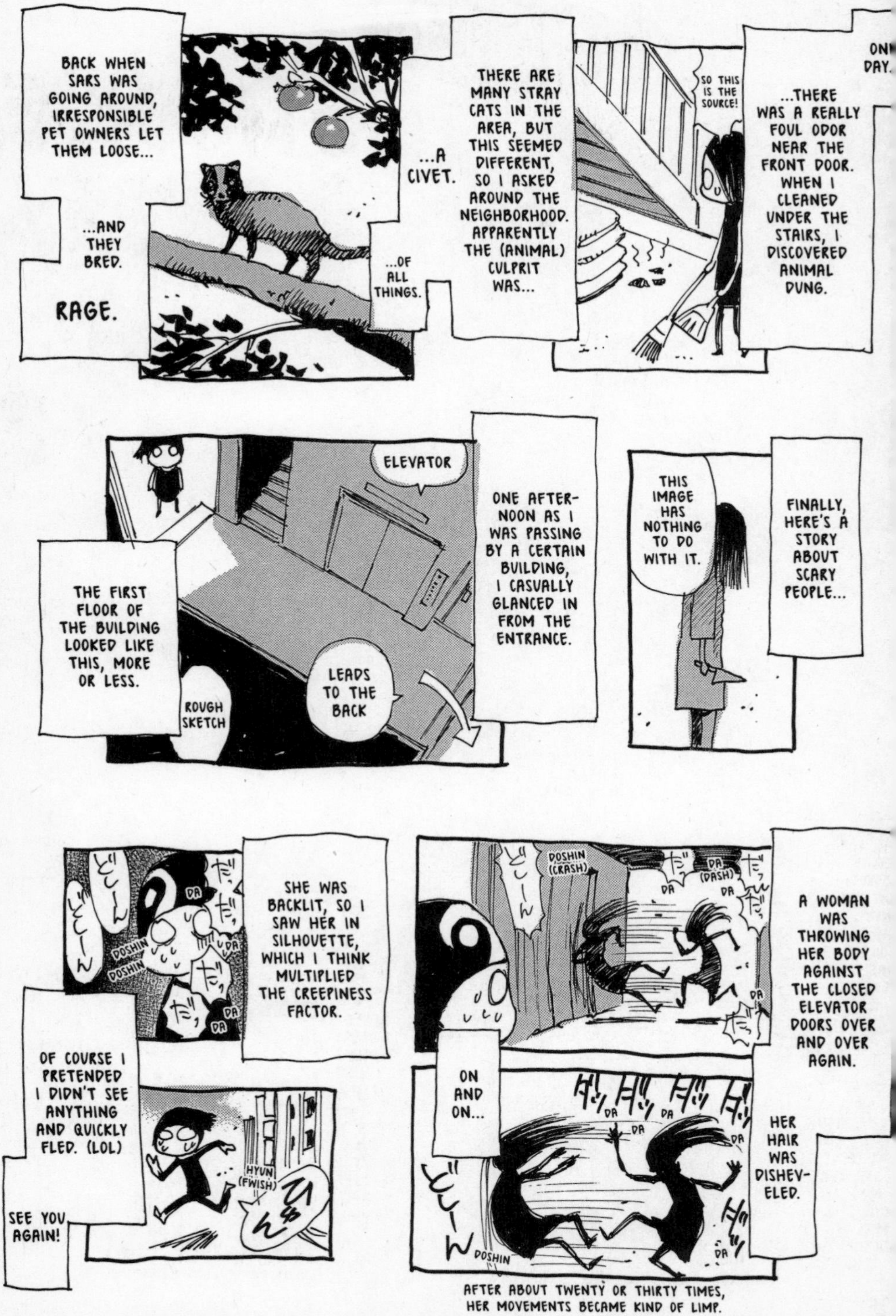

ONE DAY.
...THERE WAS A REALLY FOUL ODOR NEAR THE FRONT DOOR. WHEN I CLEANED UNDER THE STAIRS, I DISCOVERED ANIMAL DUNG.
SO THIS IS THE SOURCE!
THERE ARE MANY STRAY CATS IN THE AREA, BUT THIS SEEMED DIFFERENT, SO I ASKED AROUND THE NEIGHBORHOOD. APPARENTLY THE (ANIMAL) CULPRIT WAS...
...A CIVET.
...OF ALL THINGS.
BACK WHEN SARS WAS GOING AROUND, IRRESPONSIBLE PET OWNERS LET THEM LOOSE...
...AND THEY BRED.
RAGE.
FINALLY, HERE'S A STORY ABOUT SCARY PEOPLE...
THIS IMAGE HAS NOTHING TO DO WITH IT.
ONE AFTERNOON AS I WAS PASSING BY A CERTAIN BUILDING, I CASUALLY GLANCED IN FROM THE ENTRANCE.
ELEVATOR
LEADS TO THE BACK
ROUGH SKETCH
THE FIRST FLOOR OF THE BUILDING LOOKED LIKE THIS, MORE OR LESS.
A WOMAN WAS THROWING HER BODY AGAINST THE CLOSED ELEVATOR DOORS OVER AND OVER AGAIN.
DA (DASH)
DA
DA
DOSHIN (CRASH)
DA
SHE WAS BACKLIT, SO I SAW HER IN SILHOUETTE, WHICH I THINK MULTIPLIED THE CREEPINESS FACTOR.
DA
DA
DOSHIN
DOSHIN
DA
DA
HER HAIR WAS DISHEVELED.
ON AND ON...
DA
DA
DA
DA
DA
DOSHIN
AFTER ABOUT TWENTY OR THIRTY TIMES, HER MOVEMENTS BECAME KIND OF LIMP.
OF COURSE I PRETENDED I DIDN'T SEE ANYTHING AND QUICKLY FLED. (LOL)
HYUN (FWISH)
SEE YOU AGAIN!

erased

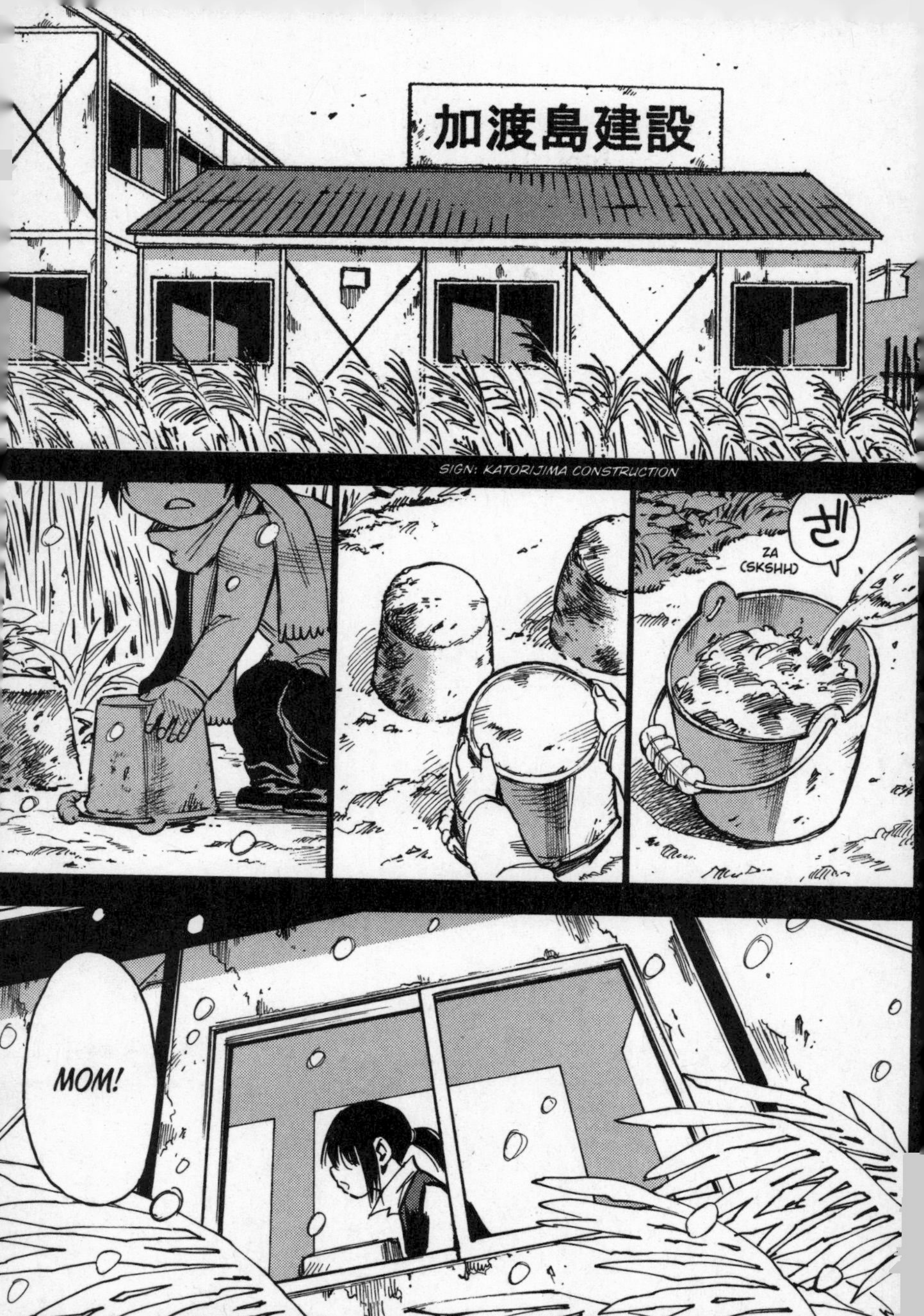
加渡島建設
SIGN: KATORIJIMA CONSTRUCTION
ざ
ZA (SKSHH)
MOM!

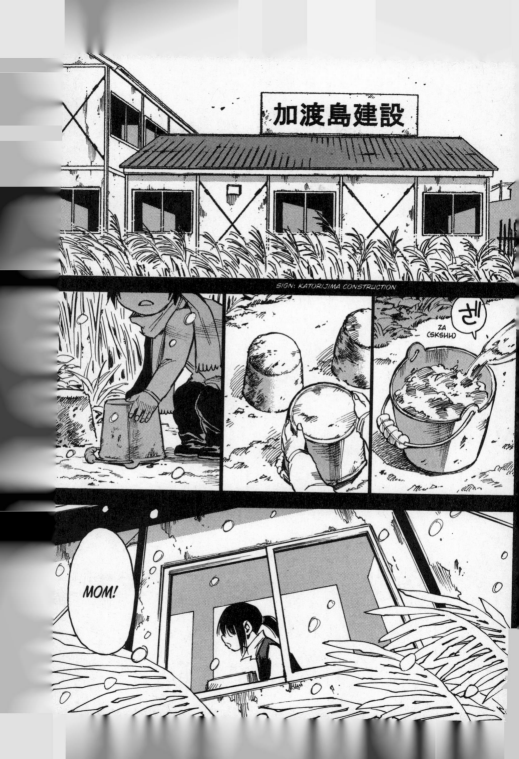

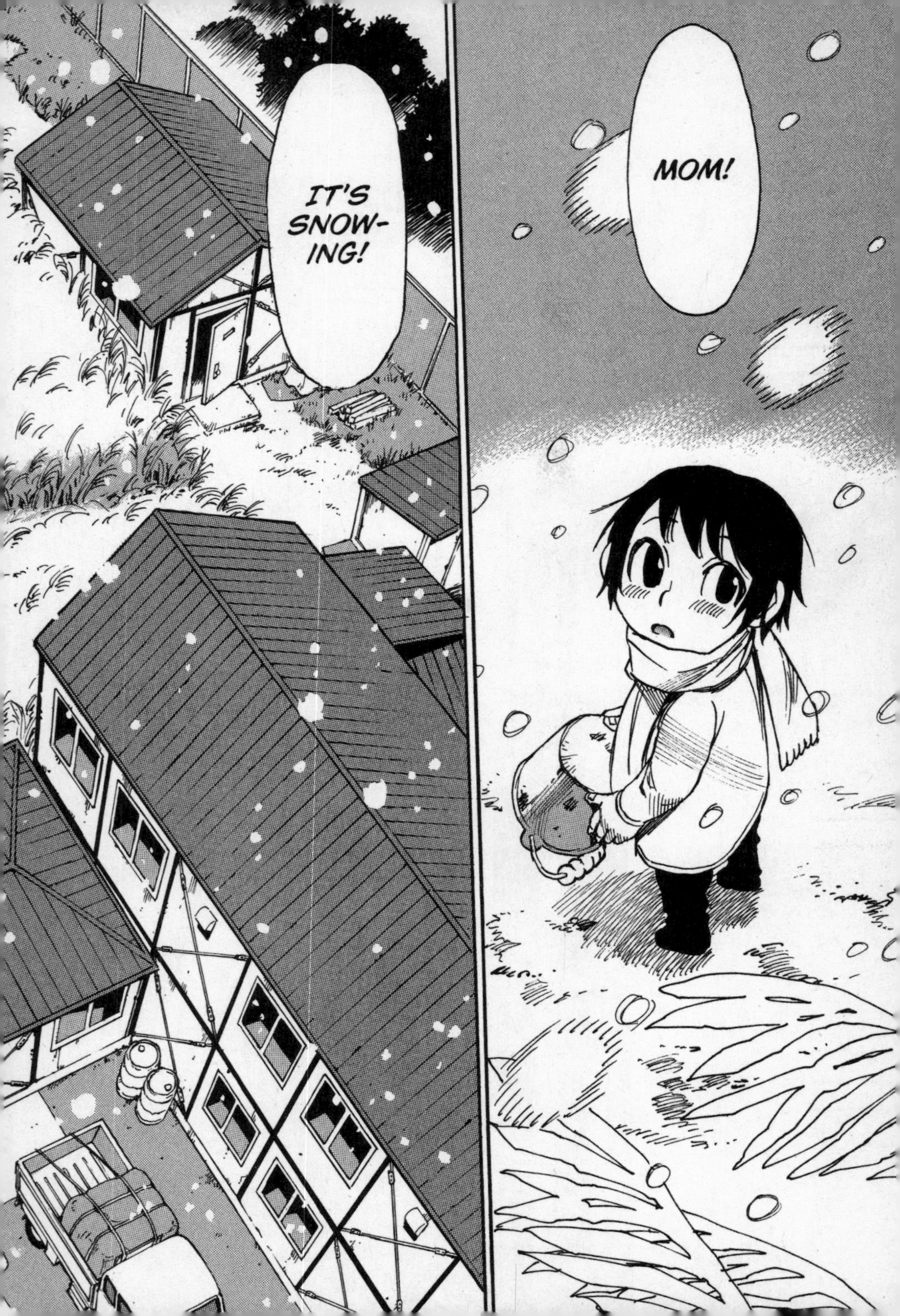
MOM!
IT'S SNOW-ING!

#19: Last Chance, February 1988

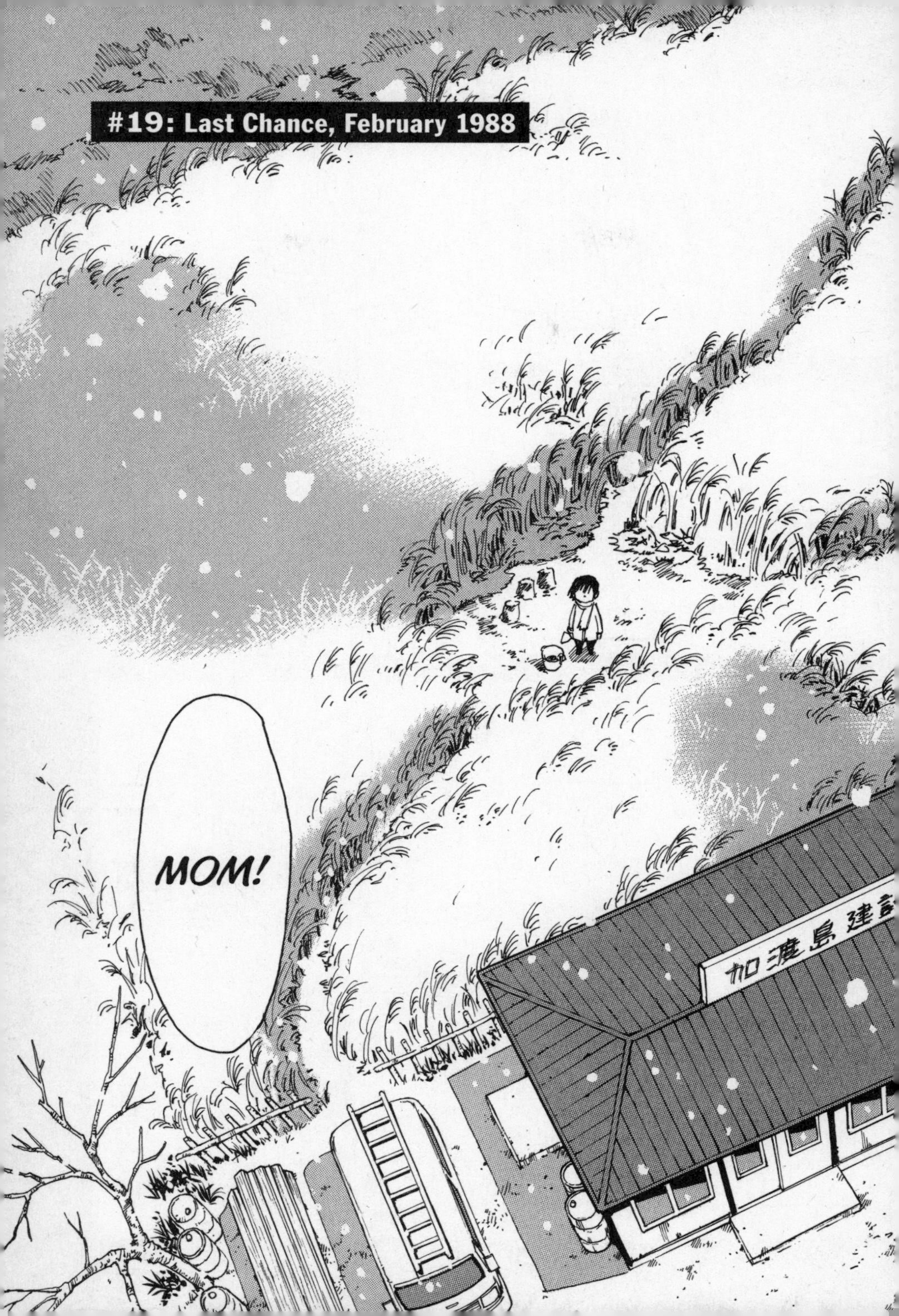
MOM!
加渡島建

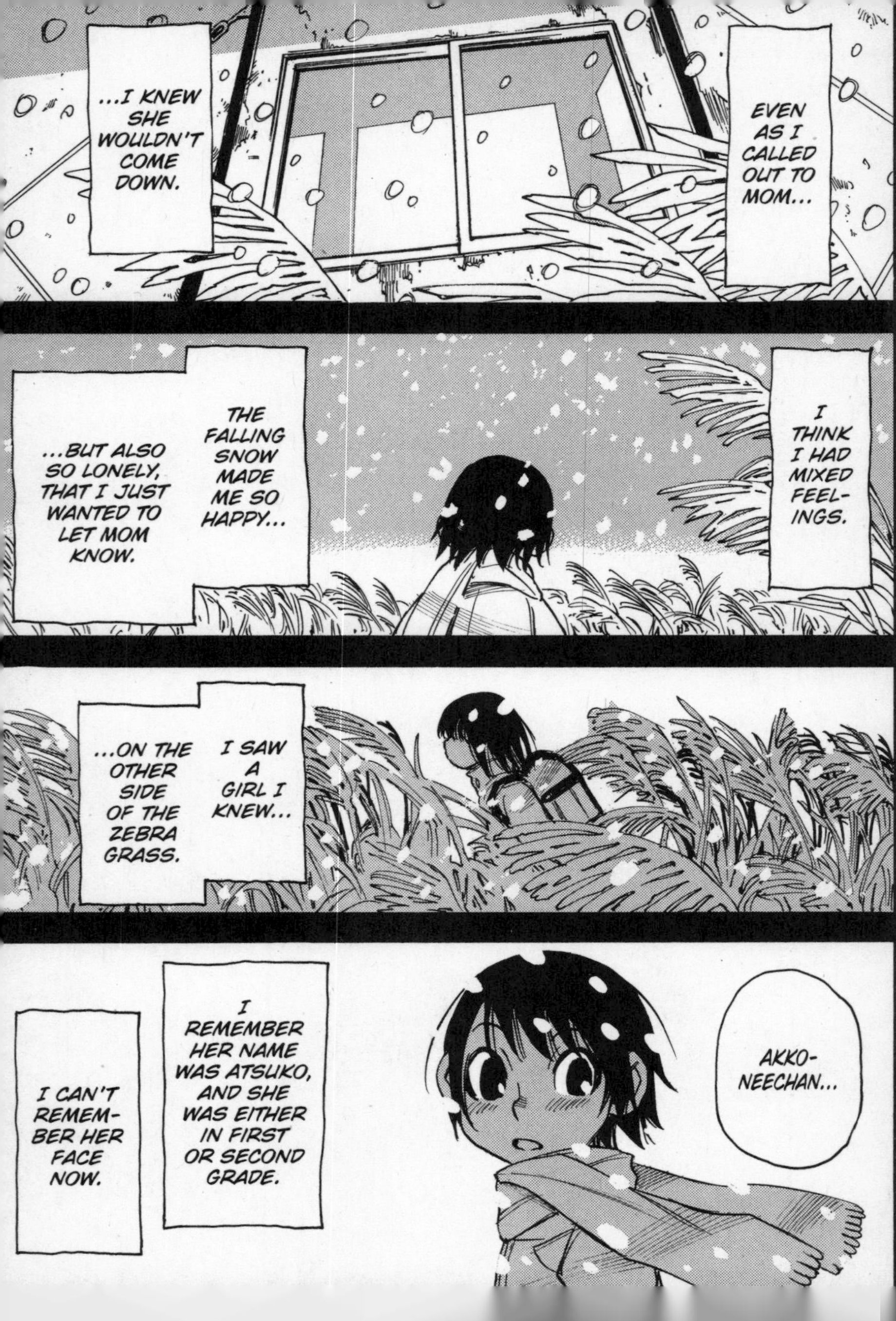
EVEN AS I CALLED OUT TO MOM...
...I KNEW SHE WOULDN'T COME DOWN.
I THINK I HAD MIXED FEEL-INGS.
THE FALLING SNOW MADE ME SO HAPPY...
...BUT ALSO SO LONELY, THAT I JUST WANTED TO LET MOM KNOW.
I SAW A GIRL I KNEW...
...ON THE OTHER SIDE OF THE ZEBRA GRASS.
AKKO-NEECHAN...
I REMEMBER HER NAME WAS ATSUKO, AND SHE WAS EITHER IN FIRST OR SECOND GRADE.
I CAN'T REMEM-BER HER FACE NOW.

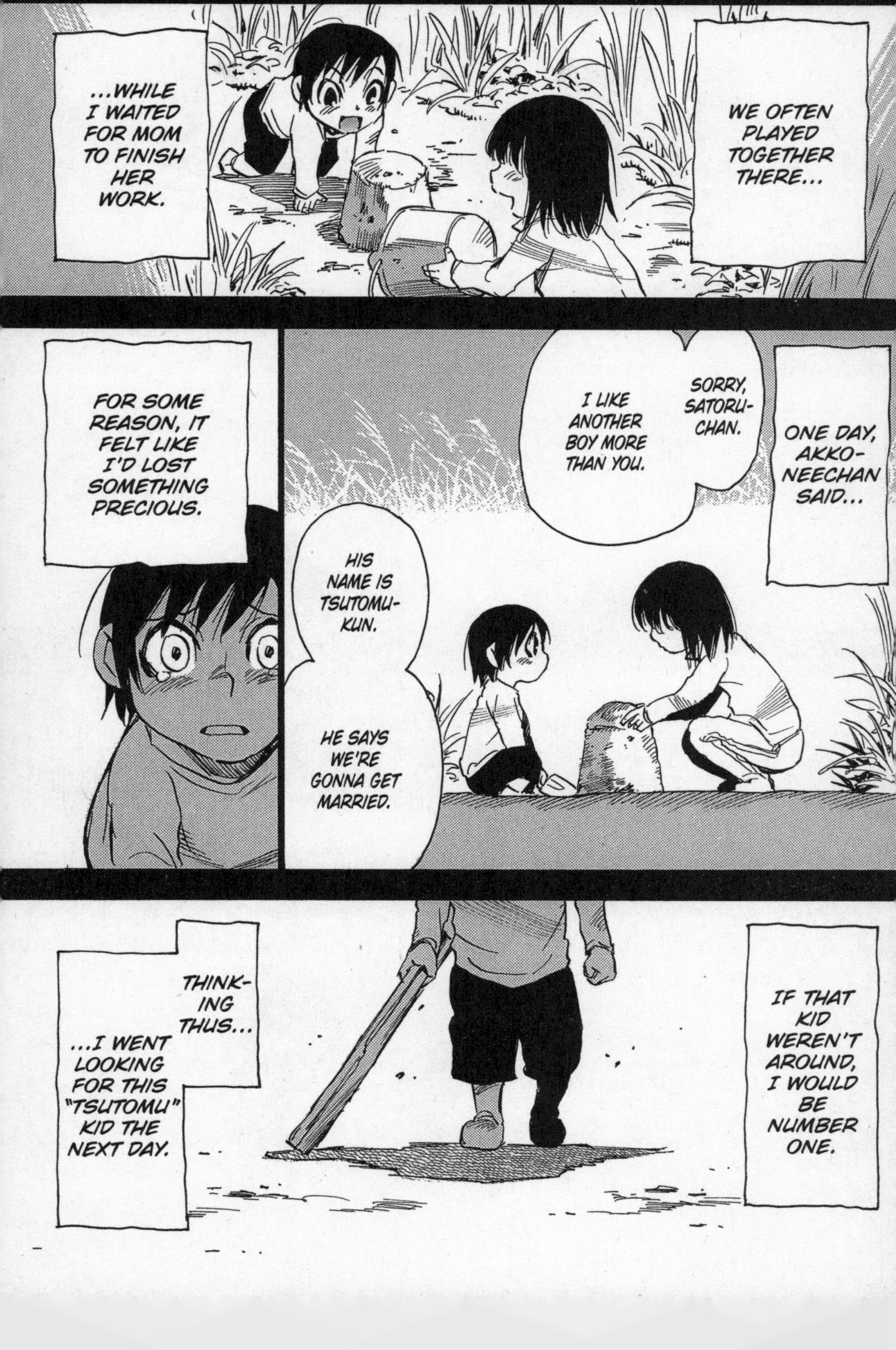
WE OFTEN PLAYED TOGETHER THERE...
...WHILE I WAITED FOR MOM TO FINISH HER WORK.
ONE DAY, AKKO-NEECHAN SAID...
SORRY, SATORU-CHAN.
I LIKE ANOTHER BOY MORE THAN YOU.
HIS NAME IS TSUTOMU-KUN.
HE SAYS WE'RE GONNA GET MARRIED.
FOR SOME REASON, IT FELT LIKE I'D LOST SOMETHING PRECIOUS.
IF THAT KID WEREN'T AROUND, I WOULD BE NUMBER ONE.
THINKING THUS...
...I WENT LOOKING FOR THIS "TSUTOMU" KID THE NEXT DAY.

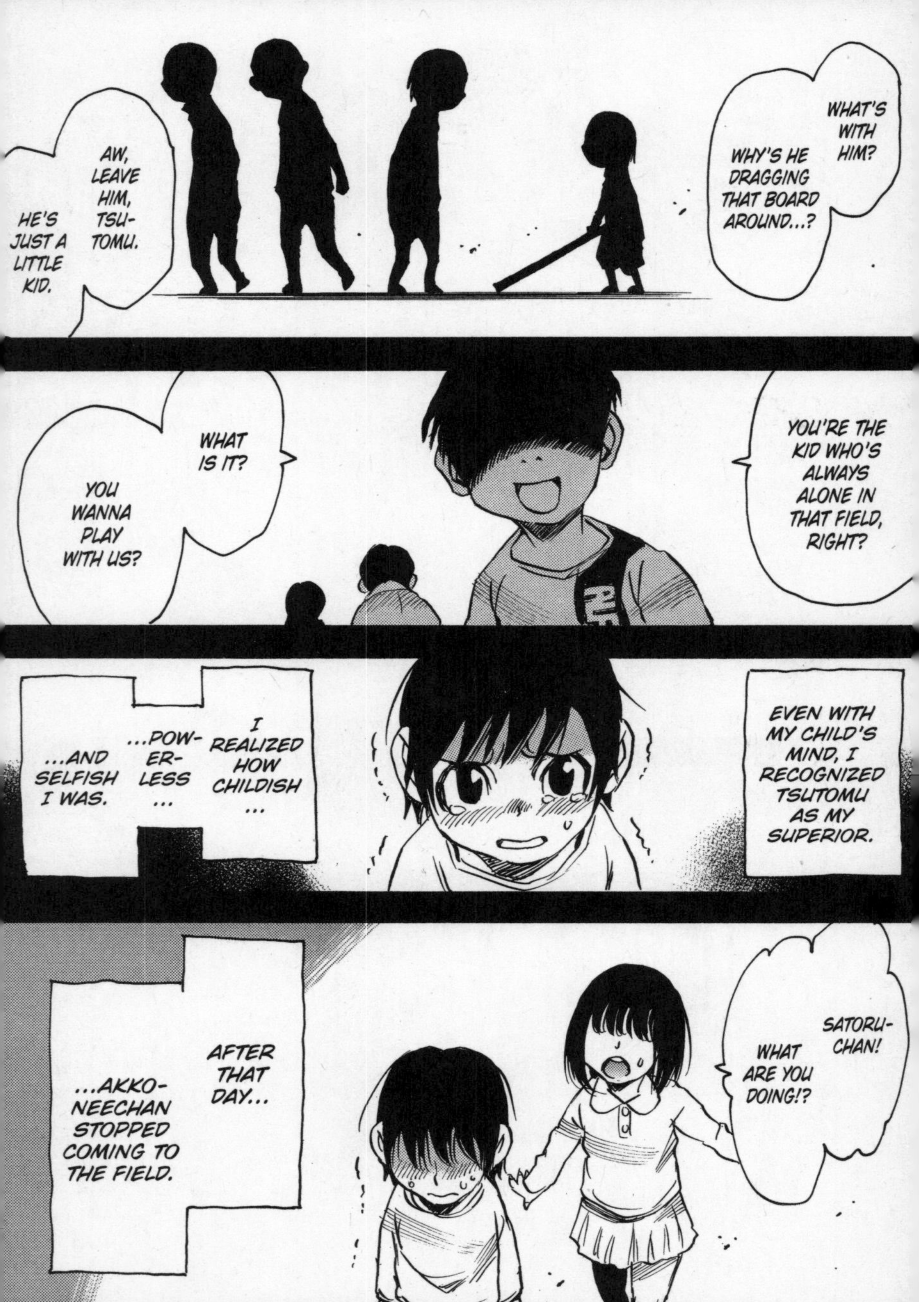
WHAT'S WITH HIM?
WHY'S HE DRAGGING THAT BOARD AROUND...?
AW, LEAVE HIM, TSU-TOMU.
HE'S JUST A LITTLE KID.
YOU'RE THE KID WHO'S ALWAYS ALONE IN THAT FIELD, RIGHT?
WHAT IS IT?
YOU WANNA PLAY WITH US?
EVEN WITH MY CHILD'S MIND, I RECOGNIZED TSUTOMU AS MY SUPERIOR.
I REALIZED HOW CHILDISH...
...POW-ER-LESS...
...AND SELFISH I WAS.
SATORU-CHAN!
WHAT ARE YOU DOING!?
AFTER THAT DAY...
...AKKO-NEECHAN STOPPED COMING TO THE FIELD.

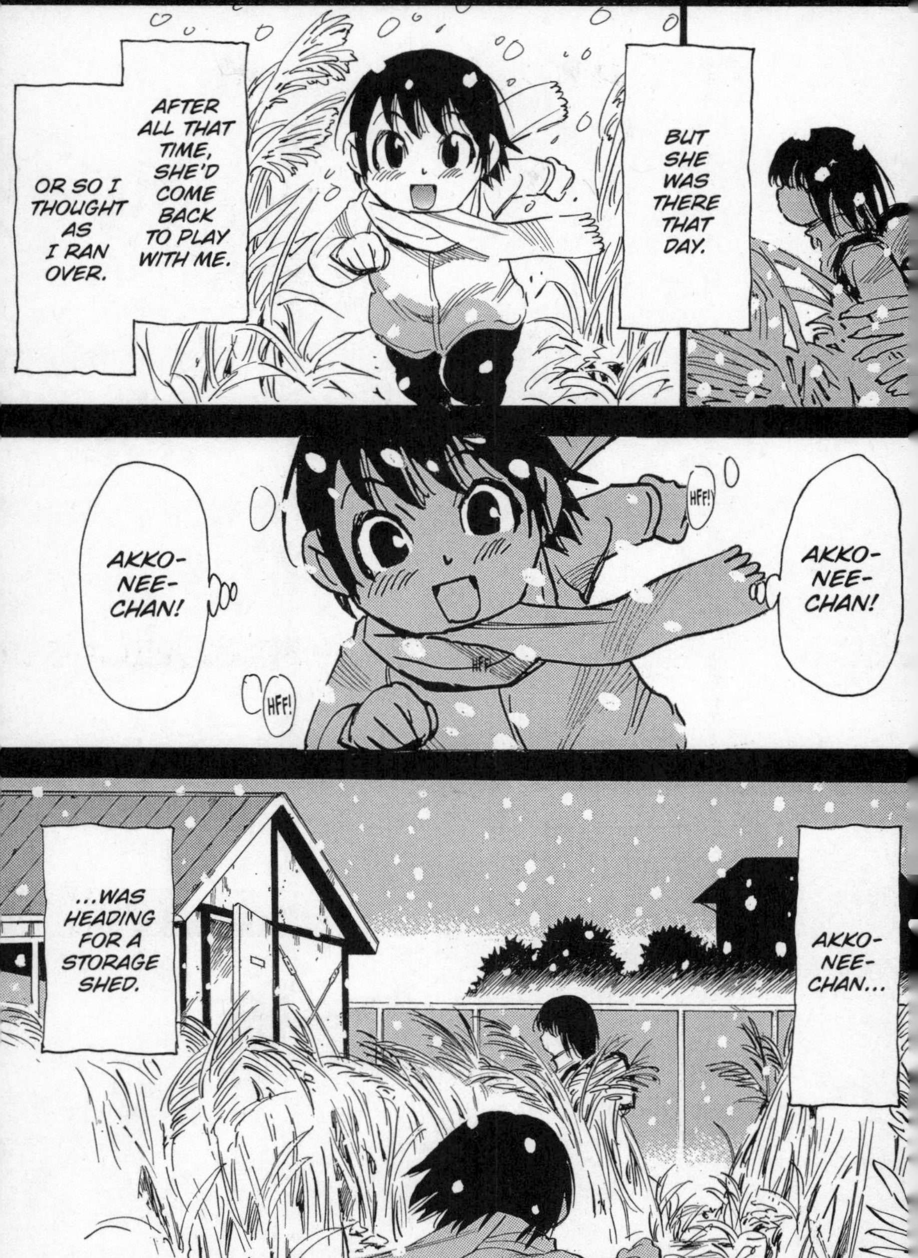
BUT SHE WAS THERE THAT DAY.
AFTER ALL THAT TIME, SHE'D COME BACK TO PLAY WITH ME.
OR SO I THOUGHT AS I RAN OVER.
AKKO-NEE-CHAN!
HFF!
AKKO-NEE-CHAN!
HFF
HFF!
AKKO-NEE-CHAN...
...WAS HEADING FOR A STORAGE SHED.

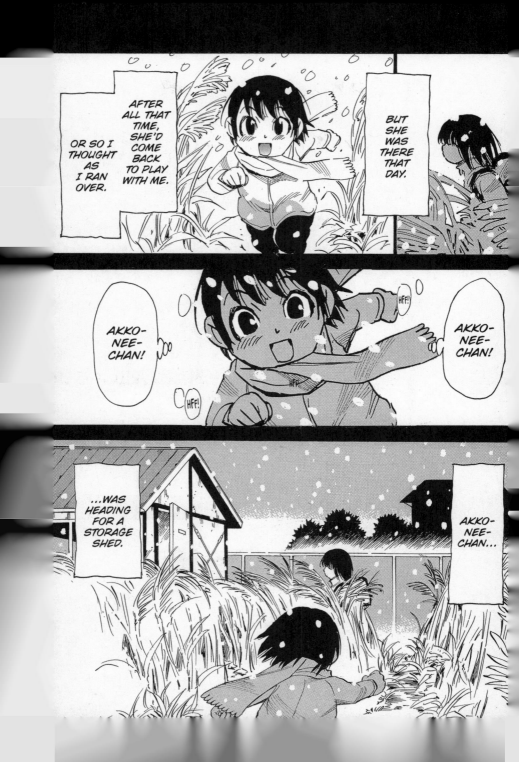

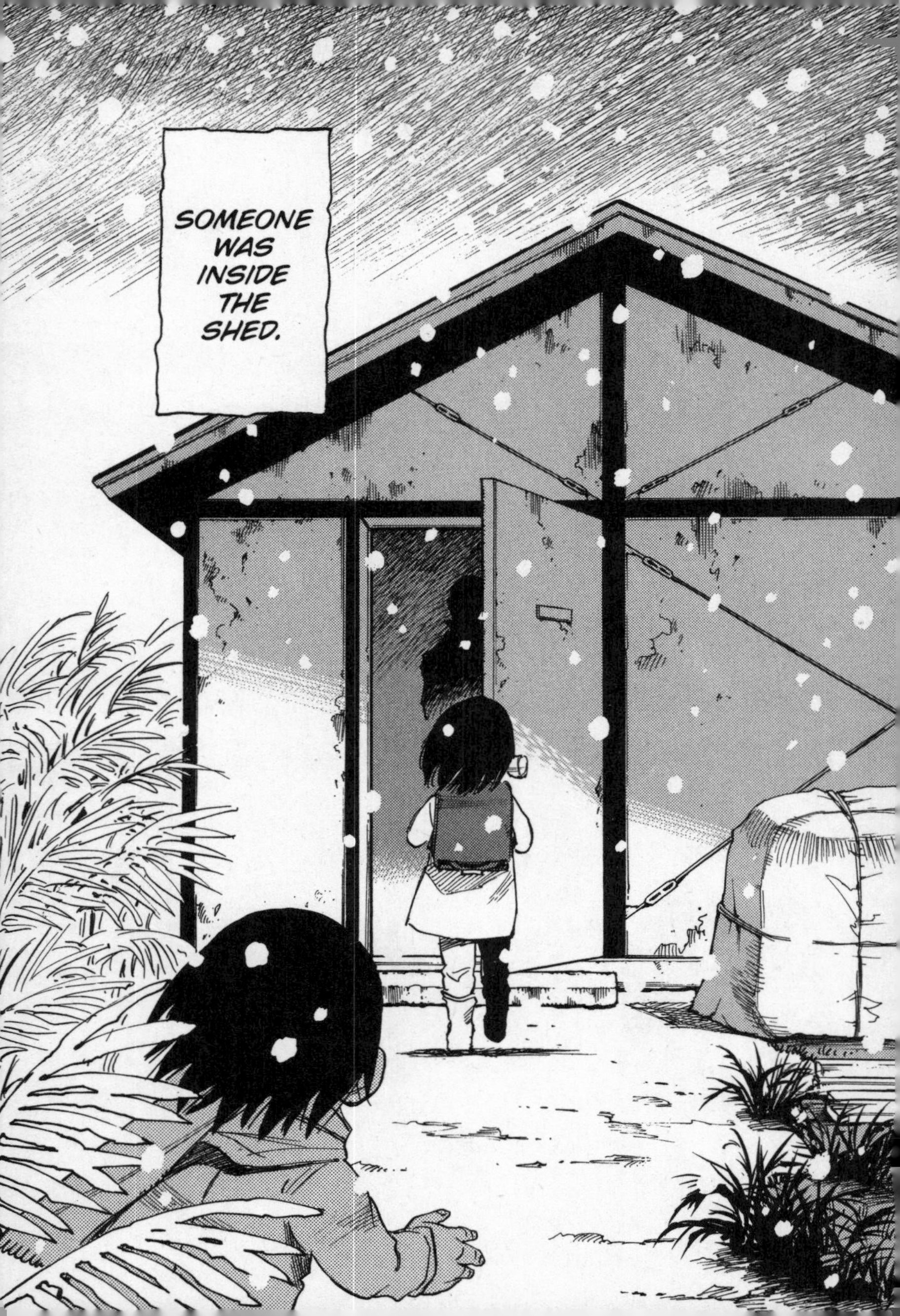
SOMEONE WAS INSIDE THE SHED.

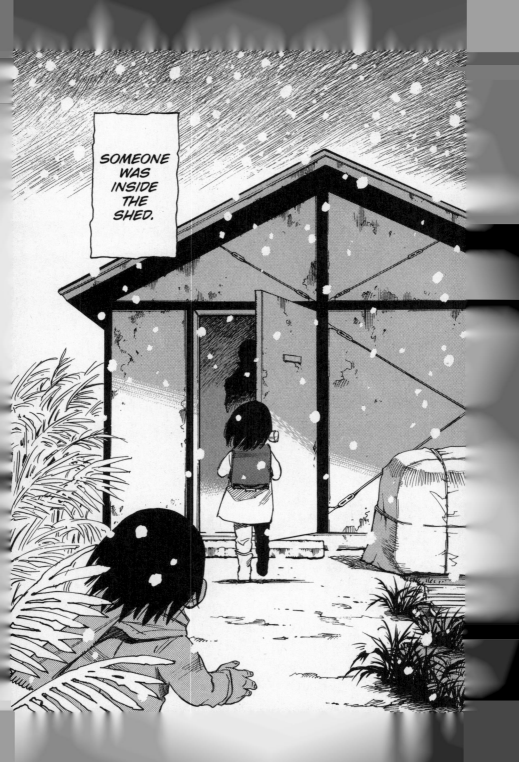

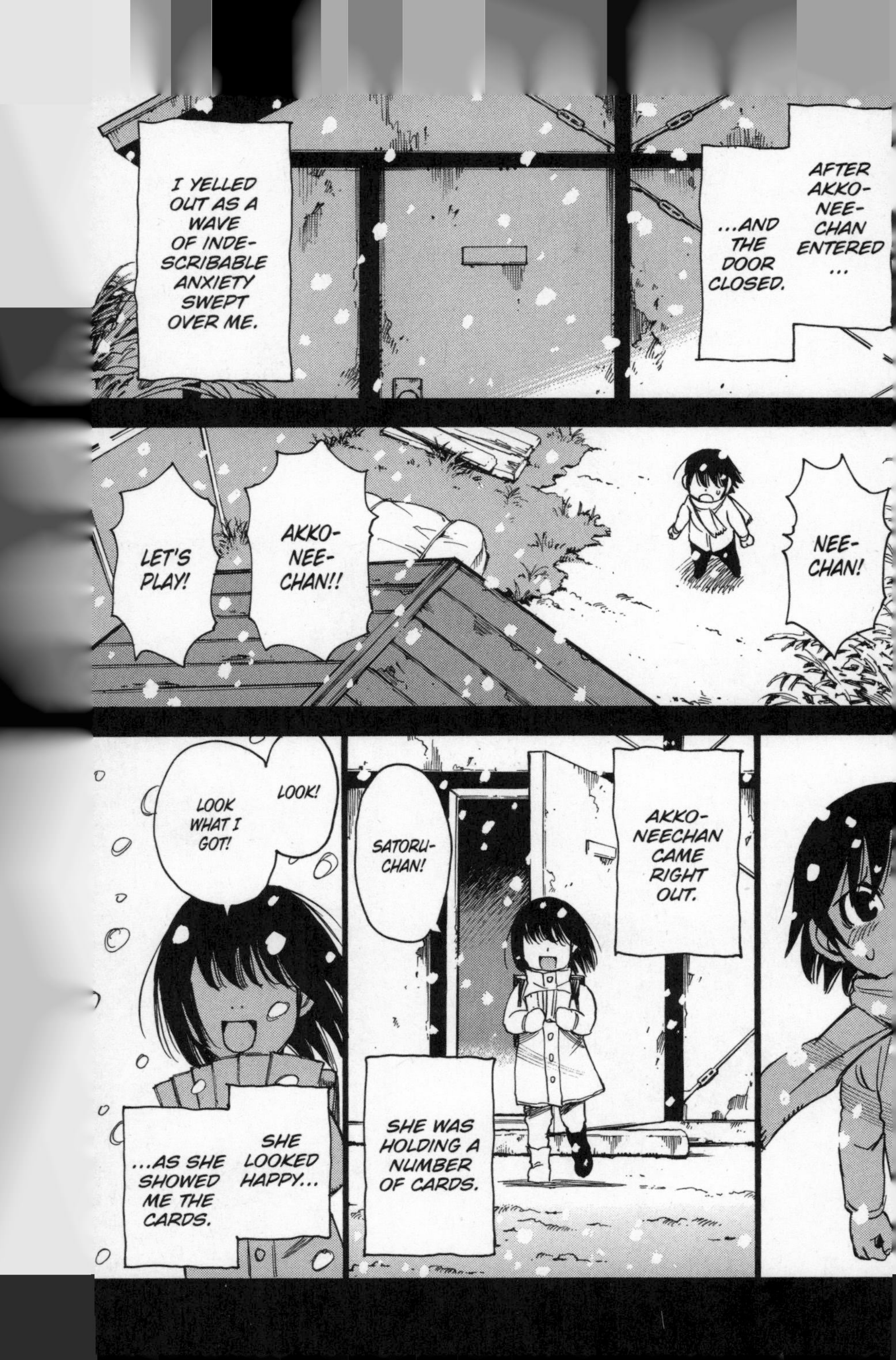
AFTER AKKO-NEE-CHAN ENTERED ...
...AND THE DOOR CLOSED.
I YELLED OUT AS A WAVE OF INDE-SCRIBABLE ANXIETY SWEPT OVER ME.
NEE-CHAN!
AKKO-NEE-CHAN!!
LET'S PLAY!
AKKO-NEECHAN CAME RIGHT OUT.
SATORU-CHAN!
SHE WAS HOLDING A NUMBER OF CARDS.
LOOK!
LOOK WHAT I GOT!
SHE LOOKED HAPPY...
...AS SHE SHOWED ME THE CARDS.

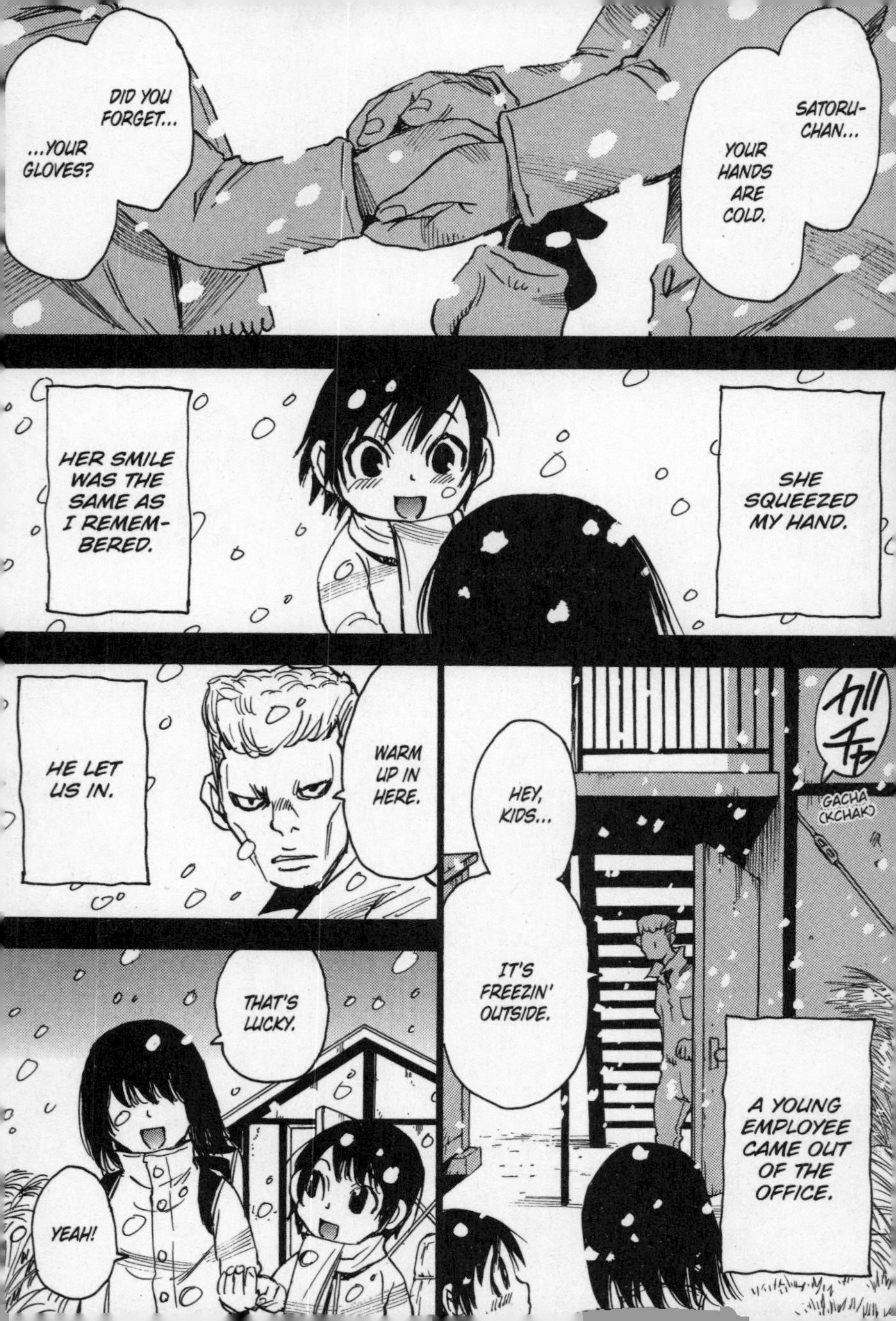
SATORU-CHAN...
YOUR HANDS ARE COLD.
DID YOU FORGET...
...YOUR GLOVES?
SHE SQUEEZED MY HAND.
HER SMILE WAS THE SAME AS I REMEMBERED.
ガチャ
GACHA (KCHAK)
HEY, KIDS...
IT'S FREEZIN' OUTSIDE.
A YOUNG EMPLOYEE CAME OUT OF THE OFFICE.
WARM UP IN HERE.
HE LET US IN.
THAT'S LUCKY.
YEAH!

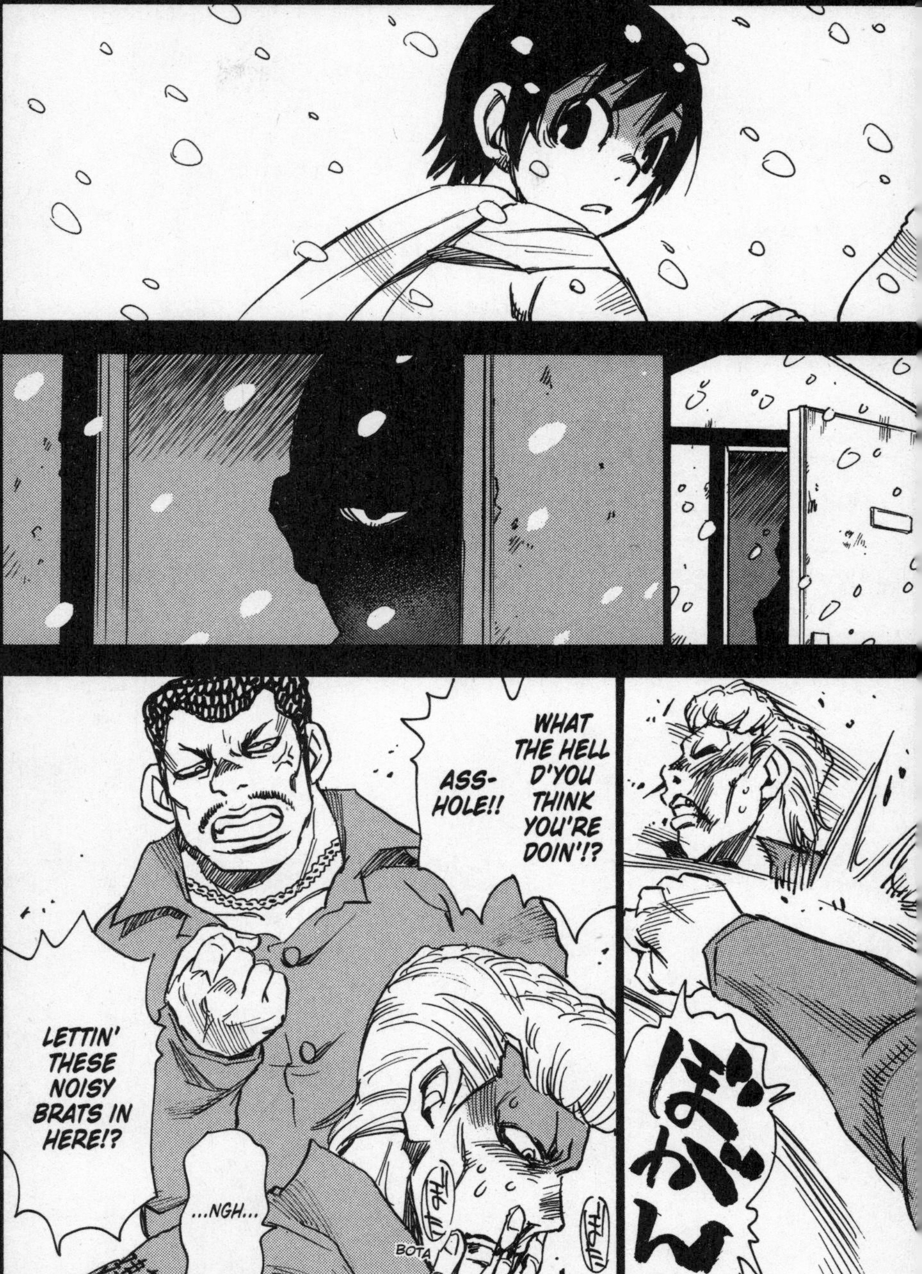

ぼがん
BOGAN (CRACK)
WHAT THE HELL D'YOU THINK YOU'RE DOIN'!?
ASS-HOLE!!
LETTIN' THESE NOISY BRATS IN HERE!?
...NGH...
BOTA (DRIP)
BOTA

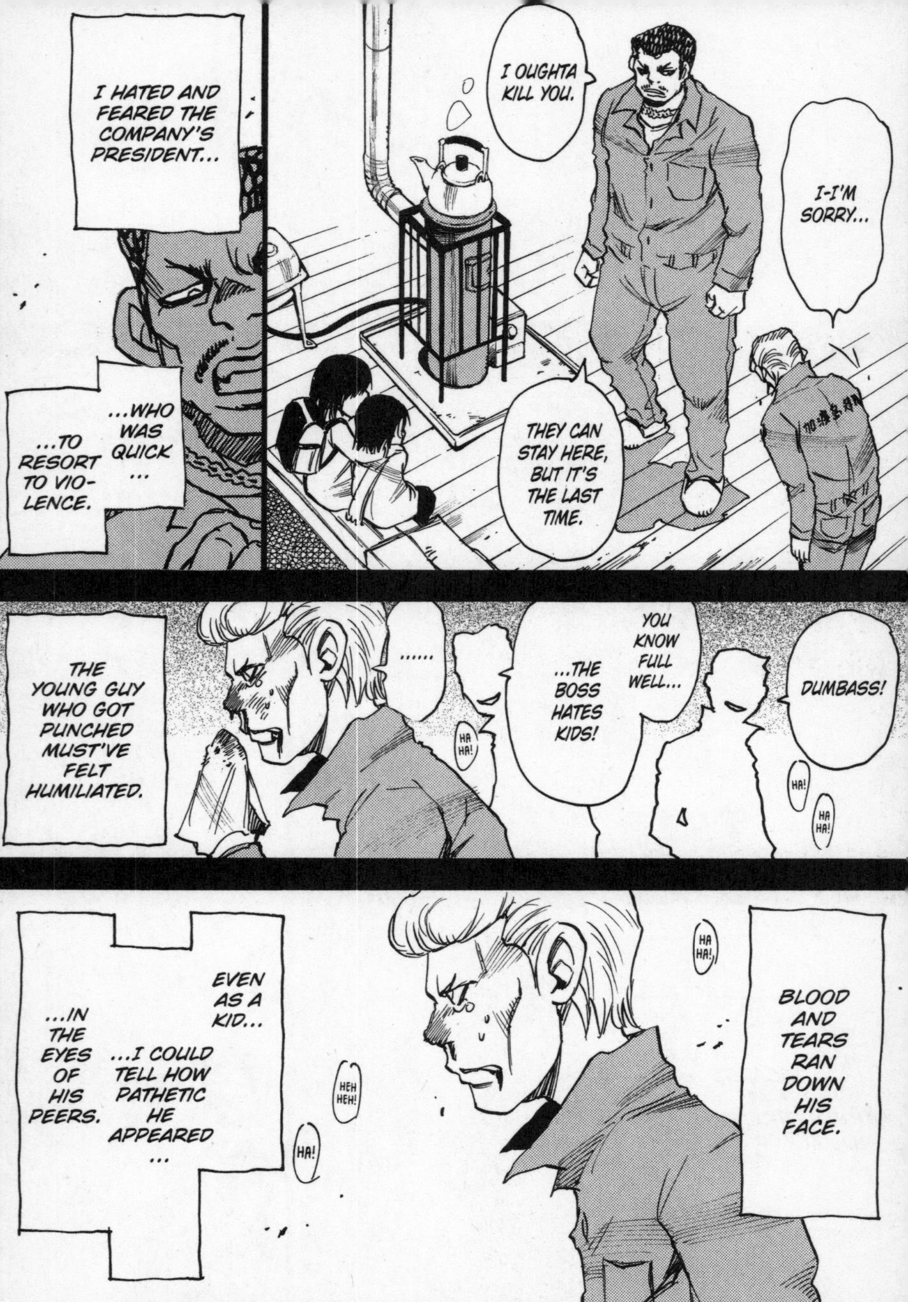
I OUGHTA KILL YOU.
I-I'M SORRY...
THEY CAN STAY HERE, BUT IT'S THE LAST TIME.
I HATED AND FEARED THE COMPANY'S PRESIDENT...
...WHO WAS QUICK...
...TO RESORT TO VIOLENCE.
DUMBASS!
HA!
HA HA!
YOU KNOW FULL WELL...
...THE BOSS HATES KIDS!
HA HA!
......
THE YOUNG GUY WHO GOT PUNCHED MUST'VE FELT HUMILIATED.
HA HA!
BLOOD AND TEARS RAN DOWN HIS FACE.
HEH HEH!
HA!
EVEN AS A KID...
...I COULD TELL HOW PATHETIC HE APPEARED...
...IN THE EYES OF HIS PEERS.

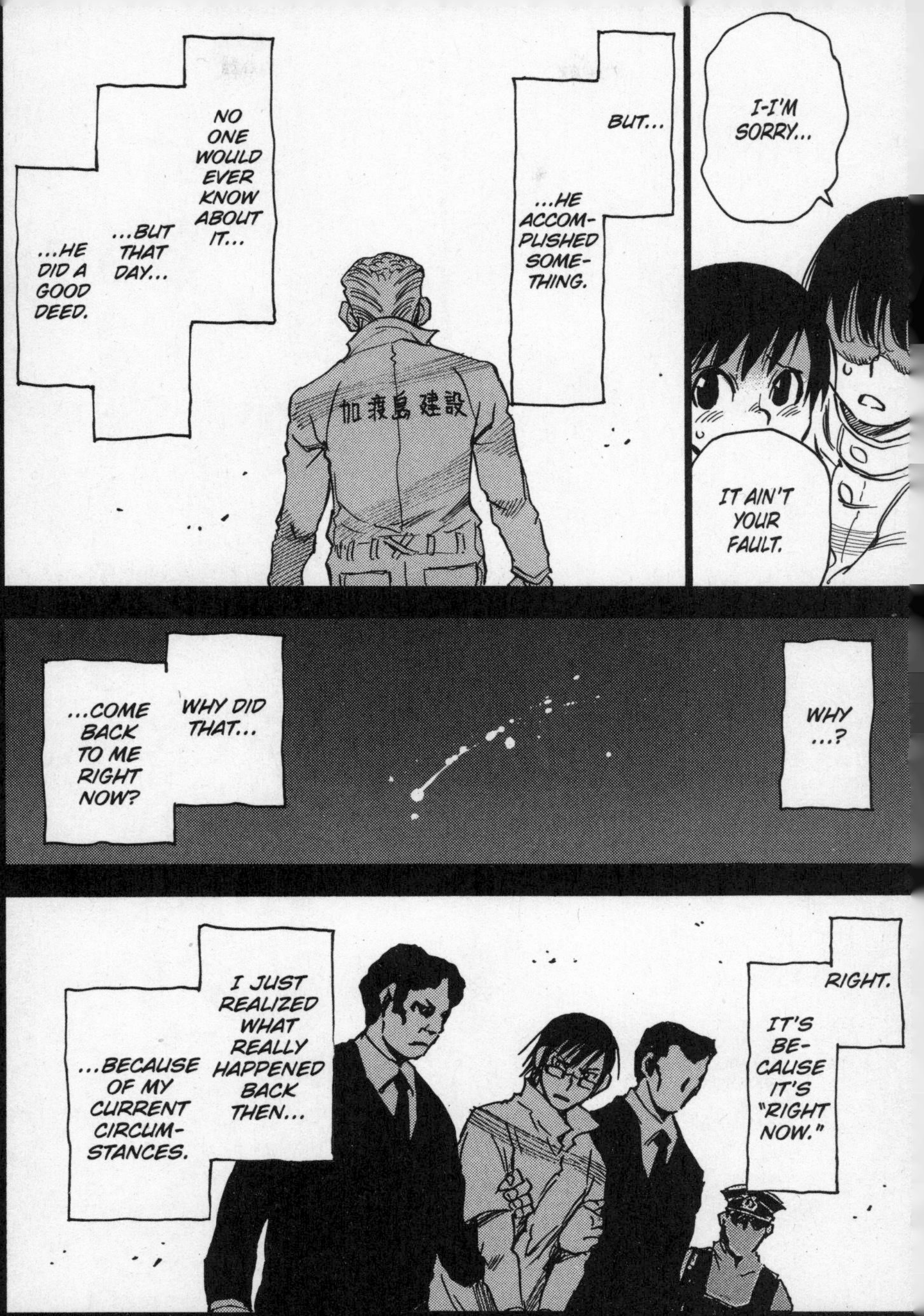
I-I'M SORRY...
IT AIN'T YOUR FAULT.
BUT...
...HE ACCOMPLISHED SOMETHING.
NO ONE WOULD EVER KNOW ABOUT IT...
...BUT THAT DAY...
...HE DID A GOOD DEED.
WHY...?
WHY DID THAT...
...COME BACK TO ME RIGHT NOW?
RIGHT.
IT'S BECAUSE IT'S "RIGHT NOW."
I JUST REALIZED WHAT REALLY HAPPENED BACK THEN...
...BECAUSE OF MY CURRENT CIRCUMSTANCES.

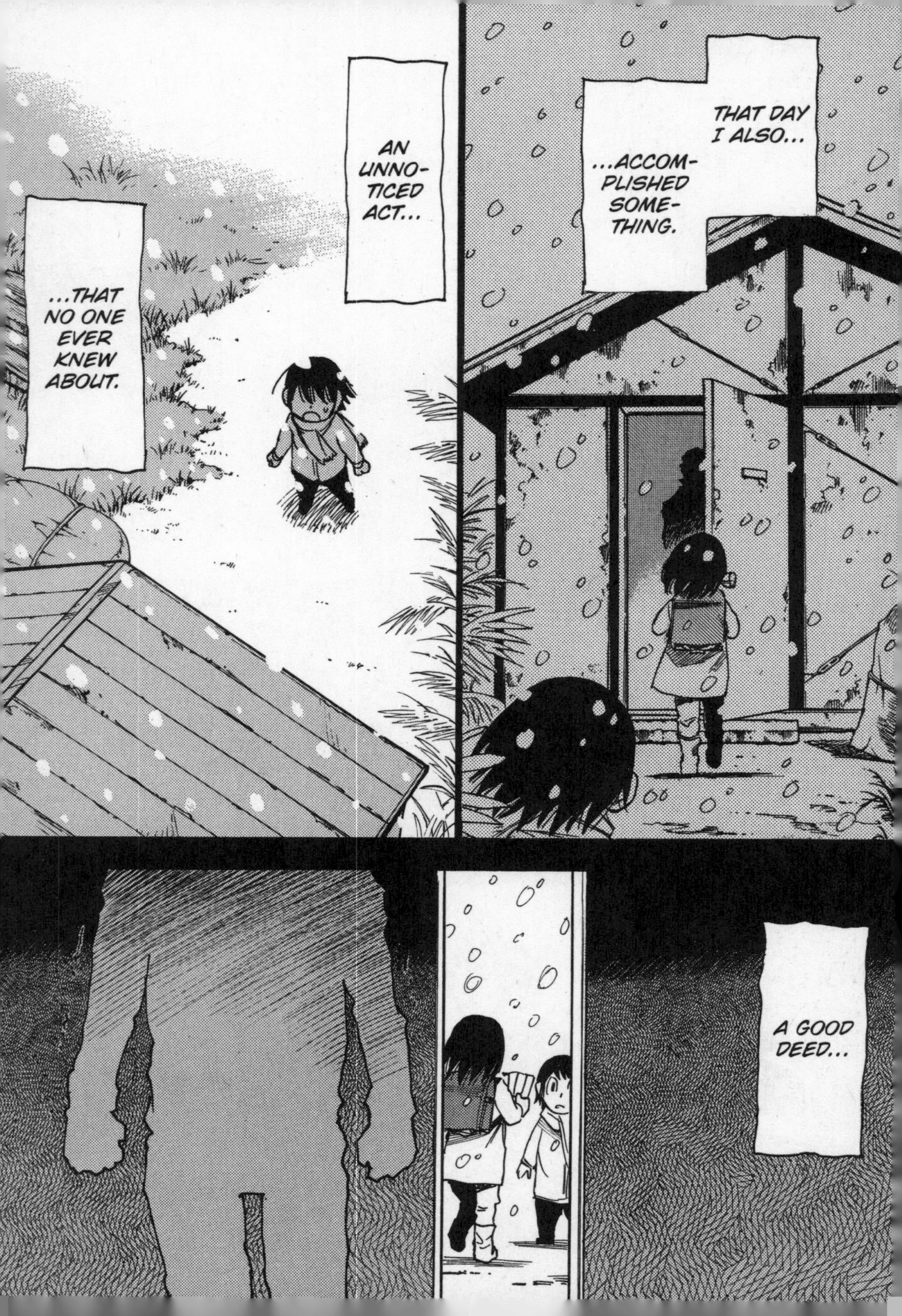
THAT DAY I ALSO...
...ACCOM-PLISHED SOME-THING.
AN UNNO-TICED ACT...
...THAT NO ONE EVER KNEW ABOUT.
A GOOD DEED...

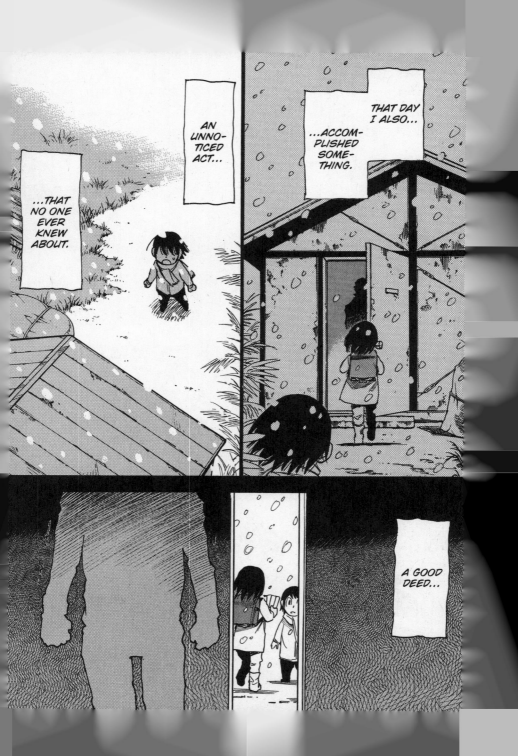

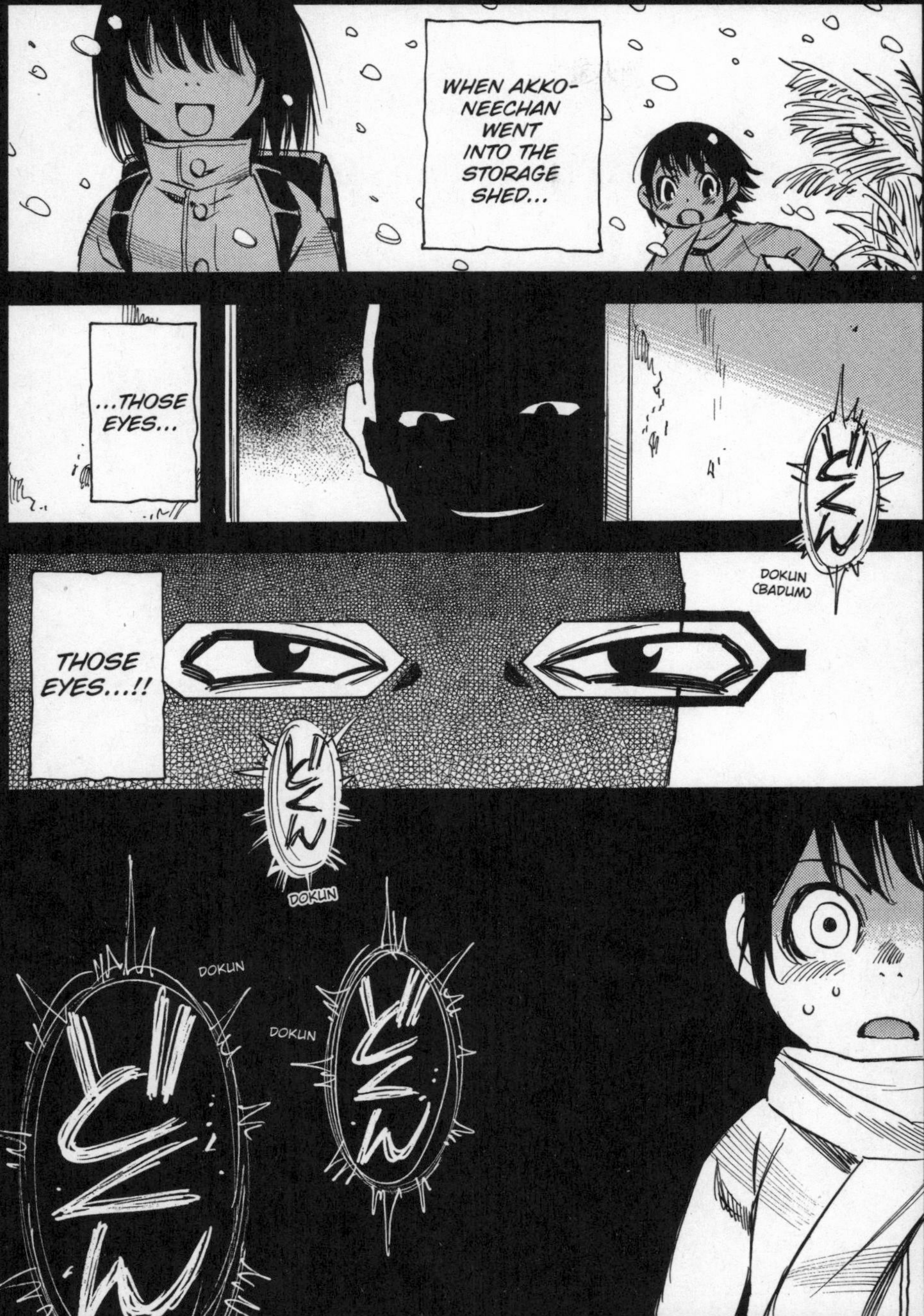
WHEN AKKO-NEECHAN WENT INTO THE STORAGE SHED...
DOKUN (BADUM)
...THOSE EYES...
THOSE EYES...!!
DOKUN
DOKUN
DOKUN

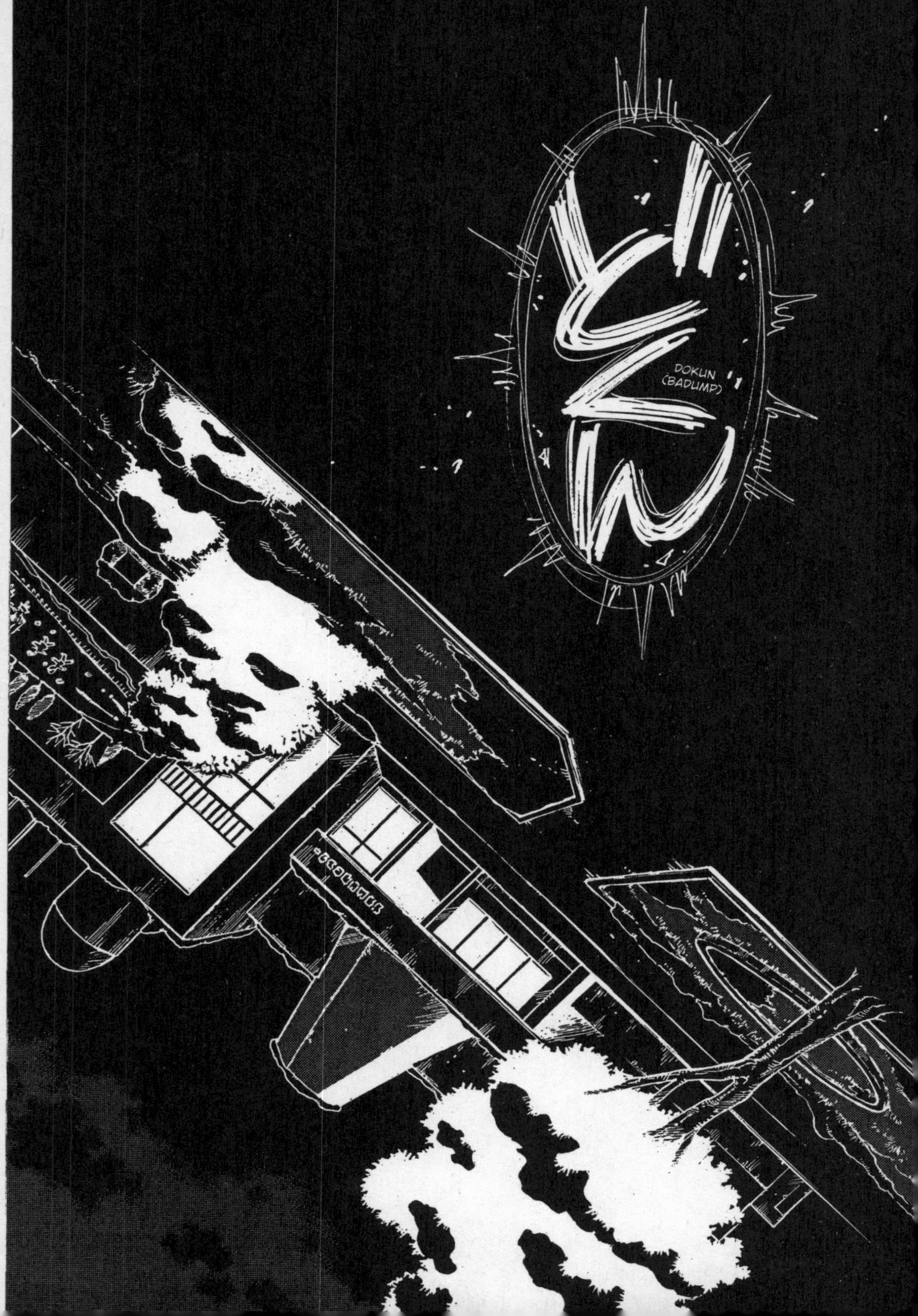
DOKUN
(BADUMP)

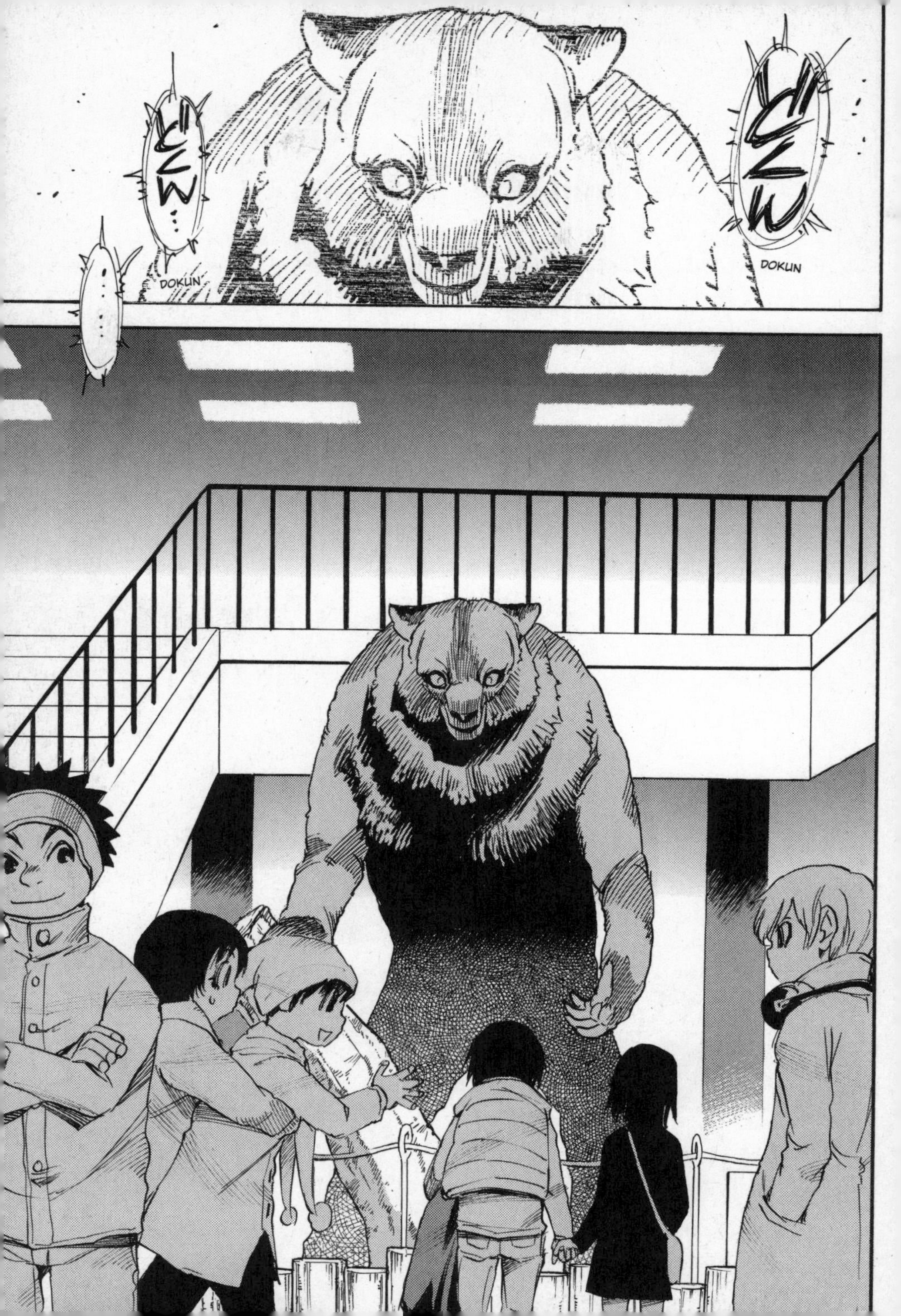
DOKUN
DOKUN
……

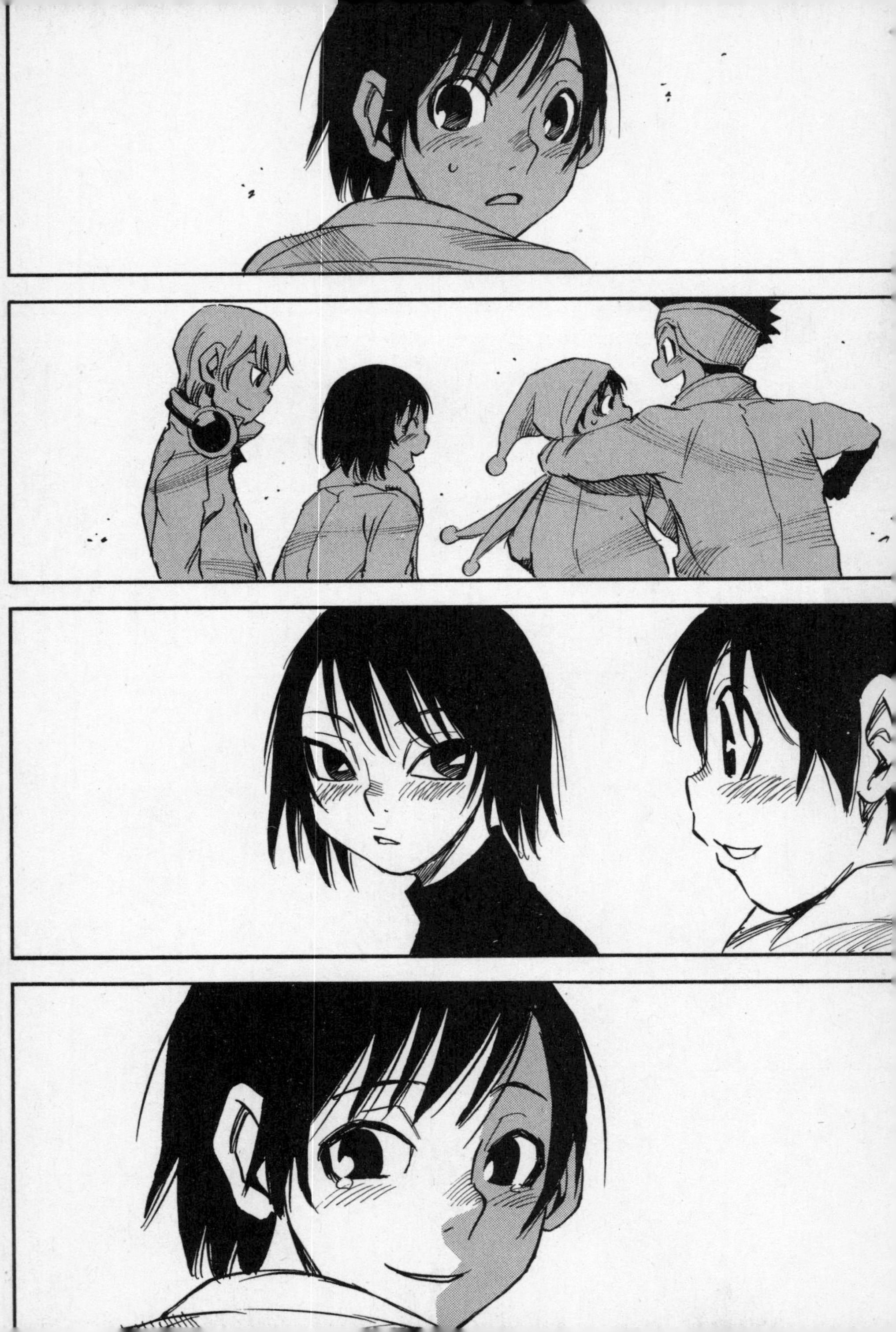

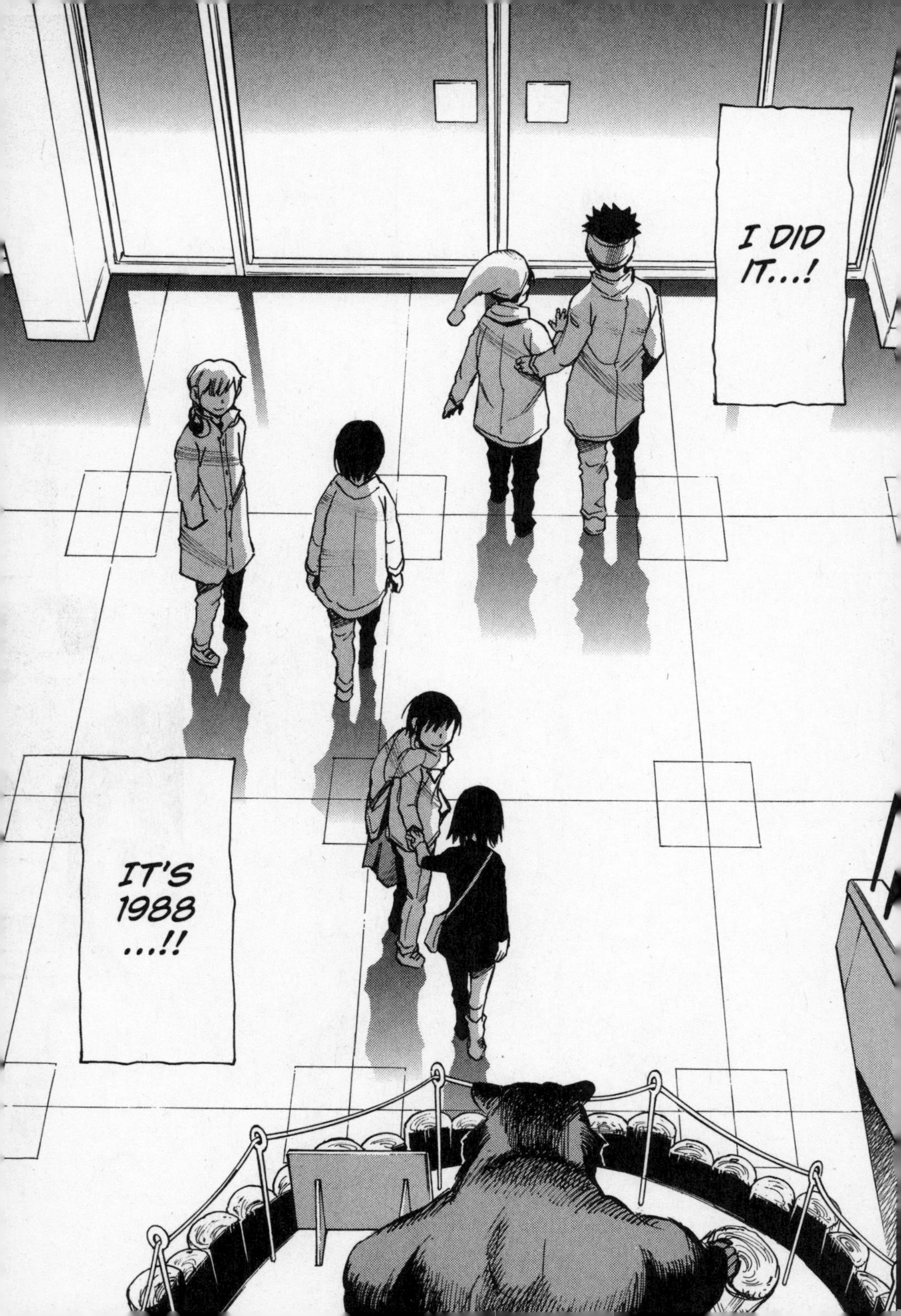
I DID IT...!
IT'S 1988 ...!!

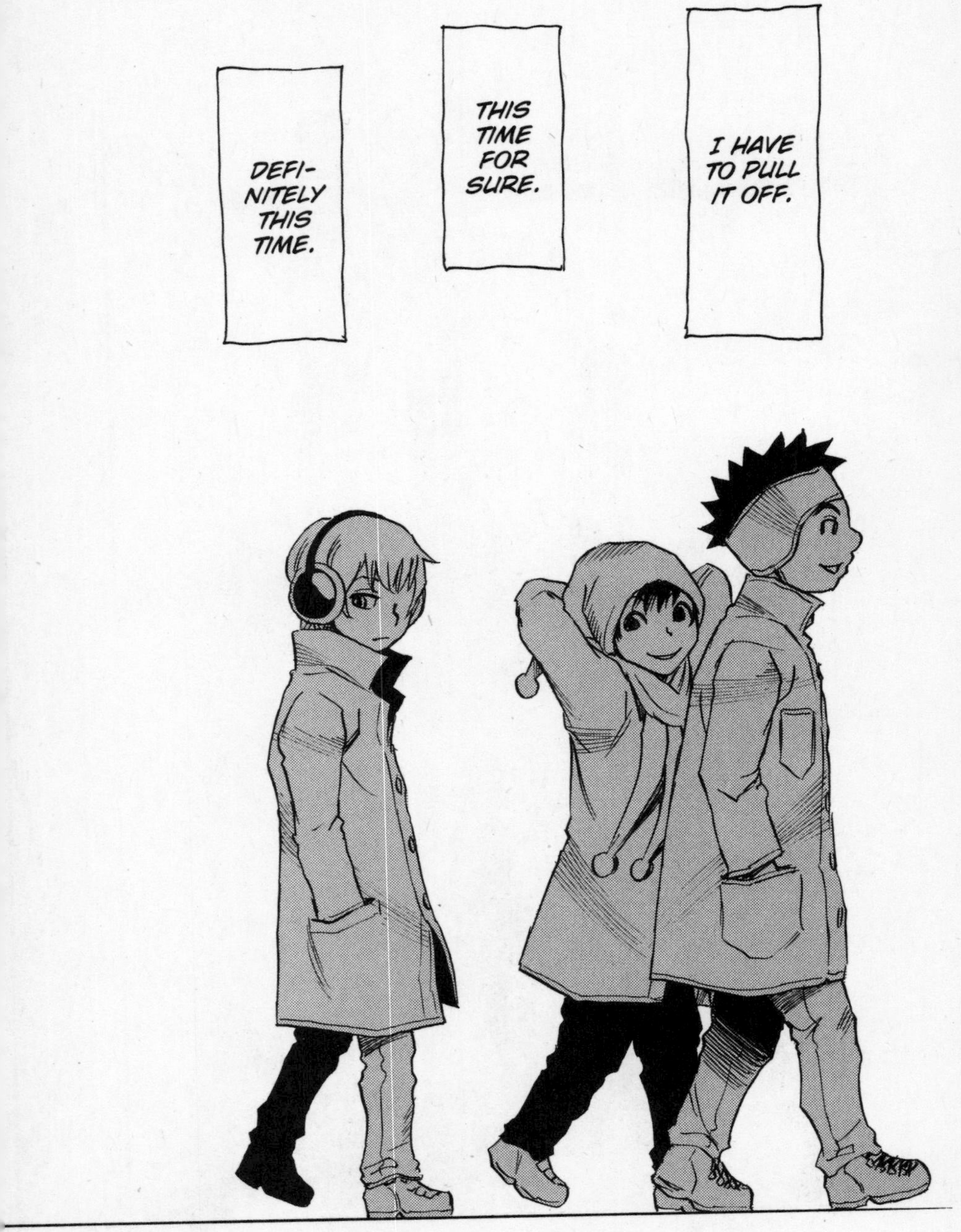
I HAVE TO PULL IT OFF.
THIS TIME FOR SURE.
DEFINITELY THIS TIME.

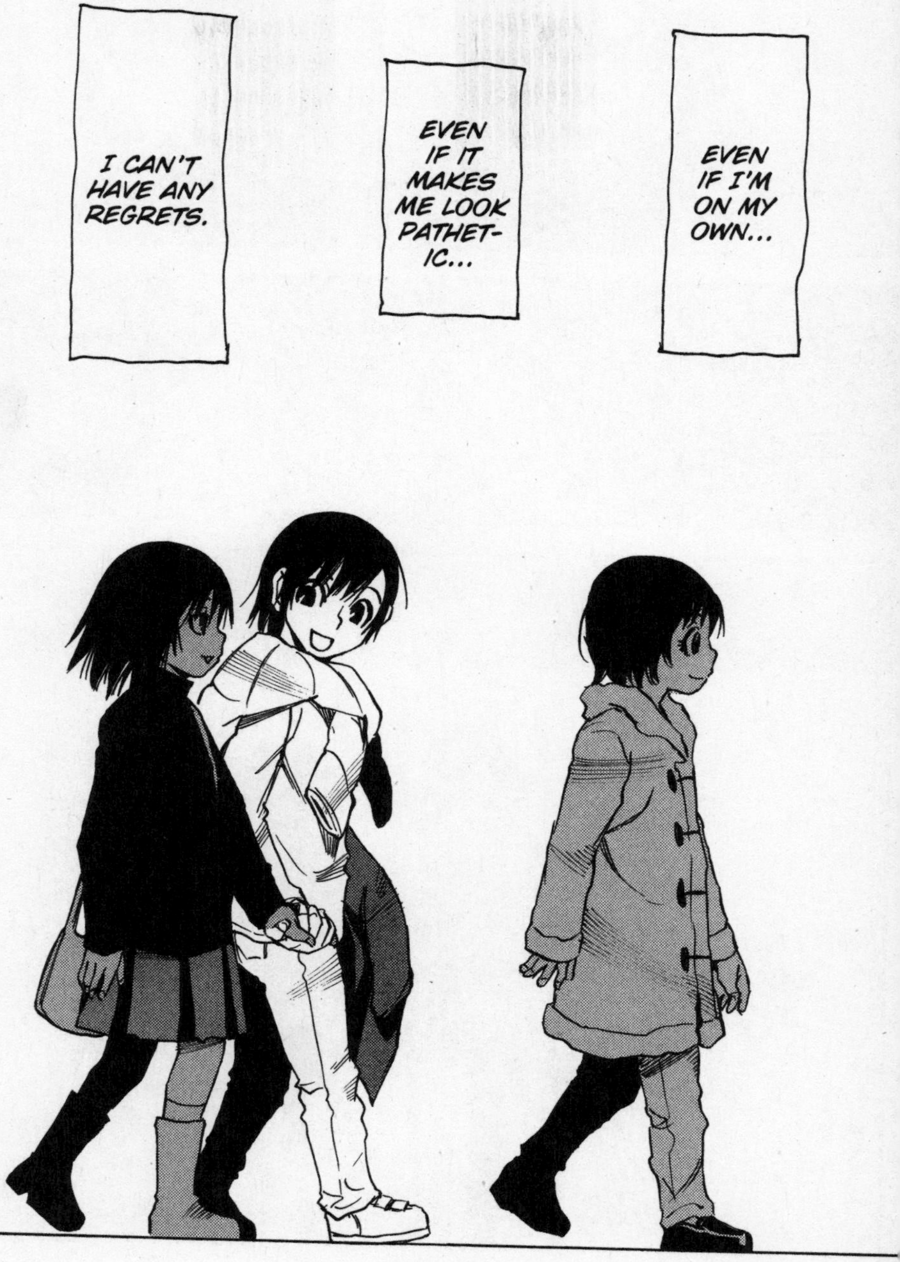
EVEN IF I'M ON MY OWN...
EVEN IF IT MAKES ME LOOK PATHETIC...
I CAN'T HAVE ANY REGRETS.

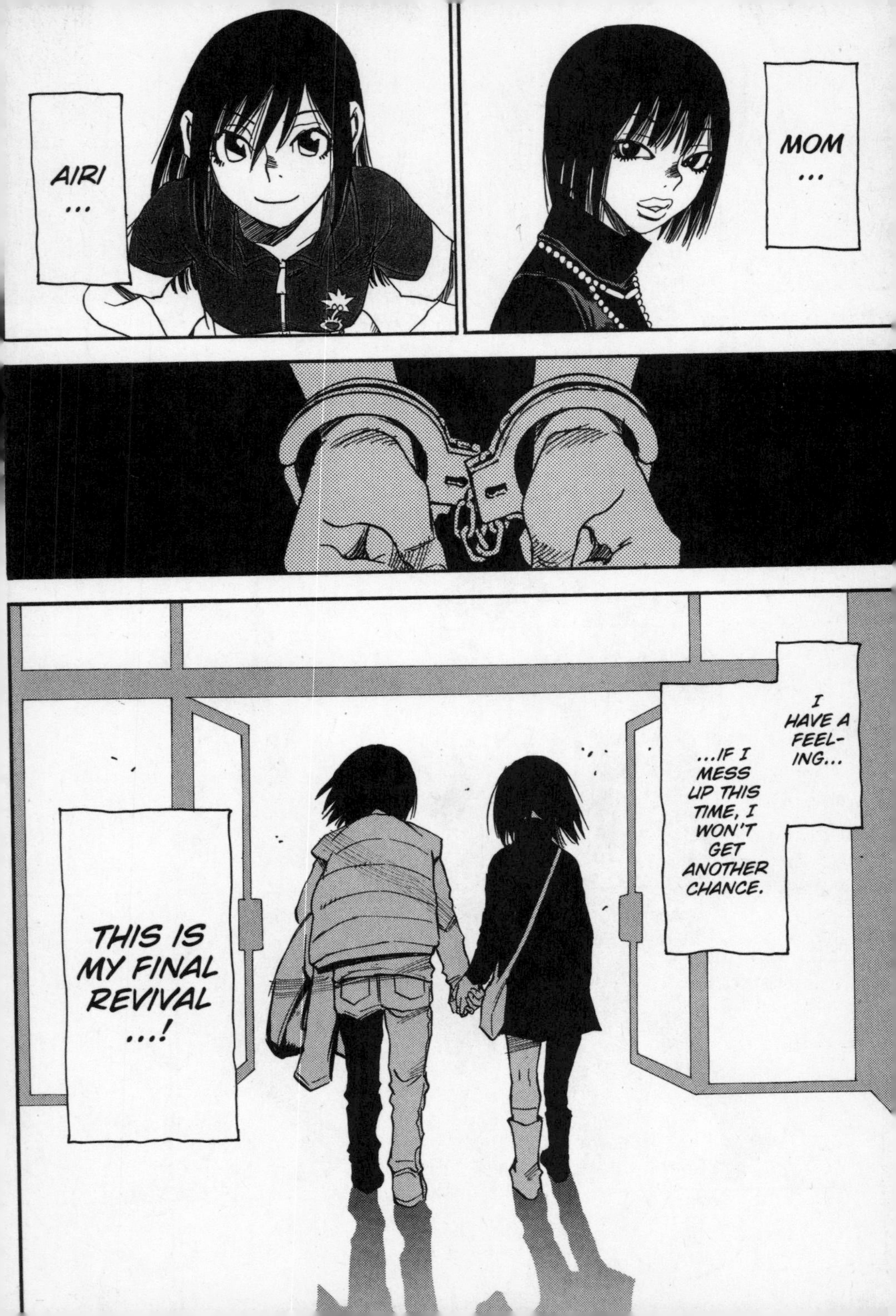
MOM ...
AIRI ...
I HAVE A FEEL-ING...
...IF I MESS UP THIS TIME, I WON'T GET ANOTHER CHANCE.
THIS IS MY FINAL REVIVAL ...!

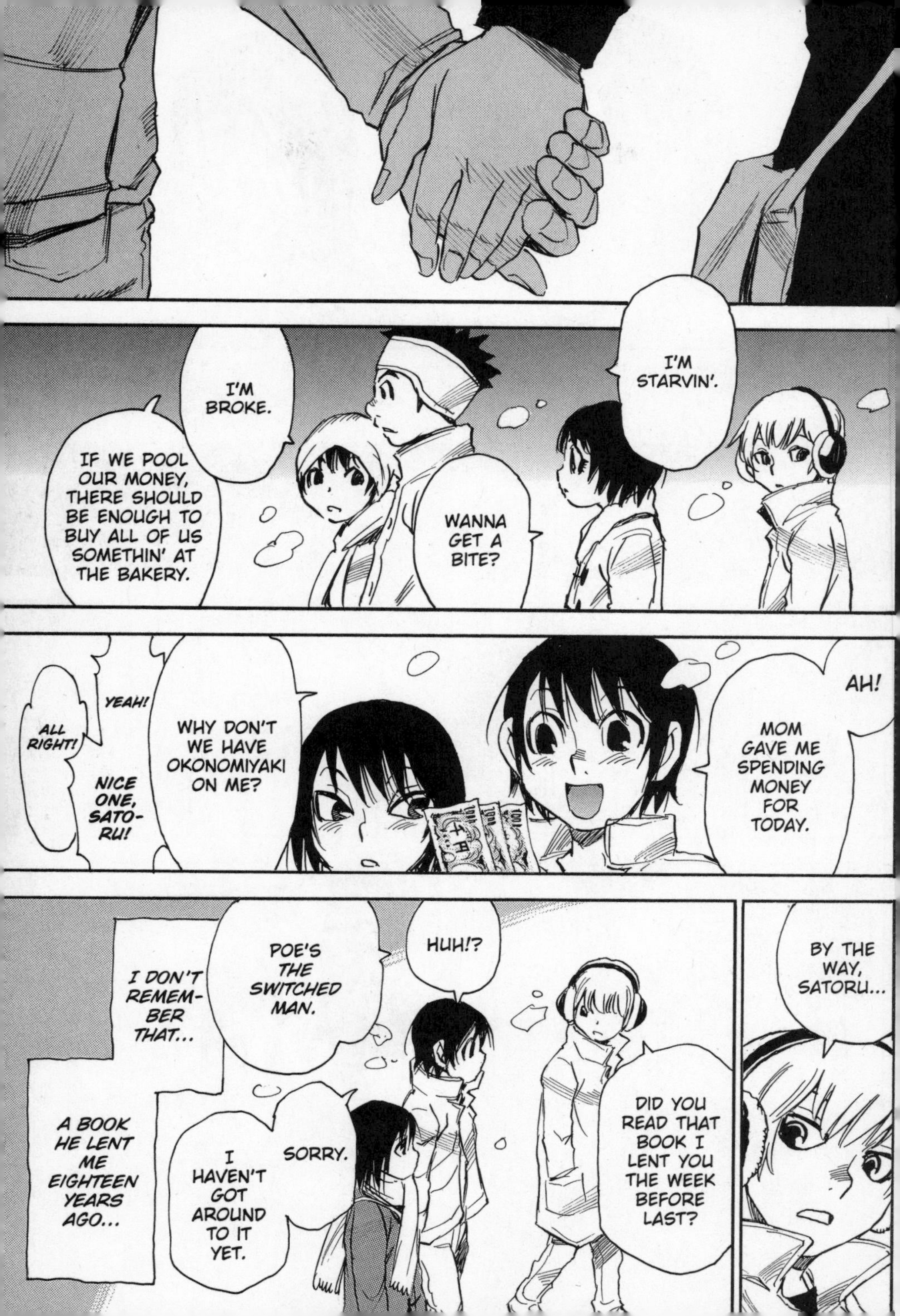
I'M STARVIN'.
WANNA GET A BITE?
I'M BROKE.
IF WE POOL OUR MONEY, THERE SHOULD BE ENOUGH TO BUY ALL OF US SOMETHIN' AT THE BAKERY.
AH!
MOM GAVE ME SPENDING MONEY FOR TODAY.
WHY DON'T WE HAVE OKONOMIYAKI ON ME?
YEAH!
NICE ONE, SATO-RU!
ALL RIGHT!
BY THE WAY, SATORU...
DID YOU READ THAT BOOK I LENT YOU THE WEEK BEFORE LAST?
SORRY.
I HAVEN'T GOT AROUND TO IT YET.
HUH!?
POE'S THE SWITCHED MAN.
I DON'T REMEM-BER THAT...
A BOOK HE LENT ME EIGHTEEN YEARS AGO...

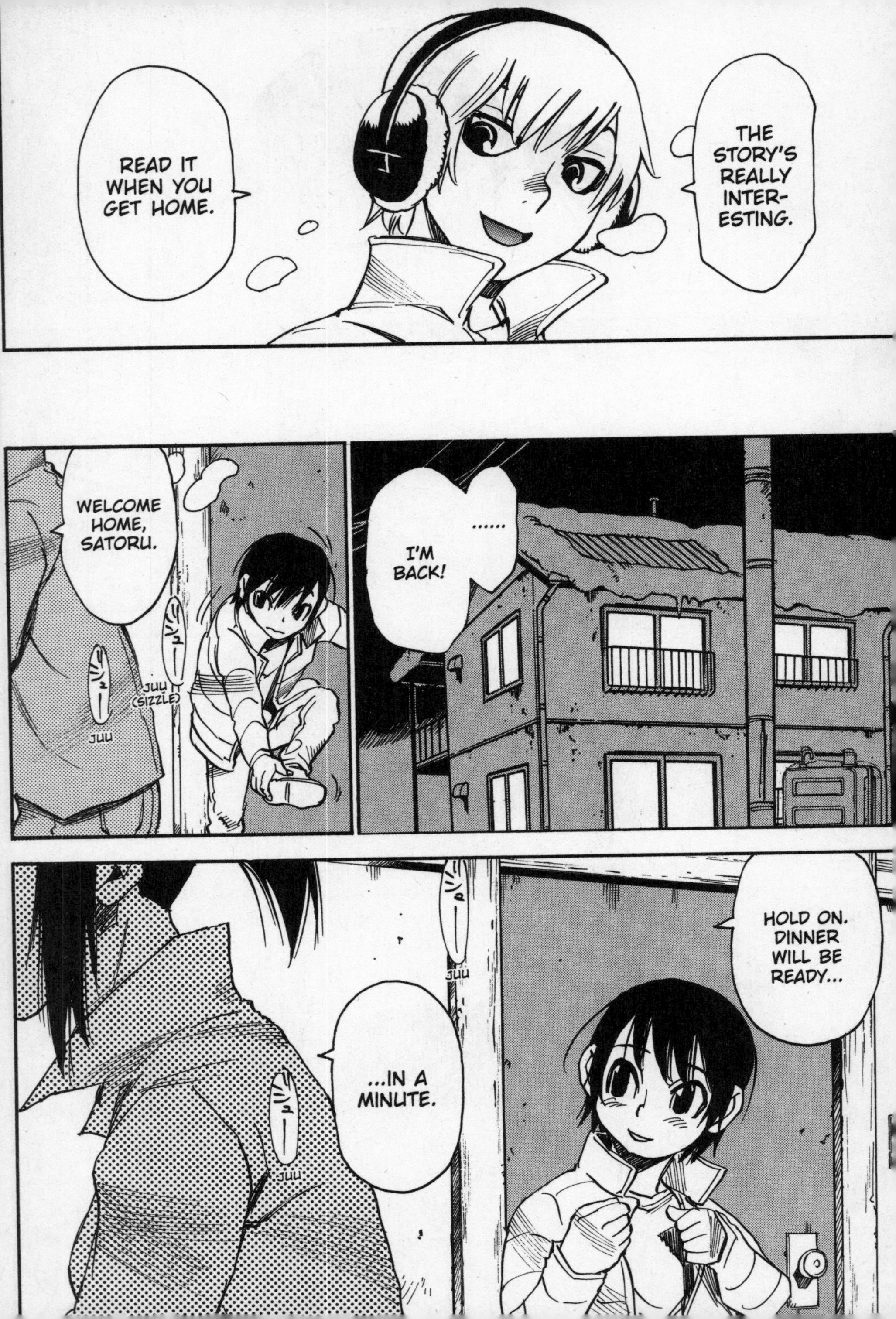
THE STORY'S REALLY INTER-ESTING.
READ IT WHEN YOU GET HOME.
......
I'M BACK!
WELCOME HOME, SATORU.
JUU (SIZZLE)
JUU
HOLD ON. DINNER WILL BE READY...
JUU
...IN A MINUTE.
JUU

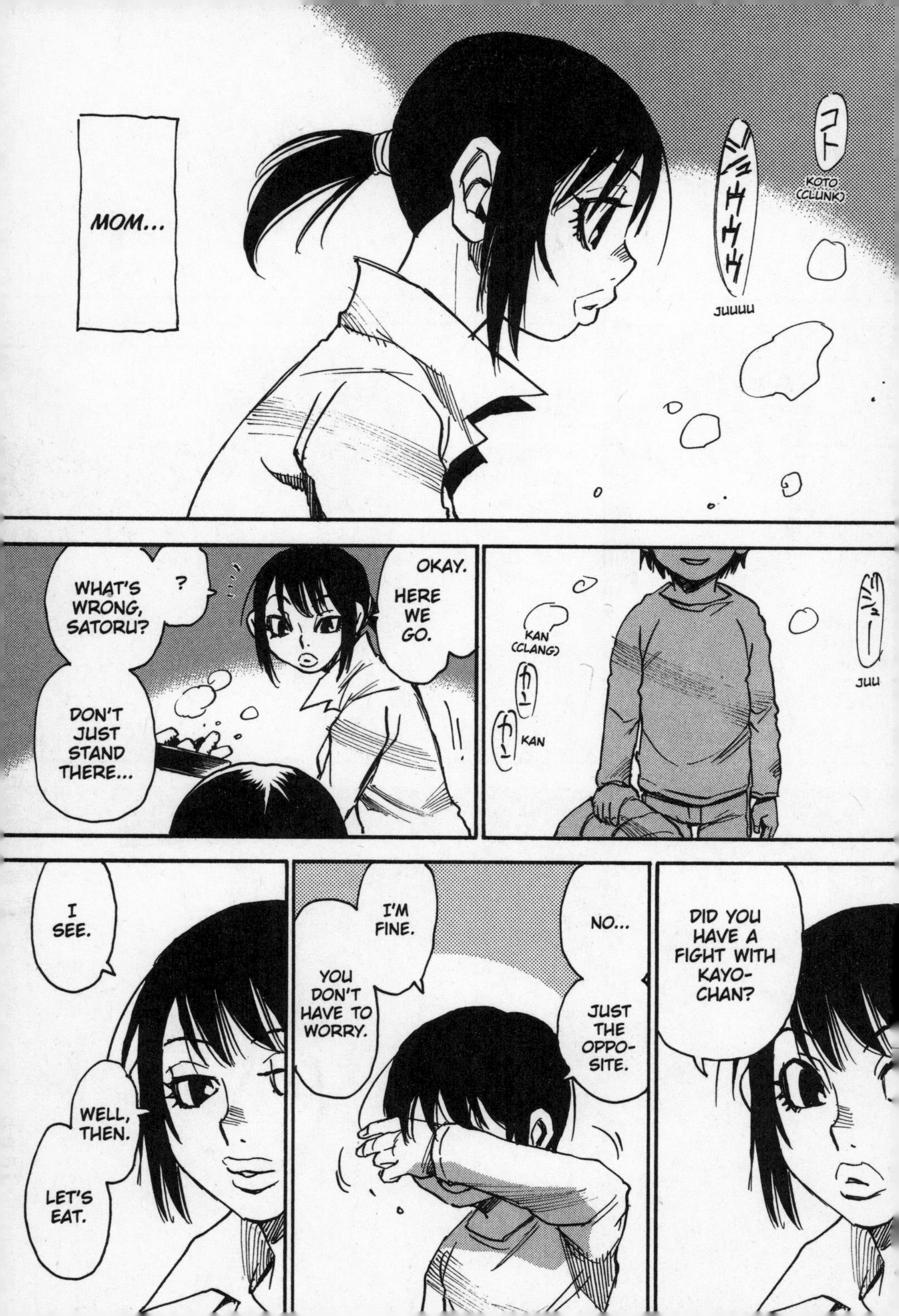

コト
KOTO (CLUNK)
JUUUU
MOM...
JUU
KAN (CLANG)
KAN
OKAY. HERE WE GO.
WHAT'S WRONG, SATORU?
?
DON'T JUST STAND THERE...
DID YOU HAVE A FIGHT WITH KAYO-CHAN?
NO...
JUST THE OPPO-SITE.
I'M FINE.
YOU DON'T HAVE TO WORRY.
I SEE.
WELL, THEN.
LET'S EAT.

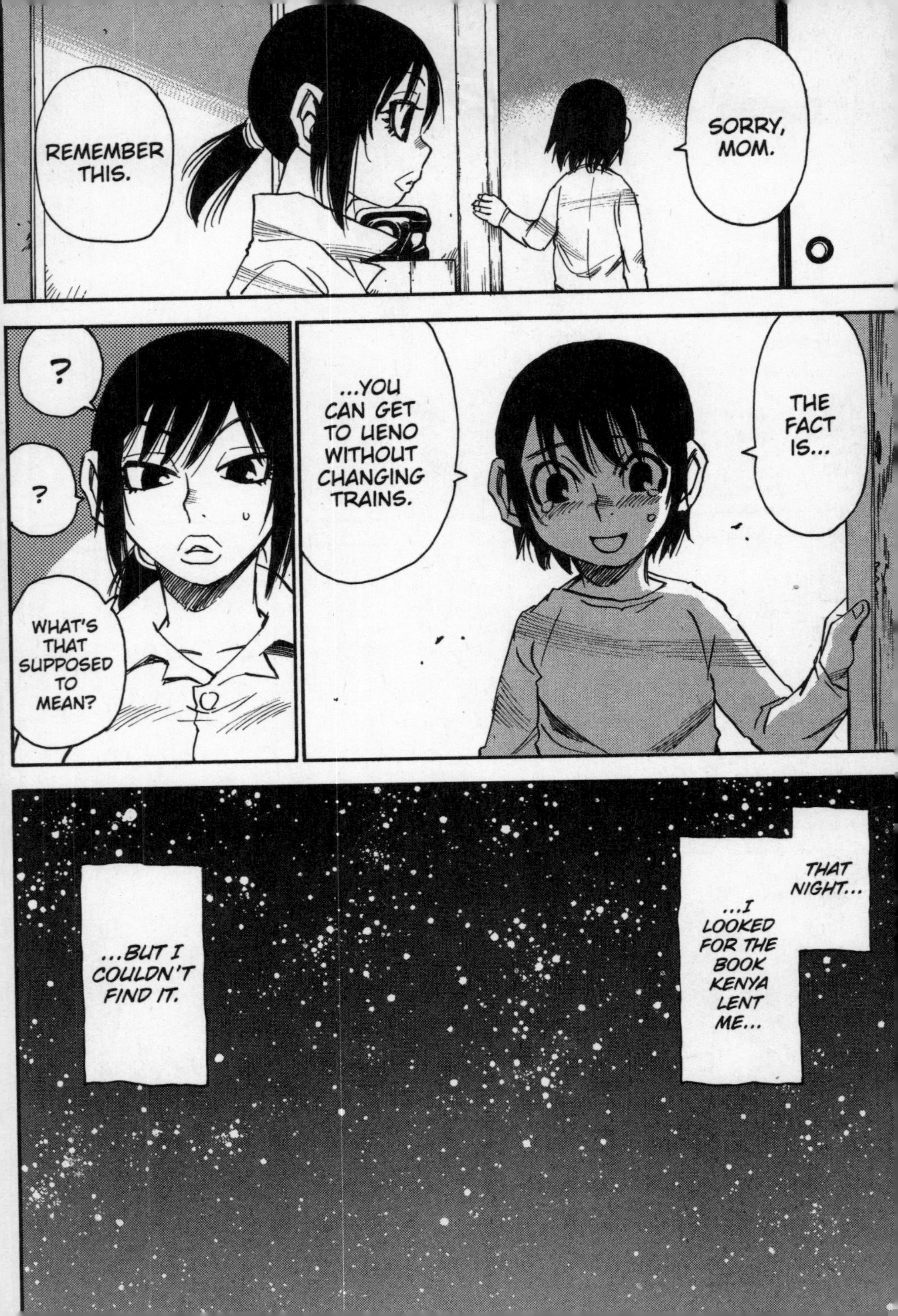
SORRY, MOM.
REMEMBER THIS.
THE FACT IS...
...YOU CAN GET TO UENO WITHOUT CHANGING TRAINS.
?
?
WHAT'S THAT SUPPOSED TO MEAN?
THAT NIGHT...
...I LOOKED FOR THE BOOK KENYA LENT ME...
...BUT I COULDN'T FIND IT.

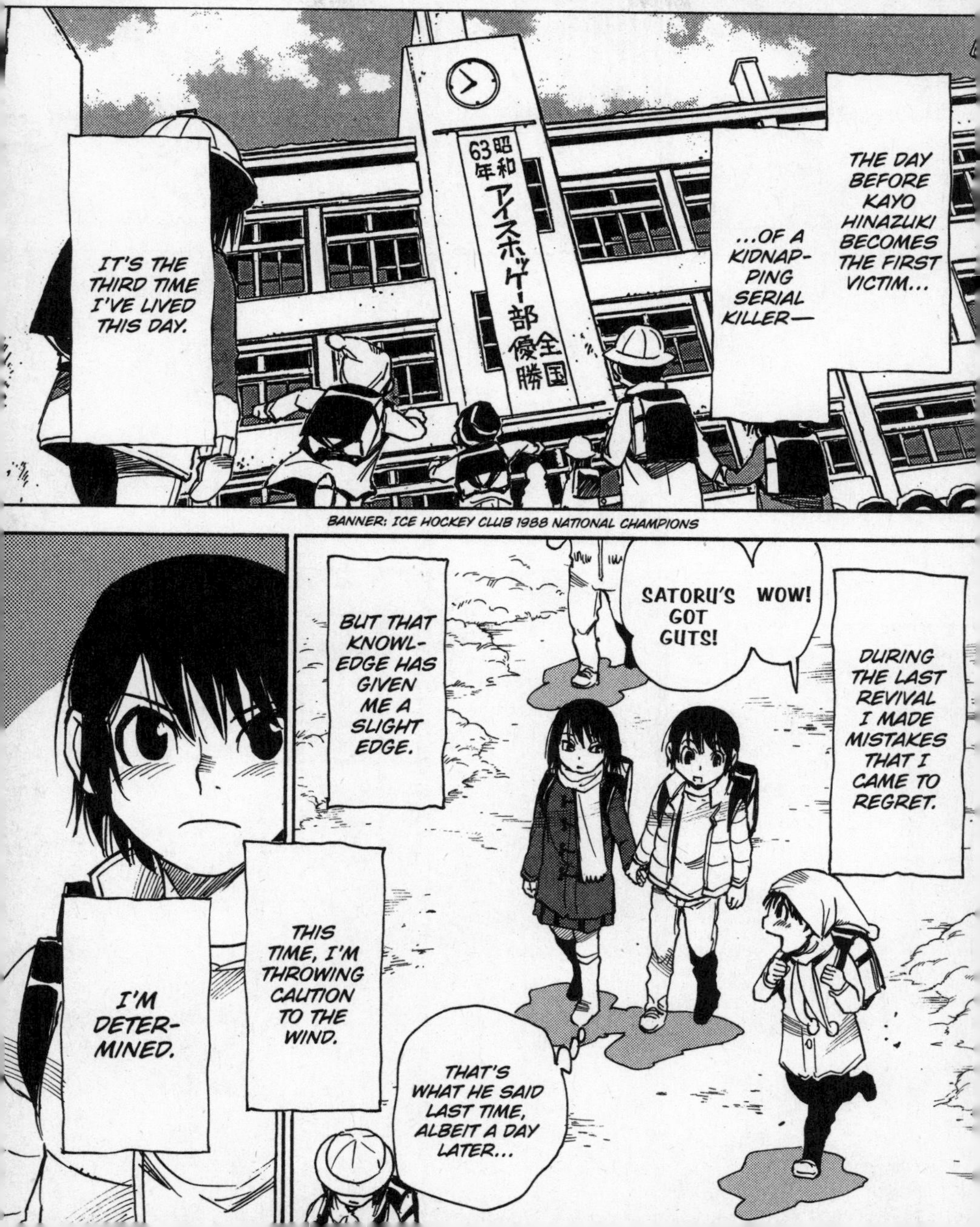
THE DAY BEFORE KAYO HINAZUKI BECOMES THE FIRST VICTIM...
...OF A KIDNAPPING SERIAL KILLER—
IT'S THE THIRD TIME I'VE LIVED THIS DAY.
昭和63年 アイスホッケー部 全国優勝
BANNER: ICE HOCKEY CLUB 1988 NATIONAL CHAMPIONS
DURING THE LAST REVIVAL I MADE MISTAKES THAT I CAME TO REGRET.
WOW! SATORU'S GOT GUTS!
BUT THAT KNOWLEDGE HAS GIVEN ME A SLIGHT EDGE.
THAT'S WHAT HE SAID LAST TIME, ALBEIT A DAY LATER...
THIS TIME, I'M THROWING CAUTION TO THE WIND.
I'M DETERMINED.

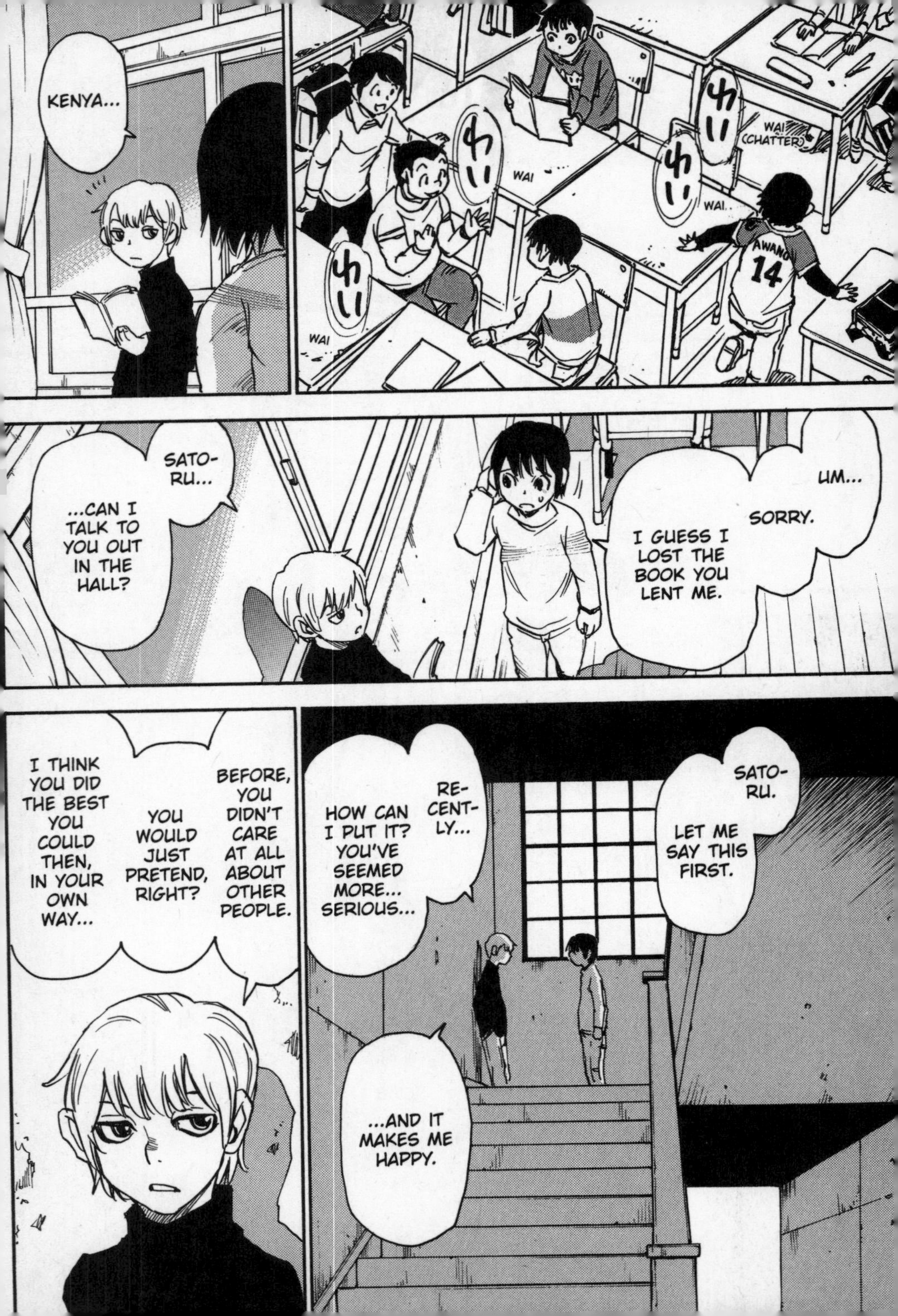

わい
WAI (CHATTER)
わい
WAI..
AWANO 14
わい
WAI
わい
WAI
KENYA...
UM... SORRY.
I GUESS I LOST THE BOOK YOU LENT ME.
SATO-RU...
...CAN I TALK TO YOU OUT IN THE HALL?
SATO-RU.
LET ME SAY THIS FIRST.
RE-CENT-LY...
HOW CAN I PUT IT? YOU'VE SEEMED MORE... SERIOUS...
...AND IT MAKES ME HAPPY.
BEFORE, YOU DIDN'T CARE AT ALL ABOUT OTHER PEOPLE.
YOU WOULD JUST PRETEND, RIGHT?
I THINK YOU DID THE BEST YOU COULD THEN, IN YOUR OWN WAY...

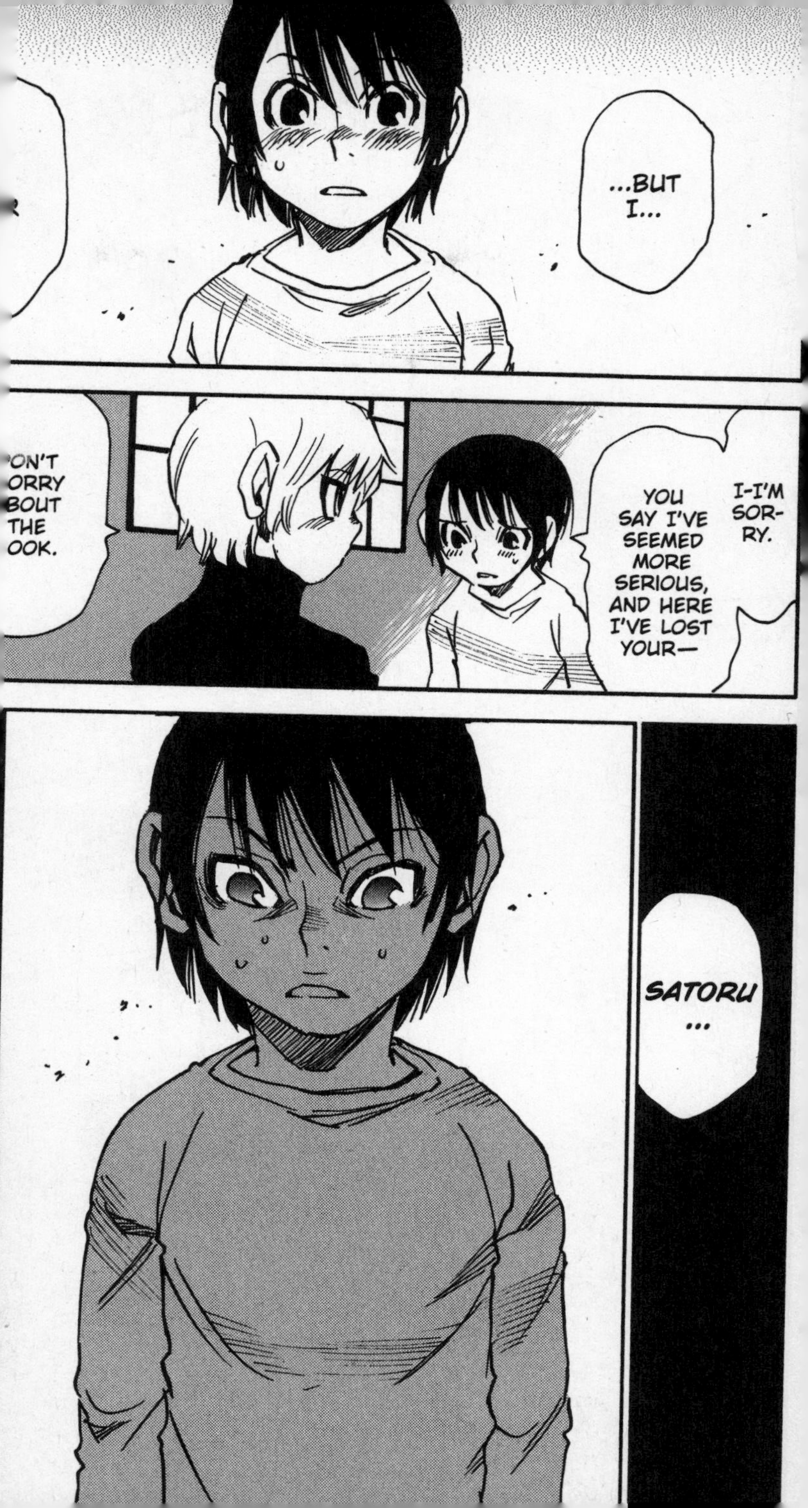
...BUT I...
I-I'M SOR-RY.
YOU SAY I'VE SEEMED MORE SERIOUS, AND HERE I'VE LOST YOUR—
ON'T ORRY BOUT THE OOK.
SATORU ...

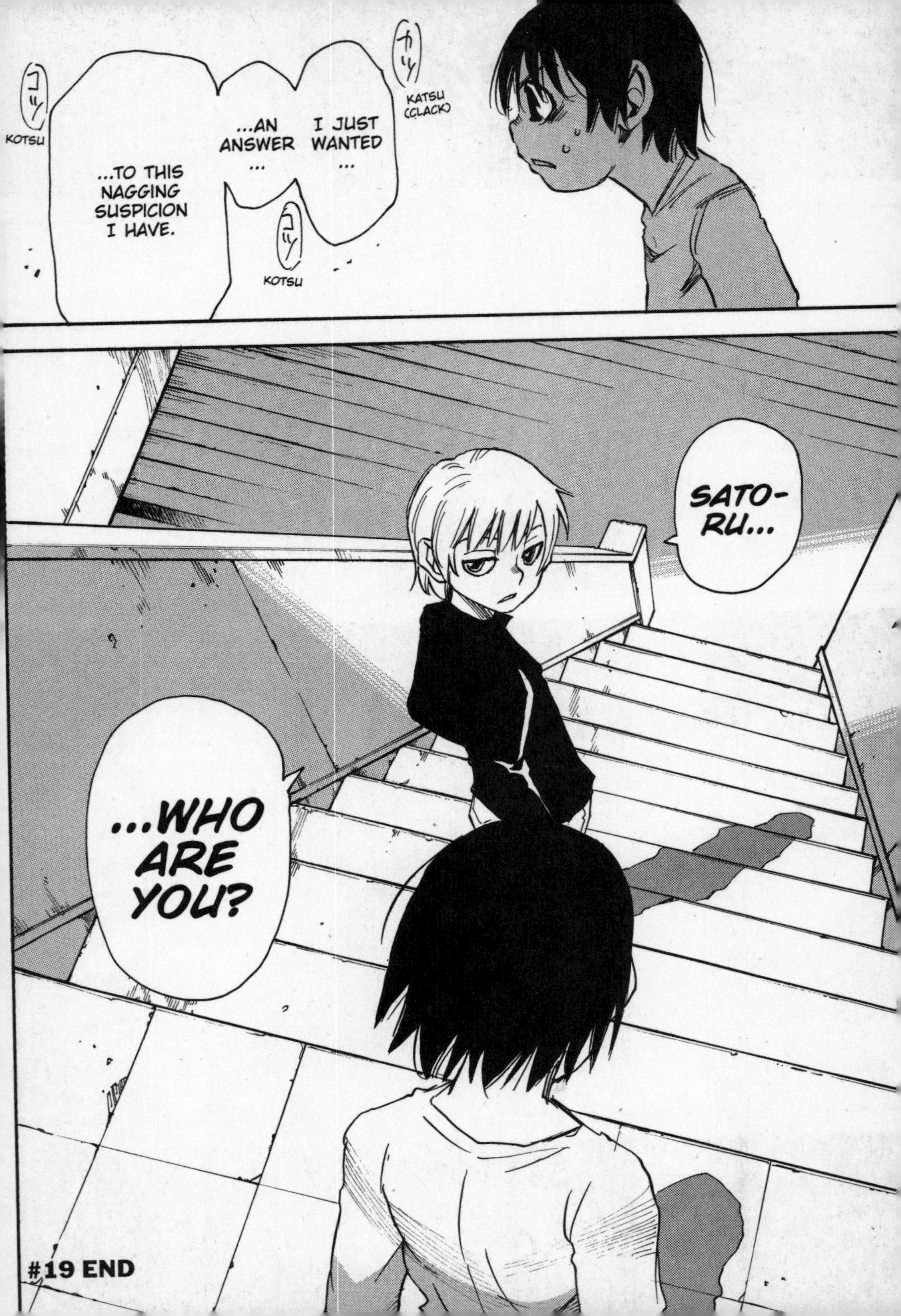
カッ
KATSU (CLACK)
I JUST WANTED ...
...AN ANSWER ...
...TO THIS NAGGING SUSPICION I HAVE.
コッ
KOTSU
コッ
KOTSU
SATO-RU...
...WHO ARE YOU?
#19 END

"SATORU, WHO ARE YOU?"??

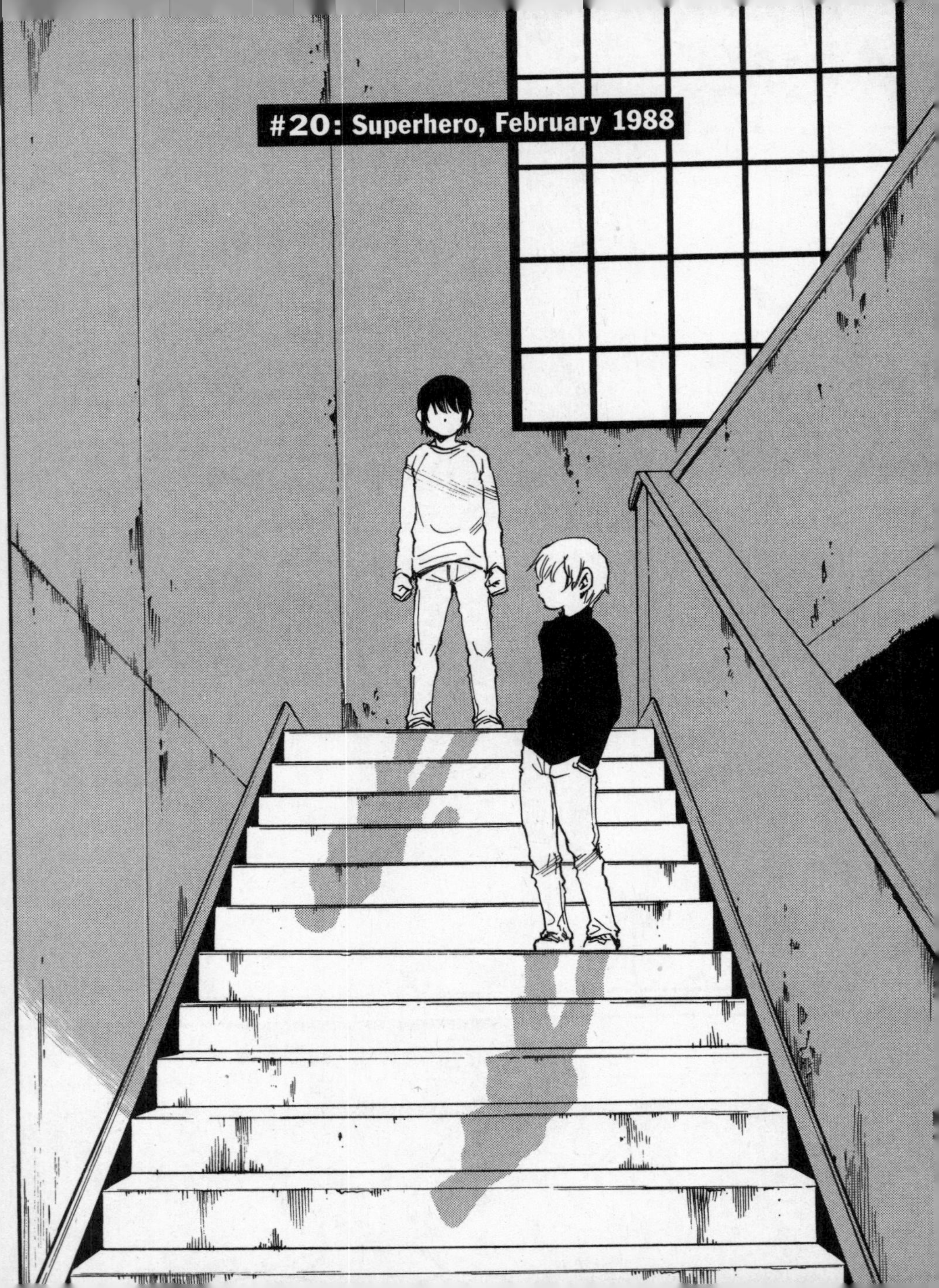
#20: Superhero, February 1988

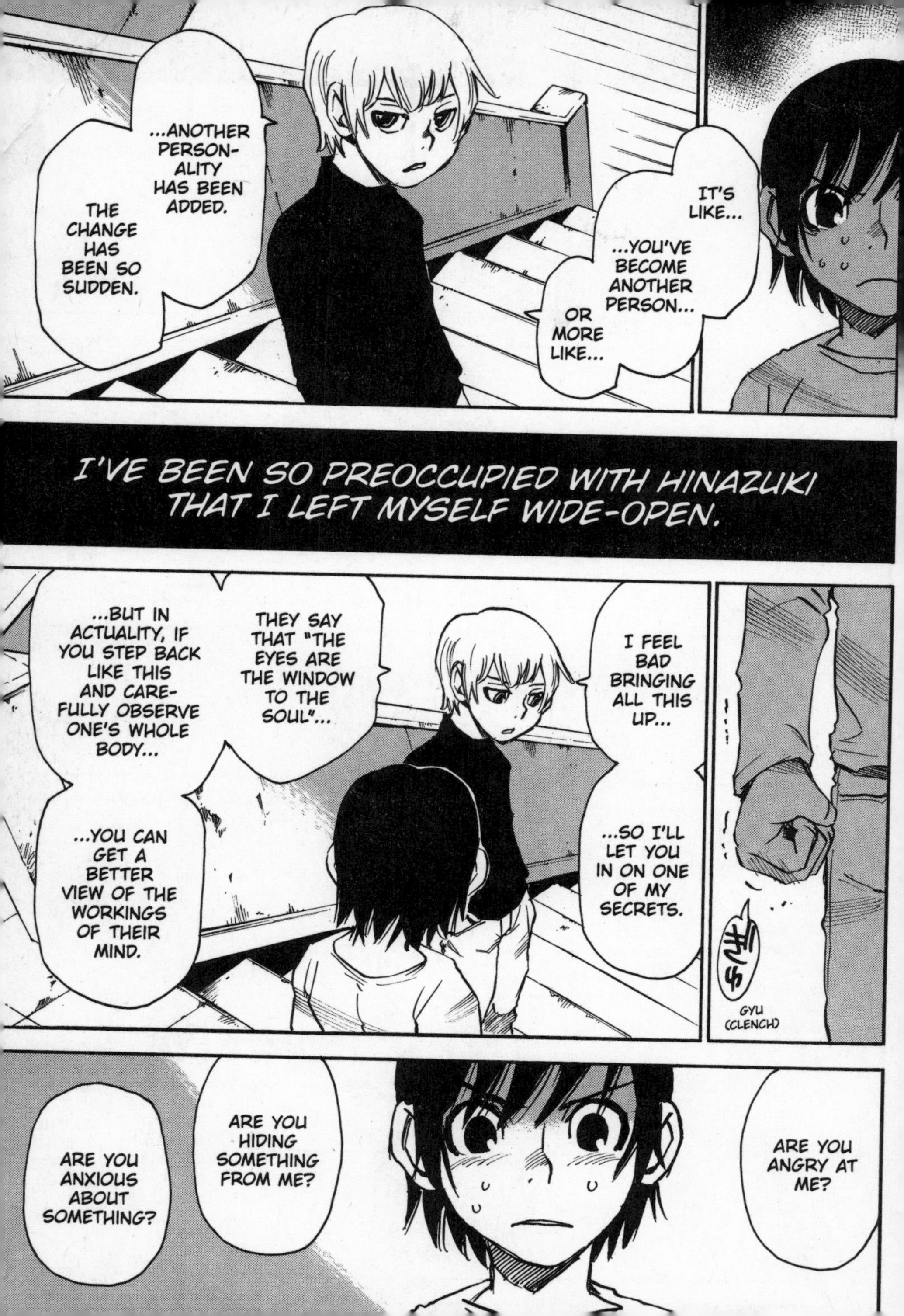
IT'S LIKE...
...YOU'VE BECOME ANOTHER PERSON...
OR MORE LIKE...
...ANOTHER PERSON-ALITY HAS BEEN ADDED.
THE CHANGE HAS BEEN SO SUDDEN.
I'VE BEEN SO PREOCCUPIED WITH HINAZUKI THAT I LEFT MYSELF WIDE-OPEN.
GYU (CLENCH)
I FEEL BAD BRINGING ALL THIS UP...
...SO I'LL LET YOU IN ON ONE OF MY SECRETS.
THEY SAY THAT "THE EYES ARE THE WINDOW TO THE SOUL"...
...BUT IN ACTUALITY, IF YOU STEP BACK LIKE THIS AND CARE-FULLY OBSERVE ONE'S WHOLE BODY...
...YOU CAN GET A BETTER VIEW OF THE WORKINGS OF THEIR MIND.
ARE YOU ANGRY AT ME?
ARE YOU HIDING SOMETHING FROM ME?
ARE YOU ANXIOUS ABOUT SOMETHING?

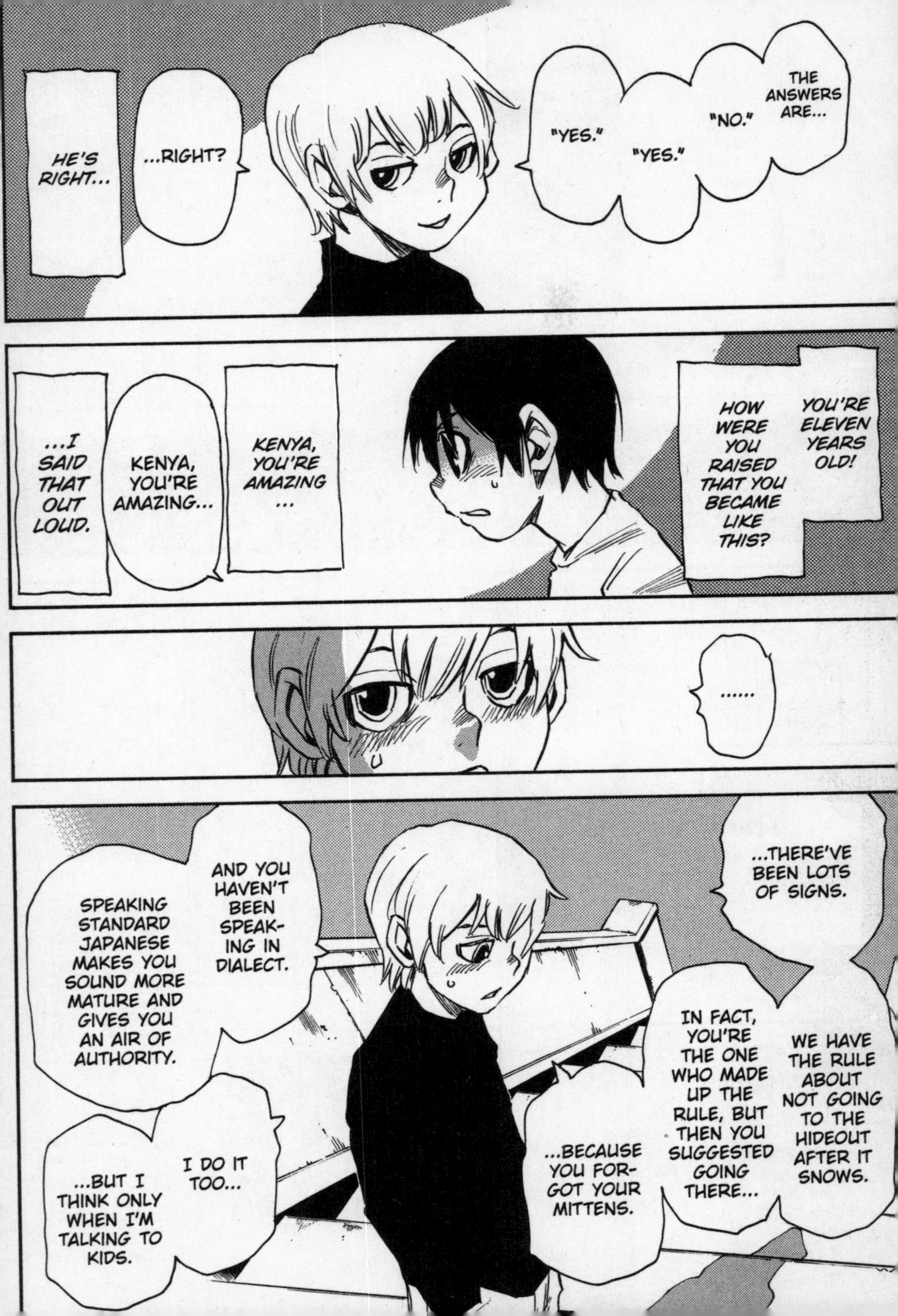
THE ANSWERS ARE...
"NO."
"YES."
"YES."
...RIGHT?
HE'S RIGHT...
YOU'RE ELEVEN YEARS OLD!
HOW WERE YOU RAISED THAT YOU BECAME LIKE THIS?
KENYA, YOU'RE AMAZING ...
KENYA, YOU'RE AMAZING...
...I SAID THAT OUT LOUD.
......
...THERE'VE BEEN LOTS OF SIGNS.
WE HAVE THE RULE ABOUT NOT GOING TO THE HIDEOUT AFTER IT SNOWS.
IN FACT, YOU'RE THE ONE WHO MADE UP THE RULE, BUT THEN YOU SUGGESTED GOING THERE...
...BECAUSE YOU FOR-GOT YOUR MITTENS.
AND YOU HAVEN'T BEEN SPEAK-ING IN DIALECT.
SPEAKING STANDARD JAPANESE MAKES YOU SOUND MORE MATURE AND GIVES YOU AN AIR OF AUTHORITY.
I DO IT TOO...
...BUT I THINK ONLY WHEN I'M TALKING TO KIDS.

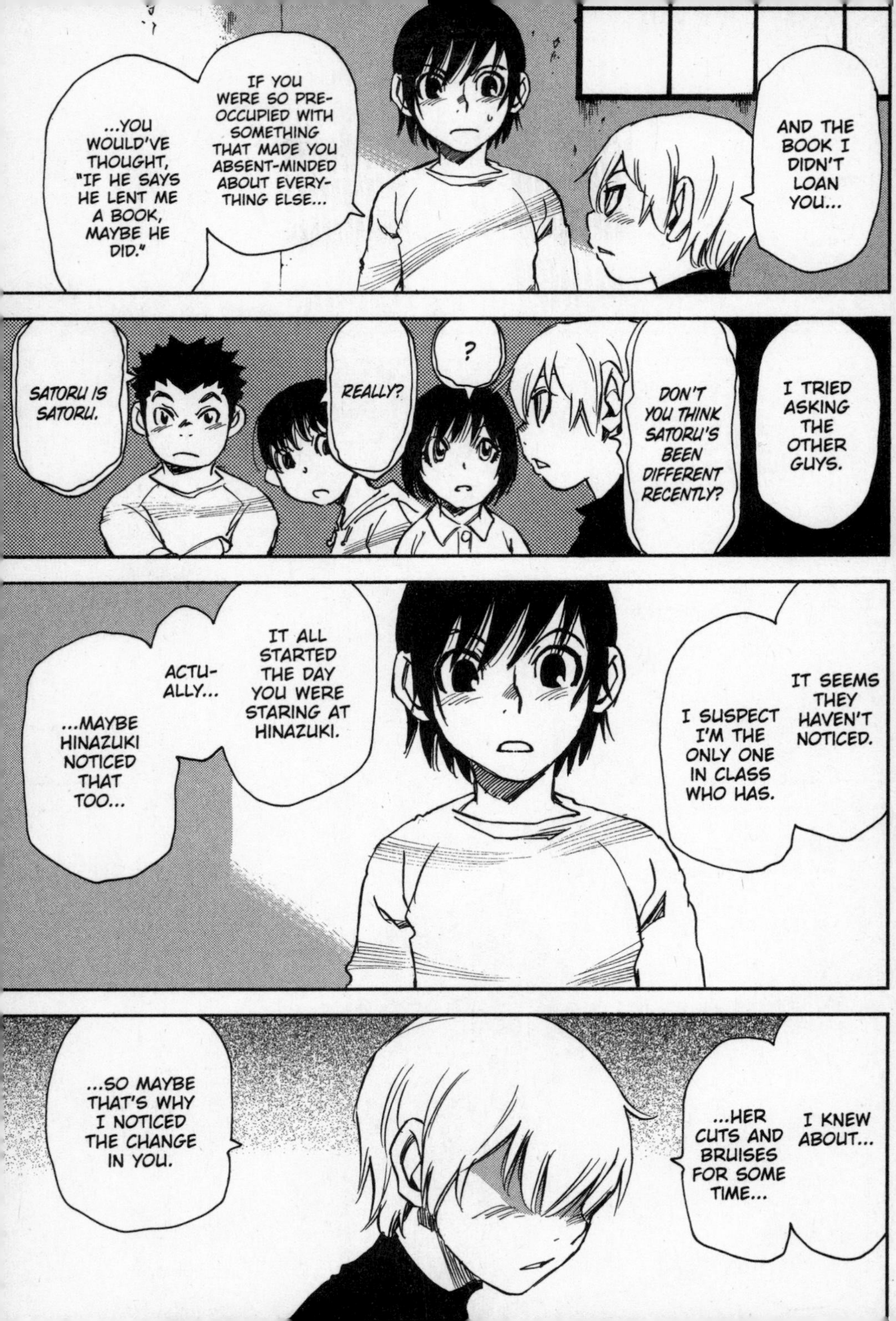
AND THE BOOK I DIDN'T LOAN YOU...
IF YOU WERE SO PRE-OCCUPIED WITH SOMETHING THAT MADE YOU ABSENT-MINDED ABOUT EVERY-THING ELSE...
...YOU WOULD'VE THOUGHT, "IF HE SAYS HE LENT ME A BOOK, MAYBE HE DID."
I TRIED ASKING THE OTHER GUYS.
DON'T YOU THINK SATORU'S BEEN DIFFERENT RECENTLY?
?
REALLY?
SATORU IS SATORU.
IT SEEMS THEY HAVEN'T NOTICED.
I SUSPECT I'M THE ONLY ONE IN CLASS WHO HAS.
IT ALL STARTED THE DAY YOU WERE STARING AT HINAZUKI.
ACTU-ALLY...
...MAYBE HINAZUKI NOTICED THAT TOO...
I KNEW ABOUT...
...HER CUTS AND BRUISES FOR SOME TIME...
...SO MAYBE THAT'S WHY I NOTICED THE CHANGE IN YOU.

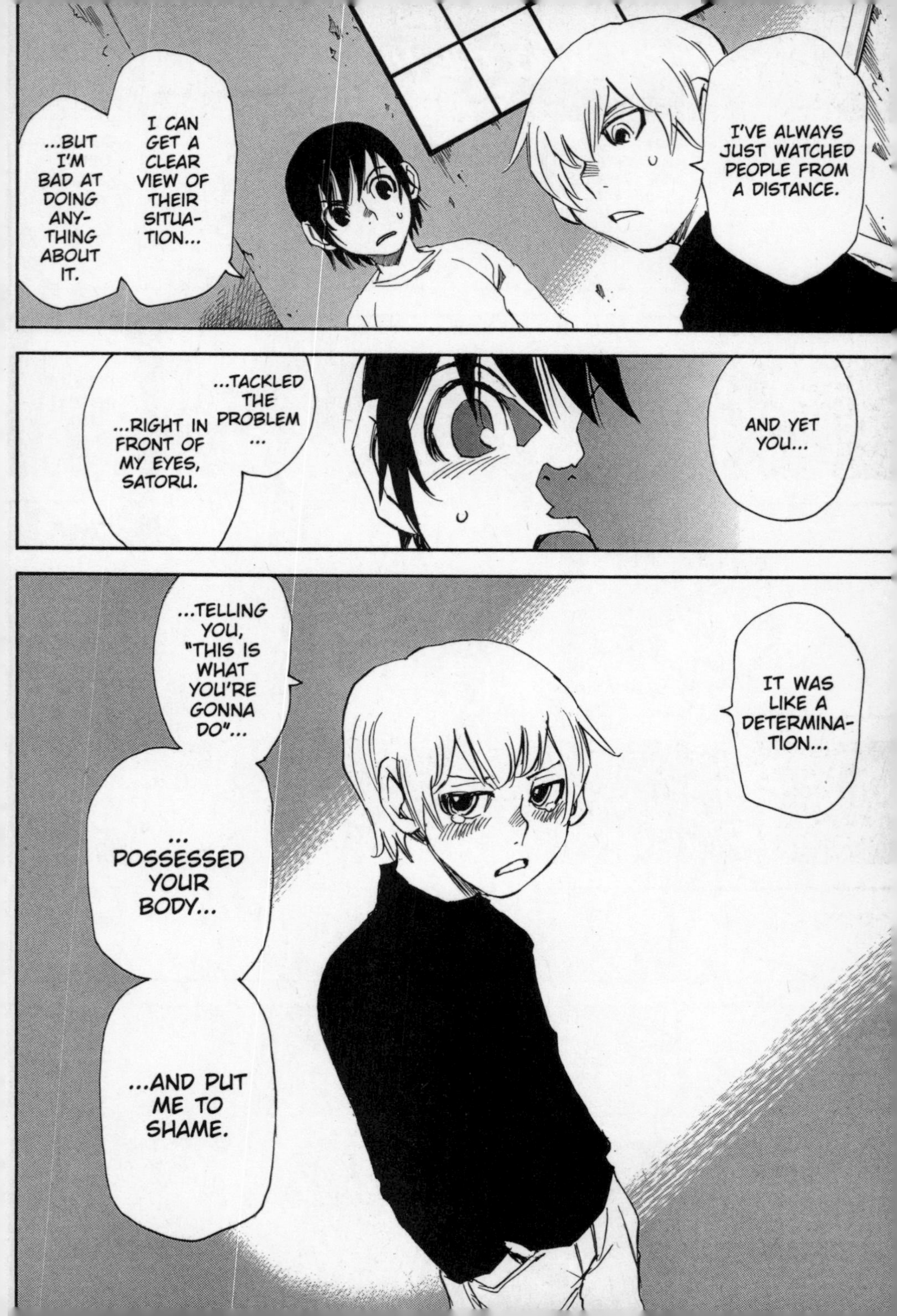
I'VE ALWAYS JUST WATCHED PEOPLE FROM A DISTANCE.
I CAN GET A CLEAR VIEW OF THEIR SITUATION...
...BUT I'M BAD AT DOING ANYTHING ABOUT IT.
AND YET YOU...
...TACKLED THE PROBLEM ...
...RIGHT IN FRONT OF MY EYES, SATORU.
IT WAS LIKE A DETERMINATION...
...TELLING YOU, "THIS IS WHAT YOU'RE GONNA DO"...
... POSSESSED YOUR BODY...
...AND PUT ME TO SHAME.

WHO AM I...? WHO THE HELL AM I?

I'M...

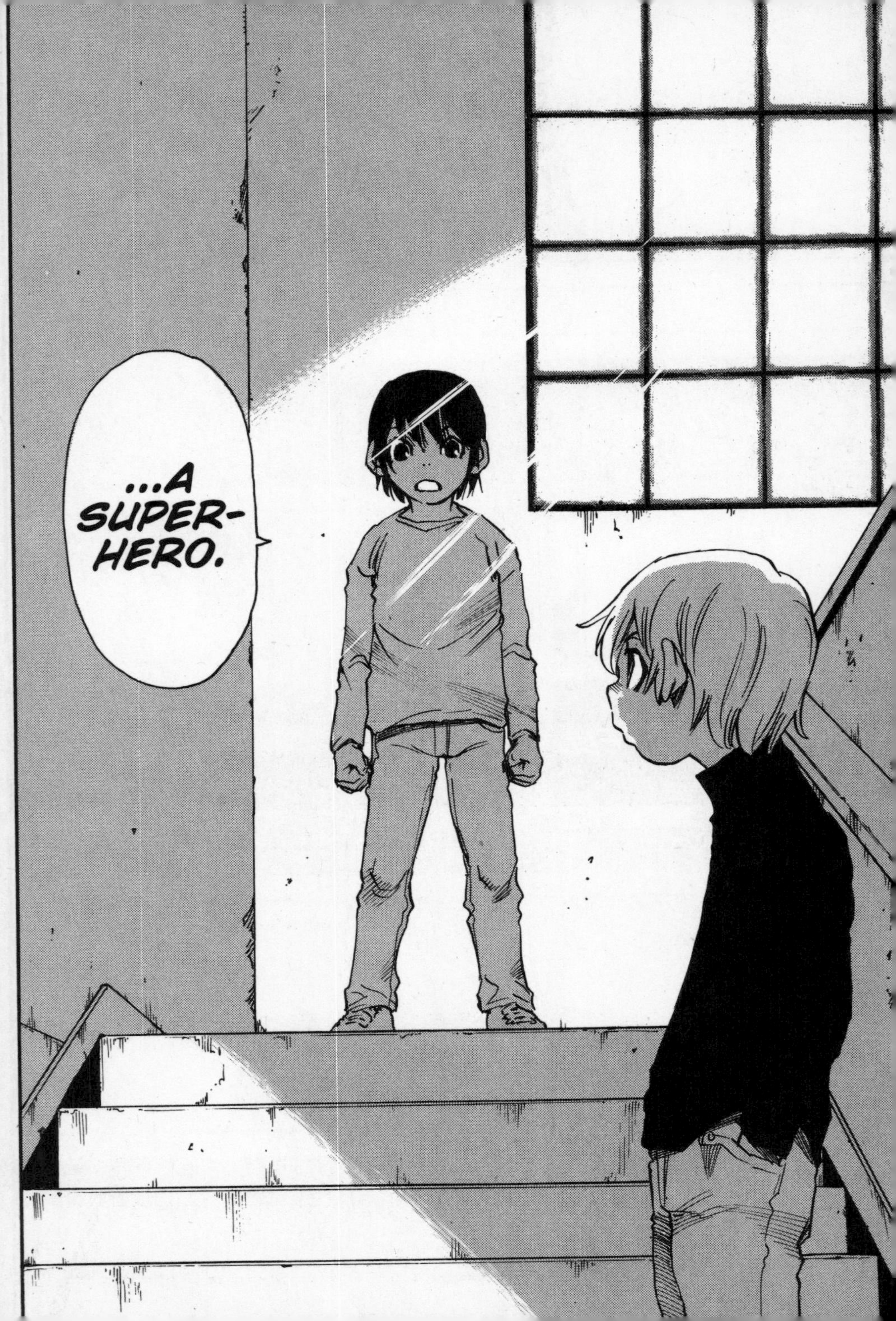
...A SUPER-HERO.

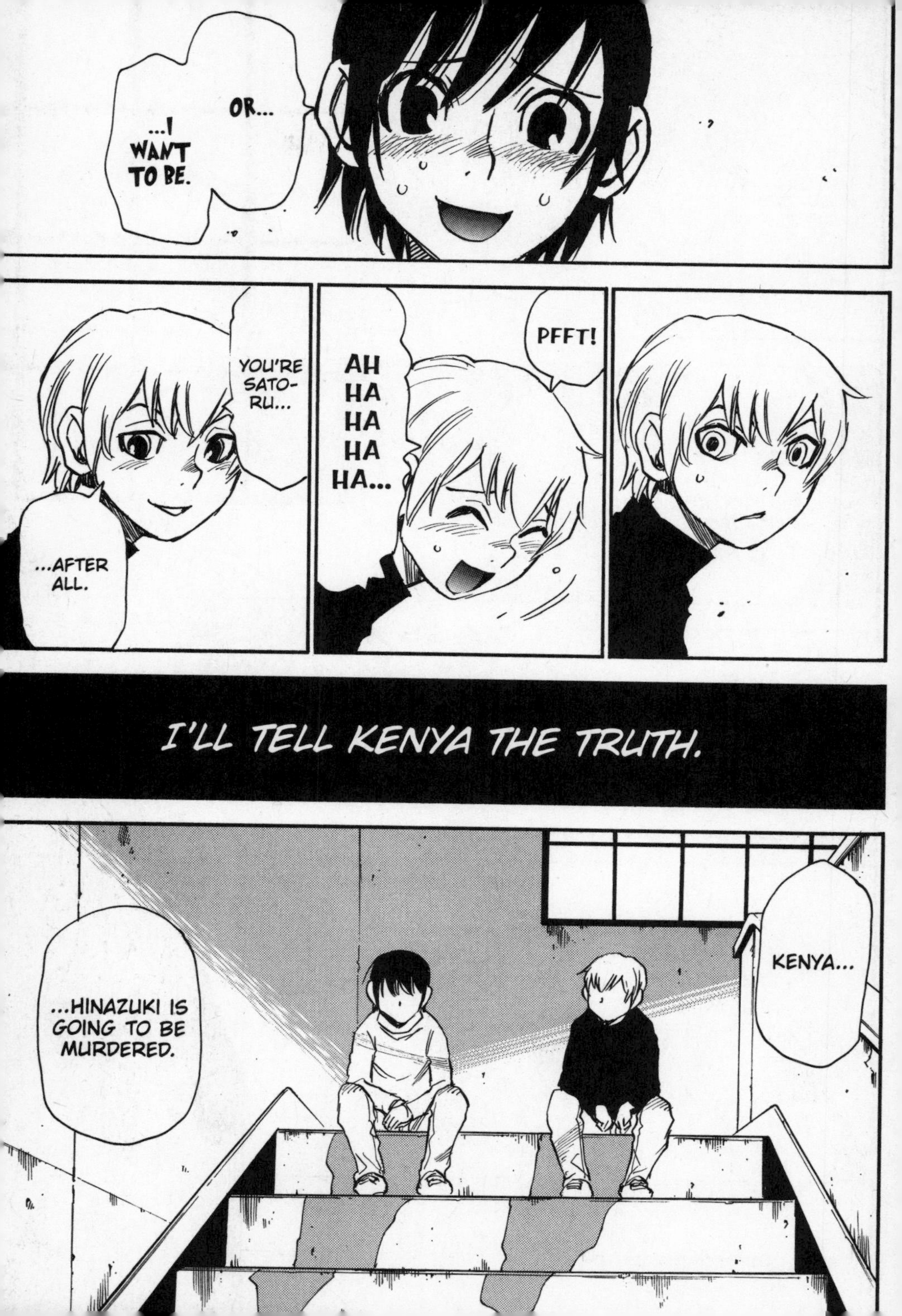
OR...
...I WANT TO BE.
PFFT!
AH HA HA HA HA...
YOU'RE SATO-RU...
...AFTER ALL.
I'LL TELL KENYA THE TRUTH.
KENYA...
...HINAZUKI IS GOING TO BE MURDERED.

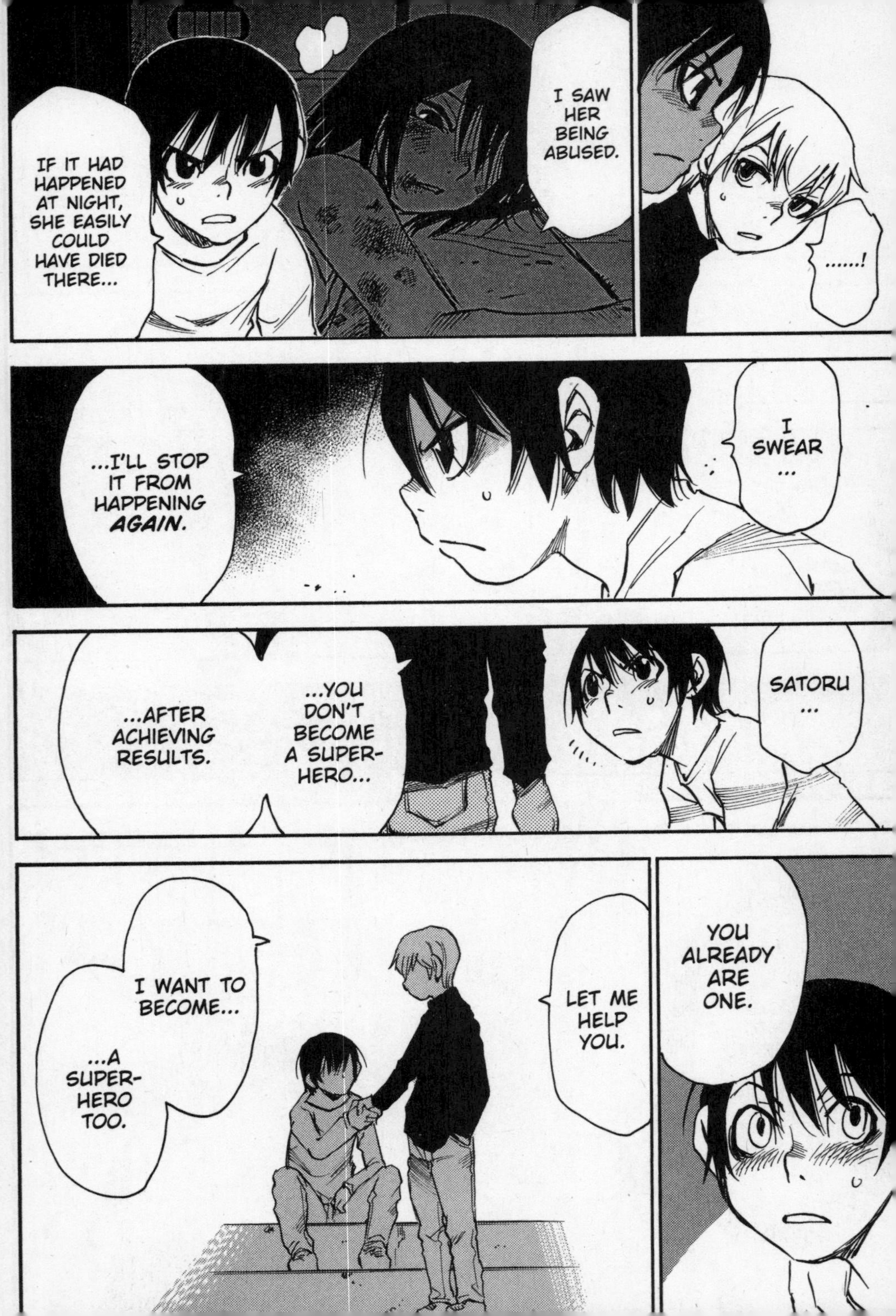

......!
I SAW HER BEING ABUSED.
IF IT HAD HAPPENED AT NIGHT, SHE EASILY COULD HAVE DIED THERE...
I SWEAR...
...I'LL STOP IT FROM HAPPENING *AGAIN*.
SATORU...
...YOU DON'T BECOME A SUPER-HERO...
...AFTER ACHIEVING RESULTS.
YOU ALREADY ARE ONE.
LET ME HELP YOU.
I WANT TO BECOME...
...A SUPER-HERO TOO.

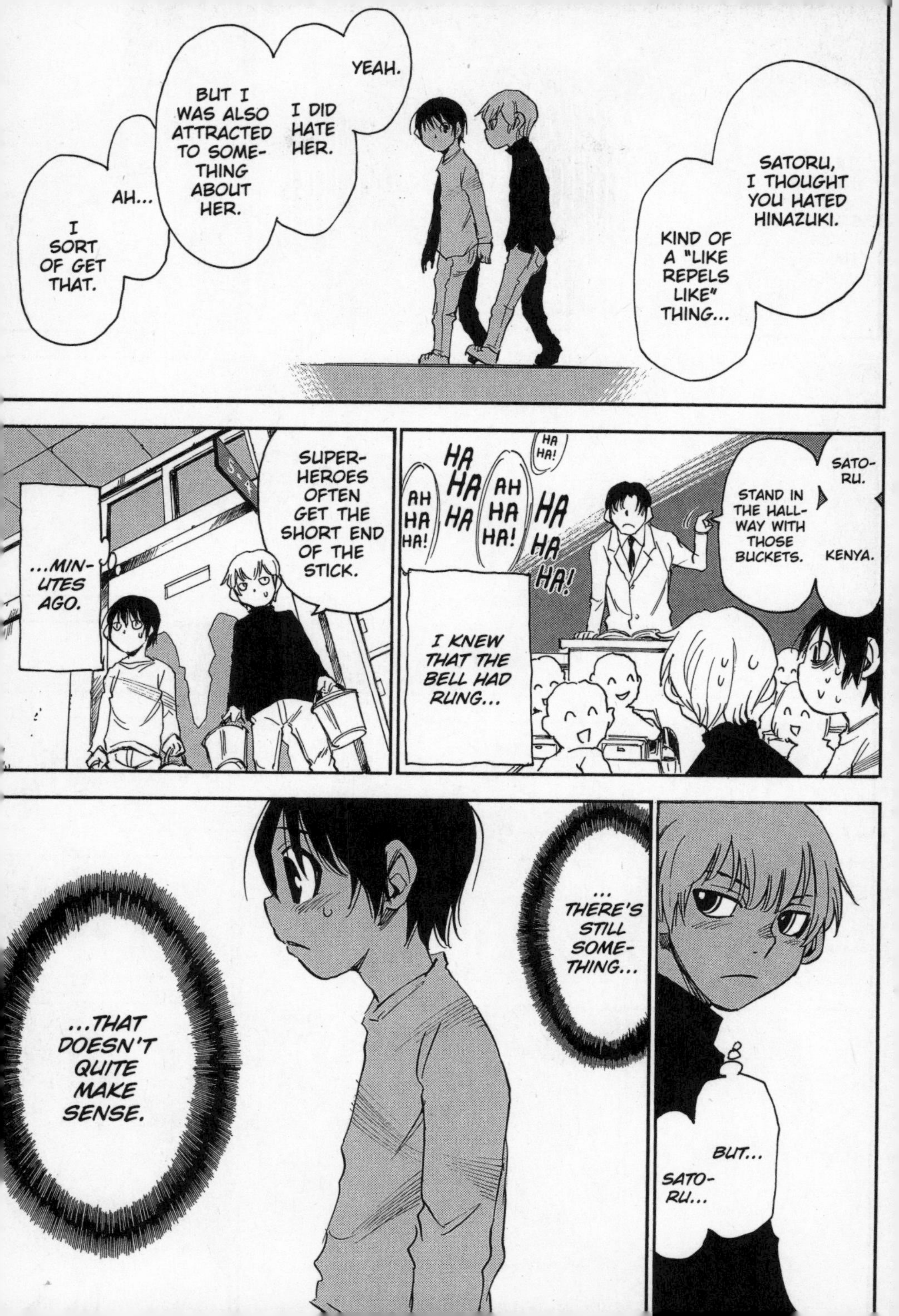
SATORU, I THOUGHT YOU HATED HINAZUKI.
KIND OF A "LIKE REPELS LIKE" THING...
YEAH.
I DID HATE HER.
BUT I WAS ALSO ATTRACTED TO SOME-THING ABOUT HER.
AH...
I SORT OF GET THAT.
SATO-RU.
KENYA.
STAND IN THE HALL-WAY WITH THOSE BUCKETS.
HA HA!
HA HA HA
HA HA HA!
AH HA HA!
AH HA HA!
HA HA HA!
I KNEW THAT THE BELL HAD RUNG...
SUPER-HEROES OFTEN GET THE SHORT END OF THE STICK.
...MIN-UTES AGO.
BUT...
SATO-RU...
...THERE'S STILL SOME-THING...
...THAT DOESN'T QUITE MAKE SENSE.

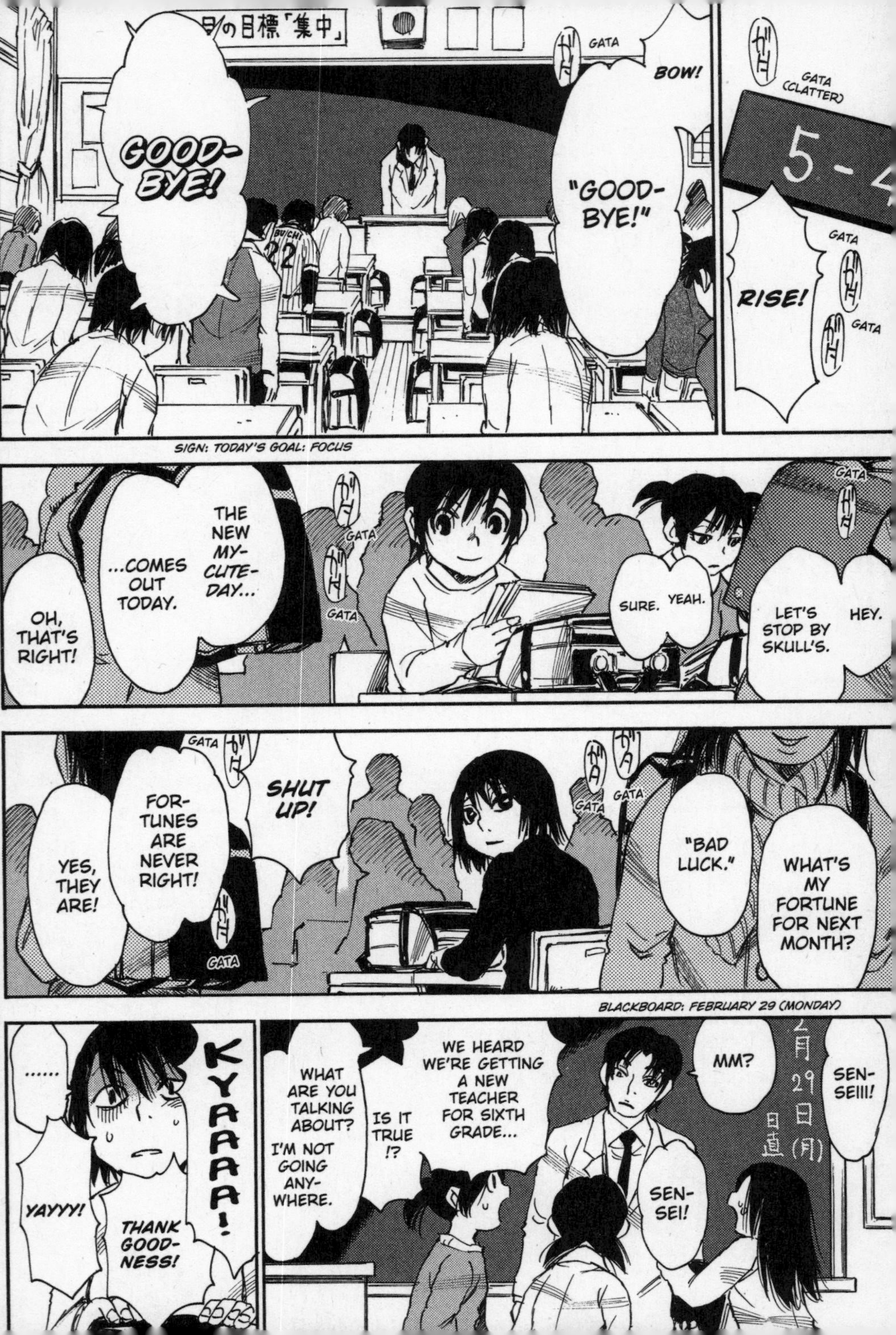
ガタ
GATA (CLATTER)
5-4
RISE!
ガタ
GATA
ガタ
GATA
ガタ
GATA
BOW!
"GOOD-BYE!"
GOOD-BYE!
日の目標「集中」
SIGN: TODAY'S GOAL: FOCUS
GATA
ガタ
HEY.
LET'S STOP BY SKULL'S.
YEAH.
SURE.
ガタ
GATA
ガタ
GATA
THE NEW MY-CUTE-DAY...
...COMES OUT TODAY.
OH, THAT'S RIGHT!
WHAT'S MY FORTUNE FOR NEXT MONTH?
"BAD LUCK."
ガタ
GATA
GATA
SHUT UP!
GATA
ガタ
FOR-TUNES ARE NEVER RIGHT!
YES, THEY ARE!
ガタ
GATA
BLACKBOARD: FEBRUARY 29 (MONDAY)
SEN-SEIII!
2月29日(月)
日直
MM?
SEN-SEI!
WE HEARD WE'RE GETTING A NEW TEACHER FOR SIXTH GRADE...
IS IT TRUE!?
WHAT ARE YOU TALKING ABOUT?
I'M NOT GOING ANY-WHERE.
KYAAAA!
......
THANK GOOD-NESS!
YAYYY!

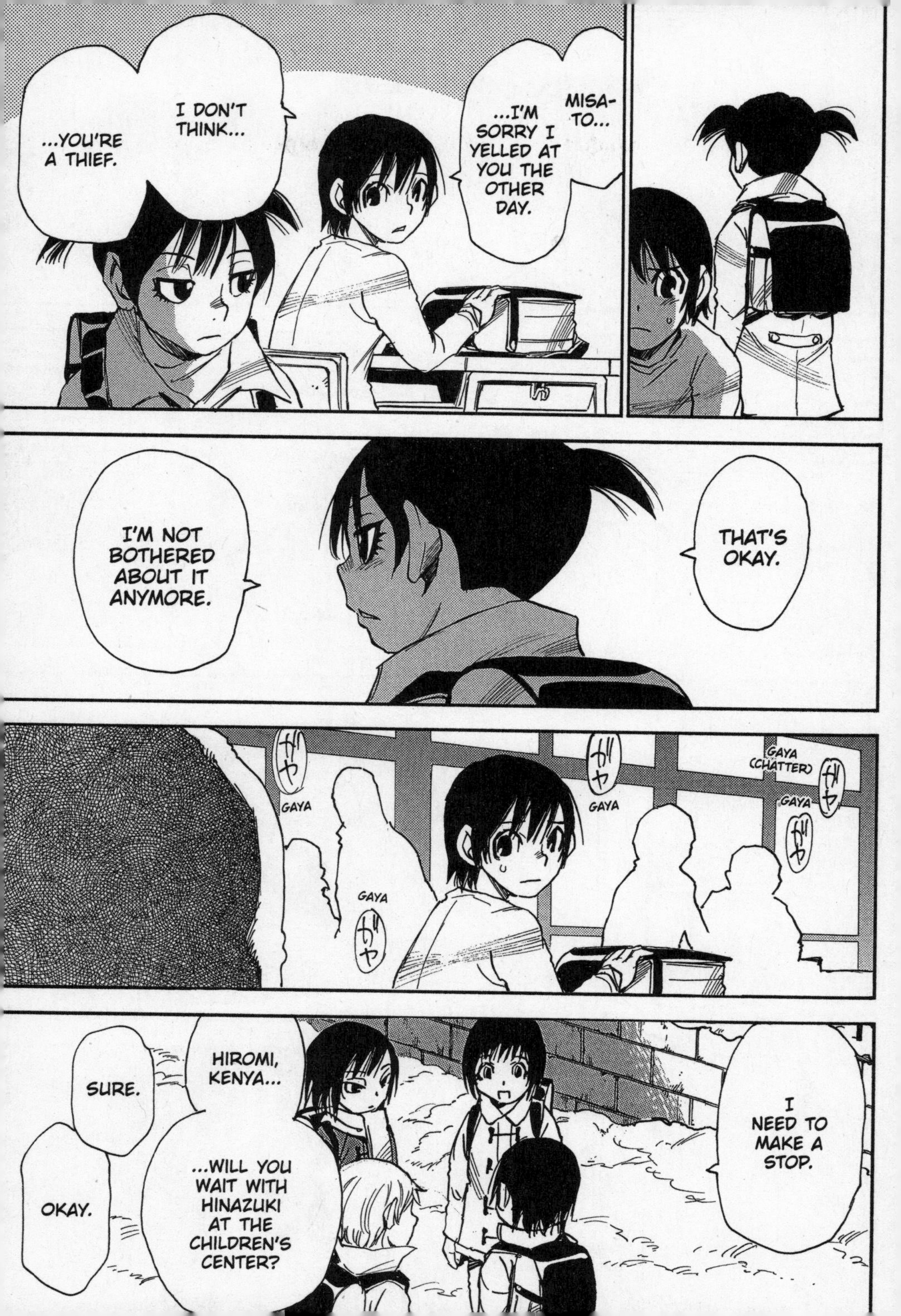
MISA-TO...
...I'M SORRY I YELLED AT YOU THE OTHER DAY.
I DON'T THINK...
...YOU'RE A THIEF.
THAT'S OKAY.
I'M NOT BOTHERED ABOUT IT ANYMORE.
がや
GAYA (CHATTER)
がや
GAYA
がや
GAYA
がや
GAYA
がや
GAYA
I NEED TO MAKE A STOP.
HIROMI, KENYA...
...WILL YOU WAIT WITH HINAZUKI AT THE CHILDREN'S CENTER?
SURE.
OKAY.

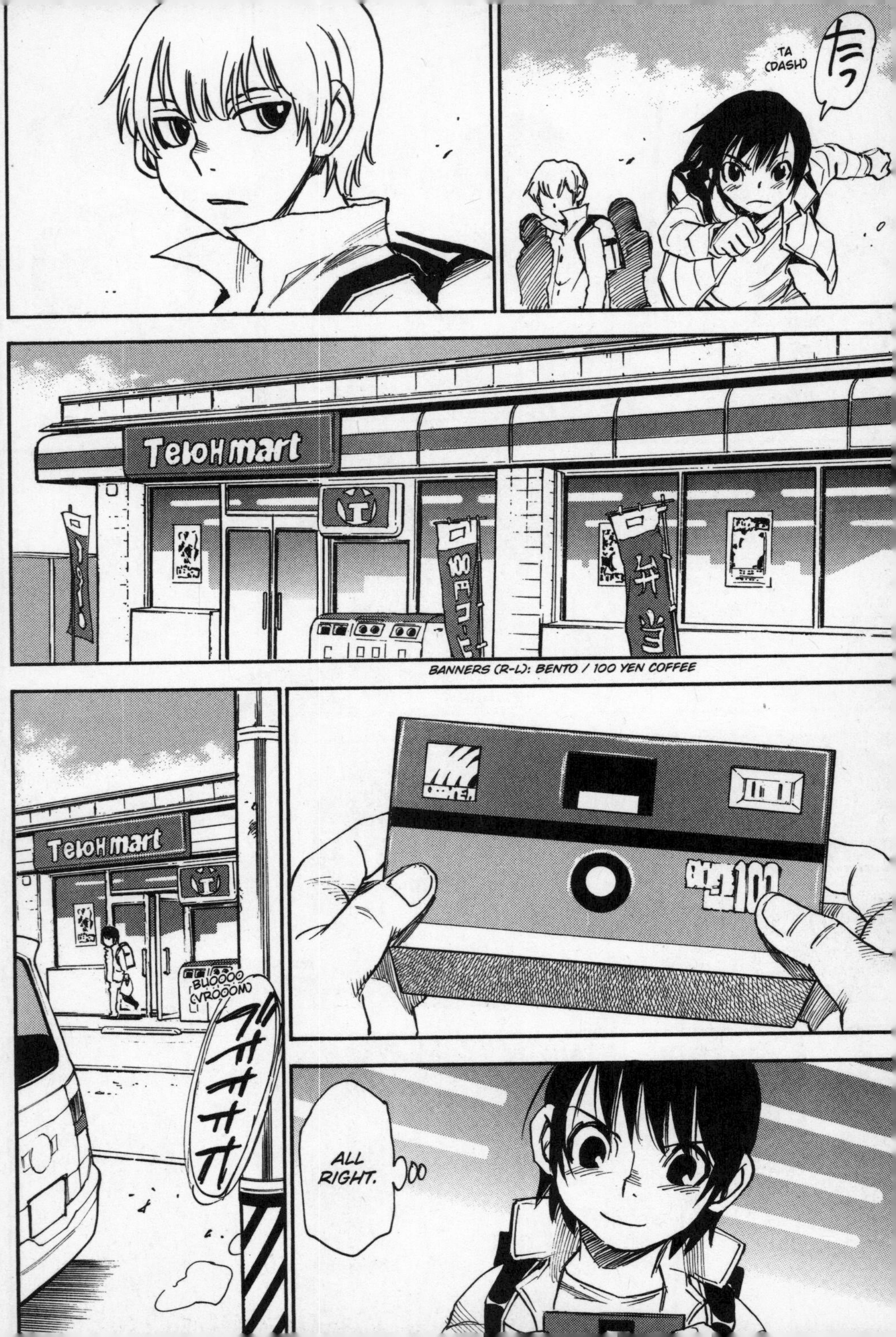
TA (DASH)
TeIOH mart
BANNERS (R-L): BENTO / 100 YEN COFFEE
ALL RIGHT.
BUOOOO (VROOOM)

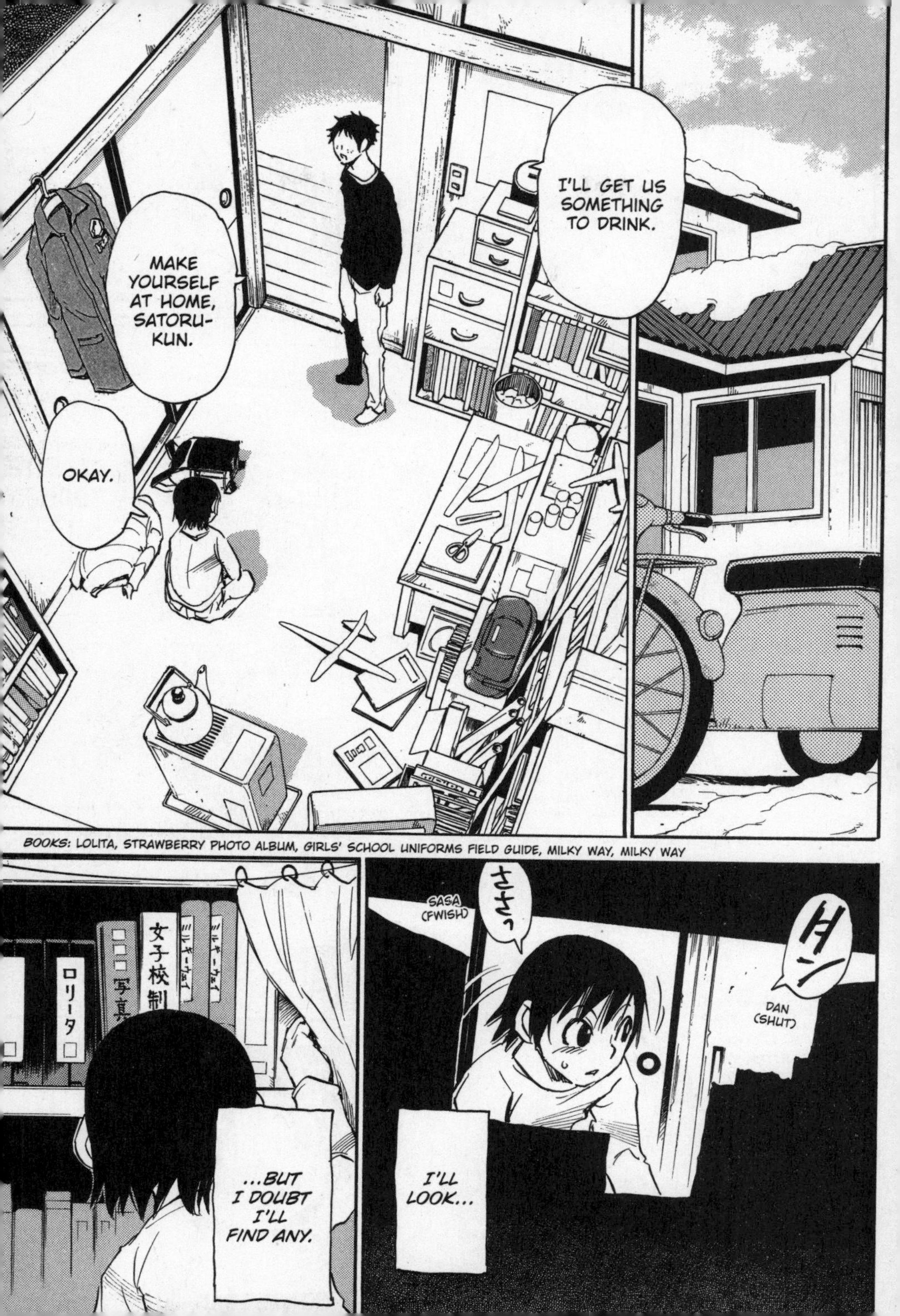
I'LL GET US SOMETHING TO DRINK.
MAKE YOURSELF AT HOME, SATORU-KUN.
OKAY.
BOOKS: LOLITA, STRAWBERRY PHOTO ALBUM, GIRLS' SCHOOL UNIFORMS FIELD GUIDE, MILKY WAY, MILKY WAY
ささっ
SASA (FWISH)
ダン
DAN (SHUT)
I'LL LOOK...
...BUT I DOUBT I'LL FIND ANY.

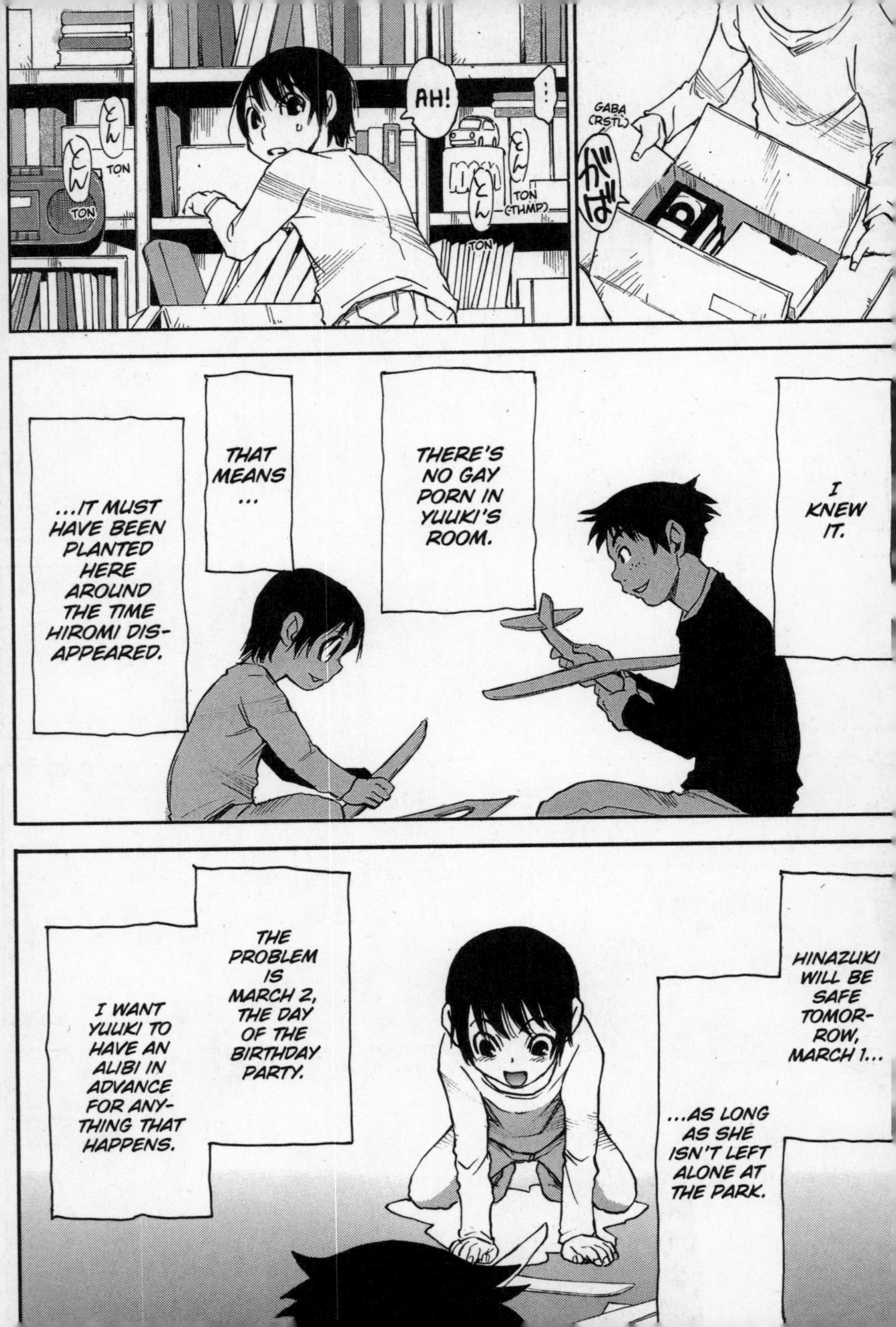
がば
GABA (RSTL)
…
AH!
とん
TON (THMP)
とん
TON
とん
TON
とん
TON
I KNEW IT.
THERE'S NO GAY PORN IN YUUKI'S ROOM.
THAT MEANS …
…IT MUST HAVE BEEN PLANTED HERE AROUND THE TIME HIROMI DIS-APPEARED.
HINAZUKI WILL BE SAFE TOMOR-ROW, MARCH 1…
…AS LONG AS SHE ISN'T LEFT ALONE AT THE PARK.
THE PROBLEM IS MARCH 2, THE DAY OF THE BIRTHDAY PARTY.
I WANT YUUKI TO HAVE AN ALIBI IN ADVANCE FOR ANY-THING THAT HAPPENS.

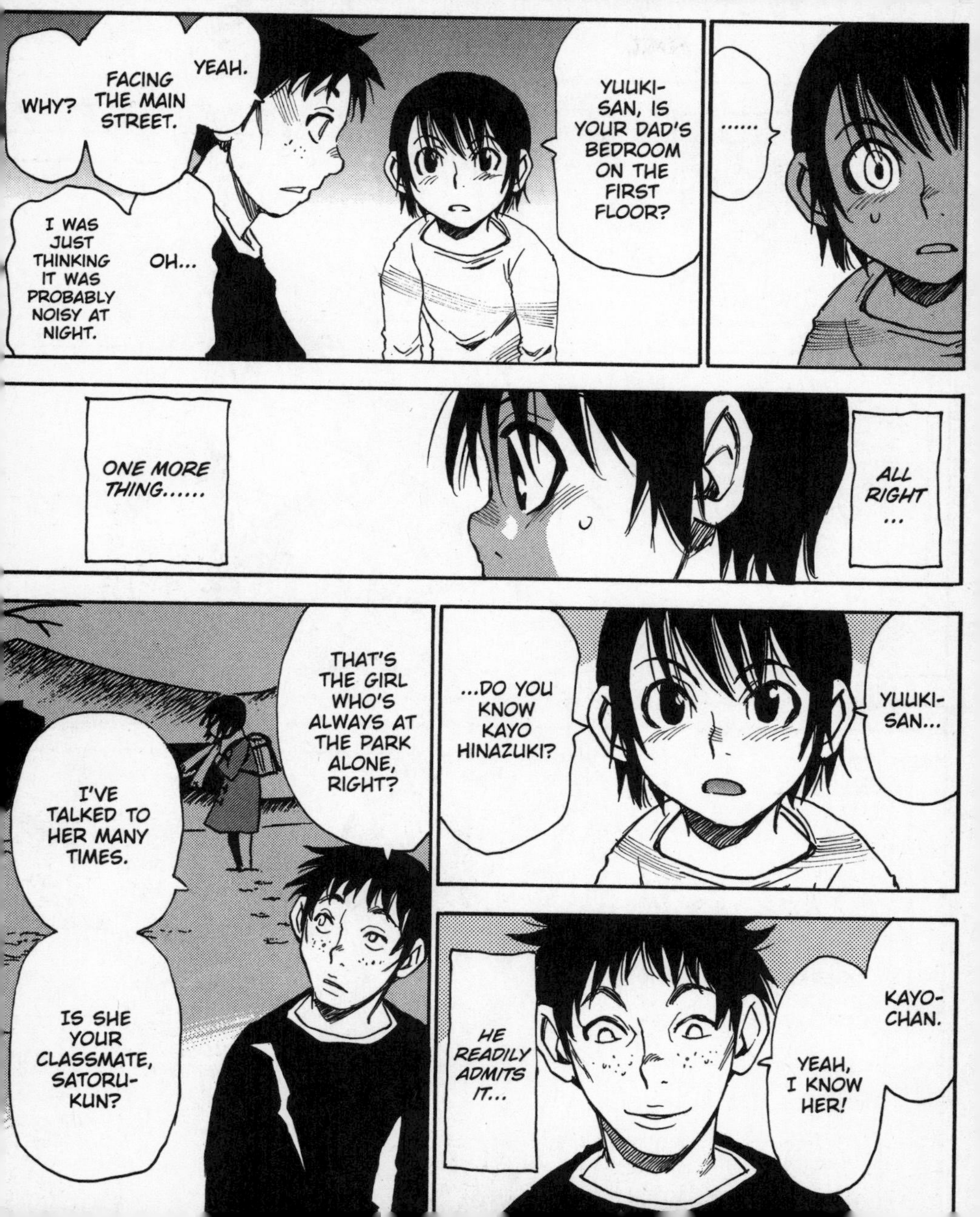
......
YUUKI-SAN, IS YOUR DAD'S BEDROOM ON THE FIRST FLOOR?
YEAH.
FACING THE MAIN STREET.
WHY?
OH...
I WAS JUST THINKING IT WAS PROBABLY NOISY AT NIGHT.
ALL RIGHT ...
ONE MORE THING......
YUUKI-SAN...
...DO YOU KNOW KAYO HINAZUKI?
KAYO-CHAN.
YEAH, I KNOW HER!
HE READILY ADMITS IT...
THAT'S THE GIRL WHO'S ALWAYS AT THE PARK ALONE, RIGHT?
I'VE TALKED TO HER MANY TIMES.
IS SHE YOUR CLASSMATE, SATORU-KUN?

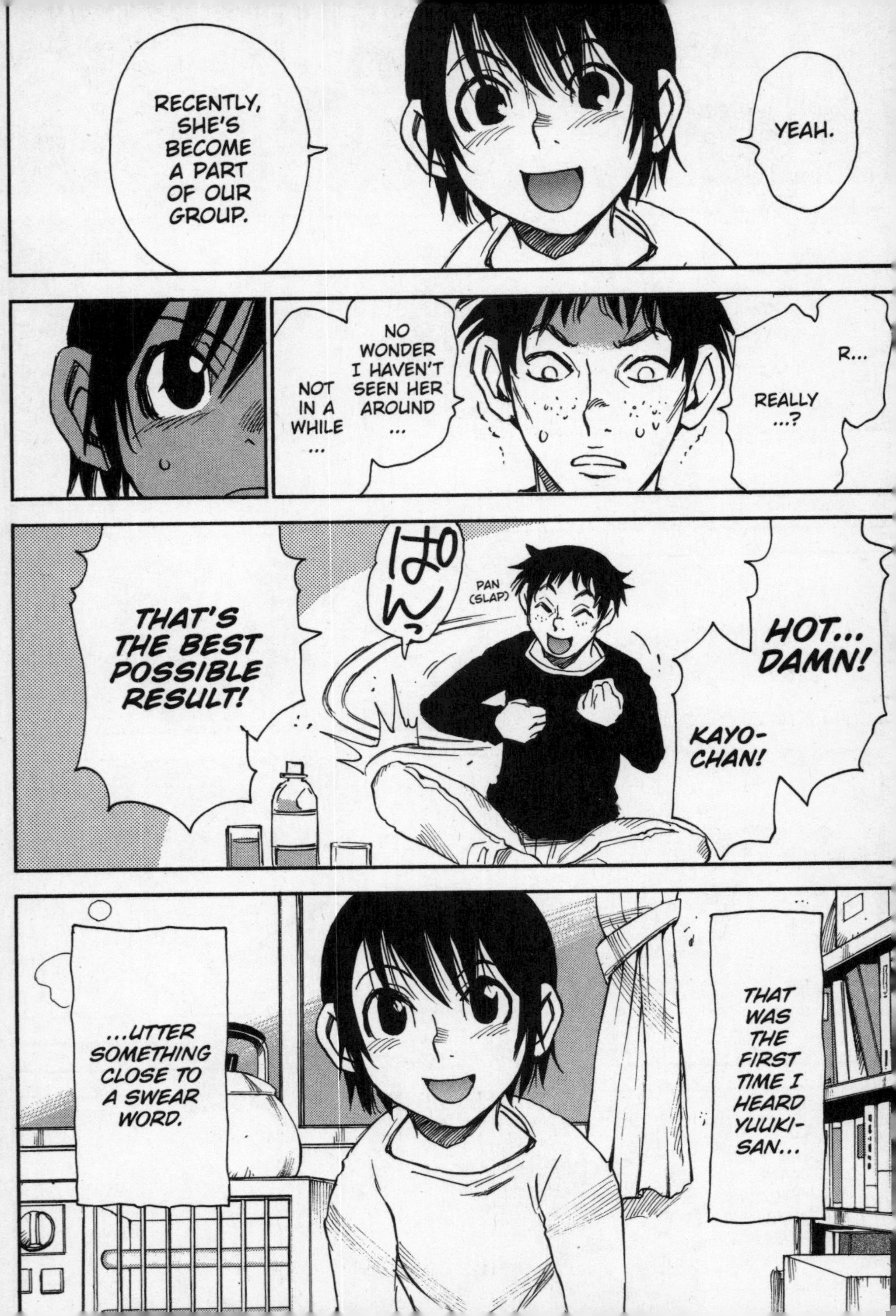
YEAH.
RECENTLY, SHE'S BECOME A PART OF OUR GROUP.
R...
REALLY ...?
NO WONDER I HAVEN'T SEEN HER AROUND ...
NOT IN A WHILE ...
HOT... DAMN!
KAYO-CHAN!
ぱんっ
PAN (SLAP)
THAT'S THE BEST POSSIBLE RESULT!
THAT WAS THE FIRST TIME I HEARD YUUKI-SAN...
...UTTER SOMETHING CLOSE TO A SWEAR WORD.

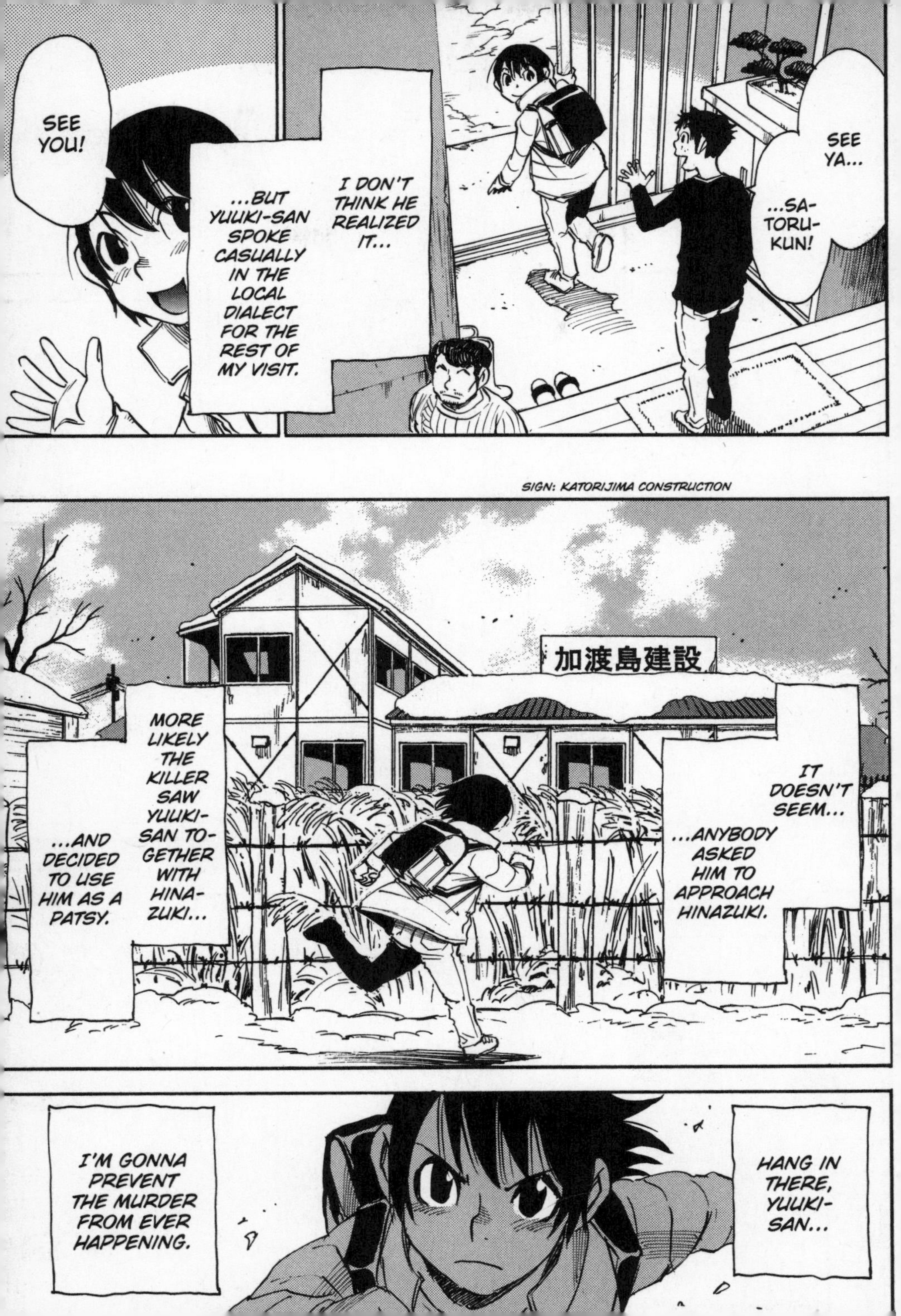
SEE YA...
...SATORU-KUN!
I DON'T THINK HE REALIZED IT...
...BUT YUUKI-SAN SPOKE CASUALLY IN THE LOCAL DIALECT FOR THE REST OF MY VISIT.
SEE YOU!
SIGN: KATORIJIMA CONSTRUCTION
加渡島建設
IT DOESN'T SEEM...
...ANYBODY ASKED HIM TO APPROACH HINAZUKI.
MORE LIKELY THE KILLER SAW YUUKI-SAN TOGETHER WITH HINAZUKI...
...AND DECIDED TO USE HIM AS A PATSY.
HANG IN THERE, YUUKI-SAN...
I'M GONNA PREVENT THE MURDER FROM EVER HAPPENING.

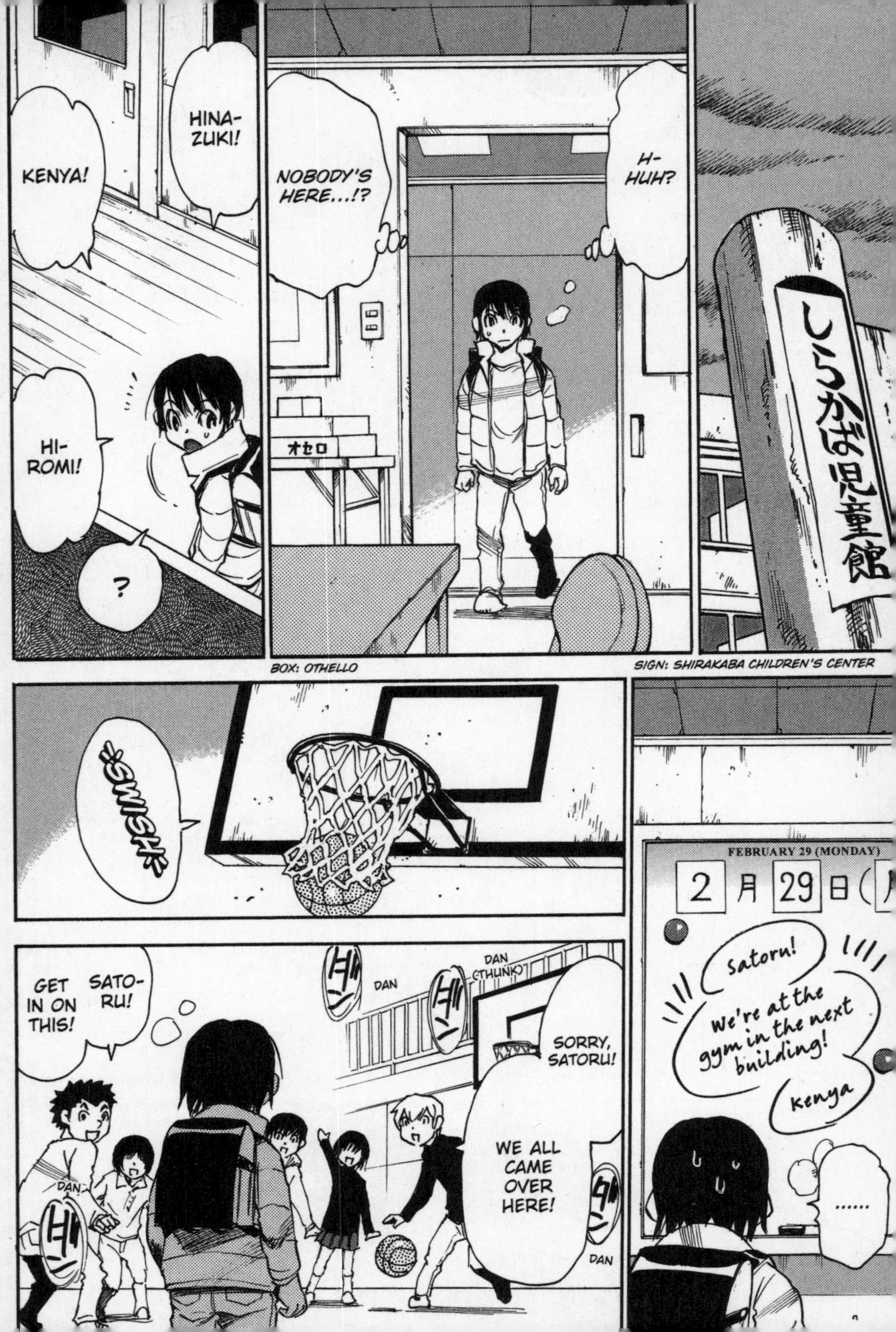
しらかば児童館
H-HUH?
NOBODY'S HERE...!?
HINA-ZUKI!
KENYA!
HI-ROMI!
?
FEBRUARY 29 (MONDAY)
2月29日(月
Satoru! We're at the gym in the next building! Kenya
......
SWISH
DAN (THUNK)
DAN
SORRY, SATORU!
WE ALL CAME OVER HERE!
SATO-RU!
GET IN ON THIS!
DAN
DAN
SIGN: SHIRAKABA CHILDREN'S CENTER

BOX: OTHELLO

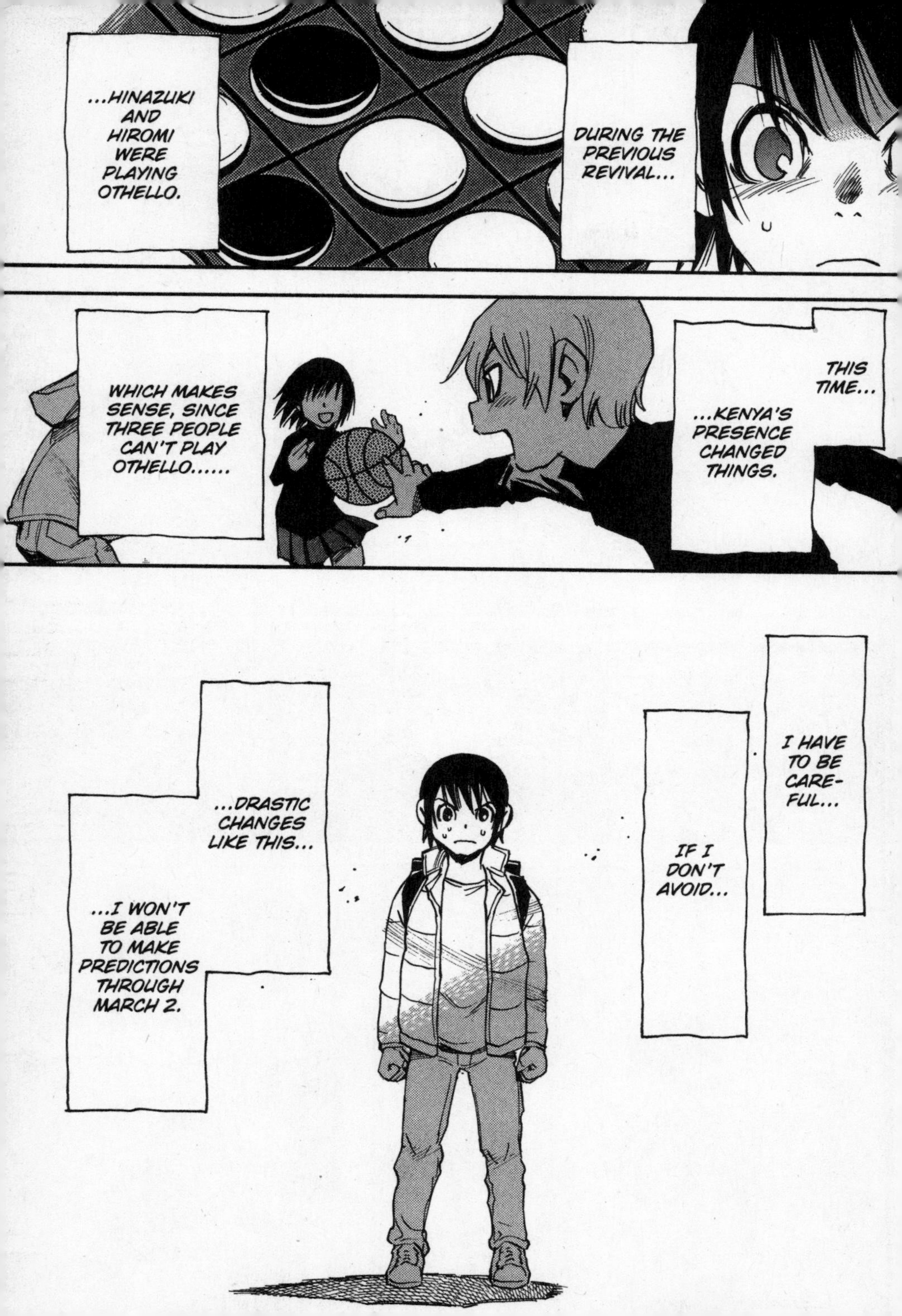
DURING THE PREVIOUS REVIVAL...
...HINAZUKI AND HIROMI WERE PLAYING OTHELLO.
THIS TIME...
...KENYA'S PRESENCE CHANGED THINGS.
WHICH MAKES SENSE, SINCE THREE PEOPLE CAN'T PLAY OTHELLO......
I HAVE TO BE CARE-FUL...
IF I DON'T AVOID...
...DRASTIC CHANGES LIKE THIS...
...I WON'T BE ABLE TO MAKE PREDICTIONS THROUGH MARCH 2.

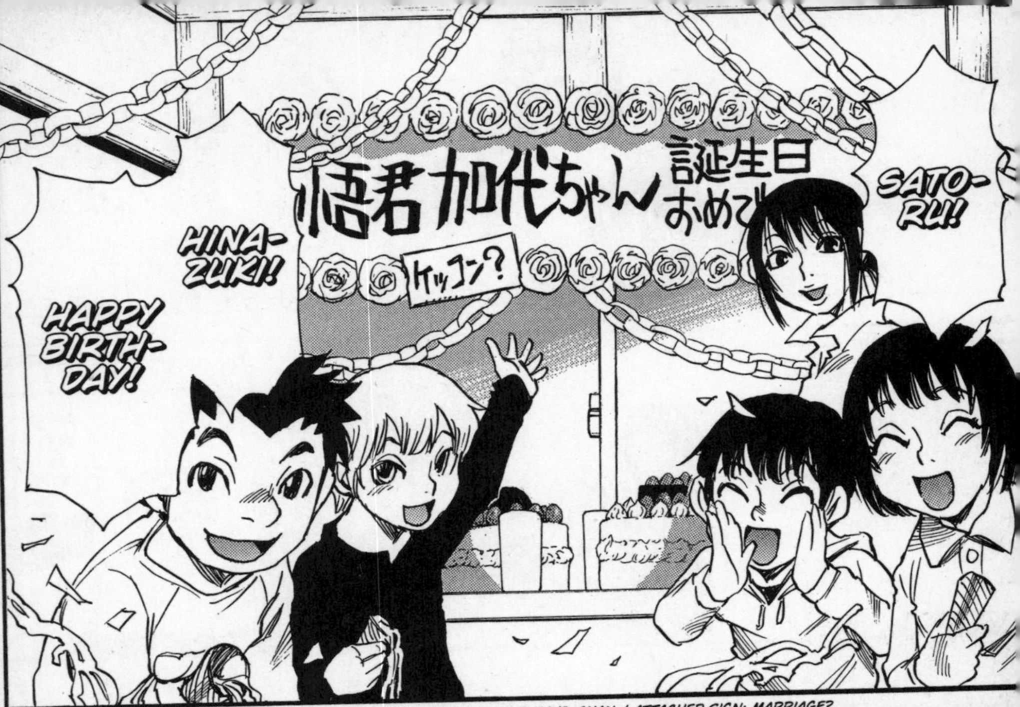
SATO-RU!
悟君加代ちゃん
誕生日
おめで
ケッコン?
HINA-ZUKI!
HAPPY BIRTH-DAY!
BANNER: HAPPY BIRTHDAY, SATORU-KUN AND KAYO-CHAN / ATTACHED SIGN: MARRIAGE?

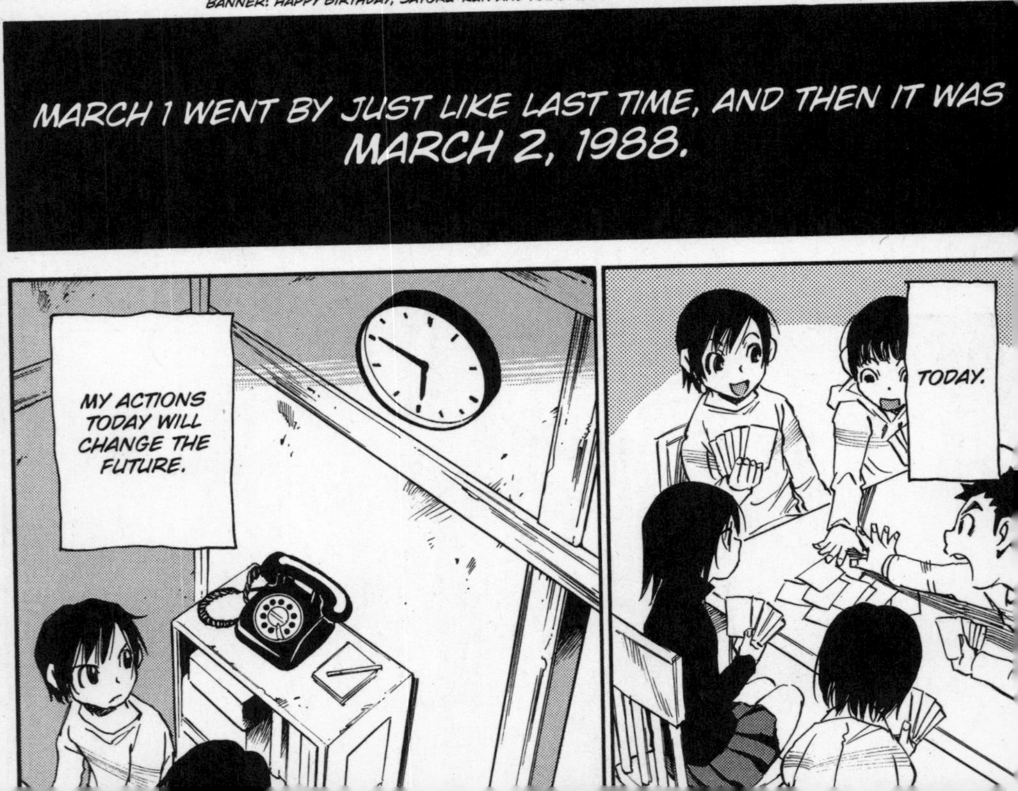
MARCH 1 WENT BY JUST LIKE LAST TIME, AND THEN IT WAS MARCH 2, 1988.
TODAY.
MY ACTIONS TODAY WILL CHANGE THE FUTURE.

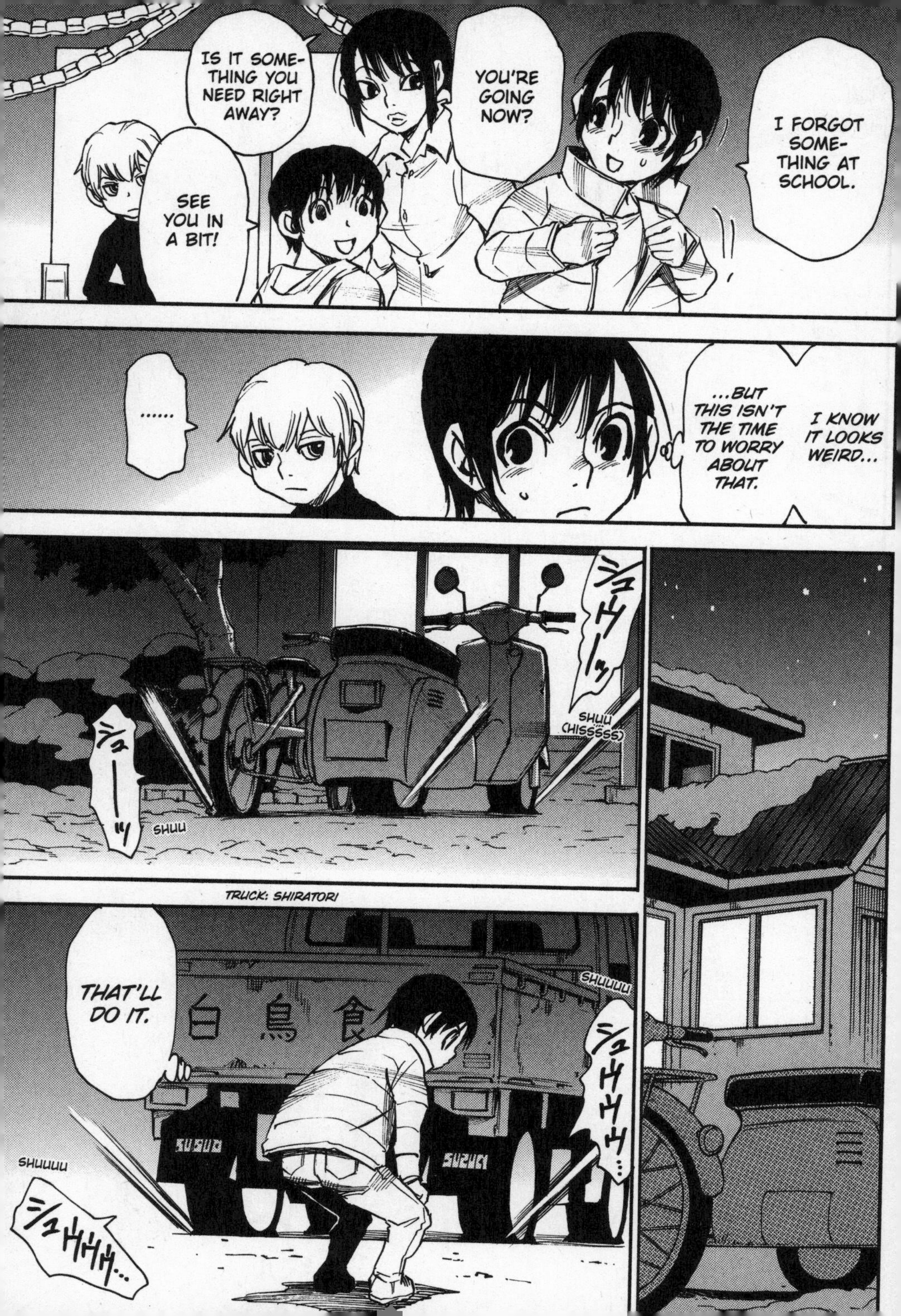
I FORGOT SOME-THING AT SCHOOL.
YOU'RE GOING NOW?
IS IT SOME-THING YOU NEED RIGHT AWAY?
SEE YOU IN A BIT!
I KNOW IT LOOKS WEIRD...
...BUT THIS ISN'T THE TIME TO WORRY ABOUT THAT.
......
シュウーッ
SHUU (HISSSSS)
シューーッ
SHUU
TRUCK: SHIRATORI
白鳥食
SHUUUU
シュウウウ…
THAT'LL DO IT.
SHUUUU
シュウウウウ…

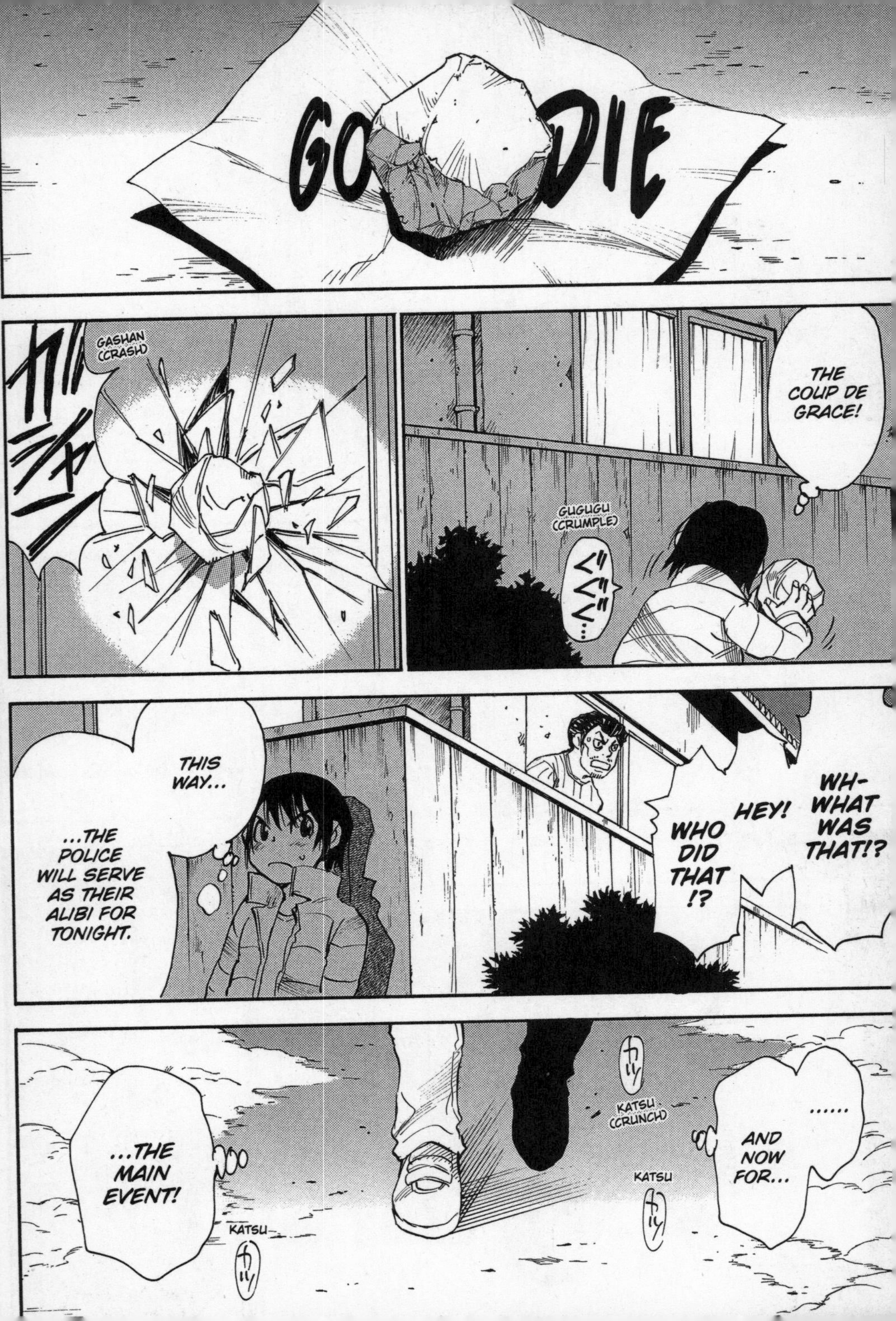
GO DIE
THE COUP DE GRACE!
GUGUGU (CRUMPLE)
ぐぐぐ…
GASHAN (CRASH)
ガシャン
WH- WHAT WAS THAT!?
HEY!
WHO DID THAT!?
THIS WAY...
...THE POLICE WILL SERVE AS THEIR ALIBI FOR TONIGHT.
......
AND NOW FOR...
KATSU (CRUNCH)
カツ
KATSU
カツ
...THE MAIN EVENT!
KATSU
カツ

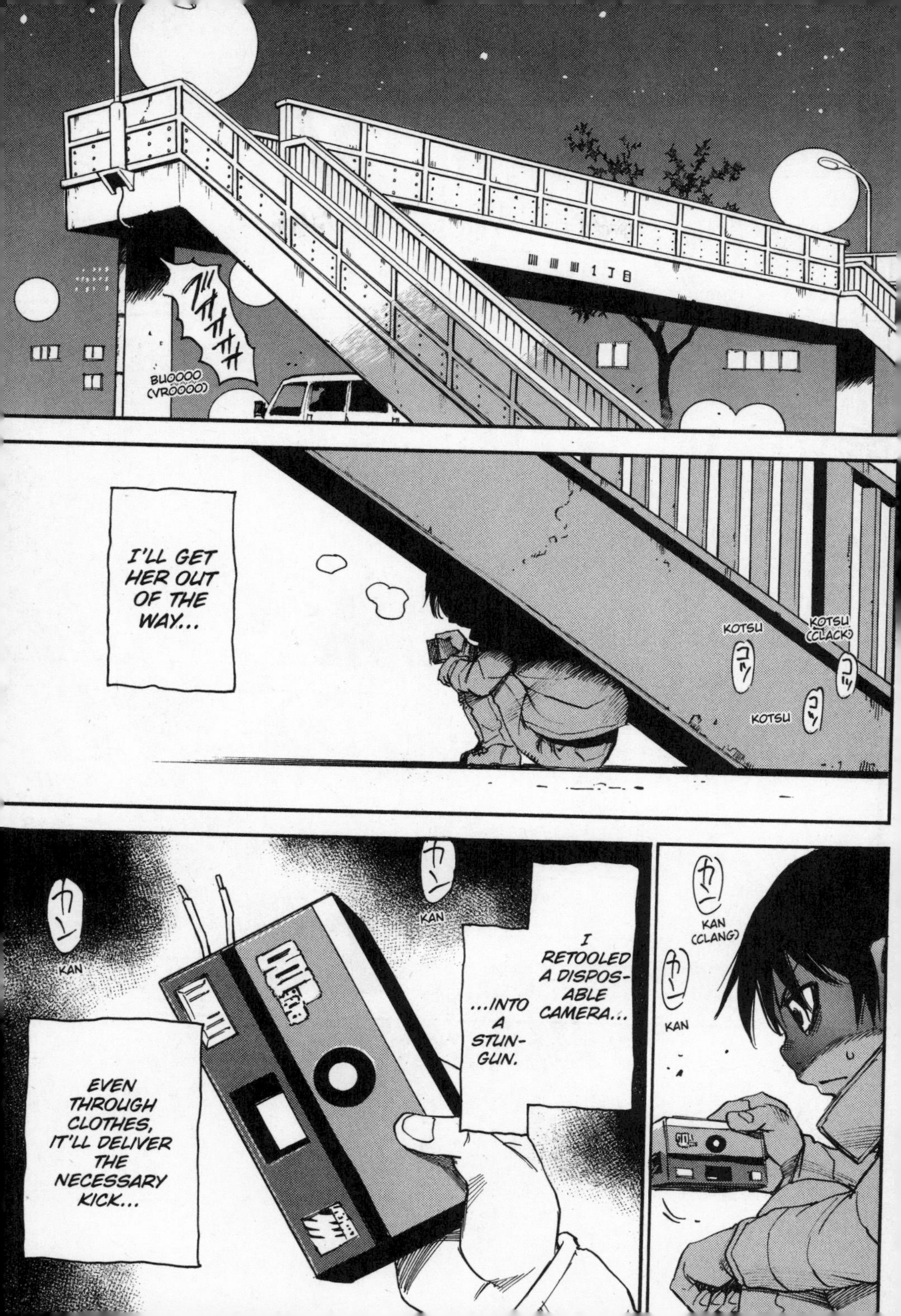
BUOOOO (VROOOO)
I'LL GET HER OUT OF THE WAY...
KOTSU (CLACK)
KOTSU
KOTSU
KAN (CLANG)
KAN
KAN
KAN
I RETOOLED A DISPOSABLE CAMERA...
...INTO A STUN-GUN.
EVEN THROUGH CLOTHES, IT'LL DELIVER THE NECESSARY KICK...

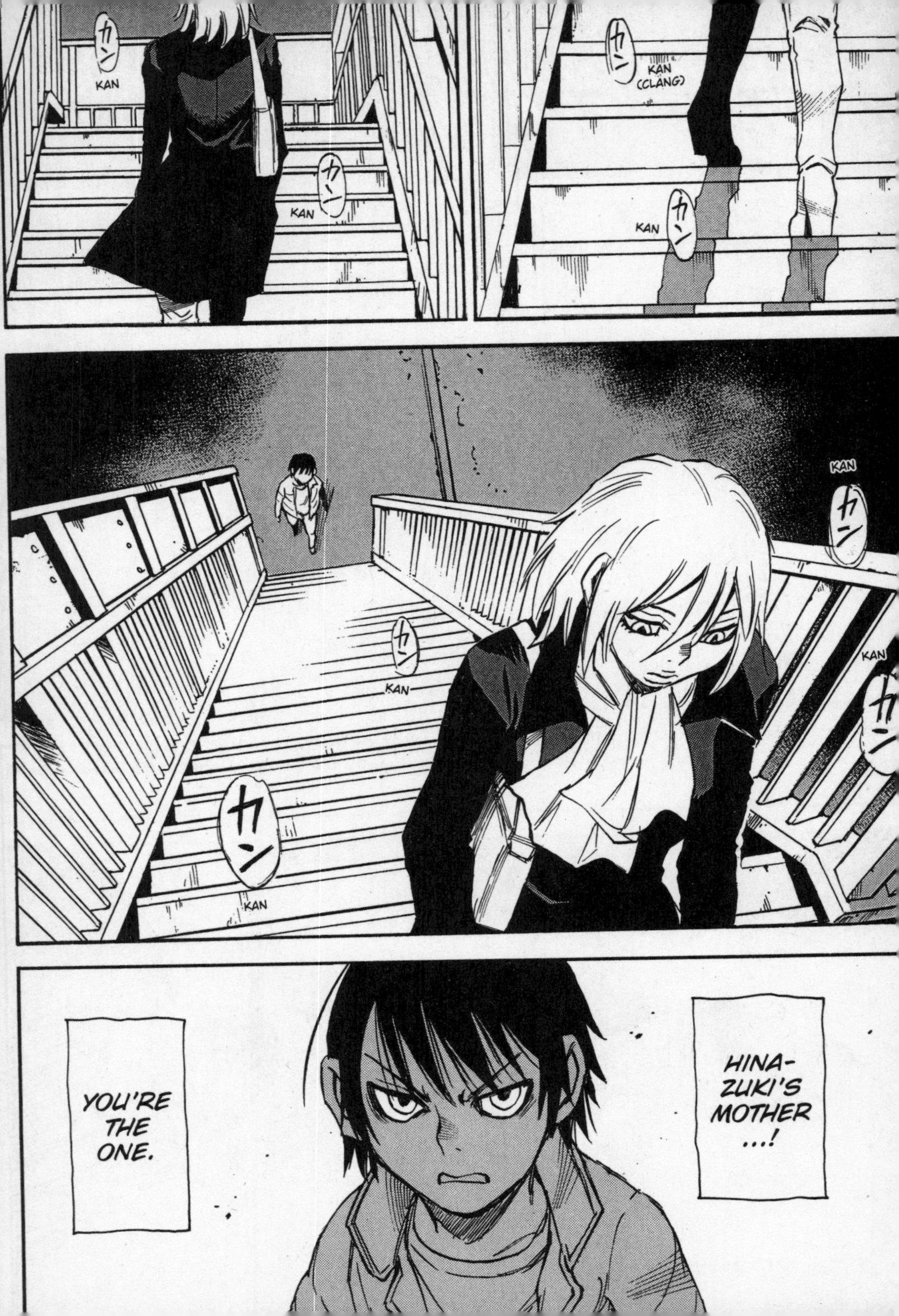
カン
KAN (CLANG)
カン
KAN
カン
KAN
カン
KAN
カン
KAN
カン
KAN
カン
KAN
カン
KAN
HINA-ZUKI'S MOTHER ...!
YOU'RE THE ONE.

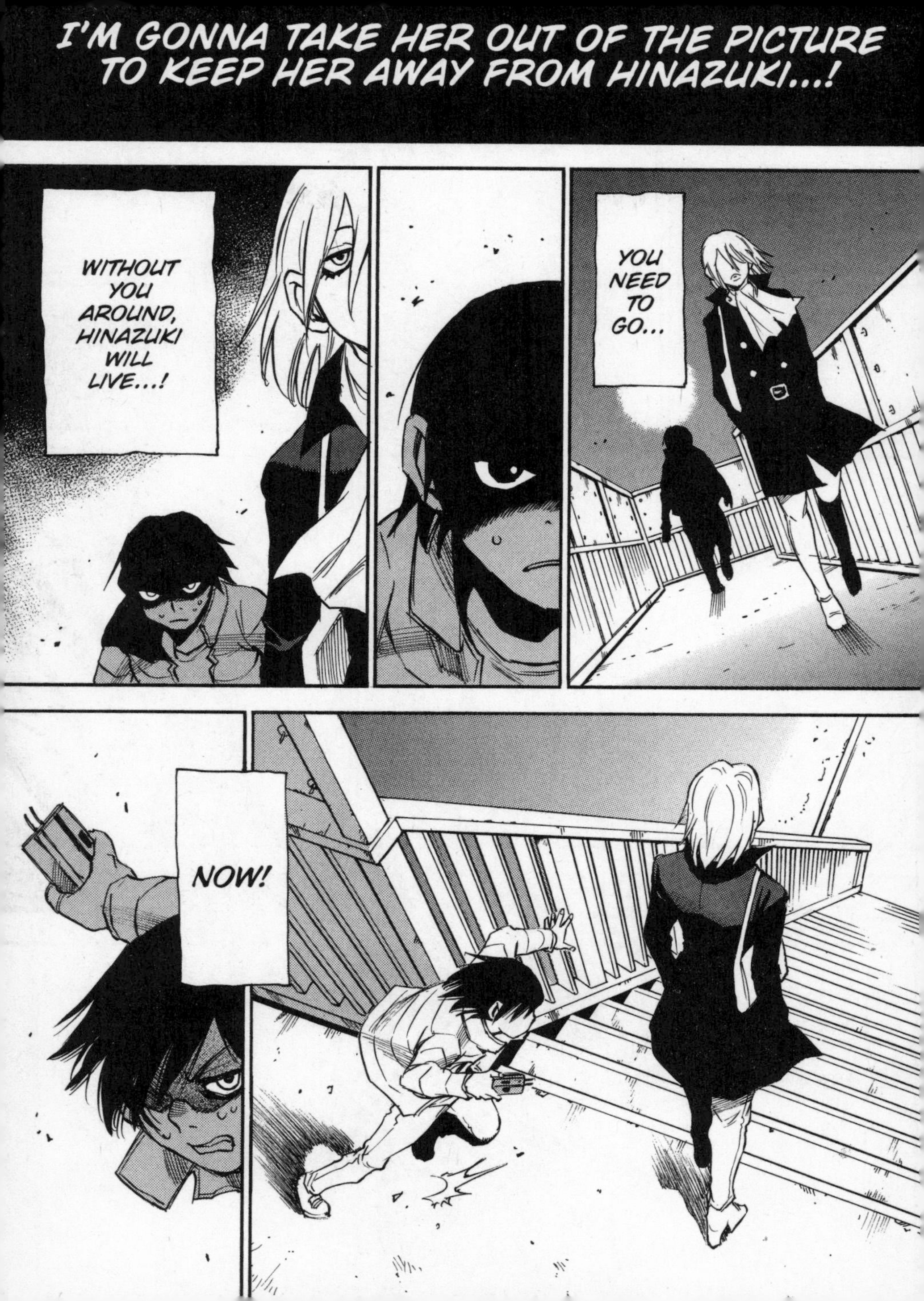
I'M GONNA TAKE HER OUT OF THE PICTURE TO KEEP HER AWAY FROM HINAZUKI...!
YOU NEED TO GO...
WITHOUT YOU AROUND, HINAZUKI WILL LIVE...!
NOW!

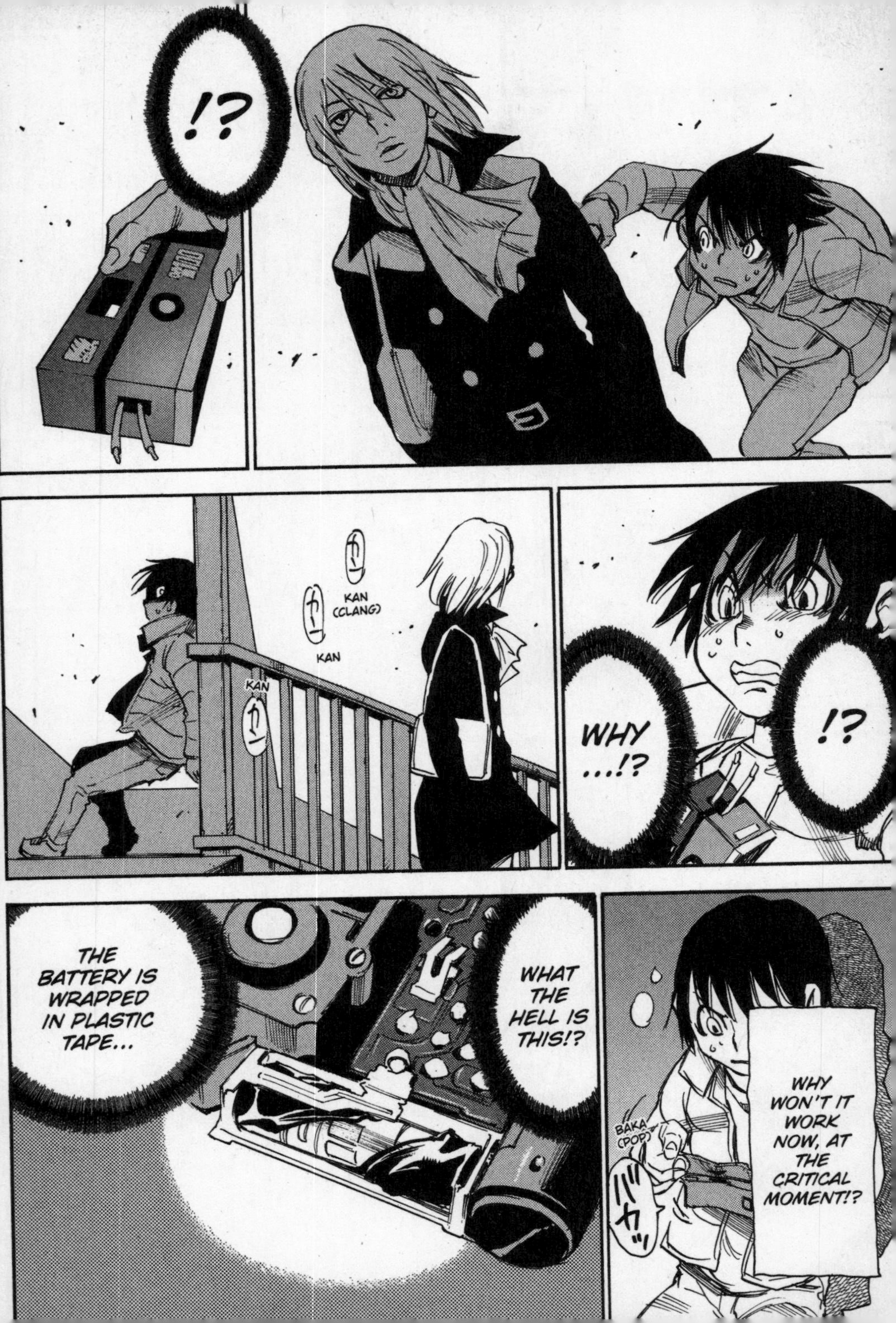
!?
!?
WHY ...!?
KAN (CLANG)
KAN
KAN
WHY WON'T IT WORK NOW, AT THE CRITICAL MOMENT!?
BAKA (POP)
バカッ
WHAT THE HELL IS THIS!?
THE BATTERY IS WRAPPED IN PLASTIC TAPE...

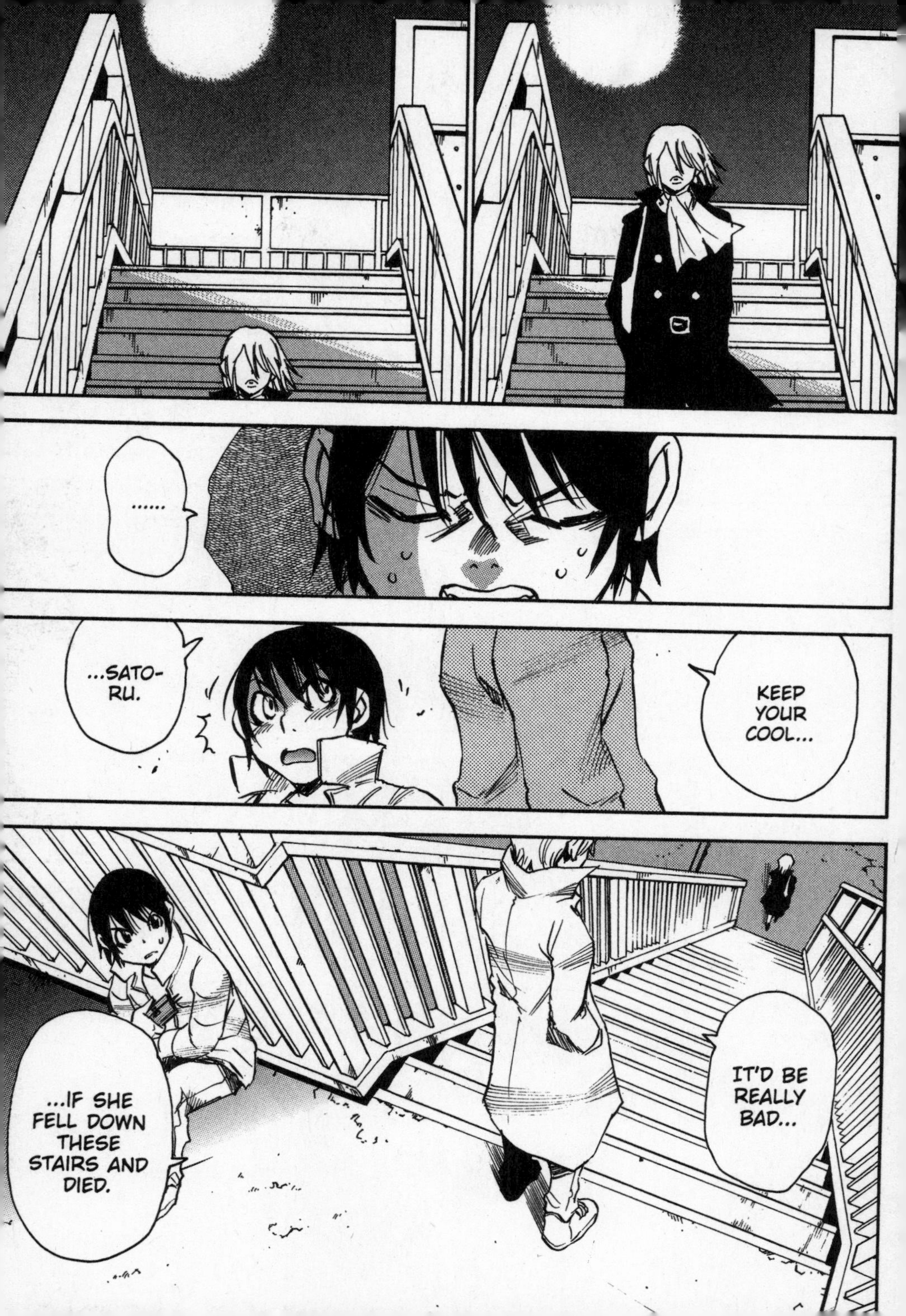
......
KEEP YOUR COOL...
...SATO-RU.
IT'D BE REALLY BAD...
...IF SHE FELL DOWN THESE STAIRS AND DIED.

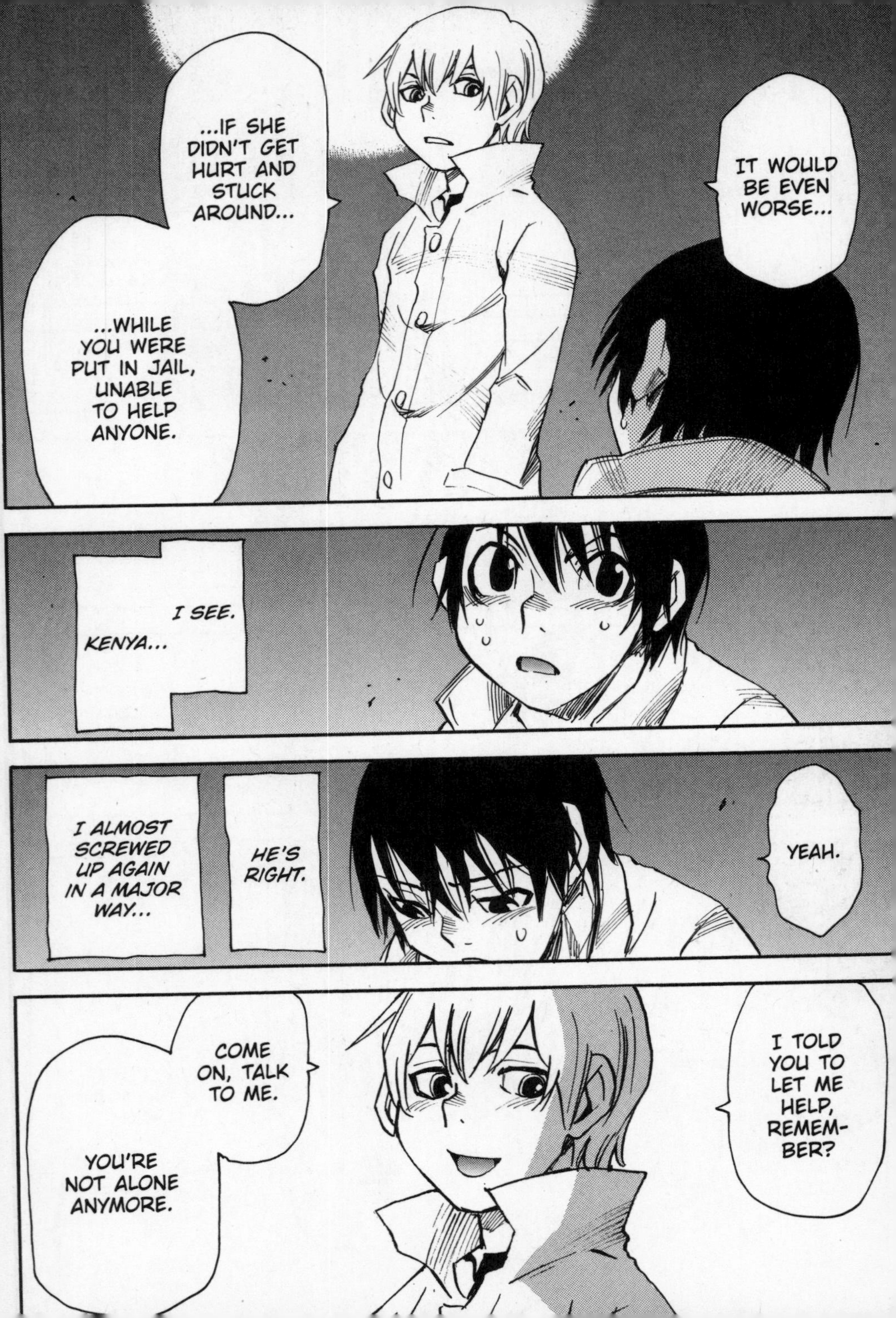
IT WOULD BE EVEN WORSE...
...IF SHE DIDN'T GET HURT AND STUCK AROUND...
...WHILE YOU WERE PUT IN JAIL, UNABLE TO HELP ANYONE.
I SEE.
KENYA...
YEAH.
HE'S RIGHT.
I ALMOST SCREWED UP AGAIN IN A MAJOR WAY...
I TOLD YOU TO LET ME HELP, REMEMBER?
COME ON, TALK TO ME.
YOU'RE NOT ALONE ANYMORE.

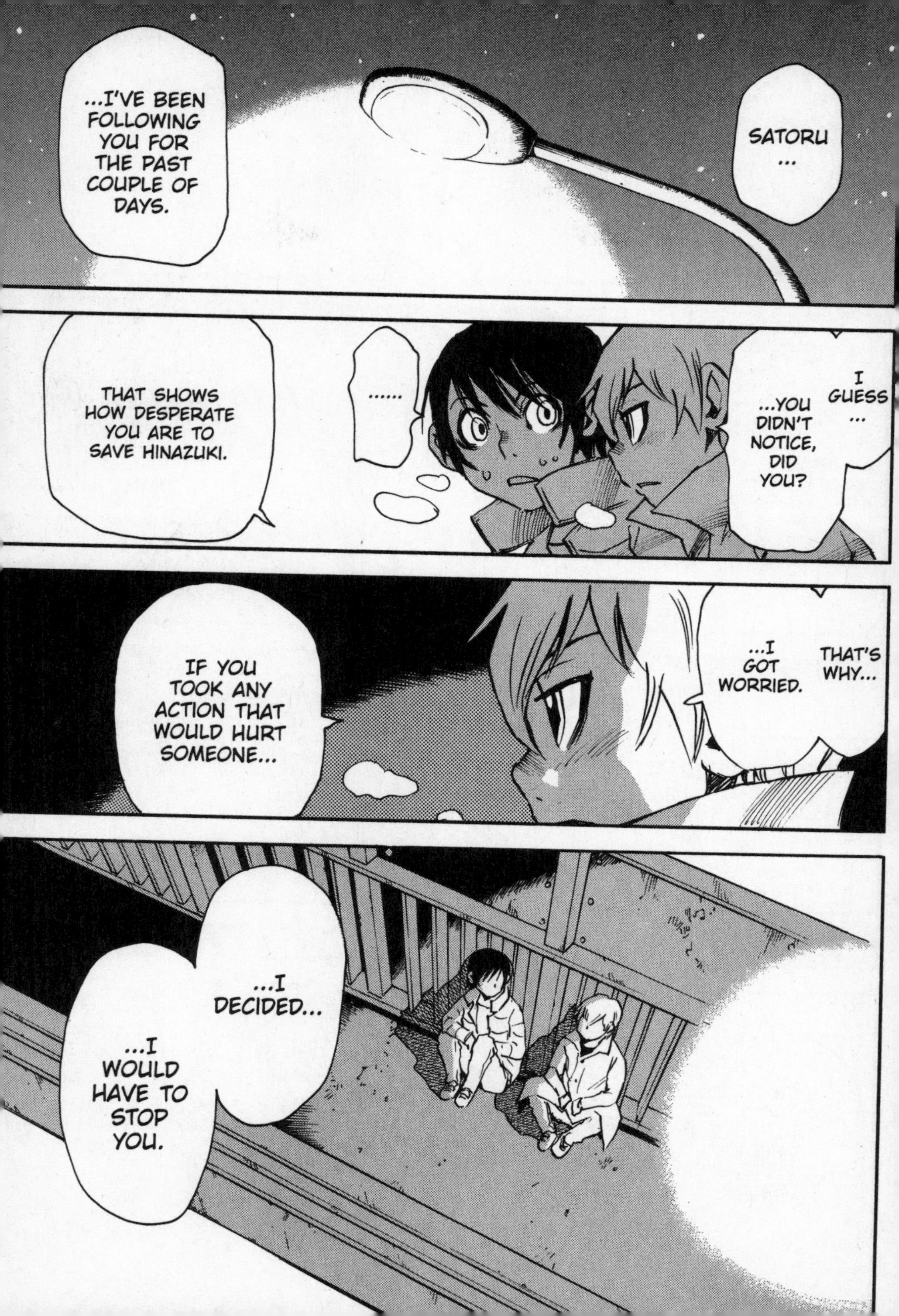
SATORU ...
...I'VE BEEN FOLLOWING YOU FOR THE PAST COUPLE OF DAYS.
I GUESS ...
...YOU DIDN'T NOTICE, DID YOU?
......
THAT SHOWS HOW DESPERATE YOU ARE TO SAVE HINAZUKI.
THAT'S WHY...
...I GOT WORRIED.
IF YOU TOOK ANY ACTION THAT WOULD HURT SOMEONE...
...I DECIDED...
...I WOULD HAVE TO STOP YOU.

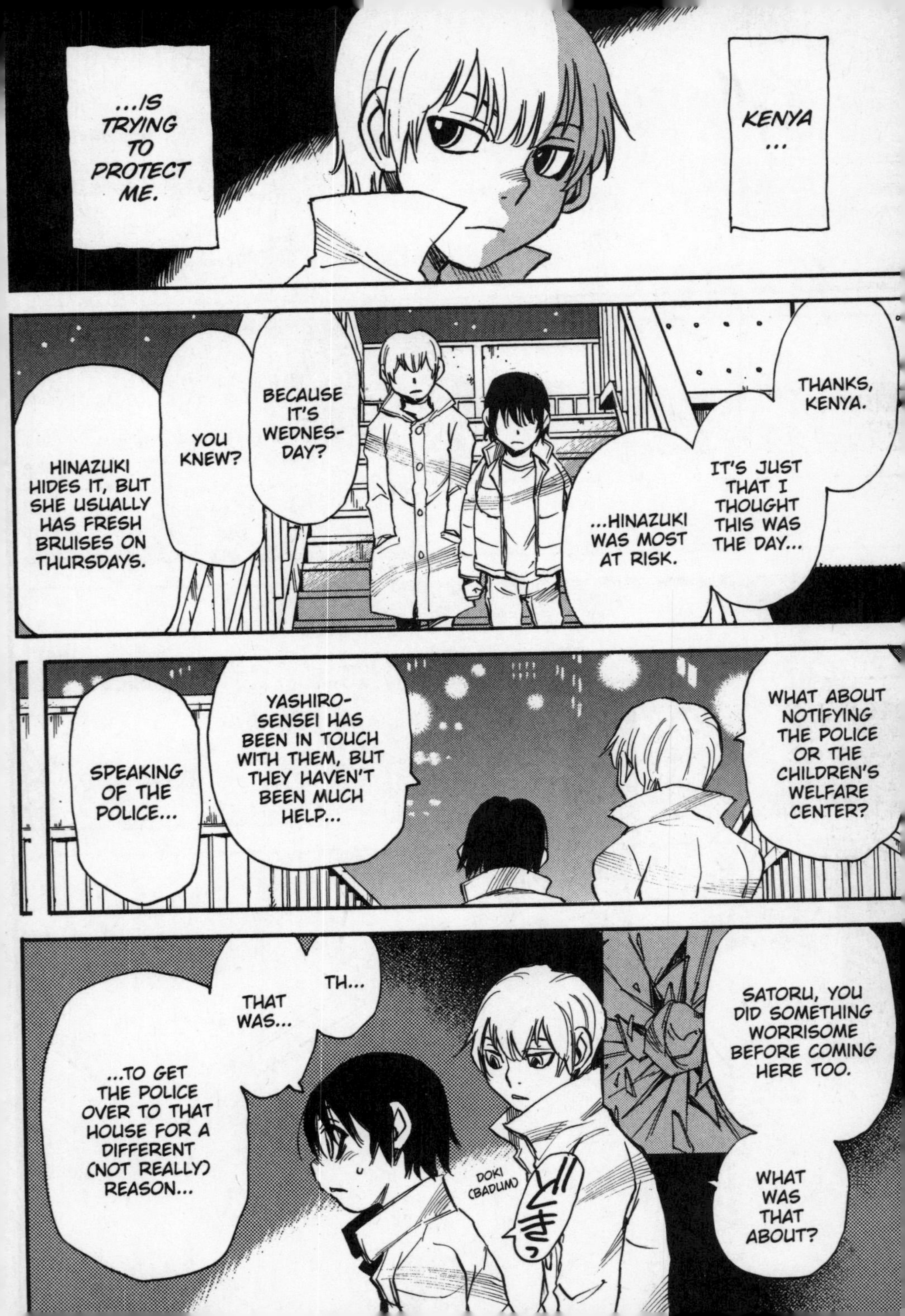
KENYA...
...IS TRYING TO PROTECT ME.
THANKS, KENYA.
IT'S JUST THAT I THOUGHT THIS WAS THE DAY...
...HINAZUKI WAS MOST AT RISK.
BECAUSE IT'S WEDNESDAY?
YOU KNEW?
HINAZUKI HIDES IT, BUT SHE USUALLY HAS FRESH BRUISES ON THURSDAYS.
WHAT ABOUT NOTIFYING THE POLICE OR THE CHILDREN'S WELFARE CENTER?
YASHIRO-SENSEI HAS BEEN IN TOUCH WITH THEM, BUT THEY HAVEN'T BEEN MUCH HELP...
SPEAKING OF THE POLICE...
SATORU, YOU DID SOMETHING WORRISOME BEFORE COMING HERE TOO.
WHAT WAS THAT ABOUT?
どきっ
DOKI (BADUM)
TH...
THAT WAS...
...TO GET THE POLICE OVER TO THAT HOUSE FOR A DIFFERENT (NOT REALLY) REASON...

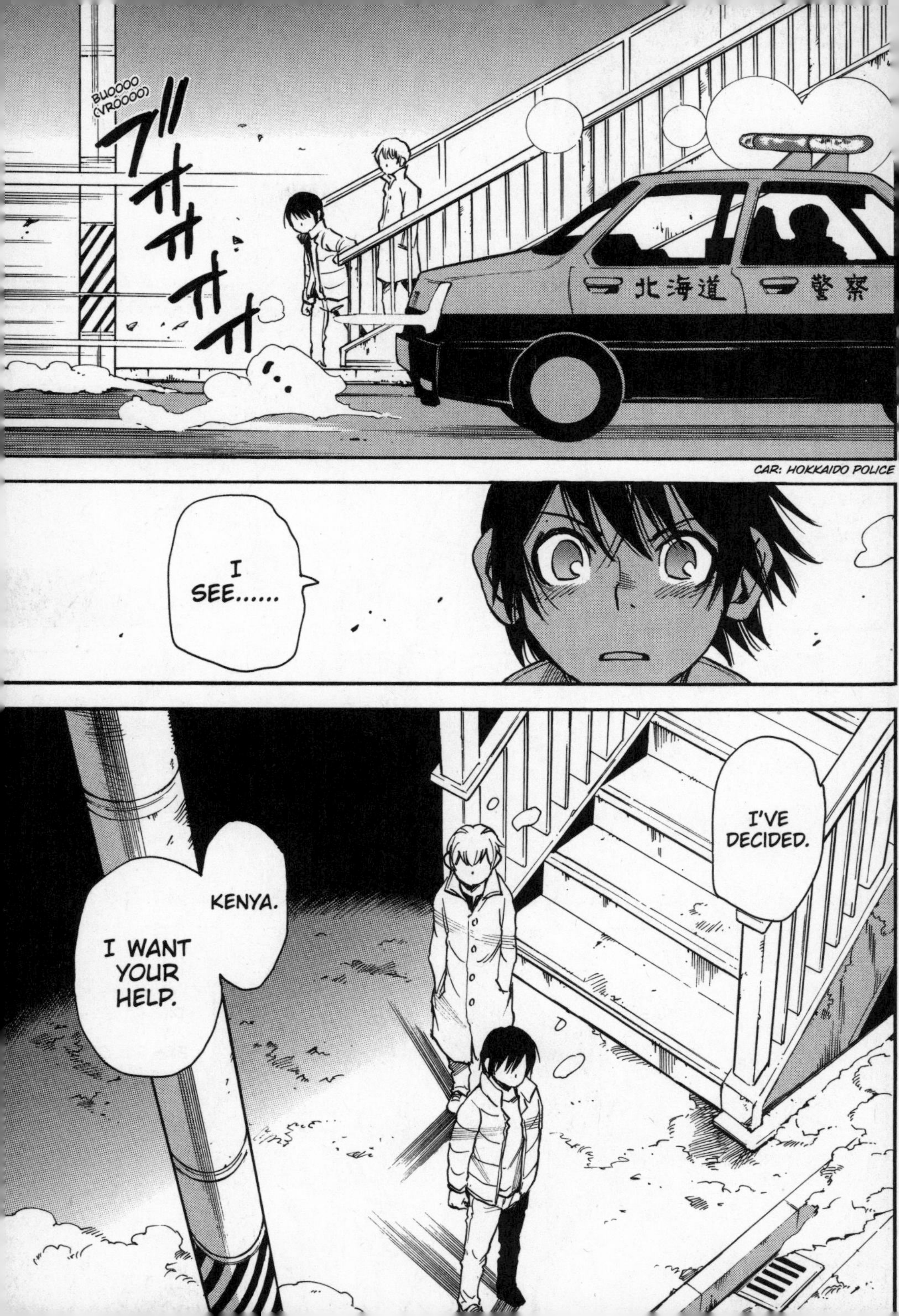
BUOOOO (VROOOO)
ブオオオオ
...
北海道 警察
CAR: HOKKAIDO POLICE
I SEE......
I'VE DECIDED.
KENYA.
I WANT YOUR HELP.

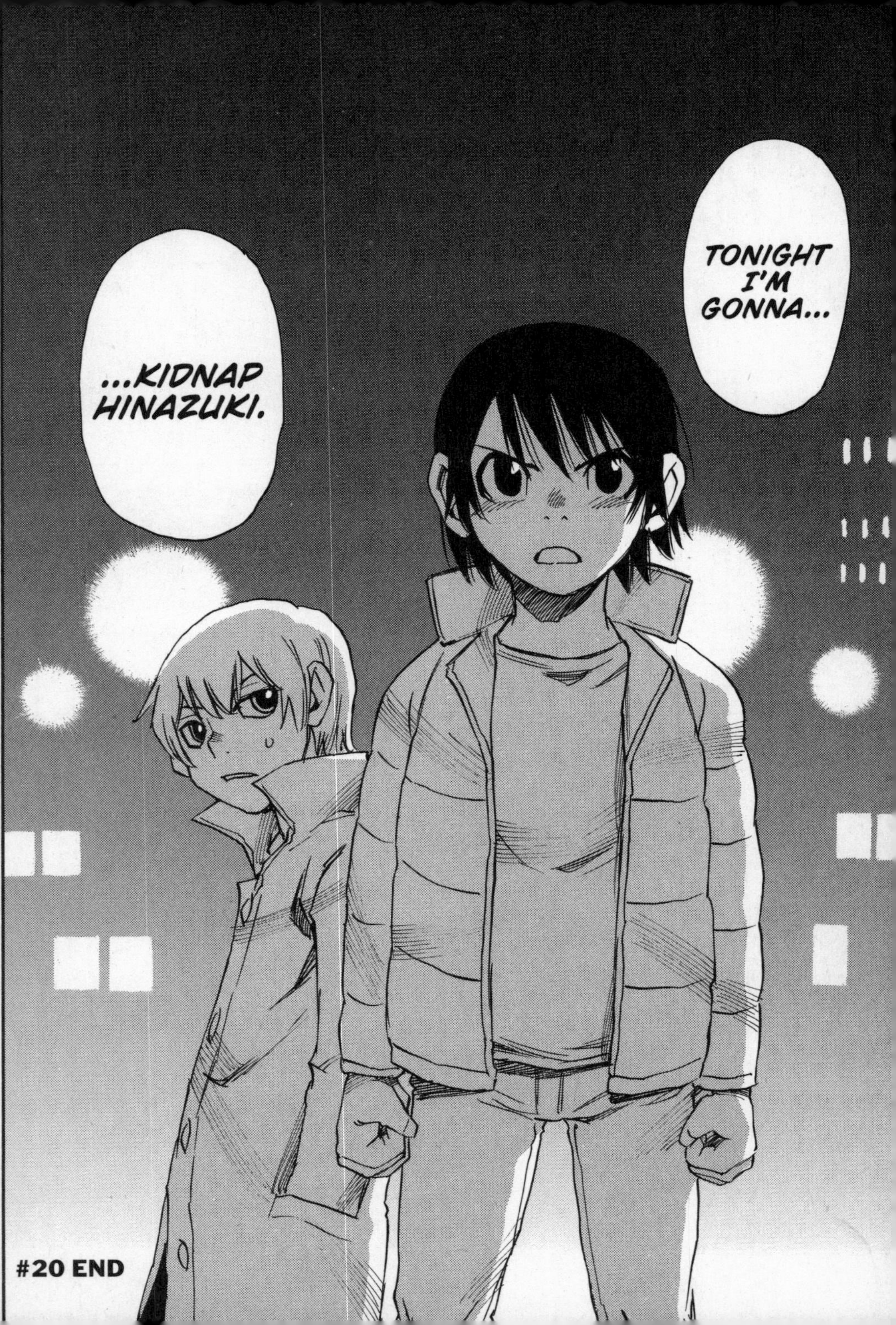
TONIGHT I'M GONNA...
...KIDNAP HINAZUKI.
#20 END

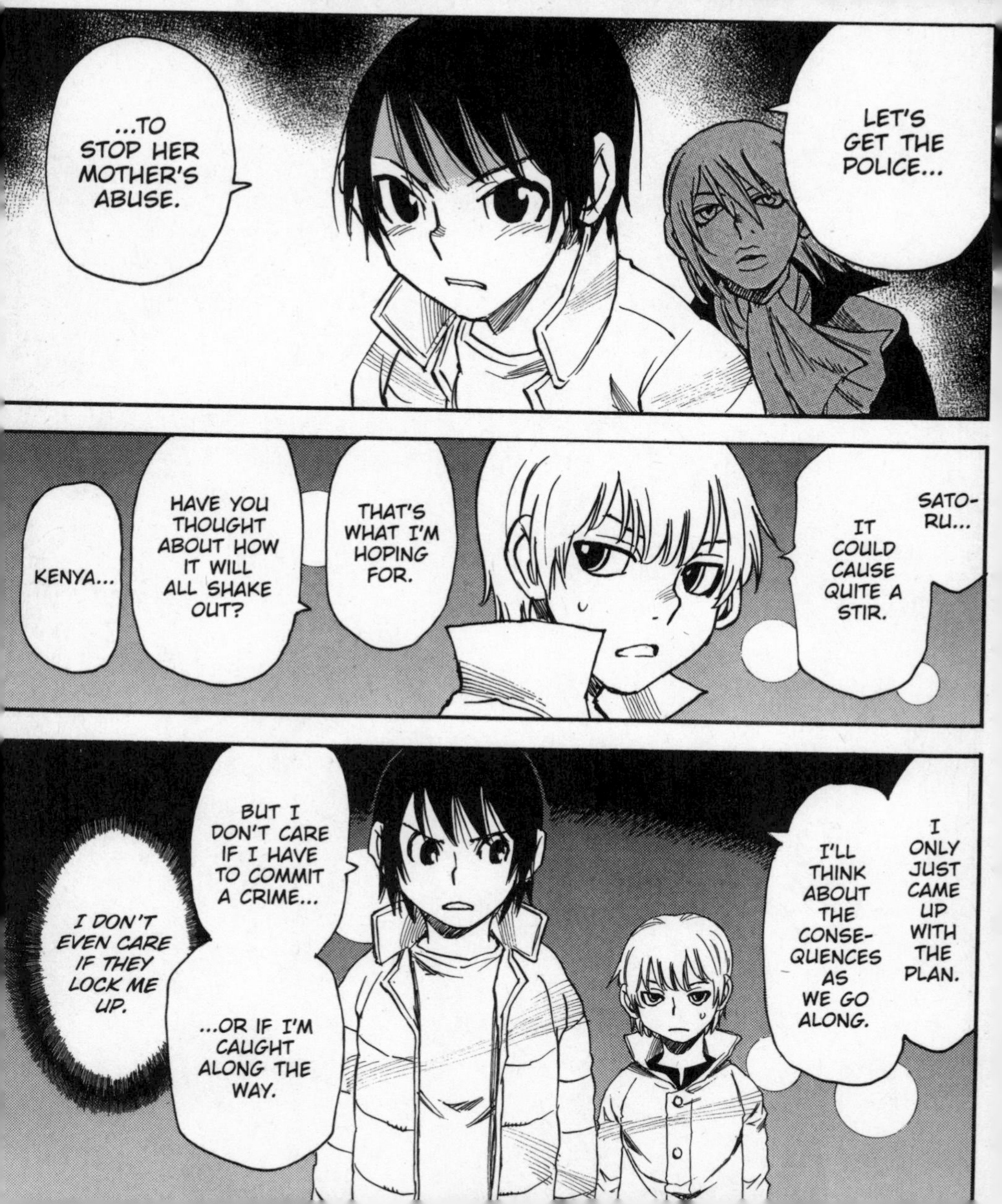
LET'S GET THE POLICE...
...TO STOP HER MOTHER'S ABUSE.
SATO-RU...
IT COULD CAUSE QUITE A STIR.
THAT'S WHAT I'M HOPING FOR.
HAVE YOU THOUGHT ABOUT HOW IT WILL ALL SHAKE OUT?
KENYA...
I ONLY JUST CAME UP WITH THE PLAN.
I'LL THINK ABOUT THE CONSE-QUENCES AS WE GO ALONG.
BUT I DON'T CARE IF I HAVE TO COMMIT A CRIME...
...OR IF I'M CAUGHT ALONG THE WAY.
I DON'T EVEN CARE IF THEY LOCK ME UP.

#21: Hiding Place, March 1988

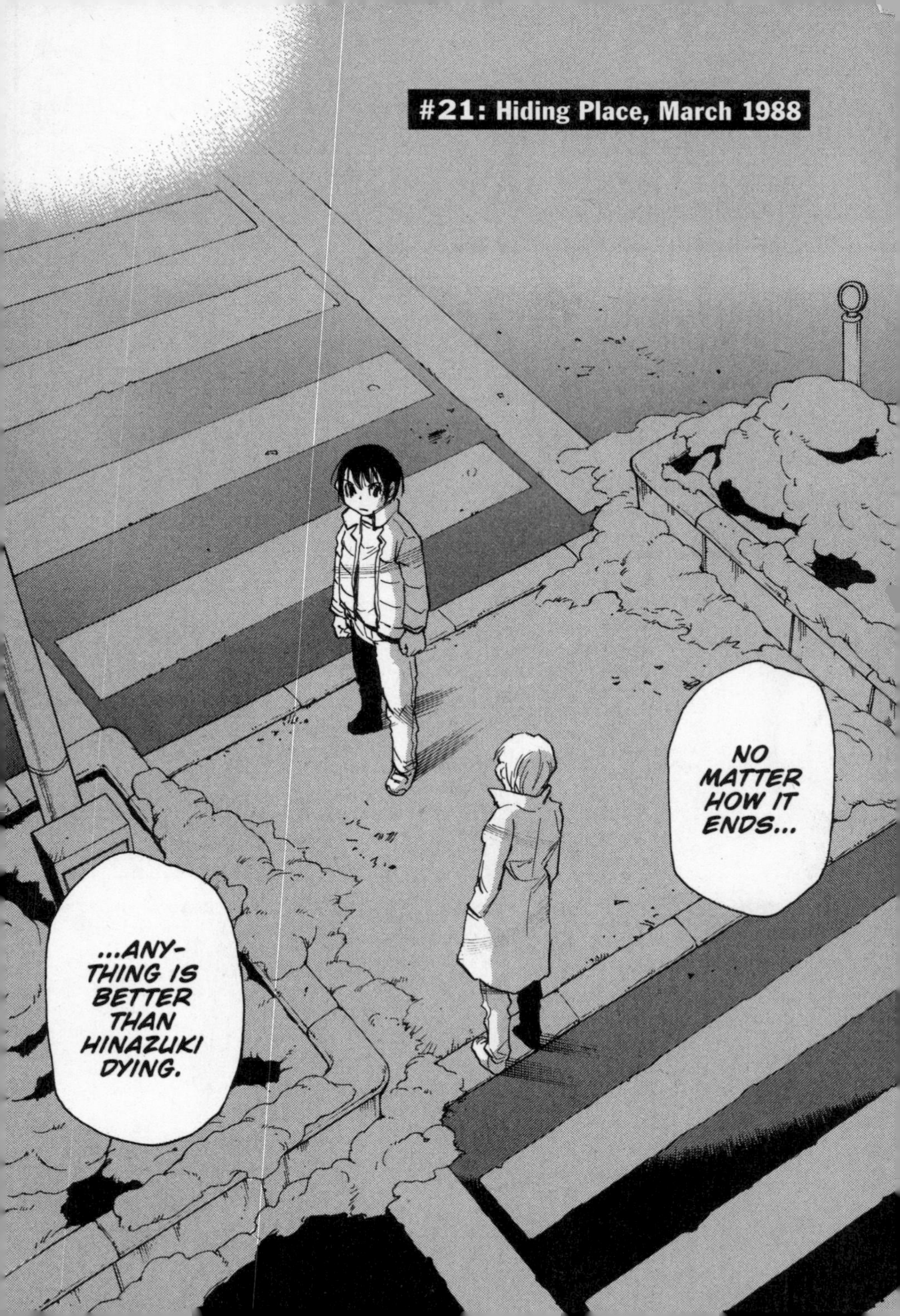
NO MATTER HOW IT ENDS...
...ANY-THING IS BETTER THAN HINAZUKI DYING.

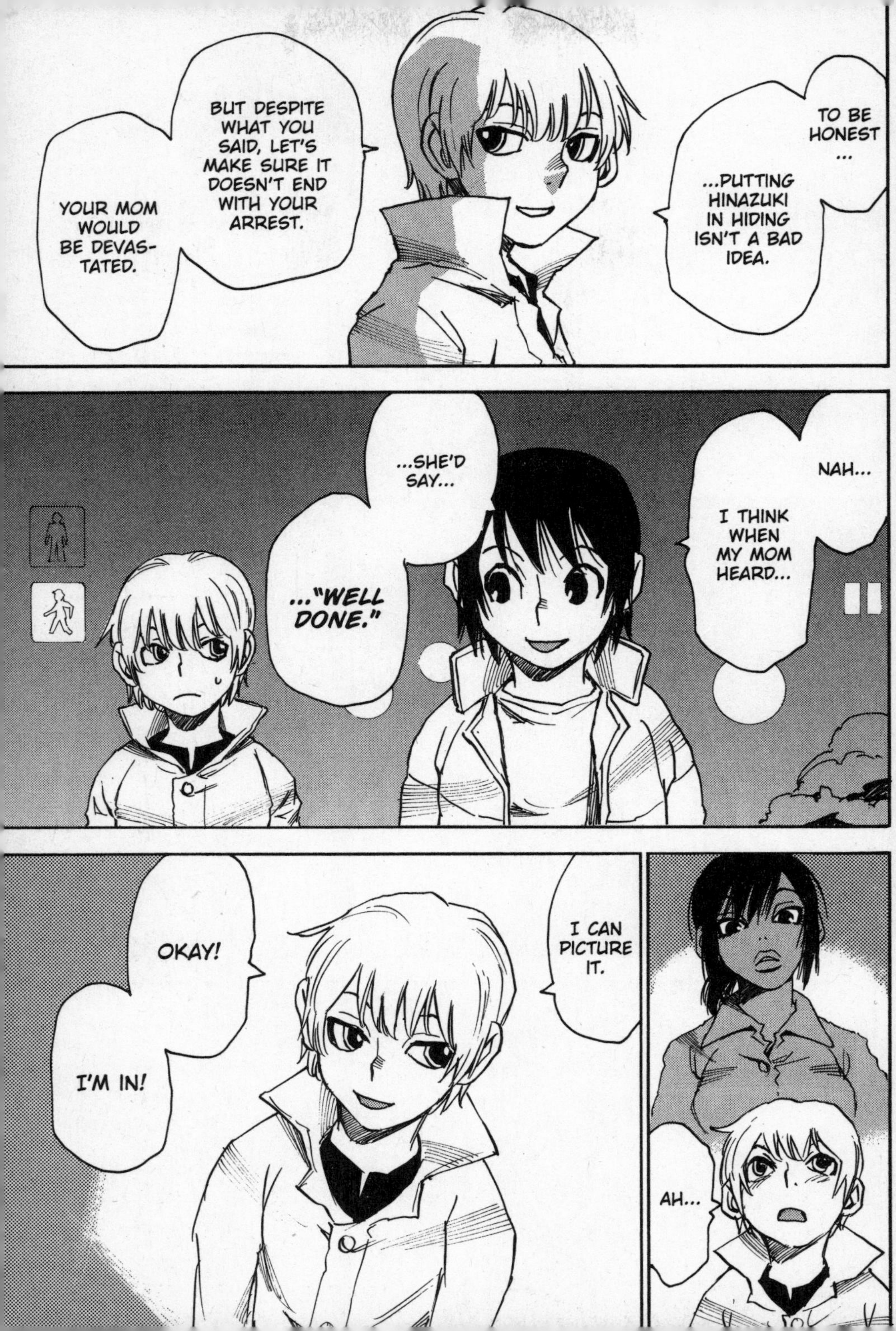
TO BE HONEST ...
...PUTTING HINAZUKI IN HIDING ISN'T A BAD IDEA.
BUT DESPITE WHAT YOU SAID, LET'S MAKE SURE IT DOESN'T END WITH YOUR ARREST.
YOUR MOM WOULD BE DEVAS-TATED.
NAH...
I THINK WHEN MY MOM HEARD...
...SHE'D SAY...
..."WELL DONE."
AH...
I CAN PICTURE IT.
OKAY!
I'M IN!

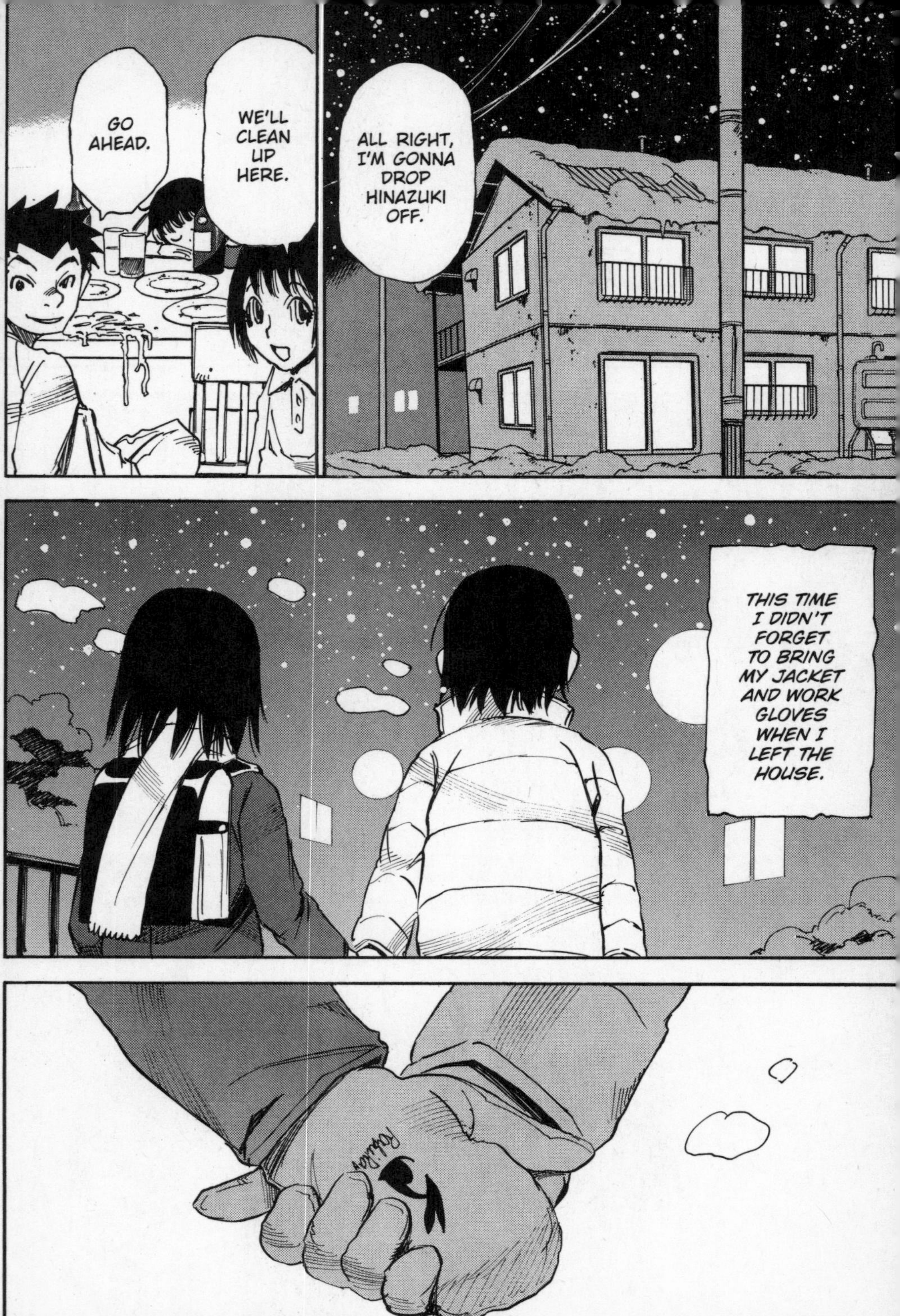
ALL RIGHT, I'M GONNA DROP HINAZUKI OFF.
WE'LL CLEAN UP HERE.
GO AHEAD.
THIS TIME I DIDN'T FORGET TO BRING MY JACKET AND WORK GLOVES WHEN I LEFT THE HOUSE.

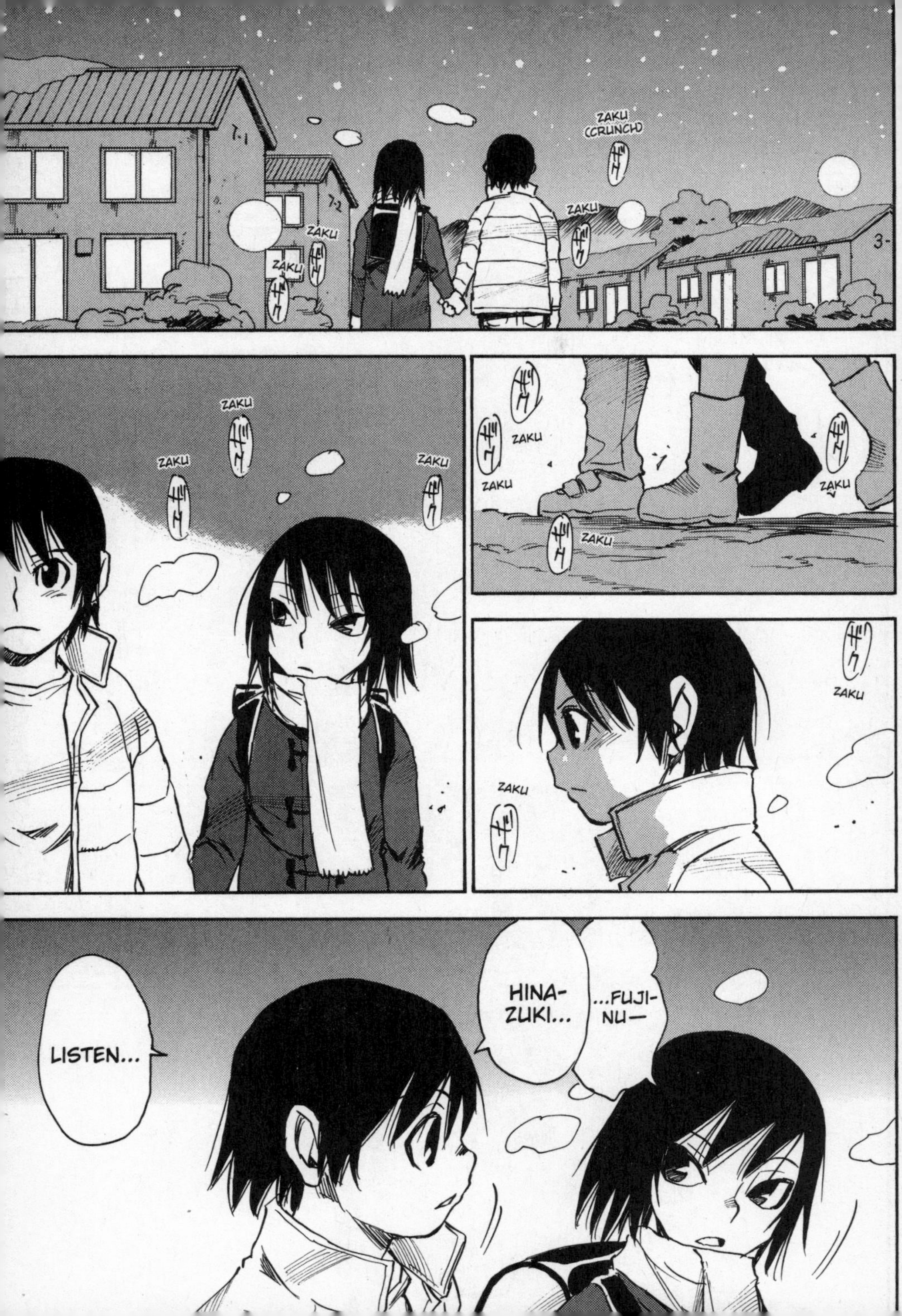
ZAKU (CRUNCH)
ZAKU
ZAKU
ZAKU
ZAKU
ZAKU
ZAKU
ZAKU
ZAKU
ZAKU
ZAKU
ZAKU
ZAKU
...FUJI-NU—
HINA-ZUKI...
LISTEN...

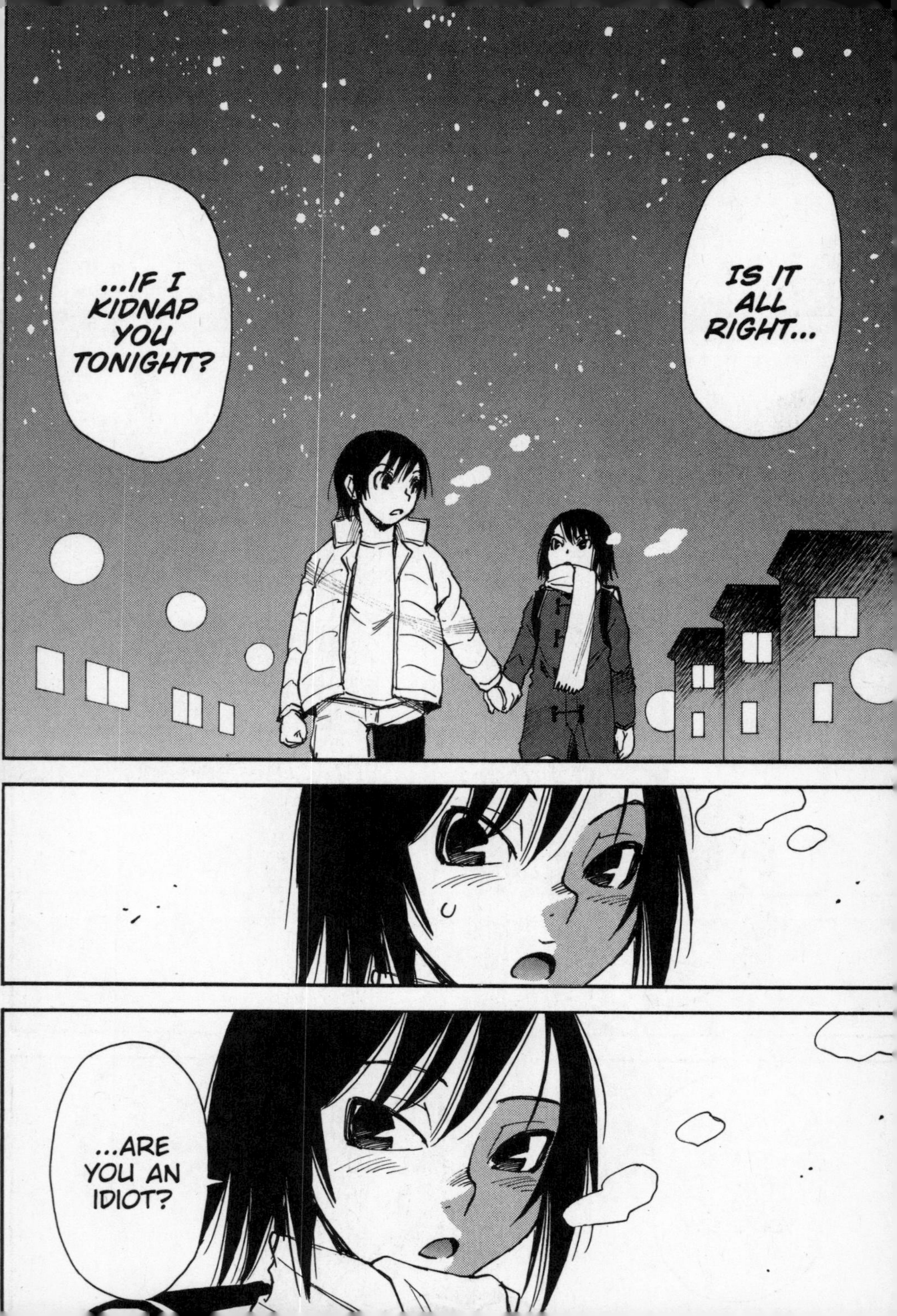
IS IT ALL RIGHT...
...IF I KIDNAP YOU TONIGHT?
...ARE YOU AN IDIOT?

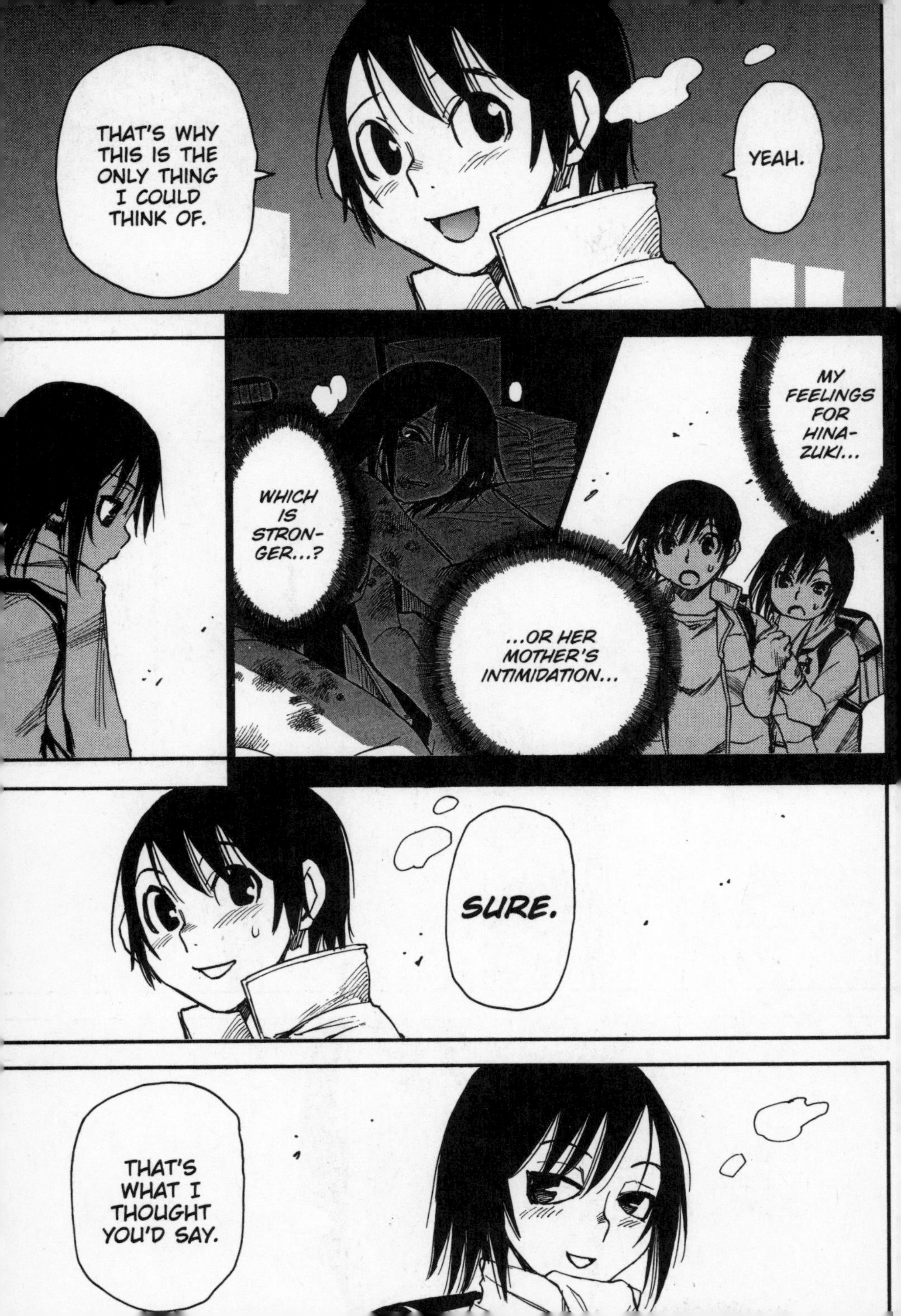
YEAH.
THAT'S WHY THIS IS THE ONLY THING I COULD THINK OF.
MY FEELINGS FOR HINA-ZUKI...
...OR HER MOTHER'S INTIMIDATION...
WHICH IS STRONGER...?
SURE.
THAT'S WHAT I THOUGHT YOU'D SAY.

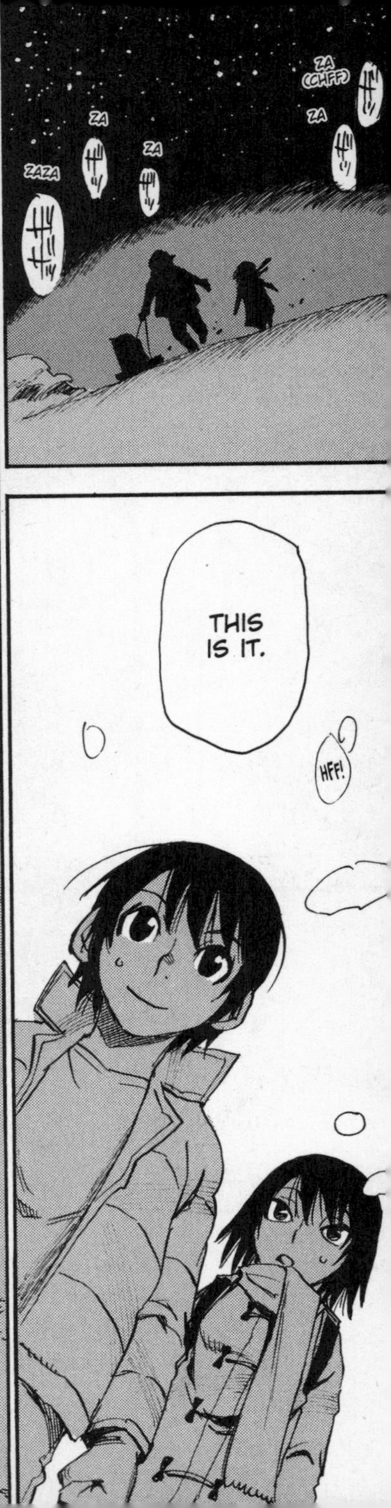
ZA (CHFF)
ZA
ZA
ZA
ZAZA
THIS IS IT.
HFF!
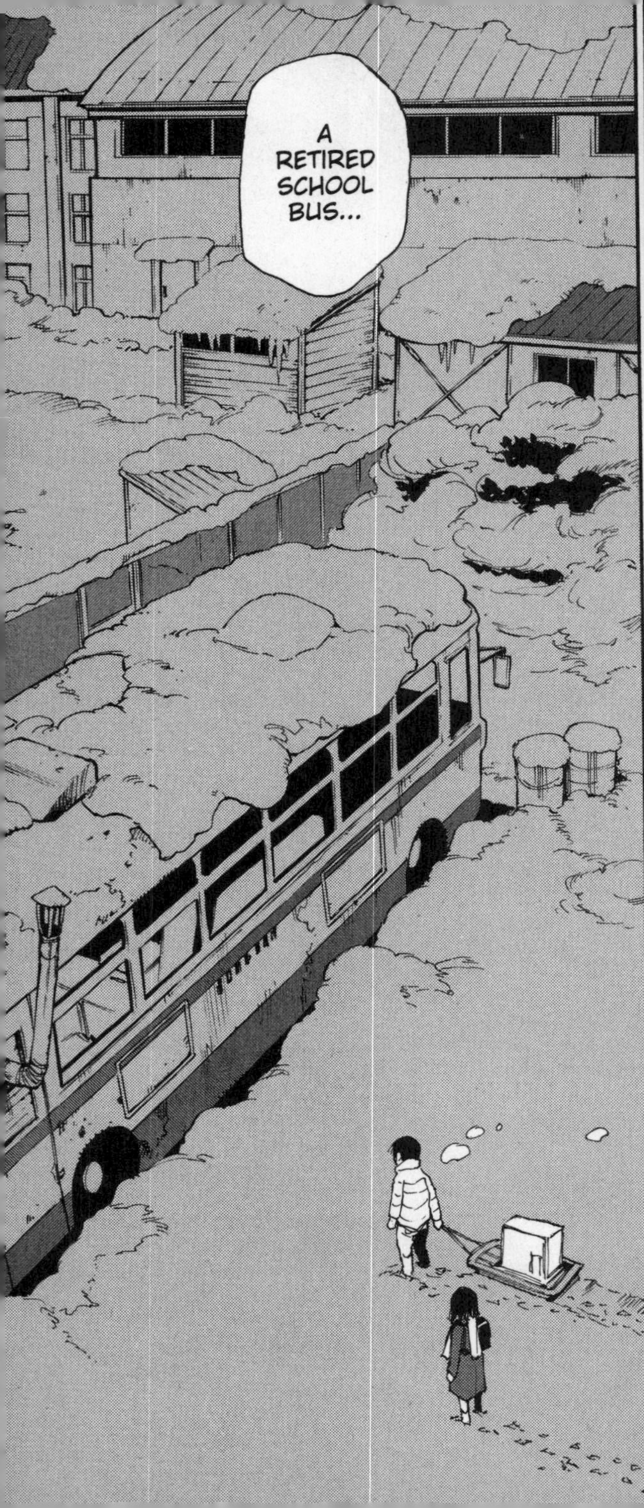
A RETIRED SCHOOL BUS...

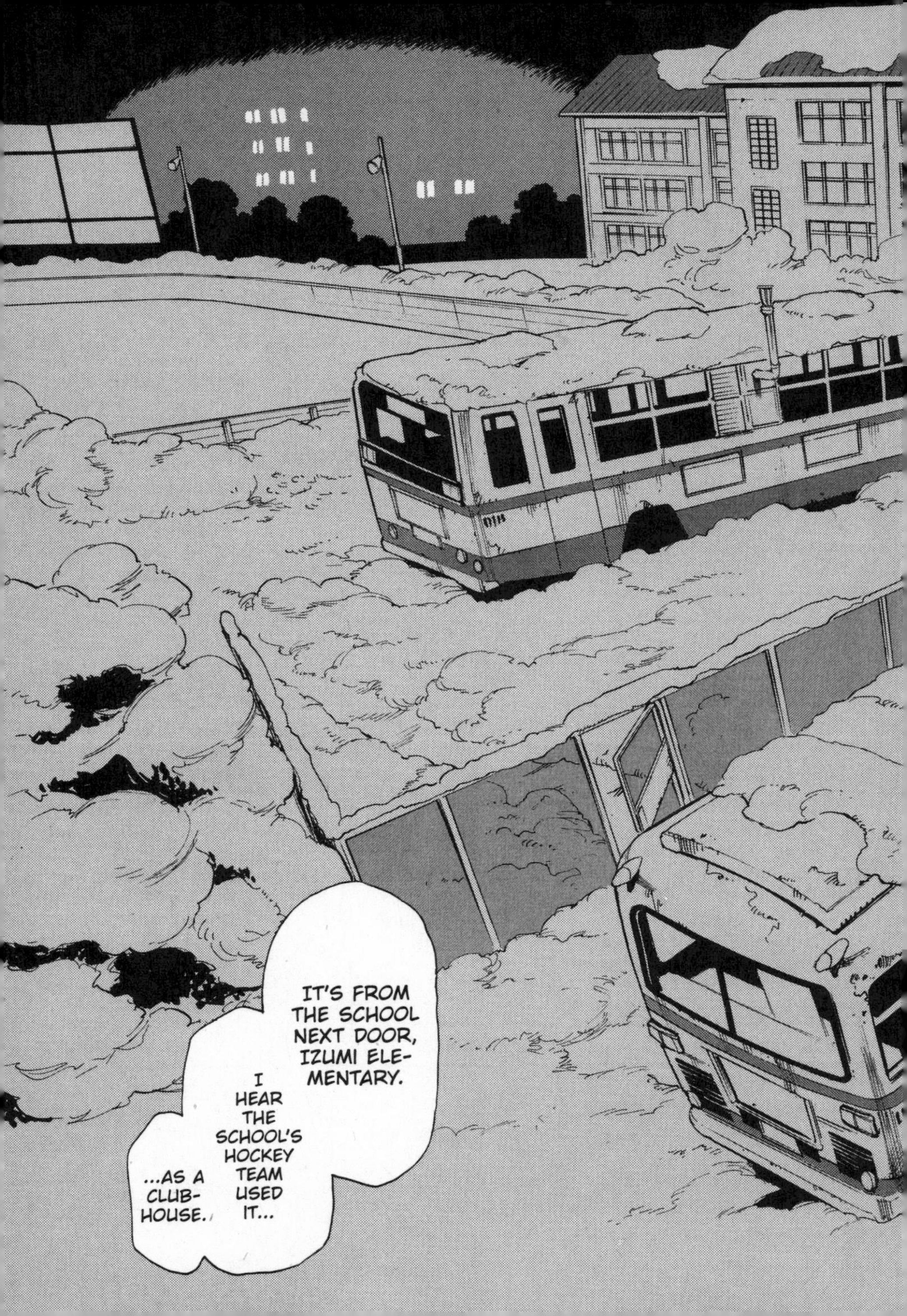
IT'S FROM THE SCHOOL NEXT DOOR, IZUMI ELEMENTARY.
I HEAR THE SCHOOL'S HOCKEY TEAM USED IT...
...AS A CLUB-HOUSE.

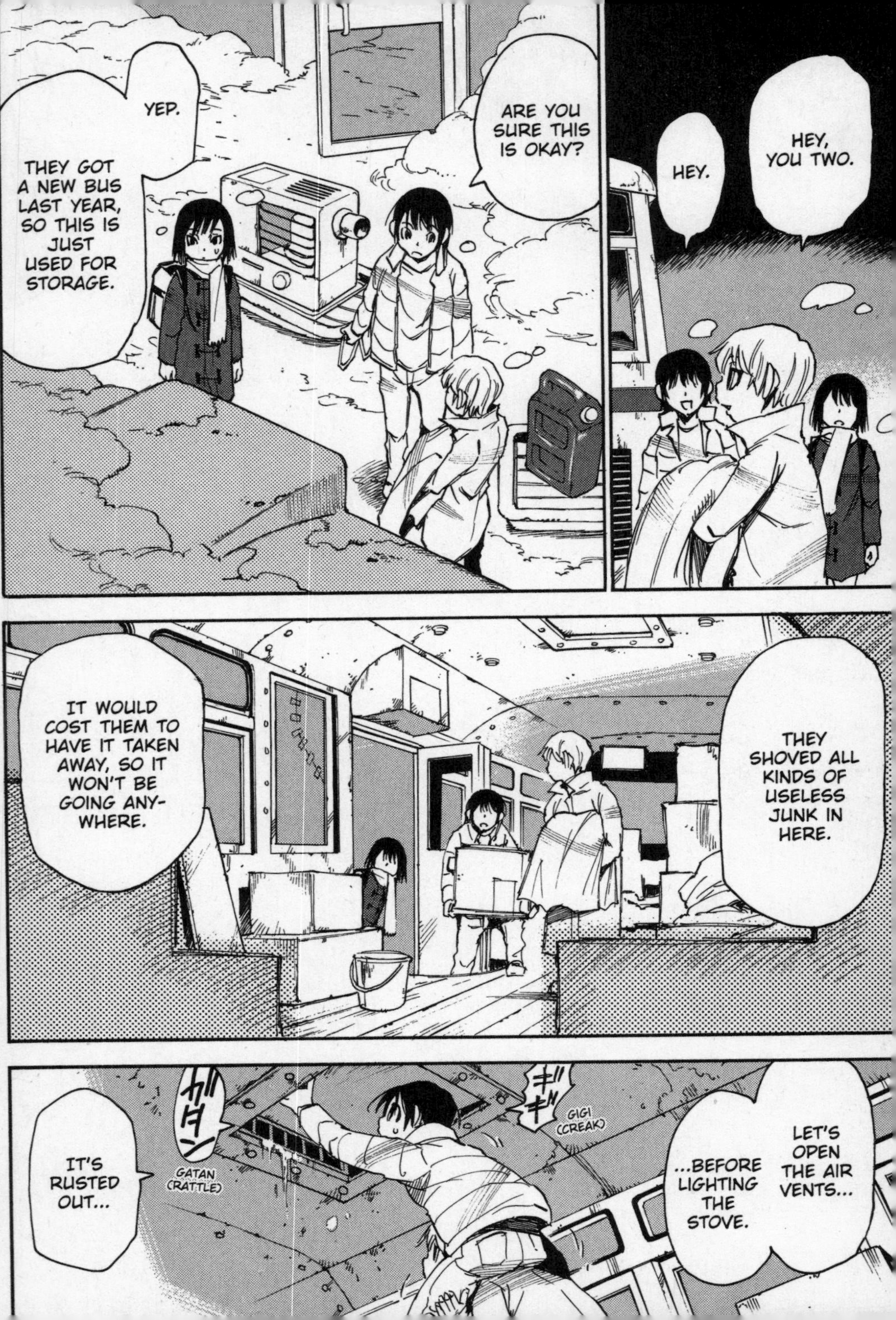
HEY, YOU TWO.
HEY.
ARE YOU SURE THIS IS OKAY?
YEP.
THEY GOT A NEW BUS LAST YEAR, SO THIS IS JUST USED FOR STORAGE.
THEY SHOVED ALL KINDS OF USELESS JUNK IN HERE.
IT WOULD COST THEM TO HAVE IT TAKEN AWAY, SO IT WON'T BE GOING ANY-WHERE.
LET'S OPEN THE AIR VENTS...
...BEFORE LIGHTING THE STOVE.
GIGI (CREAK)
GATAN (RATTLE)
IT'S RUSTED OUT...

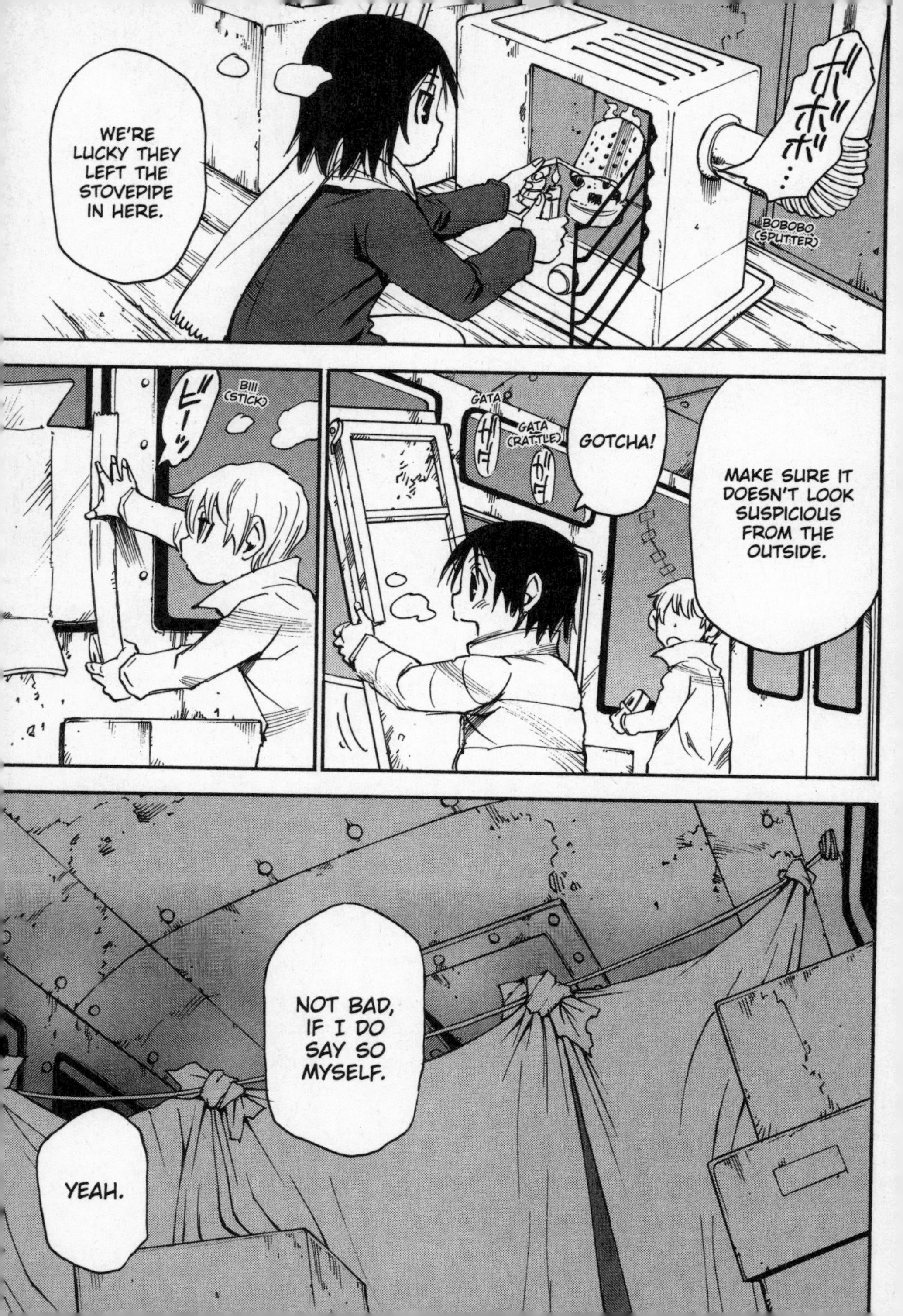
BOBOBO (SPUTTER)
WE'RE LUCKY THEY LEFT THE STOVEPIPE IN HERE.
MAKE SURE IT DOESN'T LOOK SUSPICIOUS FROM THE OUTSIDE.
GOTCHA!
GATA GATA (RATTLE)
BIII (STICK)
NOT BAD, IF I DO SAY SO MYSELF.
YEAH.

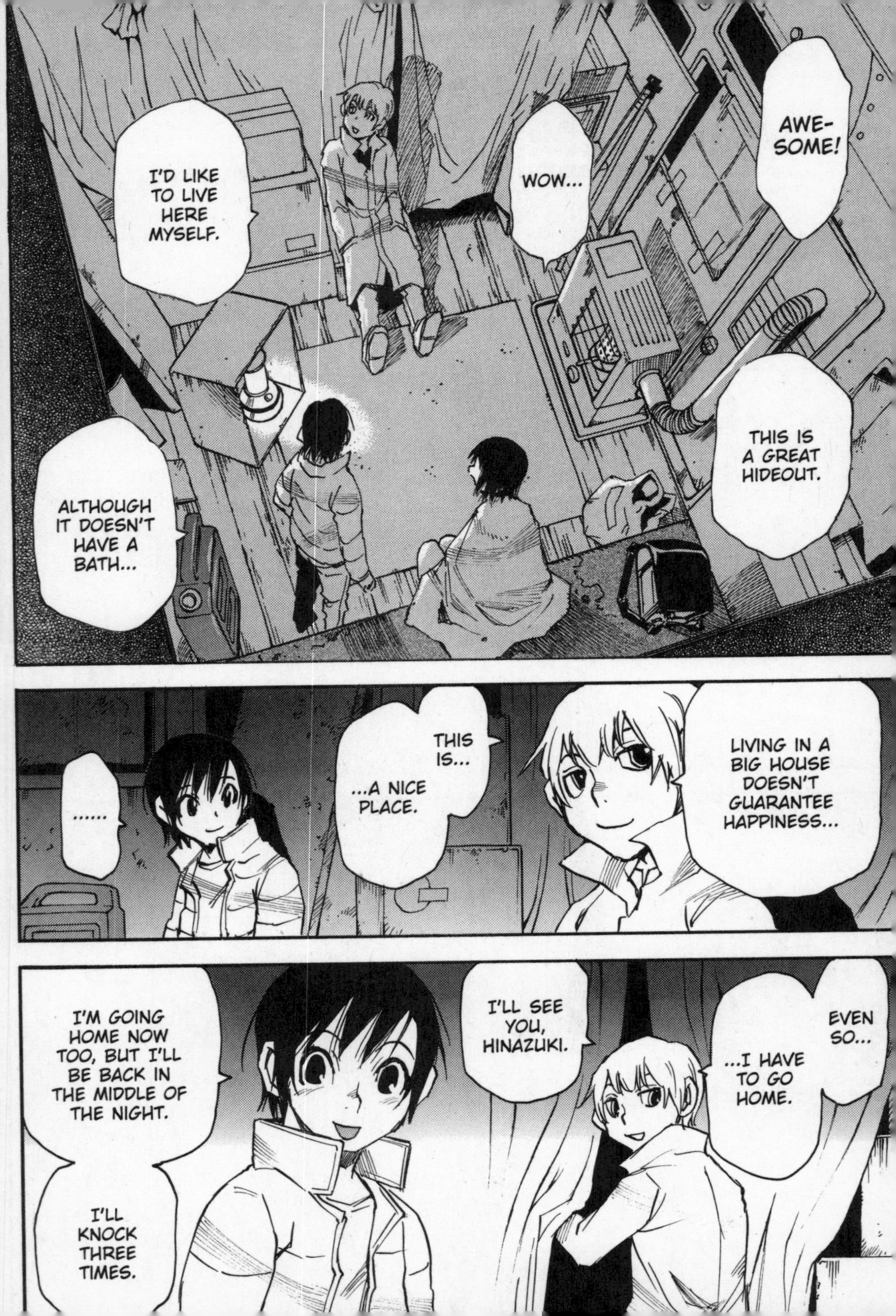
AWE-SOME!
WOW...
I'D LIKE TO LIVE HERE MYSELF.
THIS IS A GREAT HIDEOUT.
ALTHOUGH IT DOESN'T HAVE A BATH...
LIVING IN A BIG HOUSE DOESN'T GUARANTEE HAPPINESS...
THIS IS...
...A NICE PLACE.
......
EVEN SO...
...I HAVE TO GO HOME.
I'LL SEE YOU, HINAZUKI.
I'M GOING HOME NOW TOO, BUT I'LL BE BACK IN THE MIDDLE OF THE NIGHT.
I'LL KNOCK THREE TIMES.

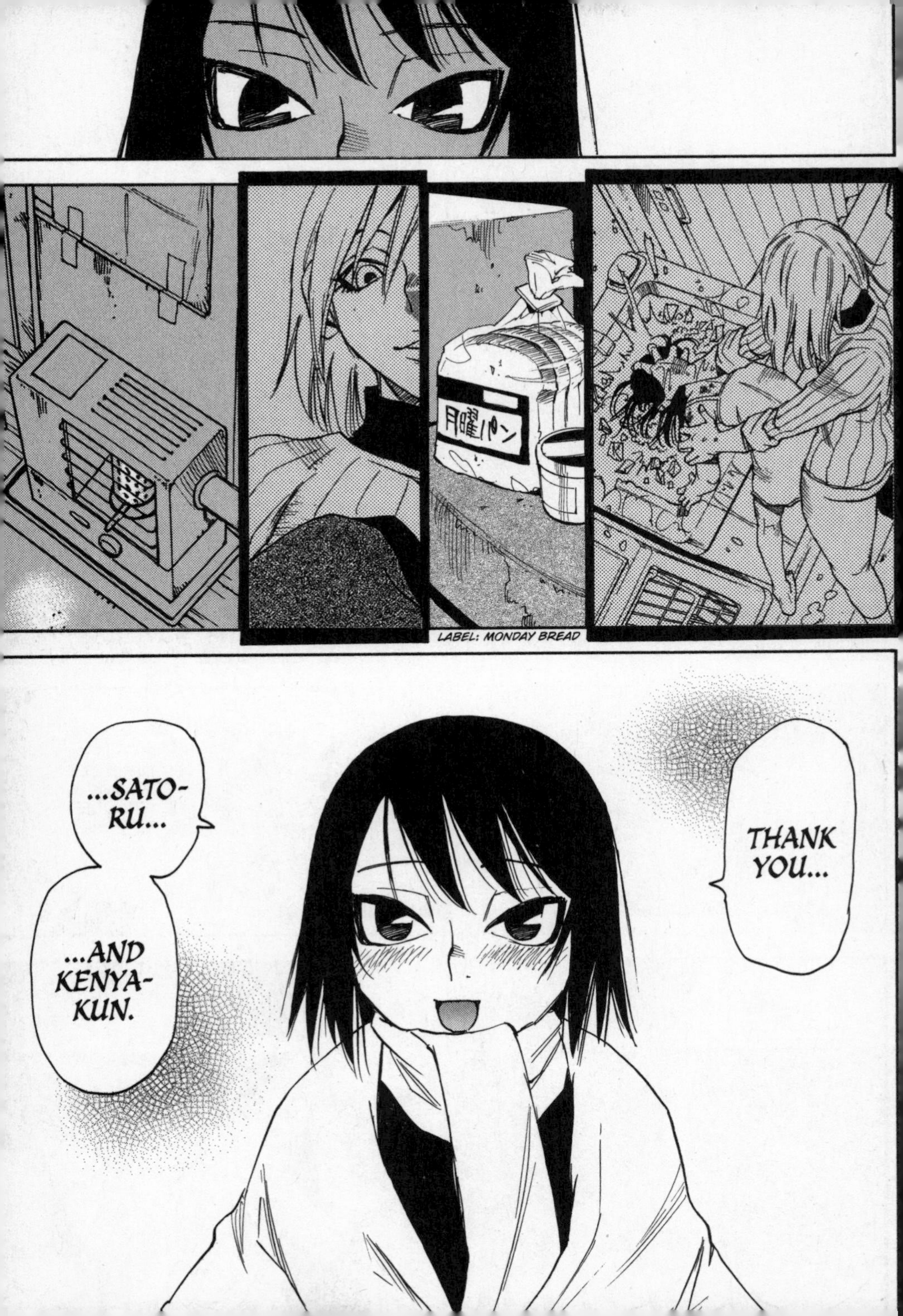
月曜パン
LABEL: MONDAY BREAD
THANK YOU...
...SATO-RU...
...AND KENYA-KUN.

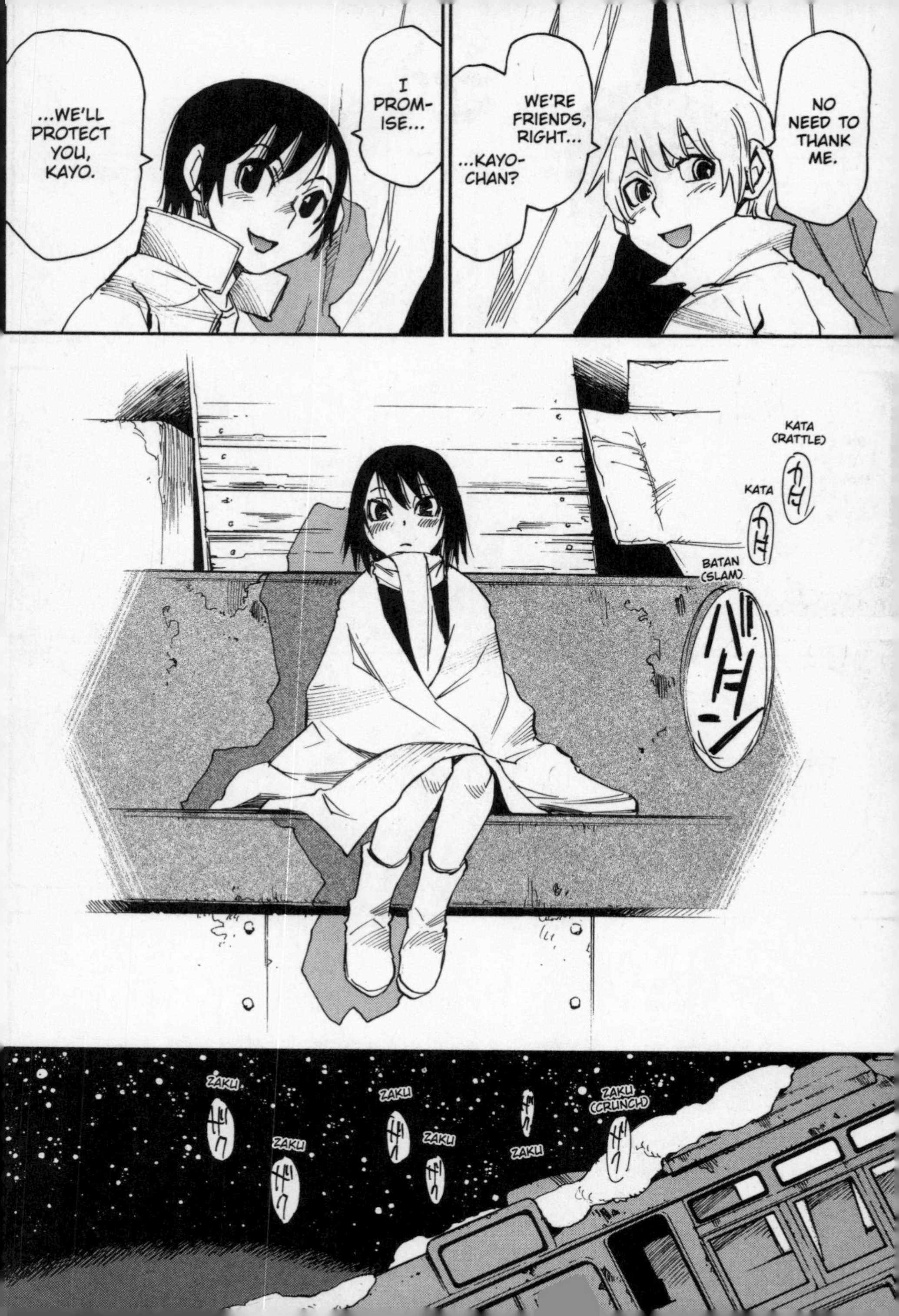
NO NEED TO THANK ME.
WE'RE FRIENDS, RIGHT...
...KAYO-CHAN?
I PROMISE...
...WE'LL PROTECT YOU, KAYO.
KATA (RATTLE)
KATA
BATAN (SLAM)
ZAKU (CRUNCH)
ZAKU
ZAKU
ZAKU
ZAKU
ZAKU

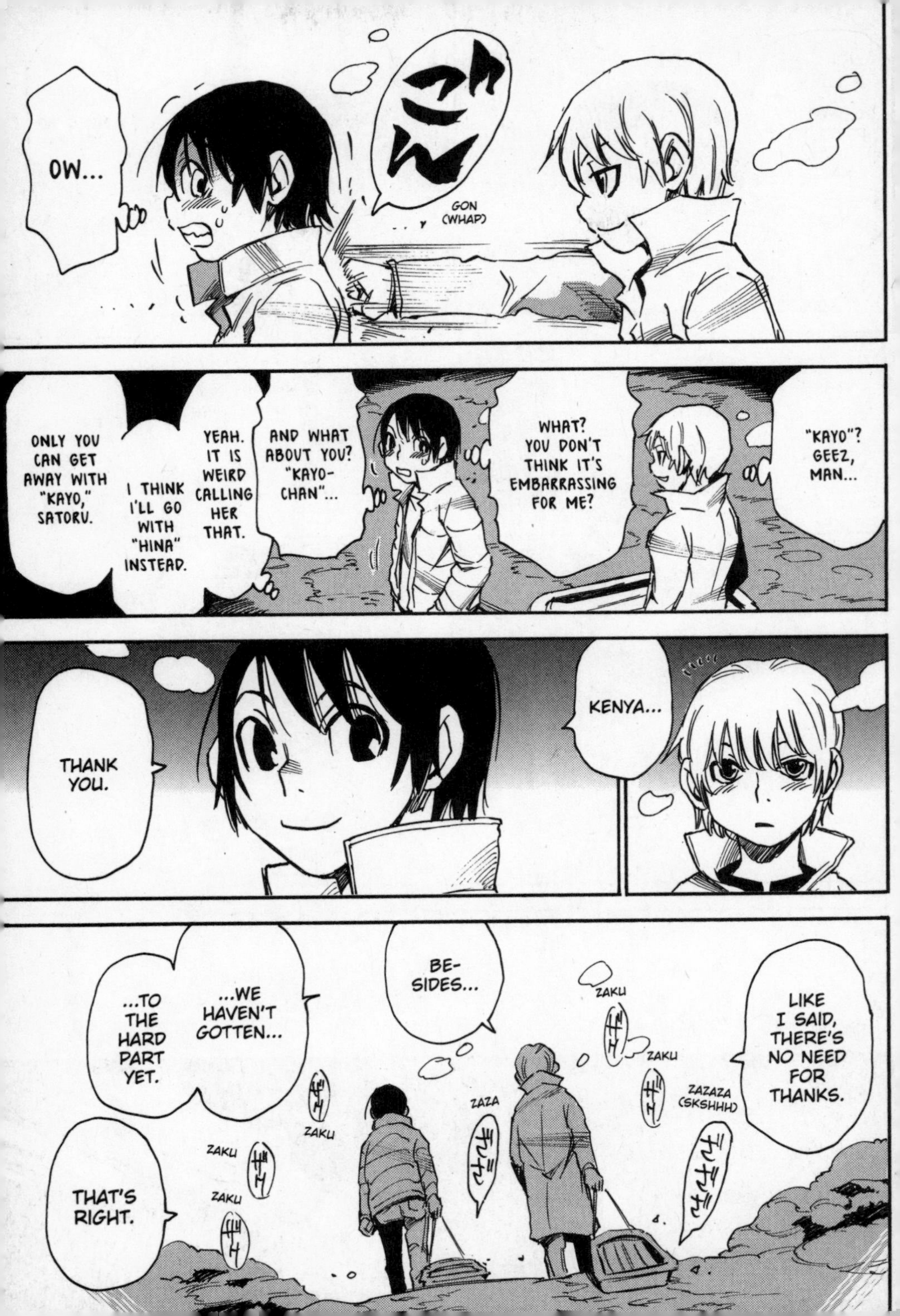

GON (WHAP)
OW...
"KAYO"? GEEZ, MAN...
WHAT? YOU DON'T THINK IT'S EMBARRASSING FOR ME?
AND WHAT ABOUT YOU? "KAYO-CHAN"...
YEAH. IT IS WEIRD CALLING HER THAT.
I THINK I'LL GO WITH "HINA" INSTEAD.
ONLY YOU CAN GET AWAY WITH "KAYO," SATORU.
KENYA...
THANK YOU.
LIKE I SAID, THERE'S NO NEED FOR THANKS.
ZAKU
ZAKU
ZAZAZA (SKSHHH)
BE-SIDES...
ZAZA
...WE HAVEN'T GOTTEN...
...TO THE HARD PART YET.
ZAKU
ZAKU
ZAKU
THAT'S RIGHT.

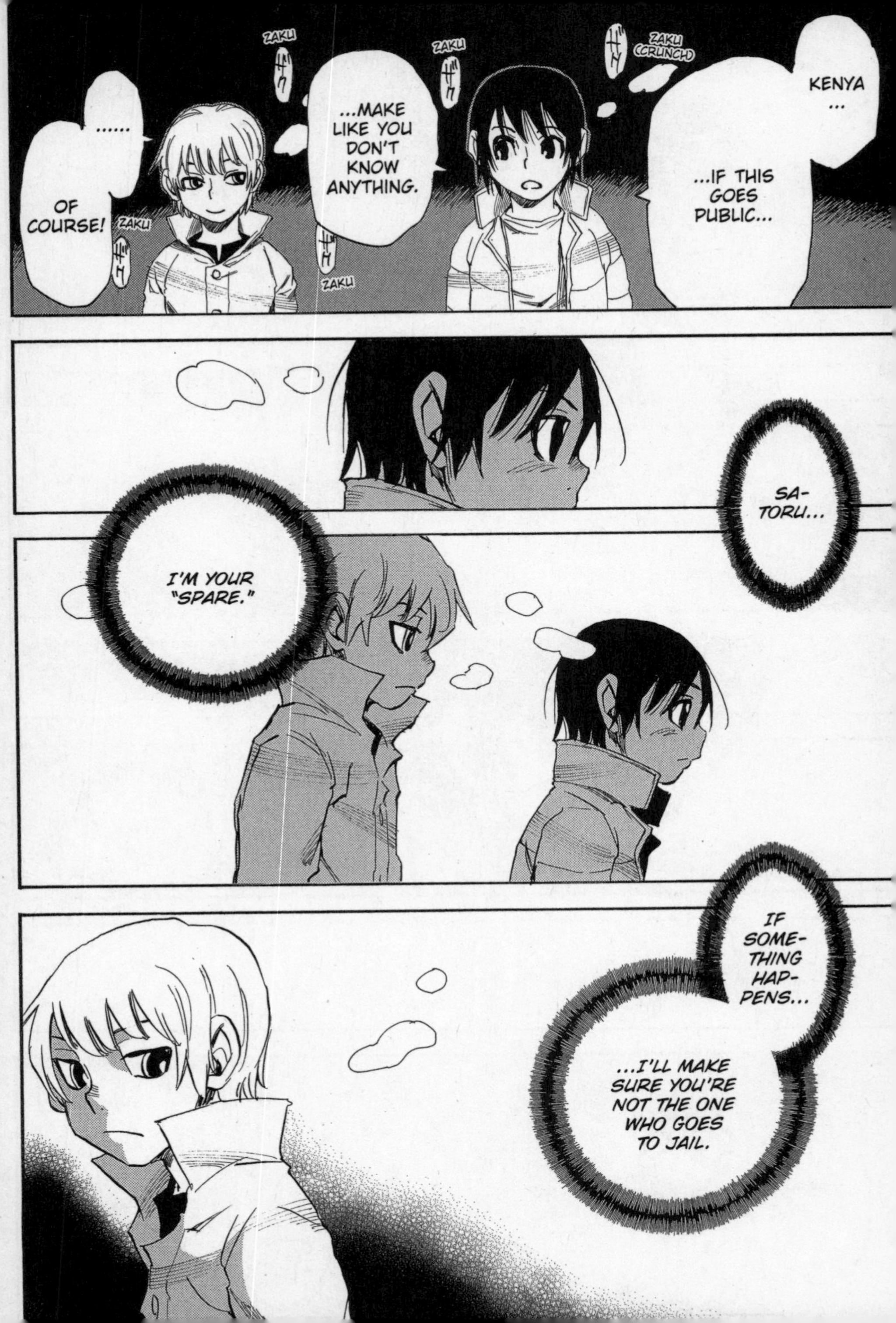
ZAKU (CRUNCH)
KENYA ...
...IF THIS GOES PUBLIC...
ZAKU
...MAKE LIKE YOU DON'T KNOW ANYTHING.
ZAKU
ZAKU
......
OF COURSE!
ZAKU
SA-TORU...
I'M YOUR "SPARE."
IF SOMETHING HAPPENS...
...I'LL MAKE SURE YOU'RE NOT THE ONE WHO GOES TO JAIL.

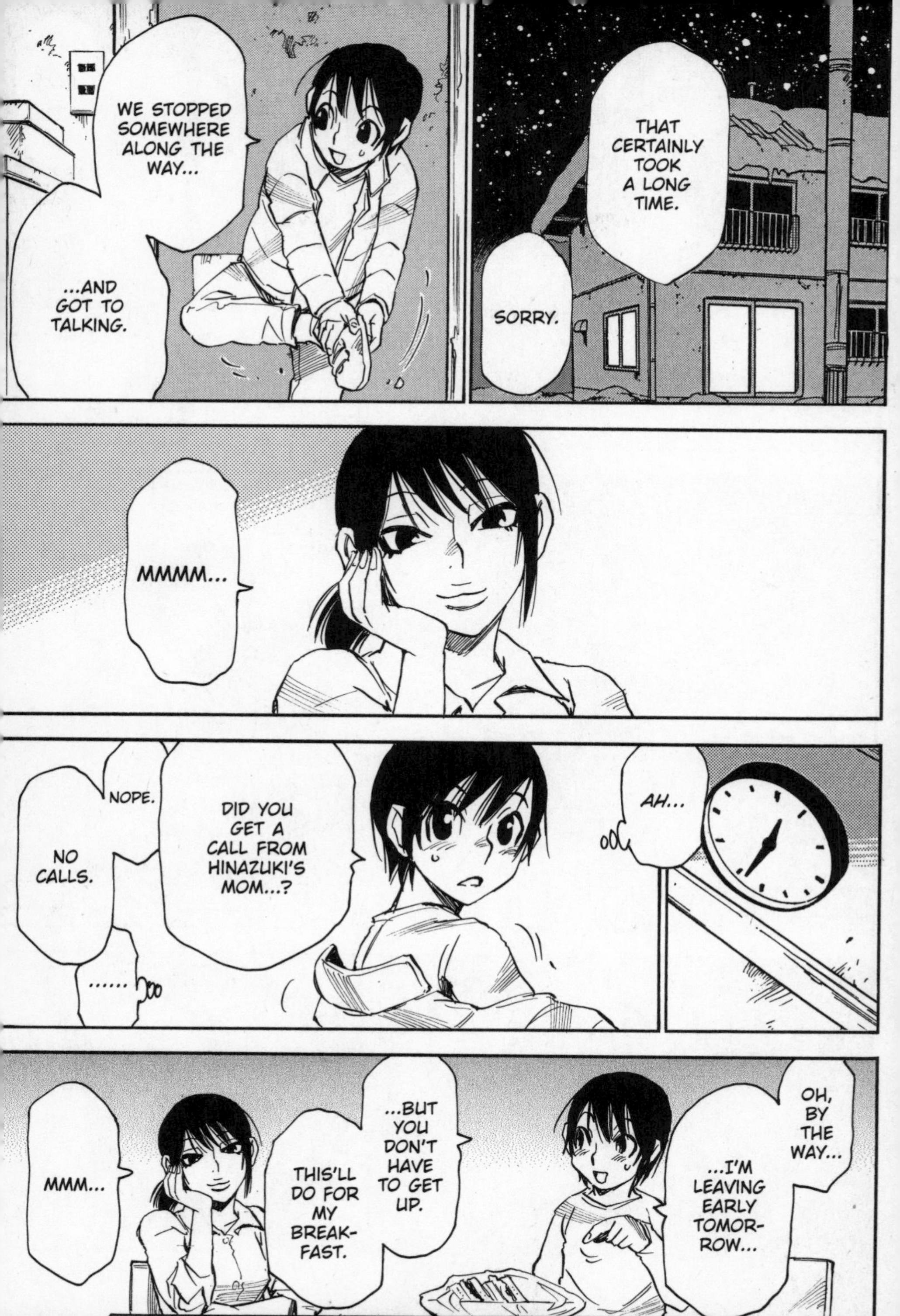
THAT CERTAINLY TOOK A LONG TIME.
SORRY.
WE STOPPED SOMEWHERE ALONG THE WAY...
...AND GOT TO TALKING.
MMMM...
AH...
DID YOU GET A CALL FROM HINAZUKI'S MOM...?
NOPE.
NO CALLS.
......
OH, BY THE WAY...
...I'M LEAVING EARLY TOMOR-ROW...
...BUT YOU DON'T HAVE TO GET UP.
THIS'LL DO FOR MY BREAK-FAST.
MMM...

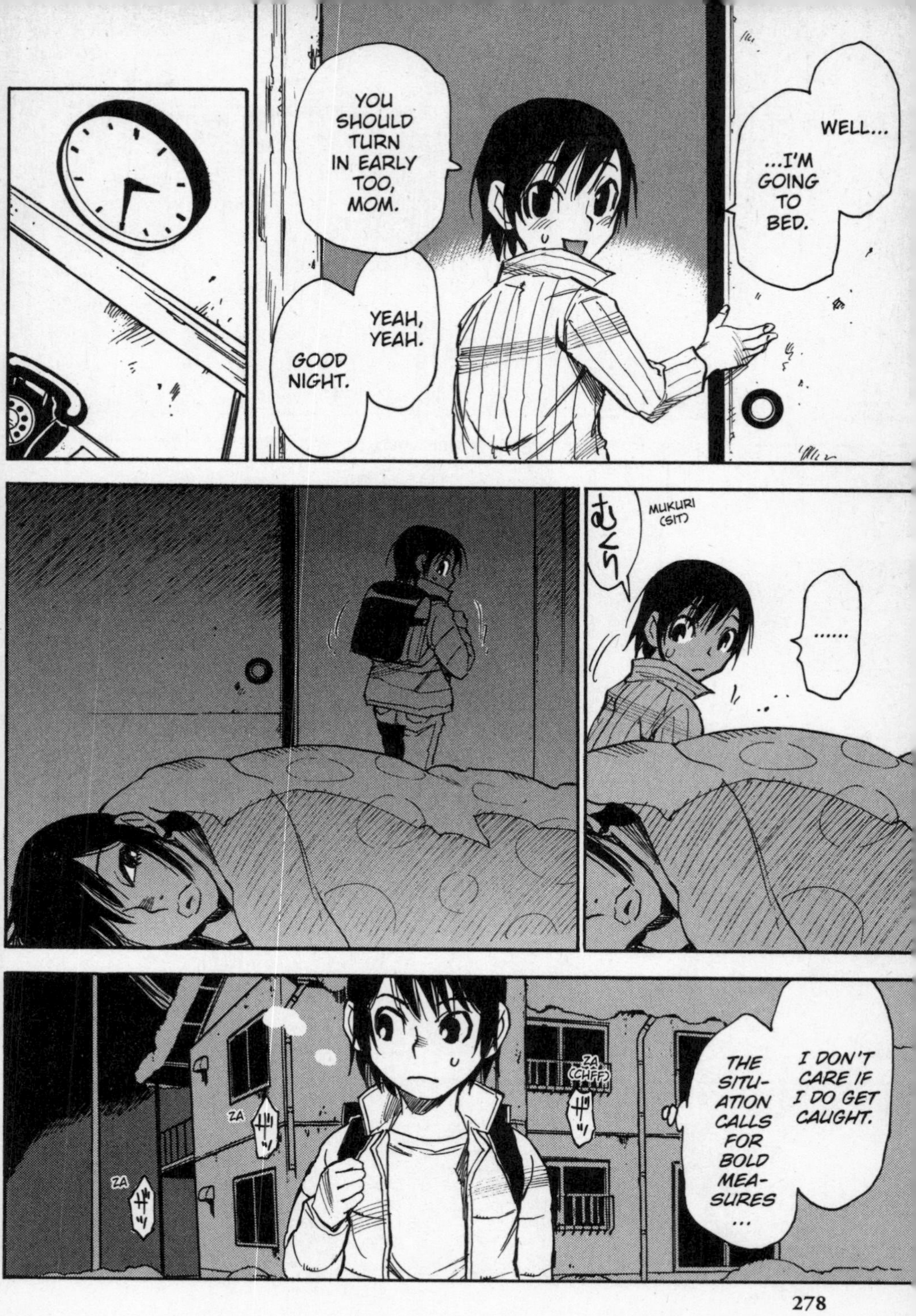
WELL...
...I'M GOING TO BED.
YOU SHOULD TURN IN EARLY TOO, MOM.
YEAH, YEAH.
GOOD NIGHT.
むくり
MUKURI (SIT)
......
I DON'T CARE IF I DO GET CAUGHT.
THE SITUATION CALLS FOR BOLD MEASURES...
ZA (CHFF)
ザッ
ZA
ザッ
ZA
ザッ

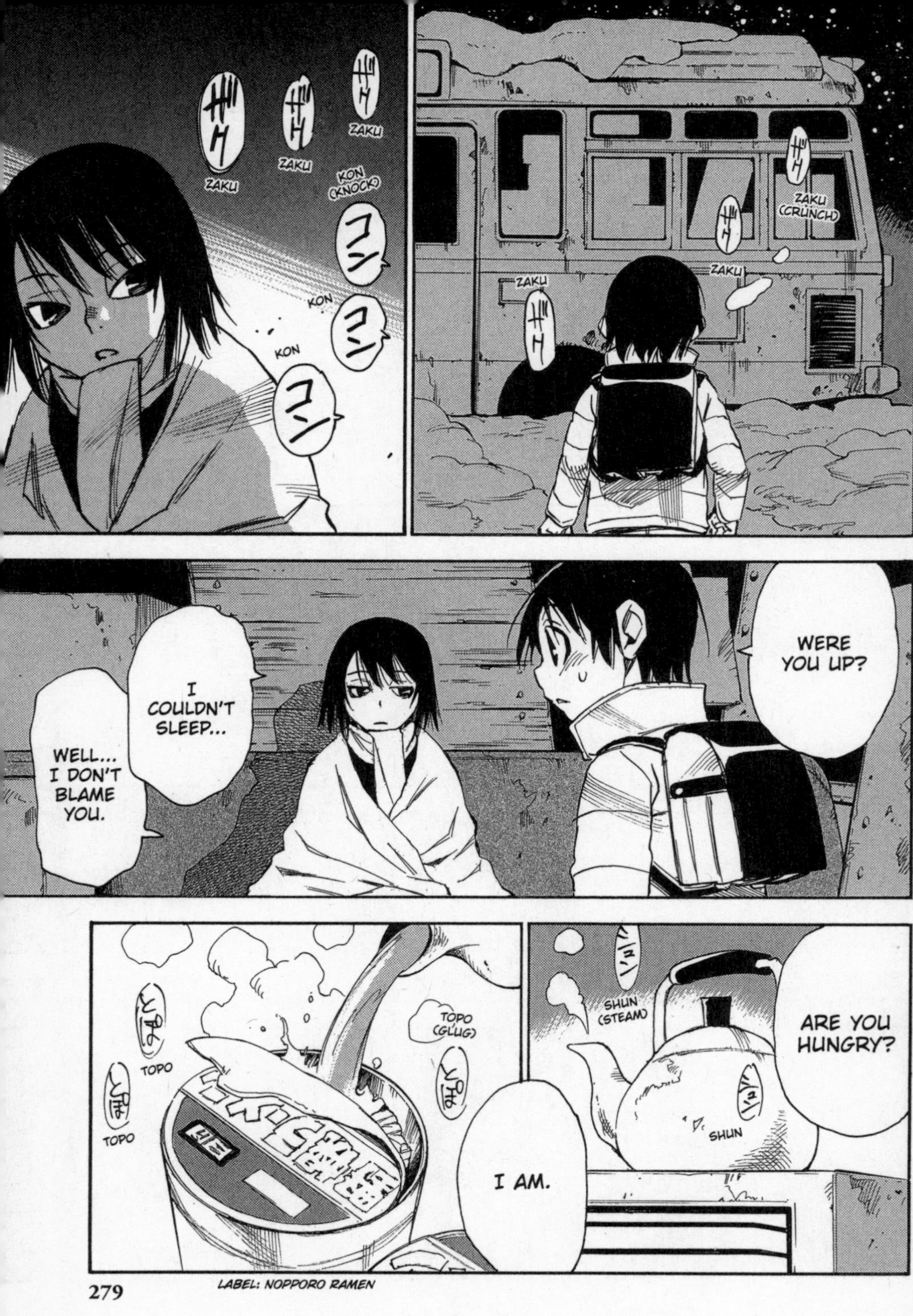
ZAKU (CRUNCH)
ZAKU
ZAKU
ZAKU
ZAKU
ZAKU
KON (KNOCK)
KON
KON
WERE YOU UP?
I COULDN'T SLEEP...
WELL... I DON'T BLAME YOU.
SHUN (STEAM)
SHUN
ARE YOU HUNGRY?
I AM.
TOPO (GLUG)
TOPO
TOPO

LABEL: NOPPORO RAMEN

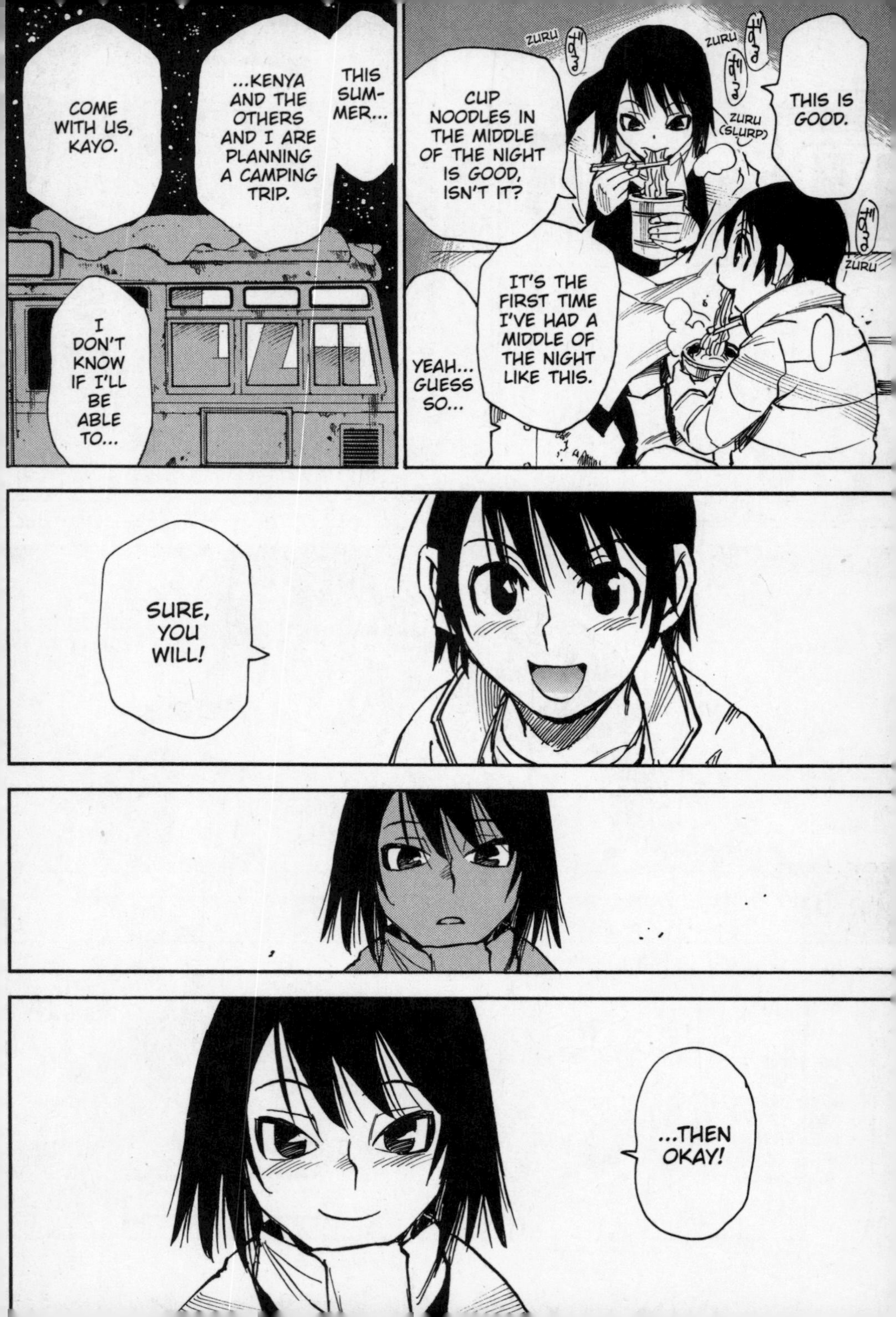
ZURU
ZURU
THIS IS GOOD.
ZURU (SLURP)
CUP NOODLES IN THE MIDDLE OF THE NIGHT IS GOOD, ISN'T IT?
ZURU
IT'S THE FIRST TIME I'VE HAD A MIDDLE OF THE NIGHT LIKE THIS.
YEAH... GUESS SO...
THIS SUMMER...
...KENYA AND THE OTHERS AND I ARE PLANNING A CAMPING TRIP.
COME WITH US, KAYO.
I DON'T KNOW IF I'LL BE ABLE TO...
SURE, YOU WILL!
...THEN OKAY!

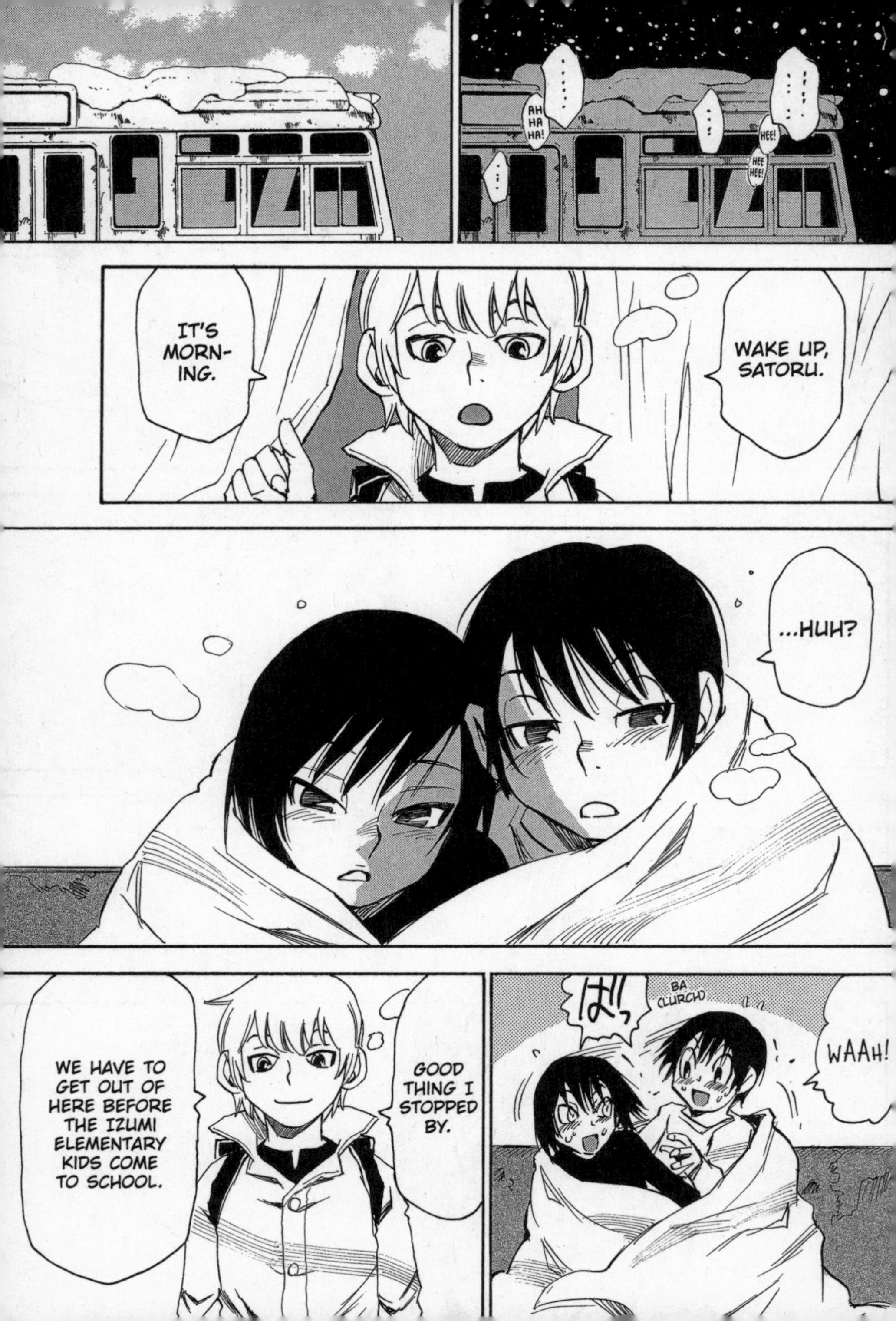
HEE!
HEE HEE!
...
...
AH HA HA!
...
WAKE UP, SATORU.
IT'S MORN-ING.
...HUH?
WAAH!
BA (LURCH)
は!,
GOOD THING I STOPPED BY.
WE HAVE TO GET OUT OF HERE BEFORE THE IZUMI ELEMENTARY KIDS COME TO SCHOOL.

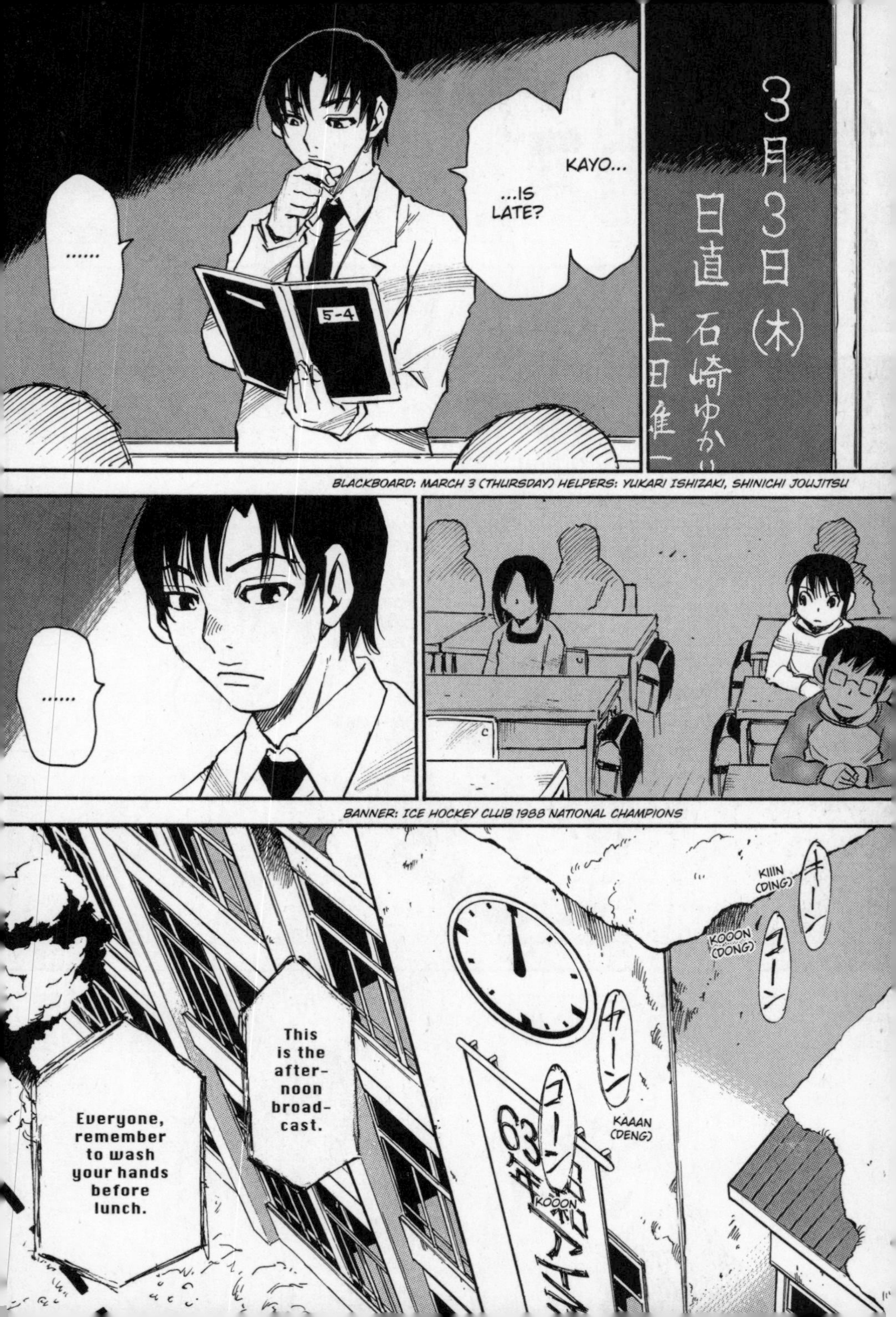
3月3日(木)
日直 石崎ゆかり
KAYO...
...IS LATE?
......
BLACKBOARD: MARCH 3 (THURSDAY) HELPERS: YUKARI ISHIZAKI, SHINICHI JOUJITSU
......
BANNER: ICE HOCKEY CLUB 1988 NATIONAL CHAMPIONS
キーン
KIIIN (DING)
コーン
KOOON (DONG)
カーン
KAAAN (DENG)
コーン
KOOON
This is the after-noon broad-cast.
Everyone, remember to wash your hands before lunch.

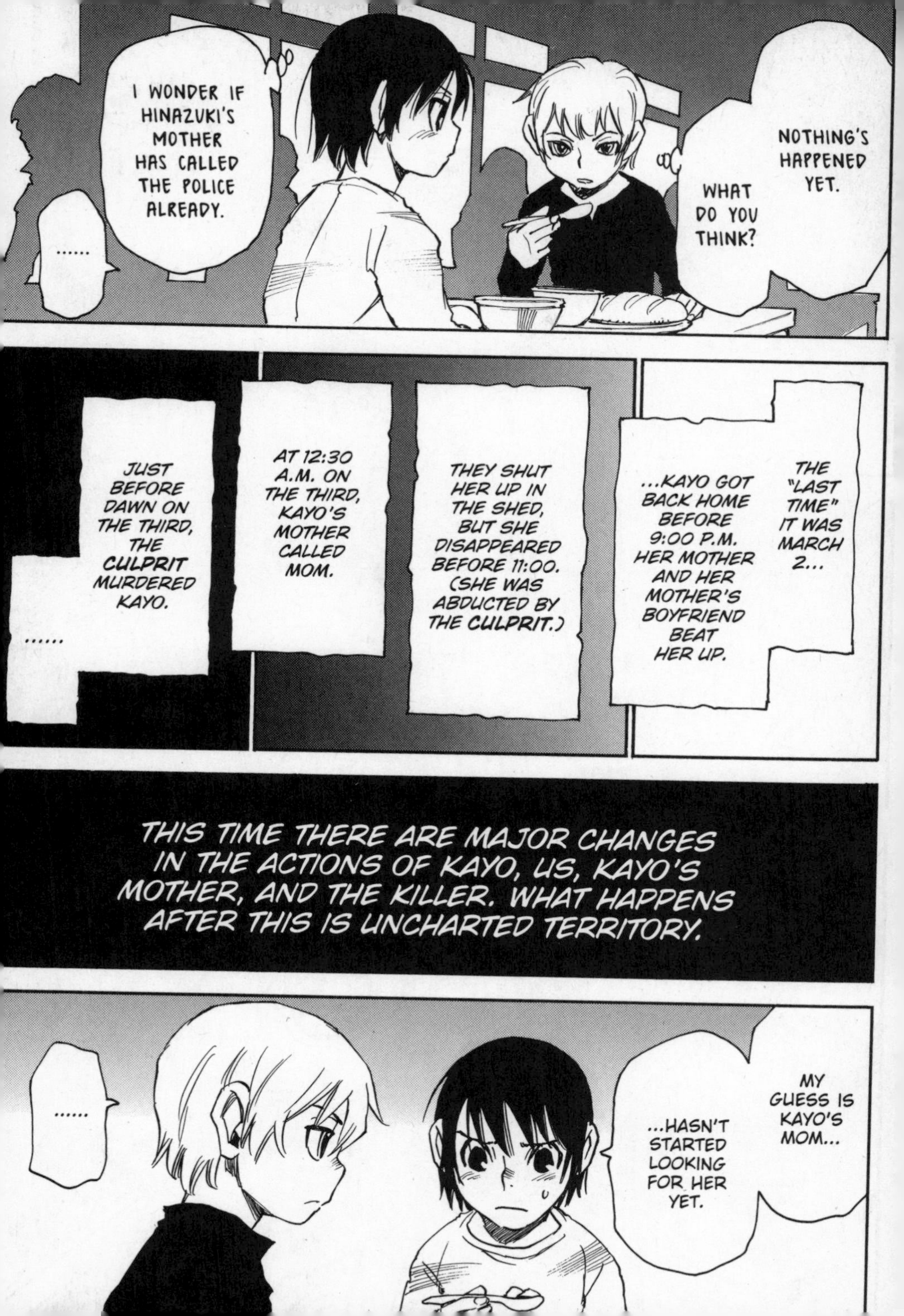
NOTHING'S HAPPENED YET.
WHAT DO YOU THINK?
I WONDER IF HINAZUKI'S MOTHER HAS CALLED THE POLICE ALREADY.
......
THE "LAST TIME" IT WAS MARCH 2...
...KAYO GOT BACK HOME BEFORE 9:00 P.M. HER MOTHER AND HER MOTHER'S BOYFRIEND BEAT HER UP.
THEY SHUT HER UP IN THE SHED, BUT SHE DISAPPEARED BEFORE 11:00. (SHE WAS ABDUCTED BY THE CULPRIT.)
AT 12:30 A.M. ON THE THIRD, KAYO'S MOTHER CALLED MOM.
JUST BEFORE DAWN ON THE THIRD, THE CULPRIT MURDERED KAYO.
......
THIS TIME THERE ARE MAJOR CHANGES IN THE ACTIONS OF KAYO, US, KAYO'S MOTHER, AND THE KILLER. WHAT HAPPENS AFTER THIS IS UNCHARTED TERRITORY.
MY GUESS IS KAYO'S MOM...
...HASN'T STARTED LOOKING FOR HER YET.
......

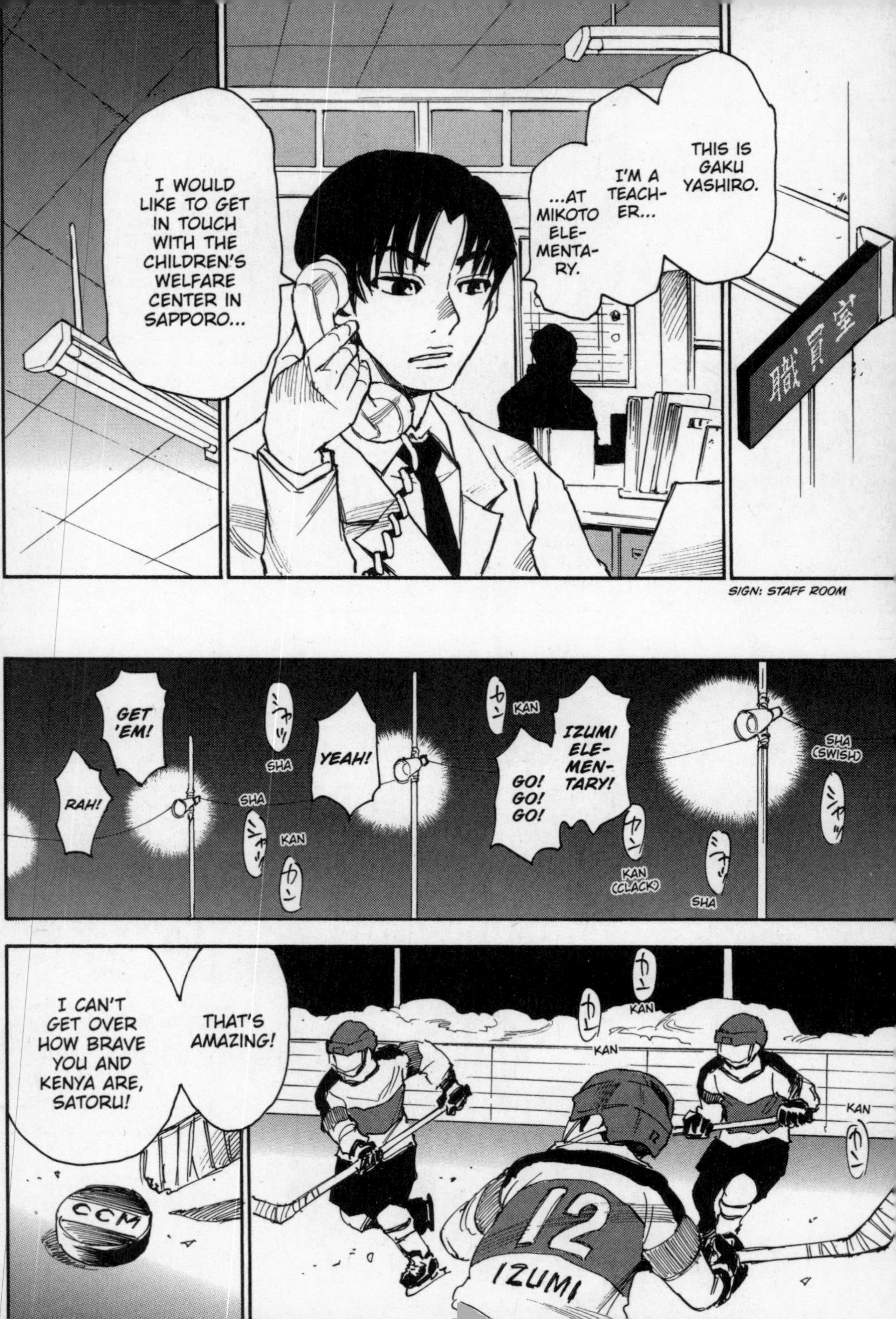
THIS IS GAKU YASHIRO.
I'M A TEACH-ER...
...AT MIKOTO ELE-MENTA-RY.
I WOULD LIKE TO GET IN TOUCH WITH THE CHILDREN'S WELFARE CENTER IN SAPPORO...
職員室
SHA (SWISH)
SHA
KAN (CLACK)
IZUMI ELE-MEN-TARY!
GO! GO! GO!
KAN
YEAH!
SHA
SHA
KAN
GET 'EM!
RAH!
KAN
KAN
KAN
KAN
THAT'S AMAZING!
I CAN'T GET OVER HOW BRAVE YOU AND KENYA ARE, SATORU!
12
IZUMI
CCM
SIGN: STAFF ROOM

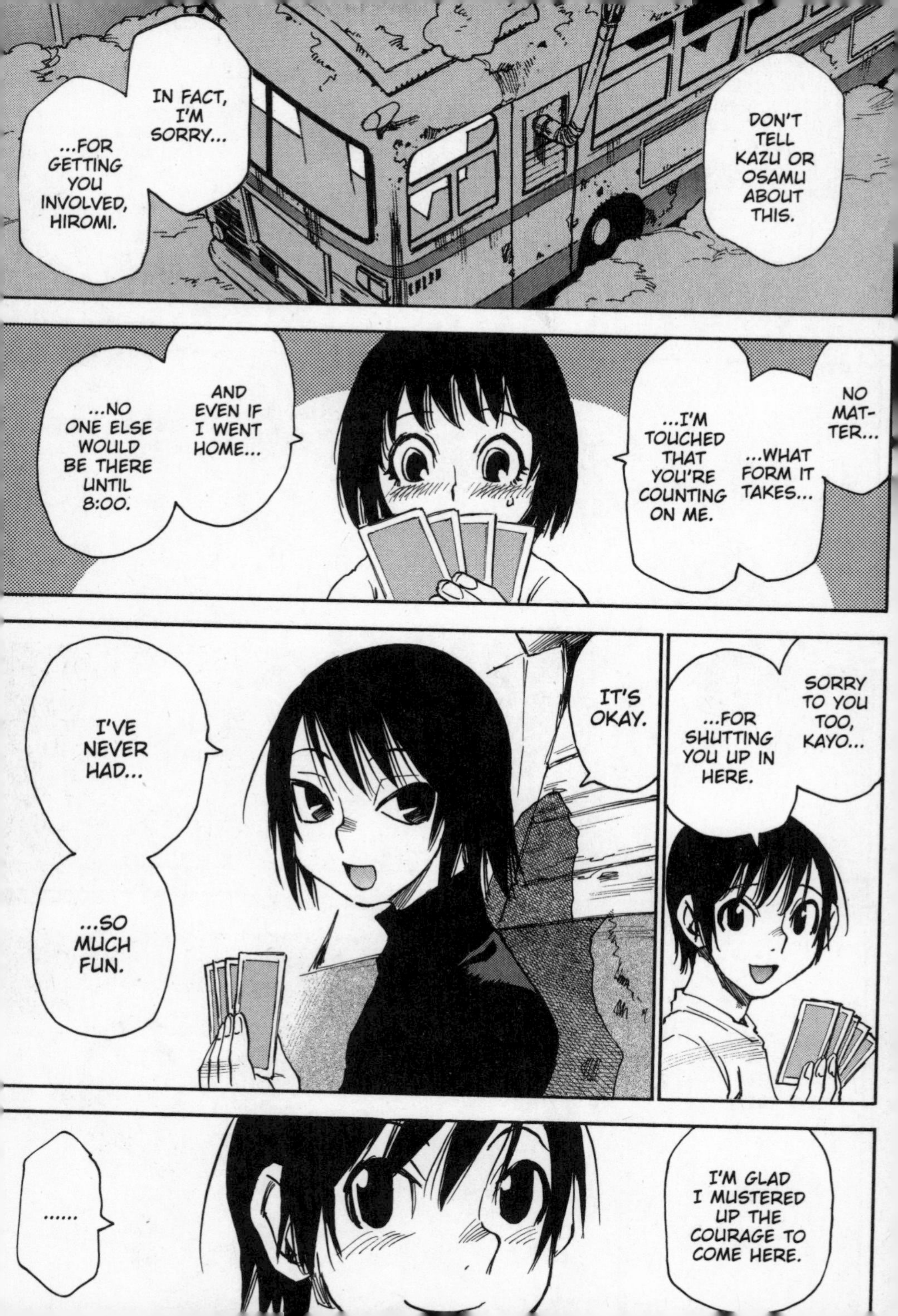
DON'T TELL KAZU OR OSAMU ABOUT THIS.
IN FACT, I'M SORRY...
...FOR GETTING YOU INVOLVED, HIROMI.
NO MAT-TER...
...WHAT FORM IT TAKES...
...I'M TOUCHED THAT YOU'RE COUNTING ON ME.
AND EVEN IF I WENT HOME...
...NO ONE ELSE WOULD BE THERE UNTIL 8:00.
SORRY TO YOU TOO, KAYO...
...FOR SHUTTING YOU UP IN HERE.
IT'S OKAY.
I'VE NEVER HAD...
...SO MUCH FUN.
I'M GLAD I MUSTERED UP THE COURAGE TO COME HERE.
......

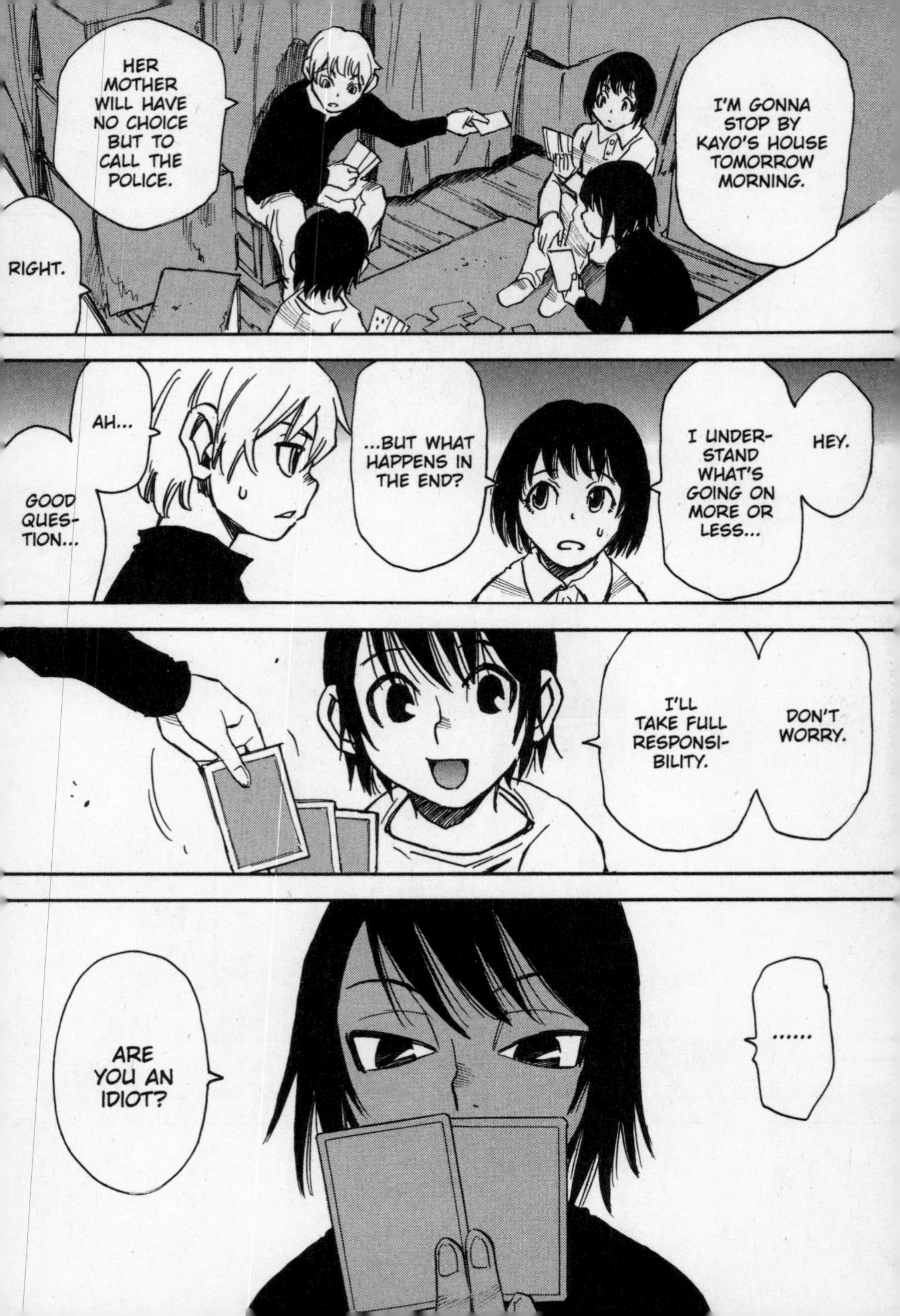
I'M GONNA STOP BY KAYO'S HOUSE TOMORROW MORNING.
HER MOTHER WILL HAVE NO CHOICE BUT TO CALL THE POLICE.
RIGHT.
HEY.
I UNDERSTAND WHAT'S GOING ON MORE OR LESS...
...BUT WHAT HAPPENS IN THE END?
AH...
GOOD QUESTION...
DON'T WORRY.
I'LL TAKE FULL RESPONSIBILITY.
......
ARE YOU AN IDIOT?

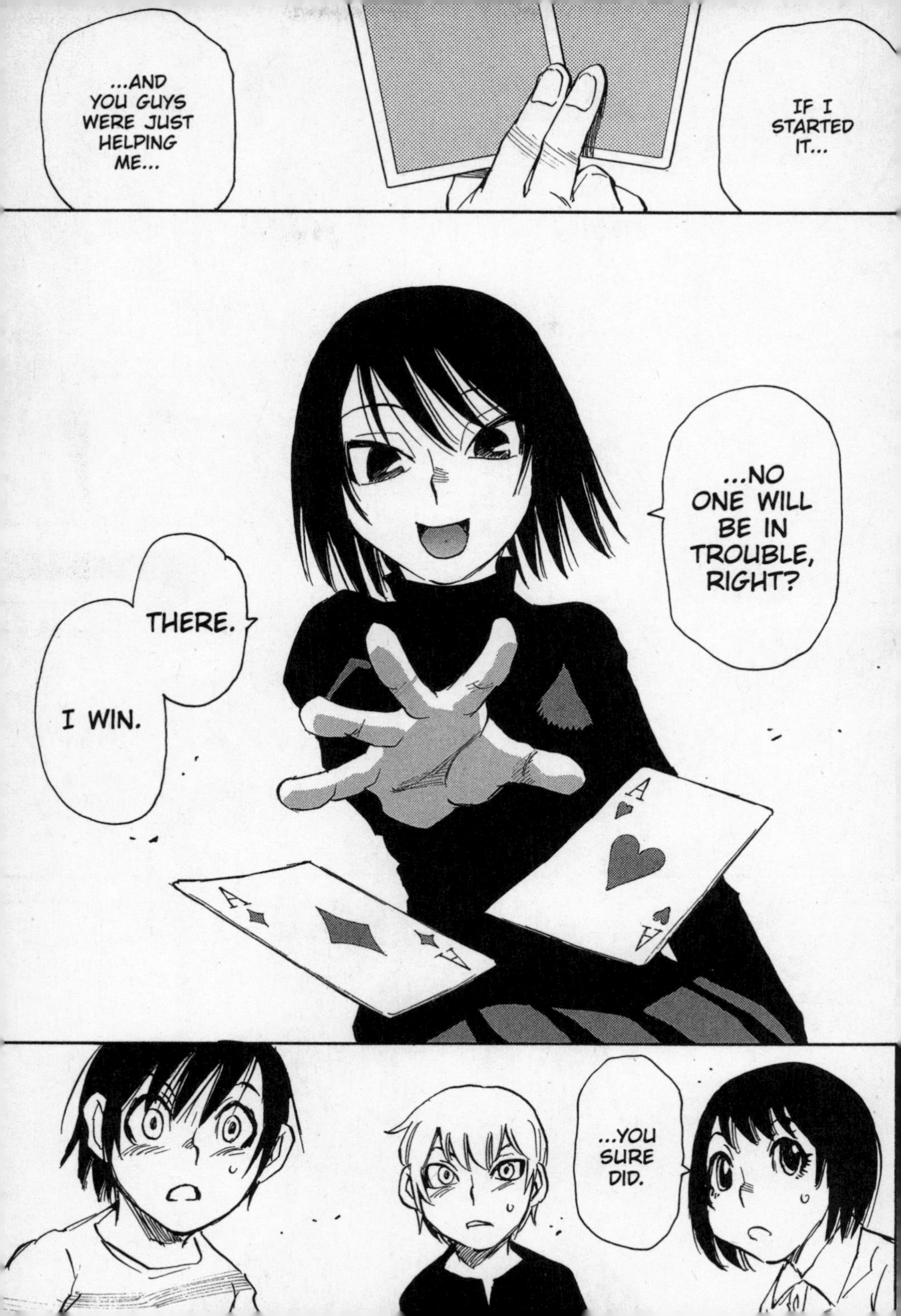
IF I STARTED IT...
...AND YOU GUYS WERE JUST HELPING ME...
...NO ONE WILL BE IN TROUBLE, RIGHT?
THERE.
I WIN.
...YOU SURE DID.

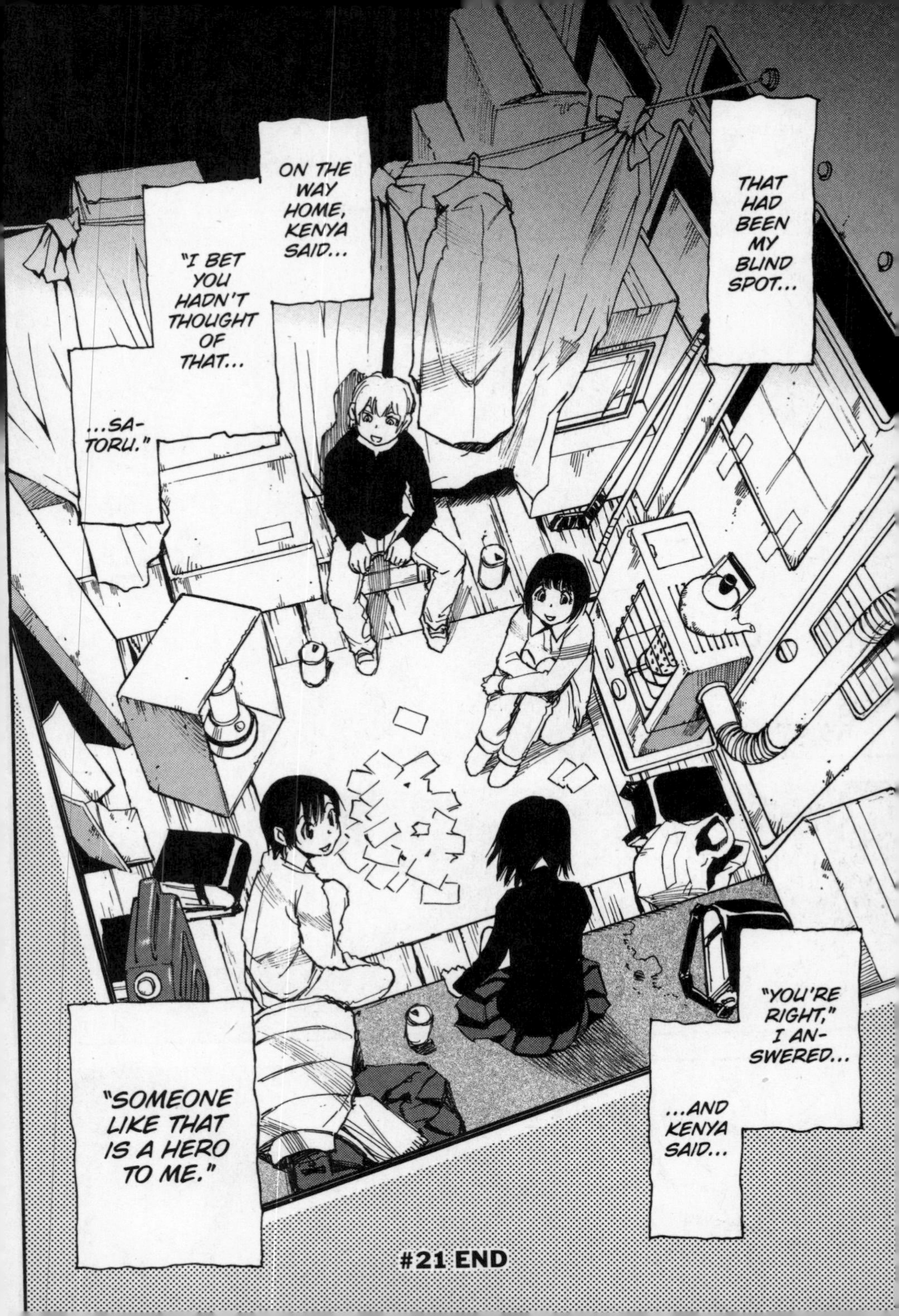
THAT HAD BEEN MY BLIND SPOT...
ON THE WAY HOME, KENYA SAID...
"I BET YOU HADN'T THOUGHT OF THAT...
...SA-TORU."
"YOU'RE RIGHT," I AN-SWERED...
...AND KENYA SAID...
"SOMEONE LIKE THAT IS A HERO TO ME."
#21 END

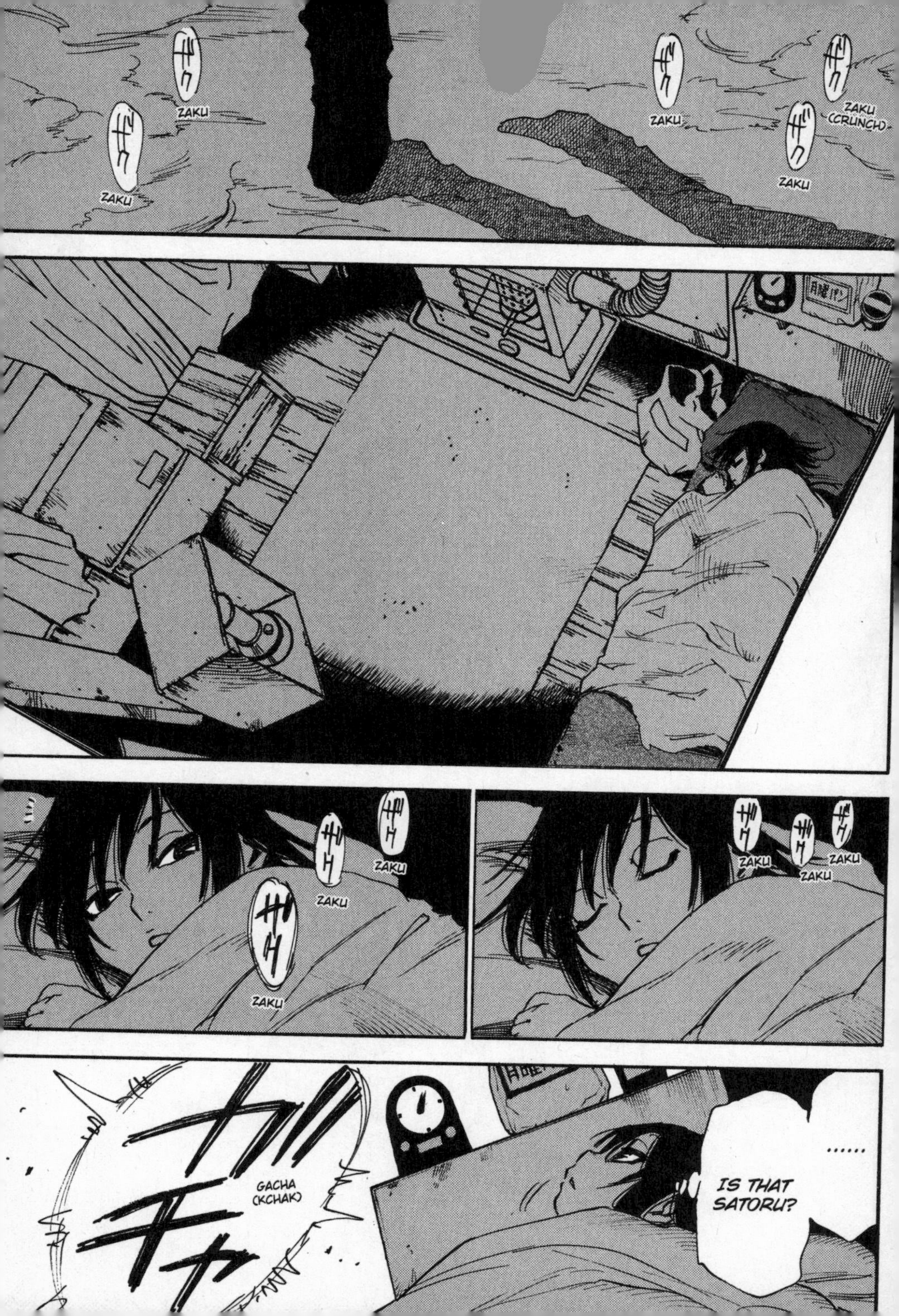
ZAKU (CRUNCH)
ZAKU
ZAKU
ZAKU
ZAKU
ZAKU
ZAKU
ZAKU
ZAKU
ZAKU
ZAKU
...
......
IS THAT SATORU?
GACHA (KCHAK)

#22: Refuge, March 1988

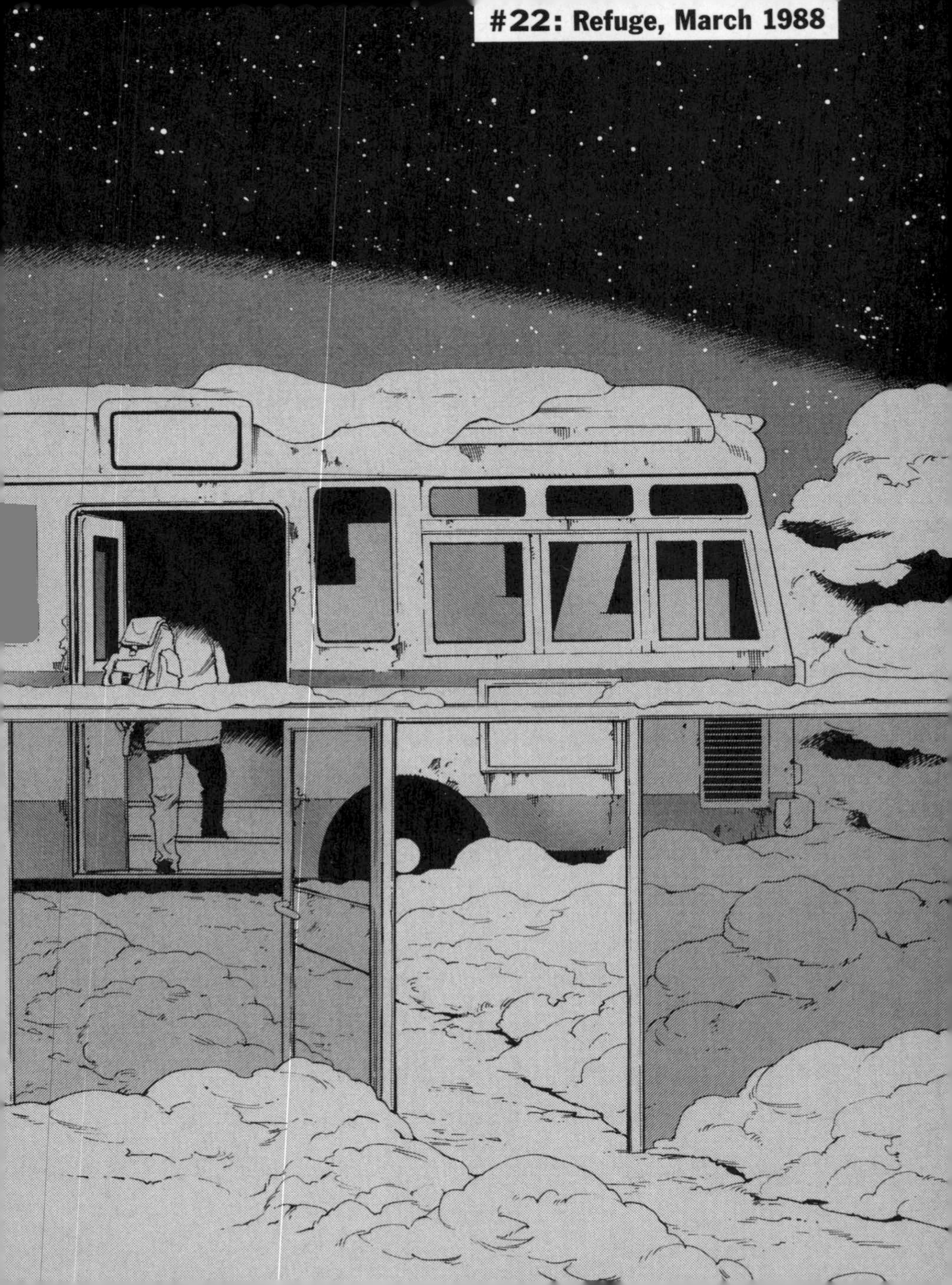

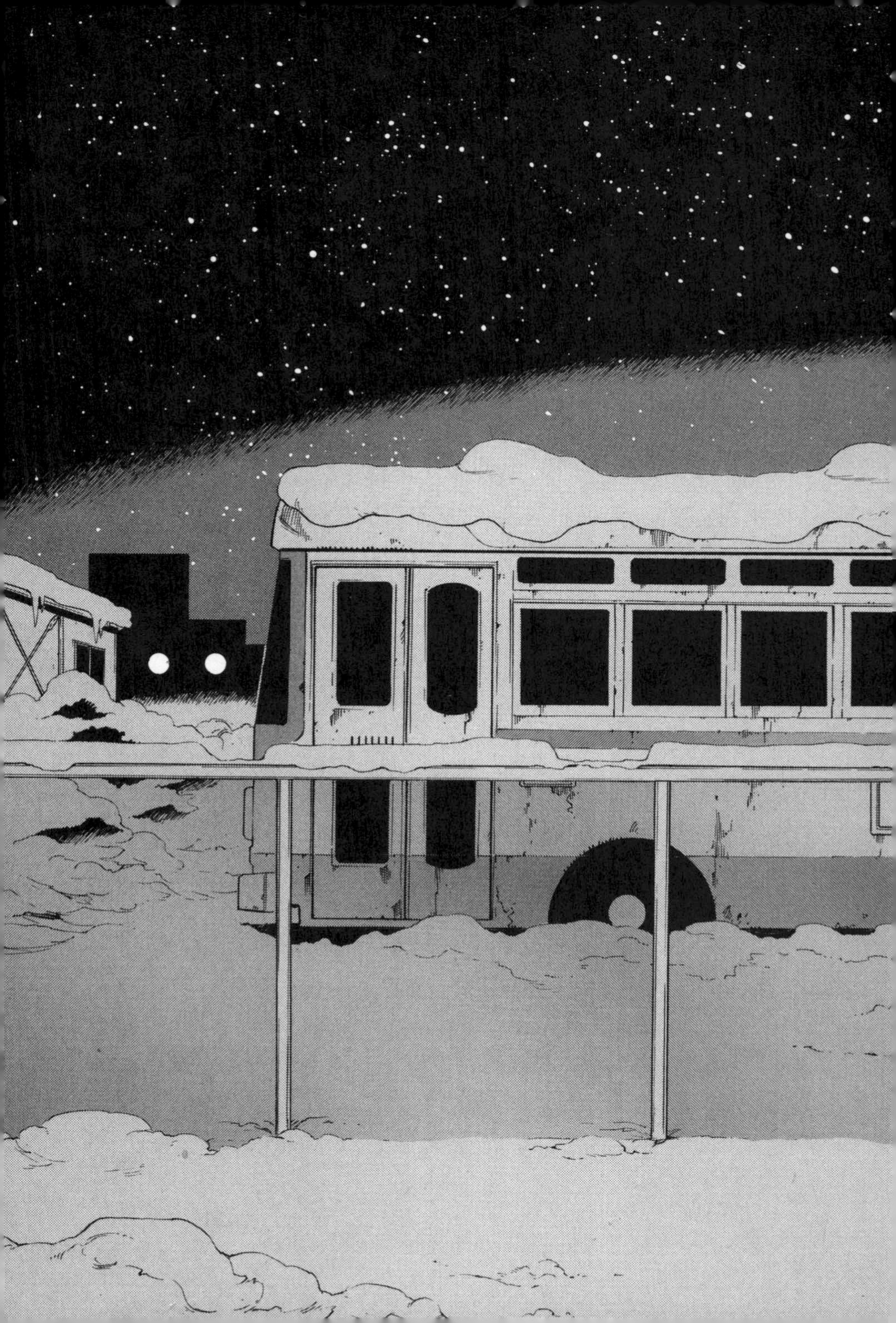

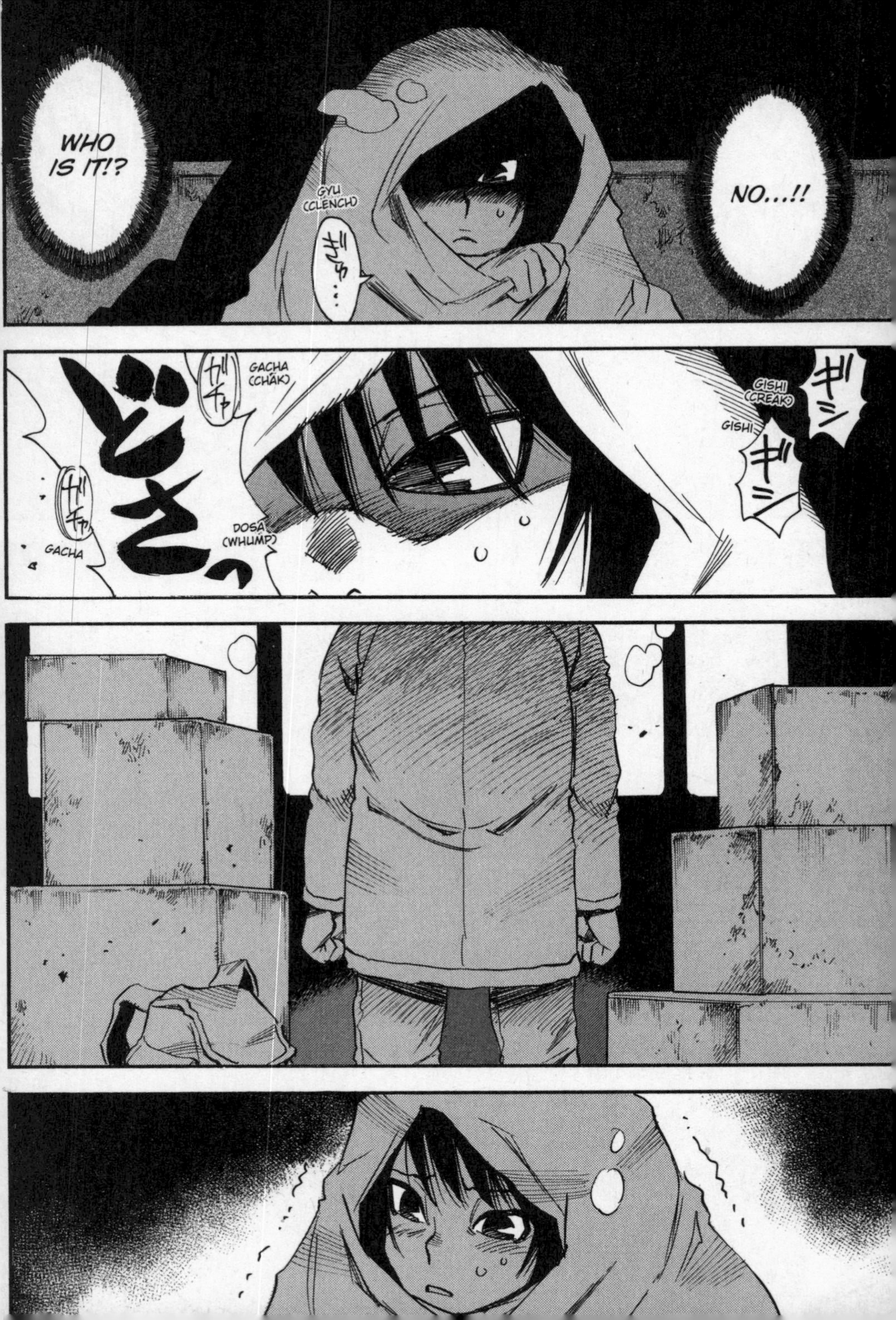
NO...!!
GYU (CLENCH)
ぎゅ…
WHO IS IT!?
ギシ
GISHI (CREAK)
ギシ
GISHI
どさっ
DOSA (WHUMP)
ガチャ
GACHA (CHAK)
ガチャ
GACHA

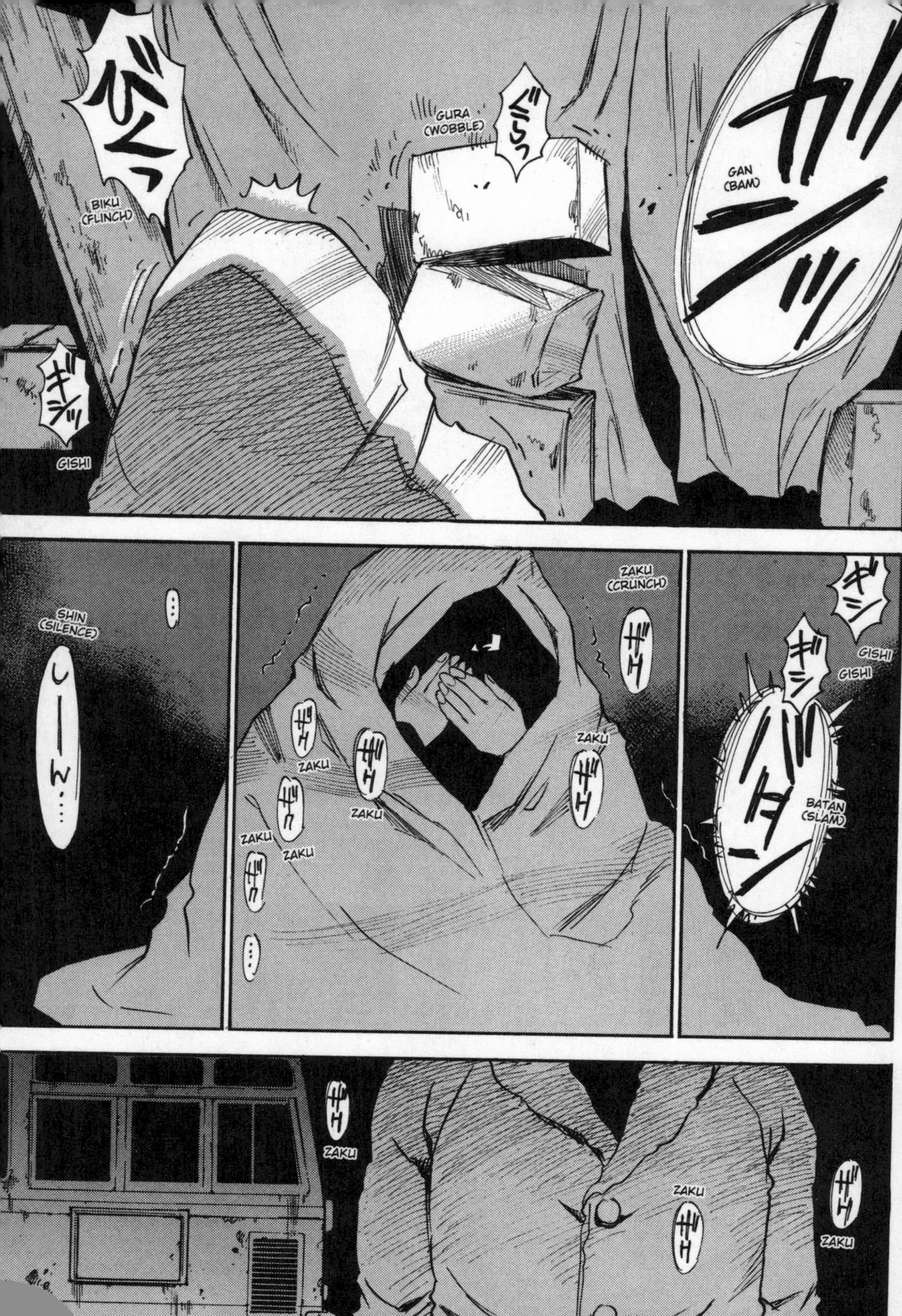
ガーンッ
GAN (BAM)
ぐらっ
GURA (WOBBLE)
びくっ
BIKU (FLINCH)
ギシッ
GISHI
ギシ
ギシ
GISHI
GISHI
バターン
BATAN (SLAM)
ザク
ZAKU (CRUNCH)
ザク
ZAKU
ザク
ZAKU
ザク
ZAKU
ザク
ZAKU
ザク
ZAKU
…
…
しーーん…
SHIN (SILENCE)
ザク
ZAKU
ザク
ZAKU
ザク
ZAKU

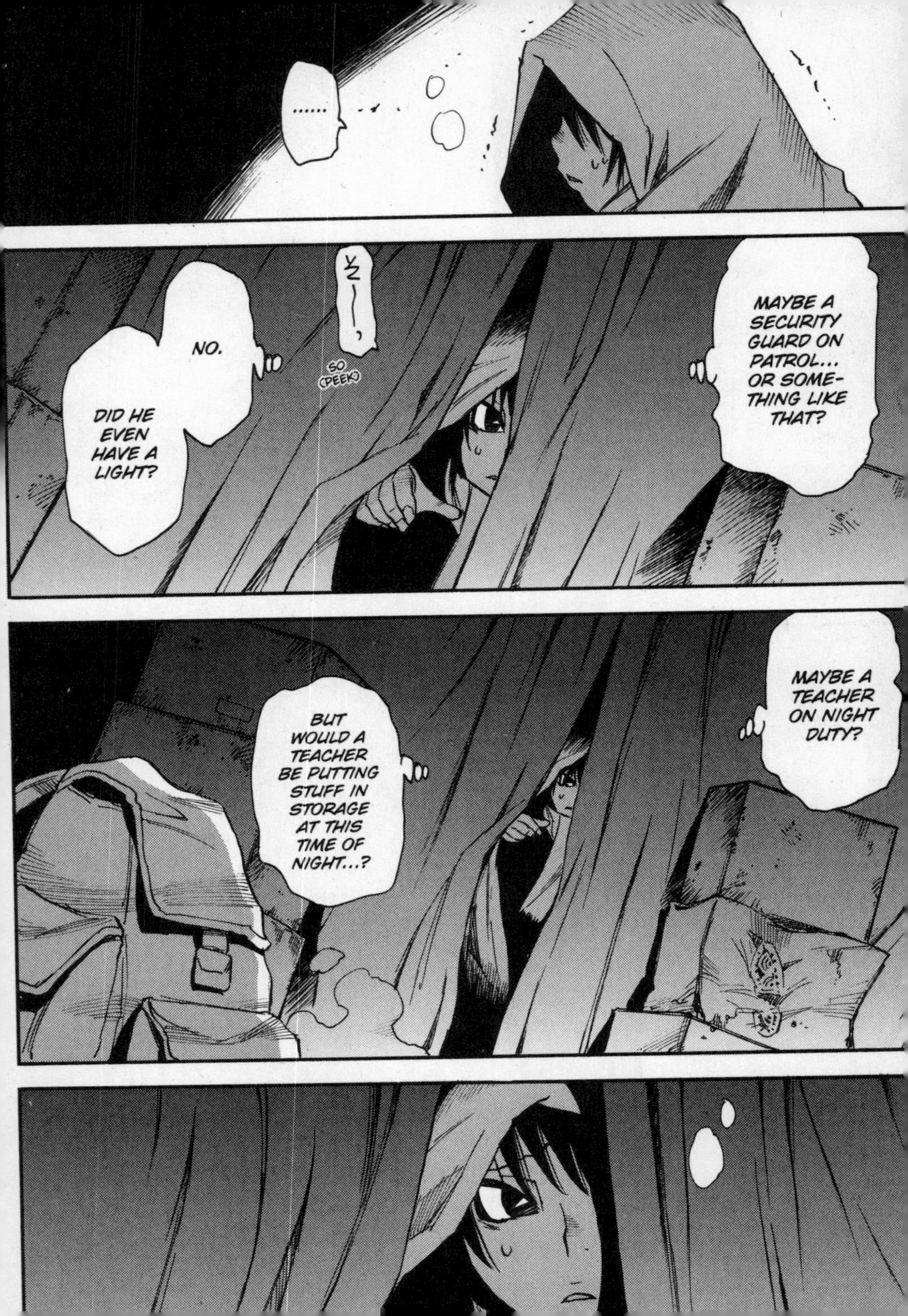
......
MAYBE A SECURITY GUARD ON PATROL... OR SOMETHING LIKE THAT?
SO (PEEK)
NO.
DID HE EVEN HAVE A LIGHT?
MAYBE A TEACHER ON NIGHT DUTY?
BUT WOULD A TEACHER BE PUTTING STUFF IN STORAGE AT THIS TIME OF NIGHT...?

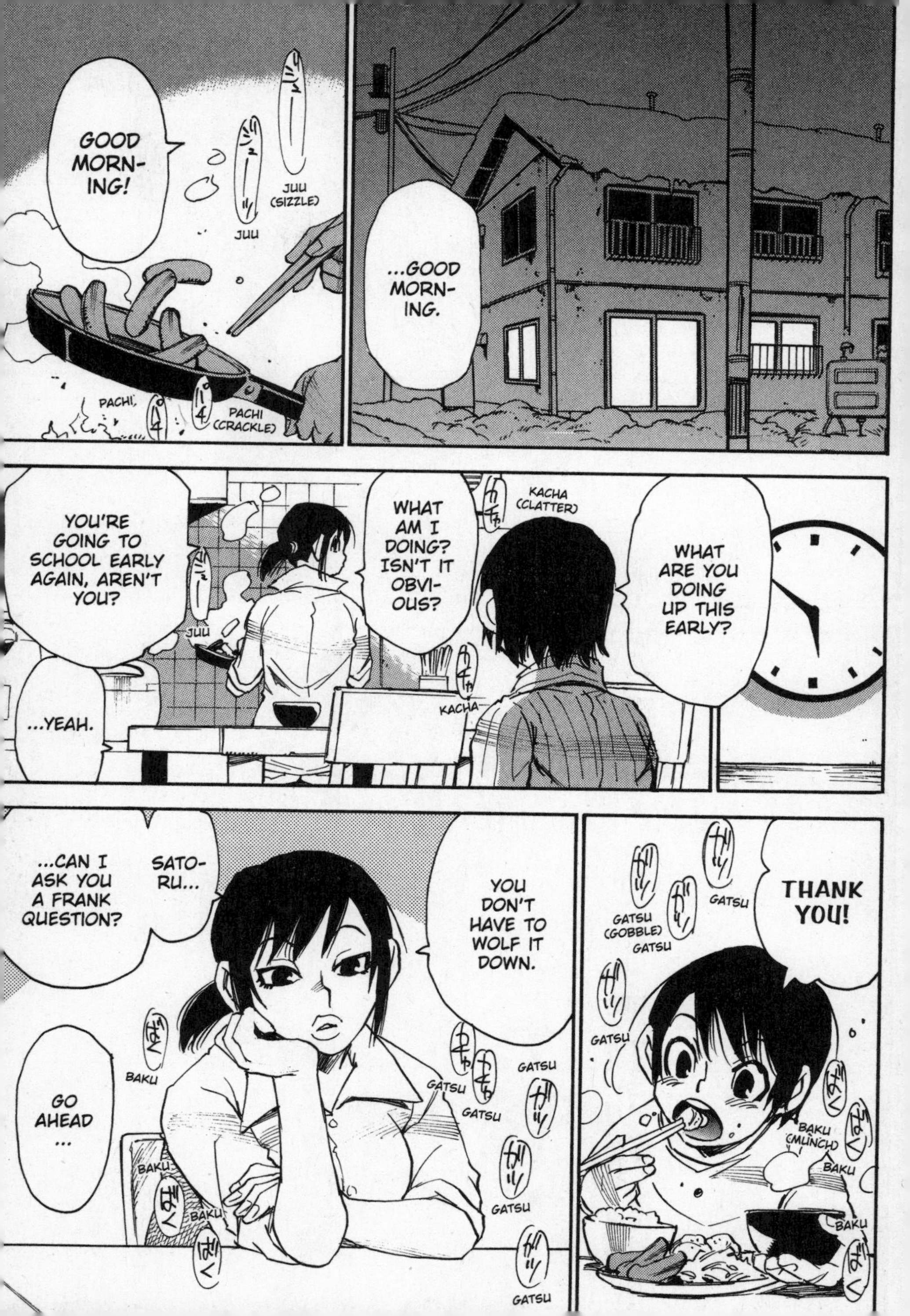
...GOOD MORNING.
GOOD MORNING!
JUU (SIZZLE)
JUU
PACHI (CRACKLE)
PACHI
WHAT ARE YOU DOING UP THIS EARLY?
KACHA (CLATTER)
WHAT AM I DOING? ISN'T IT OBVIOUS?
KACHA
YOU'RE GOING TO SCHOOL EARLY AGAIN, AREN'T YOU?
JUU
...YEAH.
THANK YOU!
GATSU
GATSU (GOBBLE)
GATSU
GATSU
BAKU (MUNCH)
BAKU
BAKU
YOU DON'T HAVE TO WOLF IT DOWN.
SATORU...
...CAN I ASK YOU A FRANK QUESTION?
GATSU
GATSU
GATSU
GO AHEAD...
BAKU
BAKU
BAKU
GATSU
GATSU

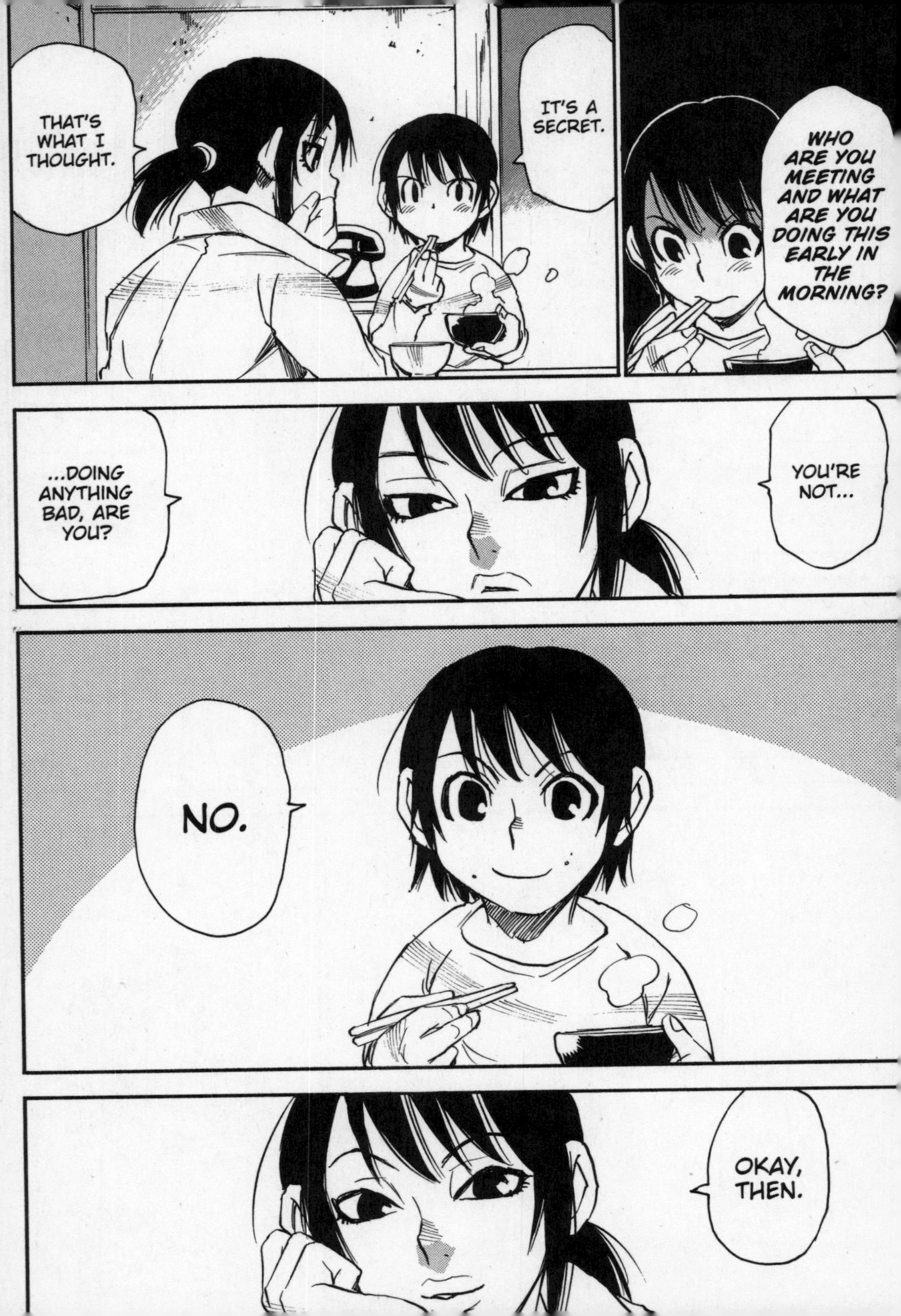
WHO ARE YOU MEETING AND WHAT ARE YOU DOING THIS EARLY IN THE MORNING?
IT'S A SECRET.
THAT'S WHAT I THOUGHT.
YOU'RE NOT...
...DOING ANYTHING BAD, ARE YOU?
NO.
OKAY, THEN.

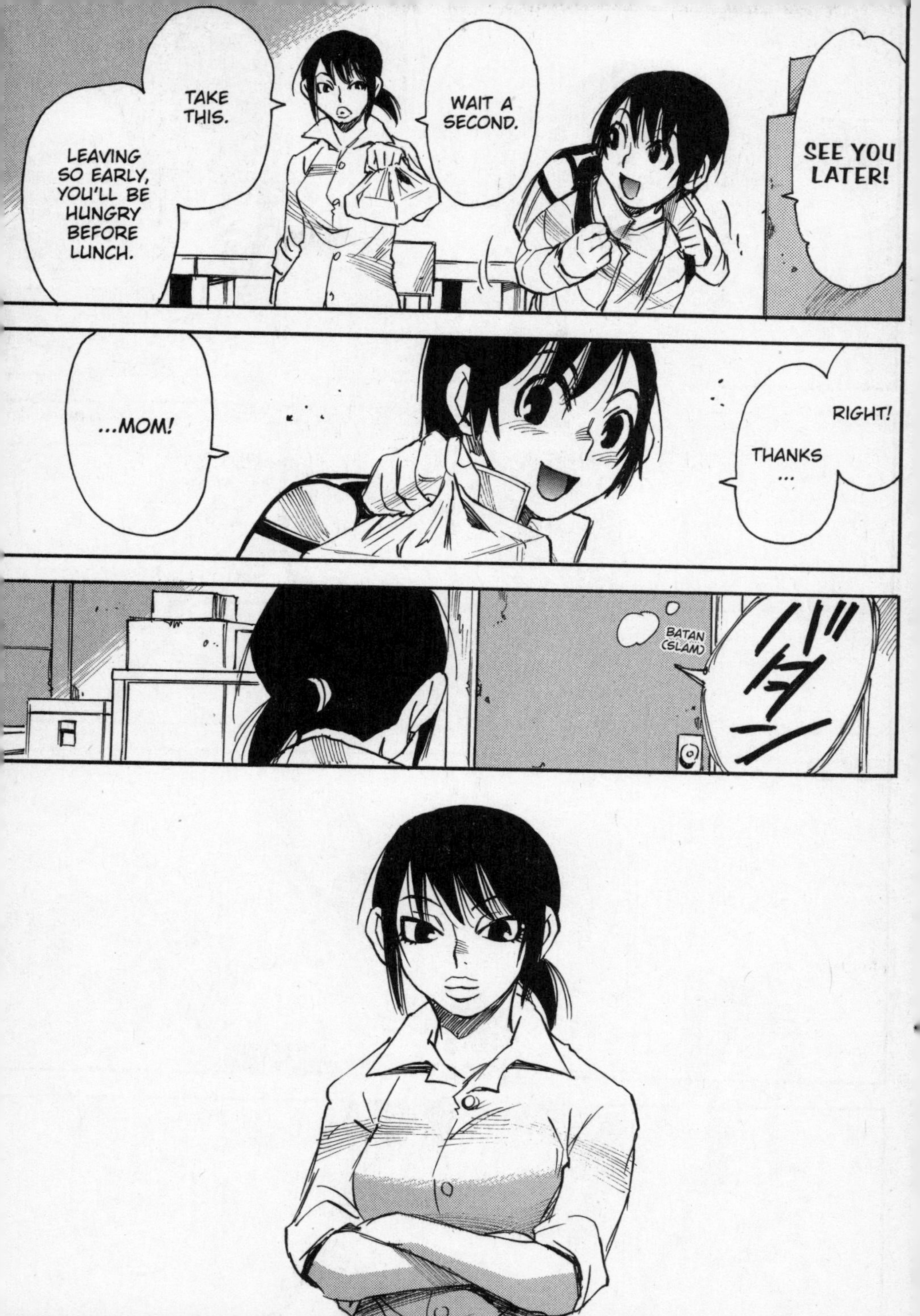
SEE YOU LATER!
WAIT A SECOND.
TAKE THIS.
LEAVING SO EARLY, YOU'LL BE HUNGRY BEFORE LUNCH.
RIGHT!
THANKS ...
...MOM!
バタン
BATAN (SLAM)

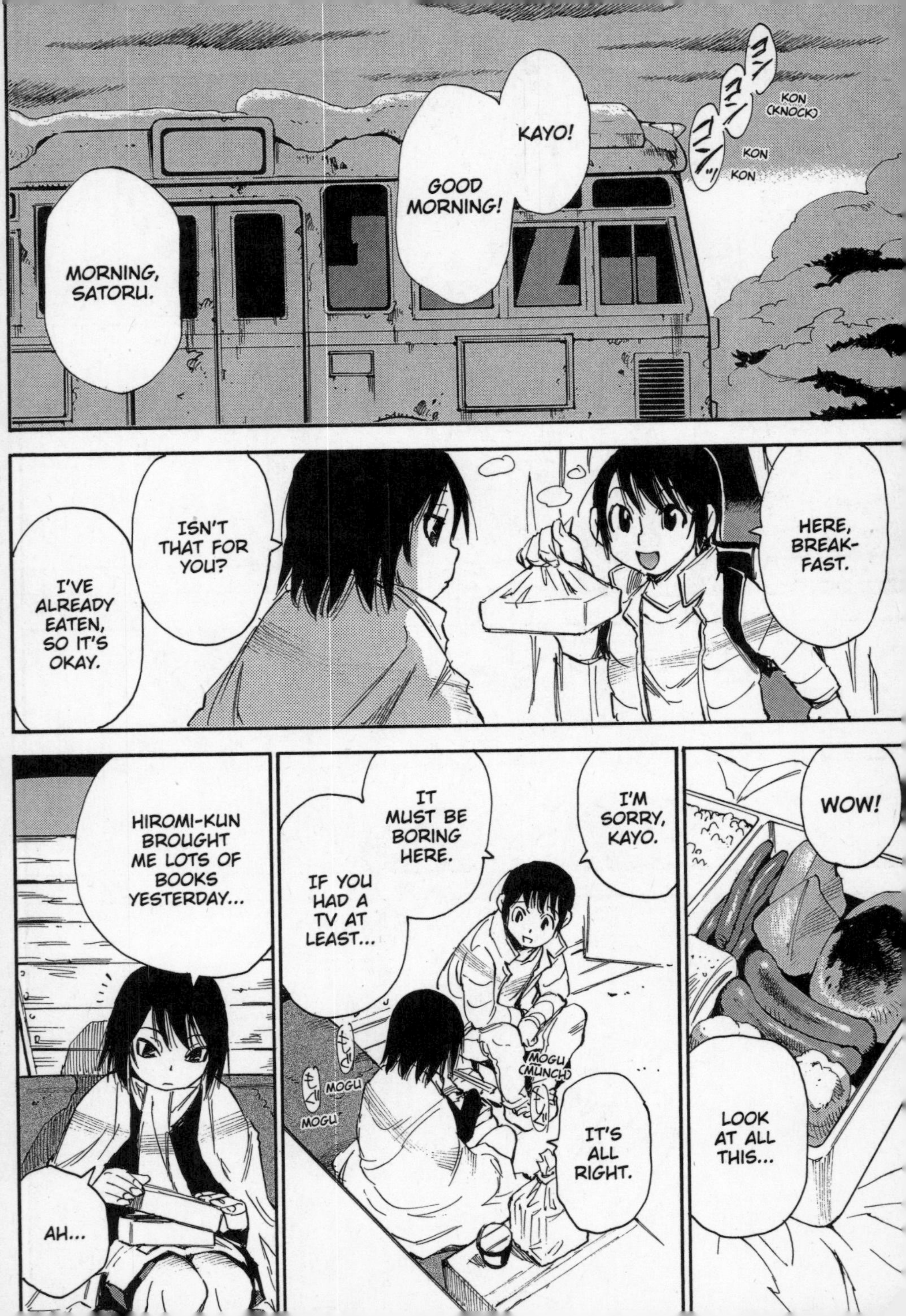
KON (KNOCK)
KON
KON
KAYO!
GOOD MORNING!
MORNING, SATORU.
HERE, BREAKFAST.
ISN'T THAT FOR YOU?
I'VE ALREADY EATEN, SO IT'S OKAY.
WOW!
LOOK AT ALL THIS...
I'M SORRY, KAYO.
IT MUST BE BORING HERE.
IF YOU HAD A TV AT LEAST...
MOGU (MUNCH)
MOGU
MOGU
IT'S ALL RIGHT.
HIROMI-KUN BROUGHT ME LOTS OF BOOKS YESTERDAY...
AH...

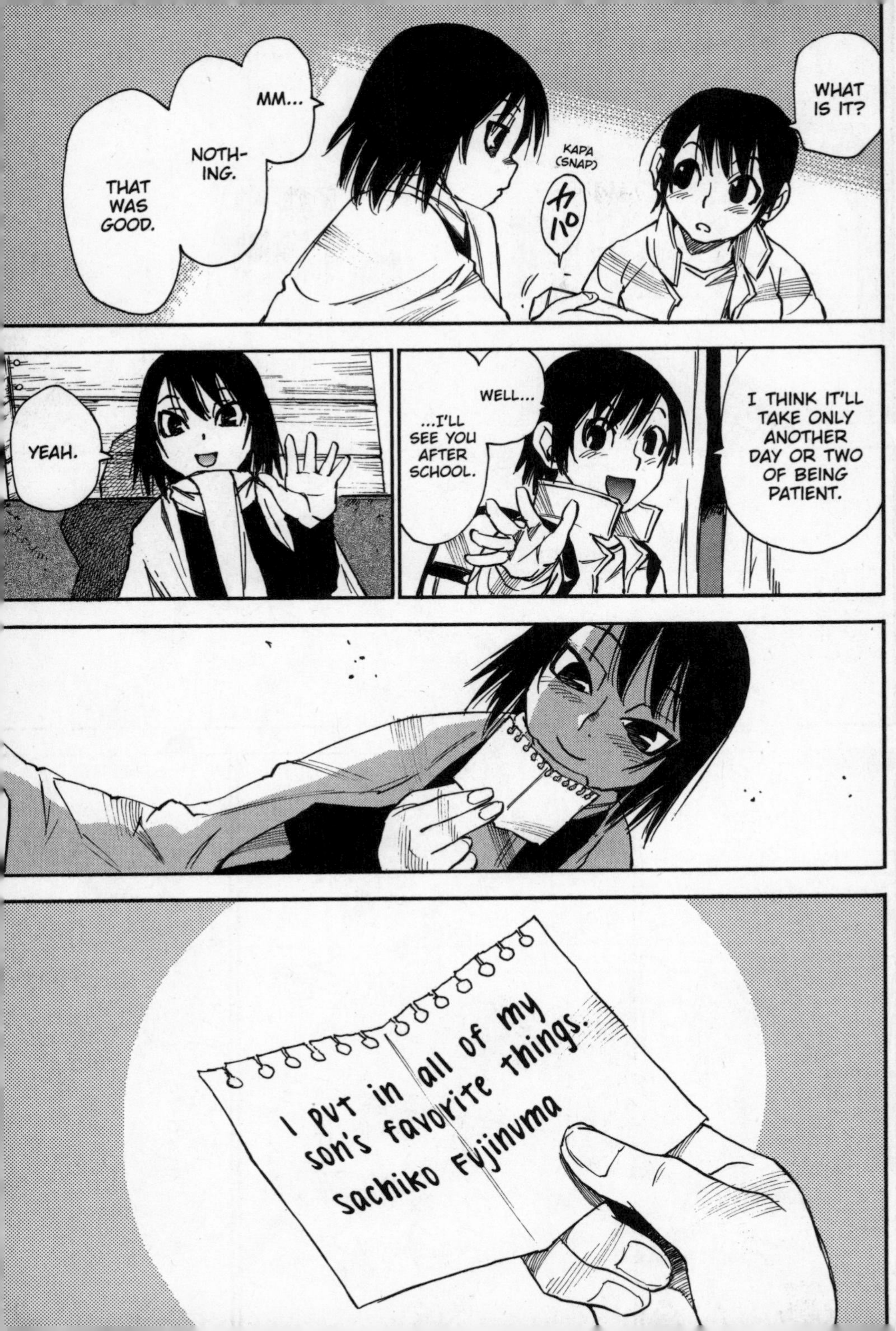
WHAT IS IT?
KAPA (SNAP)
カパ
MM...
NOTH-ING.
THAT WAS GOOD.
I THINK IT'LL TAKE ONLY ANOTHER DAY OR TWO OF BEING PATIENT.
WELL...
...I'LL SEE YOU AFTER SCHOOL.
YEAH.
I put in all of my son's favorite things.
Sachiko Fujinuma

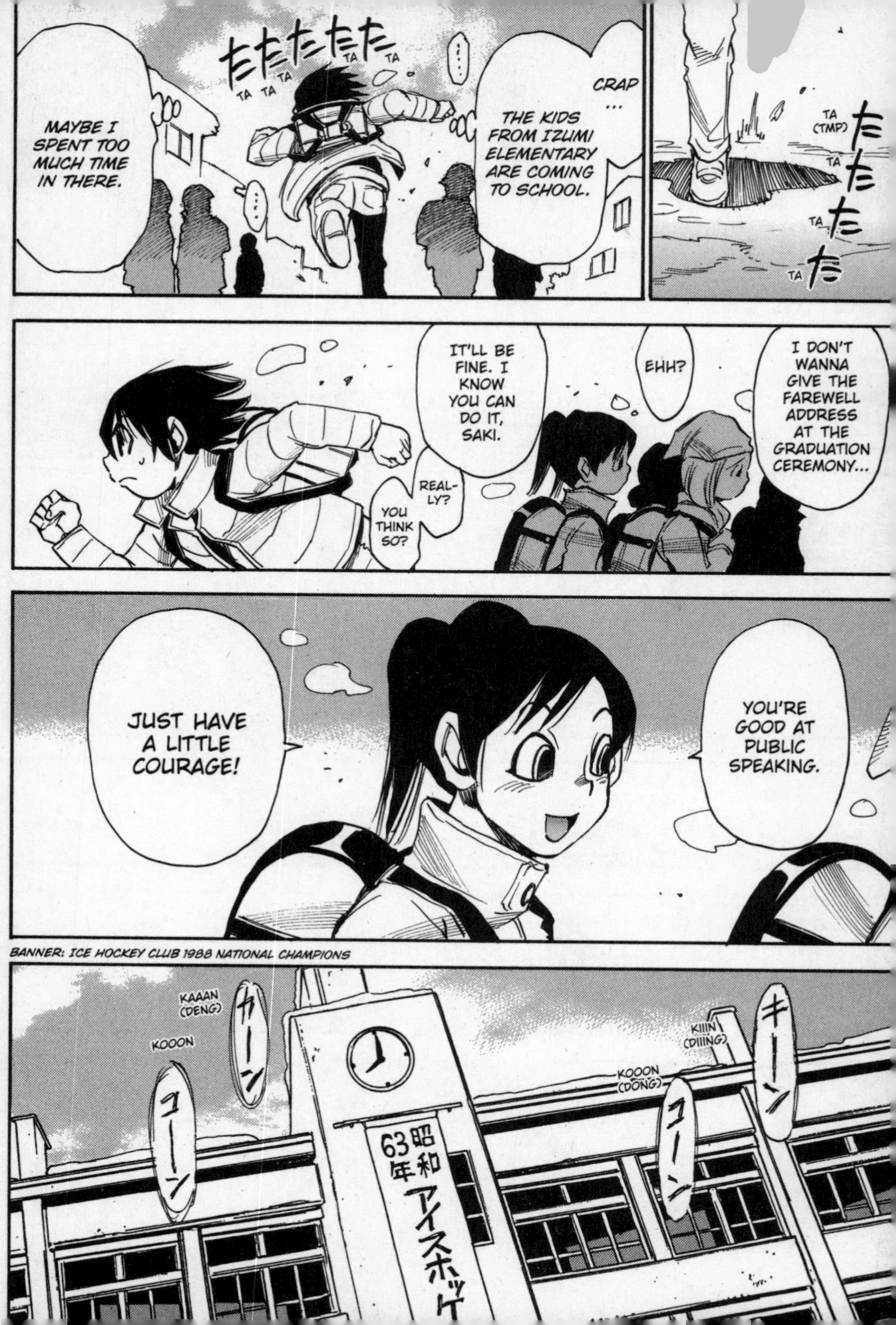
TA (TMP) たたたた TA TA TA
CRAP...
THE KIDS FROM IZUMI ELEMENTARY ARE COMING TO SCHOOL.
.....
たたたたたた TA TA TA TA TA TA
.....
MAYBE I SPENT TOO MUCH TIME IN THERE.
I DON'T WANNA GIVE THE FAREWELL ADDRESS AT THE GRADUATION CEREMONY...
EHH?
IT'LL BE FINE. I KNOW YOU CAN DO IT, SAKI.
REAL-LY?
YOU THINK SO?
YOU'RE GOOD AT PUBLIC SPEAKING.
JUST HAVE A LITTLE COURAGE!
BANNER: ICE HOCKEY CLUB 1988 NATIONAL CHAMPIONS
KIIIN (DIIING) キーン
KOOON (DONG) コーン
昭和63年アイスホッケ
KAAAN (DENG) カーン
KOOON コーン

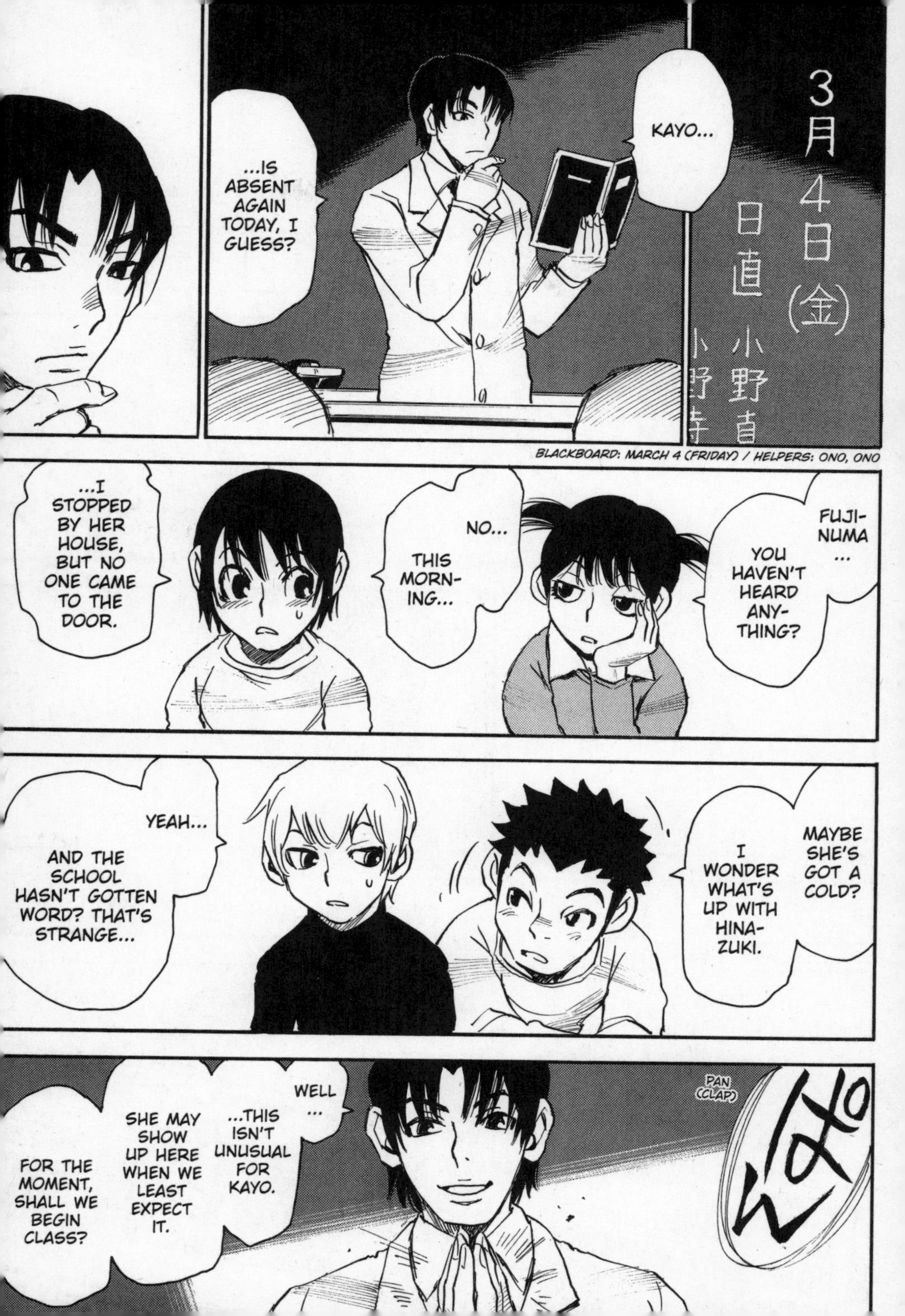
3月4日(金)
日直 小野直
小野
KAYO...
...IS ABSENT AGAIN TODAY, I GUESS?
BLACKBOARD: MARCH 4 (FRIDAY) / HELPERS: ONO, ONO
FUJI-NUMA...
YOU HAVEN'T HEARD ANY-THING?
NO...
THIS MORN-ING...
...I STOPPED BY HER HOUSE, BUT NO ONE CAME TO THE DOOR.
MAYBE SHE'S GOT A COLD?
I WONDER WHAT'S UP WITH HINA-ZUKI.
YEAH...
AND THE SCHOOL HASN'T GOTTEN WORD? THAT'S STRANGE...
ぱん。
PAN (CLAP)
WELL...
...THIS ISN'T UNUSUAL FOR KAYO.
SHE MAY SHOW UP HERE WHEN WE LEAST EXPECT IT.
FOR THE MOMENT, SHALL WE BEGIN CLASS?

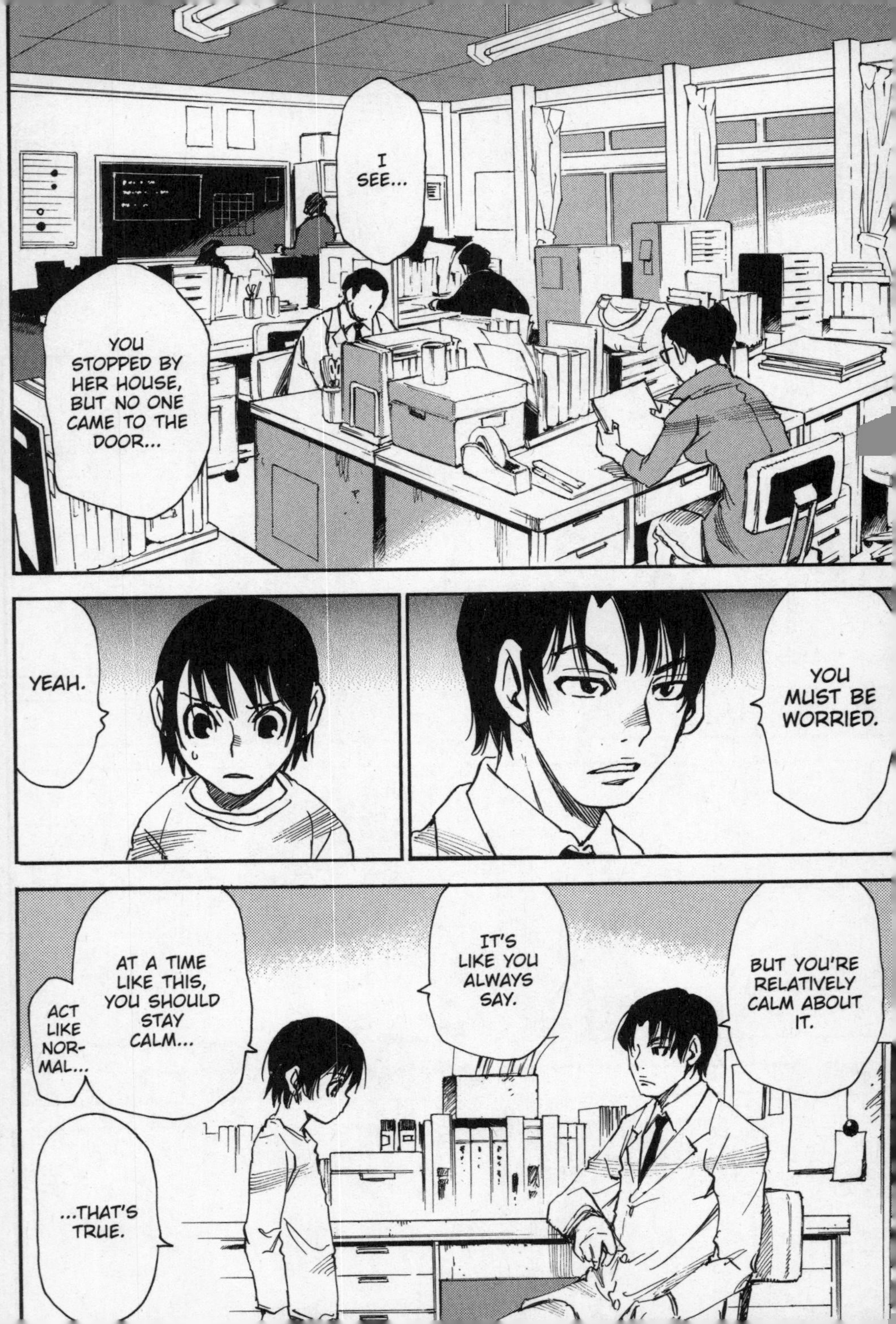
I SEE...
YOU STOPPED BY HER HOUSE, BUT NO ONE CAME TO THE DOOR...
YOU MUST BE WORRIED.
YEAH.
BUT YOU'RE RELATIVELY CALM ABOUT IT.
IT'S LIKE YOU ALWAYS SAY.
AT A TIME LIKE THIS, YOU SHOULD STAY CALM...
ACT LIKE NOR-MAL...
...THAT'S TRUE.

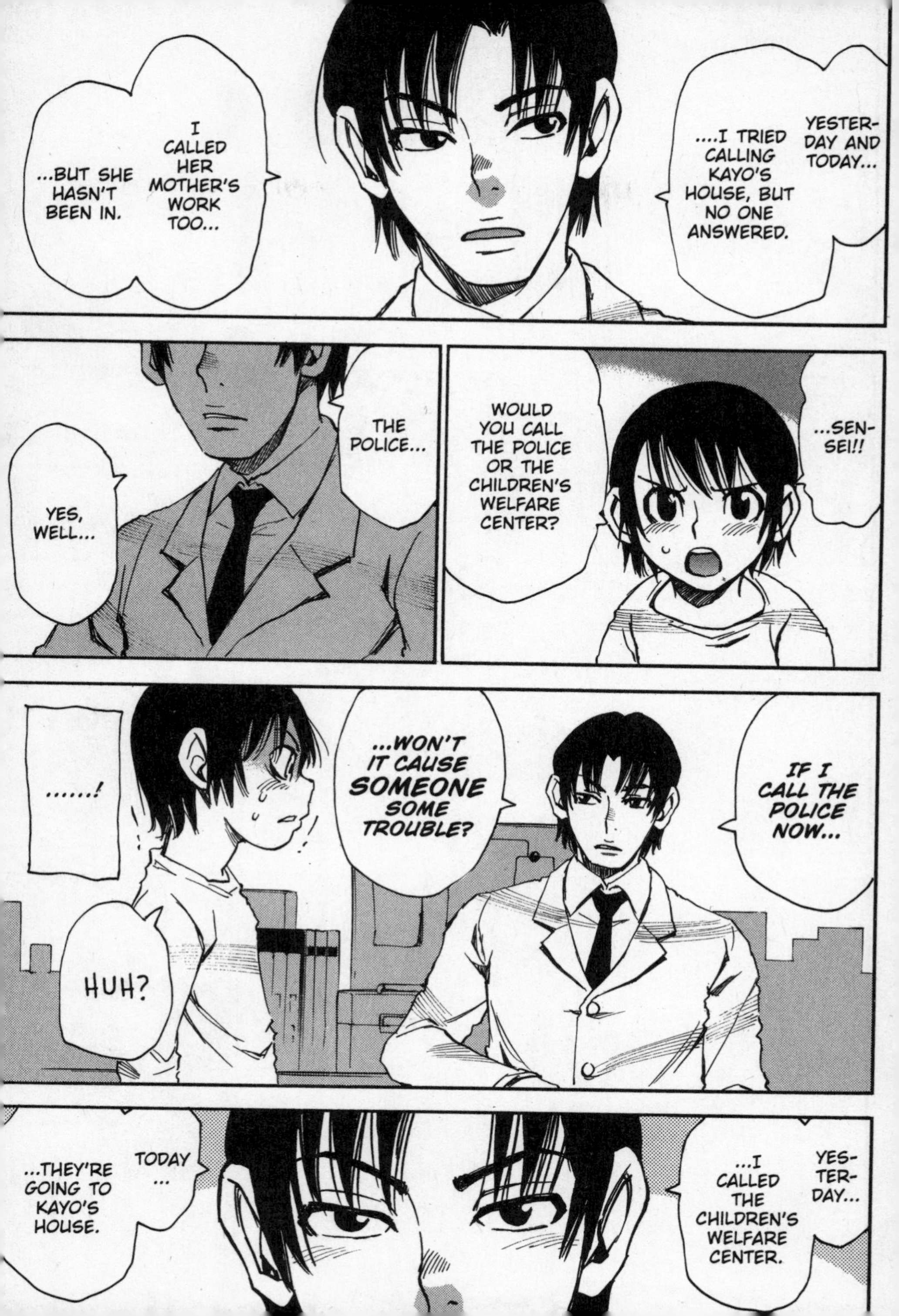
YESTER-DAY AND TODAY...
....I TRIED CALLING KAYO'S HOUSE, BUT NO ONE ANSWERED.
I CALLED HER MOTHER'S WORK TOO...
...BUT SHE HASN'T BEEN IN.
...SEN-SEI!!
WOULD YOU CALL THE POLICE OR THE CHILDREN'S WELFARE CENTER?
THE POLICE...
YES, WELL...
IF I CALL THE POLICE NOW...
...WON'T IT CAUSE SOMEONE SOME TROUBLE?
......!
HUH?
YES-TER-DAY...
...I CALLED THE CHILDREN'S WELFARE CENTER.
TODAY ...
...THEY'RE GOING TO KAYO'S HOUSE.

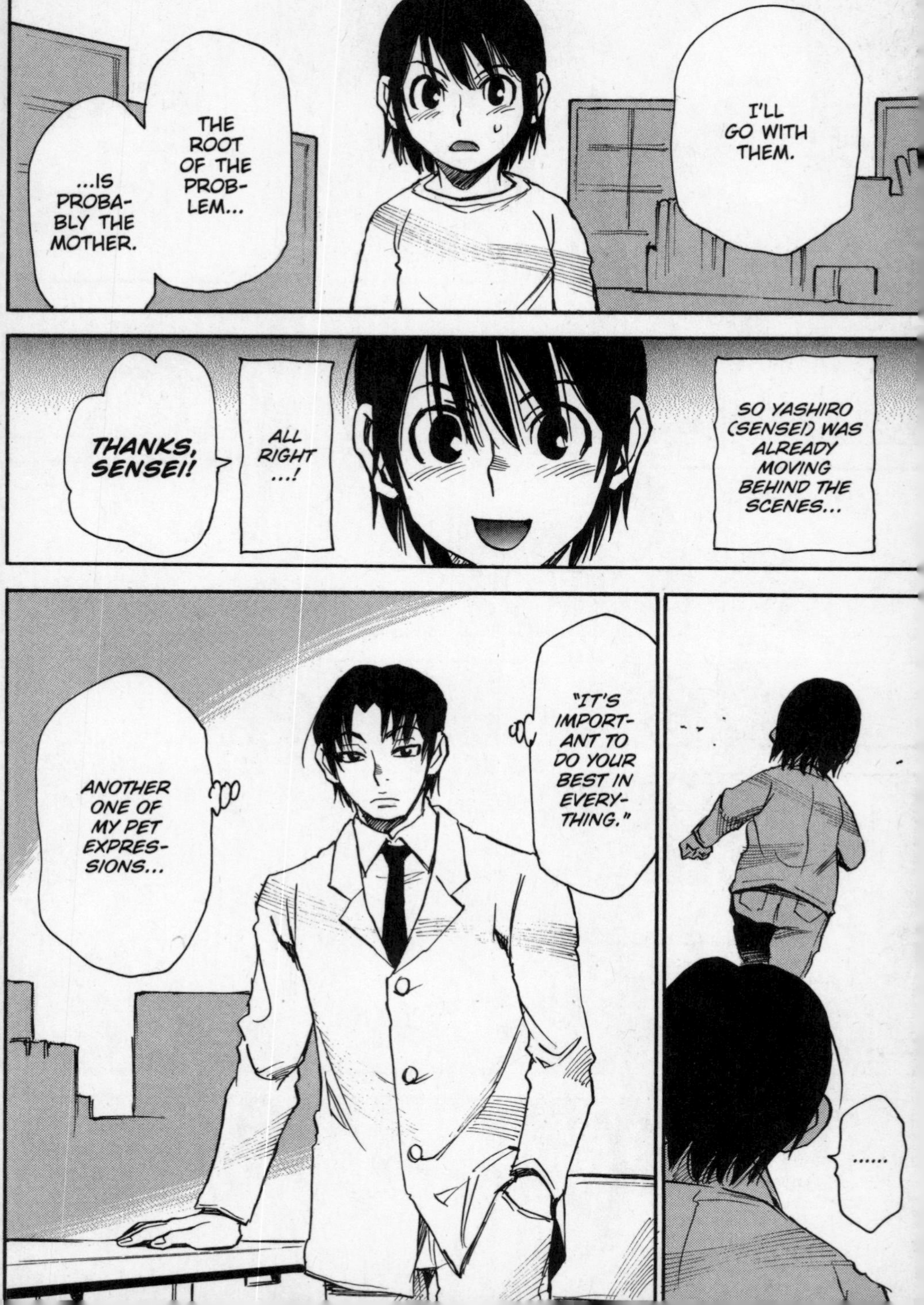
I'LL GO WITH THEM.
THE ROOT OF THE PROBLEM...
...IS PROBABLY THE MOTHER.
SO YASHIRO (SENSEI) WAS ALREADY MOVING BEHIND THE SCENES...
ALL RIGHT...!
THANKS, SENSEI!
......
"IT'S IMPORTANT TO DO YOUR BEST IN EVERYTHING."
ANOTHER ONE OF MY PET EXPRESSIONS...

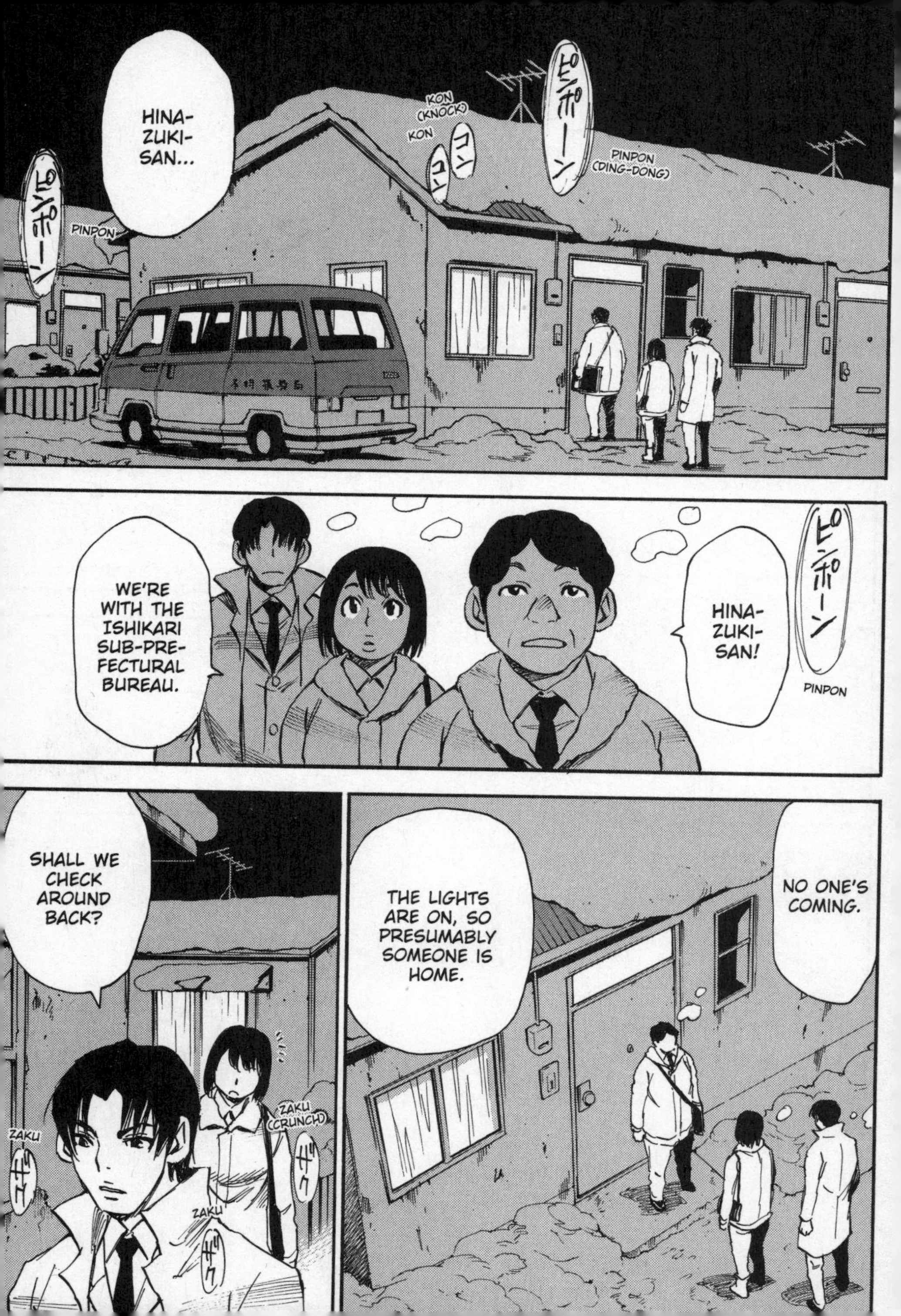
ピンポーン
PINPON (DING-DONG)
コンコン
KON (KNOCK)
KON
HINA-ZUKI-SAN...
ピンポーン
PINPON
ピンポーン
PINPON
HINA-ZUKI-SAN!
WE'RE WITH THE ISHIKARI SUB-PREFECTURAL BUREAU.
NO ONE'S COMING.
THE LIGHTS ARE ON, SO PRESUMABLY SOMEONE IS HOME.
SHALL WE CHECK AROUND BACK?
ザク
ZAKU (CRUNCH)
ザク
ZAKU
ザク
ZAKU

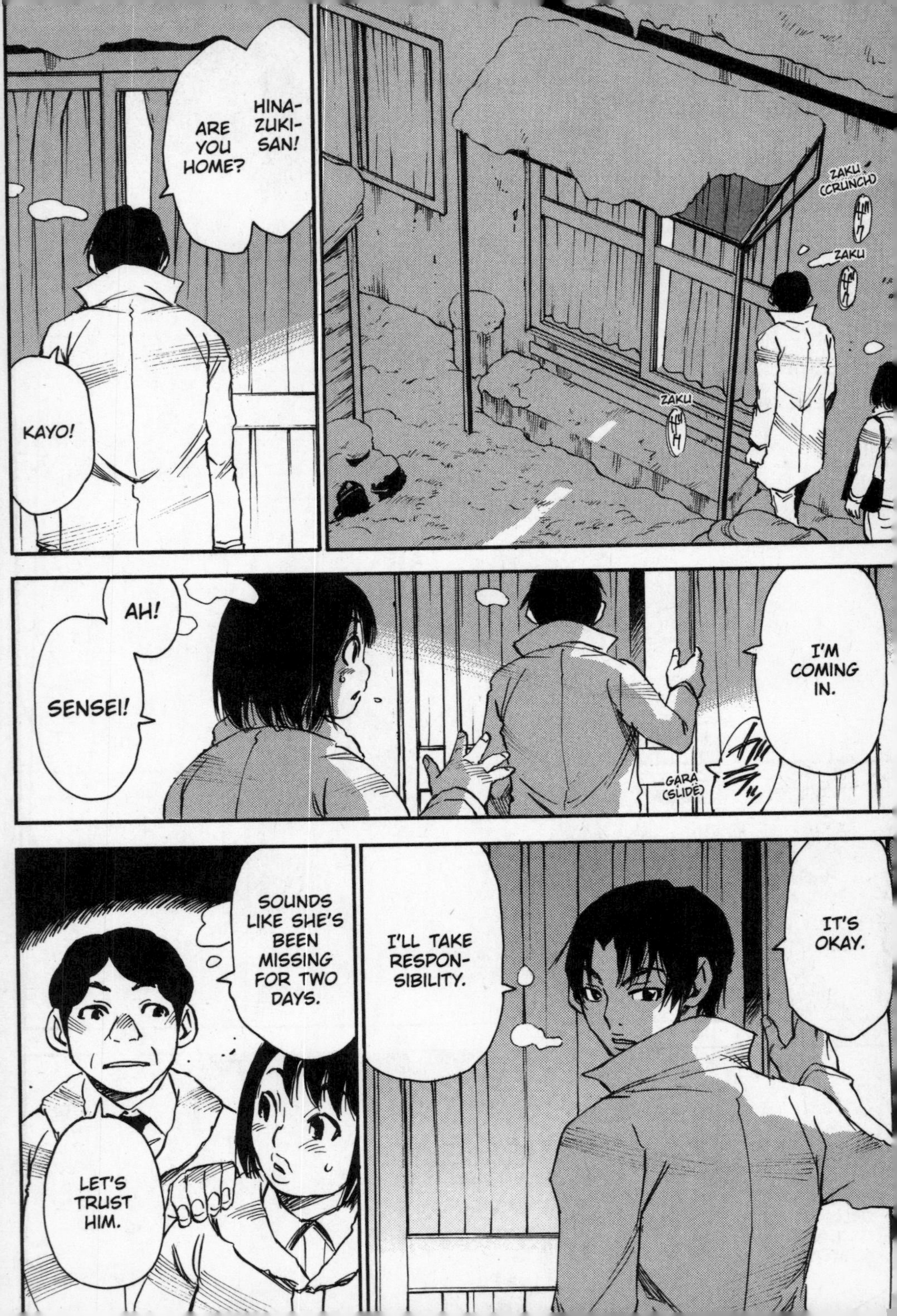
ZAKU (CRUNCH)
ZAKU
ZAKU
HINA-ZUKI-SAN!
ARE YOU HOME?
KAYO!
I'M COMING IN.
GARA (SLIDE)
AH!
SENSEI!
IT'S OKAY.
I'LL TAKE RESPON-SIBILITY.
SOUNDS LIKE SHE'S BEEN MISSING FOR TWO DAYS.
LET'S TRUST HIM.

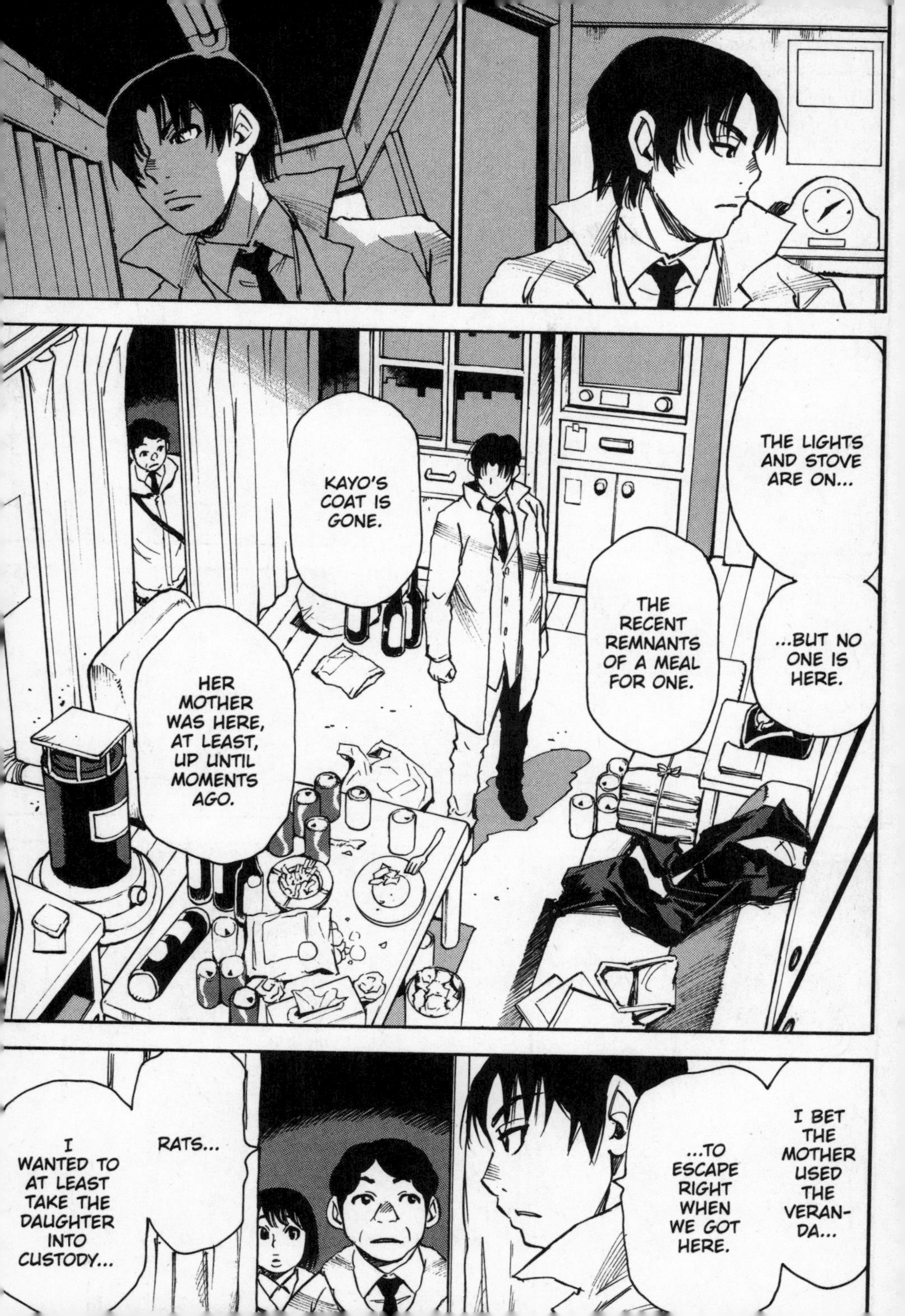
THE LIGHTS AND STOVE ARE ON...
...BUT NO ONE IS HERE.
THE RECENT REMNANTS OF A MEAL FOR ONE.
KAYO'S COAT IS GONE.
HER MOTHER WAS HERE, AT LEAST, UP UNTIL MOMENTS AGO.
I BET THE MOTHER USED THE VERAN-DA...
...TO ESCAPE RIGHT WHEN WE GOT HERE.
RATS...
I WANTED TO AT LEAST TAKE THE DAUGHTER INTO CUSTODY...

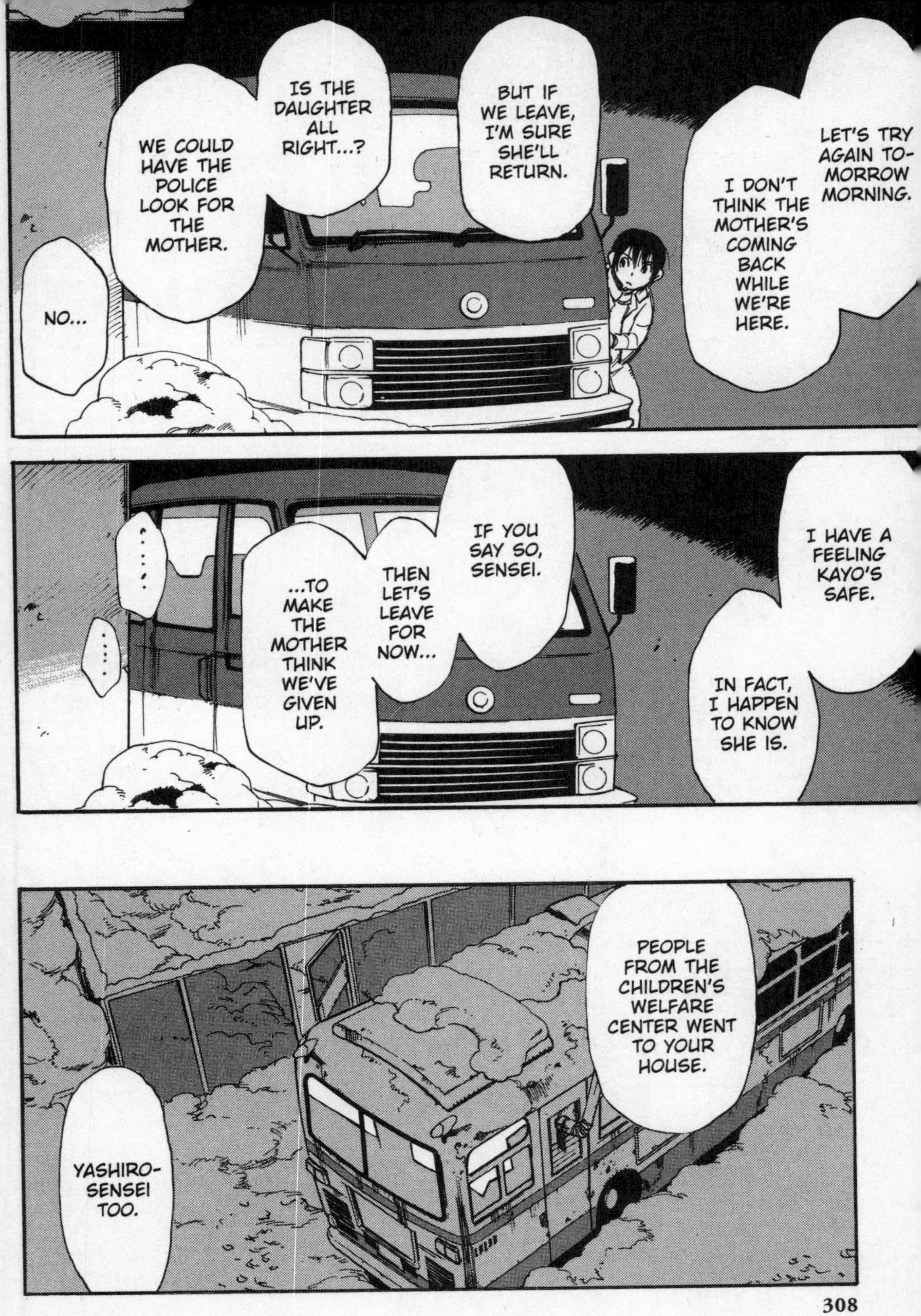
LET'S TRY AGAIN TO-MORROW MORNING.
I DON'T THINK THE MOTHER'S COMING BACK WHILE WE'RE HERE.
BUT IF WE LEAVE, I'M SURE SHE'LL RETURN.
IS THE DAUGHTER ALL RIGHT...?
WE COULD HAVE THE POLICE LOOK FOR THE MOTHER.
NO...
I HAVE A FEELING KAYO'S SAFE.
IN FACT, I HAPPEN TO KNOW SHE IS.
IF YOU SAY SO, SENSEI.
THEN LET'S LEAVE FOR NOW...
...TO MAKE THE MOTHER THINK WE'VE GIVEN UP.
......
......
PEOPLE FROM THE CHILDREN'S WELFARE CENTER WENT TO YOUR HOUSE.
YASHIRO-SENSEI TOO.

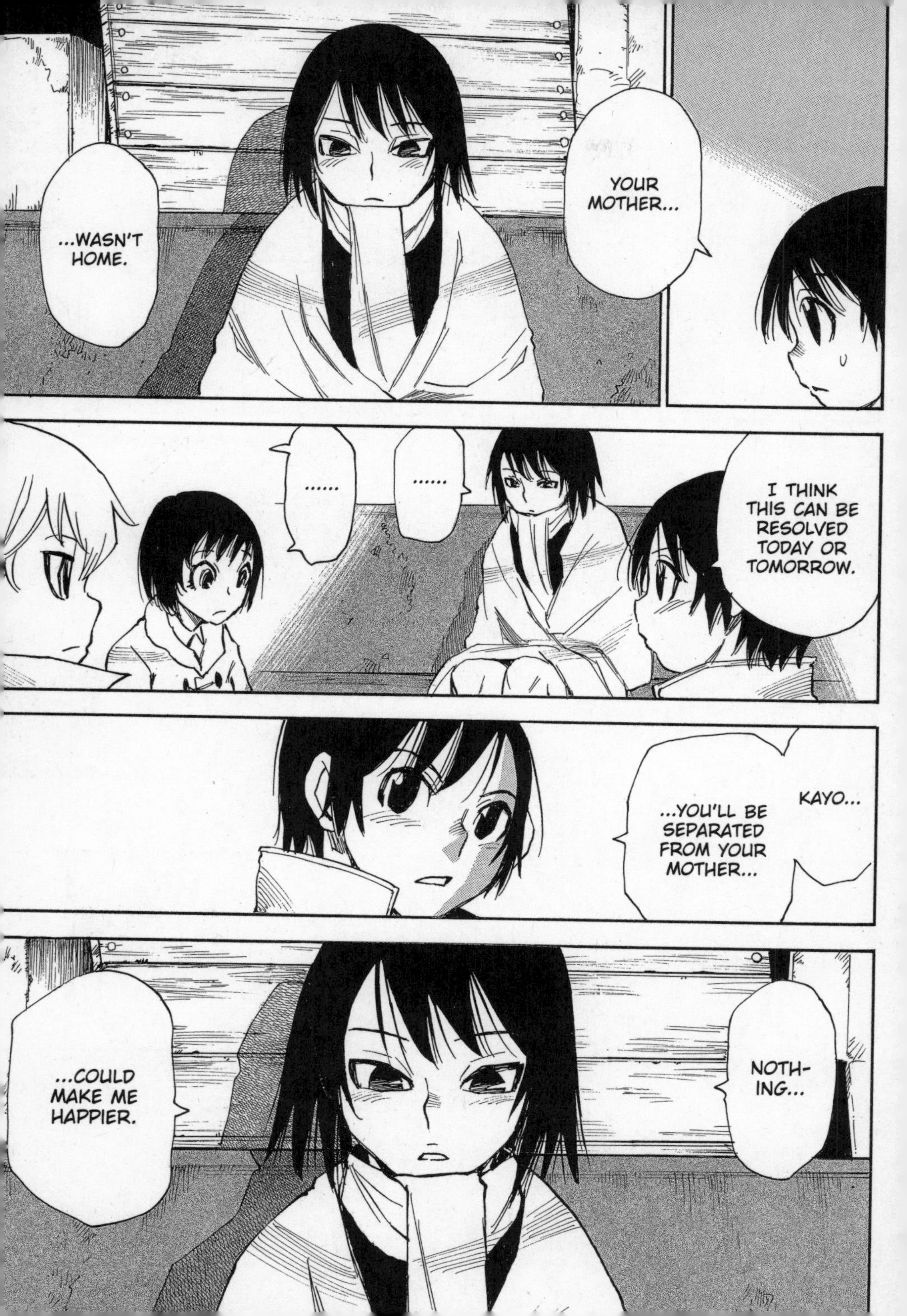
YOUR MOTHER...
...WASN'T HOME.
I THINK THIS CAN BE RESOLVED TODAY OR TOMORROW.
......
......
KAYO...
...YOU'LL BE SEPARATED FROM YOUR MOTHER...
NOTH-ING...
...COULD MAKE ME HAPPIER.

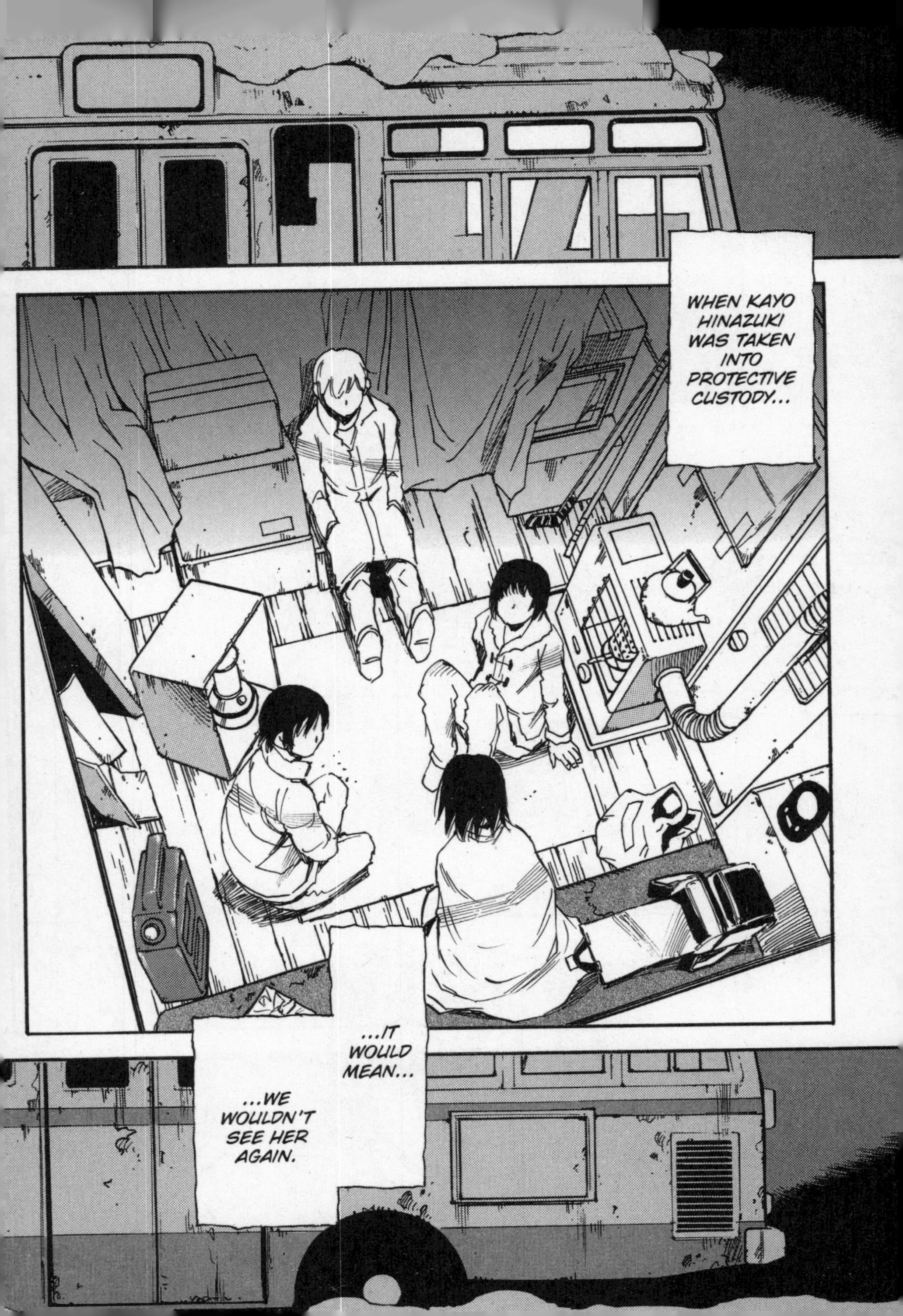
WHEN KAYO HINAZUKI WAS TAKEN INTO PROTECTIVE CUSTODY...
...IT WOULD MEAN...
...WE WOULDN'T SEE HER AGAIN.

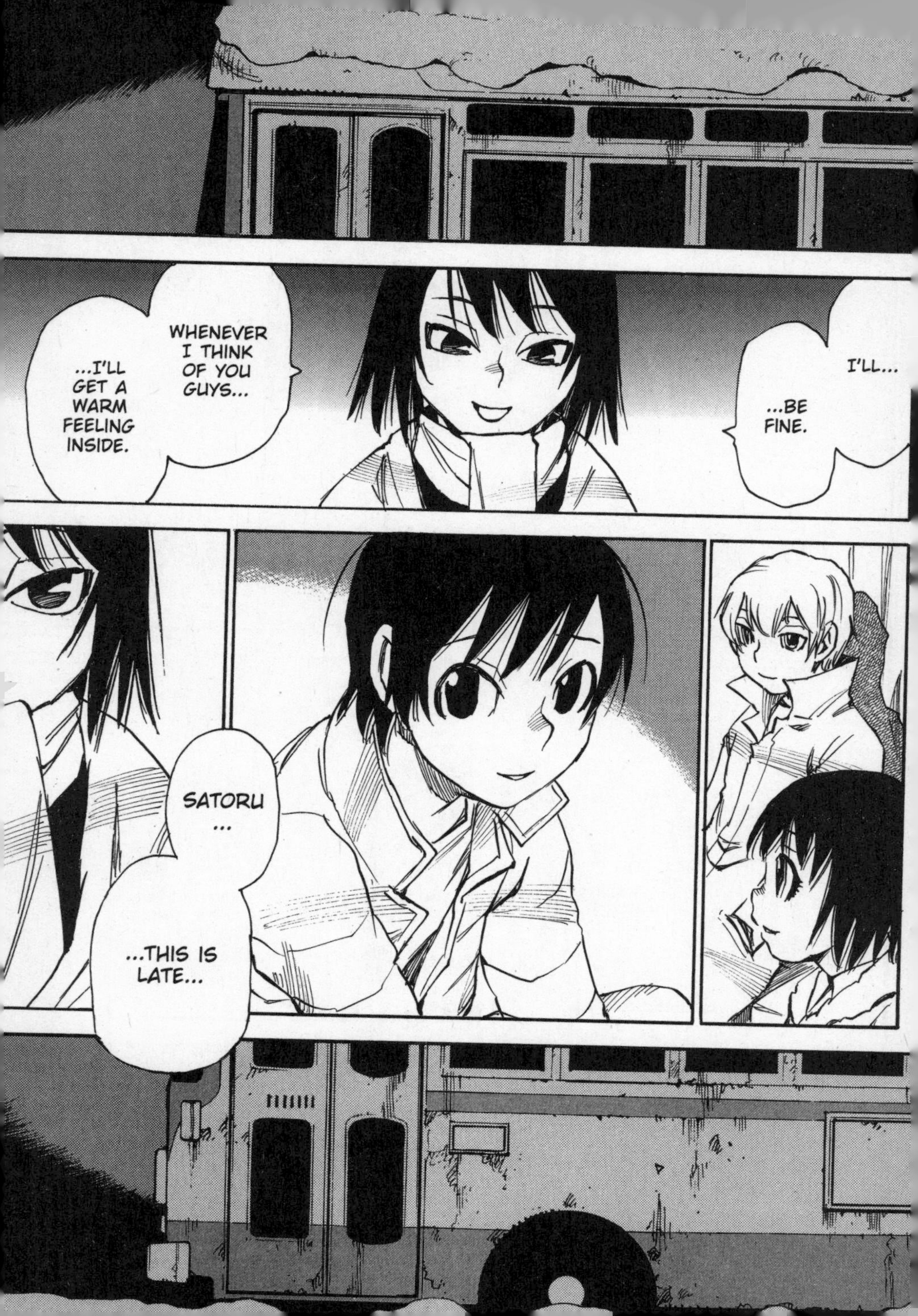
I'LL...
...BE FINE.
WHENEVER I THINK OF YOU GUYS...
...I'LL GET A WARM FEELING INSIDE.
SATORU ...
...THIS IS LATE...

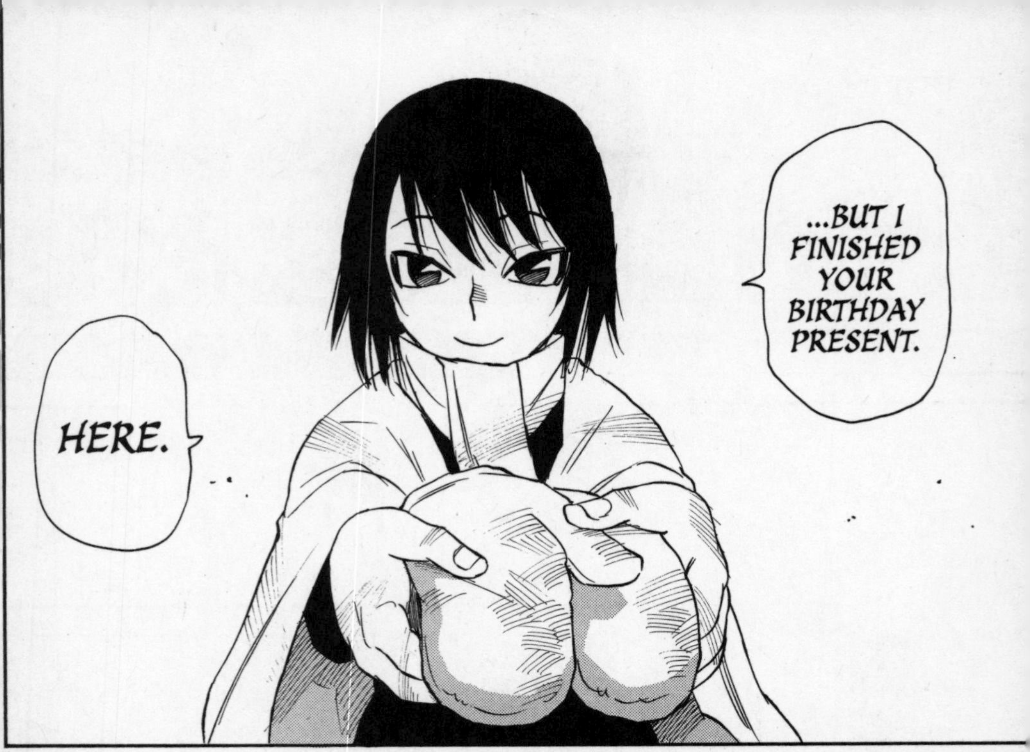
...BUT I FINISHED YOUR BIRTHDAY PRESENT.
HERE.
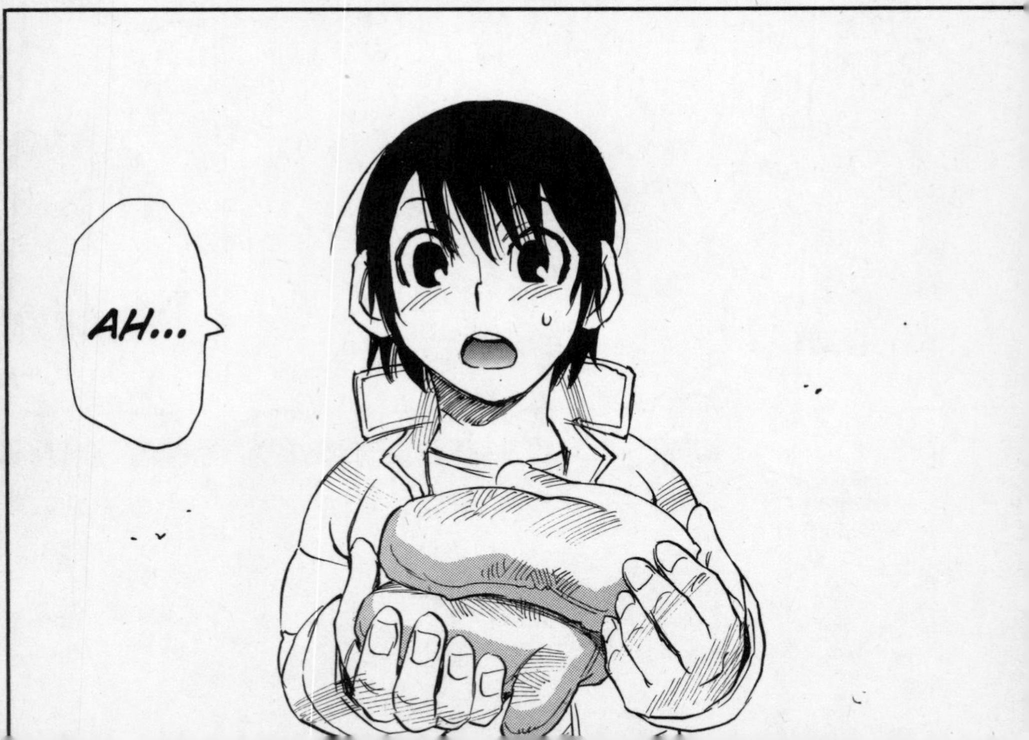
AH...

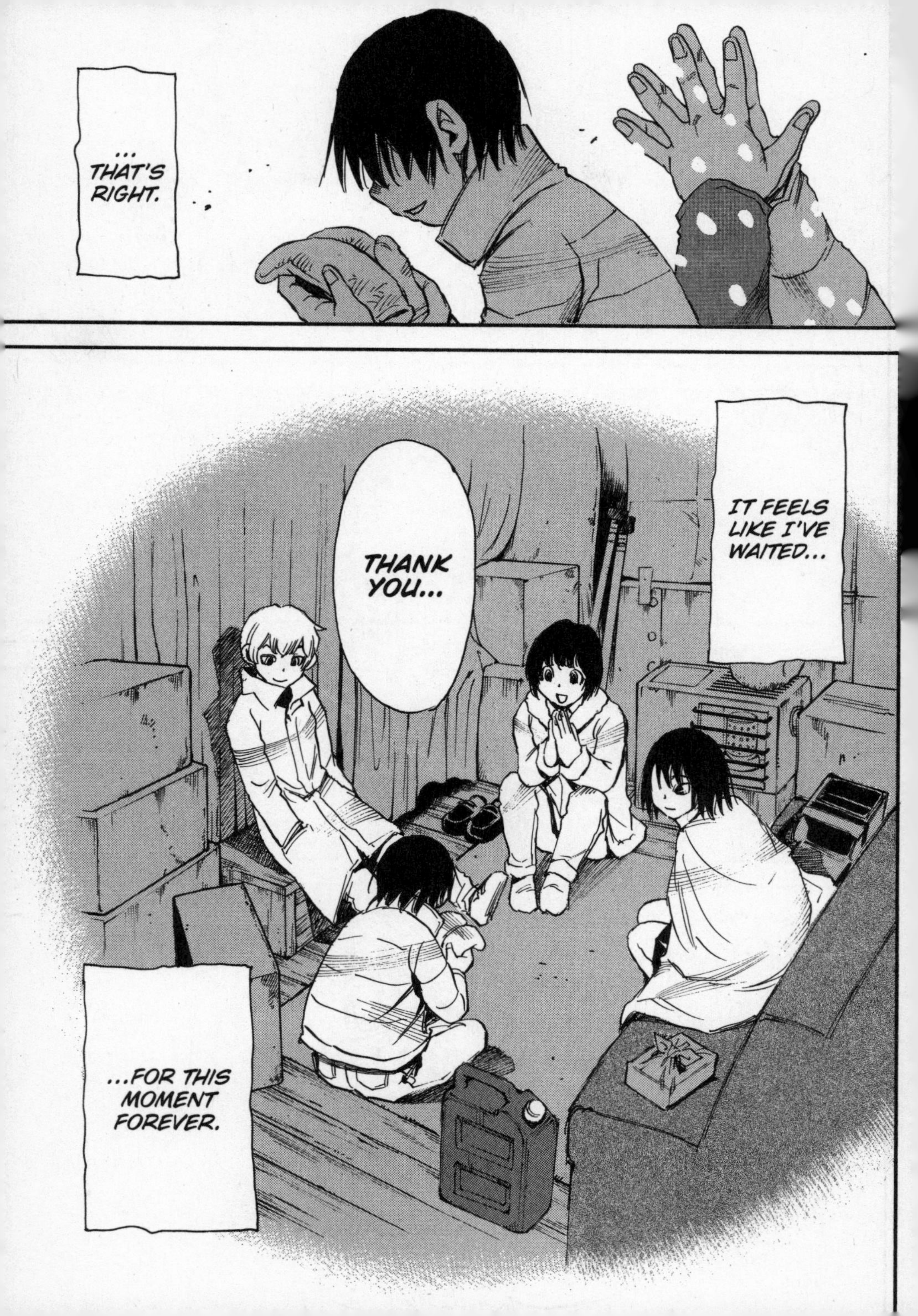
...THAT'S RIGHT.
IT FEELS LIKE I'VE WAITED...
THANK YOU...
...FOR THIS MOMENT FOREVER.

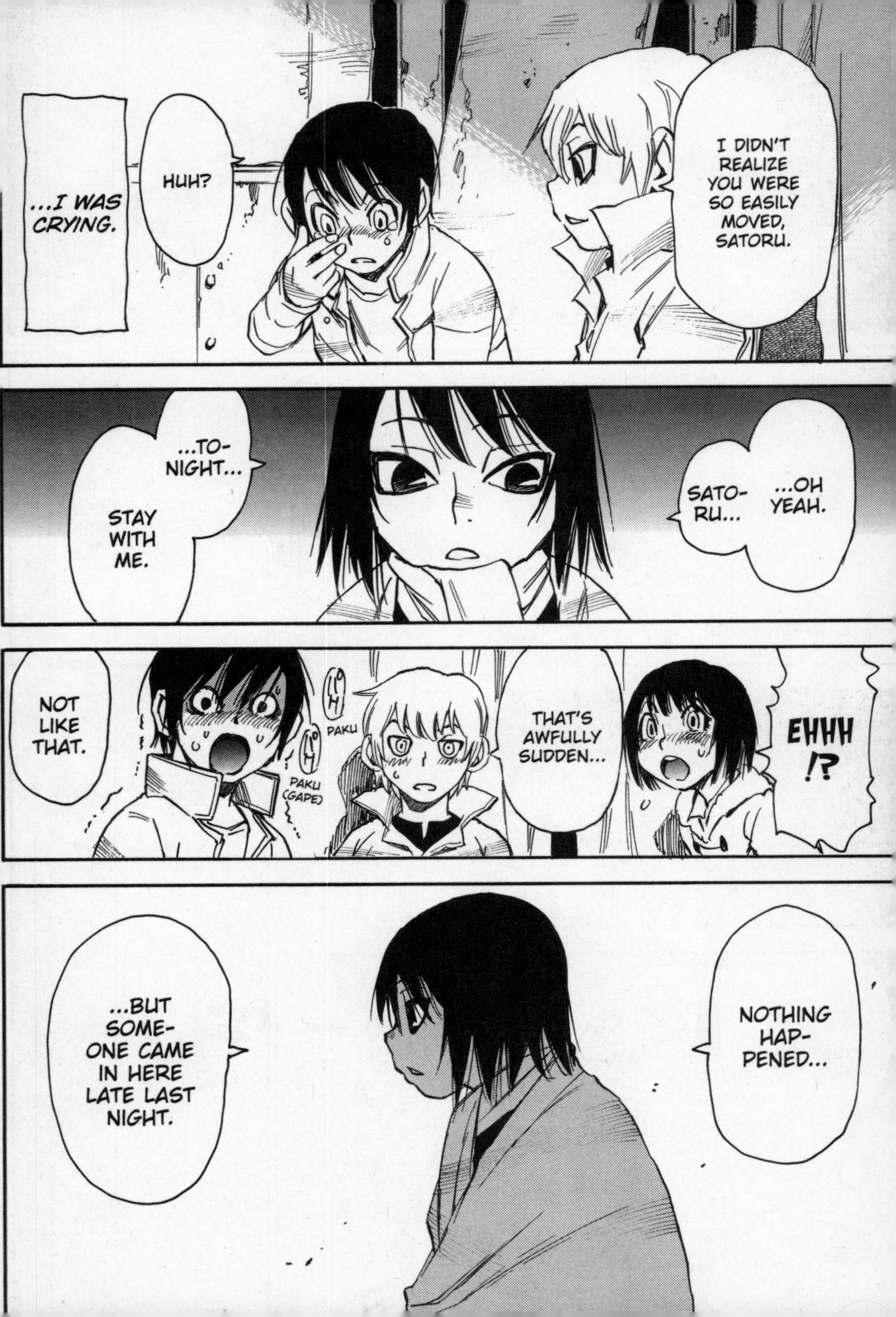
I DIDN'T REALIZE YOU WERE SO EASILY MOVED, SATORU.
HUH?
...I WAS CRYING.
...OH YEAH.
SATO-RU...
...TO-NIGHT...
STAY WITH ME.
EHHH!?
THAT'S AWFULLY SUDDEN...
PAKU
PAKU (GAPE)
NOT LIKE THAT.
NOTHING HAP-PENED...
...BUT SOME-ONE CAME IN HERE LATE LAST NIGHT.

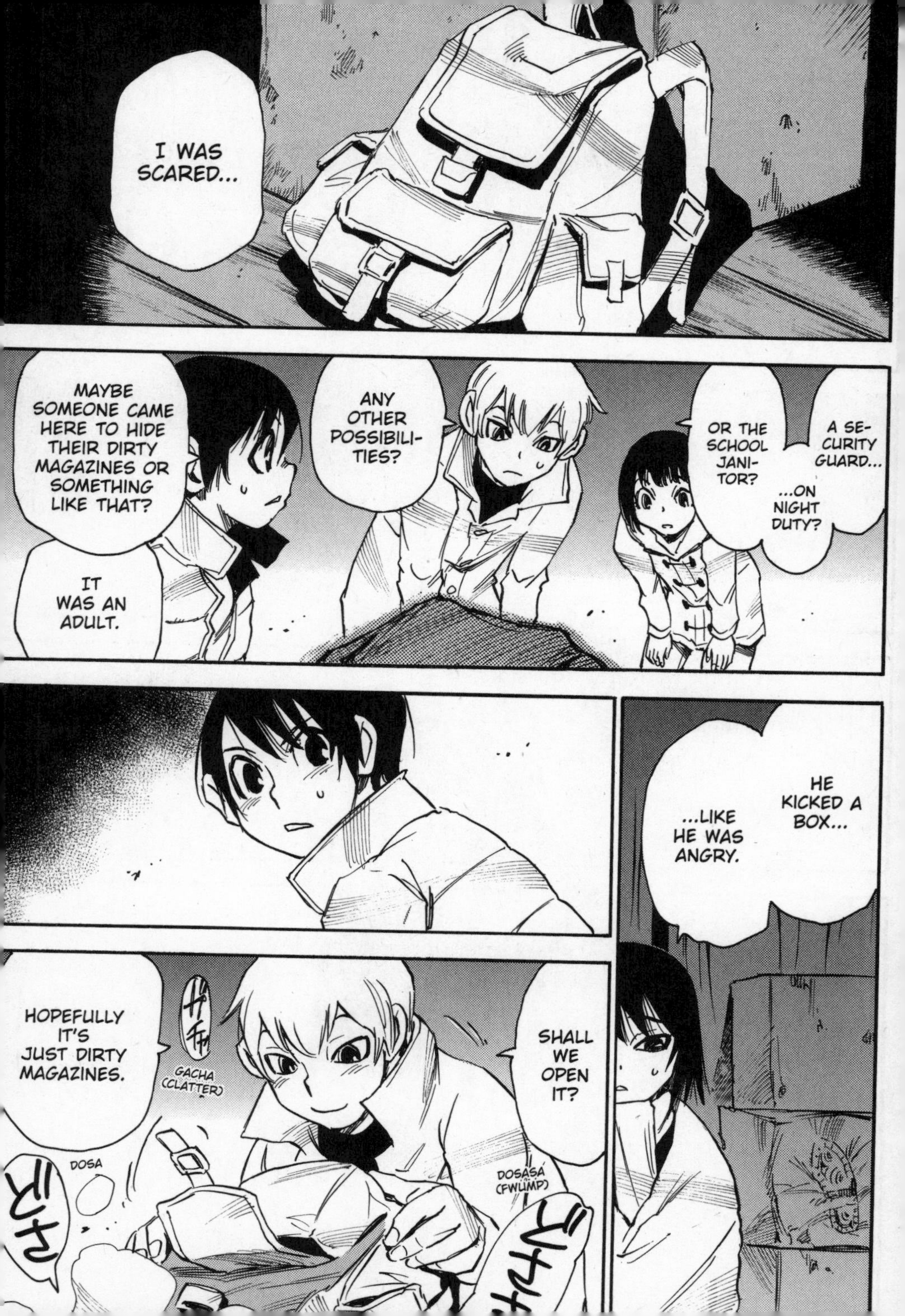
I WAS SCARED...
A SECURITY GUARD...
...ON NIGHT DUTY?
OR THE SCHOOL JANITOR?
ANY OTHER POSSIBILITIES?
MAYBE SOMEONE CAME HERE TO HIDE THEIR DIRTY MAGAZINES OR SOMETHING LIKE THAT?
IT WAS AN ADULT.
HE KICKED A BOX...
...LIKE HE WAS ANGRY.
SHALL WE OPEN IT?
HOPEFULLY IT'S JUST DIRTY MAGAZINES.
GACHA (CLATTER)
DOSASA (FWUMP)
DOSA

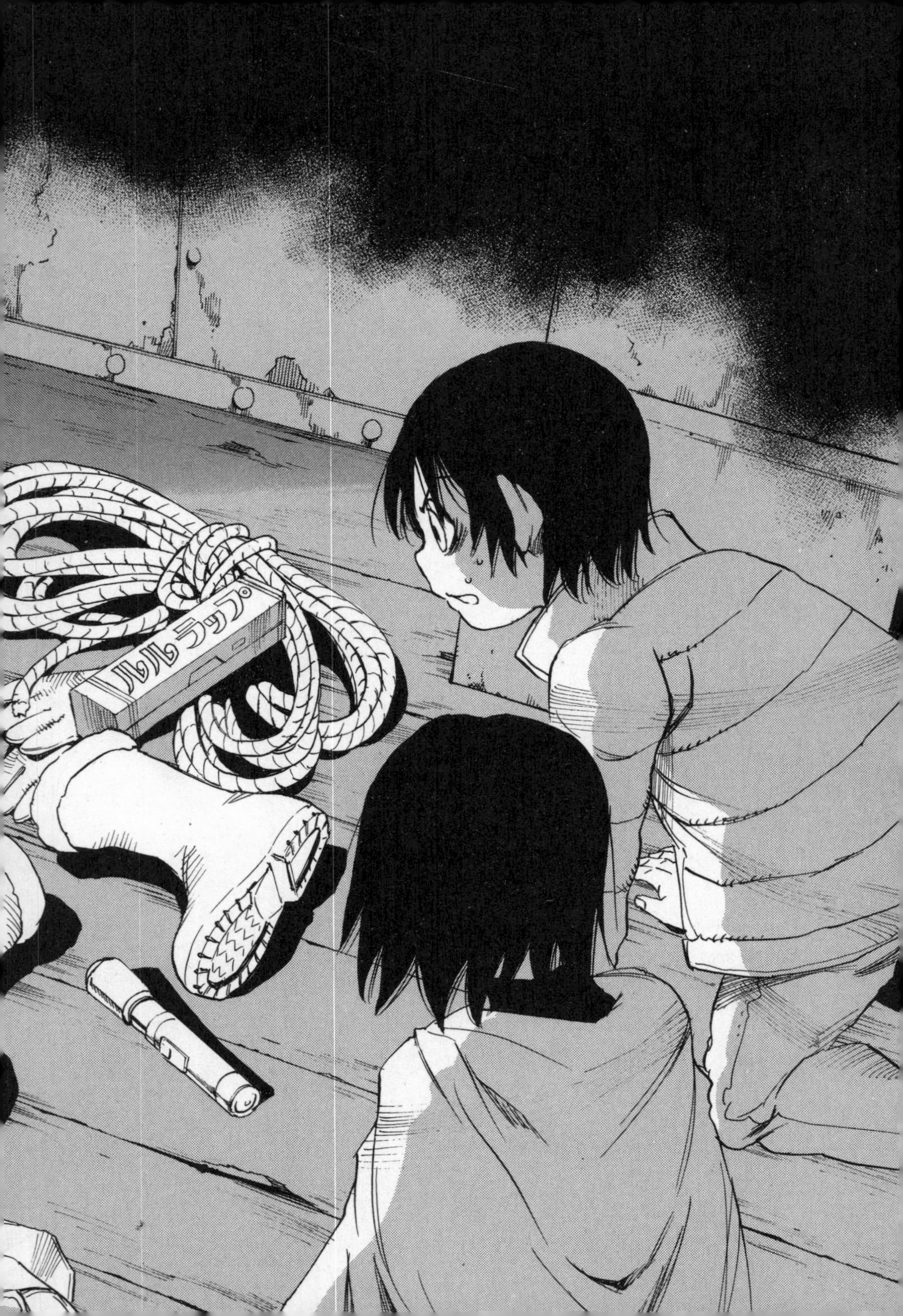
ハルラップ

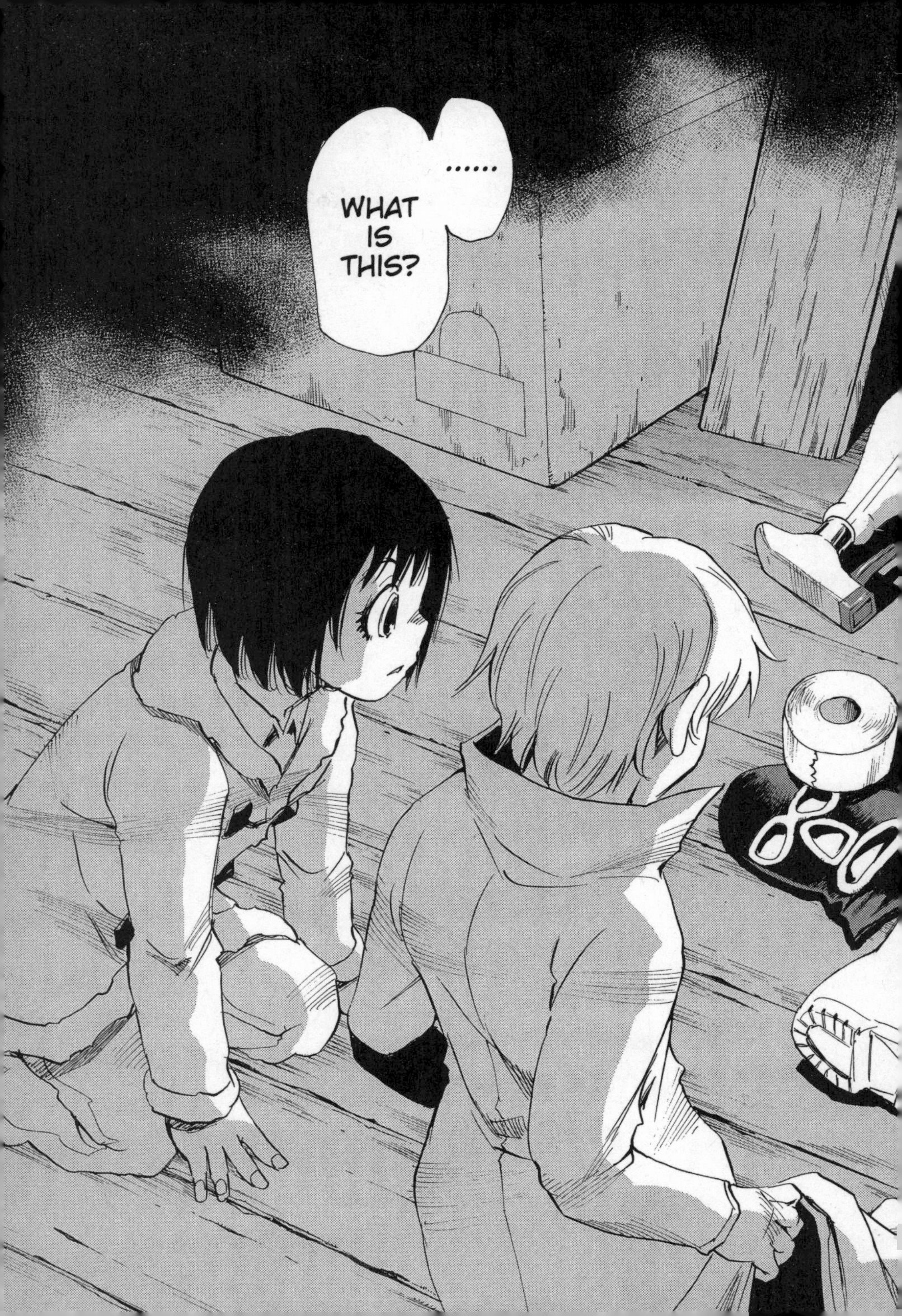
......
WHAT IS THIS?

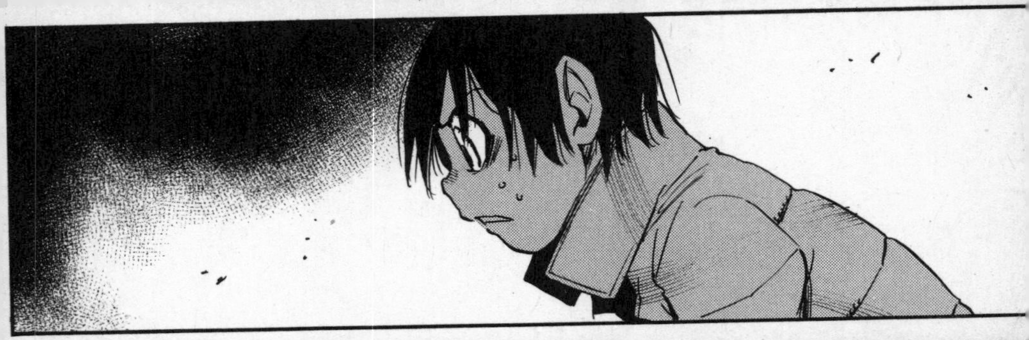

AND IT FINALLY DAWNED ON ME THAT THE SERIAL KILLER'S SECOND VICTIM, AYA NAKANISHI, IS A STUDENT HERE AT IZUMI ELEMENTARY.

BOX: RURU WRAP

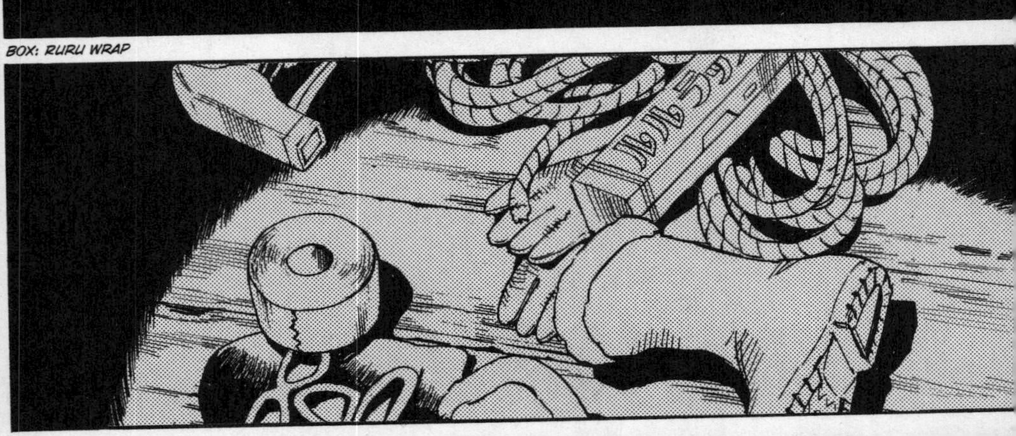

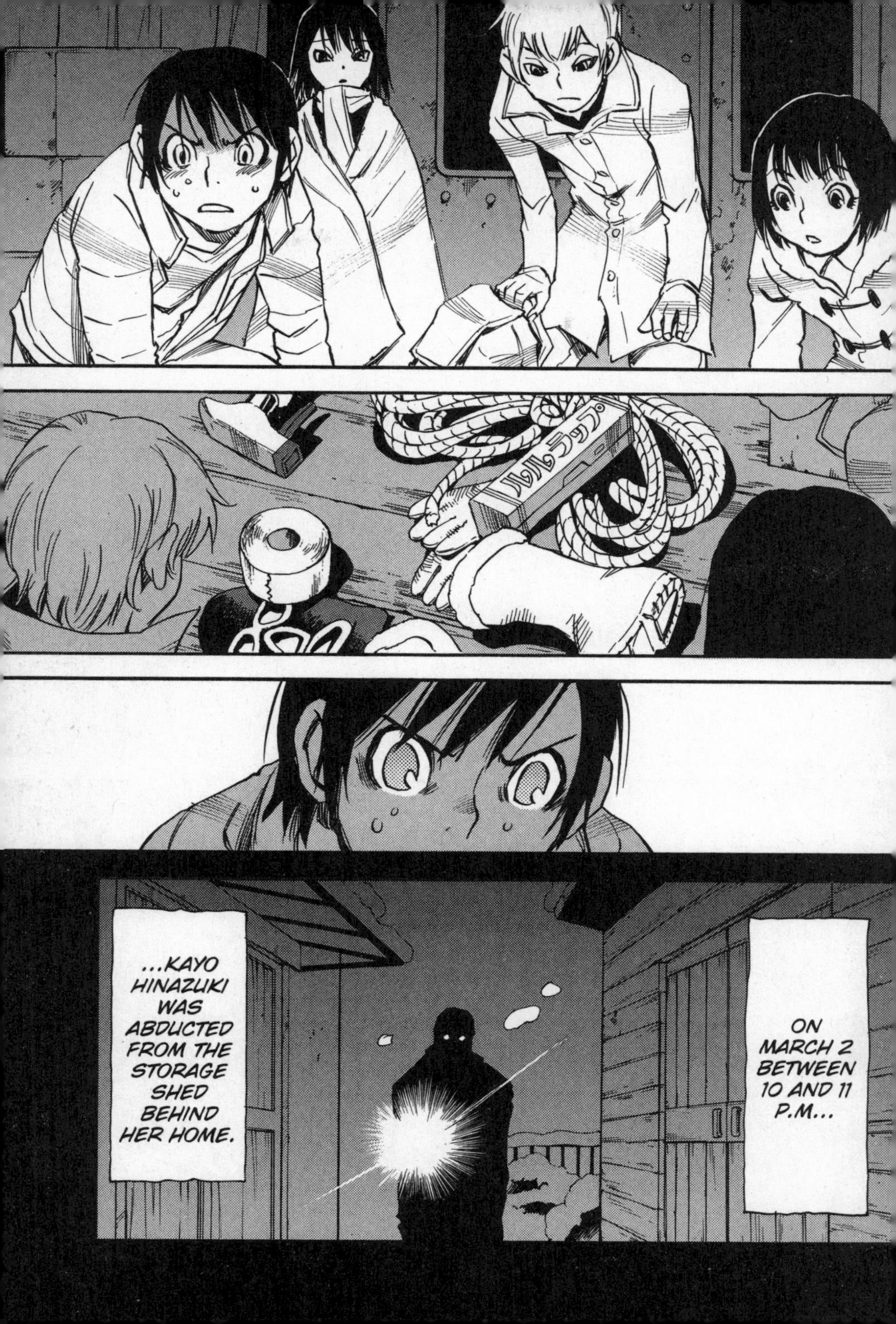
ルルラップ
ON MARCH 2 BETWEEN 10 AND 11 P.M...
...KAYO HINAZUKI WAS ABDUCTED FROM THE STORAGE SHED BEHIND HER HOME.

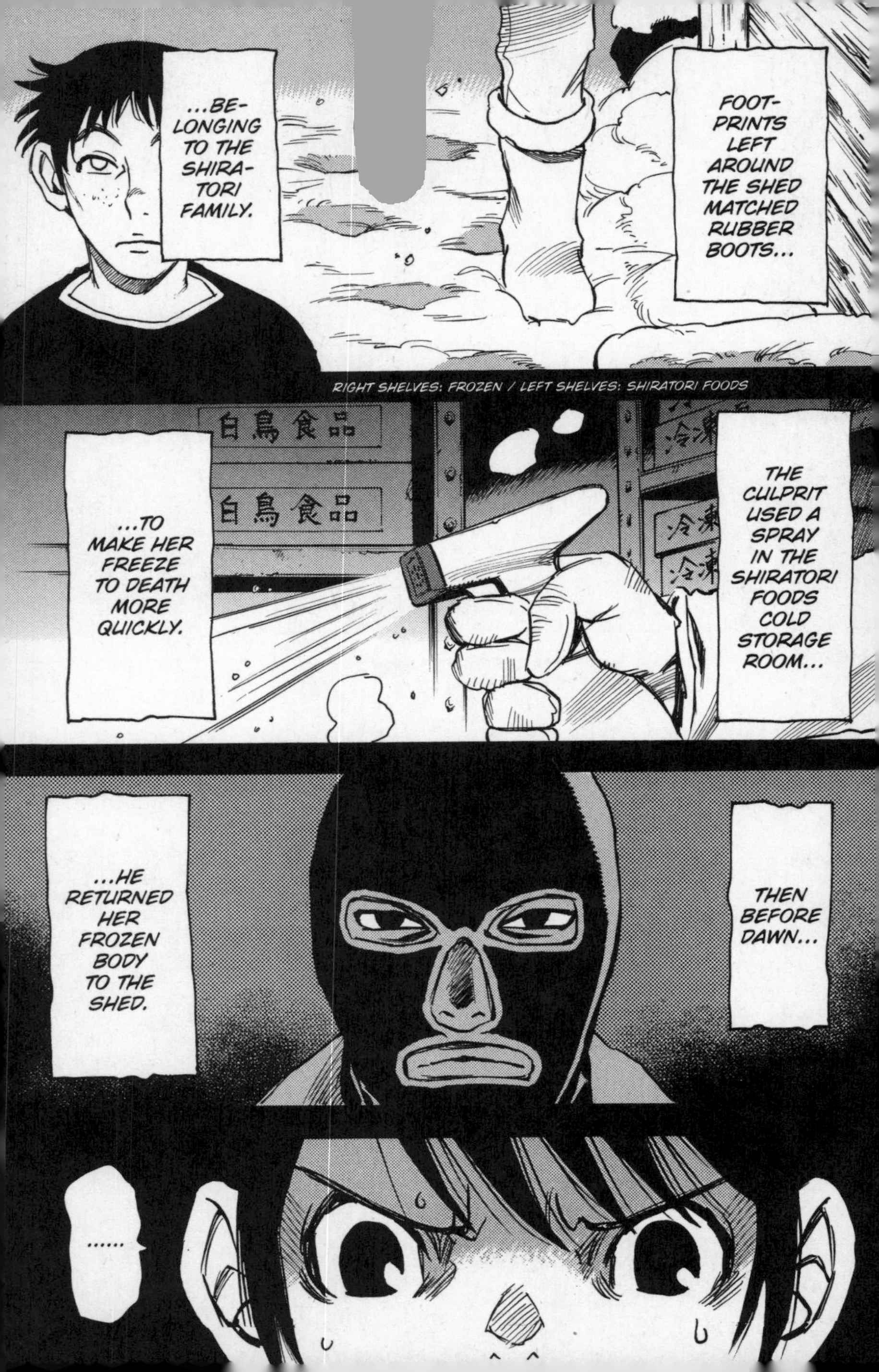
FOOTPRINTS LEFT AROUND THE SHED MATCHED RUBBER BOOTS...
...BELONGING TO THE SHIRATORI FAMILY.
RIGHT SHELVES: FROZEN / LEFT SHELVES: SHIRATORI FOODS
冷凍
白鳥食品
白鳥食品
THE CULPRIT USED A SPRAY IN THE SHIRATORI FOODS COLD STORAGE ROOM...
...TO MAKE HER FREEZE TO DEATH MORE QUICKLY.
THEN BEFORE DAWN...
...HE RETURNED HER FROZEN BODY TO THE SHED.
......

#23: Going Outside the Loop, March 1988

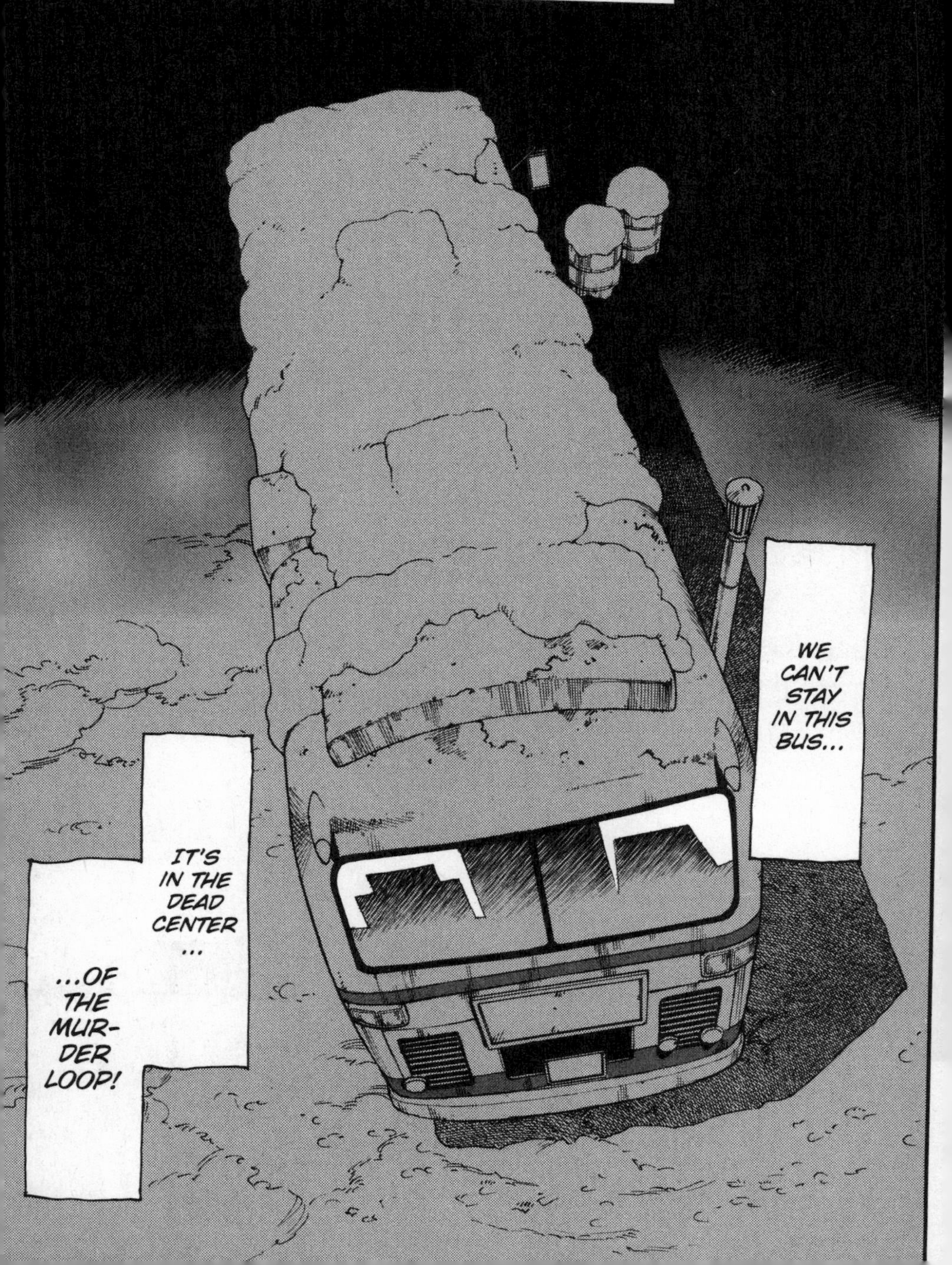
WE CAN'T STAY IN THIS BUS...
IT'S IN THE DEAD CENTER...
...OF THE MUR-DER LOOP!

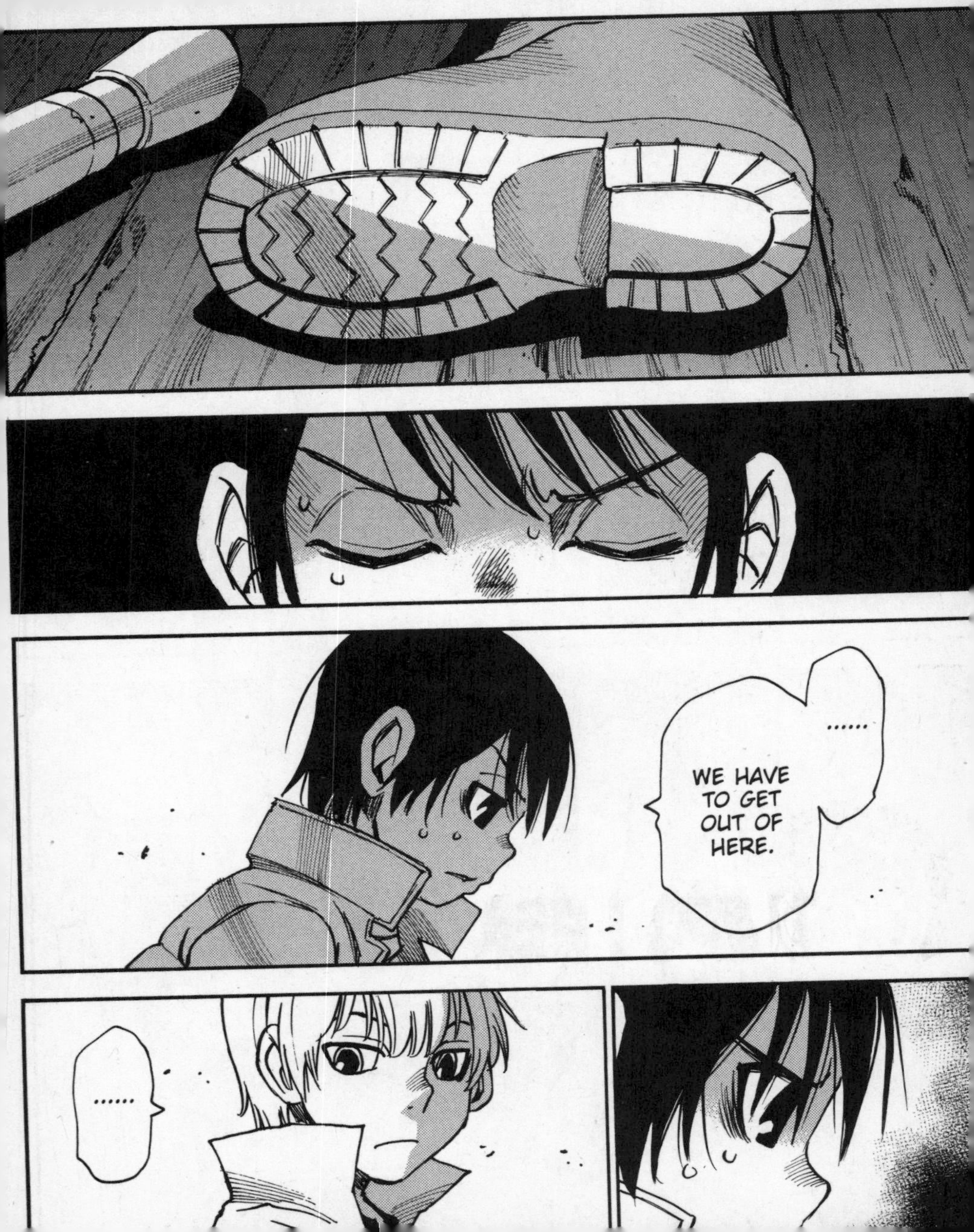
......
WE HAVE TO GET OUT OF HERE.
......

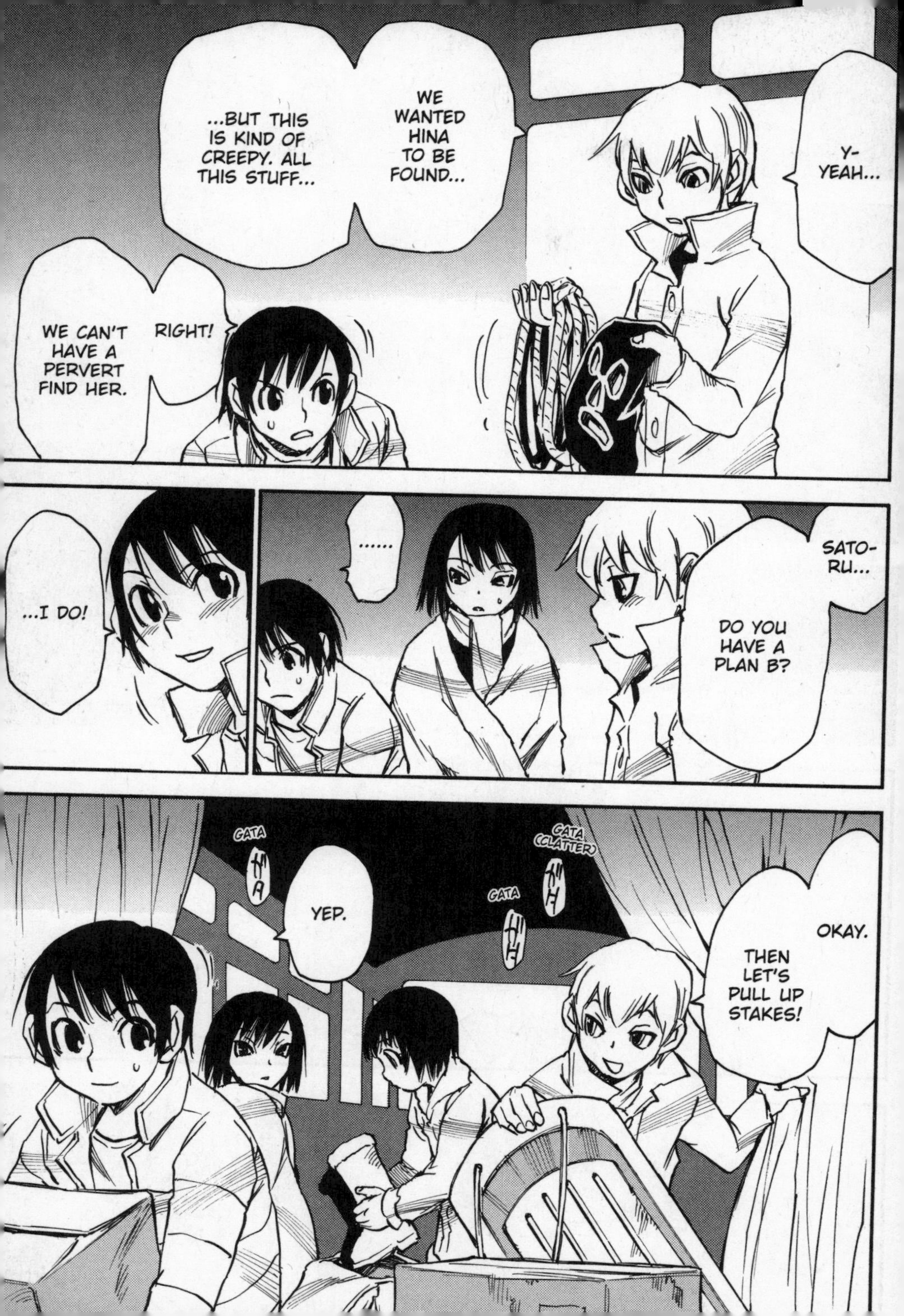
Y-YEAH...
WE WANTED HINA TO BE FOUND...
...BUT THIS IS KIND OF CREEPY. ALL THIS STUFF...
RIGHT!
WE CAN'T HAVE A PERVERT FIND HER.
SATO-RU...
DO YOU HAVE A PLAN B?
......
...I DO!
OKAY.
THEN LET'S PULL UP STAKES!
GATA (CLATTER)
GATA
YEP.
GATA

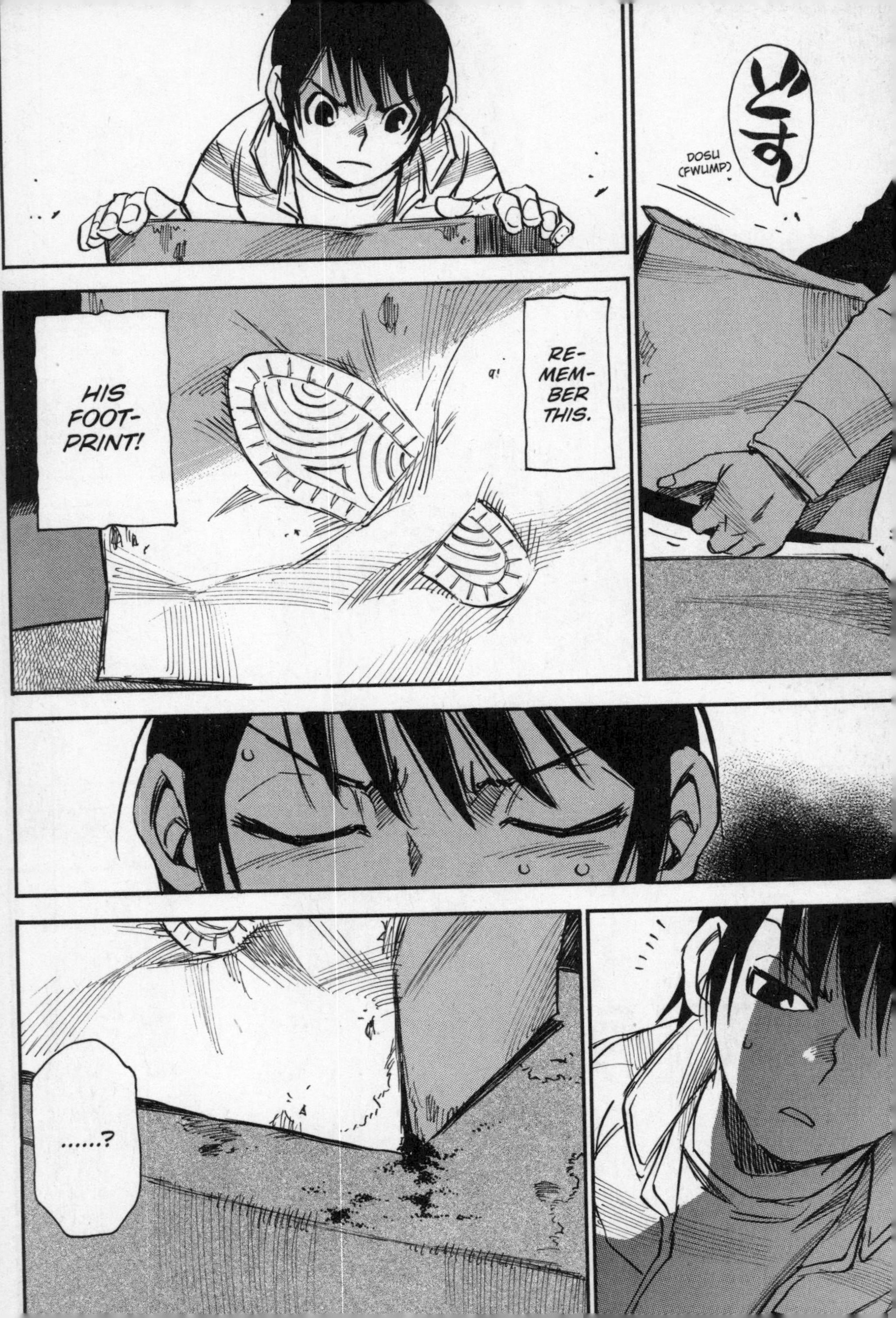
どす
DOSU (FWUMP)
RE-MEM-BER THIS.
HIS FOOT-PRINT!
......?

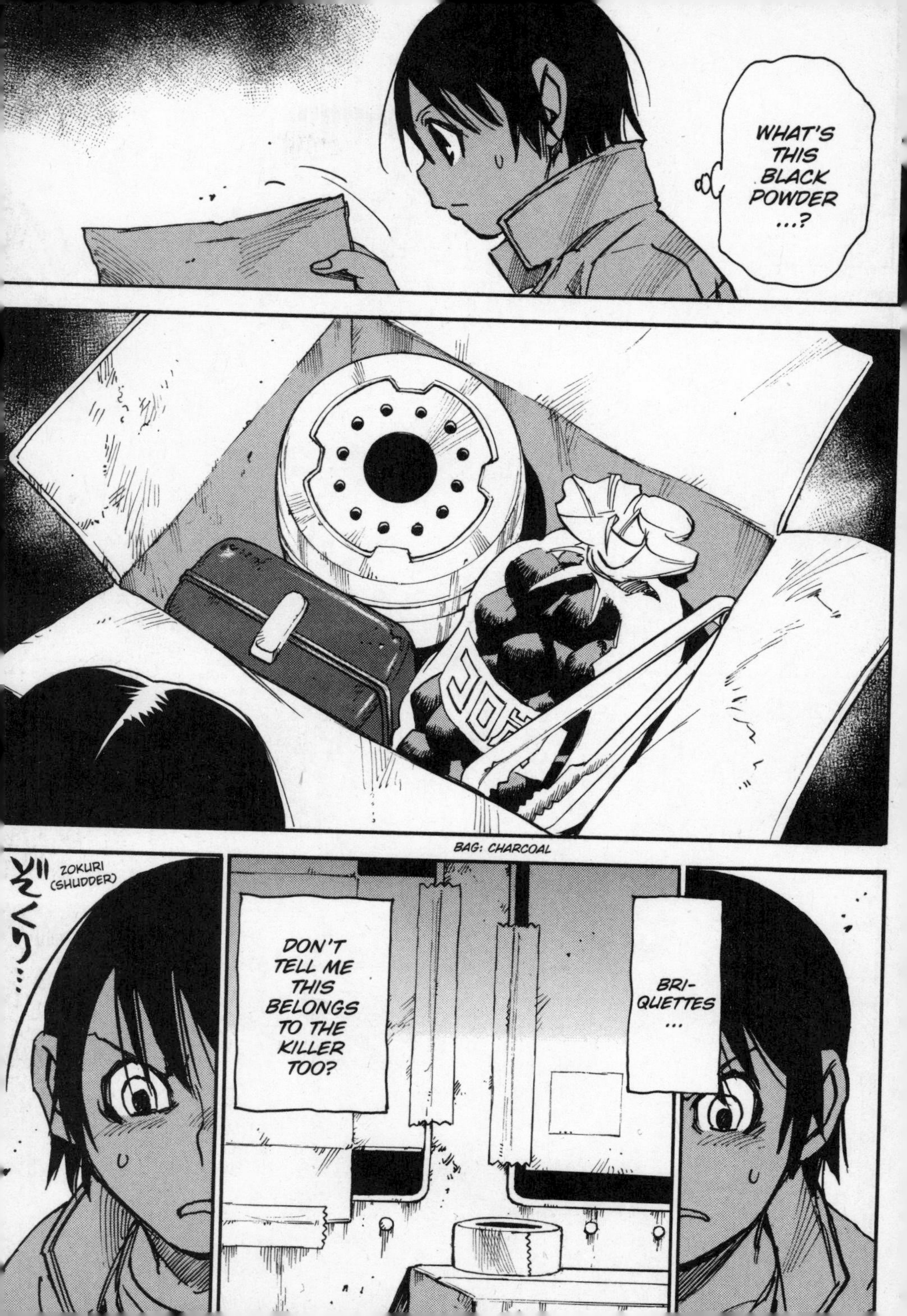
WHAT'S THIS BLACK POWDER ...?
BAG: CHARCOAL
BRI-QUETTES ...
DON'T TELL ME THIS BELONGS TO THE KILLER TOO?
ぞくっ…
ZOKURI (SHUDDER)

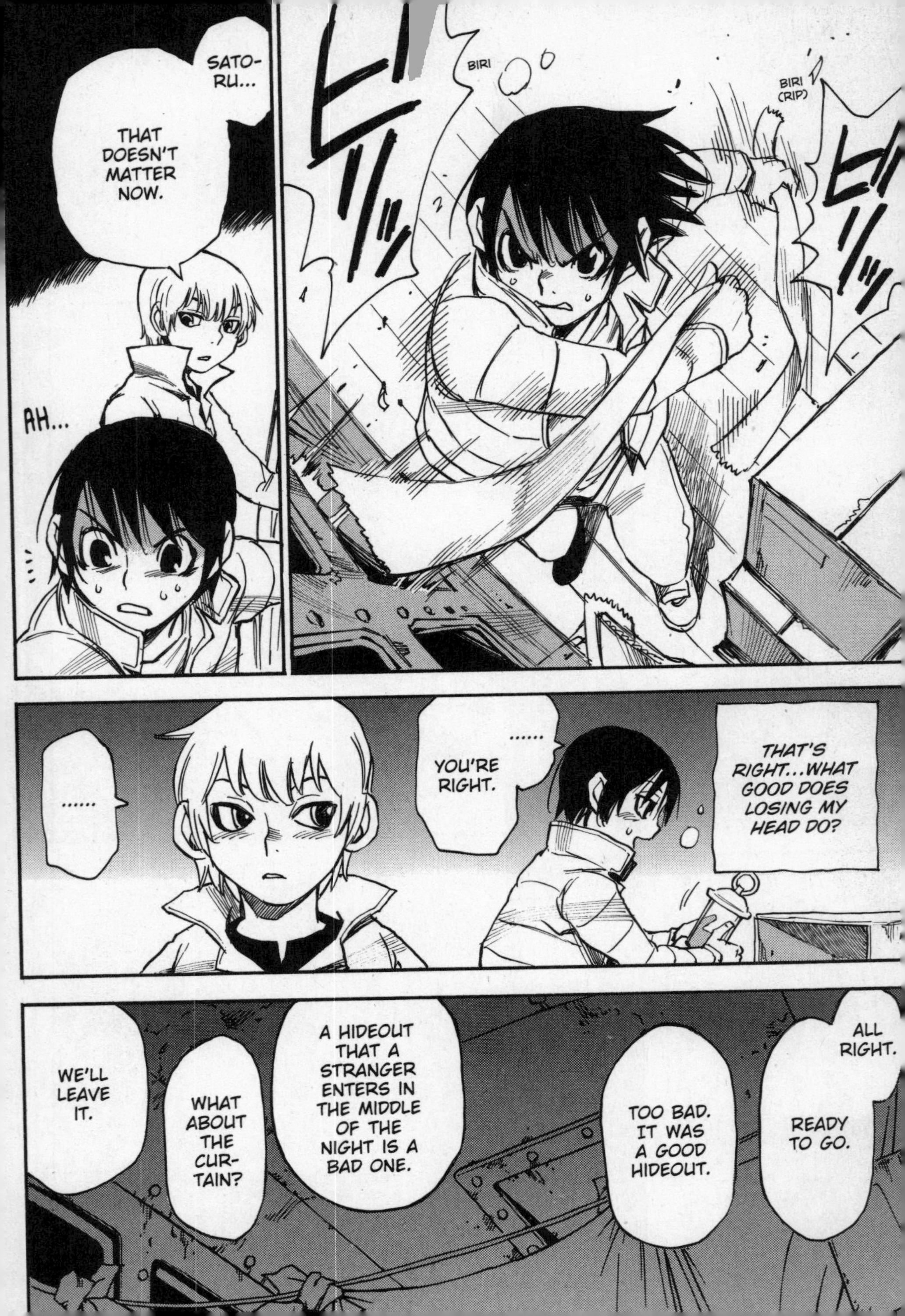
BIRI (RIP)
BIRI
SATO-RU...
THAT DOESN'T MATTER NOW.
AH...
THAT'S RIGHT...WHAT GOOD DOES LOSING MY HEAD DO?
......
YOU'RE RIGHT.
......
ALL RIGHT.
READY TO GO.
TOO BAD. IT WAS A GOOD HIDEOUT.
A HIDEOUT THAT A STRANGER ENTERS IN THE MIDDLE OF THE NIGHT IS A BAD ONE.
WHAT ABOUT THE CUR-TAIN?
WE'LL LEAVE IT.

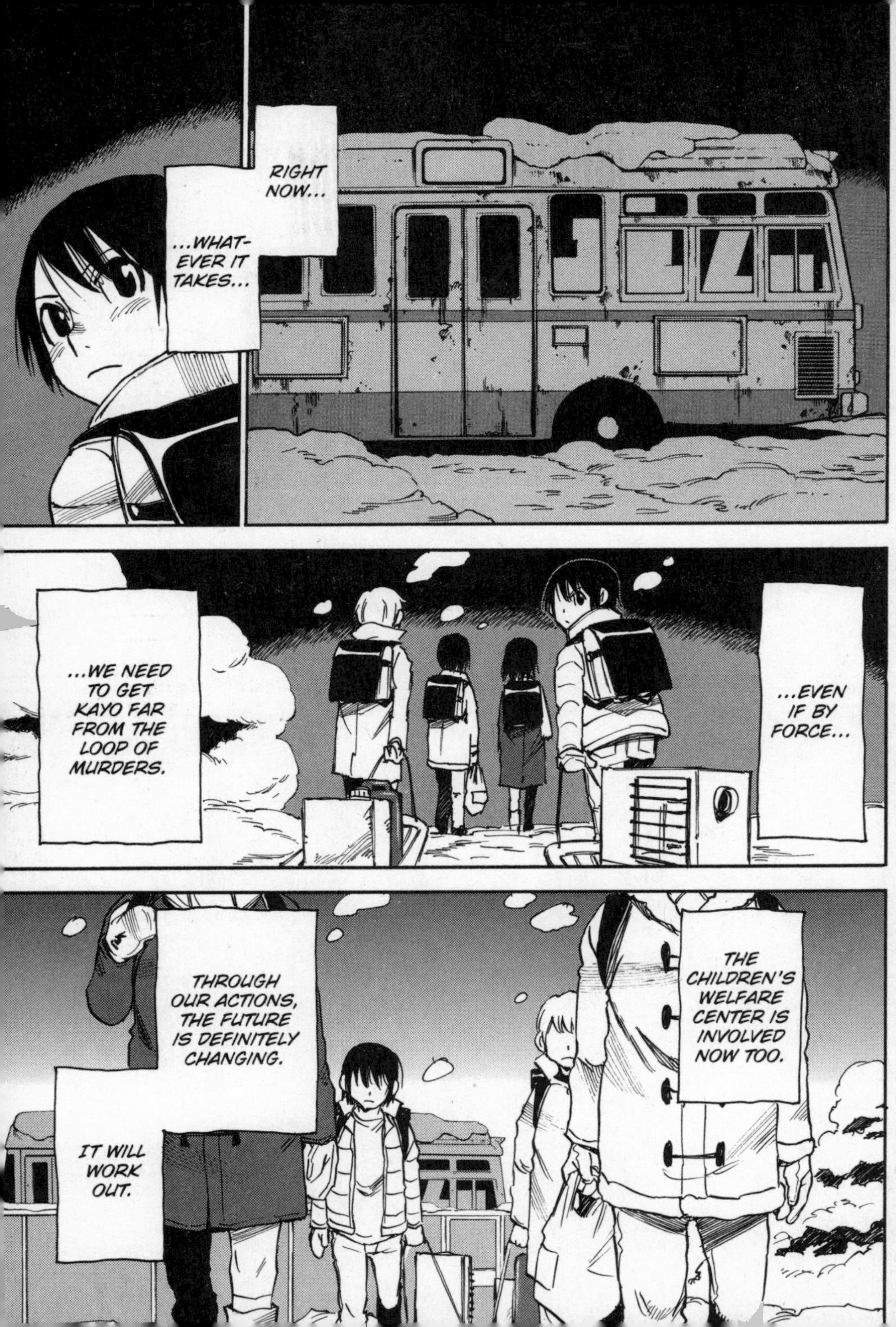
RIGHT NOW...
...WHAT-EVER IT TAKES...
...EVEN IF BY FORCE...
...WE NEED TO GET KAYO FAR FROM THE LOOP OF MURDERS.
THE CHILDREN'S WELFARE CENTER IS INVOLVED NOW TOO.
THROUGH OUR ACTIONS, THE FUTURE IS DEFINITELY CHANGING.
IT WILL WORK OUT.

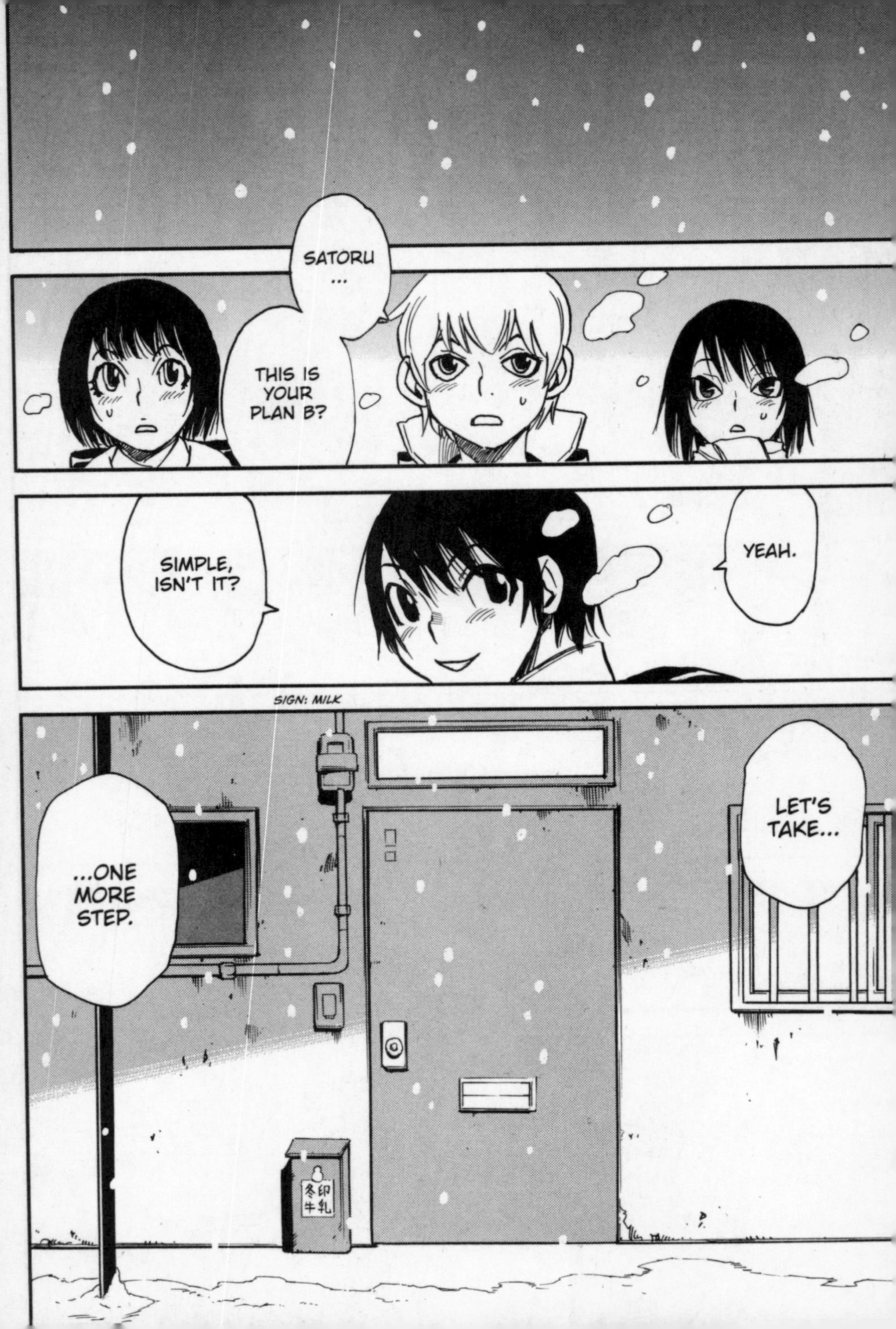
SATORU...
THIS IS YOUR PLAN B?
YEAH.
SIMPLE, ISN'T IT?
SIGN: MILK
LET'S TAKE...
...ONE MORE STEP.
冬印牛乳

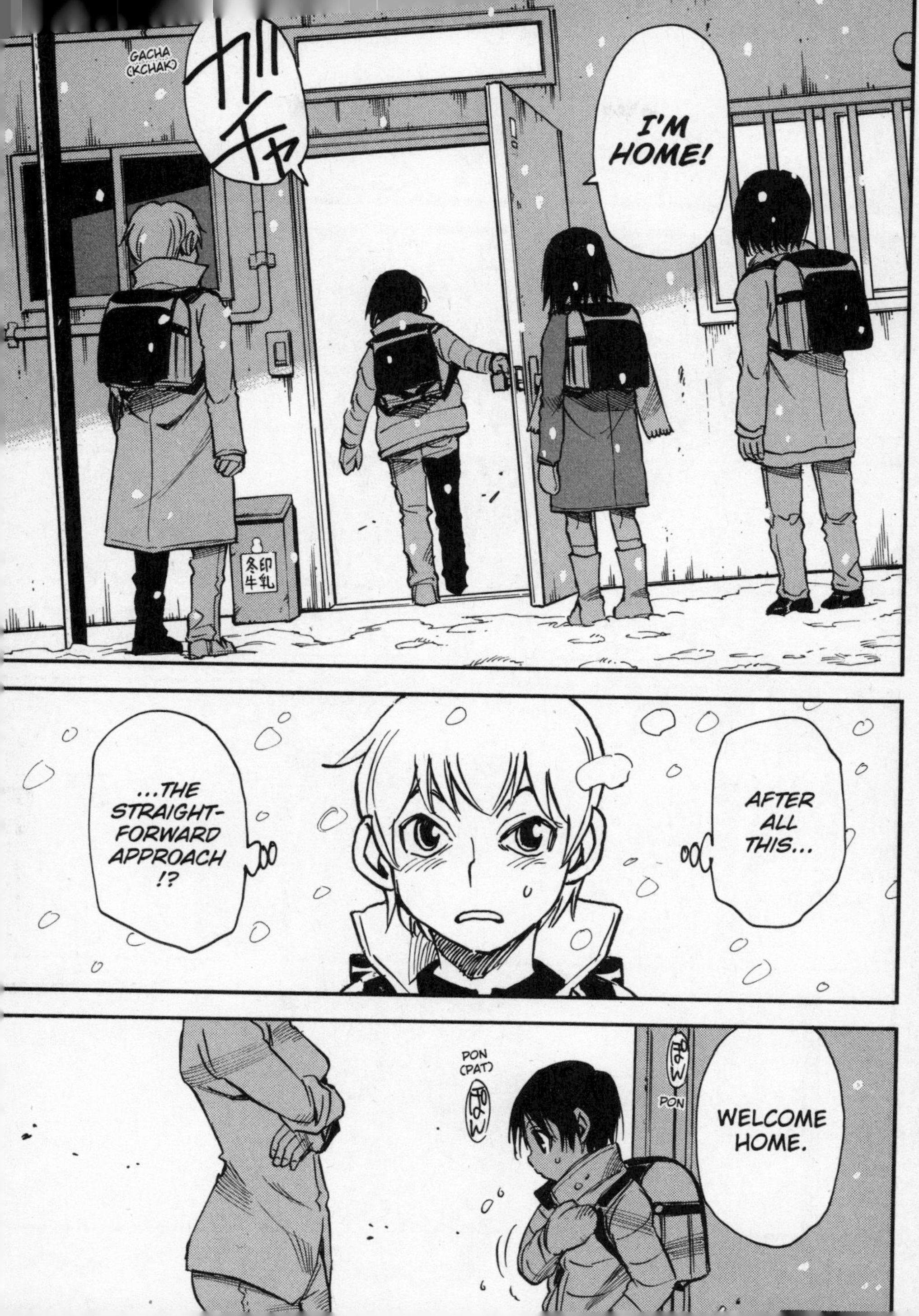
I'M HOME!
ガチャ
GACHA (KCHAK)
AFTER ALL THIS...
...THE STRAIGHT-FORWARD APPROACH!?
WELCOME HOME.
ぽん
PON
ぽん
PON (PAT)

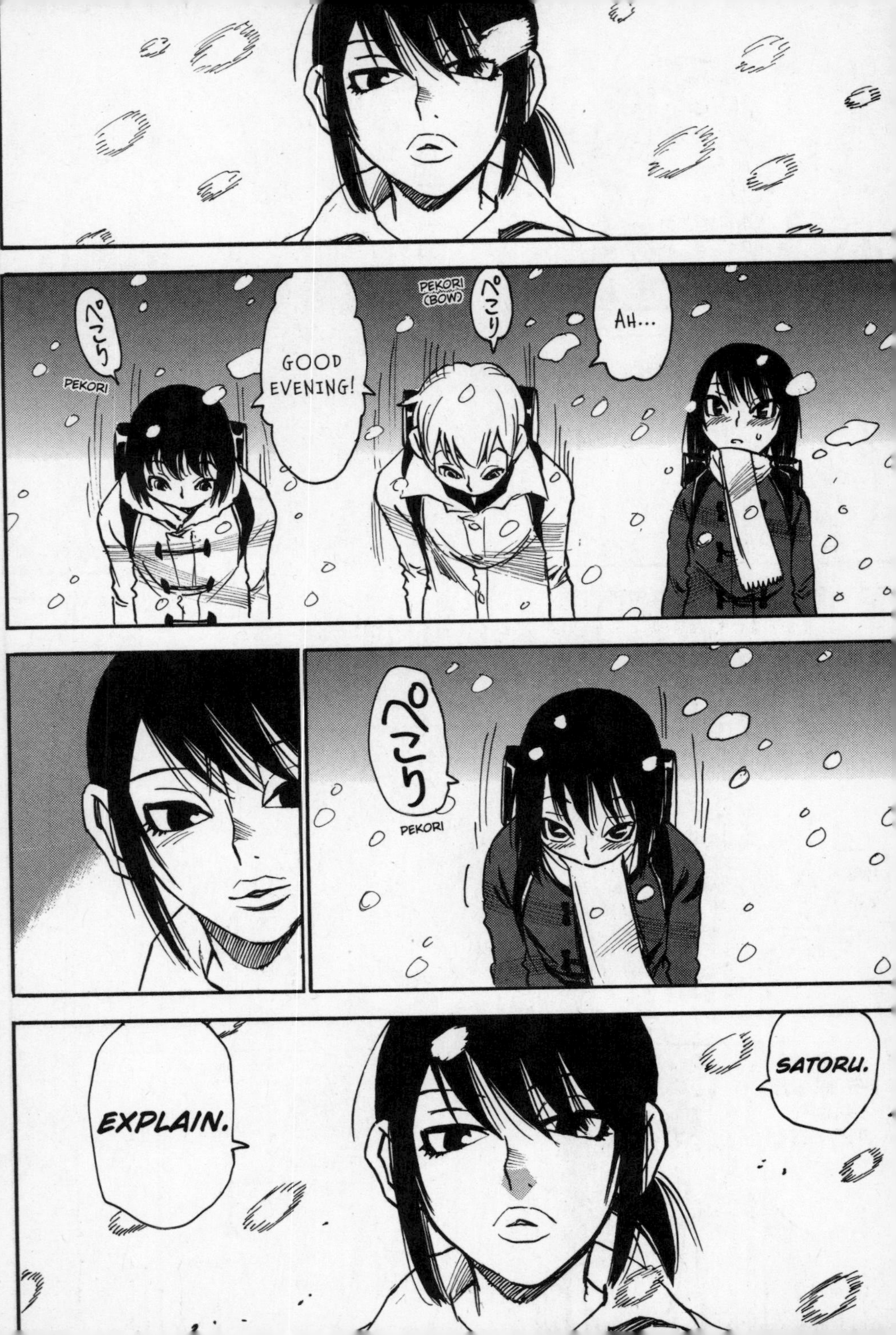
AH...
ぺこり
PEKORI (BOW)
GOOD EVENING!
ぺこり
PEKORI
ぺこり
PEKORI
SATORU.
EXPLAIN.

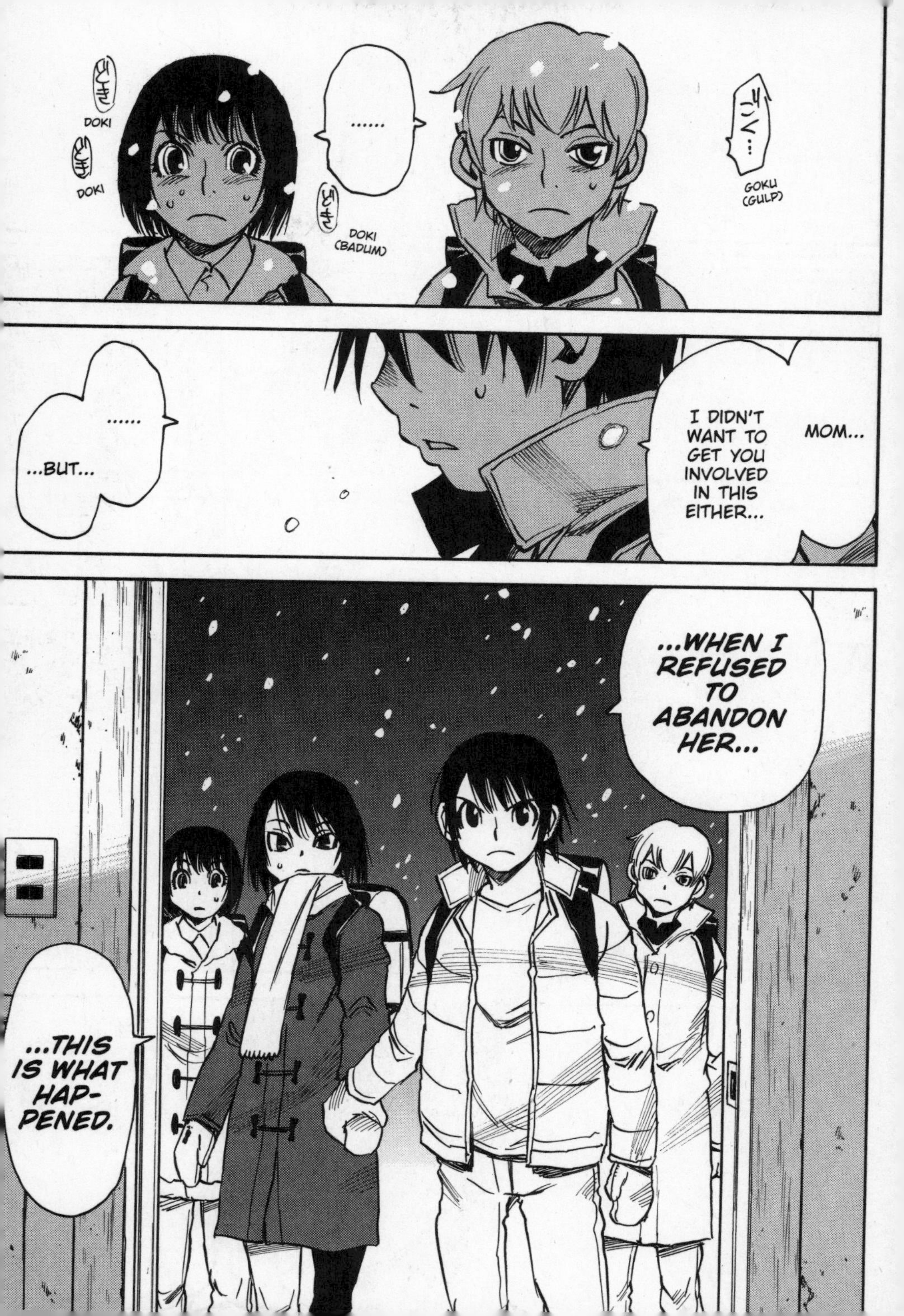
GOKU (GULP)
......
DOKI (BADUM)
DOKI
DOKI
MOM...
I DIDN'T WANT TO GET YOU INVOLVED IN THIS EITHER...
......
...BUT...
...WHEN I REFUSED TO ABANDON HER...
...THIS IS WHAT HAP-PENED.

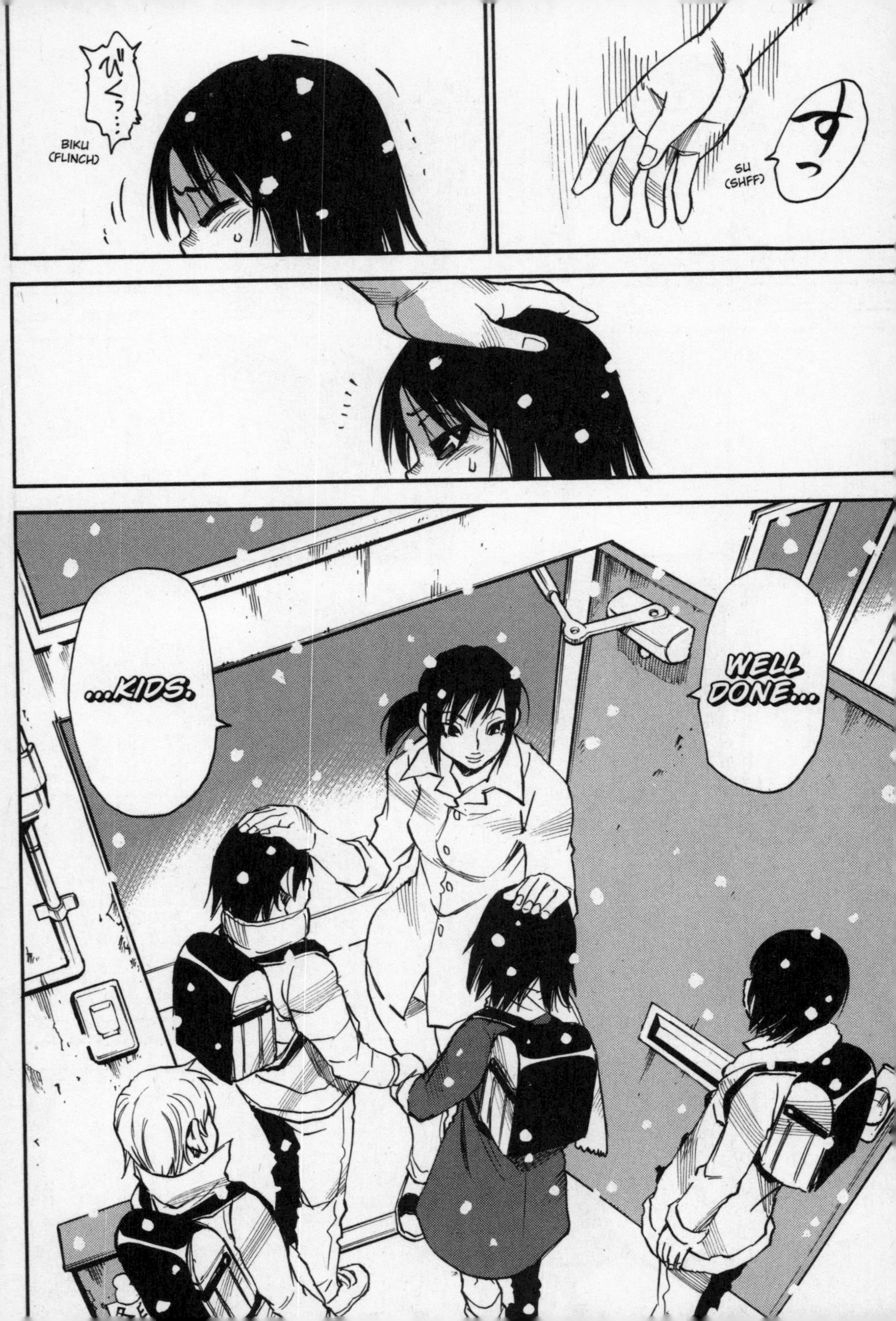
すっ
SU (SHFF)
びくっ…
BIKU (FLINCH)
WELL DONE...
...KIDS.

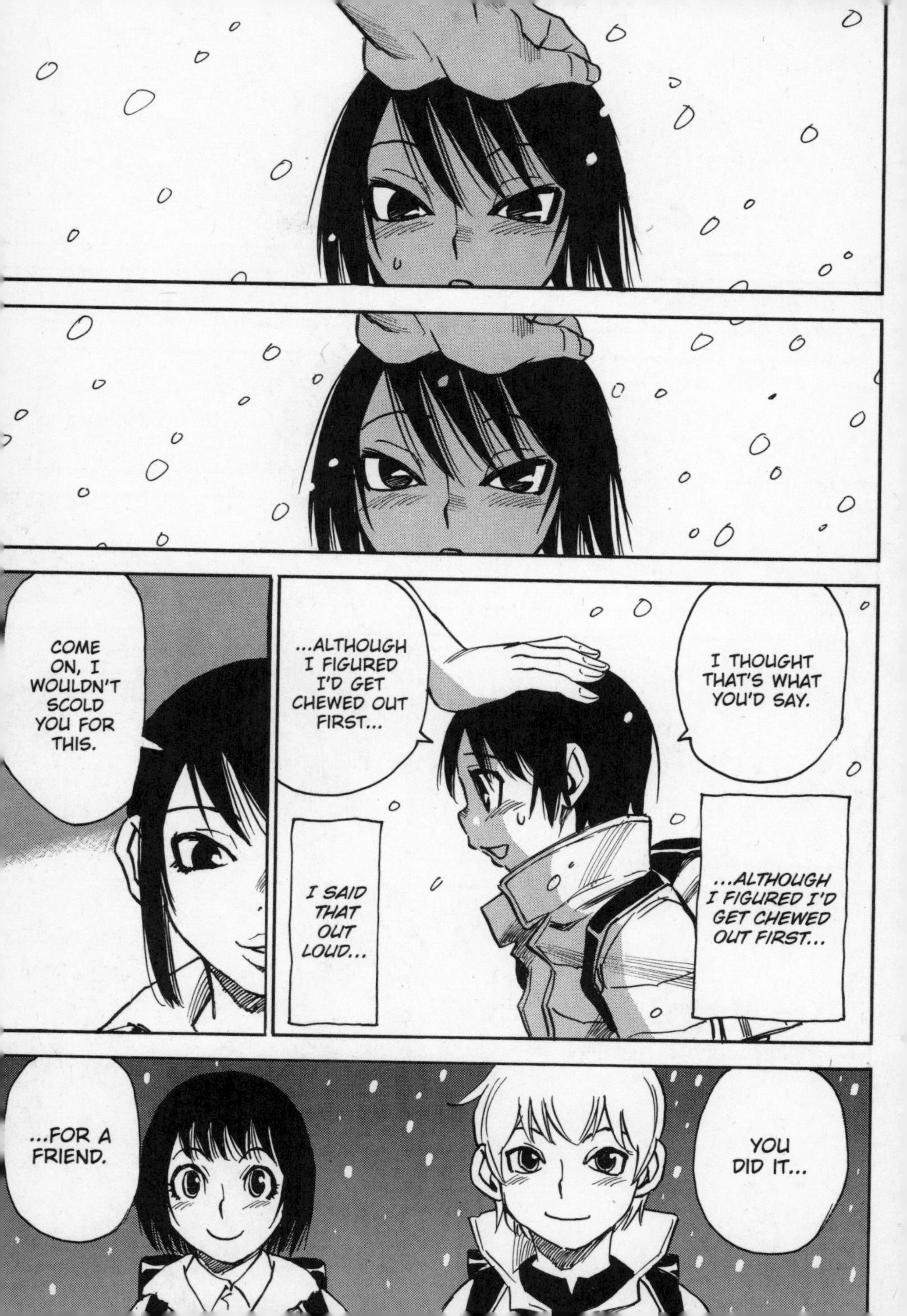
I THOUGHT THAT'S WHAT YOU'D SAY.
...ALTHOUGH I FIGURED I'D GET CHEWED OUT FIRST...
...ALTHOUGH I FIGURED I'D GET CHEWED OUT FIRST...
I SAID THAT OUT LOUD...
COME ON, I WOULDN'T SCOLD YOU FOR THIS.
YOU DID IT...
...FOR A FRIEND.

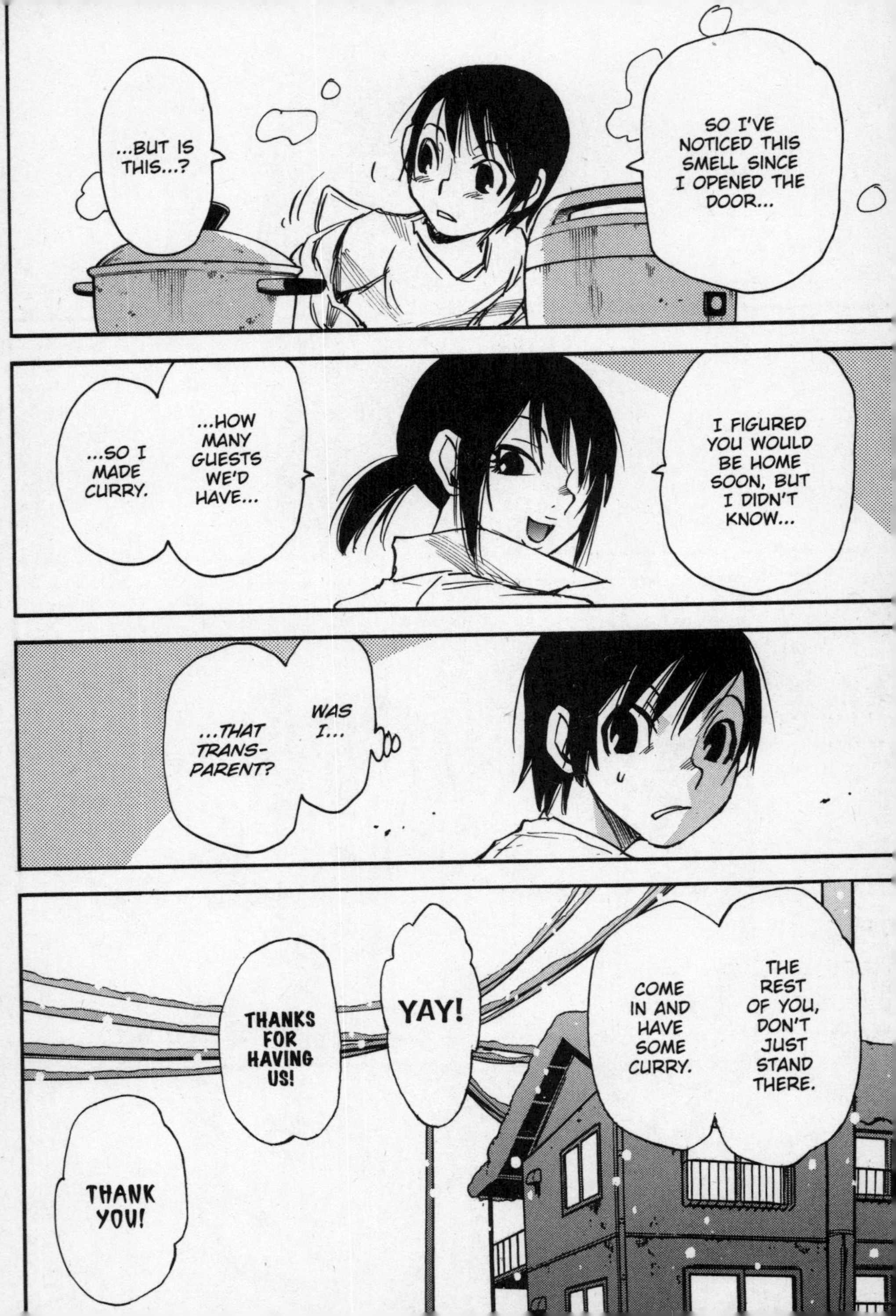
SO I'VE NOTICED THIS SMELL SINCE I OPENED THE DOOR...
...BUT IS THIS...?
I FIGURED YOU WOULD BE HOME SOON, BUT I DIDN'T KNOW...
...HOW MANY GUESTS WE'D HAVE...
...SO I MADE CURRY.
WAS I...
...THAT TRANS-PARENT?
THE REST OF YOU, DON'T JUST STAND THERE.
COME IN AND HAVE SOME CURRY.
YAY!
THANKS FOR HAVING US!
THANK YOU!

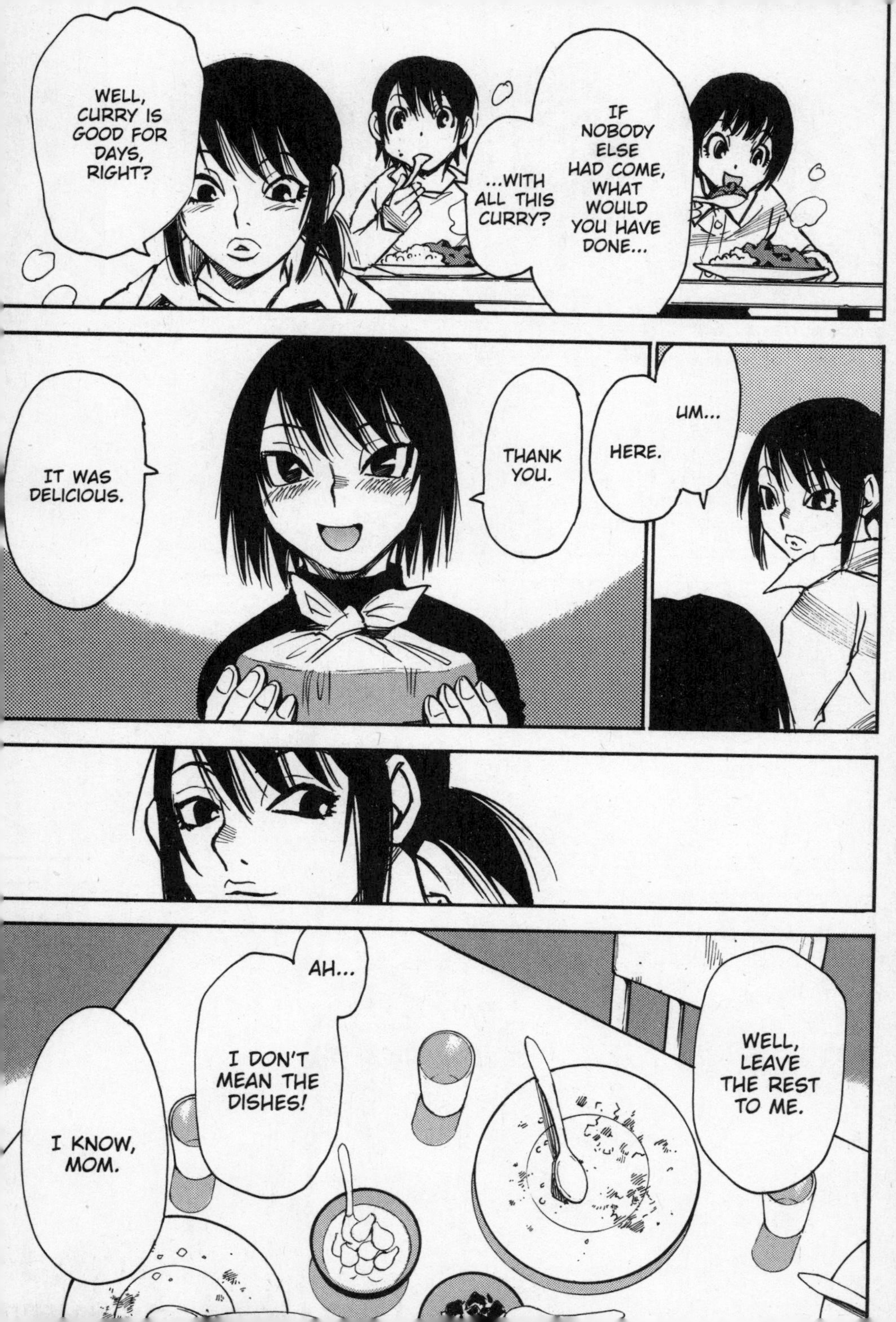
IF NOBODY ELSE HAD COME, WHAT WOULD YOU HAVE DONE...
...WITH ALL THIS CURRY?
WELL, CURRY IS GOOD FOR DAYS, RIGHT?
UM...
HERE.
THANK YOU.
IT WAS DELICIOUS.
WELL, LEAVE THE REST TO ME.
AH...
I DON'T MEAN THE DISHES!
I KNOW, MOM.

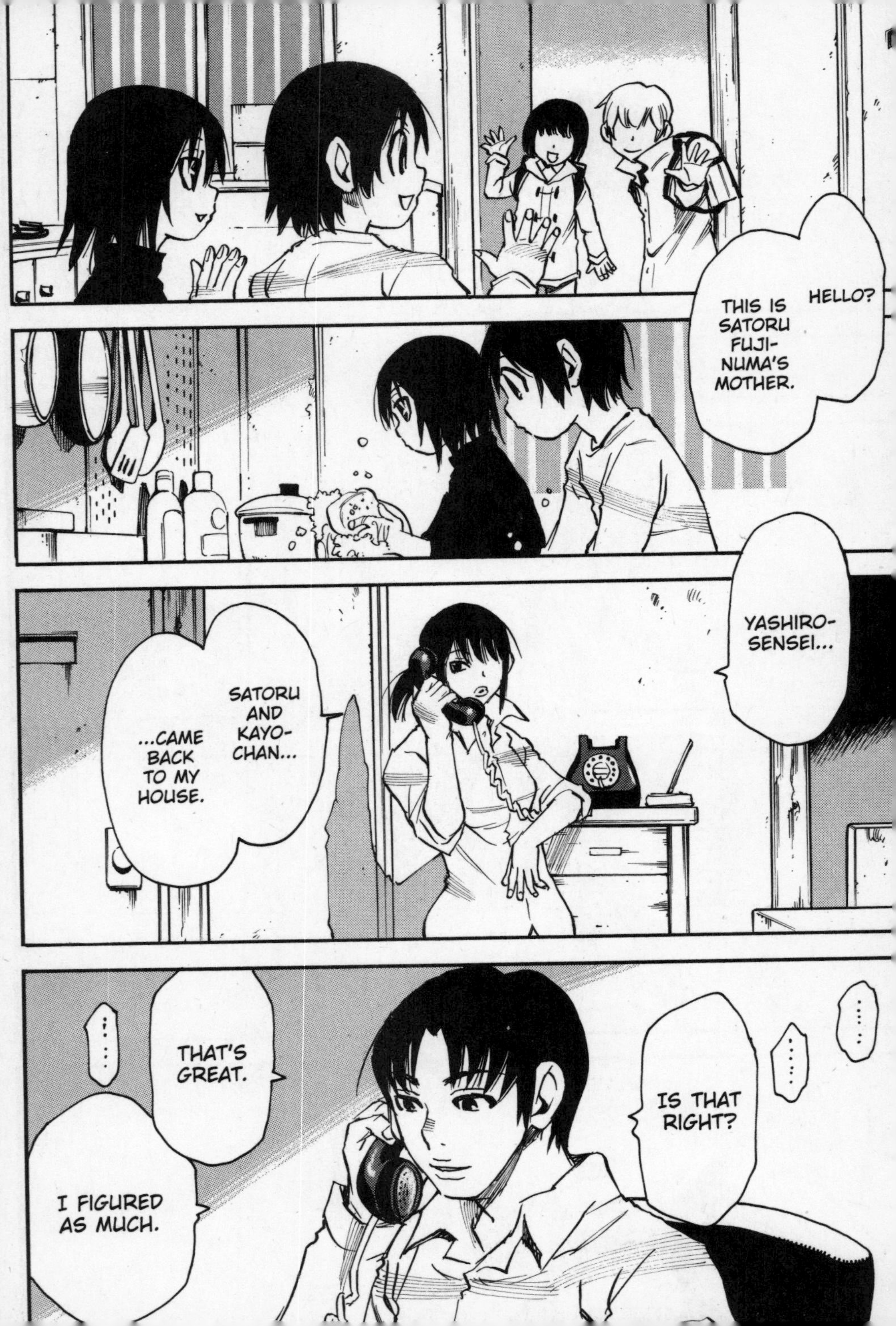
HELLO? THIS IS SATORU FUJI-NUMA'S MOTHER.
YASHIRO-SENSEI...
SATORU AND KAYO-CHAN...
...CAME BACK TO MY HOUSE.
......
......
IS THAT RIGHT?
THAT'S GREAT.
......
I FIGURED AS MUCH.

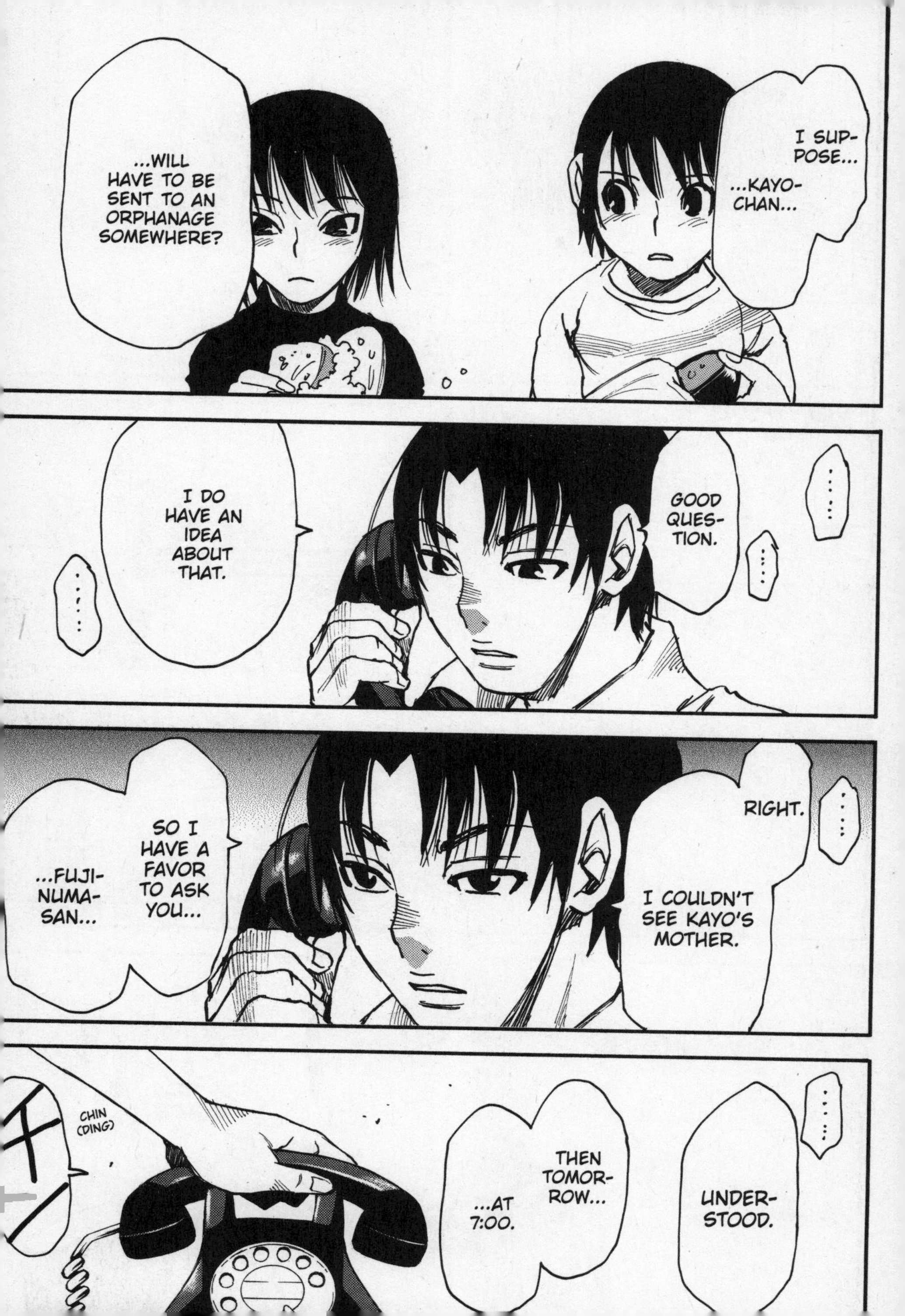
I SUP-POSE...
...KAYO-CHAN...
...WILL HAVE TO BE SENT TO AN ORPHANAGE SOMEWHERE?
......
GOOD QUES-TION.
......
I DO HAVE AN IDEA ABOUT THAT.
......
......
RIGHT.
I COULDN'T SEE KAYO'S MOTHER.
SO I HAVE A FAVOR TO ASK YOU...
...FUJI-NUMA-SAN...
......
UNDER-STOOD.
THEN TOMOR-ROW...
...AT 7:00.
CHIN (DING)

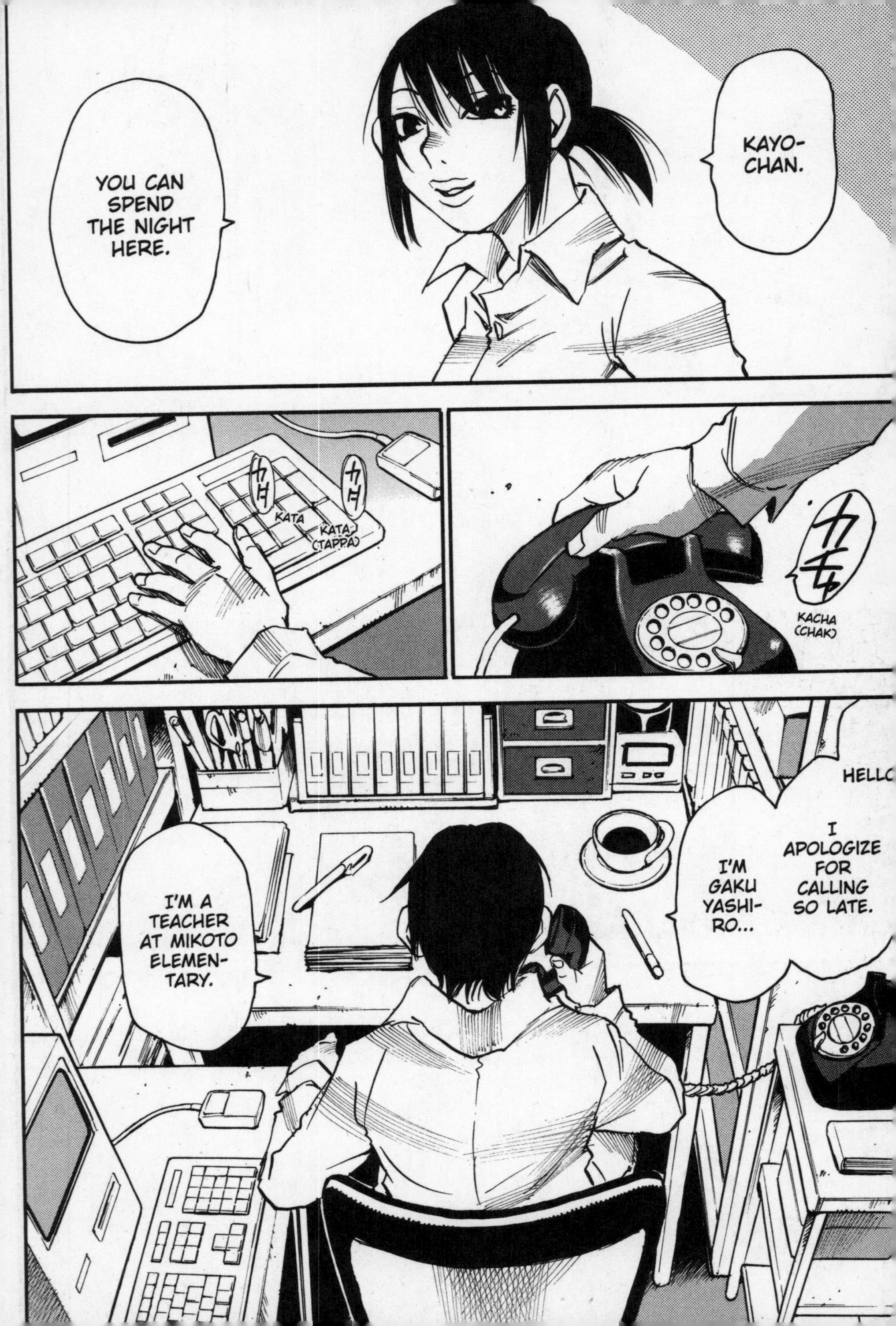
KAYO-CHAN.
YOU CAN SPEND THE NIGHT HERE.
カチャ
KACHA (CHAK)
カタ
カタ
KATA
KATA (TAPPA)
HELLO
I APOLOGIZE FOR CALLING SO LATE.
I'M GAKU YASHIRO...
I'M A TEACHER AT MIKOTO ELEMENTARY.

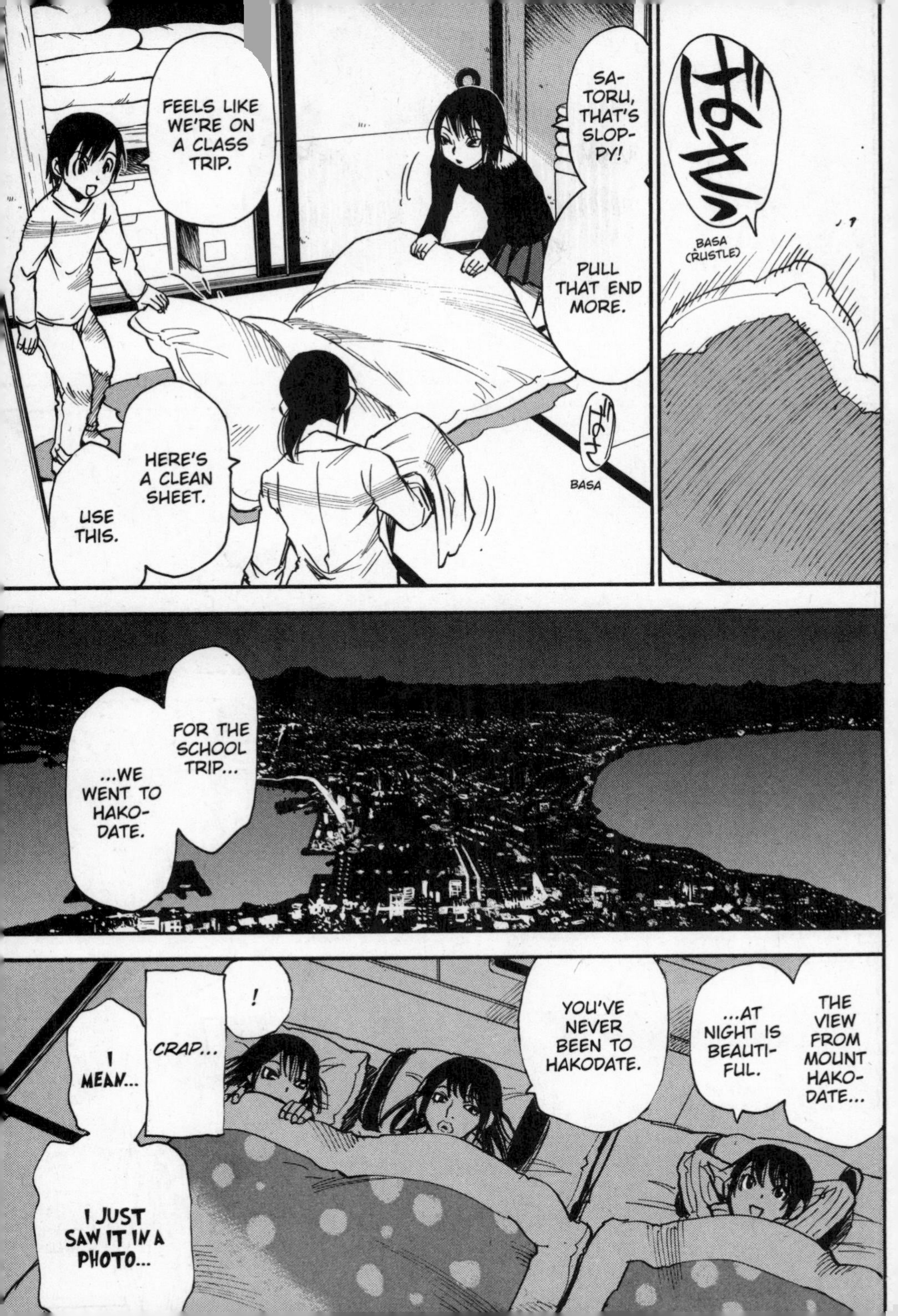
ばさっ
BASA (RUSTLE)
SA-TORU, THAT'S SLOP-PY!
PULL THAT END MORE.
FEELS LIKE WE'RE ON A CLASS TRIP.
BASA
HERE'S A CLEAN SHEET.
USE THIS.
FOR THE SCHOOL TRIP...
...WE WENT TO HAKO-DATE.
THE VIEW FROM MOUNT HAKO-DATE...
...AT NIGHT IS BEAUTI-FUL.
YOU'VE NEVER BEEN TO HAKODATE.
!
CRAP...
I MEAN...
I JUST SAW IT IN A PHOTO...

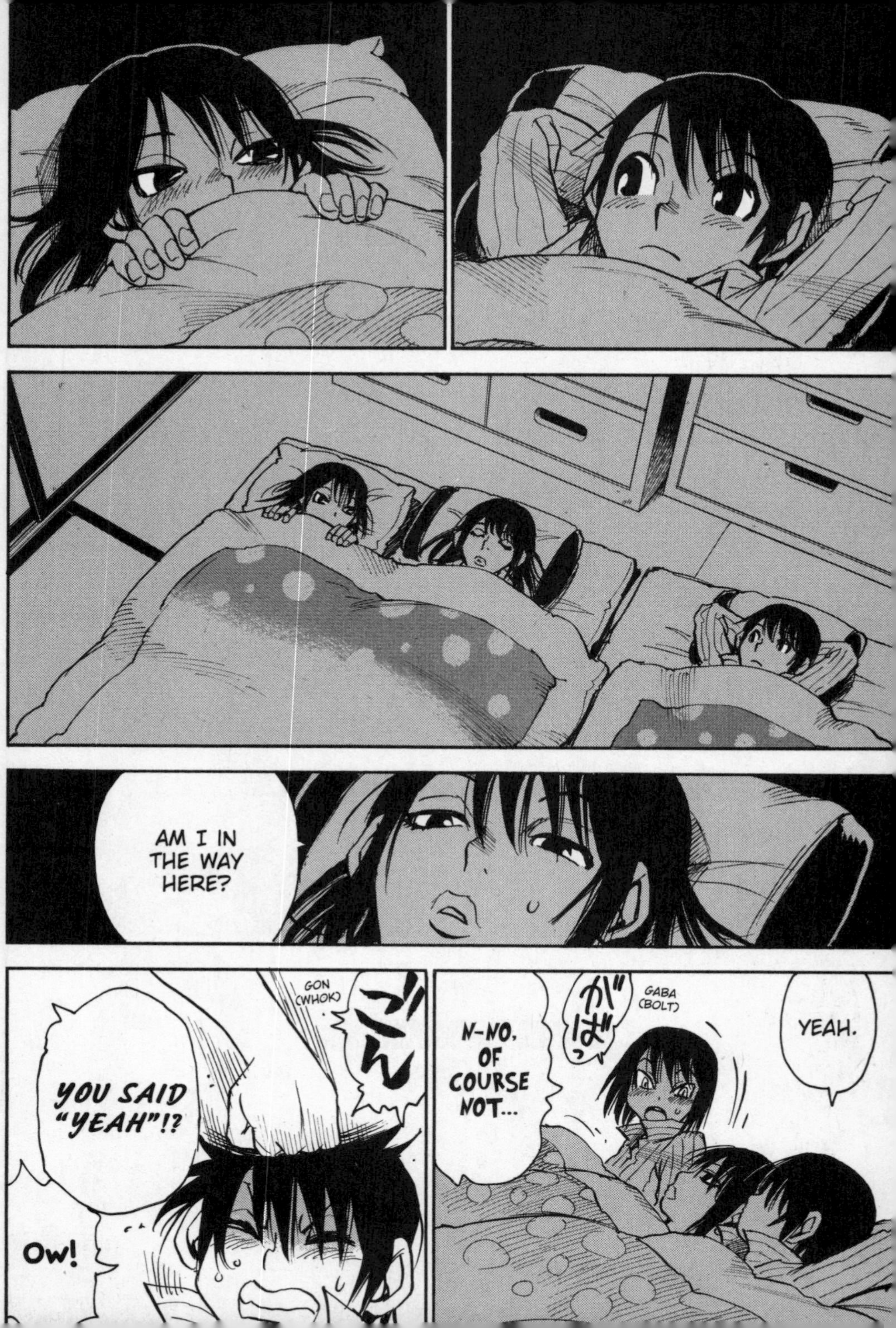
AM I IN THE WAY HERE?
YEAH.
がばっ
GABA (BOLT)
N-NO, OF COURSE NOT...
ごん
GON (WHOK)
YOU SAID "YEAH"!?
Ow!

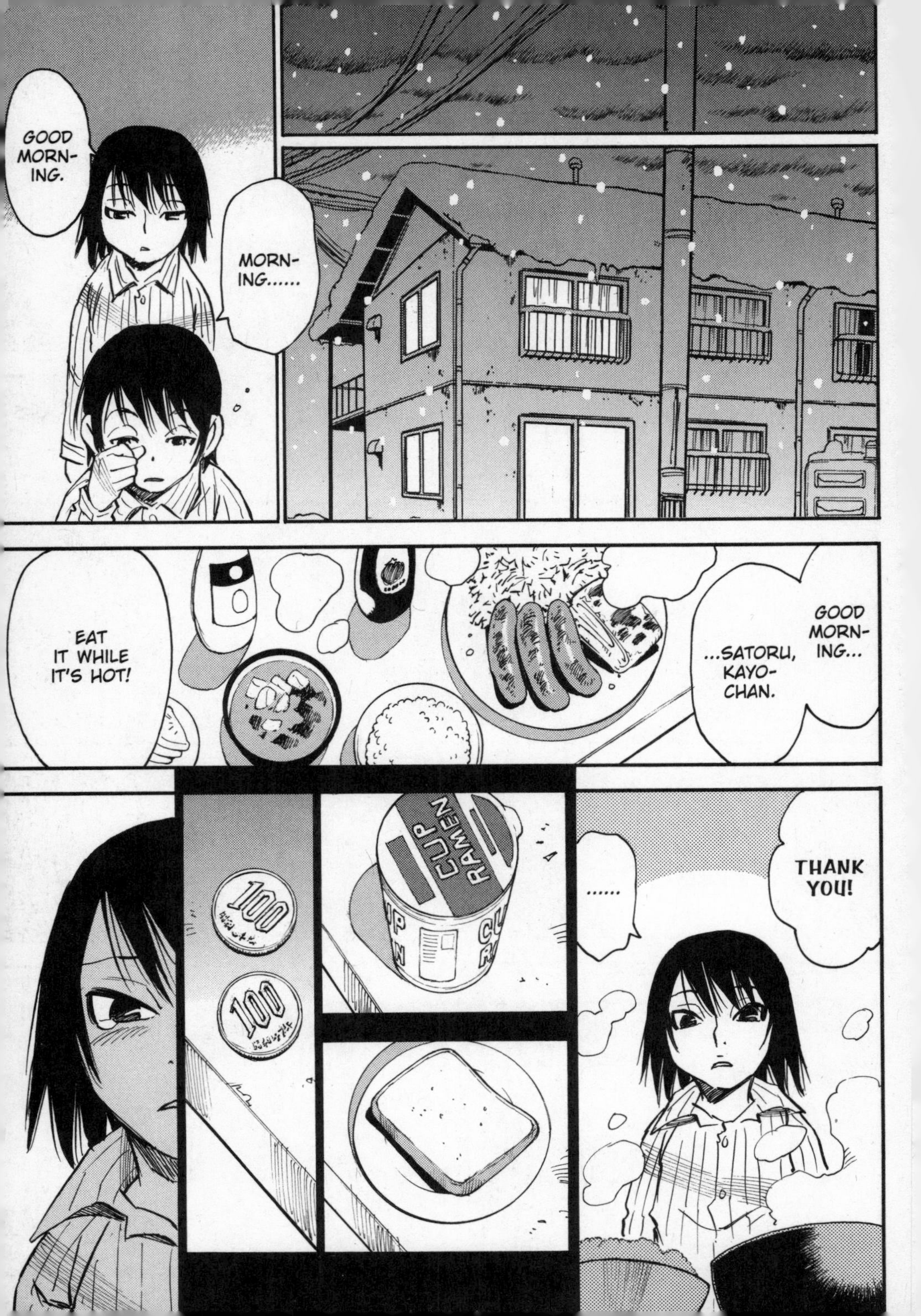
GOOD MORNING.
MORNING......
GOOD MORNING...
...SATORU, KAYO-CHAN.
EAT IT WHILE IT'S HOT!
THANK YOU!
......
CUP RAMEN

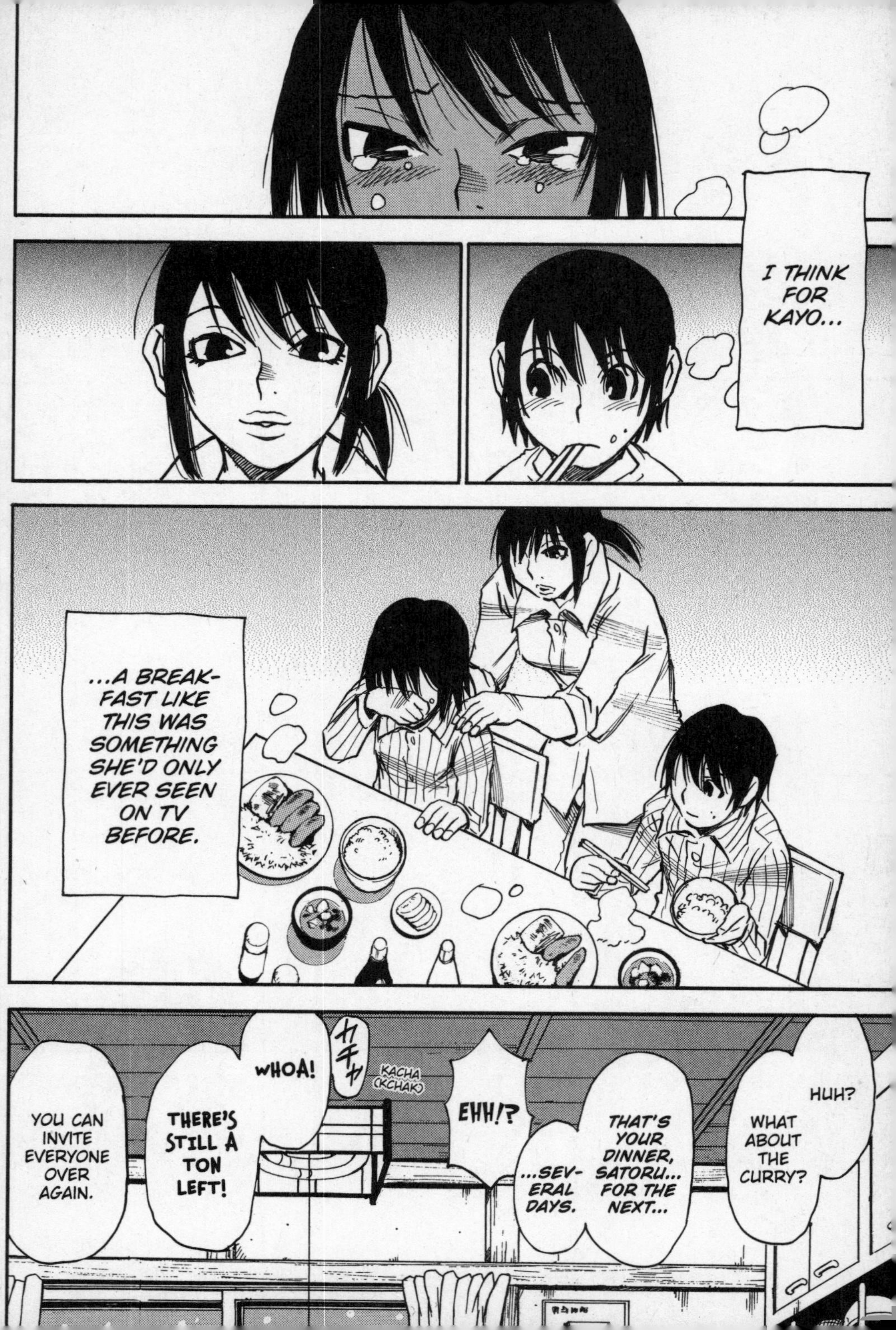
I THINK FOR KAYO...
...A BREAK-FAST LIKE THIS WAS SOMETHING SHE'D ONLY EVER SEEN ON TV BEFORE.
HUH?
WHAT ABOUT THE CURRY?
THAT'S YOUR DINNER, SATORU... FOR THE NEXT...
...SEV-ERAL DAYS.
EHH!?
カチャ
KACHA (KCHAK)
WHOA!
THERE'S STILL A TON LEFT!
YOU CAN INVITE EVERYONE OVER AGAIN.

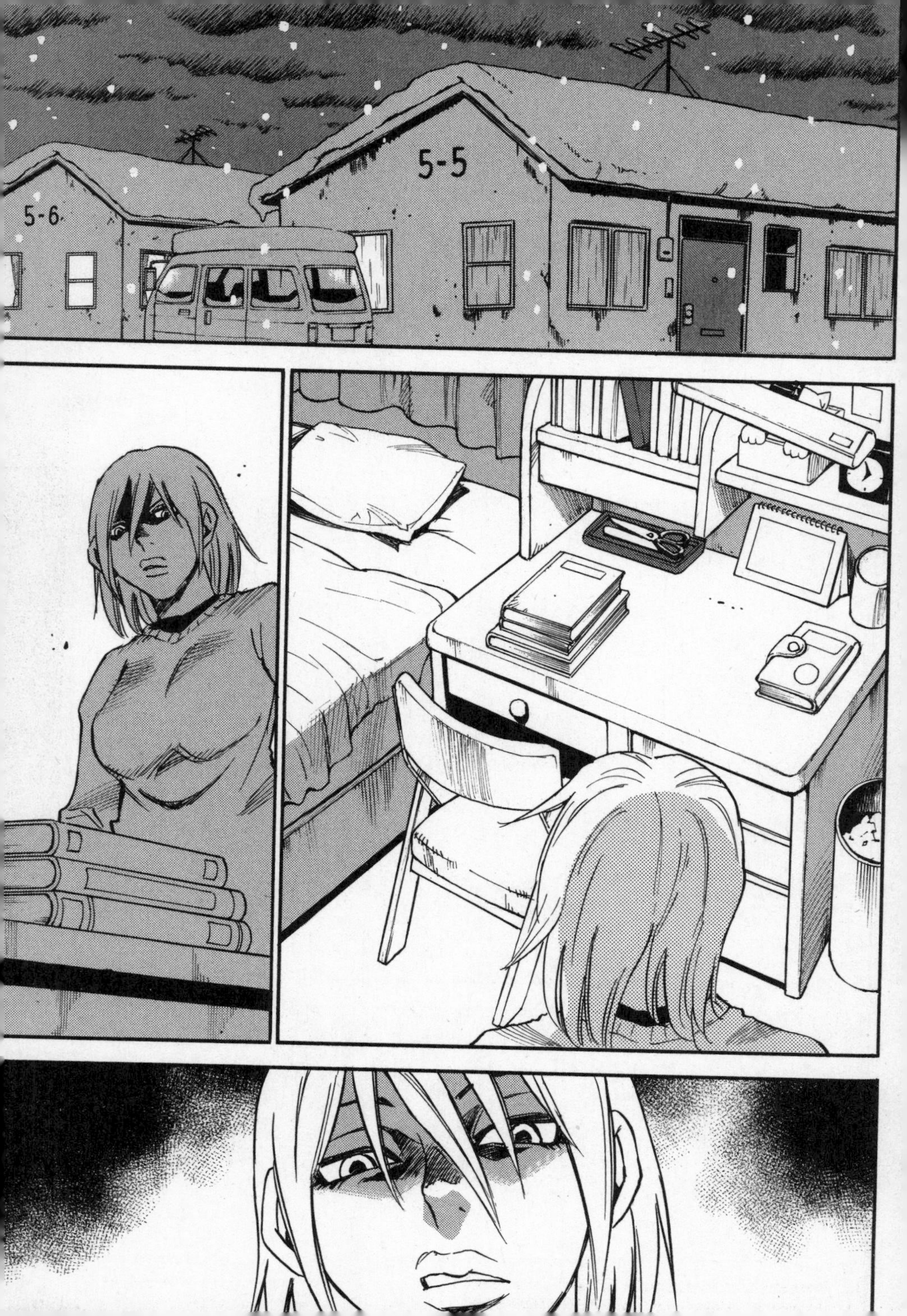
5-5
5-6

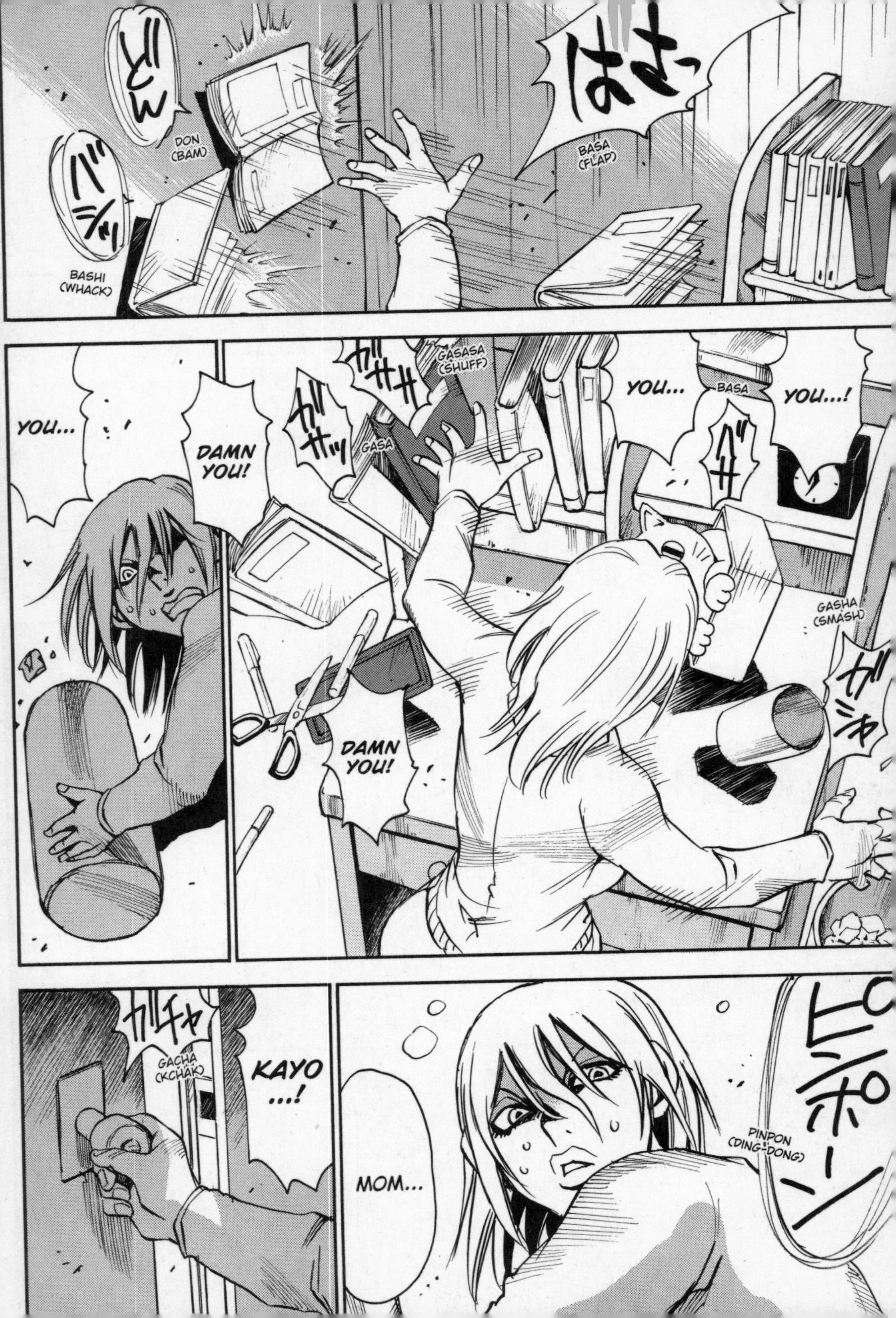
ばさっ
BASA (FLAP)
どん
DON (BAM)
バシッ
BASHI (WHACK)
YOU...!
バサ
BASA
YOU...
ガシャ
GASHA (SMASH)
ガサササ
GASASA (SHUFF)
ガサッ
GASA
DAMN YOU!
DAMN YOU!
YOU...
ピンポーン
PINPON (DING-DONG)
MOM...
カチャ
GACHA (KCHAK)
KAYO ...!

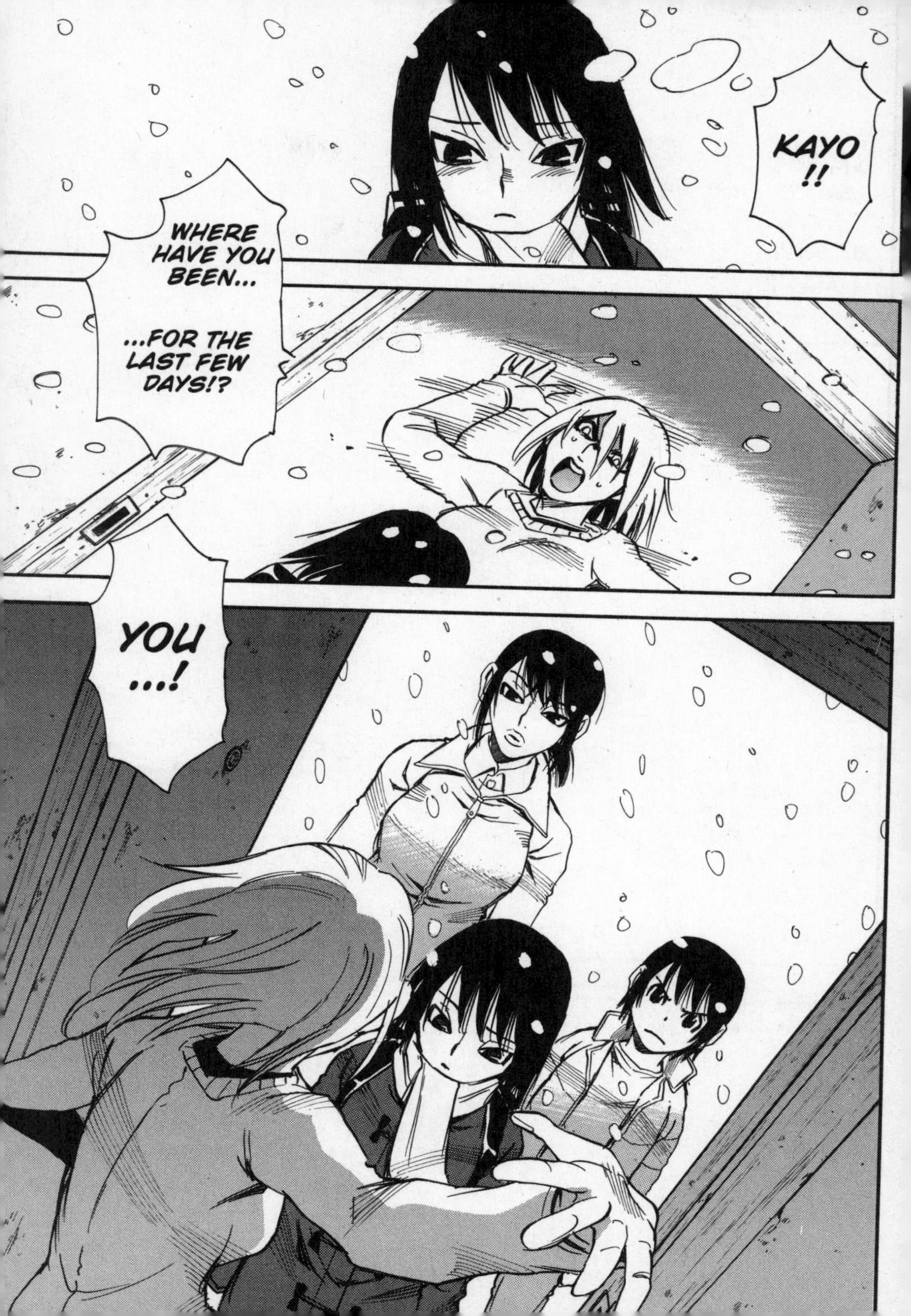
KAYO!!
WHERE HAVE YOU BEEN...
...FOR THE LAST FEW DAYS!?
YOU...!

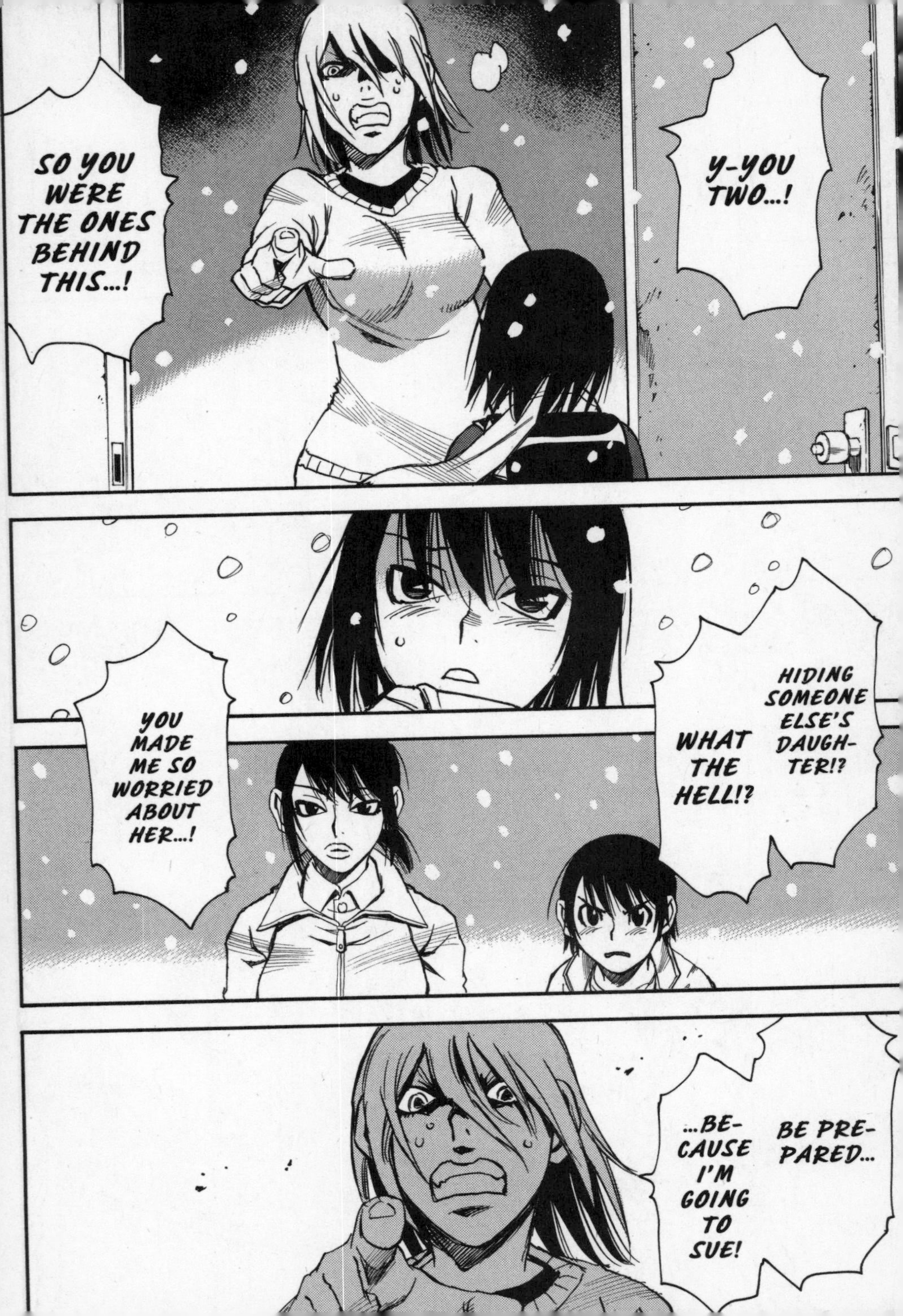
Y-YOU TWO...!
SO YOU WERE THE ONES BEHIND THIS...!
HIDING SOMEONE ELSE'S DAUGH-TER!?
WHAT THE HELL!?
YOU MADE ME SO WORRIED ABOUT HER...!
BE PRE-PARED...
...BE-CAUSE I'M GOING TO SUE!

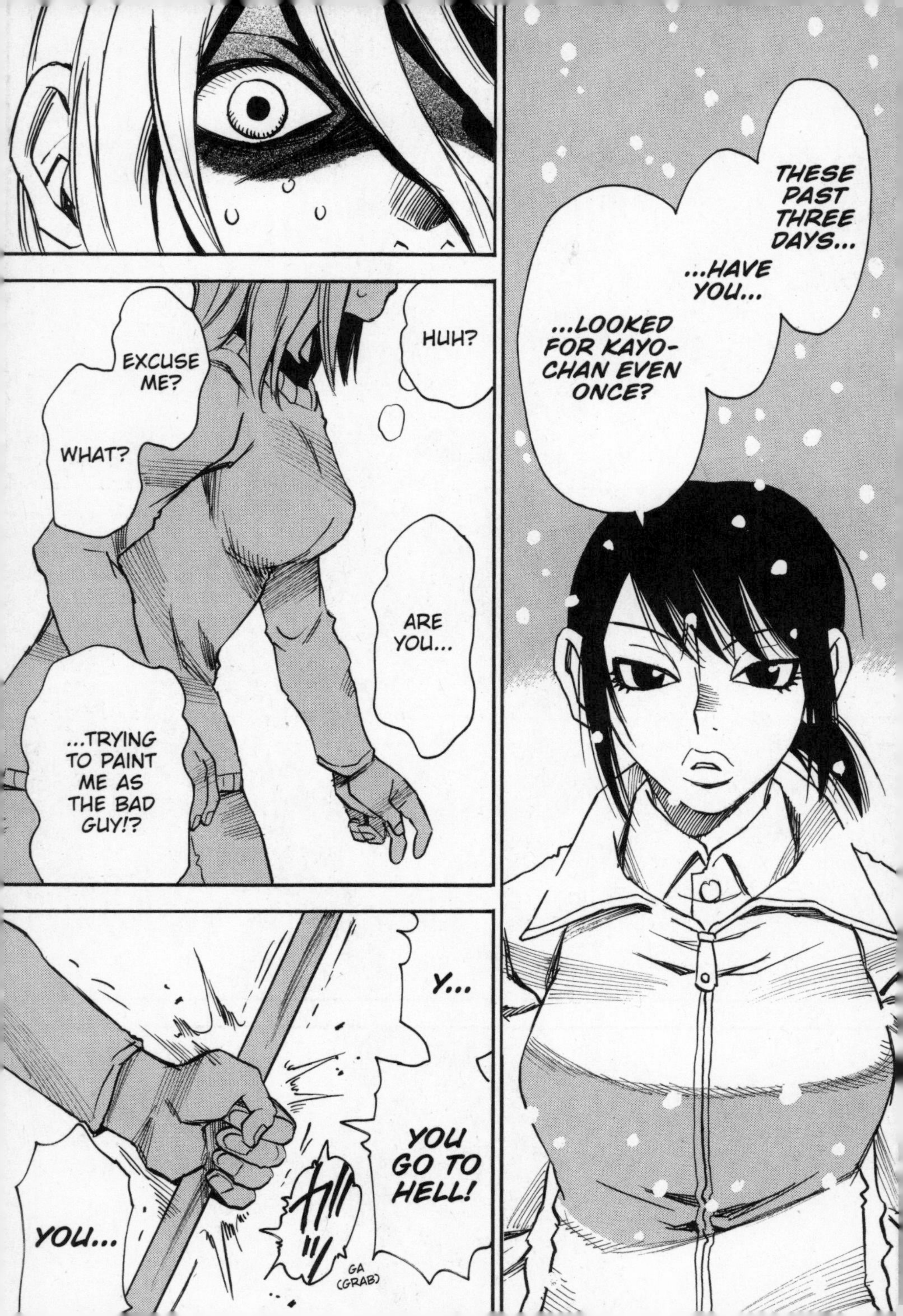
THESE PAST THREE DAYS...
...HAVE YOU...
...LOOKED FOR KAYO-CHAN EVEN ONCE?
HUH?
EXCUSE ME?
WHAT?
ARE YOU...
...TRYING TO PAINT ME AS THE BAD GUY!?
Y...
YOU GO TO HELL!
GA (GRAB)
YOU...

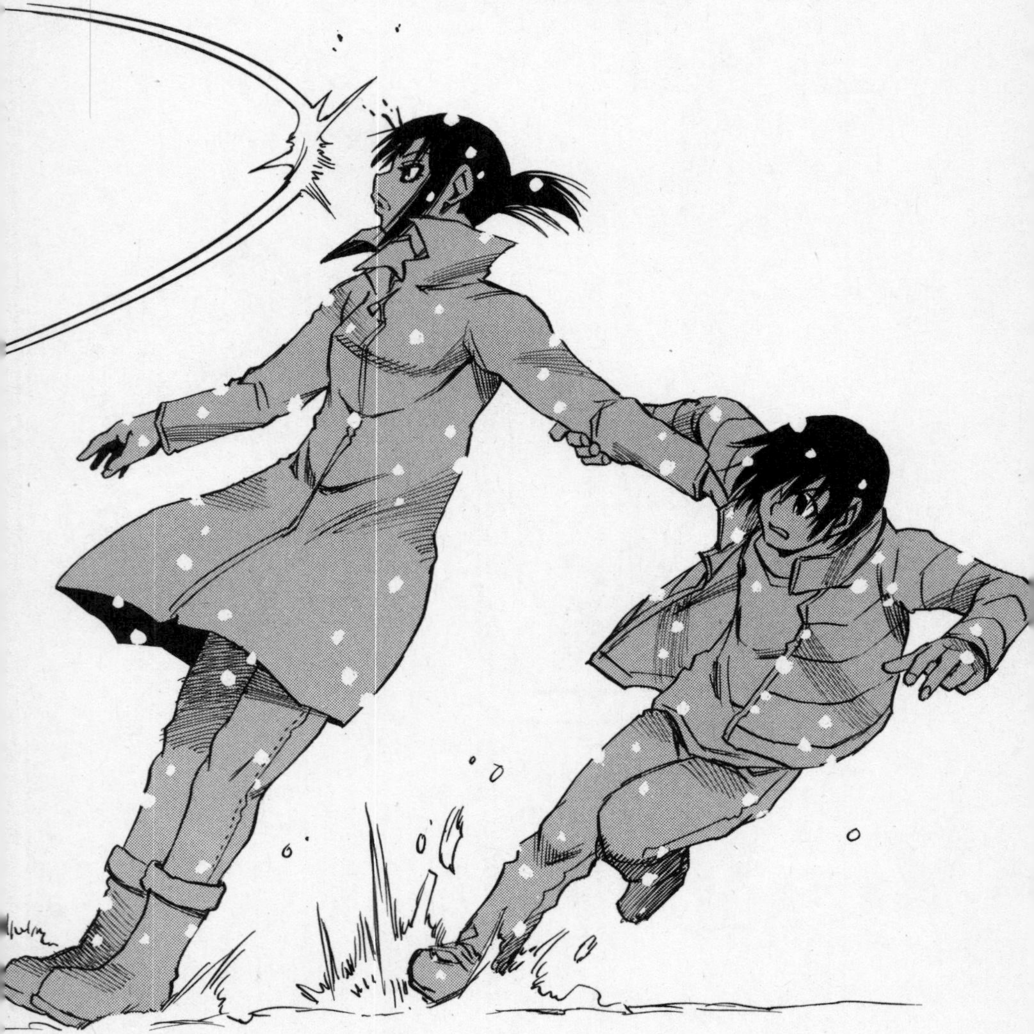

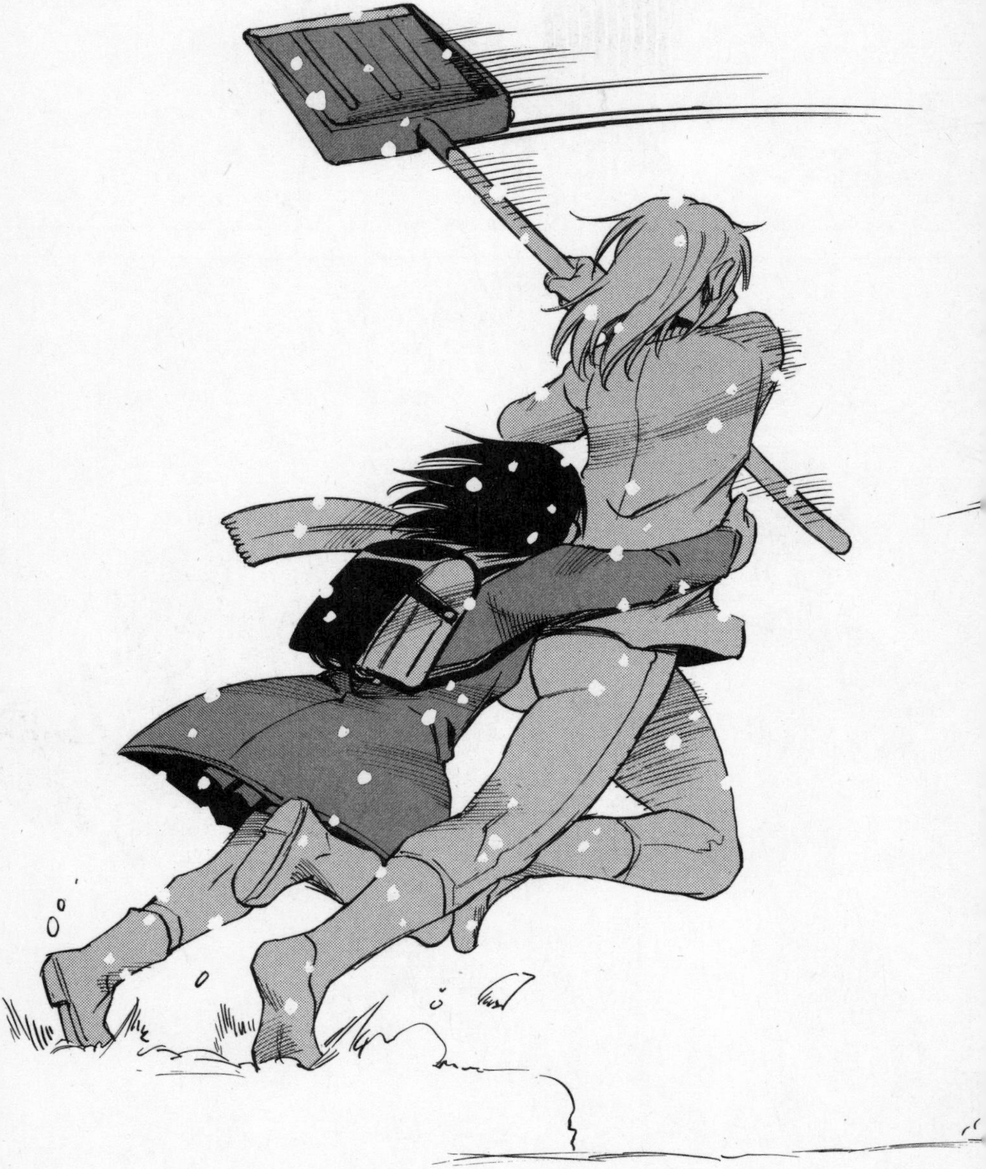

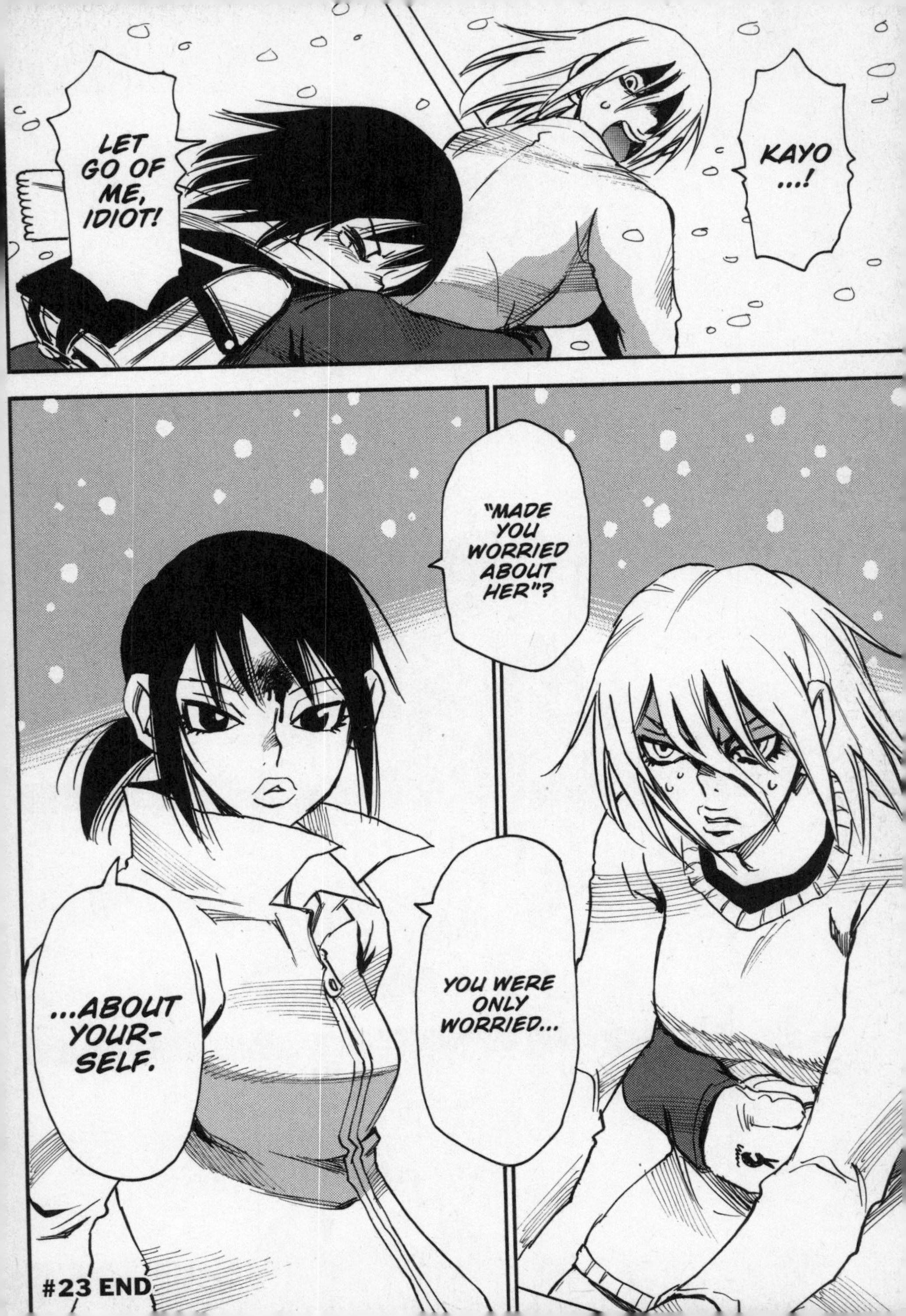
KAYO ...!
LET GO OF ME, IDIOT!
"MADE YOU WORRIED ABOUT HER"?
YOU WERE ONLY WORRIED...
...ABOUT YOURSELF.
#23 END

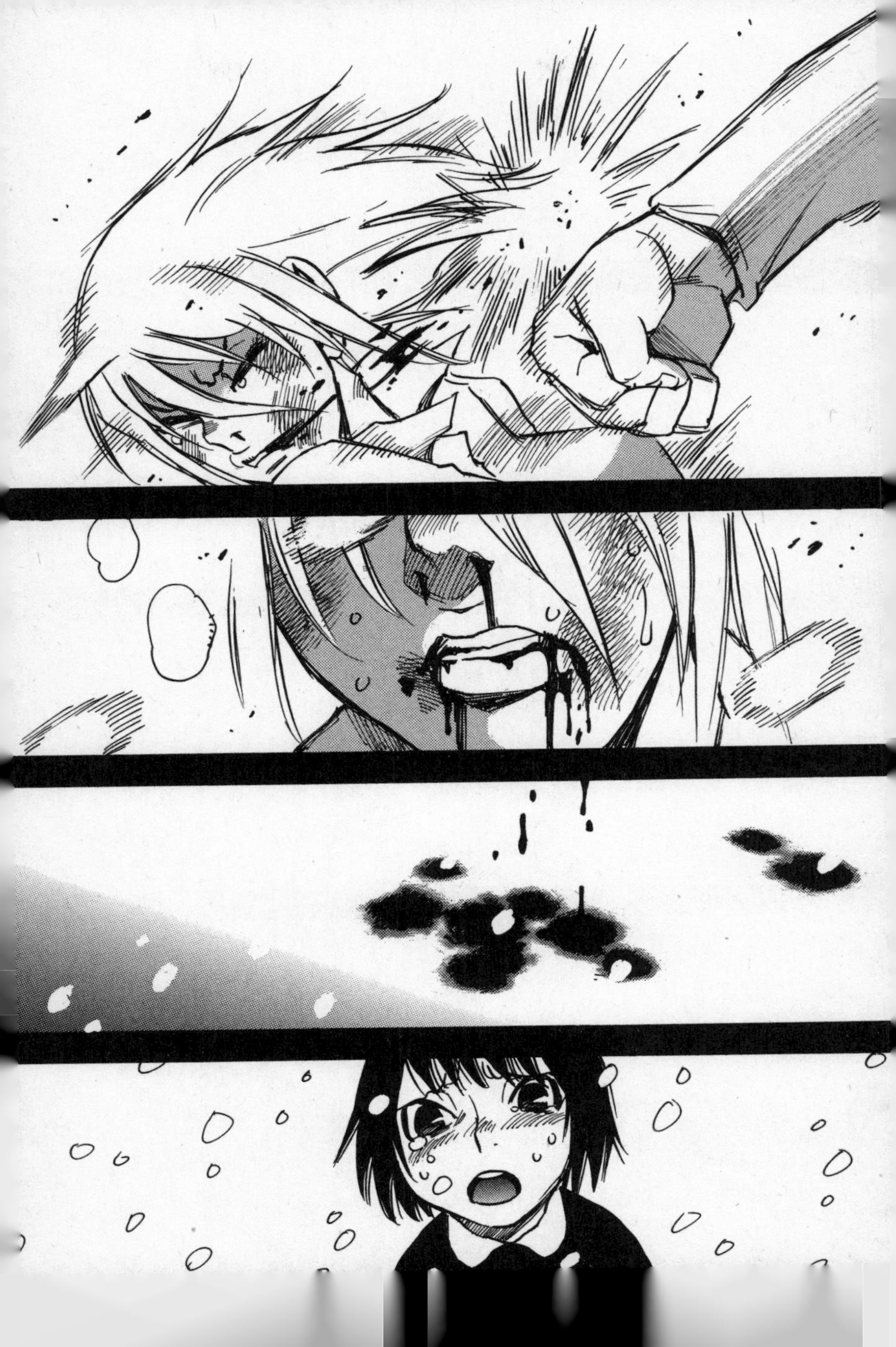

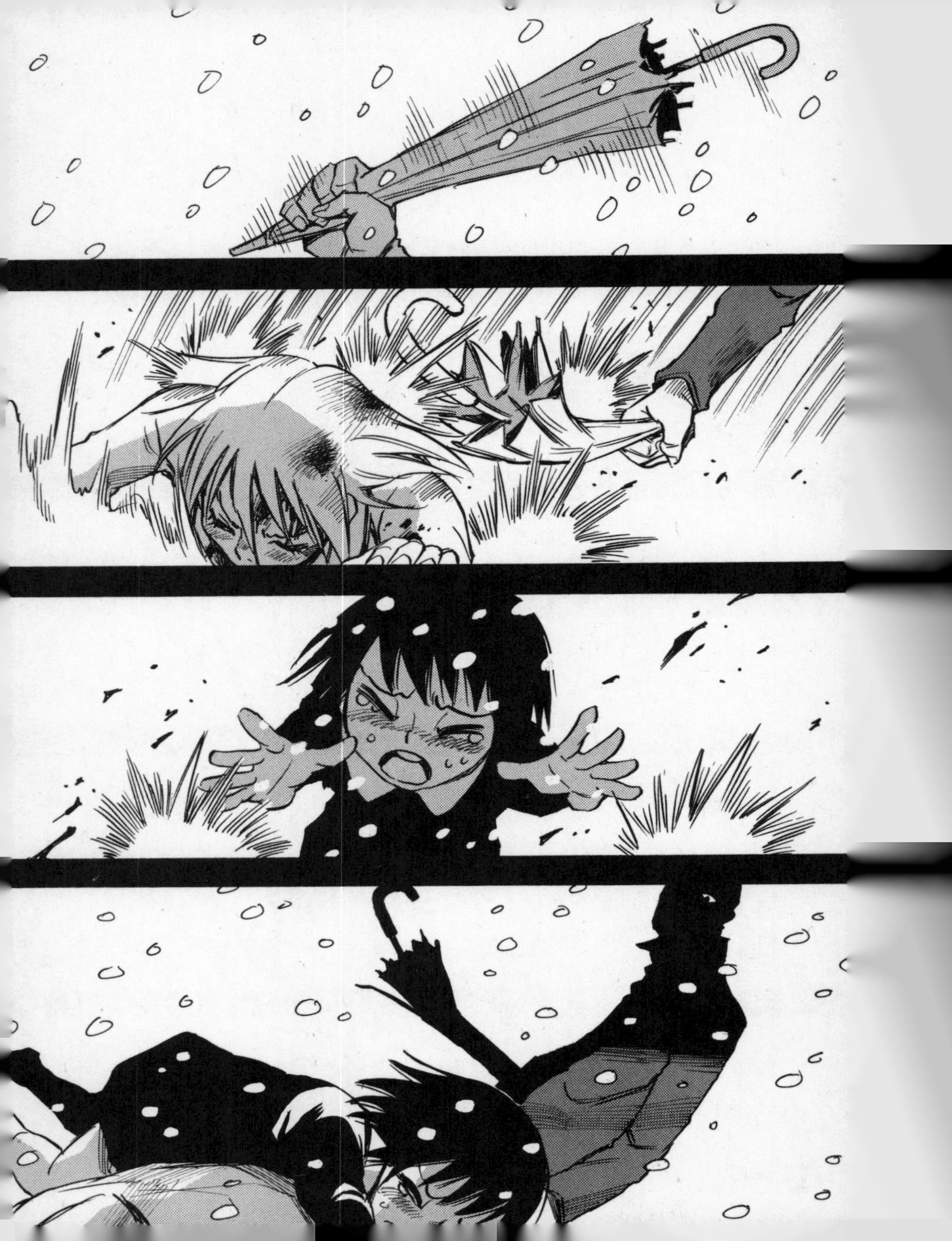

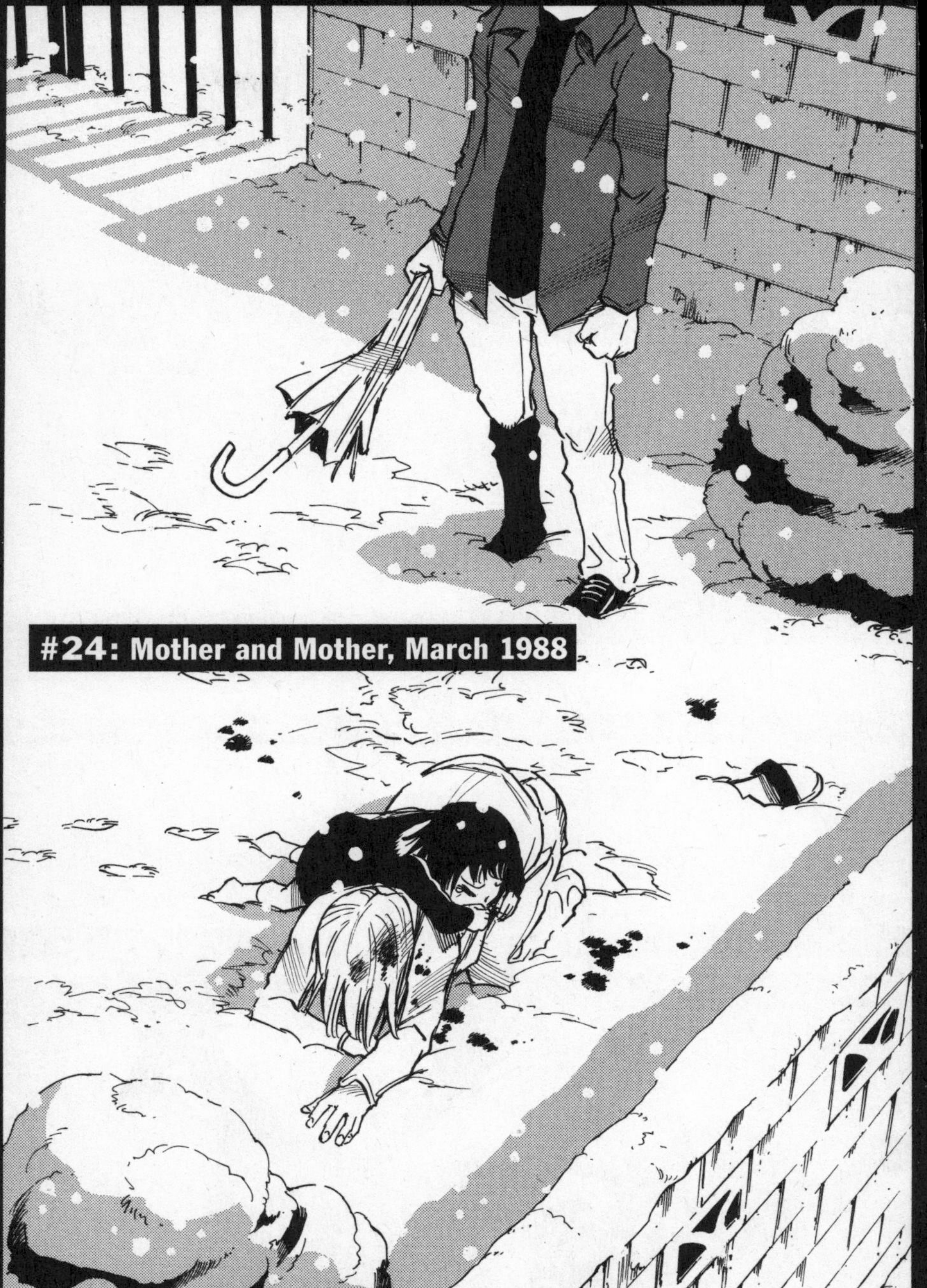
#24: Mother and Mother, March 1988

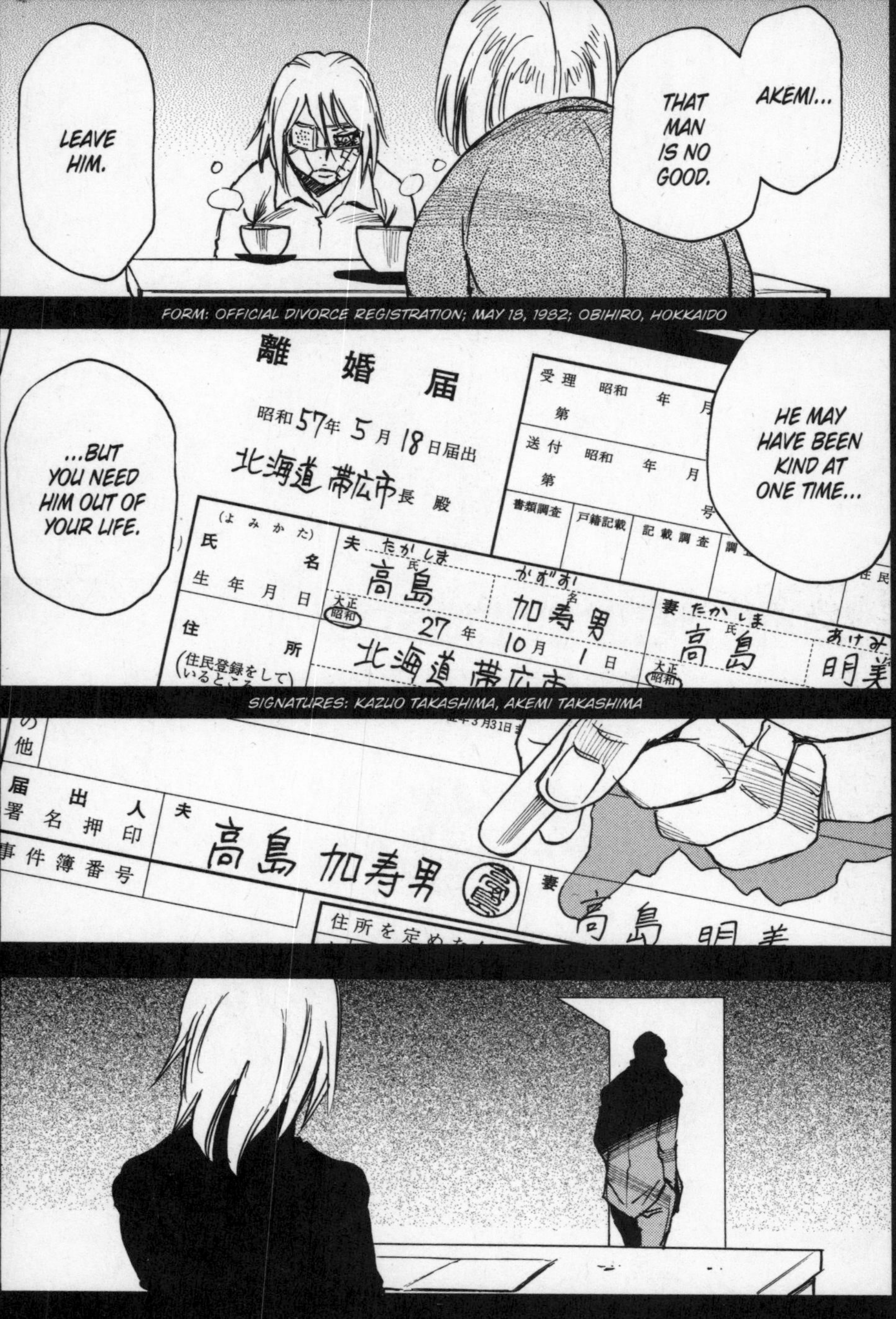
AKEMI...
THAT MAN IS NO GOOD.
LEAVE HIM.
FORM: OFFICIAL DIVORCE REGISTRATION; MAY 18, 1982; OBIHIRO, HOKKAIDO
離婚届
昭和57年5月18日届出
北海道帯広市長 殿
夫 高島 加寿男
妻 高島 明美
HE MAY HAVE BEEN KIND AT ONE TIME...
...BUT YOU NEED HIM OUT OF YOUR LIFE.
SIGNATURES: KAZUO TAKASHIMA, AKEMI TAKASHIMA
届出人署名押印
夫 高島 加寿男
妻 高島 明美

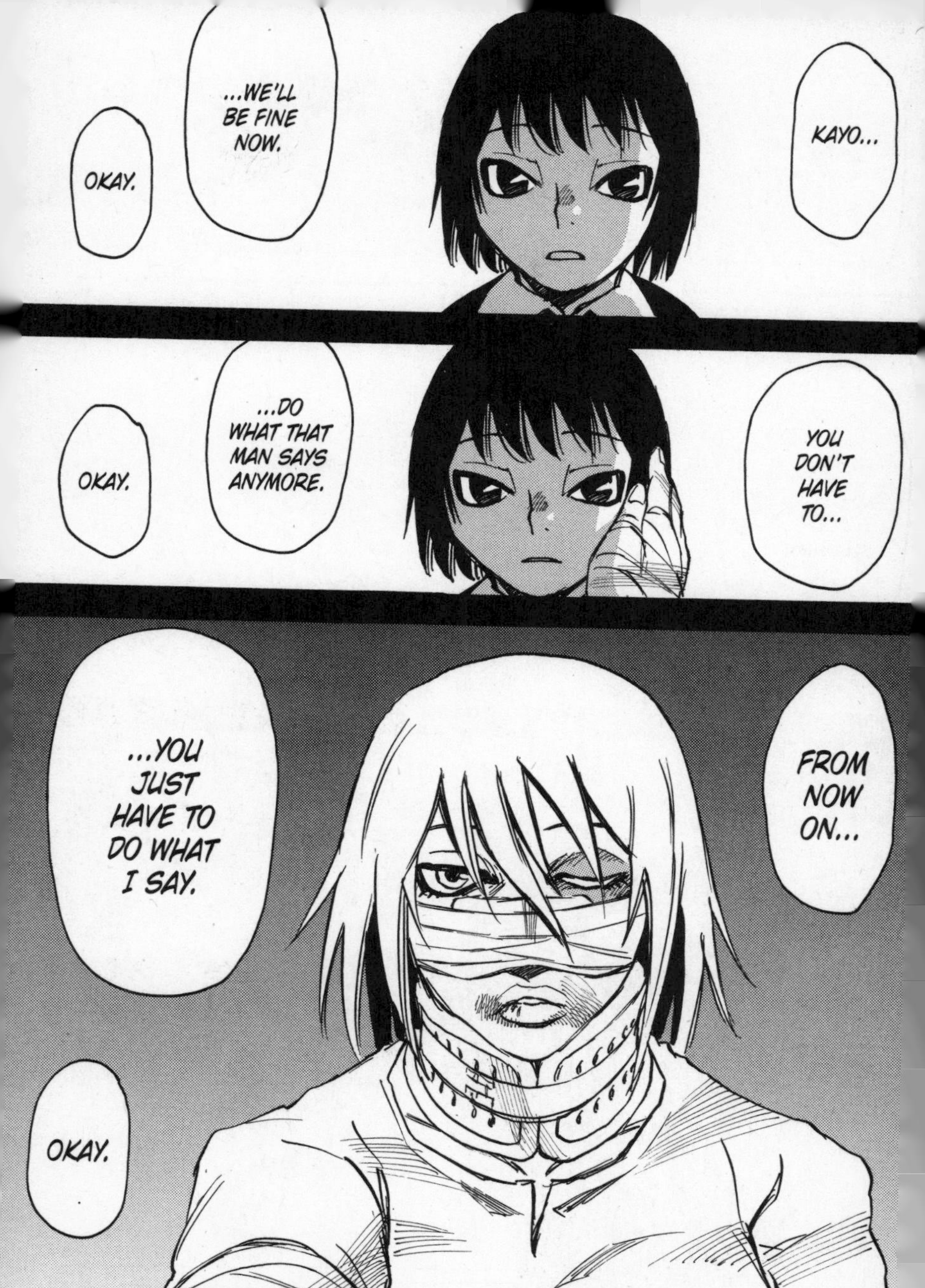
KAYO...
...WE'LL BE FINE NOW.
OKAY.
YOU DON'T HAVE TO...
...DO WHAT THAT MAN SAYS ANYMORE.
OKAY.
FROM NOW ON...
...YOU JUST HAVE TO DO WHAT I SAY.
OKAY.

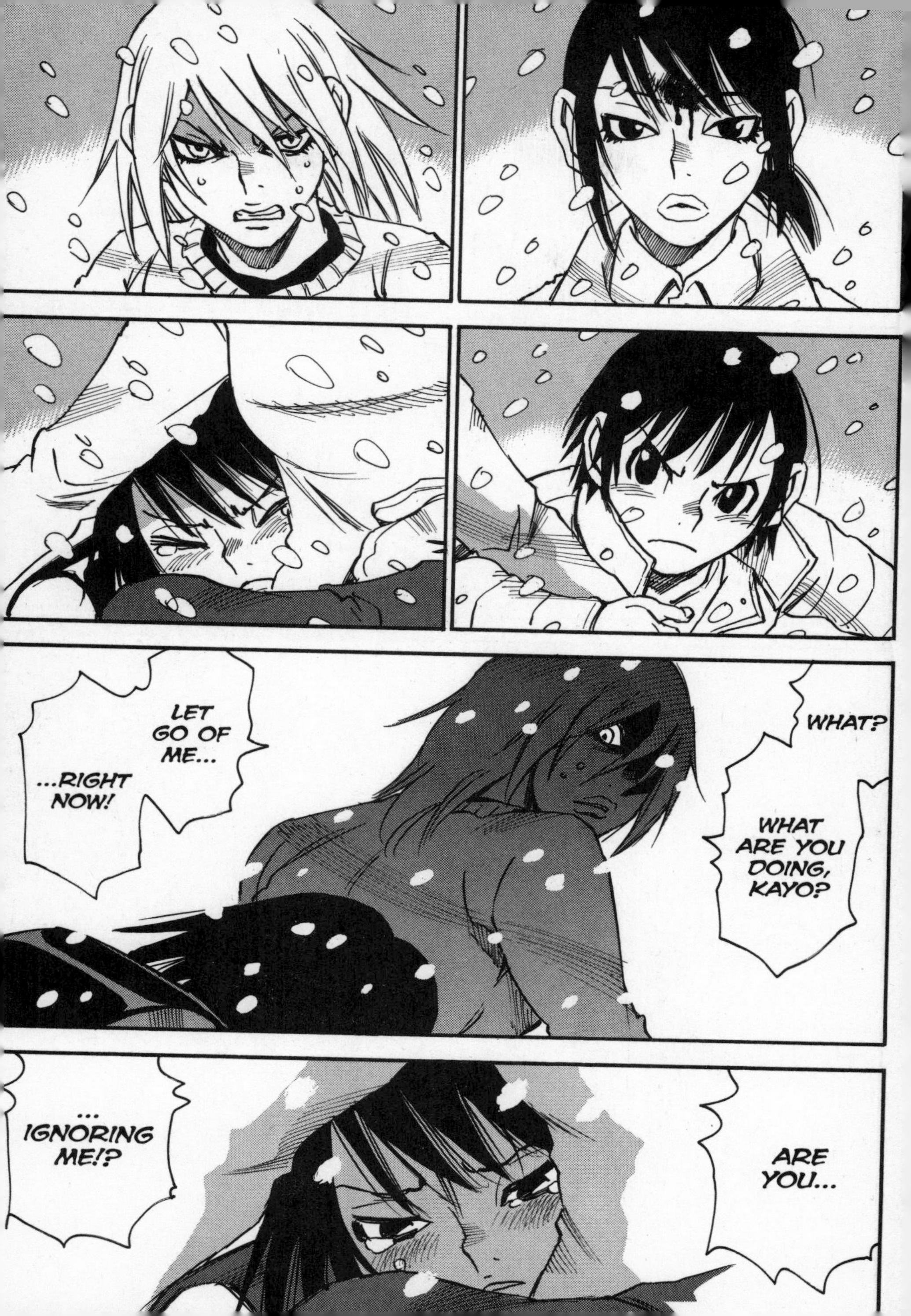
WHAT?
WHAT ARE YOU DOING, KAYO?
LET GO OF ME...
...RIGHT NOW!
ARE YOU...
...IGNORING ME!?

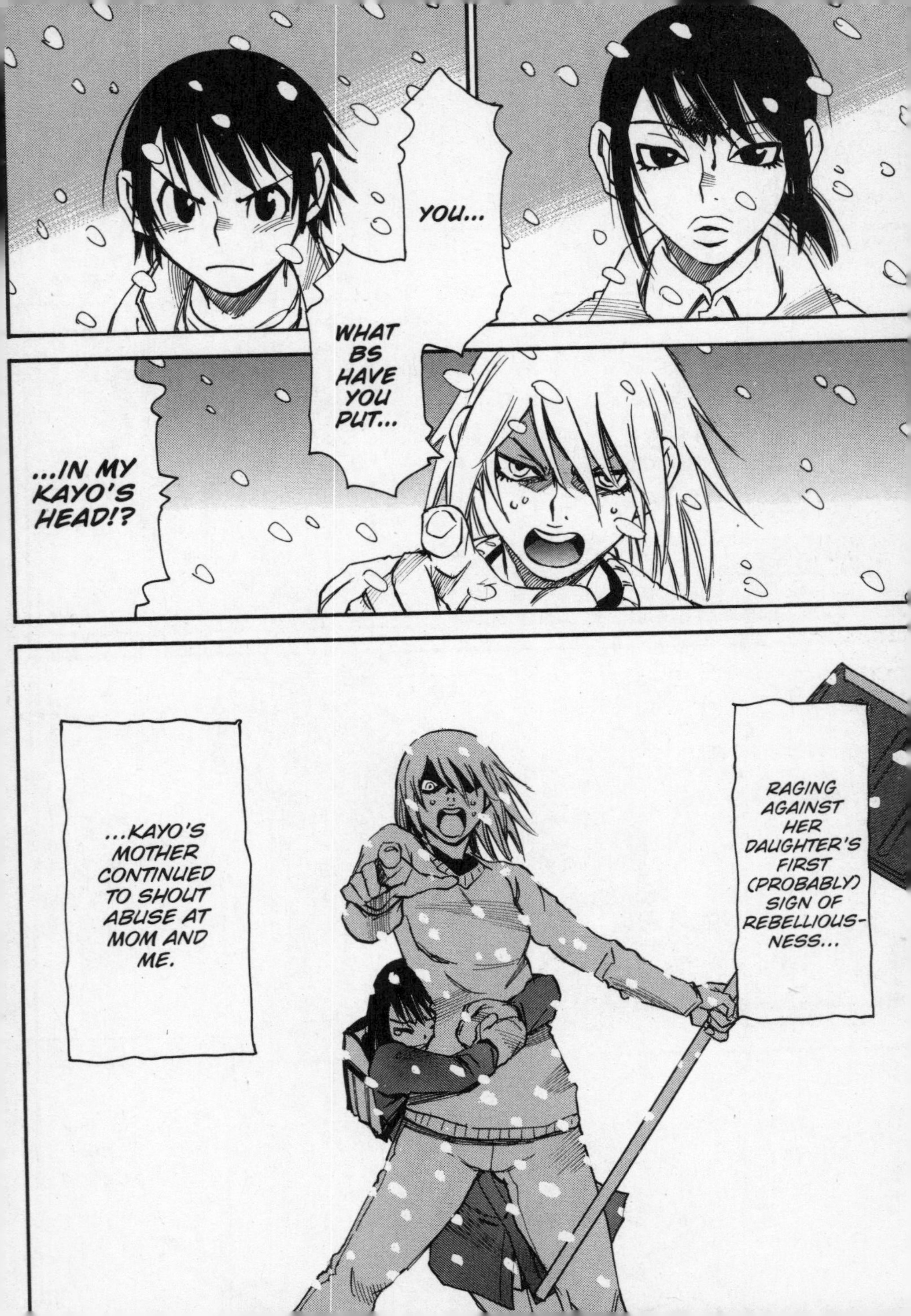
YOU...
WHAT BS HAVE YOU PUT...
...IN MY KAYO'S HEAD!?
RAGING AGAINST HER DAUGHTER'S FIRST (PROBABLY) SIGN OF REBELLIOUS-NESS...
...KAYO'S MOTHER CONTINUED TO SHOUT ABUSE AT MOM AND ME.

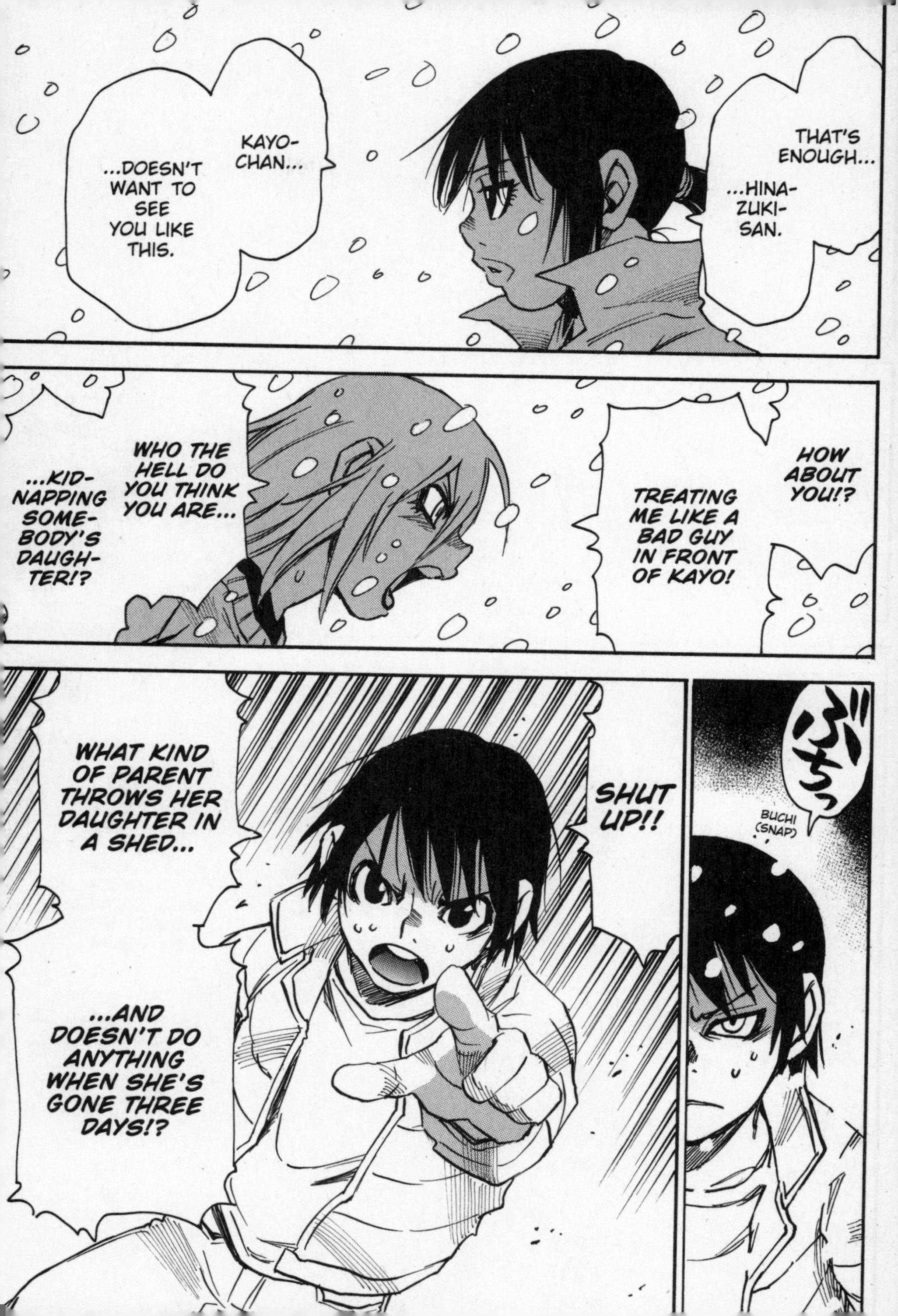
THAT'S ENOUGH... ...HINA-ZUKI-SAN.
KAYO-CHAN... ...DOESN'T WANT TO SEE YOU LIKE THIS.
HOW ABOUT YOU!? TREATING ME LIKE A BAD GUY IN FRONT OF KAYO!
WHO THE HELL DO YOU THINK YOU ARE... ...KID-NAPPING SOME-BODY'S DAUGH-TER!?
ぶちっ
BUCHI (SNAP)
SHUT UP!!
WHAT KIND OF PARENT THROWS HER DAUGHTER IN A SHED...
...AND DOESN'T DO ANYTHING WHEN SHE'S GONE THREE DAYS!?

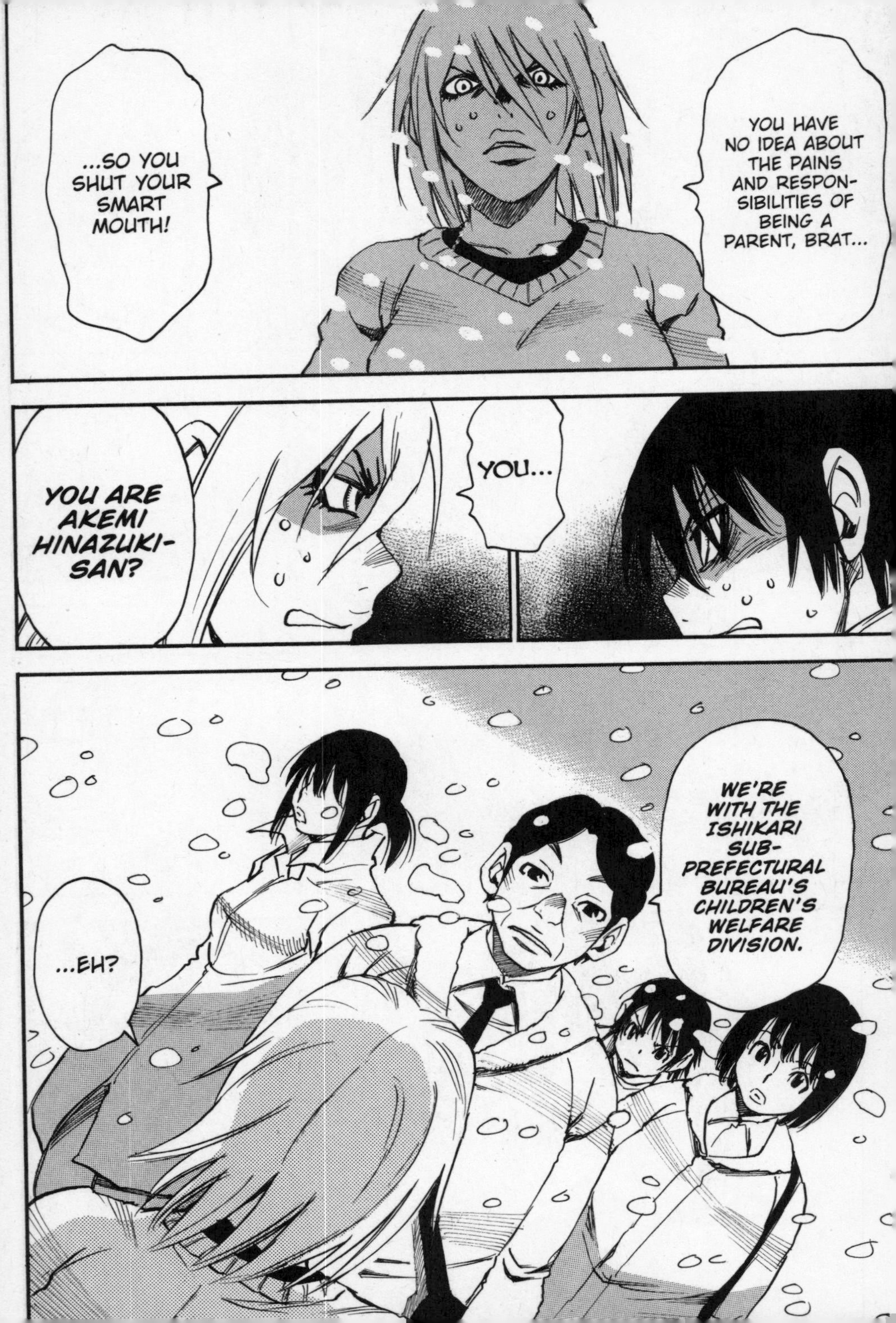
YOU HAVE NO IDEA ABOUT THE PAINS AND RESPONSIBILITIES OF BEING A PARENT, BRAT...
...SO YOU SHUT YOUR SMART MOUTH!
YOU...
YOU ARE AKEMI HINAZUKI-SAN?
WE'RE WITH THE ISHIKARI SUB-PREFECTURAL BUREAU'S CHILDREN'S WELFARE DIVISION.
...EH?

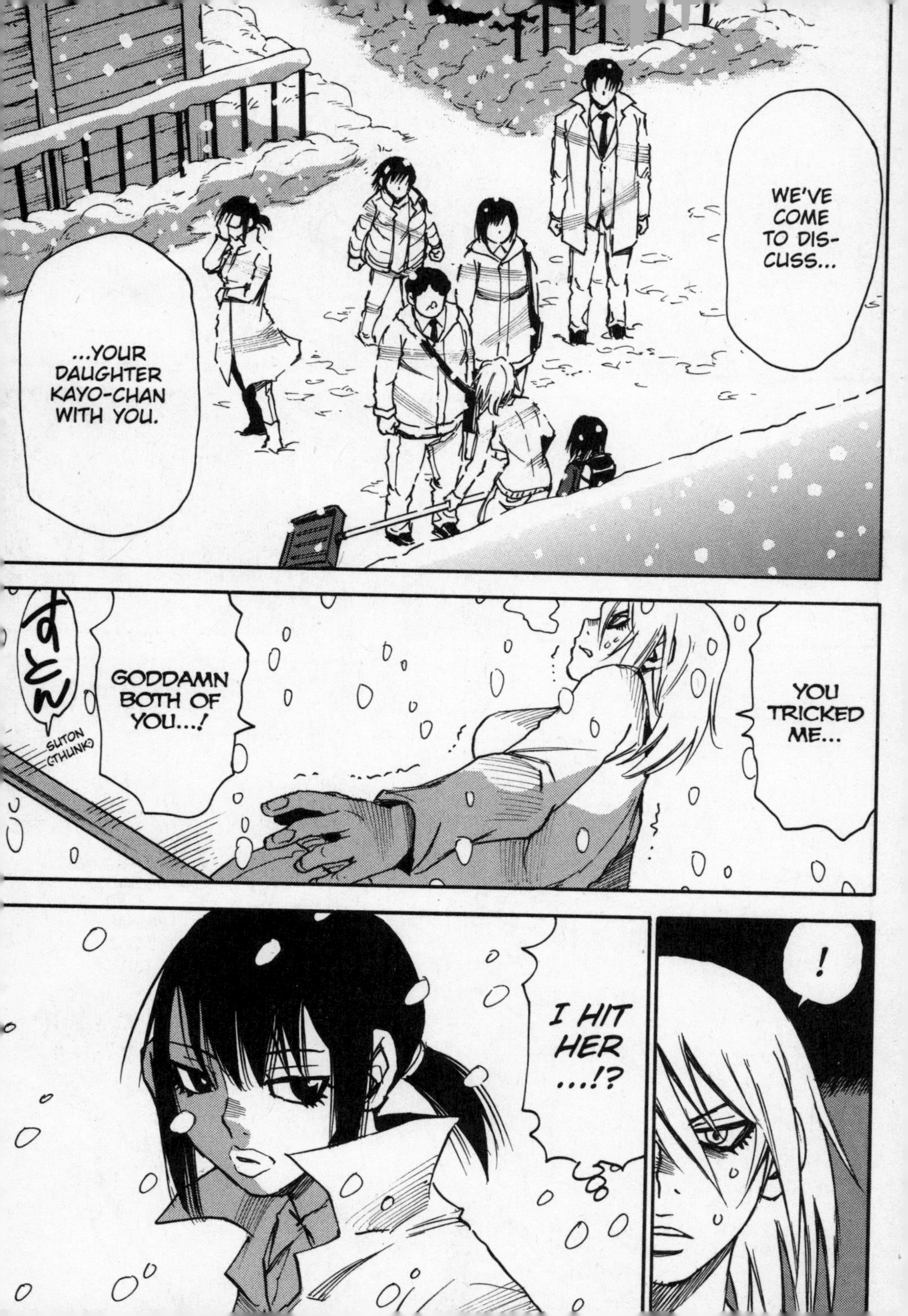
WE'VE COME TO DIS-CUSS...
...YOUR DAUGHTER KAYO-CHAN WITH YOU.
YOU TRICKED ME...
GODDAMN BOTH OF YOU...!
すとん
SUTON (THUNK)
!
I HIT HER ...!?

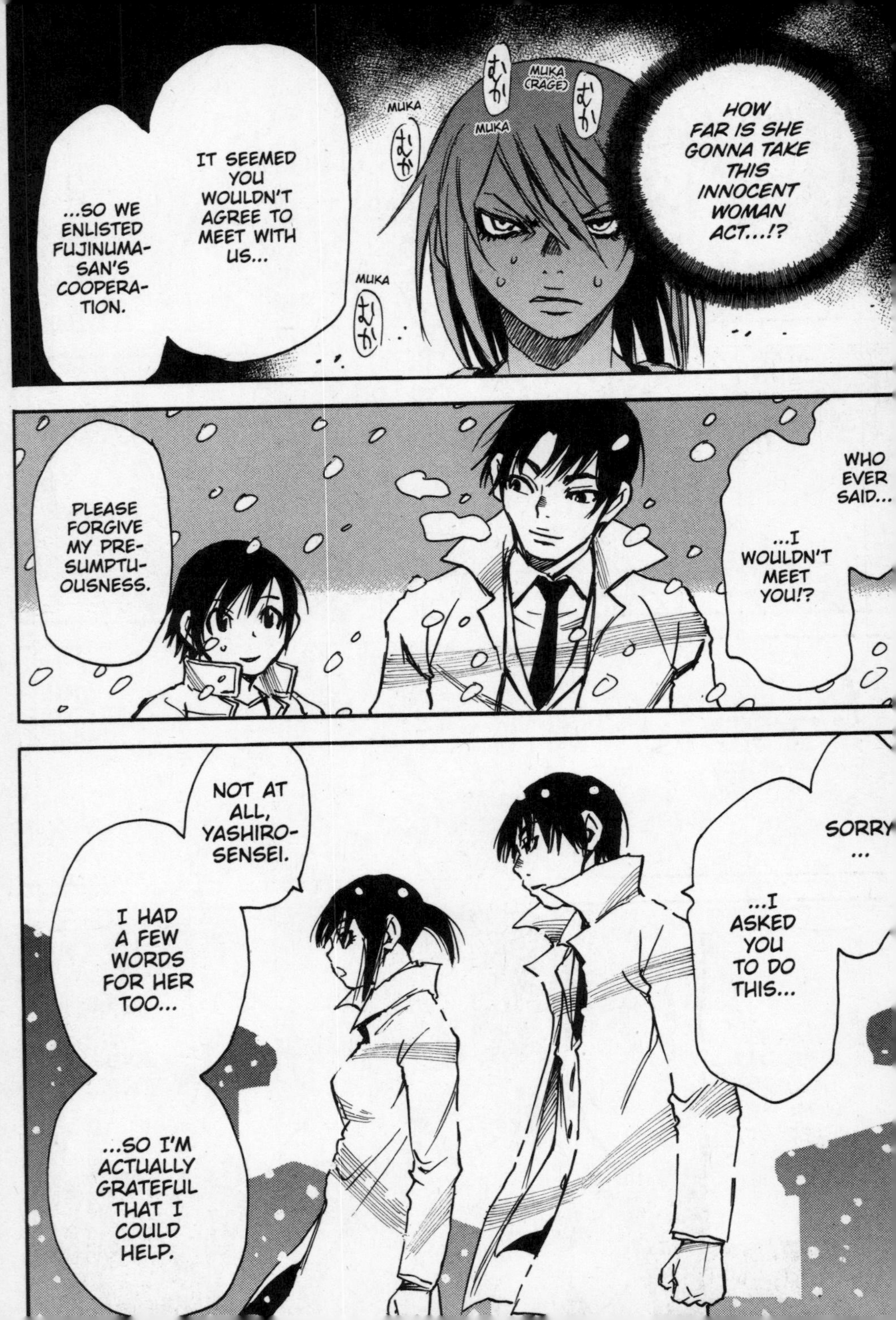
HOW FAR IS SHE GONNA TAKE THIS INNOCENT WOMAN ACT...!?
むか
MUKA (RAGE)
むか
MUKA
むか
MUKA
むか
MUKA
IT SEEMED YOU WOULDN'T AGREE TO MEET WITH US...
...SO WE ENLISTED FUJINUMA-SAN'S COOPERATION.
WHO EVER SAID...
...I WOULDN'T MEET YOU!?
PLEASE FORGIVE MY PRESUMPTUOUSNESS.
SORRY...
...I ASKED YOU TO DO THIS...
NOT AT ALL, YASHIRO-SENSEI.
I HAD A FEW WORDS FOR HER TOO...
...SO I'M ACTUALLY GRATEFUL THAT I COULD HELP.

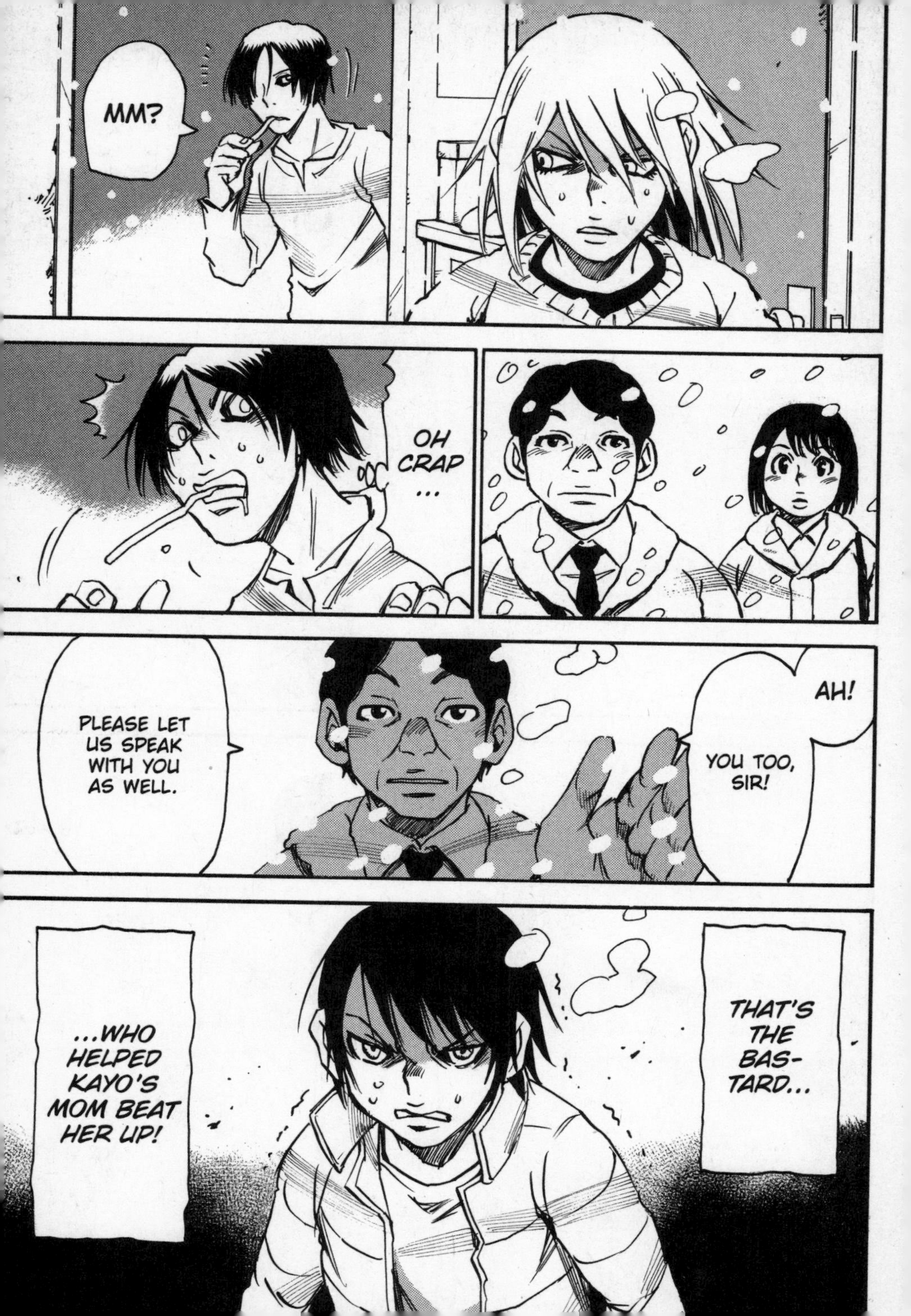
MM?
OH CRAP ...
AH! YOU TOO, SIR!
PLEASE LET US SPEAK WITH YOU AS WELL.
THAT'S THE BAS-TARD...
...WHO HELPED KAYO'S MOM BEAT HER UP!

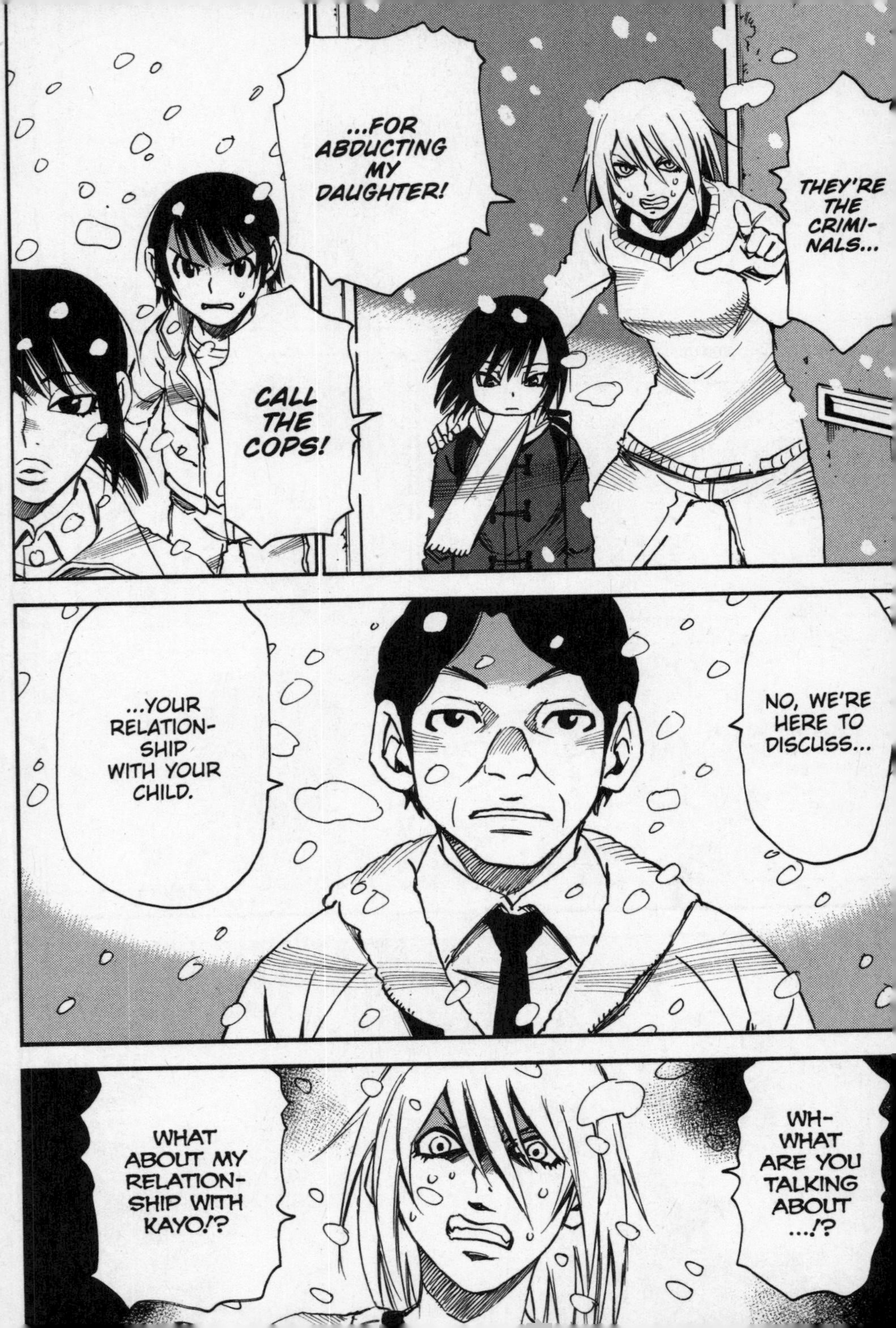
THEY'RE THE CRIMINALS...
...FOR ABDUCTING MY DAUGHTER!
CALL THE COPS!
NO, WE'RE HERE TO DISCUSS...
...YOUR RELATIONSHIP WITH YOUR CHILD.
WH-WHAT ARE YOU TALKING ABOUT ...!?
WHAT ABOUT MY RELATIONSHIP WITH KAYO!?

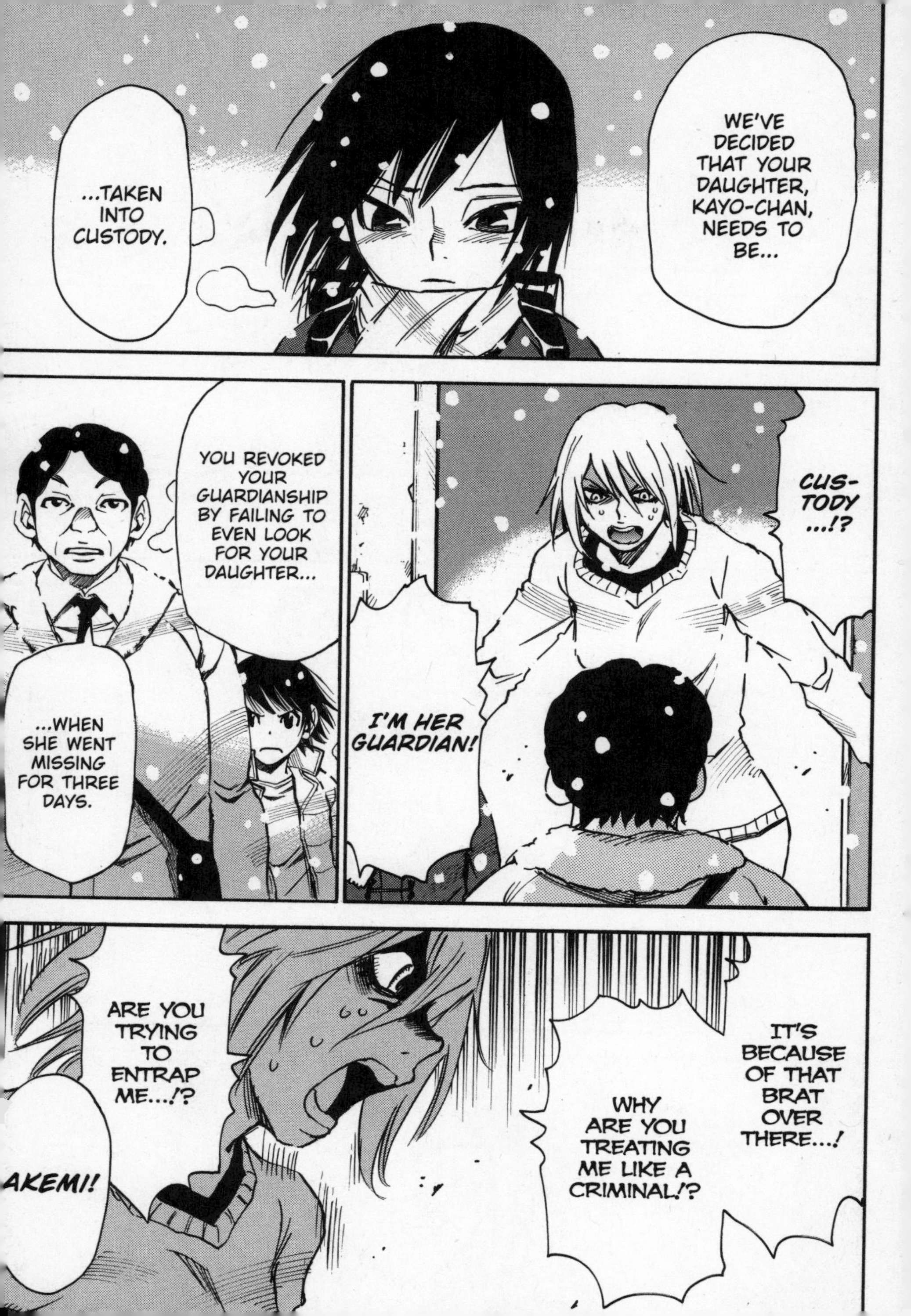
WE'VE DECIDED THAT YOUR DAUGHTER, KAYO-CHAN, NEEDS TO BE...
...TAKEN INTO CUSTODY.
CUS-TODY ...!?
I'M HER GUARDIAN!
YOU REVOKED YOUR GUARDIANSHIP BY FAILING TO EVEN LOOK FOR YOUR DAUGHTER...
...WHEN SHE WENT MISSING FOR THREE DAYS.
IT'S BECAUSE OF THAT BRAT OVER THERE...!
WHY ARE YOU TREATING ME LIKE A CRIMINAL!?
ARE YOU TRYING TO ENTRAP ME...!?
AKEMI!

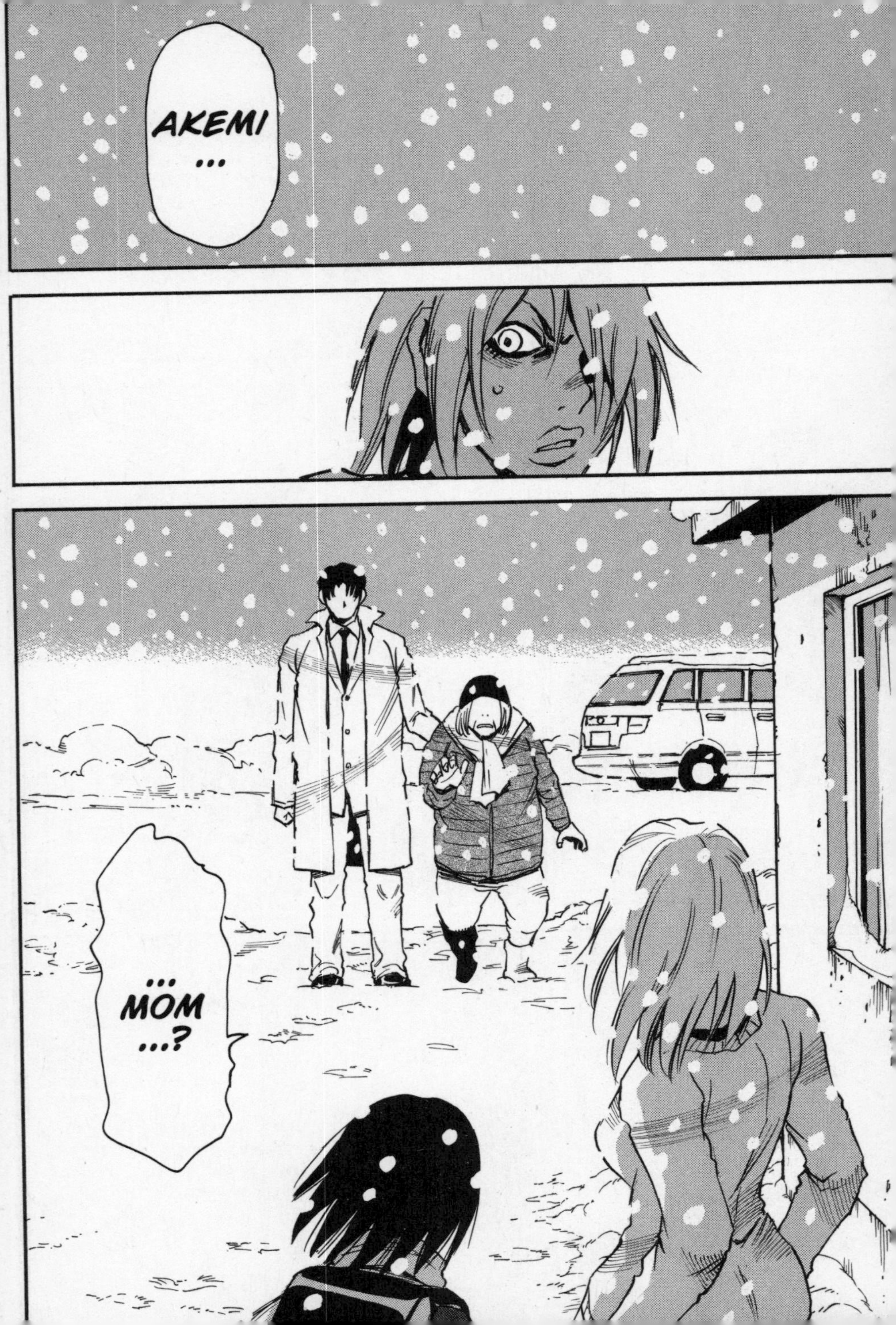
AKEMI
...
... MOM ...?

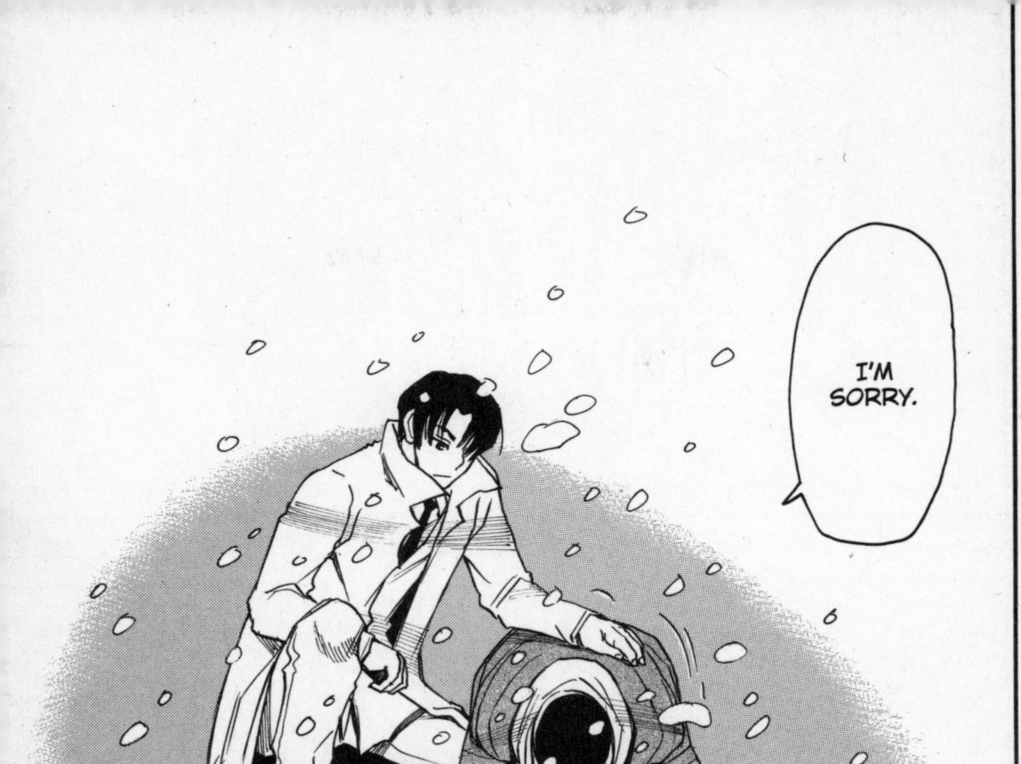
I'M SORRY.
ZA (CHFF)
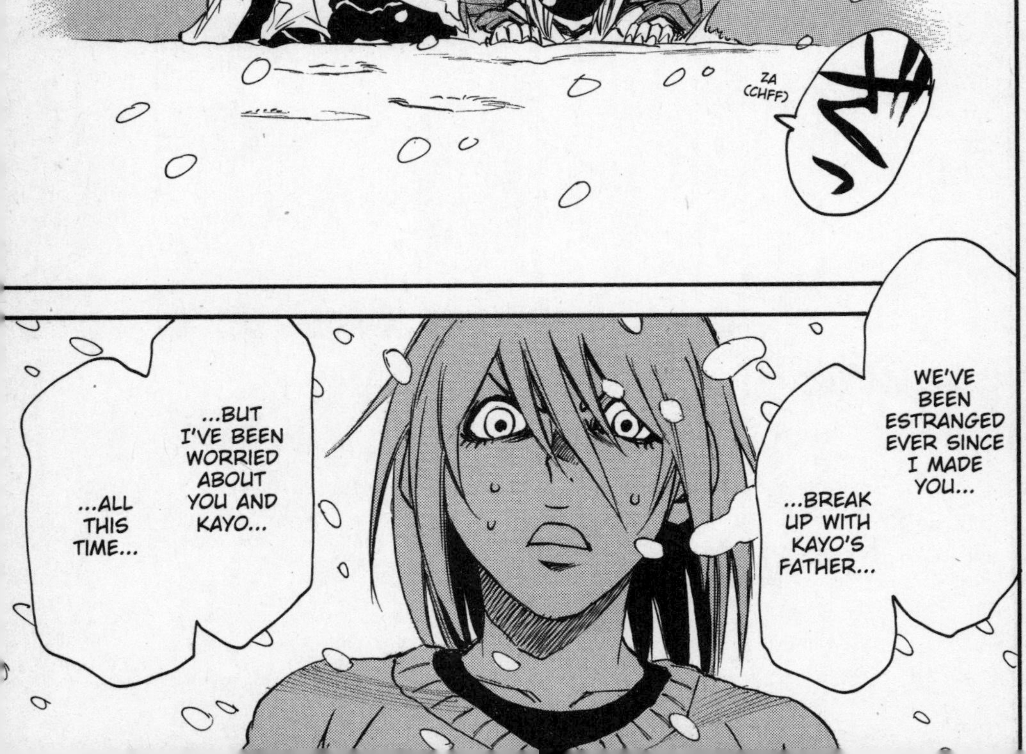
WE'VE BEEN ESTRANGED EVER SINCE I MADE YOU...
...BREAK UP WITH KAYO'S FATHER...
...BUT I'VE BEEN WORRIED ABOUT YOU AND KAYO...
...ALL THIS TIME...

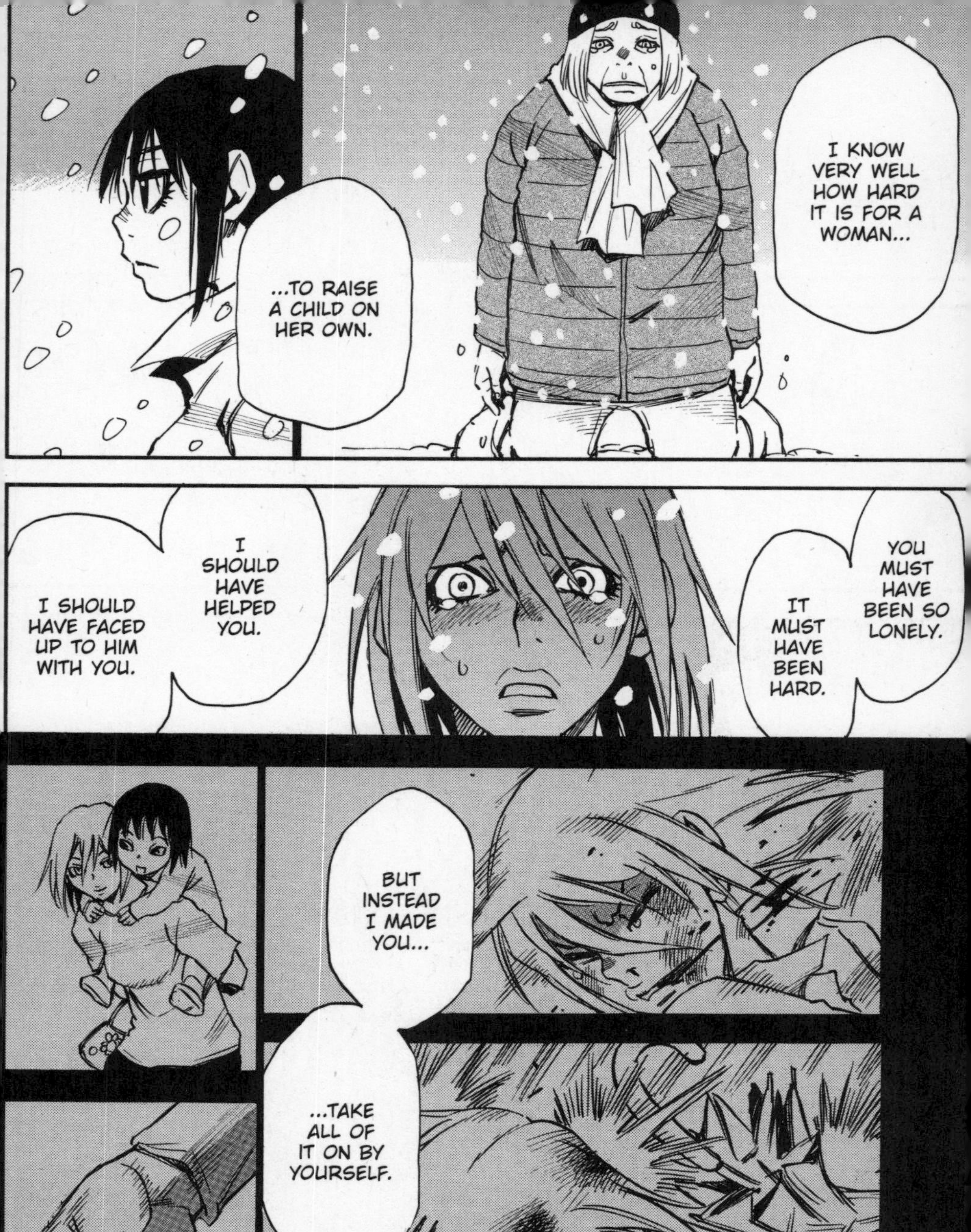
I KNOW VERY WELL HOW HARD IT IS FOR A WOMAN...
...TO RAISE A CHILD ON HER OWN.
YOU MUST HAVE BEEN SO LONELY.
IT MUST HAVE BEEN HARD.
I SHOULD HAVE HELPED YOU.
I SHOULD HAVE FACED UP TO HIM WITH YOU.
BUT INSTEAD I MADE YOU...
...TAKE ALL OF IT ON BY YOURSELF.

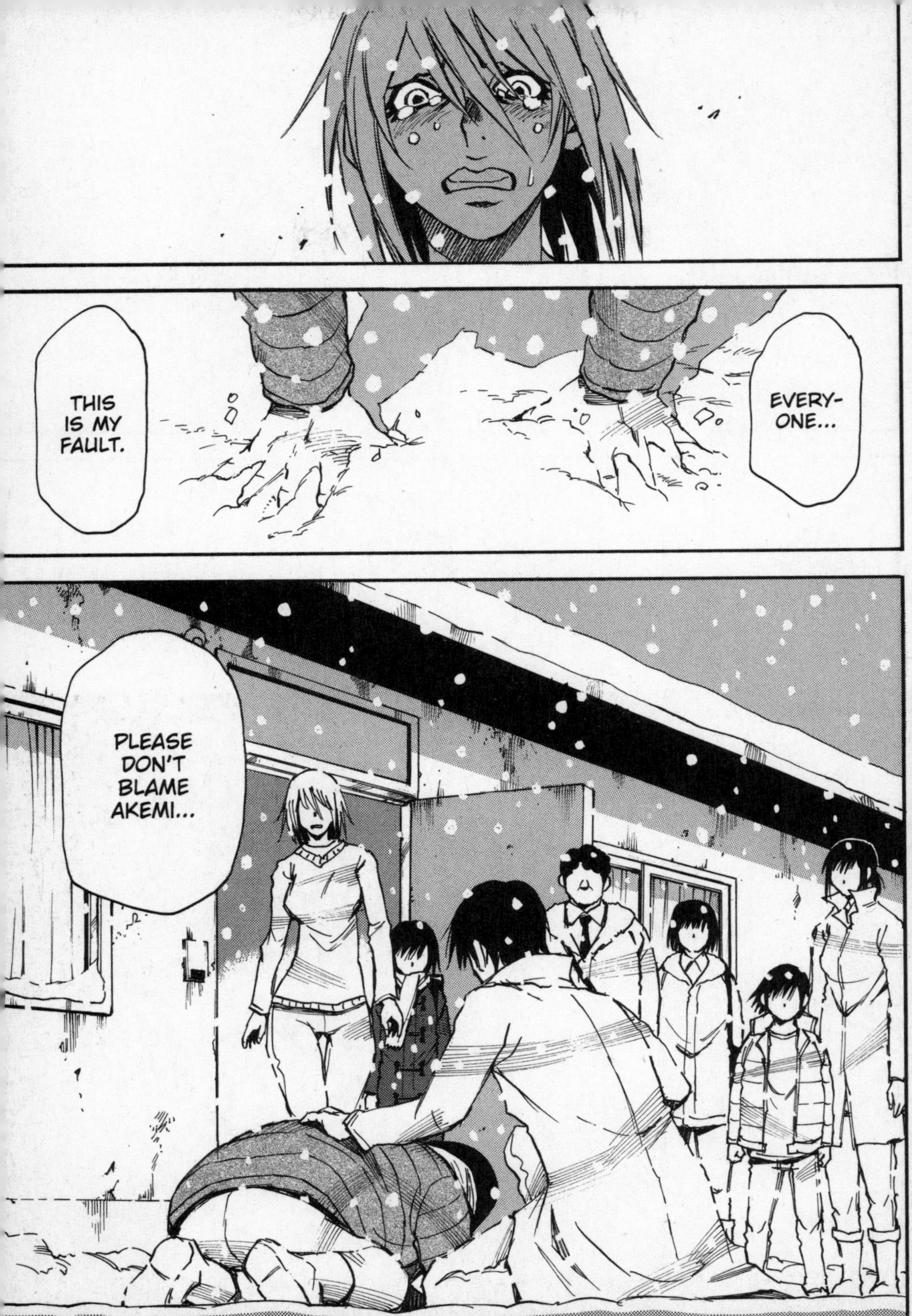
EVERY-ONE...
THIS IS MY FAULT.
PLEASE DON'T BLAME AKEMI...

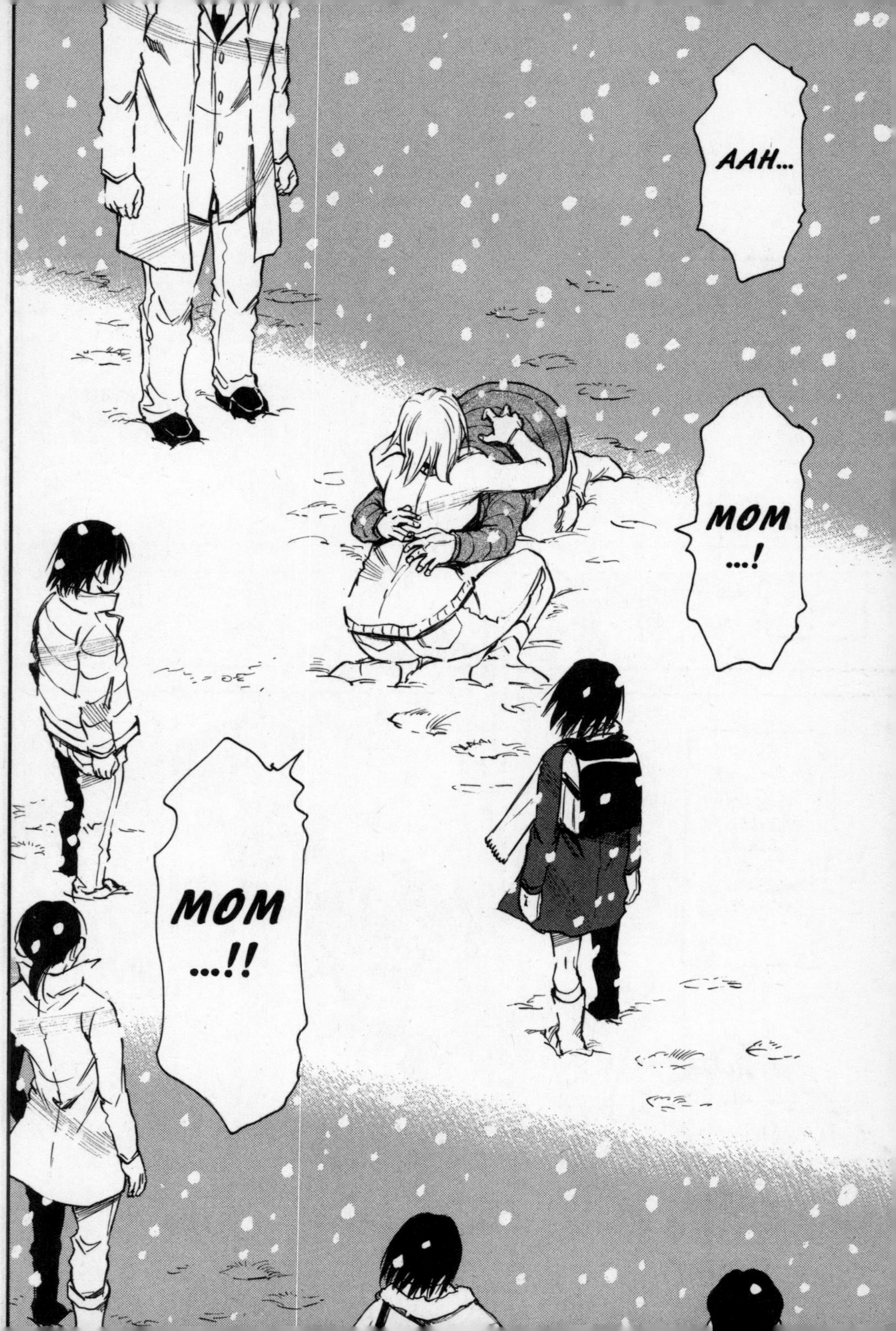
AAH...
MOM ...!
MOM ...!!

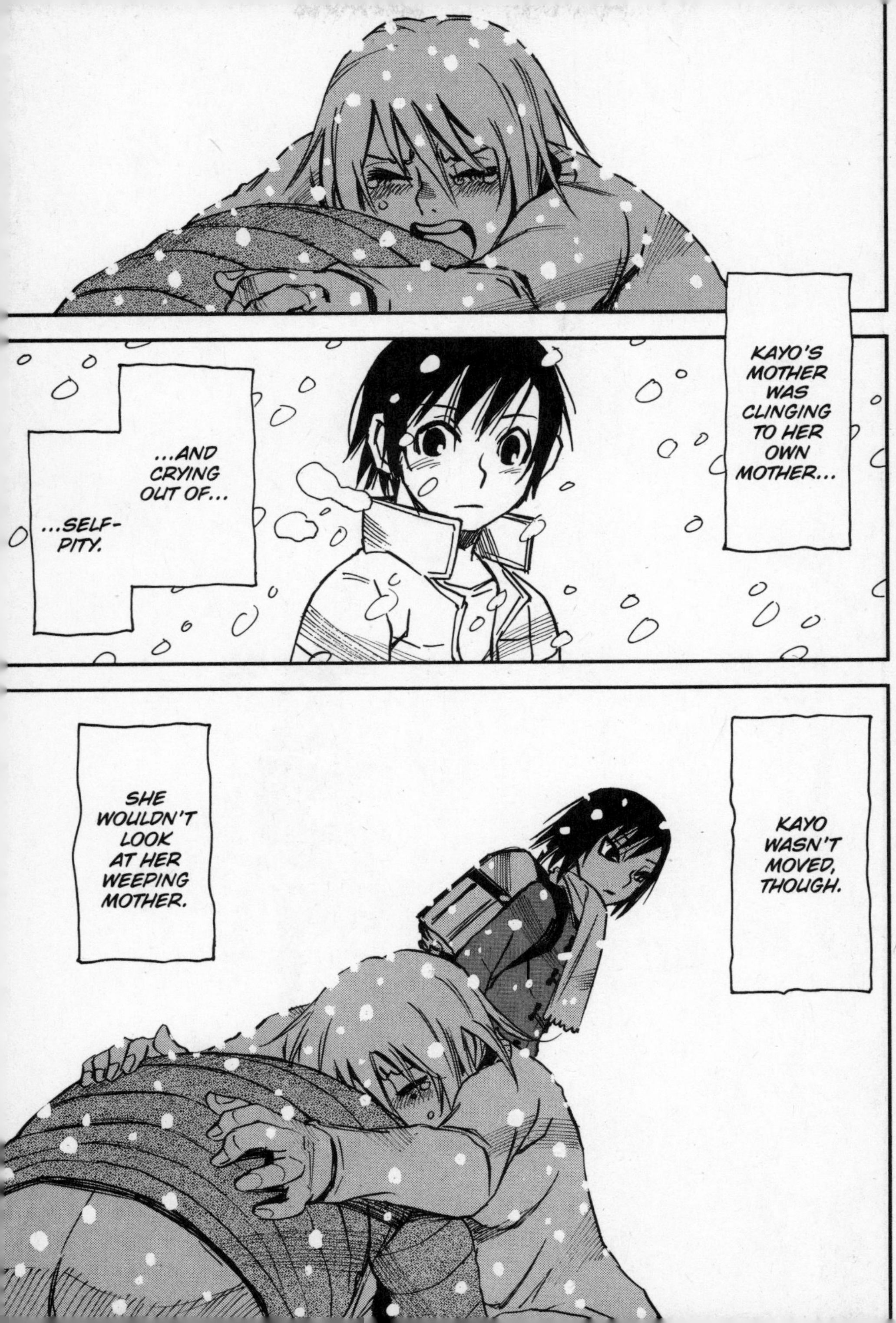
KAYO'S MOTHER WAS CLINGING TO HER OWN MOTHER...
...AND CRYING OUT OF...
...SELF-PITY.
KAYO WASN'T MOVED, THOUGH.
SHE WOULDN'T LOOK AT HER WEEPING MOTHER.

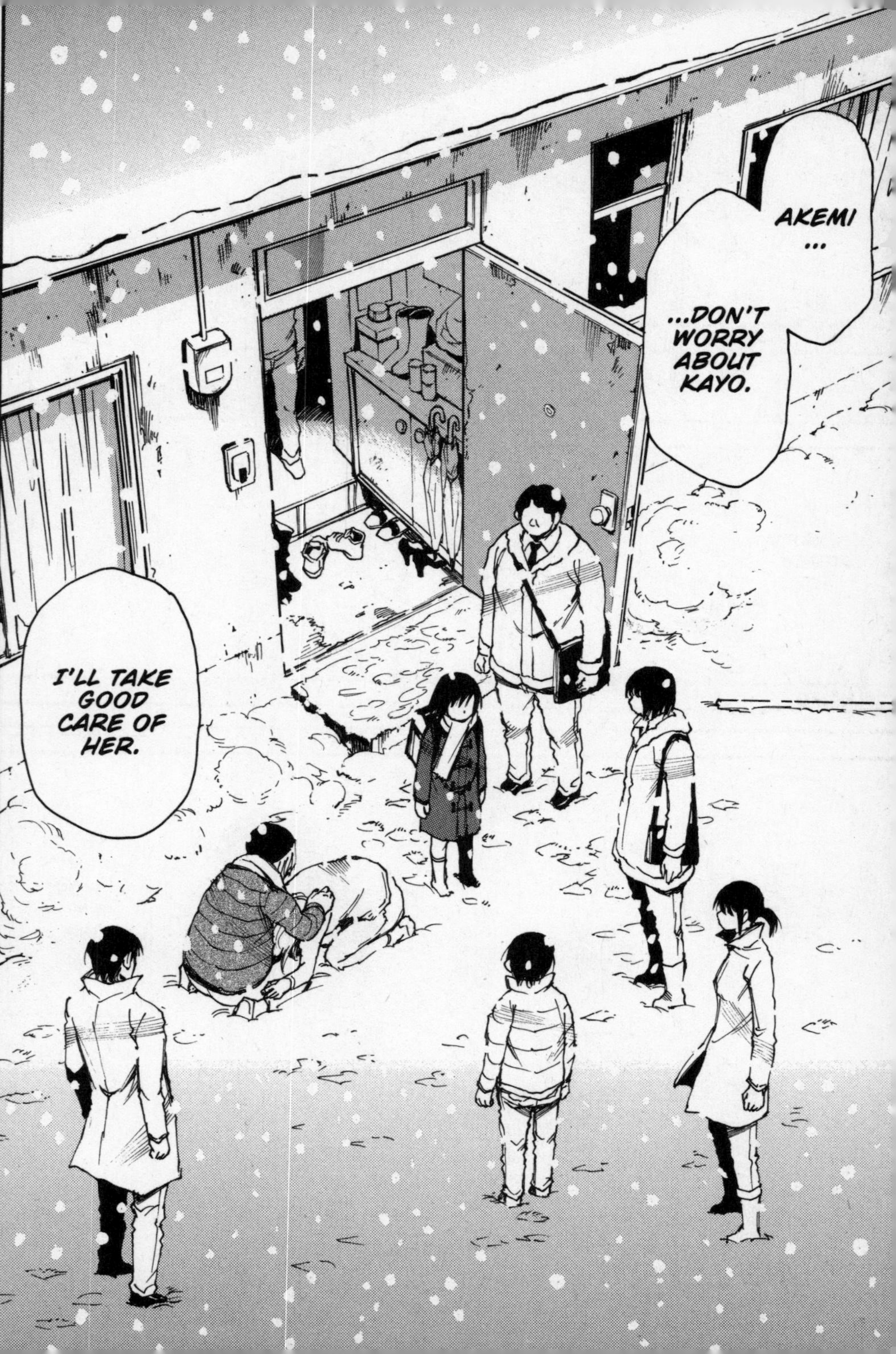
AKEMI ...
...DON'T WORRY ABOUT KAYO.
I'LL TAKE GOOD CARE OF HER.

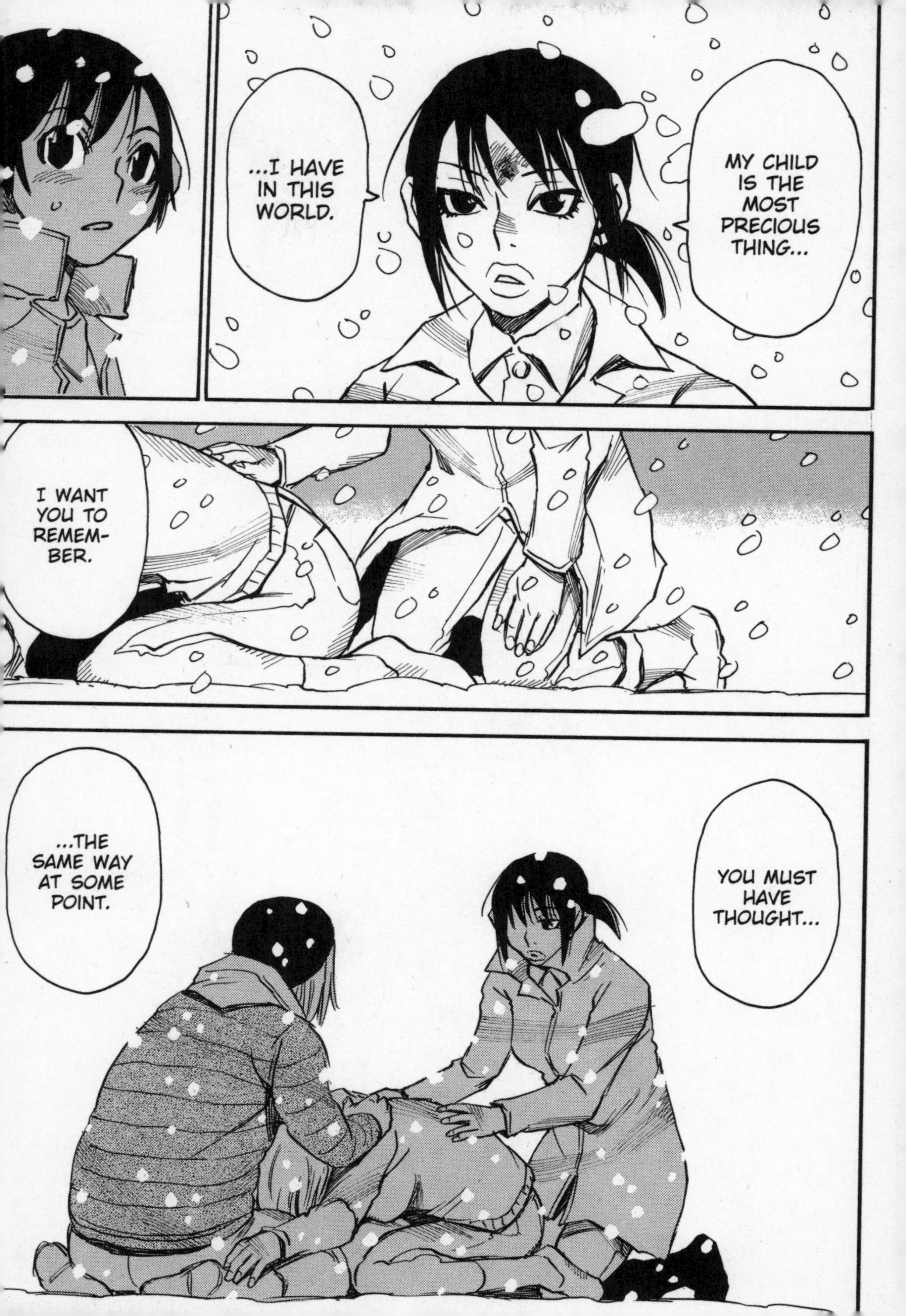
MY CHILD IS THE MOST PRECIOUS THING...
...I HAVE IN THIS WORLD.
I WANT YOU TO REMEMBER.
YOU MUST HAVE THOUGHT...
...THE SAME WAY AT SOME POINT.

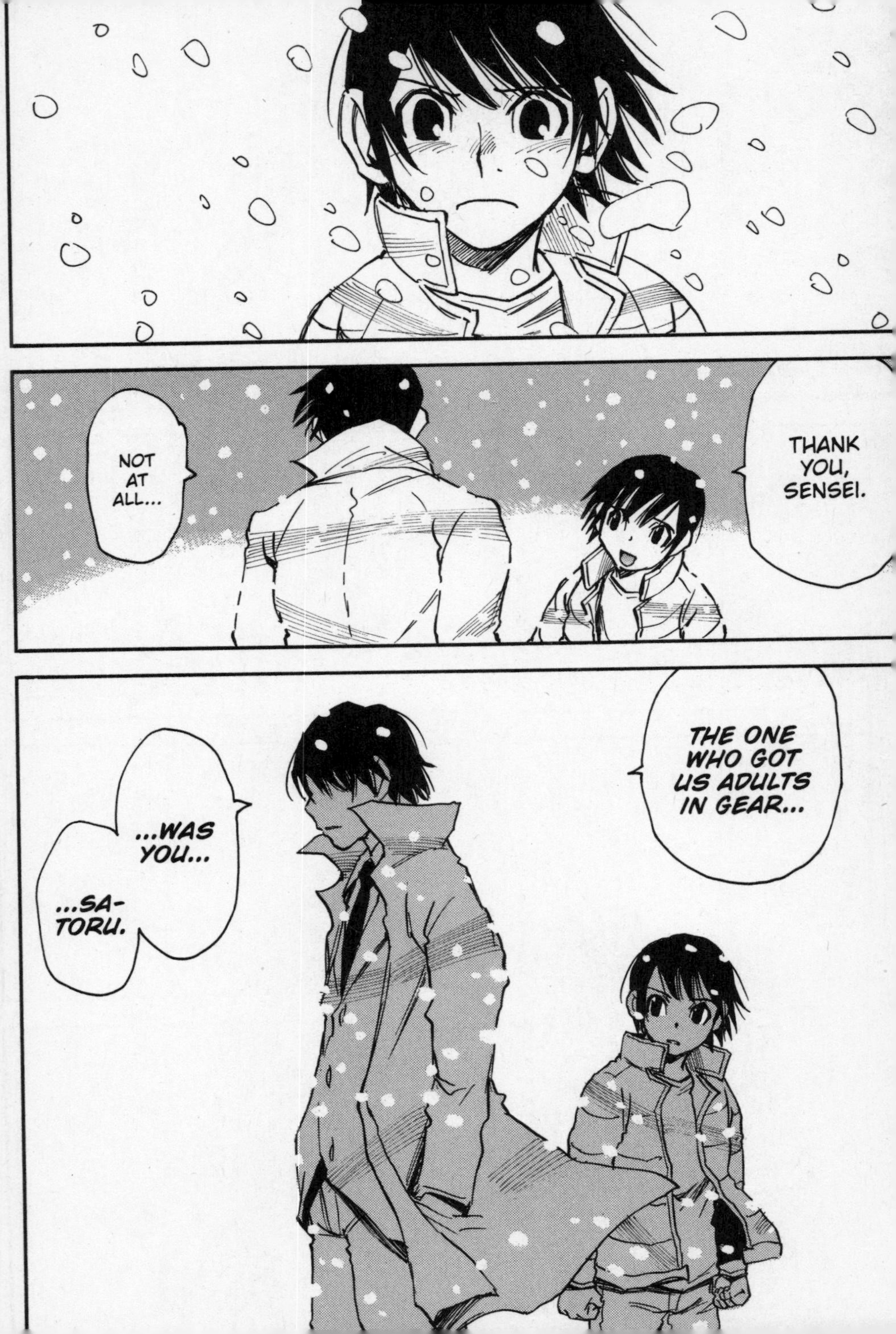
THANK YOU, SENSEI.
NOT AT ALL...
THE ONE WHO GOT US ADULTS IN GEAR...
...WAS YOU...
...SA-TORU.

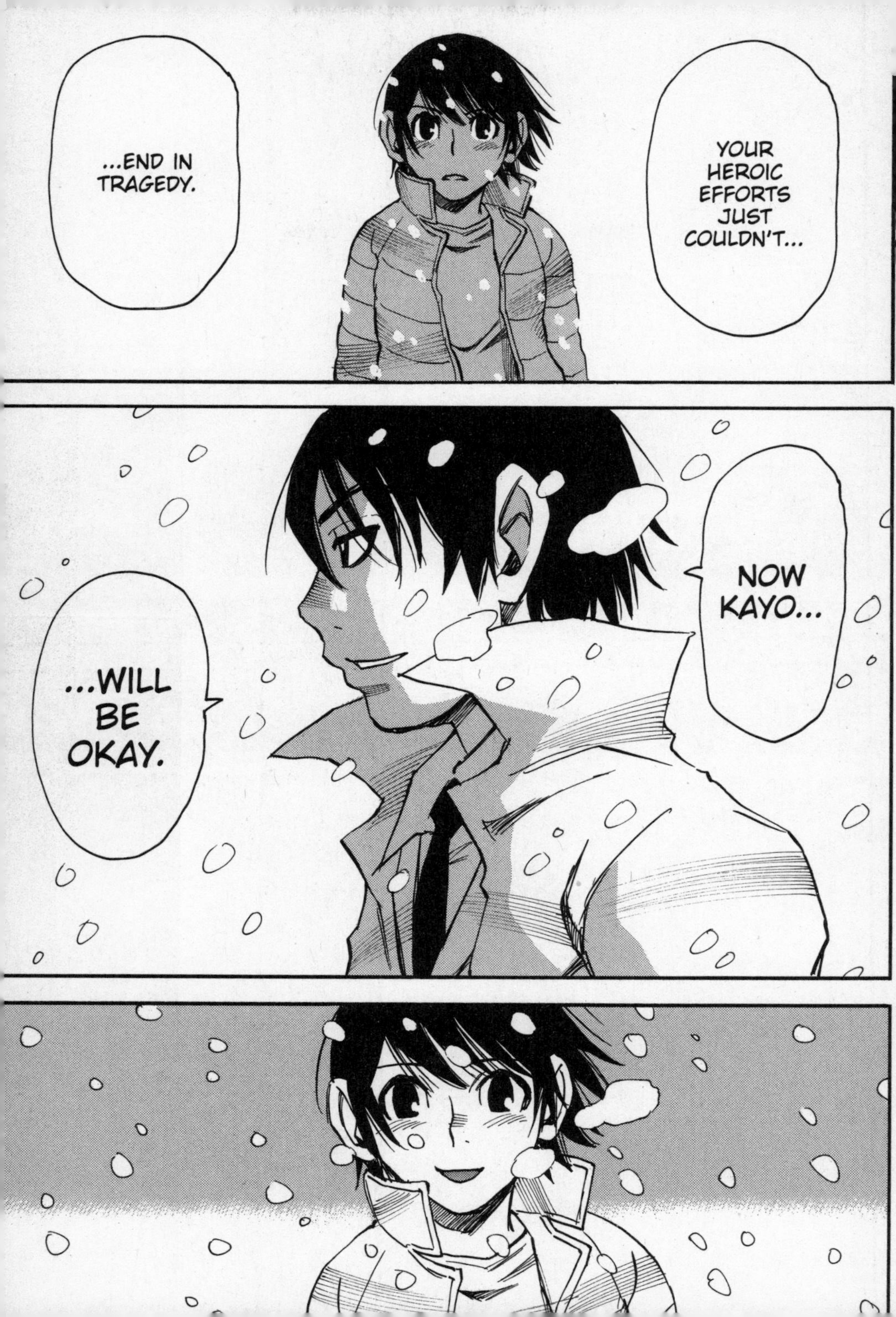
YOUR HEROIC EFFORTS JUST COULDN'T...
...END IN TRAGEDY.
NOW KAYO...
...WILL BE OKAY.

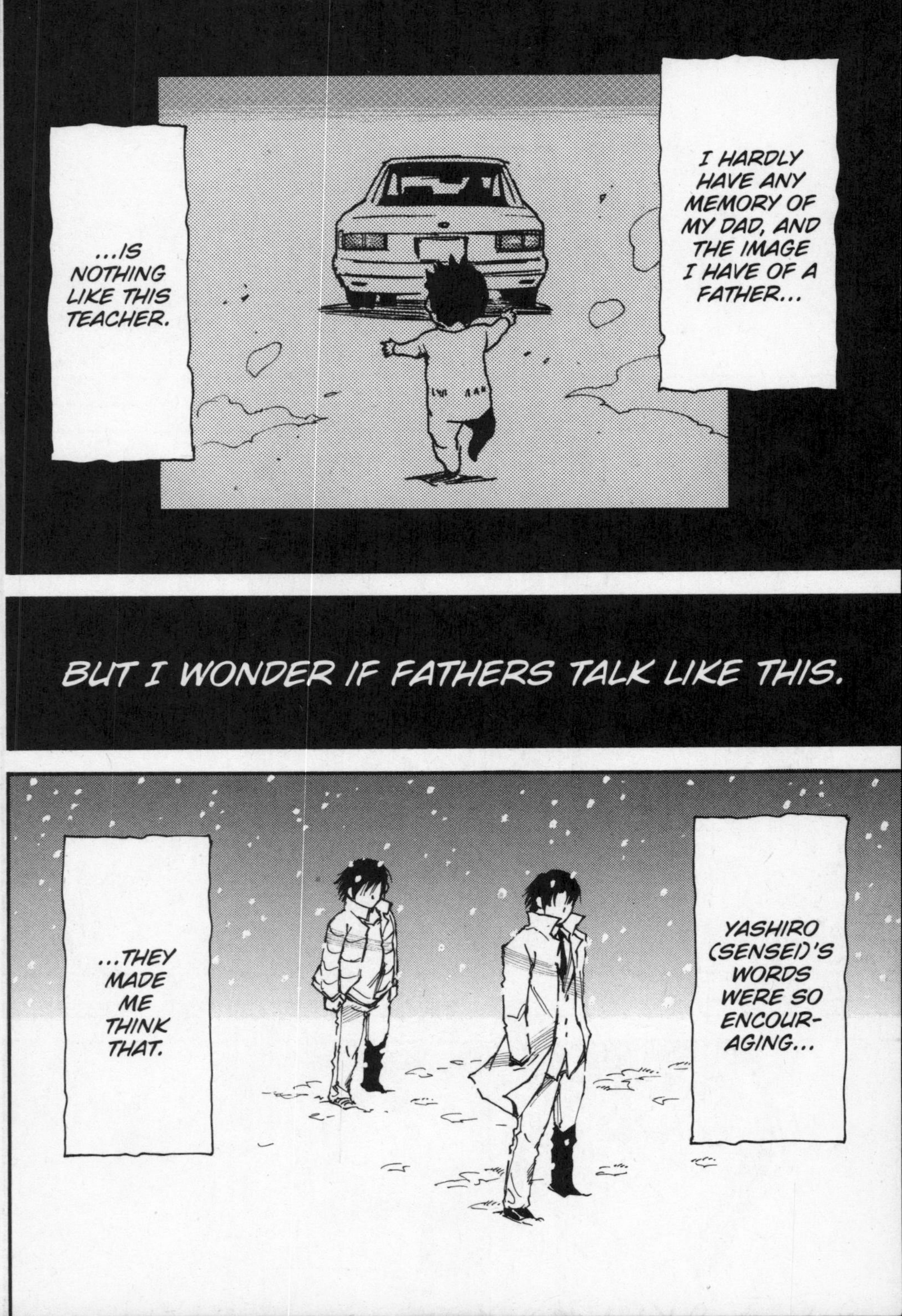
I HARDLY HAVE ANY MEMORY OF MY DAD, AND THE IMAGE I HAVE OF A FATHER...
...IS NOTHING LIKE THIS TEACHER.
BUT I WONDER IF FATHERS TALK LIKE THIS.
YASHIRO (SENSEI)'S WORDS WERE SO ENCOUR-AGING...
...THEY MADE ME THINK THAT.

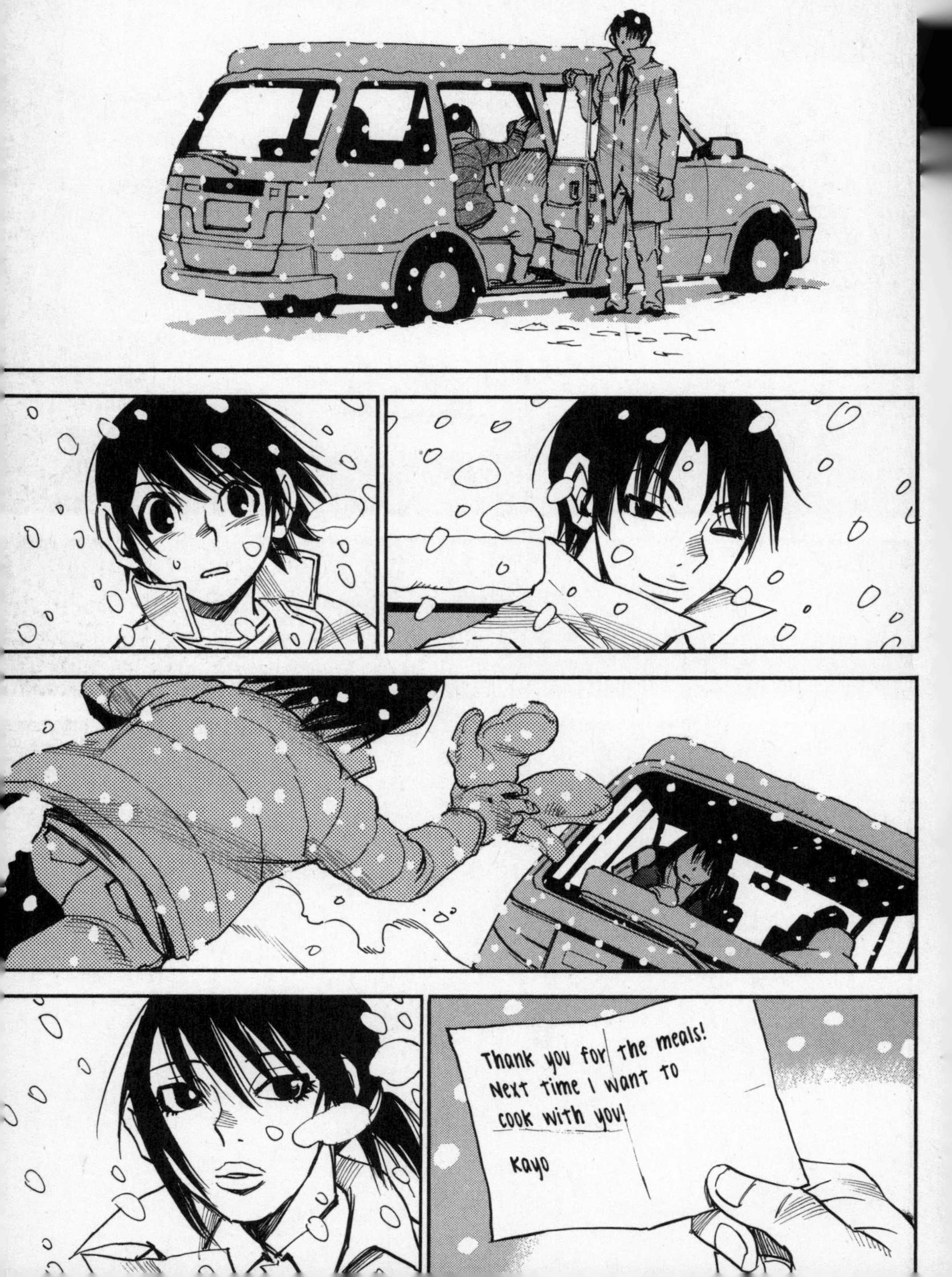
Thank you for the meals!
Next time I want to
cook with you!
Kayo

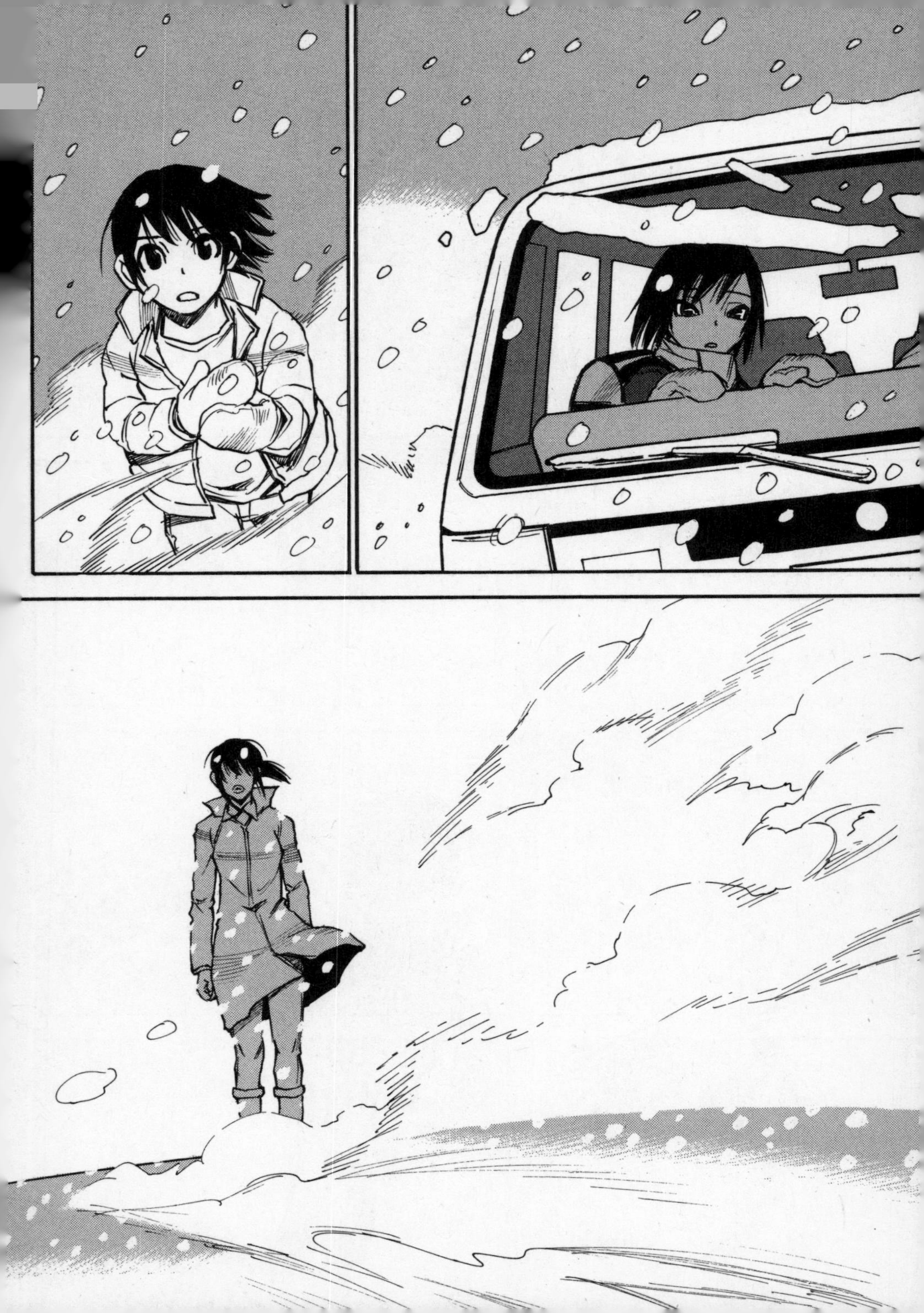

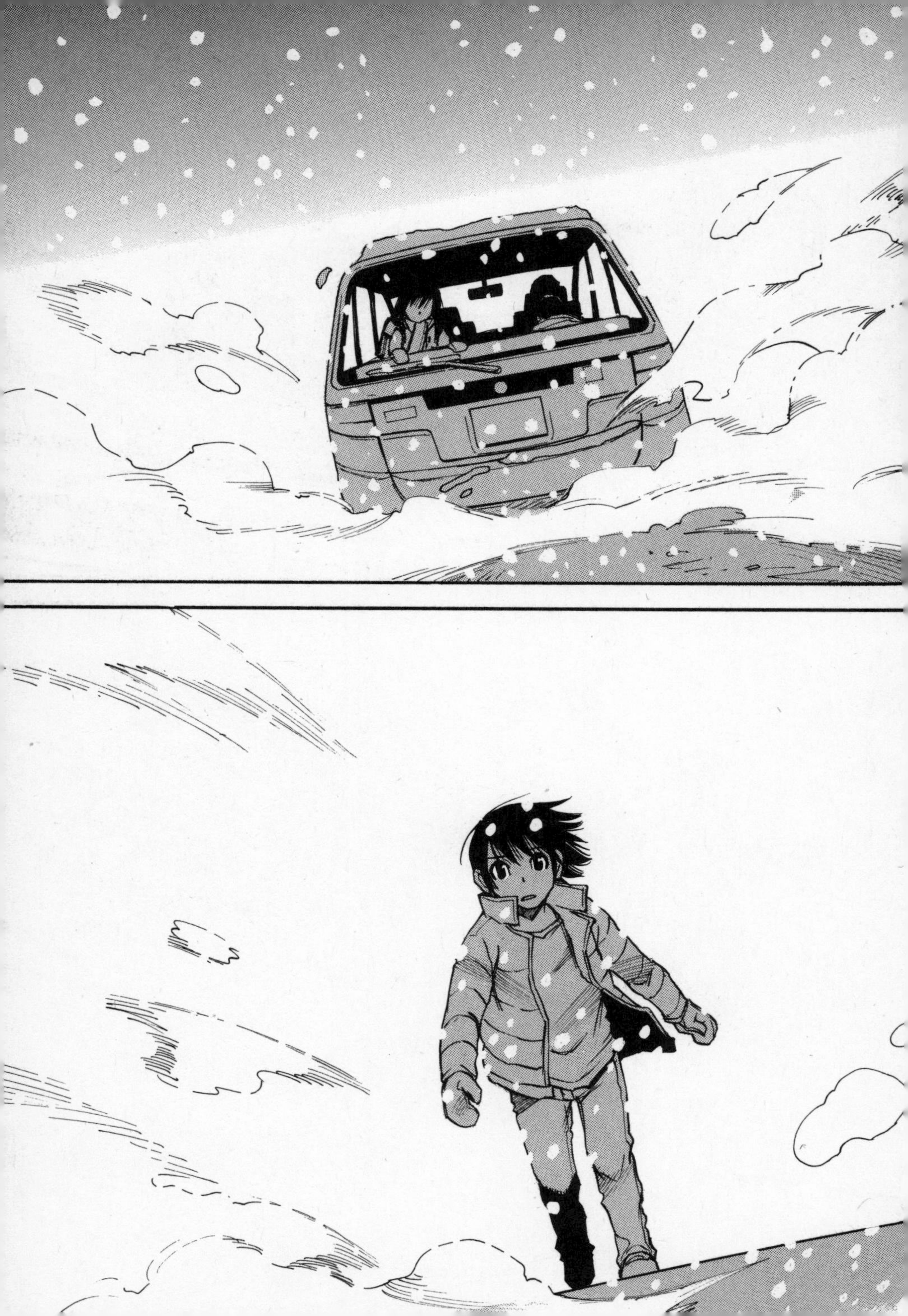

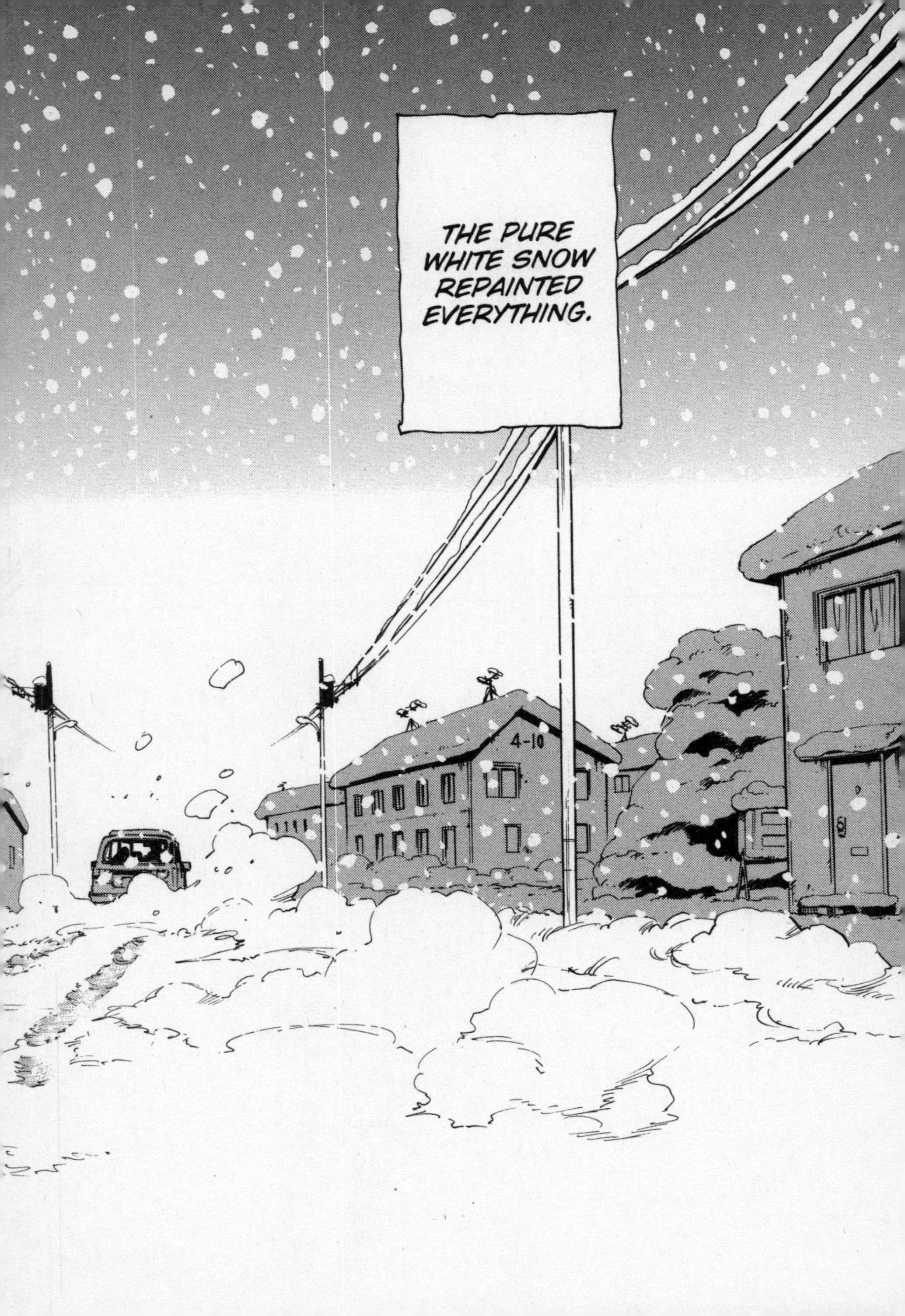
THE PURE WHITE SNOW REPAINTED EVERYTHING.
4-10

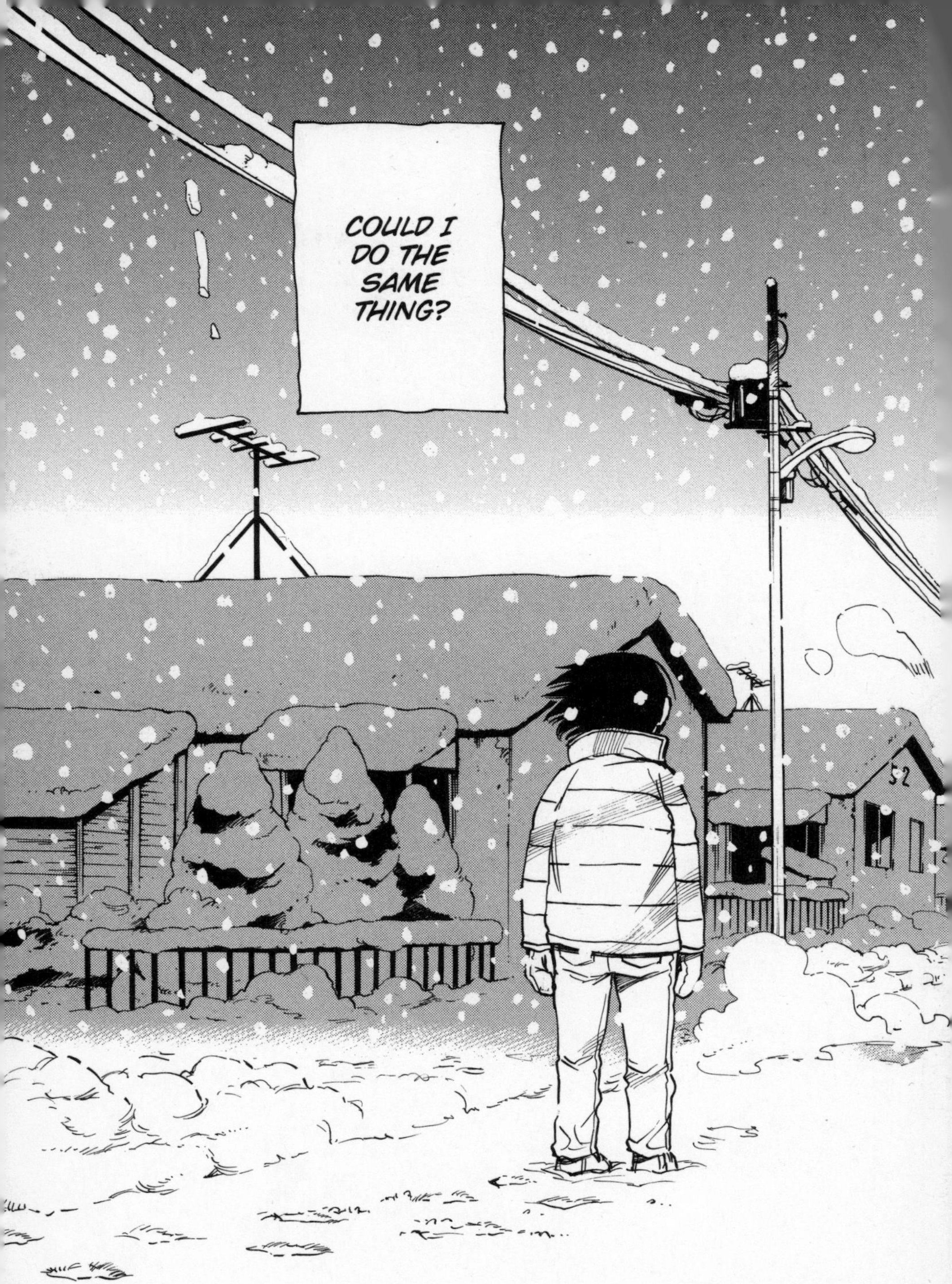
COULD I DO THE SAME THING?
52

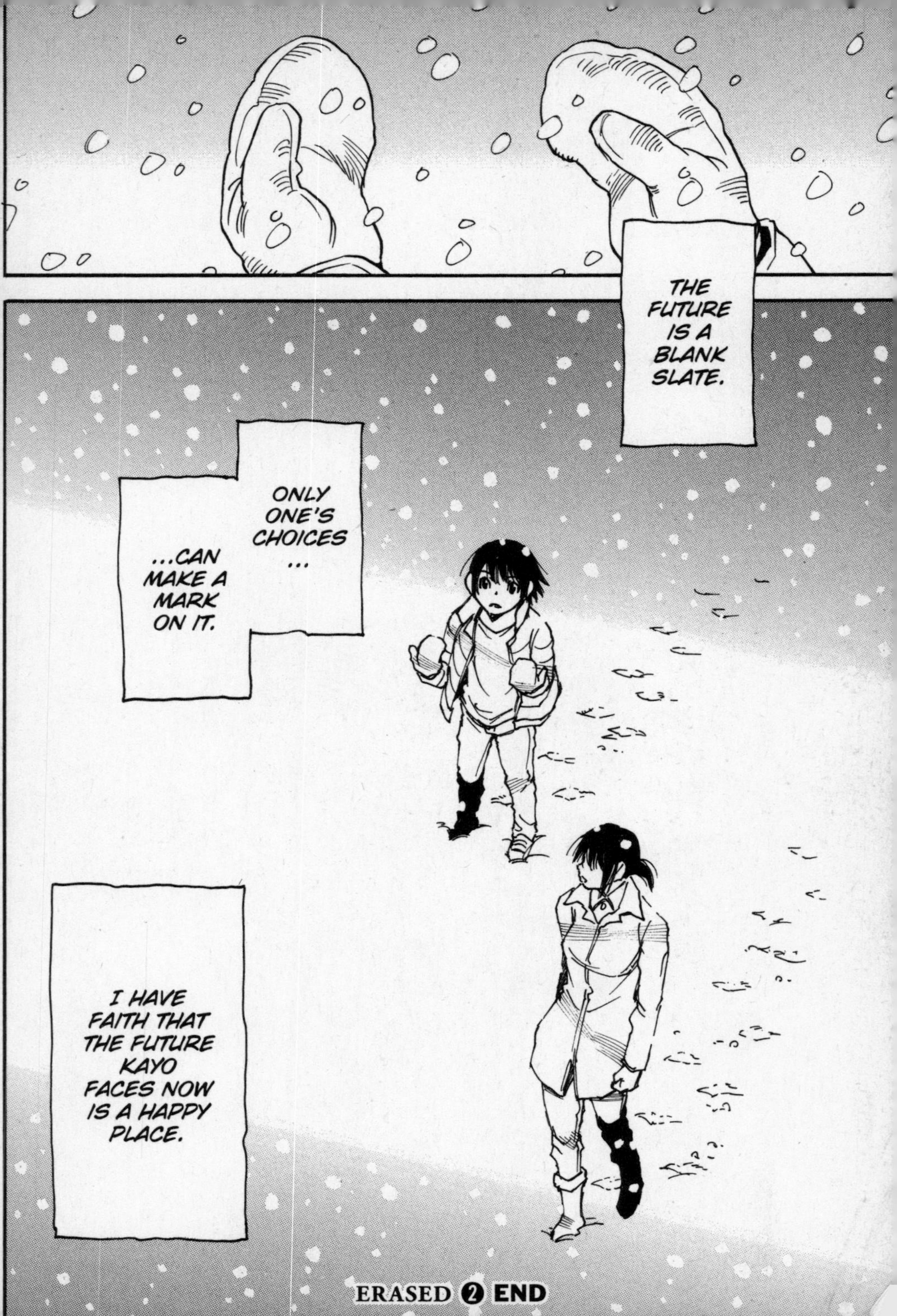
THE FUTURE IS A BLANK SLATE.
ONLY ONE'S CHOICES...
...CAN MAKE A MARK ON IT.
I HAVE FAITH THAT THE FUTURE KAYO FACES NOW IS A HAPPY PLACE.
ERASED 2 END

STAFF

Kei Sanbe

Yoichiro Tomita
Manami 18-years-old
Zukku Ozaki
Kouji Kikuta

Keishi Kanesada
Houwa Toda

BOOK DESIGN
Yukio Hoshino
VOLARE inc.

EDITOR
Tsunenori Matsumiya

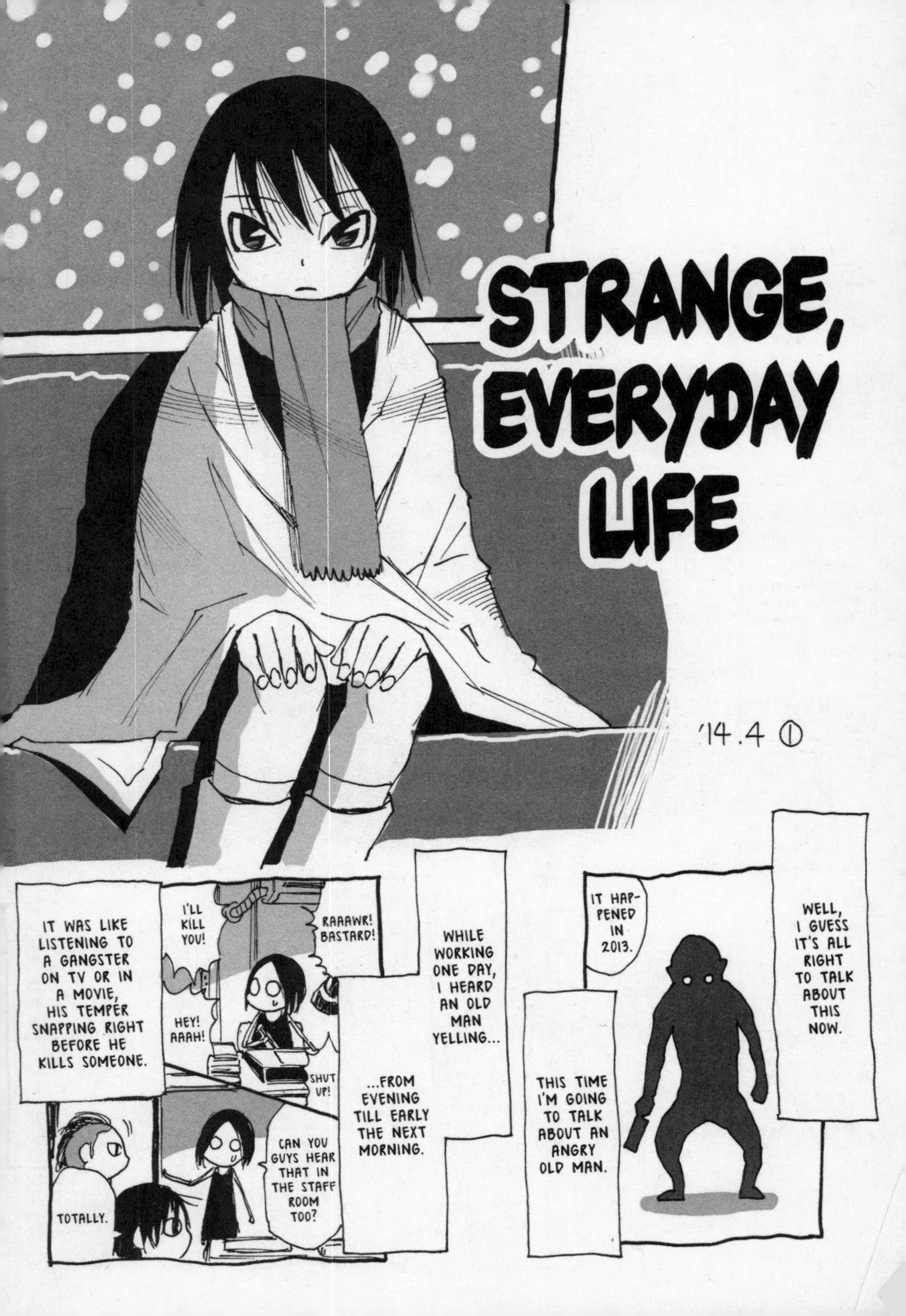
STRANGE, EVERYDAY LIFE
'14.4 ①
WELL, I GUESS IT'S ALL RIGHT TO TALK ABOUT THIS NOW.
IT HAPPENED IN 2013.
THIS TIME I'M GOING TO TALK ABOUT AN ANGRY OLD MAN.
WHILE WORKING ONE DAY, I HEARD AN OLD MAN YELLING...
...FROM EVENING TILL EARLY THE NEXT MORNING.
RAAAWR! BASTARD!
I'LL KILL YOU!
HEY! AAAH!
SHUT UP!
IT WAS LIKE LISTENING TO A GANGSTER ON TV OR IN A MOVIE, HIS TEMPER SNAPPING RIGHT BEFORE HE KILLS SOMEONE.
CAN YOU GUYS HEAR THAT IN THE STAFF ROOM TOO?
TOTALLY.

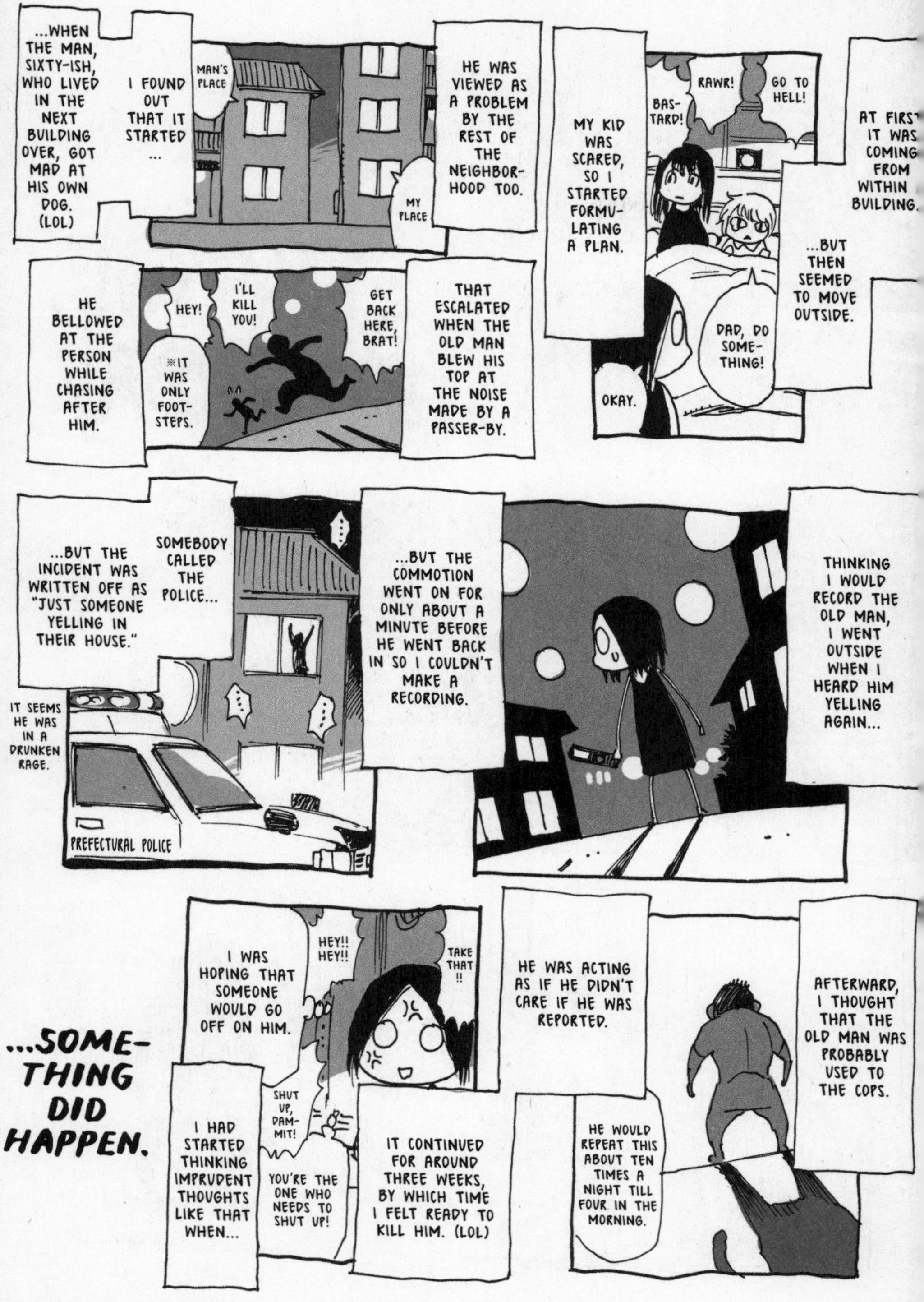

AT FIRST IT WAS COMING FROM WITHIN BUILDING.
...BUT THEN SEEMED TO MOVE OUTSIDE.
GO TO HELL!
RAWR!
BAS-TARD!
MY KID WAS SCARED, SO I STARTED FORMU-LATING A PLAN.
DAD, DO SOME-THING!
OKAY.
HE WAS VIEWED AS A PROBLEM BY THE REST OF THE NEIGHBOR-HOOD TOO.
MY PLACE
MAN'S PLACE
I FOUND OUT THAT IT STARTED ...
...WHEN THE MAN, SIXTY-ISH, WHO LIVED IN THE NEXT BUILDING OVER, GOT MAD AT HIS OWN DOG. (LOL)
THAT ESCALATED WHEN THE OLD MAN BLEW HIS TOP AT THE NOISE MADE BY A PASSER-BY.
GET BACK HERE, BRAT!
I'LL KILL YOU!
HEY!
※IT WAS ONLY FOOT-STEPS.
HE BELLOWED AT THE PERSON WHILE CHASING AFTER HIM.
THINKING I WOULD RECORD THE OLD MAN, I WENT OUTSIDE WHEN I HEARD HIM YELLING AGAIN...
...BUT THE COMMOTION WENT ON FOR ONLY ABOUT A MINUTE BEFORE HE WENT BACK IN SO I COULDN'T MAKE A RECORDING.
SOMEBODY CALLED THE POLICE...
...BUT THE INCIDENT WAS WRITTEN OFF AS "JUST SOMEONE YELLING IN THEIR HOUSE."
IT SEEMS HE WAS IN A DRUNKEN RAGE.
PREFECTURAL POLICE
AFTERWARD, I THOUGHT THAT THE OLD MAN WAS PROBABLY USED TO THE COPS.
HE WAS ACTING AS IF HE DIDN'T CARE IF HE WAS REPORTED.
HE WOULD REPEAT THIS ABOUT TEN TIMES A NIGHT TILL FOUR IN THE MORNING.
IT CONTINUED FOR AROUND THREE WEEKS, BY WHICH TIME I FELT READY TO KILL HIM. (LOL)
TAKE THAT!!
HEY!! HEY!!
I WAS HOPING THAT SOMEONE WOULD GO OFF ON HIM.
SHUT UP, DAM-MIT!
YOU'RE THE ONE WHO NEEDS TO SHUT UP!
I HAD STARTED THINKING IMPRUDENT THOUGHTS LIKE THAT WHEN...
...SOME-THING DID HAPPEN.

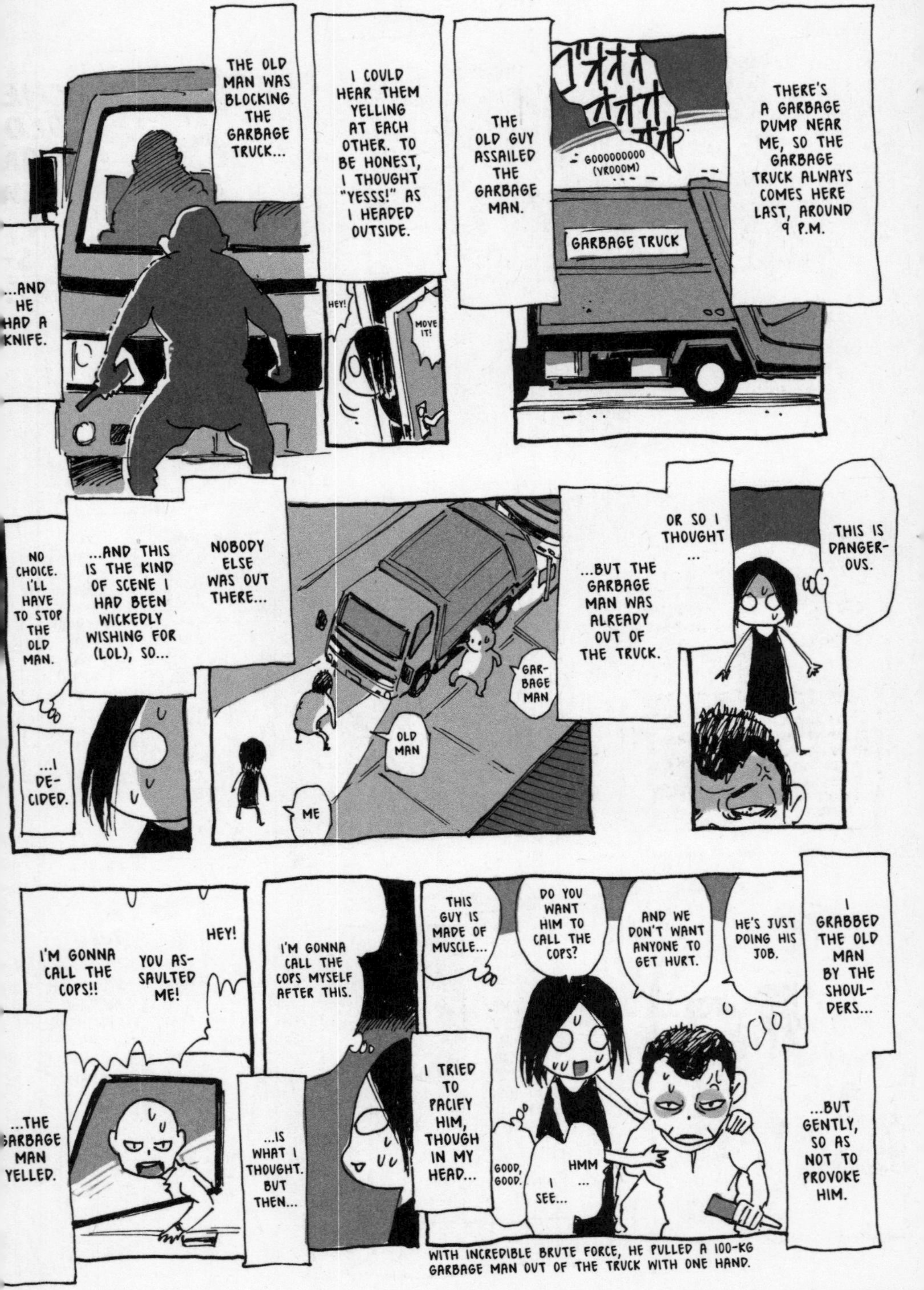
THERE'S A GARBAGE DUMP NEAR ME, SO THE GARBAGE TRUCK ALWAYS COMES HERE LAST, AROUND 9 P.M.
ゴオオオオオオオオ
GOOOOOOOOO (VROOOM)
GARBAGE TRUCK
THE OLD GUY ASSAILED THE GARBAGE MAN.
I COULD HEAR THEM YELLING AT EACH OTHER. TO BE HONEST, I THOUGHT "YESSS!" AS I HEADED OUTSIDE.
MOVE IT!
HEY!
THE OLD MAN WAS BLOCKING THE GARBAGE TRUCK...
...AND HE HAD A KNIFE.
THIS IS DANGEROUS.
OR SO I THOUGHT...
...BUT THE GARBAGE MAN WAS ALREADY OUT OF THE TRUCK.
NOBODY ELSE WAS OUT THERE...
GARBAGE MAN
OLD MAN
ME
...AND THIS IS THE KIND OF SCENE I HAD BEEN WICKEDLY WISHING FOR (LOL), SO...
NO CHOICE. I'LL HAVE TO STOP THE OLD MAN.
...I DECIDED.
I GRABBED THE OLD MAN BY THE SHOULDERS...
...BUT GENTLY, SO AS NOT TO PROVOKE HIM.
HE'S JUST DOING HIS JOB.
AND WE DON'T WANT ANYONE TO GET HURT.
DO YOU WANT HIM TO CALL THE COPS?
THIS GUY IS MADE OF MUSCLE...
HMM... I SEE...
GOOD, GOOD.
I TRIED TO PACIFY HIM, THOUGH IN MY HEAD...
WITH INCREDIBLE BRUTE FORCE, HE PULLED A 100-KG GARBAGE MAN OUT OF THE TRUCK WITH ONE HAND.
I'M GONNA CALL THE COPS MYSELF AFTER THIS.
...IS WHAT I THOUGHT. BUT THEN...
HEY!
YOU ASSAULTED ME!
I'M GONNA CALL THE COPS!!
...THE GARBAGE MAN YELLED.

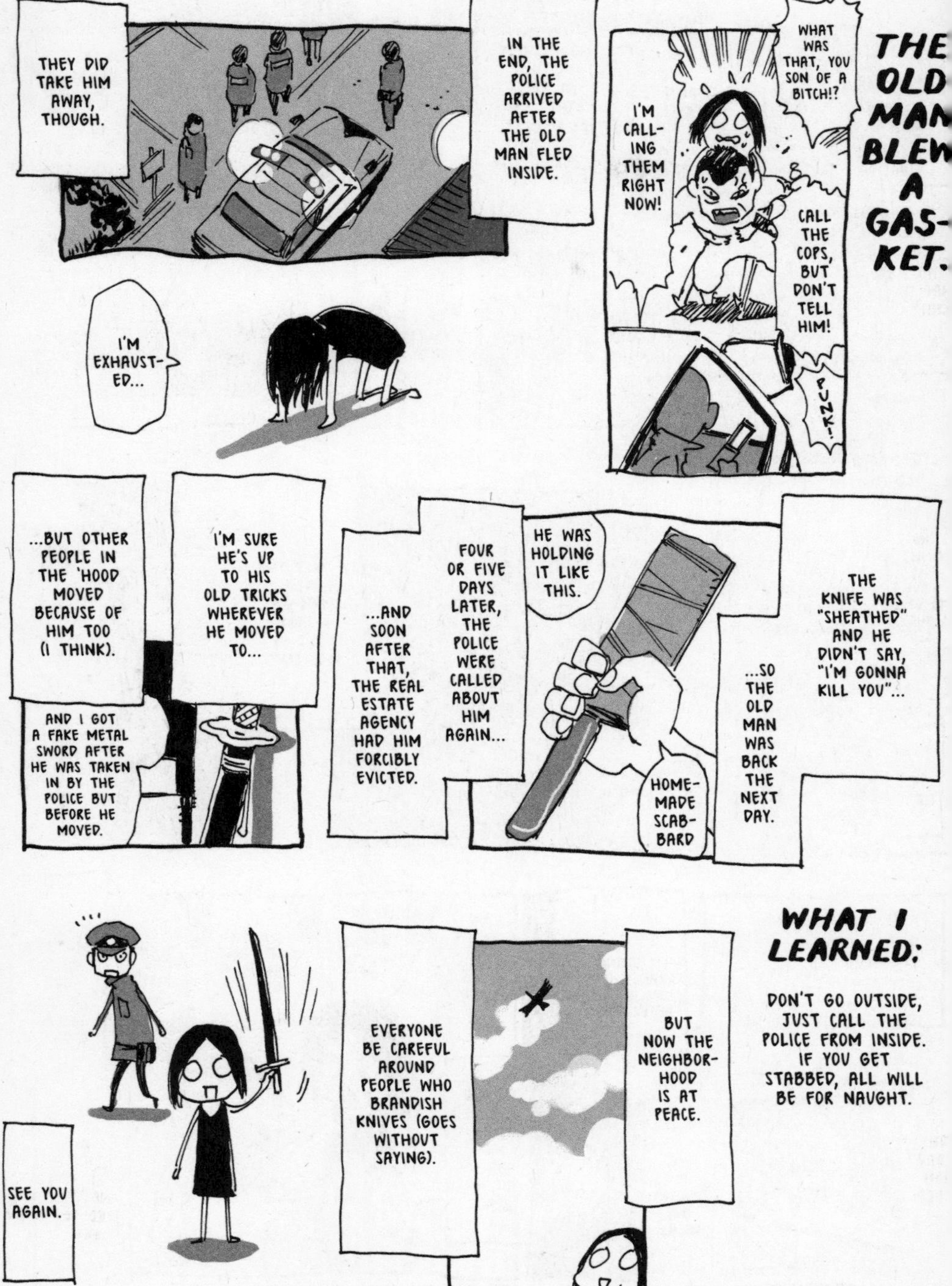
THE OLD MAN BLEW A GASKET.
WHAT WAS THAT, YOU SON OF A BITCH!?
I'M CALLING THEM RIGHT NOW!
CALL THE COPS, BUT DON'T TELL HIM!
PUNK!
IN THE END, THE POLICE ARRIVED AFTER THE OLD MAN FLED INSIDE.
THEY DID TAKE HIM AWAY, THOUGH.
I'M EXHAUSTED...
THE KNIFE WAS "SHEATHED" AND HE DIDN'T SAY, "I'M GONNA KILL YOU"...
...SO THE OLD MAN WAS BACK THE NEXT DAY.
HE WAS HOLDING IT LIKE THIS.
HOMEMADE SCABBARD
FOUR OR FIVE DAYS LATER, THE POLICE WERE CALLED ABOUT HIM AGAIN...
...AND SOON AFTER THAT, THE REAL ESTATE AGENCY HAD HIM FORCIBLY EVICTED.
I'M SURE HE'S UP TO HIS OLD TRICKS WHEREVER HE MOVED TO...
...BUT OTHER PEOPLE IN THE 'HOOD MOVED BECAUSE OF HIM TOO (I THINK).
AND I GOT A FAKE METAL SWORD AFTER HE WAS TAKEN IN BY THE POLICE BUT BEFORE HE MOVED.
WHAT I LEARNED:
DON'T GO OUTSIDE, JUST CALL THE POLICE FROM INSIDE. IF YOU GET STABBED, ALL WILL BE FOR NAUGHT.
BUT NOW THE NEIGHBORHOOD IS AT PEACE.
EVERYONE BE CAREFUL AROUND PEOPLE WHO BRANDISH KNIVES (GOES WITHOUT SAYING).
SEE YOU AGAIN.

Translation notes

Common Honorifics

no honorific: Indicates familiarity or closeness; if used without permission or reason, addressing someone in this manner would constitute an insult.

-san: The Japanese equivalent of Mr./Mrs./Miss. If a situation calls for politeness, this is the fail-safe honorific.

-sama: Conveys great respect; may also indicate the social status of the speaker is lower than that of the addressee.

-kun: Used most often when referring to boys, this indicates affection or familiarity. Occasionally used by older men among their peers, but it may also be used by anyone referring to a person of lower standing.

-chan: An affectionate honorific indicating familiarity used mostly in reference to girls; also used in reference to cute persons or animals of either gender.

-sensei: A respectful term for teachers, artists, or high-level professionals.

Currency Conversion

While conversion rates fluctuate daily, an easy estimate for Japanese Yen conversion is ¥100 to 1 USD.

Page 14

Girls' Day: Also known as the Doll Festival. Held on March 3, this holiday celebrates and promotes the growth and happiness of young girls. Families with daughters put beautiful (and expensive) traditional dolls on display.

Page 24

Hokuhokuan: A well-known *udon* noodle shop relatively close to Sapporo, Hokkaido. *Udon* is thick wheat noodles.

Page 174

God of misfortune: Traditionally a god or spirit that possesses a human being or a house, subsequently attracting poverty and misery.

Page 219

Okonomiyaki: A grilled pancake- or omelet-like dish that may include a variety of savory ingredients, depending on the region of Japan.

Page 238

New teacher: Generally middle school students have the same main "homeroom" teacher for all three years (the equivalent of U.S. grades 7-9).

Page 244

Swear word: Literally, the dialogue translates as, "the first time I heard him speak with dialect (as opposed to standard Japanese)," but this doesn't come across well in translation. He really ends his last exclamation with *-ssho*, which is an ending specific to Hokkaido dialect.

Local dialect: As noted in the previous volume, standard Japanese is taught in schools and used on TV, as well as for all official matters. Hence Satoru (as a child) considered Yuuki's usual "affected" standard Japanese manner of speech to sound mature and authoritative. In this scene, however, Yuuki was so pleased with Kayo's social improvement that he "let his guard down" and spoke using his natural local accent.

Page 275

"'Kayo'? Geez, man.": Here Kenya teases Satoru for not using an honorific with Kayo's name, which can indicate a close casualness (Kenya, Satoru and their group only use given names without honorifics for each other) and gives the impression of being cool in a mature sort of way.

Page 339

"For the school trip, we went to Hakodate.": A slip-up on Satoru's part, as school trips are a high school activity. Hakodate is an old port city in Hokkaido with western-style buildings and amazing night views. The third-largest city in Hokkaido, it's been a hub for trade with other countries since the late 1800s.